CONTEMPORARY
STRATEGY
ANALYSIS
TEXT AND CASES

CONTEMPORARY STRATEGY ANALYSIS

TEXT AND CASES

NINTH EDITION

ROBERT M. GRANT

WILEY

To Liam, Ava, Finn, Evie, Max, Lucy, and Bobby

BRIEF CONTENTS

CONTENTS

PREFACE TO NINTH EDITION

Contemporary Strategy Analysis equips managers and students of management with the concepts, frameworks, and techniques needed to make better strategic decisions. My goal is a strategy text that reflects the dynamism and intellectual rigor of this fast-developing field of management and takes account of the strategy issues that companies face today.

Contemporary Strategy Analysis endeavors to be both rigorous and relevant. While embodying the latest thinking in the strategy field, it aims to be accessible to students from different backgrounds and with varying levels of experience. I achieve this accessibility by combining clarity of exposition, concentration on the fundamentals of value creation, and an emphasis on practicality.

This ninth edition maintains the book's focus on the essential tasks of strategy: identifying the sources of superior business performance and formulating and implementing a strategy that exploits these performance drivers. At the same time, the content of the book has been revised to reflect recent developments in the business environment and in strategy research and to take account of feedback from instructors.

Distinctive features of the ninth edition include:

- an explicit guide of how to apply strategy analysis in order to generate strategy recommendations (see "Applying Strategy Analysis" in Chapter 1);
- further development of the role of stakeholder orientation and corporate social responsibility within a value creating view of the firm (see "Beyond Profit: Values and Corporate Social Responsibility" in Chapter 2);
- an increased emphasis on inter-industry linkages including complements, business ecosystems, and platform strategies, especially in digital markets (Chapters 4 and 9);
- a more comprehensive treatment of strategy implementation; while maintaining an integrated approach to strategy formulation and strategy implementation (the chapters on strategic change, technology, mature industries, global strategies, and diversification address both the formulation and implementation of strategy), Chapters 6, 14, and 15 offer a systematic approach to strategy execution;
- greater emphasis on cooperative strategies, especially strategic alliances (Chapter 15).

There is little in *Contemporary Strategy Analysis* that is original: I have plundered mercilessly the ideas, theories, and evidence of fellow scholars. My greatest debts are to my colleagues and students at the business schools where this book has been developed and tested, notably Georgetown University, Bocconi University, London Business School, City University's Cass Business School, Cal Poly, UCLA's Anderson School, and Mumbai International School of Business. I have also benefitted from feedback and suggestions from professors and students in the many other schools where *Contemporary Strategy Analysis* has been adopted. I look forward to continuing my engagement with users.

I am grateful for the professionalism and enthusiasm of the editorial, production, and sales and marketing teams at John Wiley & Sons, Ltd, especially to Steve Hardman, Juliet Booker, Joshua Poole, Catriona King, Deb Egleton, Joyce Poh, Tim Bettsworth, and Dom Wharram—I couldn't wish for better support.

Robert M. Grant

I

INTRODUCTION

1 The Concept of Strategy

Strategy is the great work of the organization. In situations of life or death, it is the Tao of survival or extinction. Its study cannot be neglected.

—SUN TZU, *THE ART OF WAR*

To shoot a great score you need a clever strategy.

—RORY MCILROY, *GOLF MONTHLY*, MAY 19, 2011

Everybody has a plan until they get punched in the mouth.

—MIKE TYSON, FORMER WORLD HEAVYWEIGHT BOXING CHAMPION

OUTLINE

Introduction and Objectives

Strategy is about achieving success. This chapter explains what strategy is and why it is important to success, for both organizations and individuals. We will distinguish strategy from planning. Strategy is not a detailed plan or program of instructions; it is a unifying theme that gives coherence and direction to the actions and decisions of an individual or an organization.

The principal task of this chapter will be to introduce the basic framework for strategy analysis that underlies this book. I will introduce the two basic components of strategy analysis: analysis of the external environment of the firm (mainly industry analysis) and analysis of the internal environment (primarily analysis of the firm's resources and capabilities).

By the time you have completed this chapter, you will be able to:

◆ Appreciate the contribution that strategy can make to successful performance, both for individuals and for organizations, and recognize the key characteristics of an effective strategy.

◆ Comprehend the basic framework of strategy analysis that underlies this book.

◆ Recognize how strategic management has evolved over the past 60 years.

◆ Identify and describe the strategy of a business enterprise.

◆ Understand how strategy is made within organizations.

◆ Recognize the distinctive features of strategic management among not-for-profit organizations.

Since the purpose of strategy is to help us to win, we start by looking at the role of strategy in success.

The Role of Strategy in Success

Strategy Capsules 1.1 and 1.2 describe the careers of two individuals, Queen Elizabeth II and Lady Gaga, who have been outstandingly successful in leading their organizations. Although these two remarkable women operate within vastly different arenas, can their success be attributed to any common factors?

For neither of these successful women can success be attributed to overwhelmingly superior resources. For all of Queen Elizabeth's formal status as head of state, she has very little real power and, in most respects, is a servant of the democratically elected British government. Lady Gaga is clearly a creative and capable entertainer, but few would claim that she has outstanding talents as a vocalist, musician, or songwriter.

Nor can their success be attributed either exclusively or primarily to luck. Indeed, Queen Elizabeth has experienced a succession of difficulties and tragedies, while Lady Gaga has experienced setbacks (e.g. the cancelation of her first recording contract and various health problems). Central to their success has been their ability to respond to events—whether positive or negative—with flexibility and clarity of direction.

My contention is that common to both the 60-year successful reign of Queen Elizabeth II and the short but stellar career of Lady Gaga is the presence of a soundly formulated and effectively implemented strategy. While these strategies did not exist as explicit plans, for both Queen Elizabeth and Lady Gaga we can discern a consistency of direction based clear goals and a keen awareness of how to maneuver into a position of advantage.

Elizabeth Windsor's strategy as queen of the UK and the Commonwealth countries may be seen in the role she has created for herself in relation to her people. As queen she is figurehead for the nation, an embodiment of the stability and continuity of the nation, a symbol of British family and cultural life, and an exemplar of service and professional dedication.

Lady Gaga's remarkable success during 2008-15 reflects a career strategy that uses music as her gateway, upon which she has built a celebrity status by combining the generic tools of star creation—shock value, fashion leadership, and media presence— with a uniquely differentiated image that has captured the imagination and affection of teenagers and young adults throughout the world.

What do these two examples tell us about the characteristics of a strategy that are conducive to success? In both stories, four common factors stand out (Figure 1.1):

- *Goals that are consistent and long term*: Both Queen Elizabeth and Lady Gaga display a focused commitment to career goals that they have pursued steadfastly.
- *Profound understanding of the competitive environment*: The ways in which both Elizabeth II and Gaga define their roles and pursue their careers reveal a deep and insightful appreciation of the external environments in which they operate. Queen Elizabeth has been alert both to the changing political environment in which the monarchy is situated and to the mood and needs of the British people. Lady Gaga's business model and strategic positioning show a keen awareness of the changing economics of the music business, the marketing potential of social networking, and the needs of Generation Y.
- *Objective appraisal of resources*: Both Queen Elizabeth and Lady Gaga have been adept at recognizing and deploying the resources at their disposal. Both, too, have been aware of the limits of those resources and drawn upon the resources of others—Queen Elizabeth through her family, the royal household, and a network of loyal supporters; Lady Gaga upon the variety of talents in her Haus of Gaga.
- *Effective implementation*: Without effective implementation, the best-laid strategies are of little use. Critical to the success of Queen Elizabeth and Lady Gaga has been their effectiveness as leaders and the creation of loyal, supportive organizations to provide decision support and operational implementation.

These observations about the role of strategy in success can be made in relation to most fields of human endeavor. Whether we look at warfare, chess, politics, sport, or business, the success of individuals and organizations is seldom the outcome

STRATEGY CAPSULE 1.1

Queen Elizabeth II and the House of Windsor

By late 2015, Elizabeth Windsor had been queen for 63 years—longer than any of her predecessors.

At her birth on April 21, 1926, hereditary monarchies were common throughout the world. Apart from the British Empire, 45 countries had this form of government. By 2015, the forces of democracy, modernity, and reform had reduced these to 26—mostly small autocracies such as Bahrain, Qatar, Oman, Kuwait, Bhutan, and Lesotho. Monarchies had also survived in Denmark, Sweden, Norway, the Netherlands, and Belgium, but these royal families had lost most of their wealth and privileges.

By contrast, the British royal family retains considerable wealth—the Queen's personal net worth was estimated by *Forbes* magazine at $500 million—not including the $10 billion worth of palaces and other real estate owned by the nation but used by her and her family. Queen Elizabeth's formal status is head of state of the UK and 15 other Commonwealth countries (including Canada and Australia), head of the Church of England, and head of the British armed forces. Yet none of these positions confers any decision making power—her influence comes from the informal role she has established for herself. According to her website, she "has a less formal role as

Head of Nation" where she "acts as a focus for national identity, unity and pride; gives a sense of stability and continuity; officially recognises success and excellence; and supports the ideal of voluntary service" (www.royal.gov.uk).

How has Queen Elizabeth been able to retain not just the formal position of the monarchy but also its status, influence, and wealth despite the challenges of the past 60 years? These challenges include the social and political changes which have swept away most of the privileges conferred by hereditary status (including the exclusion of most hereditary lords from the House of Lords, Britain's upper chamber of Parliament) and the internal challenges presented by such a famously dysfunctional family—including the failed marriages of most of her family members and the controversy that surrounded the life and death of her daughter-in-law, Diana, Princess of Wales.

At the heart of Elizabeth's sustaining of the British monarchy has been her single-minded devotion to what she regards as her duties to the monarchy and to the nation. Throughout her 60-year reign she has cultivated the role of leader of her nation—a role that she has not compromised by pursuit of personal or family interests. In pursing this role she has recognized

of a purely random process. Nor is superiority in initial endowments of skills and resources typically the determining factor. Strategies that build on these four elements almost always play an influential role.

Look at the "high achievers" in any competitive area. Whether we review the world's political leaders, the CEOs of the Fortune 500, or our own circles of friends and acquaintances, those who have achieved outstanding success in their careers are seldom those who possessed the greatest innate abilities. Success has gone to those who managed their careers most effectively, typically by combining these four strategic factors. They are goal focused; their career goals have taken primacy over the multitude of life's other goals—friendship, love, leisure, knowledge, spiritual fulfillment—which the majority of us spend most of our lives juggling the need for political neutrality—even when she has personally disagreed with her prime ministers (notably with Margaret Thatcher's "socially divisive" policies and Tony Blair's commitment of British troops to Iraq and Afghanistan).

Through her outreach activities she has played a major role in promoting British influence, British culture, and British values within the wider world. She has made multiple visits to each of the 54 Commonwealth nations, including 26 to Canada and 16 to Australia.

Maintaining her popularity with the British people has required adaptation to the wrenching changes of her era. Recognizing the growing unacceptability of hereditary privilege and the traditional British class system, she has repositioned the royal family from being the leader of the ruling class to an embodiment of the nation as a whole. To make her and her family more inclusive and less socially stereotyped she cultivated involvement with popular culture, with ordinary people engaged in social service and charitable work, and, most recently, endorsing the marriage of her grandson William to Kate Middleton—the first member of the royal family to marry outside the ranks of the aristocracy.

Elizabeth has been adept at exploiting new media. Television has provided an especially powerful medium for communicating both with her subjects and with a wider global audience. Her web page appeared in 1997, in 2009 she joined Twitter, and in 2010 Facebook. Throughout her reign, her press and public relations strategy has been carefully managed by a group of top professionals who report to her private secretary.

While respecting tradition and protocol, she adapts in the face of pressing circumstances. The death of her daughter-in-law, Diana, created difficult tensions between her responsibilities as a grandmother and her need to show leadership to a grieving nation. In responding to this time of crisis she departed from several established traditions: including bowing to the coffin of her ex-daughter-in-law as it passed the palace.

Elizabeth has made effective use of the resources available to her. First and foremost of these has been the underlying desire of the British people for continuity and their inherent distrust of their political leaders. By positioning herself above the political fray and emphasizing her lineage—including the prominent public roles of her mother and her children and grandchildren—she reinforces the legitimacy of herself, her family, and the institution they represent. She has also exploited her powers of patronage, using her formal position to cultivate informal relationships with both political and cultural leaders.

The success of Elizabeth's 63-year reign is indicated by the popular support for her personally and for the institution of the monarchy. Outside of Northern Ireland, the UK lacks any significant republican movement; republicanism is also weak in Canada and Australia.

and reconciling. They know the environments within which they play and tend to be fast learners in terms of recognizing the paths to advancement. They know themselves well in terms of both strengths and weaknesses. Finally, they implement their career strategies with commitment, consistency, and determination. As the late Peter Drucker observed: "we must learn how to be the CEO of our own careers."[1]

There is a downside, however. Focusing on a single goal may lead to outstanding success but may be matched by dismal failure in other areas of life. Many people who have reached the pinnacles of their careers have led lives scarred by poor relationships with friends and families and stunted personal development. These include Howard Hughes and Jean Paul Getty in business, Richard Nixon and

Lady Gaga and the Haus of Gaga

Stefani Joanne Angelina Germanotta, better known as Lady Gaga, is one of the most successful popular entertainers to emerge in the 21st century. Since releasing her first album, *The Fame*, in 2008 she has certified album sales of 27 million, swept leading music awards including Grammy, MTV, and Billboards, topped *Forbes Celebrity 100* list, and generated $382 million in ticket sales for her 2012 "Born this Way" tour. Her 79 concerts during her 2014 "Artrave: The Artpop Ball" tour generated $271 million.

Since dropping out of NYU's Tisch School of the Arts in 2005, Germanotta has shown total commitment to advancing her musical career, first as a songwriter, and then developing her Lady Gaga persona. Her debut album, *The Fame*, and its follow up, *The Fame Monster*, yielded a succession of number-one hits during 2009 and 2010.

Gaga's music is a catchy mix of pop and dance, well suited to dance clubs and radio airplay. It features good melodies, Gaga's capable singing voice, and her reflections on society and life, but it is hardly exceptional or innovative: music critic Simon Reynolds described it as: "ruthlessly catchy, naughties pop glazed with Auto-Tune and undergirded with R&B-ish beats."

However, music is only one element in the Lady Gaga phenomenon—her achievement is not so much as a singer or songwriter as in establishing a persona which transcends pop music. Like David Bowie and Madonna before her, Lady Gaga is famous for being Lady Gaga. To do this requires a multi-media, multi-faceted offering that comprises an integrated array of components including music, visual appearance, newsworthy events, a distinctive attitude and personality, and a set of values with which fans can identify.

Key among these is visual impact and theatricality. Her hit records were heavily promoted by the visually stunning music videos that accompanied them. *Paparazzi* and *Bad Romance* each won best video awards at the 2009 and 2010 Grammies; the latter is the second-most-downloaded YouTube video of all time. Most striking of all has been Lady Gaga's dress and overall appearance, which have set new standards in eccentricity, innovation, and impact. Individual outfits—her plastic bubble dress, meat dress, and "decapitated-corpse dress"—together with weird hairdos, extravagant hats, and extreme footwear (she met President Obama in 16-inch heels)—are as well-known

FIGURE 1.1   Common elements in successful strategies

as her hit songs. The range of visual images she projects is so varied that her every appearance creates a buzz of anticipation as to her latest incarnation.

More than any other star, Lady Gaga has developed a business model that recognizes the realities of the post-digital world of entertainment. Like Web 2.0 pioneers such as Facebook and Twitter, Gaga has followed the model: first build market presence, and then think about monetizing that presence. Her record releases are accompanied, sometimes preceded, by music videos on YouTube. With 45 million Facebook fans, 15.8 million Twitter followers, and 1.9 billion YouTube views (as of November 16, 2011), Famecount crowned her "most popular living musician online." Her networking with fans includes Gagaville, an interactive game developed by Zynga, and The Backplane, a music-based social network.

Her emphasis on visual imagery reflects the ways in which her fame is converted into revenues. While music royalties are important, concerts are her primary revenue source. Other revenue sources—endorsements, product placement in videos and concerts, merchandizing deals, and media appearances—also link closely with her visual presence.

A distinctive feature of Gaga's market presence is her relationship with her fans. The devotion of her fans—her "Little Monsters"—is based less on their desire to emulate her look as upon empathy with her values and attitudes. They recognize Gaga's images

more as social statements of non-conformity than as fashion statements. In communicating her experiences of alienation and bullying at school and her values of individuality, sexual freedom, and acceptance of differences—reinforced through her involvement in charities and gay rights events—she has built a global fan base that is unusual in its loyalty and commitment. The sense of belonging is reinforced by gestures and symbols such as the "Monster Claw" greeting and the "Manifesto of Little Monsters." As "Mother Monster," Gaga is spokesperson and guru for this community.

Lady Gaga's most outstanding talents are her showmanship and theatricality. Modeled on Andy Warhol's "Factory," The Haus of Gaga is her creative workshop and augments her own capabilities. It includes manager Troy Carter, choreographer and creative director Laurieann Gibson, fashion director Nicola Formichetti, hair stylist Frederic Aspiras, stylist and designer Anna Trevelyan, fashion photographer Nick Night, makeup artist Tara Savelo, marketing director Bobby Campbell, and others involved in designing and producing songs, videos, concert sets, photo shoots, and the whole range of Gaga's public appearances.

Sources: M. Sala, "The Strategy of Lady Gaga," BSc thesis Bocconi University, Milan, June 2011; http://www.statisticbrain.com/lady-gaga-career-statistics, accessed July 20, 2015; http://en.wikipedia.org/wiki/Lady_Gaga, accessed July 20, 2015.

Joseph Stalin in politics, Elvis Presley and Marilyn Monroe in entertainment, Mike Tyson and O. J. Simpson in sport, and Bobby Fischer in chess. Fulfillment in our personal lives is likely to require broad-based lifetime strategies.[2]

These same ingredients of successful strategies—clear goals, understanding the competitive environment, resource appraisal, and effective implementation—form the key components of our analysis of business strategy.

The Basic Framework for Strategy Analysis

Figure 1.2 shows the basic framework for strategy analysis that we shall use throughout the book. The four elements of a successful strategy shown in Figure 1.1 are recast into two groups—the firm and the industry environment—with strategy

FIGURE 1.2 The basic framework: Strategy as a link between the firm and its environment

forming a link between the two. The firm embodies three of these elements: goals and values ("simple, consistent, long-term goals"), resources and capabilities ("objective appraisal of resources"), and structure and systems ("effective implementation"). The industry environment embodies the fourth ("profound understanding of the competitive environment") and is defined by the firm's relationships with competitors, customers, and suppliers.

This view of strategy as a link between the firm and its industry environment has close similarities with the widely used **SWOT framework**. However, as I explain in Strategy Capsule 1.3, a two-way classification of internal and external forces is superior to the four-way SWOT framework.

The task of business strategy, then, is to determine how the firm will deploy its resources within its environment and so satisfy its long-term goals, and how it will organize itself to implement that strategy.

Strategic Fit

Fundamental to this view of strategy as a link between the firm and its external environment is the notion of **strategic fit**. This refers to the consistency of a firm's strategy, first, with the firm's external environment and, second, with its internal environment, especially with its goals and values and resources and capabilities. A major reason for the decline and failure of some companies comes from their having a strategy that lacks consistency with either the internal or the external environment. The decline of Nokia (which lost over 90% of its stock market value in the four years up to July 2012) may be attributed to a strategy which failed to take account of a major change in its external environment: the growing consumer demand for smartphones. Other companies struggle to align their strategies to their internal resources and capabilities. A critical issue for Nintendo will be whether it possesses the financial and technological resources to continue to compete head-to-head with Sony and Microsoft in the market for video game consoles.

The concept of strategic fit also relates to the internal consistency among the different elements of a firm's strategy. Effective strategies are ones where functional strategies and individual decisions are aligned with one another to create a consistent strategic position and direction of development. This notion of internal fit is central to Michael Porter's conceptualization of the firm as an **activity system**.

STRATEGY CAPSULE 1.3
What's Wrong with SWOT?

Distinguishing between the external and the internal environment of the firm is common to most approaches to strategy analysis. The best-known and most widely used of these approaches is the "SWOT" framework, which classifies the various influences on a firm's strategy into four categories: Strengths, Weaknesses, Opportunities, and Threats. The first two—strengths and weaknesses—relate to the internal environment of the firm, primarily its resources and capabilities; the last two—opportunities and threats—relate to the external environment.

Which is better, a two-way distinction between internal and external influences or the four-way SWOT taxonomy? The key issue is whether it is sensible and worthwhile to classify internal factors into strengths and weaknesses and external factors into opportunities and threats. In practice, such distinctions are difficult.

Is LeBron James a strength or a weakness for the Cleveland Cavaliers? As one of the NBA's most accomplished and acclaimed players he is a strength. As a 30-year-old player whose best days are behind him and who may intimidate his younger team members, he is a weakness.

Is global warming a threat or an opportunity for the world's automobile producers? By encouraging higher taxes on motor fuels and restrictions on car use, it is a threat. By encouraging consumers to switch to fuel-efficient and electric cars, it offers an opportunity for new sales.

The lesson here is that classifying external factors into opportunities and threats, and internal factors into strengths and weaknesses, is arbitrary. What is important is to carefully identify the external and internal forces that impact the firm, and then analyze their implications.

In this book I will follow a simple two-way classification of internal and external factors and avoid any superficial categorization into strengths or weaknesses, and opportunities or threats.

Note: For more on SWOT see: T. Hill and R. Westbrook, "SWOT Analysis: It's Time For A Product Recall," *Long Range Planning*, 30 (February 1997): 46–52; and M. Venzin, "SWOT Analysis: Such a Waste of Time?" (February 2015) http://ideas.sdabocconi.it/strategy/archives/3405.

Porter states that "Strategy is the creation of a unique and differentiated position involving a different set of activities."[3] The key is how these activities fit together to form a consistent, mutually reinforcing system. Ryanair's strategic position is as Europe's lowest-cost airline providing no-frills flights to budget-conscious travelers. This is achieved by a set of activities which fit together to support that positioning (Figure 1.3).

The concept of strategic fit is one component of a set of ideas known as **contingency theory**. Contingency theory postulates that there is no single best way of organizing or managing. The best way to design, manage, and lead an organization depends upon circumstances—in particular the characteristics of that organization's environment.[4]

FIGURE 1.3 Ryanair's activity system

A Brief History of Business Strategy

Origins and Military Antecedents

Enterprises need business strategies for much the same reason that armies need military strategies—to give direction and purpose, to deploy resources in the most effective manner, and to coordinate the decisions made by different individuals. Many of the concepts and theories of business strategy have their antecedents in military strategy. The term *strategy* derives from the Greek word *strategia*, meaning "generalship." However, the concept of strategy did not originate with the Greeks: Sun Tzu's classic, *The Art of War*, from about 500 BC is regarded as the first treatise on strategy.[5]

Military strategy and business strategy share a number of common concepts and principles, the most basic being the distinction between strategy and tactics. Strategy is the overall plan for deploying resources to establish a favorable position; a tactic is a scheme for a specific action. Whereas tactics are concerned with the maneuvers necessary to win battles, strategy is concerned with winning the war. Strategic decisions, whether in military or business spheres, share three common characteristics:

- they are important
- they involve a significant commitment of resources
- they are not easily reversible.

Many of the principles of military strategy have been applied to business situations. These include the relative strengths of offensive and defensive strategies; the merits of outflanking over frontal assault; the roles of graduated responses to aggressive initiatives; the benefits of surprise; and the potential for deception, envelopment, escalation, and attrition.[6] At the same time, there are major differences between business competition and military conflict. The objective of war is (usually) to defeat the enemy. The purpose of business rivalry is seldom so aggressive: most business enterprises seek to coexist with their rivals rather than to destroy them.

The tendency for the principles of military and business strategy to develop along separate paths indicates the absence of a general theory of strategy. The publication of Von Neumann and Morgenstern's *Theory of Games* in 1944 gave rise to the hope that a general theory of competitive behavior would emerge. During the subsequent six decades, **game theory** has revolutionized the study of competitive interaction, not just in business but in politics, military conflict, and international relations as well. Yet, as we shall see in Chapter 4, game theory has achieved only limited success as a broadly applicable general theory of strategy.[7]

From Corporate Planning to Strategic Management

The evolution of business strategy has been driven more by the practical needs of business than by the development of theory. During the 1950s and 1960s, senior executives experienced increasing difficulty in coordinating decisions and maintaining control in companies that were growing in size and complexity. While new techniques of discounted cash flow analysis allowed more rational choices over individual investment projects, firms lacked systematic approaches to their long-term development. **Corporate planning** (also known as *long-term planning*) was developed during the late-1950s to serve this purpose. Macroeconomic forecasts provided the foundation for the new corporate planning. The typical format was a five-year corporate planning document that set goals and objectives, forecasted key economic trends (including market demand, the company's market share, revenue, costs, and margins), established priorities for different products and business areas of the firm, and allocated capital expenditures. The diffusion of corporate planning was accelerated by a flood of articles and books addressing this new science.[8] The new techniques of corporate planning proved particularly useful for guiding the diversification strategies that many large companies pursued during the 1960s.[9] By the mid-1960s, most large US and European companies had set up corporate planning departments. Strategy Capsule 1.4 provides an example of this formalized corporate planning.

During the 1970s and early 1980s, confidence in corporate planning was severely shaken. Not only did diversification fail to deliver the anticipated synergies but the oil shocks of 1974 and 1979 ushered in a new era of macroeconomic instability, while increased international competition intensified as Japanese, Korean, and Southeast Asian firms stepped onto the world stage. The new turbulence meant that firms could no longer plan their investments and resource requirements three to five years ahead—they couldn't forecast that far ahead.

The result was a shift in emphasis from planning to strategy making, where the focus was less on the detailed management of a company's growth path as on market selection and competitive positioning in order to maximize the potential for profit. This transition from corporate planning to what became called *strategic management* involved a focus on competition as the central characteristic of the business environment, and on performance maximization as the primary goal of strategy.

This emphasis on strategy as a quest for performance directed attention to the sources of profitability. During the late 1970s and into the 1980s, the focus was upon how a firm's competitive environment determined its potential for profit. Michael Porter of Harvard Business School pioneered the application of industrial organization economics to analyzing the profit potential of different industries and markets.[10] Other studies examined how strategic variables—notably market share—determined how profits were distributed between the different firms in an industry.[11]

STRATEGY CAPSULE 1.4
Corporate Planning in a Large US Steel Company, 1965

The first step in developing long-range plans was to forecast the product demand for future years. After calculating the tonnage needed in each sales district to provide the "target" fraction of the total forecast demand, the optimal production level for each area was determined. A computer program that incorporated the projected demand, existing production capacity, freight costs, etc. was used for this purpose.

When the optimum production rate in each area was found, the additional facilities needed to produce the desired tonnage were specified. Then the capital costs for the necessary equipment, buildings, and layout were estimated by the chief engineer of the corporation and various district engineers. Alternative plans for achieving company goals were also developed for some areas, and investment proposals were formulated after considering the amount of available capital and the company debt policy. The vice president who was responsible for long-range planning recommended certain plans to the president and, after the top executives and the board of directors reviewed alternative plans, they made the necessary decisions about future activities.

Source: H. W. Henry, *Long Range Planning Processes in 45 Industrial Companies* (Englewood Cliffs, NJ: Prentice-Hall, 1967): 65.

During the 1990s, the focus of strategy analysis shifted from the sources of profit in the external environment to the sources of profit within the firm. Increasingly the resources and capabilities of the firm became regarded as the main source of competitive advantage and the primary basis for formulating strategy.[12] This emphasis on what has been called the **resource-based view of the firm** represented a substantial shift in thinking about strategy. While the quest for attractive industries and market leadership encouraged firms to adopt similar strategies, emphasis on internal resources and capabilities has encouraged firms to identify how they are *different* from their competitors and design strategies that exploit these differences.

During the 21st century, new challenges have continued to shape the principles and practice of strategy. Digital technologies have had a massive impact on the competitive dynamics of many industries, creating winner-take-all markets and standards wars.[13] Disruptive technologies[14] and accelerating rates of change have meant that strategy has become less and less about plans and more about creating options of the future,[15] fostering strategic innovation,[16] and seeking the "blue oceans" of uncontested market space.[17] The complexity of these challenges have meant that being self-sufficient is no longer viable for most firms—alliances and other forms of collaboration are an increasingly common feature of firms' strategies.

The 2008–2009 financial crisis triggered new thinking about the strategy and purpose of business. Disillusion with the excesses and unfairness of market capitalism has renewed interest in corporate social responsibility, ethics, sustainability, and the role of legitimacy in long-term corporate success.[18]

Figure 1.4 summarizes the main developments in strategic management since the mid-20th century.

FIGURE 1.4   Evolution of strategic management

Strategy Today

What Is Strategy?

In its broadest sense, strategy is the means by which individuals or organizations achieve their objectives. Table 1.1 presents a number of definitions of the term strategy. Common to most definitions is the notion that strategy is focused on achieving certain goals; that it involves allocating resources; and that it implies some consistency, integration, or cohesiveness of decisions and actions.

Yet, as we have seen, the conception of firm strategy has changed greatly over the past half-century. As the business environment has become more unstable and unpredictable, so strategy has become less concerned with detailed plans and more about guidelines for success. This is consistent with the examples that began this chapter. Neither Queen Elizabeth nor Lady Gaga appears to have articulated any explicit strategic plan, but the consistency we discern in their actions suggests both possessed clear ideas of what they wanted to achieve and how they would achieve it. This shift in emphasis from strategy as plan to strategy as direction does not imply any downgrading of the role of strategy. The more turbulent the environment, the more must strategy embrace flexibility and responsiveness. But it is precisely in these conditions that strategy becomes more, rather than less, important. When the firm is buffeted by unforeseen threats and where new opportunities are constantly

TABLE 1.1 Some definitions of strategy

● Strategy: a plan, method, or series of actions designed to achieve a specific goal or effect.
>   —*Wordsmyth Dictionary* (http://www.wordsmyth.net)

● The determination of the long-run goals and objectives of an enterprise, and the adoption of courses of action and the allocation of resources necessary for carrying out these goals.
>   —Alfred Chandler, *Strategy and Structure*
>   (Cambridge, MA: MIT Press, 1962)

● Strategy: "a cohesive response to an important challenge."
>   —Richard Rumelt, *Good Strategy/Bad Strategy*
>   (New York: Crown Business, 2011): 6.

● Lost Boy: "Injuns! Let's go get 'em!"
  John Darling: "Hold on a minute. First we must have a strategy."
  Lost Boy: "Uhh? What's a strategy?"
  John Darling: "It's, er . . . it's a plan of attack."

>   —Walt Disney's *Peter Pan*

---

appearing, then strategy becomes the compass that can navigate the firm through stormy seas.

Why Do Firms Need Strategy?

This transition from strategy as plan to strategy as direction raises the question of why firms (or any type of organization) need strategy. Strategy assists the effective management of organizations, first, by enhancing the quality of decision making, second, by facilitating coordination, and, third, by focusing organizations on the pursuit of long-term goals.

Strategy as Decision Support   Strategy is a pattern or theme that gives coherence to the decisions of an individual or organization. But why can't individuals or organizations make optimal decisions in the absence of such a unifying theme? Consider the 1997 "man versus machine" chess epic in which Garry Kasparov was defeated by IBM's "Deep Blue" computer. Deep Blue did not need strategy. Its phenomenal memory and computing power allowed it to identify its optimal moves based on a huge decision tree.[19] Kasparov—although the world's greatest chess player—was subject to *bounded rationality*: his decision analysis was subject to the cognitive limitations that constrain all human beings.[20] For him, a strategy offered guidance that assisted positioning and helped create opportunities. Strategy improves decision making in several ways:

● It simplifies decision making by constraining the range of decision alternatives considered and acts as a *heuristic*—a rule of thumb that reduces the search required to find an acceptable solution to a decision problem.

● The strategy-making process permits the knowledge of different individuals to be pooled and integrated.

● It facilitates the use of analytic tools—the frameworks and techniques that we will encounter in the ensuing chapters of this book.

Strategy as a Coordinating Device   The central challenge of management is coordinating the actions of different organizational members. Strategy acts as a communication device to promote coordination. Statements of strategy are a means by which the CEO can communicate the identity, goals, and positioning of the company to all organizational members. The strategic planning process acts as a forum in which views are exchanged and consensus developed; once formulated, strategy can be translated into goals, commitments, and performance targets that ensure that the organization moves forward in a consistent direction.

Strategy as Target   Strategy is forward looking. It is concerned not only with how the firm will compete now but also with what the firm will become in the future. A key purpose of a forward-looking strategy is not only to establish a direction for the firm's development but also to set aspirations that can motivate and inspire members of the organization. Gary Hamel and C. K. Prahalad use the term **strategic intent** to describe this desired strategic position: "strategic intent creates an extreme misfit between resources and ambitions. Top management then challenges the organization to close the gap by building new competitive advantages."[21] The implication is that strategy should be less about fit and resource allocation and more about stretch and resource leverage.[22] Jim Collins and Jerry Porras make a similar point: US companies that have been sector leaders for 50 years or more—Merck, Walt Disney, 3M, IBM, and Ford—have all generated commitment and drive through setting "Big, Hairy, Ambitious Goals."[23] Striving, inspirational goals are found in most organizations' statements of vision and mission. One of the best known is that set by President Kennedy for NASA's space program: "before this decade is out, to land a man on the moon and return him safely to Earth." However, Richard Rumelt warns us not to confuse strategy with goal setting: "Strategy cannot be a useful … tool if it is confused with ambition, determination, inspirational leadership, and innovation … strategy should mean a cohesive response to an important challenge."[24]

Where Do We Find Strategy?

A company's strategy can be found in three places: in the heads of managers, in their articulations of strategy in speeches and written documents, and in the decisions through which strategy is enacted. Only the last two are observable.

Strategy has its origins in the thought processes of entrepreneurs and senior managers. For the entrepreneur the starting point of strategy is the idea for a new business. In most small companies, strategy remains in the heads of business proprietors: there is little need for any explicit statement of strategy. For large companies statements of strategy are found in board minutes and strategic planning documents, which are invariably confidential. However, most companies—public companies in particular—see value in communicating their strategy to employees, customers, investors, and business partners. Collis and Rukstad identify four types of statement through which companies communicate their strategies:

- The mission statement describes organizational purpose; it addresses "Why we exist."
- A statement of principles or values outlines "What we believe in and how we will behave."

- The vision statement projects "What we want to be."
- The strategy statement articulates the company's competitive game plan, which typically describe objectives, business scope, and advantage.[25]

These statements can be found on the corporate pages of companies' websites. More detailed statements of strategy—including qualitative and quantitative medium-term targets—are often found in top management presentations to analysts, which are typically included in the "for investors" pages of company websites.

Further information on a firm's business scope (products and its markets) and how it competes within these markets can be found in a company's annual reports. For US corporations, the description of the business that forms Item 1 of the 10-K annual report to the Securities and Exchange Commission (SEC) is particularly informative about strategy.

Strategy Capsule 1.5 provides statements of strategy by McDonald's, the global fast-food giant, and Twitter, the online messaging service.

Ultimately, strategy becomes enacted in the decisions and actions of an organization's members. Indeed, checking strategy statements against decisions and actions may reveal a gap between rhetoric and reality. As a reality check upon grandiose and platitudinous sentiments of vision and mission, it is useful to ask:

- Where is the company investing its money? Notes to financial statements provide detailed breakdowns of capital expenditure by region and by business segment.
- What technologies is the company developing? Identifying the patents that a company has filed (using the online databases of the US and EU patent offices) indicates the technological trajectory it is pursuing.
- What new products have been released, major investment projects initiated, and top management hired? These strategic decisions are typically announced in press releases and reported in trade journals.

To identify a firm's strategy it is necessary to draw upon multiple sources of information in order to build an overall picture of what the company says it is doing and what it is actually doing. We will return to this topic when we discuss *competitive intelligence* in Chapter 4.

Corporate and Business Strategy

Strategic choices can be distilled into two basic questions:

- Where to compete?
- How to compete?

The answers to these questions define the two major areas of a firm's strategy: **corporate strategy** and **business strategy**.

Corporate strategy defines the scope of the firm in terms of the industries and markets in which it competes. Corporate strategy decisions include choices over diversification, vertical integration, acquisitions, and new ventures, and the allocation of resources between the different businesses of the firm.

Statements of Company Strategy: McDonald's and Twitter

McDONALD'S CORPORATION

Our goal is to become customers' favorite place and way to eat and drink by serving core favorites such as our World Famous Fries, Big Mac, Quarter Pounder and Chicken McNuggets.

The strength of the alignment among the Company, its franchisees and suppliers (collectively referred to as the "System") has been key to McDonald's success. By leveraging our System, we are able to identify, implement and scale ideas that meet customers' changing needs and preferences.

McDonald's customer-focused Plan to Win ("Plan") provides a common framework that aligns our global business and allows for local adaptation. We continue to focus on our three global growth priorities of optimizing our menu, modernizing the customer experience, and broadening accessibility to Brand McDonald's within the framework of our Plan. Our initiatives support these priorities, and are executed with a focus on the Plan's five pillars—People, Products, Place, Price and Promotion—to enhance our customers' experience and build shareholder value over the long term. We believe these priorities align with our customers' evolving needs, and—combined with our competitive advantages of convenience, menu variety, geographic diversification and System alignment—will drive long-term sustainable growth.

Source: www.mcdonalds.com.

TWITTER, INC.

We have aligned our growth strategy around the three primary constituents of our platform:

Users. We believe that there is a significant opportunity to expand our user base…

- Geographic Expansion. We plan to develop a broad set of partnerships globally to increase relevant local content … and make Twitter more accessible in new and emerging markets.

- Mobile Applications. We plan to continue to develop and improve our mobile applications…

- Product Development. We plan to continue to build and acquire new technologies to develop and improve our products and services…

Platform Partners. We believe growth in our platform partners is complementary to our user growth strategy…

- Expand the Twitter Platform to Integrate More Content. We plan to continue to build and acquire new technologies to enable our platform partners to distribute content of all forms.

- Partner with Traditional Media … to drive more content distribution on our platform …

Advertisers … [I]ncrease the value of our platform for our advertisers by enhancing our advertising services and making our platform more accessible.

- Targeting. We plan to continue to improve the targeting capabilities of our advertising services.

- Opening our Platform to Additional Advertisers. We believe that advertisers outside of the United States represent a substantial opportunity …

- New Advertising Formats.

Source: Twitter, Inc. Amendment no. 4 to Form S-1, Registration Statement, SEC, November 4, 2013.

Business strategy is concerned with how the firm competes within a particular industry or market. If the firm is to prosper within an industry, it must establish a competitive advantage over its rivals. Hence, this area of strategy is also referred to as *competitive strategy*.

The distinction between corporate strategy and business strategy corresponds to the organizational structure of most large companies. Corporate strategy is the responsibility of corporate top management. Business strategy is primarily the responsibility of the senior managers of divisions and subsidiaries.

This distinction between corporate and business strategy also corresponds to the primary sources of superior profit for a firm. As we have noted, the purpose of strategy is to achieve superior performance. Basic to this is the need to survive and prosper, which in turn requires that over the long term the firm earn a rate of return on its capital that exceeds its cost of capital. There are two possible ways of achieving this. First, by choosing to locate within industries where overall rates of return are attractive (corporate strategy). Second, by attaining a position of advantage vis-à-vis competitors within an industry, allowing it to earn a return that exceeds the industry average (Figure 1.5).

This distinction may be expressed in even simpler terms. The basic question facing the firm is "How do we make money?" The answer to this question corresponds to the two basic strategic choices we identified above: "Where to compete?" ("In which industries and markets should we be?") and "How to compete?"

As an integrated approach to firm strategy, this book deals with both business and corporate strategy. However, my primary emphasis will be on business strategy. This is because the critical requirement for a company's success is its ability to establish competitive advantage. Hence, issues of business strategy precede those of corporate strategy. At the same time, these two dimensions of strategy are intertwined: the scope of a firm's business has implications for the sources of competitive advantage, and the nature of a firm's competitive advantage determines the industries and markets it can be successful in.

FIGURE 1.5   The sources of superior profitability

FIGURE 1.6 Describing firm strategy: Competing in the present, preparing for the future

Strategy as Positioning	**Strategy as Direction**

• *Where are we competing?*
  -Product market scope
  -Geographical scope
  -Vertical scope
• *How are we competing?*
  -What is the basis of our
  competitive advantage?
	• *What do we want to become?*
	  -Vision statement
	• *What do we want to achieve?*
	  -Mission statement
	  -Performance goals
	• *How will we get there?*
	  -Guidelines for development
	  -Priorities for capital expenditure,
	  R & D
	  -Growth modes: organic growth,
	  M & A, alliances

COMPETING FOR THE PRESENT	*PREPARING FOR THE FUTURE*

Describing Strategy

These same two questions—"Where is the firm competing?" and "How is it competing?"—also provide the basis upon which we can describe the strategy that a firm is pursuing. The *where* question has multiple dimensions. It relates to the products the firm supplies, the customers it serves, the countries and localities where it operates, and the vertical range of activities it undertakes.

However, strategy is not simply about "competing for today"; it is also concerned with "competing for tomorrow." This dynamic aspect of strategy involves establishing objectives for the future and determining how they will be achieved. Future objectives relate to the overall purpose of the firm (mission), what it seeks to become (vision), and how it will meet specific performance targets.

These two dimensions of strategy—the static and the dynamic—are depicted in Figure 1.6 and are illustrated by the Coca-Cola Company. As we shall see in Chapter 8, reconciling these two dimensions of strategy—what Derek Abell calls "competing with dual strategies"—is one of the central dilemmas of strategic management.[26]

How Is Strategy Made? The Strategy Process

How companies make strategy and how they should make strategy are among the most hotly debated issues in strategic management. The corporate planning undertaken by large companies during the 1960s was a highly formalized approach to strategy making. Strategy may also be made informally: emerging through adaptation to circumstances. In our opening discussion of Queen Elizabeth and Lady Gaga, I discerned a consistency and pattern to their career decisions that I identified as strategy, even though there is no evidence that either of them engaged in any systematic process of strategy formulation. Similarly, most successful companies are not products of grand designs. The rise of Apple Inc. to become the world's most valuable company (in terms of stock market capitalization) has often been attributed to a brilliant strategy of integrating hardware, software, and aesthetics to create consumer electronic products that offered a unique consumer experience. Yet, there is little evidence that Apple's incredible success since 2004 was the result of any grand design. Dick Rumelt reports when Steve Jobs was reappointed as Apple's CEO in 1997, his first actions were to cut costs, slash investment spending, and prune the product range. When asked in 1998 about his strategy for Apple, he replied: "I'm going to wait for the next big thing."[27]

Clearly, Apple's remarkable success since 2001 with its iPod, iPhone, and iPad was not the result of a preconceived plan. It was the outcome of a set of strategic decisions that combined penetrating insight into consumer preferences and technological trends with Apple's own design and development capabilities, and astute responses to unfolding circumstances.

So, what does this mean for strategy making by companies and other organizations? Should managers seek to formulate strategy through a rational systematic process, or is the best approach in a turbulent world to respond to events while maintaining some sense of direction in the form of goals and guidelines?

Design versus Emergence

Henry Mintzberg is a leading critic of rational approaches to strategy design. He distinguishes *intended*, *emergent*, and *realized* strategies. **Intended strategy** is strategy as conceived of by the leader or top management team. Even here, intended strategy may be less a product of rational deliberation and more an outcome of negotiation, bargaining, and compromise among the many individuals and groups involved in the strategy-making process. However, **realized strategy**—the actual strategy that is implemented—is only partly related to that which was intended (Mintzberg suggests only 10–30% of intended strategy is realized). The primary determinant of realized strategy is what Mintzberg terms **emergent strategy**—the decisions that emerge from the complex processes in which individual managers interpret the intended strategy and adapt to changing circumstances.[28]

According to Mintzberg, rational design is not only an inaccurate account of how strategies are actually formulated but also a poor way of making strategy: "The notion that strategy is something that should happen way up there, far removed from the details of running an organization on a daily basis, is one of the great fallacies of conventional strategic management."[29] The emergent approaches to strategy making permit adaptation and learning through a continuous interaction between strategy formulation and strategy implementation in which strategy is constantly being adjusted and revised in the light of experience.

The debate between those who view strategy making as a rational, analytical process of deliberate planning (the *design school*) and those who envisage strategy making as an emergent process (the *emergence* or *learning school* of strategy) has centered on the case of Honda's successful entry into the US motorcycle market during the early 1960s.[30] The Boston Consulting Group lauded Honda for its single-minded pursuit of a global strategy based on exploiting economies of scale and learning to establish unassailable cost leadership.[31] However, subsequent interviews with the Honda managers in charge of its US market entry revealed a different story: a haphazard, experimental approach with little analysis and no clear plan.[32] As Mintzberg observes: "Brilliant as its strategy may have looked after the fact, Honda's managers made almost every conceivable mistake until the market finally hit them over the head with the right formula."[33]

In practice, strategy making involves both thought and action: "Strategy exists in the cognition of managers but also is reified in what companies do."[34] This is typically through a process in which top-down rational design is combined with decentralized adaptation. The design aspect of strategy comprises a number of organizational processes through which strategy is deliberated, discussed, and decided. In larger companies these include board meetings and a formalized process of strategic planning supplemented by more broadly participative events, such as strategy workshops. I will discuss processes of strategic planning more fully in Chapter 6.

At the same time, strategy is being continually enacted through decisions that are made by every member of the organization—by middle managers especially. The decentralized, bottom-up process of strategy emergence often precedes more formalized top-down strategy formulation. Intel's historic decision to abandon memory chips and concentrate on microprocessors was initiated in the decisions taken by business unit and plant managers that were subsequently promulgated by top management as strategy.[35]

In all the companies I am familiar with, strategy making combines design and emergence—a process that I have referred to as "planned emergence."[36] The balance between the two depends greatly upon the stability and predictability of the organization's business environment. The Roman Catholic Church and La Poste, the French postal service, inhabit relatively stable environments; they can plan activities and resource allocations in some detail quite far into the future. For WikiLeaks, Credit Bank of Iraq, or Somali pirate gangs, strategic planning will inevitably be restricted to a few guidelines; most strategic decisions must be responses to unfolding circumstances.

As the business environment becomes more turbulent and less predictable, so strategy making becomes less about detailed decisions and more about guidelines and general direction. Bain & Company advocates the use of strategic principles—"pithy, memorable distillations of strategy that guide and empower employees"—to combine consistent focus with adaptability and responsiveness.[37] McDonald's strategy statement in Strategy Capsule 1.5 is an example of such strategic principles. Similarly, Southwest Airlines encapsulates its strategy in a simple statement: "Meet customers' short-haul travel needs at fares competitive with the cost of automobile travel." For fast-moving businesses, strategy may be little more than a set of "simple rules." For example, Lego evaluates new product proposals by applying a checklist of rules: "Does the product have the Lego look?" "Will children learn while having fun?" "Does it stimulate creativity?"[38]

We shall return to the role of rules and principles to guide an organization's evolution and coordination in our final chapter, where we explore some of the implications of complexity theory for strategic management.

The Role of Analysis in Strategy Formulation

Despite the criticism of rational, analytical approaches to strategy formulation by Henry Mintzberg and others, the approach of this book is to emphasize analytic approaches to strategy formulation. This is not because I wish to downplay the role of intuition, creativity, or spontaneity—these qualities are essential ingredients of successful strategies. Nevertheless, whether strategy formulation is formal or informal, whether strategies are deliberate or emergent, systematic analysis is a vital input into the strategy process. Without analysis, strategic decisions are susceptible to power battles, individual whims, fads, and wishful thinking. Concepts, theories, and analytic tools are complements of, and not substitutes for, intuition and creativity. Their role is to provide frameworks for organizing discussion, processing information, and developing consensus.

This is not to endorse current approaches to strategy analysis. Strategic management is still a young field and the existing toolbox of concepts and techniques remains woefully inadequate. Our challenge is to do better. If existing analytical techniques do not adequately address the problems of strategy making and strategy implementation under conditions of uncertainty, technological change, and complexity, we need to augment and extend our strategy toolkits. In the course of this book, you will encounter concepts such as *real options, tacit knowledge, hypercompetition, complementarity,* and *complexity* that will help you address more effectively the challenges that firms are facing in today's turbulent business environment. We must also recognize the role and the limitations of strategy analysis. Unlike many of the analytical techniques in accounting, finance, market research, or production management, strategy analysis does not generate solutions to problems. It does not offer algorithms or formulae that tell us the optimal strategy to adopt. The strategic questions that companies face (like those that we face in our own careers and lives) are simply too complex to be programmed.

The purpose of strategy analysis is not to provide answers but to help us understand the issues. Most of the analytic techniques introduced in this book are frameworks that allow us to identify, classify, and understand the principal factors relevant to strategic decisions. Such frameworks are invaluable in allowing us to come to terms with the complexities of strategy decisions. In some instances, the most useful contribution may be in assisting us to make a start on the problem. By guiding us to the questions we need to answer and by providing a framework for organizing the information gathered, strategy analysis places us in a superior position to a manager who relies exclusively on experience and intuition. Finally, analytic frameworks and techniques can improve our flexibility as managers. The concepts and frameworks we shall cover are not specific to particular industries, companies, or situations. Hence, they can help increase our confidence and effectiveness in understanding and responding to new situations and new circumstances.

Applying Strategy Analysis

So, how do we go about applying our tools of strategy analysis in a systematic and productive way that allows us to make sound strategy recommendations?

Inevitably, the procedure we follow depends upon the situation being addressed—in particular whether we are developing a strategy for a firm as a whole or making a specific strategic decision: acquiring a competitor, entering a foreign market, or outsourcing manufacturing. Let us consider a typical strategy situation that we shall encounter, either as students tackling a strategy case study or as consultants on a client engagement: recommending a business strategy.[39]

Let us consider the principal steps of such an analysis (which are displayed in Figure 1.7):

FIGURE 1.7 Applying strategy analysis

1 *Identify the current strategy.* Assuming we are dealing with an existing business, as opposed to a new venture, the first task is to identify the current strategy of the business (drawing upon the sections above on "Where do We Find Strategy?" and "Describing Strategy").

2 *Appraise performance.* How well is the current strategy performing? In the next chapter we shall consider the use of financial analysis to measure firm performance.

3 *Diagnose performance.* Having determined the level and trend of the firm's performance, the next challenge is *diagnosis*: in the case of poor performance, can we use a combination of financial and strategic analysis to determine the sources of unsatisfactory performance? In the case of good performance, can we identify the factors driving this? As Dick Rumelt observes, the core question in most strategy situations is: "What's going on here?"[40] Chapter 2 offers guidance on such diagnosis.

4 *Industry analysis.* Analyzing the fit between strategy and the firm's industry environment is a fundamental input into both diagnosing recent performance and generating future strategic options. Chapters 3 and 4 address industry analysis.

5 *Analysis of resources and capabilities.* Equivalently, analyzing the fit between strategy and the firm's resources and capabilities is a fundamental input into both diagnosing recent performance and generating future strategic options. Chapter 5 describes the analysis of resources and capabilities.

6 *Formulate strategy.* Performance diagnosis, industry analysis, and the analysis of resources and capabilities provide a basis for generating strategic options for the future, the most promising of which can be developed into a recommended strategy. Chapter 7 outlines how the intersection of internal strengths and external success factors combine to offer a basis for competitive advantage.

7 *Implement strategy.* Executing the chosen strategy requires linking the strategy to performance goals and resource allocations and establishing appropriate organizational structure and management systems. Chapter 6 outlines how this can be done.

Strategic Management of Not-For-Profit Organizations

When strategic management meant top-down, long-range planning, there was little distinction between business corporations and not-for-profit organizations: the techniques of forecast-based planning applied equally to both. As strategic management has become increasingly oriented toward the identification and exploitation of sources of profit, it has become more closely identified with for-profit organizations. So, can the concepts and tools of corporate and business strategy be applied to not-for-profit organizations?

The short answer is yes. Strategy is as important in not-for-profit organizations as it is in business firms. The benefits I have attributed to strategic management in terms of improved decision making, achieving coordination, and setting performance targets (see the section "Why Do Firms Need Strategy?" above) may be even more important in the non-profit sector. Moreover, many of the same concepts and tools of strategic analysis are readily applicable to not-for-profits—albeit with some adaptation. However, the not-for-profit sector encompasses a vast range of organizations. Both the nature of strategic planning and the appropriate tools for strategy analysis differ among these organizations.

The basic distinction here is between those not-for-profits that operate in competitive environments (most non-governmental, non-profit organizations) and those that do not (most government departments and government agencies). Among the not-for-profits that inhabit competitive environments we may distinguish between those that charge for the services they provide (most private schools, non-profit-making private hospitals, social and sports clubs, etc.) and those that provide their services free—most charities and NGOs (non-governmental organizations). Table 1.2 summarizes some key differences between each of these organizations with regard to the applicability of the basic tools of strategy analysis.

TABLE 1.2 The applicability of the concepts and tools of strategic analysis to different types of not-for-profit organizations

	Organizations in competitive environments that charge users	Organizations in competitive environments that provide free services	Organizations sheltered from competition
Examples	Royal Opera House Guggenheim Museum Stanford University	Salvation Army Habitat for Humanity Greenpeace Linux	UK Ministry of Defence European Central Bank New York Police Department World Health Organization
Analysis of goals and performance	Identification of mission, goals, and performance indicators and establishing consistency between them is a critical area of strategy analysis for all not-for-profits		
Analysis of the competitive environment	Main tools of competitive analysis are the same as for for-profit firms	Main arena for competition and competitive strategy is the market for funding	Not important. However, there is interagency competition for public funding
Analysis of resources and capabilities	Identifying and exploiting distinctive resources and capabilities critical to designing strategies that confer competitive advantage		Analysis of resources and capabilities essential for determining priorities and designing strategies
Strategy implementation	The basic principles of organizational design, performance management, and leadership are common to all organizational types		

Among the tools of strategy analysis that are applicable to all types of not-for-profit organizations, those which relate to the role of strategy in specifying organizational goals and linking goals to resource-allocation decisions are especially important. For businesses, profit is always a key goal since it ensures survival and fuels development. But for not-for-profits, goals are typically complex. The mission of Harvard University is to "create knowledge, to open the minds of students to that knowledge, and to enable students to take best advantage of their educational opportunities." But how are these multiple objectives to be reconciled in practice? How should Harvard's budget be allocated between research and financial aid for students? Is Harvard's mission better served by investing in graduate or undergraduate education? The strategic planning process of not-for-profits needs to be designed so that mission, goals, resource allocation, and performance targets are closely aligned. Strategy Capsule 1.6 shows the strategic planning framework for the US State Department.

STRATEGY CAPSULE 1.6
US State Department Strategic Plan, 2014–2018

MISSION

Shape and sustain a peaceful, prosperous, just, and democratic world, and foster conditions for stability and progress for the benefit of the American people and people everywhere.

STRATEGIC GOALS

SG 1: Strengthen America's economic reach and positive economic impact

SG 2: Strengthen America's foreign policy impact on our strategic challenges

SG 3: Promote the transition to a low-emission, climate-resilient world while expanding global access to sustainable energy

SG 4: Protect core US interests by advancing democracy and human rights and strengthening civil society

SG 5: Modernize the way we do diplomacy and development

OPERATIONALIZING THE GOALS

These strategic goals were further specified into a set of strategic objectives which were then translated into specific performance goals. For example, SG3's strategic objectives included: "Building on strong domestic action, lead international actions to combat climate change." The corresponding performance goal was: "By September 30, 2015, US bilateral assistance under Low Emission Development Strategies (LEDS) will reach at least 25 countries and will result in the achievement of at least 45 major individual country milestones, each reflecting a significant, measureable improvement in a country's development or implementation of LEDS. Also by the end of 2015, at least 1200 additional developing country government officials and practitioners will strengthen their LEDS capacity through participation in the LEDS Global Partnership..."

Source: US Department of State and US Agency for International Development, *Strategic Plan for Fiscal Years 2014–2018*.

Similarly, most of the principles and tools of strategy implementation—especially in relation to organizational structure, management systems, techniques of performance management, and choice of leadership styles—are common to both for-profit and not-for-profit organizations.

In terms of the analysis of the external environment, there is little difference between the techniques of industry analysis applied to business enterprises and those relevant to not-for-profits that inhabit competitive environments and charge for their services. In many markets (theaters, sports clubs, vocational training) for-profits and not-for-profits may be in competition with one another. Indeed, for these types of not-for-profit organizations, the pressing need to break even in order to survive may mean that their strategies do not differ significantly from those of for-profit firms.

In the case of not-for-profits that do not charge users for the services they offer (mostly charities), competition does not really exist at the final market level: different homeless shelters in San Francisco cannot really be said to be competing for the homeless. However, these organizations compete for funding—raising donations from individuals, winning grants from foundations, or obtaining contracts from funding agencies. Competing in the market for funding is a key area of strategy for most not-for-profits.

The analysis of resources and capabilities is important to all organizations that inhabit competitive environments and must deploy their internal resources and capabilities to establish a competitive advantage; however, even for those organizations that are monopolists—many government departments and other public agencies—performance is enhanced by aligning strategy with internal strengths in resources and capabilities.

Summary

This chapter has covered a great deal of ground—I hope that you are not suffering from indigestion. If you are feeling a little overwhelmed, not to worry: we shall be returning to the themes and issues raised in this chapter in the subsequent chapters of this book.

The key lessons from this chapter are:

◆ Strategy is a key ingredient of success both for individuals and organizations. A sound strategy cannot guarantee success, but it can improve the odds. Successful strategies tend to embody four elements: clear, long-term goals; profound understanding of the external environment; astute appraisal of internal resources and capabilities; and effective implementation.

◆ The above four elements form the primary components of strategy analysis: goals, industry analysis, analysis of resources and capabilities, and strategy implementation through the design of structures and systems.

◆ Strategy is no longer concerned with detailed planning based upon forecasts; it is increasingly about direction, identity, and exploiting the sources of superior profitability.

◆ To describe the strategy of a firm (or any other type of organization) we need to recognize where the firm is competing, how it is competing, and the direction in which it is developing.

◆ Developing a strategy for an organization requires a combination of purpose-led planning (rational design) and a flexible response to changing circumstances (emergence).

◆ The principles and tools of strategic management have been developed primarily for business enterprises; however, they are also applicable to the strategic management of not-for-profit organizations, especially those that inhabit competitive environments.

Our next stage is to delve further into the basic strategy framework shown in Figure 1.2. The elements of this framework—goals and values, the industry environment, resources and capabilities, and structure and systems—are the subjects of the five chapters that form Part II of the book. We then deploy these tools to analyze the quest for competitive advantages in different industry contexts (Part III), and then in the development of corporate strategy (Part IV). Figure 1.8 shows the framework for the book.

FIGURE 1.8   The structure of the book

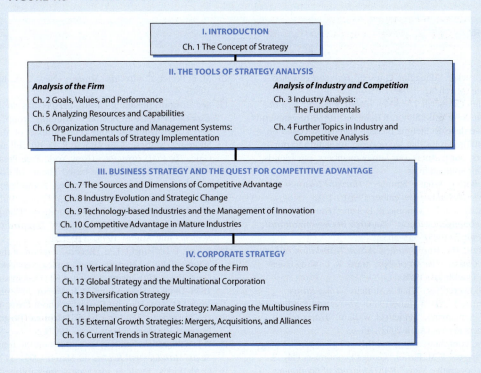

Self-Study Questions

1. In relation to the four characteristics of successful strategies in Figure 1.1, assess the US government's Middle East strategy during 2009–2015.

2. The discussion of the evolution of business strategy (see the section "From Corporate Planning to Strategic Management") established that the characteristics of a firm's strategic plans and its

strategic planning process are strongly influenced by the volatility and unpredictability of its external environment. On this basis, what differences would you expect in the strategic plans and strategic planning processes of Coca-Cola Company and Uber Technologies Inc.?

3. I have noted that a firm's strategy can be described in terms of the answers to two questions: "Where are we competing?" and "How are we competing?" Applying these two questions, provide a concise description of Lady Gaga's career strategy (see Strategy Capsule 1.2).

4. Using the framework of Figure 1.6, describe the strategy of the university or school you attend.

5. What is your career strategy for the next five years? To what extent does your strategy fit with your long-term goals, the characteristics of the external environment, and your own strengths and weaknesses?

Notes

1. P. F. Drucker, "Managing Oneself," *Harvard Business Review* (March/April 1999): 65–74.
2. Stephen Covey (in *The Seven Habits of Highly Effective People*, New York: Simon & Schuster, 1989) recommends that we develop lifetime mission statements based on the multiple roles that we occupy: in relation to our careers, our partners, our family members, our friends, and our spiritual lives.
3. M. E. Porter, "What is Strategy?" *Harvard Business Review* (November/December 1996): 61–78.
4. See A. H. Van De Ven and R. Drazin,' "The concept of fit in contingency theory" *Research in Organizational Behavior* 7 (1985): 333–365.
5. Sun Tzu, *The Art of Strategy: A New Translation of Sun Tzu's Classic "The Art of War,"* trans. R. L. Wing (New York: Doubleday, 1988).
6. See R. Evered, "So What Is Strategy?" *Long Range Planning* 16, no. 3 (June 1983): 57–72; and E. Clemons and J. Santamaria, "Maneuver Warfare," *Harvard Business Review* (April 2002): 46–53.
7. On the contribution of game theory to business strategy analysis, see F. M. Fisher, "Games Economists Play: A Non-cooperative View," *RAND Journal of Economics* 20 (Spring 1989): 113–124; C. F. Camerer, "Does Strategy Research Need Game Theory?" *Strategic Management Journal* 12 (Winter 1991): 137–152; A. K. Dixit and B. J. Nalebuff, *The Art of Strategy: A Game Theorist's Guide to Success in Business and Life* (New York: W. W. Norton, 2008).
8. For example, D. W. Ewing, "Looking Around: Long-range Business Planning," *Harvard Business Review* (July/August 1956): 135–146; and B. Payne, "Steps in Long-range Planning," *Harvard Business Review* (March/April 1957): 95–101.
9. H. I. Ansoff, "Strategies for diversification," *Harvard Business Review* (September/October, 1957): 113–124.
10. M. E. Porter, *Competitive Strategy* (New York: Free Press, 1980).
11. See Boston Consulting Group, *Perspectives on Experience* (Boston: Boston Consulting Group, 1978) and studies using the PIMS (Profit Impact of Market Strategy) database, for example R. D. Buzzell and B. T. Gale, *The PIMS Principles* (New York: Free Press, 1987).
12. R. M. Grant, "The Resource-based Theory of Competitive Advantage: Implications for Strategy Formulation," *California Management Review* 33 (Spring 1991): 114–135; D. J. Collis and C. Montgomery, "Competing on Resources: Strategy in the 1990s," *Harvard Business Review* (July/August 1995): 119–128.
13. E. Lee, J. Lee, and J. Lee, "Reconsideration of the Winner-Take-All Hypothesis: Complex Networks and Local Bias," *Management Science* 52 (December 2006): 1838–1848; C. Shapiro and H. R. Varian, *Information Rules* (Boston: Harvard Business School Press, 1998).
14. C. Christensen, *The Innovator's Dilemma* (Boston: Harvard Business School Press, 1997).
15. P. J. Williamson, "Strategy as options on the future," *Sloan Management Review* 40 (March 1999): 117–126.
16. C. Markides, "Strategic innovation in established companies," *Sloan Management Review* (June 1998): 31–42.
17. W. C. Kim and R. Mauborgne, "Creating new market space," *Harvard Business Review* (January/February 1999): 83–93.
18. See, for example, N. Koehn, "The Brain—and Soul—of Capitalism." *Harvard Business Review*, November 2013; and T. Piketty, *Capital in the Twenty-First Century* (Cambridge, MA: Harvard University Press, 2014).
19. "Strategic Intensity: A Conversation with Garry Kasparov," *Harvard Business Review* (April 2005): 105–113.
20. The concept of bounded rationality was developed by Herbert Simon ("A Behavioral Model of Rational

Choice," *Quarterly Journal of Economics* 69 (1955): 99–118.

21. G. Hamel and C. K. Prahalad, "Strategic Intent," *Harvard Business Review* (May/June 1989): 63–77.
22. G. Hamel and C. K. Prahalad, "Strategy as Stretch and Leverage," *Harvard Business Review* (March/April 1993): 75–84.
23. J. C. Collins and J. I. Porras, *Built to Last: Successful Habits of Visionary Companies* (New York: HarperCollins, 1995).
24. R. Rumelt, *Good Strategy/Bad Strategy: The Difference and Why it Matters* (New York: Crown Business, 2011): 5–6.
25. D. J. Collis and M. G. Rukstad, "Can You Say What Your Strategy Is?" *Harvard Business Review* (April 2008): 63–73.
26. D. F. Abell, *Managing with Dual Strategies* (New York: Free Press, 1993).
27. Rumelt, op cit.: 14.
28. H. Mintzberg, "Patterns of Strategy Formulation," *Management Science* 24 (1978): 934–948; "Of Strategies: Deliberate and Emergent," *Strategic Management Journal* 6 (1985): 257–272.
29. H. Mintzberg, "The Fall and Rise of Strategic Planning," *Harvard Business Review* (January/February 1994): 107–114.
30. The two views of Honda are captured in two Harvard cases: Honda [A] and [B] (Boston: Harvard Business School, Cases 384049 and 384050, 1989).
31. Boston Consulting Group, *Strategy Alternatives for the British Motorcycle Industry* (London: Her Majesty's Stationery Office, 1975).
32. R. T. Pascale, "Perspective on Strategy: The Real Story Behind Honda's Success," *California Management Review* 26, no. 3 (Spring 1984): 47–72.
33. H. Mintzberg, "Crafting Strategy," *Harvard Business Review* (July/August 1987): 70.
34. G. Gavetti and J. Rivkin, "On the origin of strategy: Action and cognition over time." *Organization Science*, 18, 420–439.
35. R. A. Burgelman and A. Grove, "Strategic Dissonance," *California Management Review* 38 (Winter 1996): 8–28.
36. R. M. Grant, "Strategic Planning in a Turbulent Environment: Evidence from the Oil and Gas Majors," *Strategic Management Journal* 14 (June 2003): 491–517.
37. O. Gadiesh and J. Gilbert, "Transforming Corner-office Strategy into Frontline Action," *Harvard Business Review* (May 2001): 73–80.
38. K. M. Eisenhardt and D. N. Sull, "Strategy as Simple Rules," *Harvard Business Review* (January 2001): 107–116.
39. A similar, but more detailed, approach is proposed by Markus Venzin. See M. Venzin, C. Rasner, and V. Mahnke, *The Strategy Process: A Practical Handbook for Implementation in Business* (Cyan, 2005).
40. Rumelt, op cit., 79.

II

THE TOOLS
OF STRATEGY
ANALYSIS

2 Goals, Values, and Performance

> The strategic aim of a business is to earn a return on capital, and if in any particular case the return in the long run is not satisfactory, then the deficiency should be corrected or the activity abandoned for a more favorable one.
>
> —ALFRED P. SLOAN JR., PRESIDENT AND THEN CHAIRMAN OF GENERAL MOTORS, 1923 TO 1956.[1]

> Profits are to business as breathing is to life. Breathing is essential to life, but is not the purpose for living. Similarly, profits are essential for the existence of the corporation, but they are not the reason for its existence.
>
> —DENNIS BAKKE, FOUNDER AND FORMER CEO, AES CORPORATION

OUTLINE

Introduction and Objectives

Our framework for strategy analysis (Figure 1.2) comprises four components: the firm's goals and values, its resources and capabilities, its structure and management systems, and its industry environment. The chapters that form Part II of this book develop these four components of strategy analysis. We begin with goals and values of the firm and, by extension, the performance of the firm in attaining its goals.

As the opening quotations to this chapter indicate, there is fierce debate over the appropriate goals for business enterprises. In this chapter we will consider the extent to which the firm should pursue the interests of its owners, of its stakeholders, and of society as a whole. Our approach will be pragmatic. While acknowledging that firms pursue multiple goals and that each possesses a unique purpose, we focus upon a single goal: the quest for value. This I interpret as the pursuit of profit over the lifetime of the firm. Hence, the focus of our strategy analysis is upon concepts and techniques that are concerned with identifying and exploiting the sources of profitability available to the firm. Our emphasis on profitability and value creation allows us to draw upon the tools of financial analysis for the purposes of performance appraisal, performance diagnosis, and target setting.

Although profitability is the most useful indicator of firm performance, we shall acknowledge that firms are motivated by goals other than profit. Indeed, the pursuit of these alternative goals may be conducive to a superior generation of profit. Profit may be the lifeblood of the enterprise, but it is not a goal that inspires organizational members to outstanding achievement. Moreover, for a firm to survive and generate profit over the long run requires responsiveness and adaptability to its social, political, and natural environments.

By the time you have completed this chapter, you will be able to:

◆ Recognize that, while every firm has a distinct purpose, the common goal for all firms is creating value, and appreciate how the debate over shareholder versus stakeholder goals involves different definitions of value creation.

◆ Understand how profit, cash flow, and enterprise value relate to one another.

◆ Use the tools of financial analysis to appraise firm performance, diagnose the sources of performance problems, and set performance targets.

◆ Appreciate how a firm's values, principles, and pursuit of corporate social responsibility can help define its strategy and support its creation of value.

◆ Understand how real options contribute to firm value and how options thinking can contribute to strategy analysis.

Strategy as a Quest for Value

There is more to business than making money. For the entrepreneurs who create business enterprises, personal wealth appears to be a less important motivation than the wish for autonomy, the desire for achievement, and lust for excitement. Over 80 years ago, the economist Joseph Schumpeter observed: "The entrepreneur–innovator's motivation includes such aspects as the dream to found a private kingdom, the will to conquer and to succeed for the sake of success itself, and the joy of creating and getting things done."[2] Business enterprises are creative organizations which offer individuals unsurpassed opportunity to make a difference in the world. Certainly, making money was not the goal that inspired Henry Ford to build a business that precipitated a social revolution:

> I will build a motor car for the great multitude … It will be so low in price that no man making good wages will be unable to own one and to enjoy with his family the blessing of hours of pleasure in God's great open spaces … When I'm through, everyone will be able to afford one, and everyone will have one.[3]

Each entrepreneur is inspired by a goal that is personal and unique—family cars for the multitude (Henry Ford), bringing the power of personal computing to the individual (Steve Jobs), reducing deaths from infection after surgery (Johnson & Johnson), or revolutionizing vacuum cleaning (James Dyson). In the case of established companies, Cynthia Montgomery argues that "forging a compelling organizational purpose" is the ongoing job of company leaders and the "crowning responsibility of the CEO."[4] Organizational purpose is articulated in companies' statements of mission and vision:

- Google's mission is "to organize the world's information and make it universally accessible and useful."
- "The IKEA vision is to create a better everyday life for the many people. We make this possible by offering a wide range of well-designed, functional home furnishing products at prices so low that as many people as possible will be able to afford them."
- The Lego Group's mission is "To inspire and develop the builders of tomorrow."

Within this vast variety of organizational purposes, there is a common denominator: the desire, and the need, to create value. Value is the monetary worth of a product or asset. Hence, we can generalize by saying that the purpose of business is, first, to create value for customers and, second, to appropriate some of that customer value in the form of profit—thereby creating value for the firm.

Value can be created in two ways: by production and by commerce. Production creates value by physically transforming products that are less valued by consumers into products that are more valued by consumers—turning coffee beans and milk into cappuccinos, for example. Commerce creates value not by physically transforming products but by repositioning them in space and time. Trade involves transferring products from individuals and locations where they are less valued to individuals and locations where they are more valued. Similarly, speculation involves transferring products from a point in time where a product is valued less to a point in time where it is valued more. Thus, commerce creates value through arbitrage across time and space.[5]

How can this value creation be measured? **Value added**—the difference between the value of a firm's output and the cost of its material inputs—is one measure. Value added is equal to the sum of all the income paid to the suppliers of factors of production. Thus:

$$\text{Value Added} = \text{Sales revenue from output} - \text{Cost of material inputs}$$
$$= \text{Wages/Salaries} + \text{Interest} + \text{Rent} + \text{Royalties/License fees}$$
$$+ \text{Taxes} + \text{Dividends} + \text{Retained profit}$$

However, value added typically understates a firm's value creation since consumers normally pay less for the goods and services they buy than the value they derive from these purchases (i.e., they derive **consumer surplus**).

Value for Whom? Shareholders versus Stakeholders

The value created by firms is distributed among different parties: employees (wages and salaries), lenders (interest), landlords (rent), government (taxes), owners (profit) and customers (consumer surplus). It is tempting, therefore, to think of the firm as operating for the benefit of multiple constituencies. This view of the business enterprise as a coalition of interest groups where top management's role is to balance these different—often conflicting—interests is referred to as the **stakeholder approach to the firm**.[6]

The idea that the corporation should balance the interests of multiple stakeholders has a long tradition, especially in Asia and continental Europe. By contrast, most English-speaking countries have endorsed shareholder capitalism, where companies' overriding duty is to produce profits for owners. These differences are reflected in international differences in companies' legal obligations. In the US, Canada, the UK, and Australia, company boards are required to act in the interests of shareholders. In most continental European countries, companies are legally required to take account of the interests of employees, the state, and the enterprise as a whole.[7]

There is an ongoing debate as to whether companies should operate exclusively in the interests of their owners or should also pursue the goals of multiple stakeholders. During the late 20th century, "Anglo-Saxon" shareholder capitalism was in the ascendant—many continental European and Asian companies changed their strategies and **corporate governance** to give primacy to shareholder interests. However, during the 21st century, shareholder value maximization has become tainted by its association with short-termism, financial manipulation, excessive CEO compensation, and the failures of risk management that precipitated the 2008–2009 financial crisis.

Clearly, companies have legal and ethical responsibilities to employees, customers, society, and the natural environment, but should companies go beyond these responsibilities and manage their businesses in the interests of these diverse stakeholders? While the concept of the firm operating in the interests of all their stakeholders is inherently appealing, in practice the stakeholder approach encounters two serious difficulties:

1 *Measuring performance.* In principle pursuing stakeholder interests means maximizing the value created for all stakeholders. In practice, estimating such value creation is impossible.[8] Hence, managing for stakeholders requires specifying the goals of each stakeholder group then establishing tradeoffs among them. According to Michael Jensen: "multiple objectives is no objective."[9]

2 *Corporate governance.* If top management is charged to pursue and balance the interests of different stakeholders, how can management's performance be assessed and by whom? Does it imply that boards of directors must comprise the representatives of every stakeholder group? The resulting conflicts, political wrangling, and vagueness around performance objectives is likely to place top management in a good position to substitute its own interests for those of stakeholders.

To simplify our analysis of strategy formulation I make the assumption that the primary goal of strategy is to maximize the value of the enterprise through seeking to maximize profits over the long term. Having extolled the virtues of business enterprises as creative institutions, how can I rationalize this unedifying focus on money making? I have three justifications:

- *Competition*: Competition erodes profitability. As competition increases, the interests of different stakeholders converge around the goal of survival. To survive a firm must over the long term, earn a rate of profit that covers its cost of capital; otherwise, it will not be able to replace its assets. When weak demand and fierce international competition depress return on capital, few companies have the luxury of sacrificing profits for other goals.
- *Threat of acquisition*: Management teams that fail to maximize the profits of their companies tend to be replaced by teams that do. In the "market for corporate control," companies that underperform financially suffer a declining share price, which attracts acquirers—both other public companies and private equity funds. Despite the admirable record of British chocolate maker Cadbury in relation to employees and local communities, its dismal return to shareholders between 2004 and 2009 meant that it was unable to resist acquisition by Kraft Foods. In addition, activist investors—both individuals and institutions—pressure boards of directors to dismiss CEOs who fail to create value for shareholders.[10]
- *Convergence of stakeholder interests*: There is likely to be more community of interests than conflict of interests among different stakeholders. Profitability over the long term requires loyalty from employees, trusting relationships with suppliers and customers, and support from governments and communities. Indeed, the instrumental theory of stakeholder management argues that pursuit of stakeholder interests is essential to creating competitive advantage, which in turn leads to superior financial performance.[11] Empirical evidence shows that firms which take account of a broader set of interests, including that of society, achieve superior financial performance.[12]

Hence, the issue of whether firms should operate in the interests of shareholders or of all stakeholders matters more in principle than in practice. According to Jensen:

"enlightened shareholder value maximization … is identical to enlightened stake-holder theory." We shall return to this issue later in this chapter when we consider explicitly the social and environmental responsibilities of firms.

What Is Profit?

Thus far, I have referred to firms' quest for profit in general terms. It is time to look more carefully at what we mean by **profit** and how it relates to value creation.

Profit is the surplus of revenues over costs available for distribution to the owners of the firm. But if profit maximization is to be a realistic goal, the firm must know what profit is and how to measure it; otherwise, instructing managers to maximize profit offers little guidance. What is the firm to maximize: total profit or rate of profit? Over what period? With what kind of adjustment for risk? And what is profit any-way—accounting profit, cash flow, or economic profit? These ambiguities become apparent once we compare the profit performance of companies. Table 2.1 shows that ranking companies by profitability depends critically on what profitability mea-sure is used.

Accounting Profit and Economic Profit

A major problem of *accounting profit* is that it combines two types of returns: the nor-mal return to capital, which rewards investors for the use of their capital, and **economic profit**, which is the surplus available after all inputs (including capital) have been paid for. Economic profit is a purer measure of profit which is a more precise measure of a firm's ability to generate surplus value. To distinguish economic profit from accounting profit, economic profit is often referred to as *rent* or *economic rent*.

TABLE 2.1 Profitability measures for some of the world's largest companies, 2014

Company	Market capitalization[a] ($ billion)	Net income ($ billion)	ROS[b] (%)	ROE[c] (%)	ROA[d] (%)	Return to shareholders[e] (%)
Apple	750	14.0	29.7	35.2	24.5	+68.5
ExxonMobil	354	30.5	12.5	27.6	17.6	−6.9
Wal-Mart Stores, Inc.	278	16.0	5.5	20.4	13.1	+2.6
Industrial & Commercial Bank of China	270	22.9	56.6	20.5	1.6	+12.3
General Electric	254	15.2	12.1	11.9	2.7	−3.4
JPMorgan Chase	222	21.8	31.6	9.8	1.2	+2.7
Volkswagen	118	11.8	6.3	12.3	3.6	+8.4

Notes:
[a]Shares outstanding × closing price of shares on February 18, 2015.
[b]Return on sales = Operating profit as a percentage of sales revenues.
[c]Return on equity = Net income as a percentage of year-end shareholder equity.
[d]Return on assets = Operating income as a percentage of year-end total assets.
[e]Dividend + share price appreciation during 2014.

STRATEGY CAPSULE 2.1
Economic Value Added at Diageo plc.

At Guinness-to-Johnny-Walker drinks giant Diageo, EVA transformed the way in which Diageo measured its performance, allocated its capital and advertising expenditures, and evaluated its managers.

Taking account of the costs of the capital tied up in slow-maturing, vintage drinks such as Talisker and Lagavulin malt whisky, Hennessey cognac, and Dom Perignon champagne showed that these high-margin drinks were often not as profitable as the company had believed. The result was that Diageo's advertising expenditures were reallocated toward Smirnoff vodka, Gordon's gin, Baileys, and other drinks that could be sold within weeks of distillation.

Once managers had to report profits after deduction of the cost of the capital tied up in their businesses, they took measures to reduce their capital bases and make their assets work harder. At Diageo's Pillsbury food business, the economic profit of every product and every major customer was scrutinized. The result was the elimination of many products and efforts to make marginal customers more profitable. Ultimately, EVA analysis resulted in Diageo selling Pillsbury to General Foods. This was followed by the sale of Diageo's Burger King chain to Texas Pacific, a private equity group.

Value-based management was extended throughout the organization by making EVA the primary determinant of the incentive pay earned by 1400 Diageo managers.

Sources: John McGrath, "Tracking Down Value," *Financial Times Mastering Management Review* (December 1998); www.diageo.com.

A widely used measure of economic profit is **economic value added (EVA)**, devised and popularized by the consulting firm Stern Stewart & Company.[13] Economic value added is measured as follows:

$$\text{EVA} = \text{Net operating profit after tax (NOPAT)} - \text{Cost of capital}$$

where,

$$\text{Cost of capital} = \text{Capital employed} \times \text{Weighted average cost of capital (WACC)}$$

Economic profit has two main advantages over accounting profit as a performance measure. First, it sets a more demanding performance discipline for managers. At many capital-intensive companies seemingly healthy profits disappear once cost of capital is taken into account. Second, it improves the allocation of capital between the different businesses of the firm by taking account of the real costs of more capital-intensive businesses (Strategy Capsule 2.1).

Linking Profit to Enterprise Value

There is also the problem of time. Once we consider multiple periods of time, then profit maximization means maximizing the net present value of the stream of profits over the lifetime of the firm.

Hence, profit maximization translates into maximizing the value of the firm. The value of the firm is calculated in the same way as any other asset: it is the *net present value* (NPV) of the returns that the asset generates. The relevant returns are the cash flows to the firm. Hence, firms are valued using the same *discounted cash flow* (DCF) methodology that we apply to the valuation of investment projects. Thus, the value of an enterprise (*V*) is the sum of its free cash flows (C) in each year *t*, discounted at the enterprise's cost of capital.[14] The relevant cost of capital is the weighted average cost of capital (WACC) that averages the cost of equity and the cost of debt:

$$V = \sum_t \frac{C_t}{(1 + \text{WACC})^t}$$

where C is measured as:

Net operating profit + Depreciation − Taxes − Investment in fixed
and working capital

Thus, to maximize its value, a firm must maximize its future net cash flows while managing its risk to minimize its cost of capital.

This value-maximizing approach identifies cash flow rather than profit as the relevant performance measure for the value-maximizing firm. In practice, valuing companies by discounting economic profit gives the same result as by discounting net cash flows. The difference is in the treatment of the capital consumed by the business. The cash flow approach deducts capital at the time when the capital expenditure is made; the economic profit approach follows the accounting convention of charging capital as it is consumed (through charging depreciation). While the DCF approach is the technically correct approach to valuing companies, in practice, it requires forecasting cash flows several years ahead. DCF valuation is especially problematic for young, growing companies because their level of capital investment typically means they often have negative free cash flows for many years. If financial forecasts can only be made for a few years out, then profit (net of depreciation) may offer a better basis for valuation than cash flow does.

The difficulties of forecasting cash flows or profits far into the future have encouraged the search for approximations to DCF valuation. McKinsey & Company argues that enterprise value depends upon three key variables: return on capital employed (ROCE), weighted average cost of capital (WACC), and growth of operating profit. Hence, creating enterprise value requires increasing ROCE, reducing WACC, and increasing the rate of growth of profits.[15]

Enterprise Value and Shareholder Value

How does maximizing the value of the firm (enterprise value) relate to the much-lauded and widely vilified goal of maximizing shareholder value? At the foundation of modern financial theory is the principle that the net present value of a firm's profit stream is equal to the market value of its securities—both equity and debt.[16] Hence:

Enterprise value = Market capitalization of equity + Market value of debt[17]

Therefore, for the equity financed firm, maximizing the present value of the firm's profits over its lifetime also means maximizing the firm's current market capitalization.

If maximizing profits over the life of the firm also means maximizing the stock market value of the firm, why is it that shareholder value maximization has attracted so much criticism in recent years? The problems arise from the fact that the stock market cannot see the future with much clarity, hence its valuations of companies are strongly influenced by short-term and psychological factors. This then creates the possibility for a top management to boost their firm's stock market value by means other than increasing profits over the lifetime of the firm. For example, if stock markets are myopic, management may be encouraged to maximize short-term profits to the detriment of long-run profitability. This in turn may tempt top management to boost short-term earnings through financial manipulation rather than by growing the firm's operating profits. Such manipulation may include adjustments to financial structure, earnings smoothing, and the use of asset sales to flatter reported profits.

To avoid some of the criticisms that shareholder value maximization has attracted, my emphasis will be on maximizing enterprise value rather than on maximizing shareholder value. This is partly for convenience: distinguishing debt from equity is not always straightforward, due to the presence of preference stock and convertible debt, while junk bonds share the characteristics of both equity and debt. More importantly, focusing on the value of the enterprise as a whole supports our emphasis of the fundamental drivers of firm value in preference to the distractions and distortions that result from a preoccupation with stock market value.

Putting Performance Analysis into Practice

Our discussion so far has established that every business enterprise has a distinct purpose. Yet, for all businesses, the profits earned over the life of the business—enterprise value—are a sound indicator of a business's success in creating value. They also offer a sound criterion for selecting the strategies to achieve that business purpose.

So, how do we apply these principles to appraise and develop business strategies? There are four key areas where our analysis of profit performance can guide strategy: first, in appraising a firm's (or business unit's) performance; second, in diagnosing the sources of poor performance; third, in selecting strategies on the basis of their profit prospects; and, finally, setting performance targets.

Appraising Current and Past Performance

The first task of any strategy formulation exercise is to assess the current situation. This means identifying the current strategy of the firm and assessing how well that strategy is doing in terms of the performance of the firm. The next stage is diagnosis—identifying the sources of unsatisfactory performance. Thus, good strategic practice emulates good medical practice: first, assess the patient's state of health, and then determine the causes of any sickness.

Forward-Looking Performance Measures: Stock Market Value   If our goal is to maximize profit over the lifetime of the firm, then to evaluate the performance of a firm we need to look at its stream of profit (or cash flows) over the rest of its life. The problem, of course, is that we can only make reasonable estimates of these a few years ahead. For public companies stock market valuation represents the best available estimate of the NPV of future cash flows. Thus, to evaluate the performance

TABLE 2.2   The comparative performance of UPS and Federal Express

Company	Market capitalization, end 2014 ($ billion)	Enterprise value, end 2014[a] ($ billion)	Return to shareholders, 2010–2014[b] (%)	Operating margin, 2010–2014[c] (%)	ROE, 2010–2014[d] (%)	ROCE, 2010–2014[e] (%)	ROA, 2010–2014[f] (%)
UPS	96.0	105.8	104.3	10.1	58.6	33.3	15.3
Federal Express	48.5	53.2	110.7	6.5	11.0	15.3	5.7

Notes:
[a]Market capitalization + Book value of long-term debt.
[b]Percentage increase in share price + Dividend yield.
[c]Operating income/Sales revenue.
[d]Net income/Shareholders' equity.
[e]Operating income/(Shareholders' equity + long-term debt).
[f]Operating income/Total assets.

of a firm in value creation we can compare the change in the market value of the firm relative to that of competitors over a period (preferably several years). At the end of 2014, United Parcel Services, Inc. (UPS) had a market capitalization of $96.0 billion (enterprise value $105.8 bn.), compared to $48.5 billion for FedEx Corp. (enterprise value $53.2 bn). This indicates that UPS is expected to generate almost twice as much value as FedEx in the future. Table 2.2 shows that, from 2010 to 2014, UPS generated a total shareholder return of 104.3% compared to 110.7% for FedEx, indicating that the two companies have been similarly effective in value creation over the past five years. Clearly, stock market valuation is an imperfect performance indicator—particularly in terms of its sensitivity to new information and its vulnerability to market psychology and disequilibrium—but it is the best indictor we have of intrinsic value.

Backward-Looking Performance Measures: Accounting Ratios   Because of the volatility of stock market values, evaluations of firm performance for the purposes of assessing the current strategy or evaluating management effectiveness tend to use accounting measures of performance. These are inevitably historical: financial reports appear at least three weeks after the period to which they relate. That said, many firms offer *earnings guidance*—forecasts of profit for the next 12 months (or longer).

The McKinsey valuation framework identifies three drivers of enterprise value: rate of return on capital, cost of capital, and profit growth (see page 42). Among these, return on capital is the key indicator of the invested firm's effectiveness in generating profits from its assets. Hence, return on capital employed (ROCE), or its closely related measures, such as return on equity (ROE) and return on assets (ROA), are valuable performance indicators. Although different profitability measures tend to converge over the longer term,[18] over shorter periods it is important to be aware of the limitations and biases inherent in any particular profitability measure and to use multiple measures of profitability so that their consistency can be judged. Table 2.3 outlines some widely used profitability indicators.

Interpreting probability ratios requires benchmarks. Comparisons over time tell us whether performance is improving or deteriorating. Interfirm comparisons tell us

TABLE 2.3   Profitability ratios

Ratio	Formula	Comments
Return on Capital Employed (ROCE)	$$\dfrac{\text{Operating profit before interest after tax}}{\text{Equity} + \text{Long-term debt}}$$	ROCE is also known as return on invested capital (ROIC). The numerator is typically operating profit or earnings before interest and tax (EBIT), and can be pre-tax or post-tax. The denominator can also be measured as fixed assets *plus* net current assets.
Return on Equity (ROE)	$$\dfrac{\text{Net income}}{\text{Shareholders' equity}}$$	ROE measures the firm's success in using shareholders' capital to generate profits that are available to remunerate investors. Net income may be adjusted to exclude discontinued operations and special items.
Return on Assets (ROA)	$$\dfrac{\text{Operating profit}}{\text{Total assets}}$$	The numerator should correspond to the return on all the firm's assets—e.g., operating profit, EBIT, or EBITDA (earnings before interest, tax, depreciation, and amortization).
Gross margin	$$\dfrac{\text{Sales} - \text{Cost of bought-in goods and services}}{\text{Sales}}$$	Gross margin measures the extent to which a firm adds value to the goods and services it buys in.
Operating margin	$$\dfrac{\text{Operating profit}}{\text{Sales}}$$	Operating margin and net margin measure a firm's ability to extract profit from its sales, but for appraising firm performance, these ratios reveal little because margins vary greatly between sectors according to capital intensity.
Net margin	$$\dfrac{\text{Net income}}{\text{Sales}}$$	Margins are useful to compare the performance of firms within the same industry, but are not useful for comparing firms in different industries because margins depend on an industry's capital intensity (see Table 2.1).

Notes:
Few accounting ratios have standard definitions, hence, it is advisable to be explicit about how you have calculated the ratio you are using. A general guideline for rate of return ratios is that the numerator should be the profits that are available to remunerate the owners of the assets in the denominator.
Profits are measured over a period of time (typically over a year). Assets are valued at a point of time. Hence, in rate of return calculations, assets, equity, and capital employed should to be averaged between the beginning and end of the period.

how a firm is performing relative to a competitor, relative to its industry average, or relative to firms in general (e.g., relative to the Fortune 500, S&P 500, or FT 500). Another key benchmark is cost of capital. ROCE should be compared with WACC, and ROE compared with the cost of equity capital. Table 2.2 shows that, during 2010–2014, UPS earned an operating margin, ROE, ROCE, and ROA that were substantially higher than those earned by FedEx. UPS's greater market capitalization and enterprise value reflects expectations that UPS's superior profit performance will be sustained into the future.

Performance Diagnosis

If profit performance is unsatisfactory, we need to identify the sources of poor performance so that management can take corrective action. The main tool of diagnosis is disaggregation of return on capital in order to identify the fundamental *value drivers*. A starting point is to apply the Du Pont Formula to disaggregate return on invested

FIGURE 2.1 Disaggregating return on capital employed

Notes:
ROCE: Return on capital employed.
COGS: Cost of goods sold.
PPE: Property, plant, and equipment.

For further discussion, see T. Koller *et al.*, *Valuation*, 5th edn (Chichester: John Wiley & Sons, Ltd, 2010).

capital into sales margin and capital turnover. We can then further disaggregate both sales margin and capital productivity into their component items (Figure 2.1). This points us toward the specific activities that are the sources of poor performance.

Strategy Capsule 2.2 disaggregates the return on assets for UPS and FedEx so that we can begin to pinpoint the sources of UPS's superior profitability. If we combine the financial data with the qualitative data on the two companies' business strategies, operations, and organization together with information on conditions within the industry in which the two companies compete, we can begin to diagnose why UPS has outperformed FedEx.

Using Performance Diagnosis to Guide Strategy Formulation

A probing diagnosis of a firm's recent performance—as outlined above—provides a useful input into strategy formulation. If we can establish why a company has been performing badly then we have a basis for corrective actions. These corrective actions are likely to be both strategic (i.e., focused on the medium to long term) and operational (focused on the short term). The worse a company's performance, the

Diagnosing Performance: UPS vs. FedEx

Between 2010 and 2014, United Parcel Service (UPS) has earned more than double the return on assets as its closest rival, FedEx Corporation. What insights can financial analysis offer into the sources of this performance differential?

Disaggregating the companies' return on capital employed into operating margin and capital turnover shows that differences in ROCE are due to UPS's superior operating margin and higher capital turnover. See Figure 2.2.

Probing UPS's higher operating margin highlights major differences in the cost structure of the two companies: UPS is more labor intensive with a much higher ratio of employee costs to sales (however, UPS's average compensation per employee is much lower than FedEx's).

FedEx has higher costs of fuel, maintenance, depreciation, and "other." UPS's higher capital turnover is mainly due to its higher turnover of fixed assets (property, plant, and equipment).

These differences reflect the different composition of the two companies' businesses. UPS is more heavily involved in ground transportation (UPS has 103,000 vehicles; FedEx has 55,000), which tends to be more labor intensive. FedEx is more oriented toward air transportation (UPS has 620 aircraft; FedEx has 650). Express delivery services tend to be less profitable than ground delivery. However, the differences in business mix do not appear to completely explain the wide discrepancy in fuel, maintenance, and other costs between FedEx and UPS. The likelihood is that UPS has superior operational efficiency.

FIGURE 2.2   Analyzing why UPS earns a higher return on capital employed (ROCE) than FedEx greater the need to concentrate on the short term. For companies teetering on the brink of bankruptcy long-term strategy takes a back seat; survival is the dominant concern.

For companies that are performing well, financial analysis allows us to understand the sources of superior performance so that strategy can protect and enhance these determinants of success. For example, in the case of UPS (see Strategy Capsule 2.2), financial analysis points to the efficiency benefits that arise from being the US's biggest package delivery company and having an integrated system of collection and delivery that optimizes operational efficiency. The superior profitability of UPS's international business points to its ability to successfully enter foreign markets and integrate overseas operations within its global system.

However, analyzing the past only takes us so far. The world of business is one of constant change and the role of strategy is to help the firm to adapt to change. The challenge is to look into the future and identify factors that threaten performance or create new opportunities for profit. In making strategy recommendations to UPS, our financial analysis can tell us some of the reasons why UPS has been doing well up until now, but the key to sustaining UPS's performance is to recognize how its industry environment will be changing in terms of customer requirements, competition, technology, and energy costs and to assess UPS's capacity to adapt to these new conditions. While financial analysis is inevitably backward looking, strategic analysis allows us to look forward and understand some of the critical factors impacting a firm's success in the future.

Setting Performance Targets

We noted in Chapter 1 that an important role for strategic planning systems is to translate strategic goals into performance targets then monitor the performance achieved against these targets. To be effective, performance targets need to be consistent with long-term goals, linked to strategy, and relevant to the tasks and responsibilities of individual organizational members. Goals need to be actionable. Translating goals into actionable performance targets presents major problems for the stakeholder-focused firm. Even for the shareholder-focused firm, the goal of maximizing the value of the firm offers little guidance to the managers entrusted with that goal. The three main approaches to setting performance targets are:

Financial Disaggregation   If the goal of the firm is to maximize profitability, we can use the same financial disaggregation in Figure 2.1 to cascade targets down the organization. Thus, for the top management team, the key financial goals are likely to be maximizing ROCE on existing assets together with investing in new projects whose return on capital exceeds their cost of capital. For functional vice presidents, these goals imply maximizing sales and market shares (marketing and sales), minimizing raw material and component costs (purchasing), minimizing production costs (operations), maximizing inventory turns (logistics/supply chain), and minimizing the cost of capital (finance). These functional goals can be further disaggregated to the department level (e.g., plant maintenance is required to minimize machine downtime in order to increase capacity utilization, customer accounts are required to minimize the number of days of outstanding receivables, and so on).

The dilemma with any system of performance management is that the performance goals are long term (e.g., maximizing profits over the lifetime of the company), but to act as an effective control mechanism performance targets need to be monitored over the short term. For financial targets the problem is that their short-term pursuit may undermine long-term profit maximization.

Balanced Scorecards   One solution to the dilemma of financial targets undermining long-term financial performance is to combine financial targets with strategic and operational targets. The most widely used method for doing this is the **balanced scorecard** developed by Robert Kaplan and David Norton.[19] The balanced scorecard methodology provides an integrated framework for balancing financial and strategic goals and cascading performance measures down the organization to individual business units and departments. The performance measures included in the balanced scorecard derive from answers to four questions:

- How do we look to shareholders? The financial perspective is composed of measures such as cash flow, sales and income growth, and return on equity.
- How do customers see us? The customer perspective comprises measures such as goals for new products, on-time delivery, and defect and failure levels.
- What must we excel at? The internal business perspective relates to internal business processes such as productivity, employee skills, cycle time, yield rates, and quality and cost measures.
- Can we continue to improve and create value? The innovation and learning perspective includes measures related to new product development cycle times, technological leadership, and rates of improvement.

By balancing a set of strategic and financial goals, the scorecard methodology allows the strategy of the business to be linked with the creation of shareholder value while providing a set of measurable targets to guide this process. Moreover, because the balanced scorecard allows explicit consideration of the goals of customers, employees, and other interested parties, scorecards can also be used to implement stakeholder-focused management. Figure 2.3 shows the balanced scorecard for a US regional airline.

Strategic Profit Drivers   Financial value drivers and balanced scorecards are systematic techniques of performance management based upon the assumption that, if overall goals can be disaggregated into precise, quantitative, time-specific targets, each member of the organization knows what is expected of him or her and is motivated toward achieving the targets set. However, a mounting body of evidence points to the unintended consequences of managing through performance targets.

Performance targets create two types of problem. The first problem is the one we acknowledged in relation to profit maximization: targeting the goal itself may undermine that goal's attainment. Thus, many of the firms that are most successful at creating shareholder value are those which emphasize purpose over profit. Conversely, many of the firms most committed to maximizing shareholder value—Enron, for example—have been spectacularly unsuccessful in achieving that goal.[20] The experiences of Boeing illustrate this problem (see Strategy Capsule 2.3).[21]

FIGURE 2.3   Balanced scorecard for a regional airline

Simplified Strategy Map	Performance Measures	Targets	Initiatives
Financial — Increase Profitability; Lower Cost; Increase Revenue	• Market Value • Seat Revenue • Plane Lease Cost	• 25% per year • 20% per year • 5% per year	• Optimize routes • Standardize planes
Customer — More Customers; On-time Flights; Low Prices	• FAA on-time arrival rating • Customer ranking • No. customers	• First in industry • 98% satisfaction • % change	• Quality management • Customer loyalty program
Internal — Improve turnaround time	• On Ground Time • On-Time Departure	• <25 Minutes • 93%	• Cycle time optimization program
Learning — Align Ground Crews	• % Ground crew stockholders • % Ground crew trained	• Year 1, 70% • Year 4, 90% • Year 6, 100%	• Stock ownership plan • Ground crew training

Source: Reproduced from www.balancedscorecard.org with permission.

STRATEGY CAPSULE 2.3
The Pitfalls of Pursuing Shareholder Value: Boeing

Boeing was one of the most financially successful members of the Dow Jones Industrial Index between 1960 and 1990. Yet Boeing gave little attention to financial management. CEO Bill Allen was interested in building great planes and leading the world market with them: "Boeing is always reaching out for tomorrow. This can only be accomplished by people who live, breathe, eat and sleep what they are doing." At a board meeting to approve Boeing's biggest ever investment, the 747, Allen was asked by non-executive director Crawford Greenwalt for Boeing's financial projections on the project. In response to Allen's vague reply, Greenwalt buried his head in his hands. "My God," he muttered, "these guys don't even know what the return on investment will be on this thing."

The change came in the mid-1990s when Boeing acquired McDonnell Douglas and a new management team of Harry Stonecipher and Phil Condit took over. Mr Condit proudly talked of taking the company into "a value-based environment where unit cost, return on investment, and shareholder return are the measures by which you'll be judged."

The result was lack of investment in major new civil aviation projects and diversification into defense and satellites. Under Condit, Boeing relinquished market leadership in passenger aircraft to Airbus, while faltering as a defense contractor due partly to ethical lapses by key executives. When Condit resigned on December 1, 2003, Boeing's stock price was 20% lower than when he was appointed.

Sources: John Kay, "Forget How the Crow Flies," *Financial Times Magazine* (January 17, 2004): 17–27; R. Perlstein, *The Stock Ticker and the Superjumbo* (Prickly Paradigm Press, 2005).

The alternative to making the goal the target is to disaggregate the goal into specific quantitative targets (e.g., using value drivers or a balanced scorecard). However, this presents our second problem: the means by which the targets are attained conflict with the desired goal. The problem is vividly illustrated by the problems of performance targets in the public sector. In Soviet shoe factories, quantitative monthly targets would be met by producing low-quality shoes of a single size.[22] In the British National Health Service the target of eight-minute ambulance response times was achieved by substituting single paramedics in cars and partially trained volunteers for regular ambulance crews.[23]

Given these challenges, the approach we shall adopt in this book is to focus on the strategic factors that drive long-run profitability. Once we have identified the primary sources of profit available to the firm we have a basis, first, for formulating a strategy to exploit these sources of profit and, second, for implementing that strategy through performance guidelines and targets based upon those strategic variables. This notion that pursuing profitability requires focusing upon the fundamental strategic drivers of profit can also bring clarity to the complex and contentious issue of the social responsibilities of business firms.

Beyond Profit: Values and Corporate Social Responsibility

At the beginning of this chapter, I argued that, while every company has a distinct organizational purpose, a common goal for every business enterprise is to create value, and the best indicator of value creation is profit over the lifetime of the company—or, equivalently, maximizing enterprise value. Although the corporate scandals of the 21st century—from Enron in 2001 to Lehman Brothers in 2008—have discredited the pursuit of profit and shareholder value maximization, I have justified long-run profit maximization as an appropriate and practical goal for the strategic management of firms.

This justification was based largely on the alignment which I perceived, first, between profits and the interests of society as a whole (reflecting Adam Smith's principle of the "invisible hand" which guides self-interest toward the common good) and, second, between the pursuit of stakeholder and shareholder interests (both are reliant on the firm earning profit over the long-term). But what about when the pursuit of profit conflicts with the social good or with widely held ethical principles? How are such inconsistencies and conflicts to be managed? Is it sufficient to follow Milton Friedman's dictum that:

> There is one and only one social responsibility of business—to use its resources and engage in activities designed to increase its profits so long as it stays within the rules of the game, which is to say, engage in open and free competition without deception or fraud.[24]

Under this doctrine, it is the role of government to intervene in the economy where the pursuit of profit conflicts with the interest of society, using taxes and regulations to align profit incentives with social goals and legislation to criminalize unethical behavior. Conversely, others have argued that business enterprises should take the initiative to establish principles and values that extend beyond the limits of the law, and pursue strategies that are explicitly oriented toward the interests of society. Let us discuss each of these areas in turn.

Values and Principles

A sense of purpose—as articulated in statements of mission and vision—is often complemented by beliefs about how this purpose should be achieved. These organizational beliefs typically comprise a set of **values**—in the form of commitments to certain ethical precepts and to different stakeholder interests—and a set of principles to guide the decisions and actions of organizational members. Strategy Capsule 2.4 displays the values statement of Accenture plc, the world's biggest consulting company.

At one level, statements of values and principles may be regarded as instruments of companies' external image management. Yet, to the extent that companies are consistent and sincere in their adherence to values and principles, these ideals can be a critical component of organizational identity and an important influence on employees' commitment and behavior. When values are shared among organizational members, they form a central component of corporate culture.

STRATEGY CAPSULE 2.4
Accenture: Our Core Values

Since its inception, Accenture has been governed by its core values. They shape the culture and define the character of our company. They guide how we behave and make decisions.

♦ **Stewardship** Fulfilling our obligation of building a better, stronger and more durable company for future generations, protecting the Accenture brand, meeting our commitments to stakeholders, acting with an owner mentality, developing our people and helping improve communities and the global environment.

♦ **Best People** Attracting, developing and retaining the best talent for our business, challenging our people, demonstrating a "can-do" attitude and fostering a collaborative and mutually supportive environment.

♦ **Client Value Creation** Enabling clients to become high-performance businesses and creating long-term relationships by being responsive and relevant and by consistently delivering value.

♦ **One Global Network** Leveraging the power of global insight, relationships, collaboration and learning to deliver exceptional service to clients wherever they do business.

♦ **Respect for the Individual** Valuing diversity and unique contributions, fostering a trusting, open and inclusive environment and treating each person in a manner that reflects Accenture's values.

♦ **Integrity** Being ethically unyielding and honest and inspiring trust by saying what we mean, matching our behaviors to our words and taking responsibility for our actions.

Source: http://www.accenture.com/us-en/company/overview/values/Pages/index.aspx, accessed July 20, 2015.

The evidence that commitment to values and principles influences organizational performance is overwhelming. McKinsey & Company places "shared values" at the center of its "7-S framework.[25] Jim Collins and Jerry Porras argue that "core values" and "core purpose" unite to form an organization's "core ideology" which "defines an organization's timeless character" and is "the glue that holds the organization together."[26] They argue that when core ideology is put together with an "envisioned future" for the enterprise the result is a powerful sense of strategic direction that provides the foundation for long-term success.

Corporate Social Responsibility

The debate over the social responsibilities of companies has been both contentious and confused. Underlying the debate are different conceptions of the public corporation: "the property conception," which views the firm as a set of assets owned by the shareholders, and the "social entity conception," which views the firm as the community of individuals that is sustained and supported by its relationships with its social, political, economic, and natural environment.[27] While the "firm as property" view implies that management's sole responsibility is to operate in the interests of shareholders, the "firm as social entity" implies a responsibility to maintain the firm within its overall network of relationships and dependencies.

However, even from a pure efficacy viewpoint, it is clear that both poles of the spectrum of opinions are untenable. The proponents of the view that the sole purpose of the business enterprise is to make profit fail to recognize that to survive and earn profit an organization must maintain social legitimacy. The near-elimination of investment banks during the financial crisis of 2008–2009—including the transformation of Goldman Sachs and other investment banks into commercial banks—was caused less by their commercial failure as by a collapse of legitimacy. The phone hacking scandal that caused the closure of a British newspaper owned by Rupert Murdoch's News Corporation represented less than 1% of News Corp's revenues. However, in the five weeks after the scandal broke in July 2011, News Corp's market capitalization declined by 25%—a loss of $11 billion.

At the other end of the spectrum, the argument that the primary responsibility of business enterprises should be the pursuit of social goals is likely to be similarly dysfunctional. To extend Adam Smith's observation that it "is not from the benevolence of the butcher, the brewer or the baker, that we expect our dinner, but from their regard to their own interest,"[28] it is likely that if the butcher becomes an animal rights activist, the brewer joins the Temperance League, and the baker signs up to Weight Watchers none of us has much hope of getting dinner.

Somewhere in the middle of this spectrum therefore lies a region of sustainability where business enterprises are aligned with the requirements of their social and natural environment but are closely in touch with both their business purpose and their generation of long-run profitability. A number of contributions to the management literature have allowed us to define more precisely this intermediate region of sustainability and to outline the considerations that should guide the pursuit of social responsibility.

The key consideration here is the firm's responsiveness to a changing business environment. The efficacy argument for **corporate social responsibility (CSR)** views the firm as embedded within an ecosystem of its social and natural environments, implying a need to adapt to and maintain the surrounding ecosystem. Thus, according to former Shell executive Arie de Geus, long-living companies are those that build strong communities, have a strong sense of identity, commit to learning, and are sensitive to the world around them. In short, they recognize they are living organisms whose life spans depend upon effective adaptation to a changing environment.[29]

This view of the firm jointly pursuing its own interests and those of its ecosystem has been developed by Michael Porter and Mark Kramer into guidelines for a focused and pragmatic approach to CSR.[30] Putting aside ethical arguments (what they call "the moral imperative"), they identify three reasons why CSR might also be in the interests of a company: the *sustainability* argument—CSR is in firms' interests due to a mutual interest in sustaining the ecosystem; the *reputation* argument—CSR enhances a firm's reputation with consumers and other third parties; and the *license-to-operate* argument—to conduct their businesses firms need the support of the constituencies upon which they depend. The critical task, in selecting which CSR initiatives firms should pursue is to identify specific intersections between the interests of the firm and those of society (i.e., projects and activities that create competitive advantage for the firm while generating positive social outcomes)—what they term *strategic CSR*.

At the intersection between corporate and social interests is what Porter and Kramer refer to as *shared value*: "creating economic value in a way which also creates value for society."[31] Shared value, they argue, is not about redistributing the value already created; it is about expanding the total pool of economic and social value. For example, fair trade is about the redistribution of value by paying farmers a higher price for their crops—in the case of Ivory Coast cocoa growers, it increases their incomes by 10–20%. By contrast, efforts by the major buyers to improve the efficiency of cocoa growing through improved growing methods, better quality control, and improved infrastructure can increase growers' incomes by 300%. Creating shared value involves reconceptualizing the firm's boundaries and its relationship with its environment. Rather than seeing itself as a separate entity which transacts with the external environment, the firm recognizes that it is co-dependent upon and intimately involved with its environment and the organizations and individuals it comprises. This offers three types of opportunity for shared value creation: reconceiving products and markets, redefining productivity within the value chain, and building local clusters of suppliers, distributors, and related businesses at the places where the firm does business. Unilever's Sustainable Growth Plan exemplifies this shared value creation (see Strategy Capsule 2.5).

This notion of shared value is embedded in the **bottom of the pyramid** initiatives—the potential for multinational companies to create profitable business and promote social and economic development through serving the world's poor—especially the four billion people living off less than $2 a day.[32] Again, the key is a switch of perception: rather than viewing the poor as victims or a burden, if multinationals recognize them as potential consumers, resilient workers, and creative entrepreneurs then a whole world of opportunity opens up.

Beyond Profit: Strategy and Real Options

So far, we have identified the value of the firm with the net present value (NPV) of its profit earnings (or, equivalently, free cash flows). But NPV is not the only source of

STRATEGY CAPSULE 2.5
Unilever's Sustainable Living Plan

Since launching its Sustainable Living Plan in November 2010, Unilever—the Anglo-Dutch multinational supplying over 400 brands of food, personal care, and household products—has become established as a world leader in environment sustainability and, according to the *Economist,* Unilever "reckoned to have the most comprehensive strategy of enlightened capitalism of any global firm." The program—with its goals of reducing Unilever's environmental footprint, increasing its positive social impact, doubling sales, and increasing long-term profitability—has been the centerpiece of CEO Paul Polman's strategy for the company. More than most other companies, Unilever has embedded its sustainability program within its strategic, operational, and human resource management: the plan is overseen by the board and incentive bonuses are linked to its quantitative targets for improvements in emissions, waste reduction, and energy and water conservation.

While Polman emphasizes that Unilever's commitment to sustainability is because it is "the right thing to do" he is also clear that the primary motivation is the fact that the Sustainable Living Plan is in the long-term interests of Unilever itself. In an interview with McKinsey and Company, Polman noted that the benefits to Unilever included improved access to raw materials, greater employee commitment, a stronger drive toward innovation throughout the company, greatly increased numbers of applications for jobs at Unilever, and improvement in efficiency in Unilever plants and throughout its supply chain. Shareholders appear to have benefitted as well: in the five years following the launch of the Sustainable Living Plan, Unilever's share price rose by 40%, well ahead of rivals Procter & Gamble and Nestlé.

However, when Polman announced, en route for the January 2015 Davos meetings, that he planned to "use the size and scale of Unilever" to lobby global leaders for a binding agreement on climate change and poverty eradication, some wondered whether he was putting global interests ahead of Unilever's—especially given Unilever's disappointing sales performance during 2014.

Sources: McKinsey & Company, "Committing to sustainability: An interview with Unilever's Paul Polman," http://www.mckinsey.com/videos/video?vid=3564008886001&plyrid=2399849255001&Height=270&Width=480, accessed July 20, 2015; "Unilever: In search of the good business," *Economist,* August 9, 2014.

value available to the firm. The simple idea that an option—the choice of whether to do something or not—has value has important implications for how we value firms. In recent years, the principles of option pricing have been extended from valuing financial securities to valuing investment projects and companies. The resulting field of **real option analysis** has emerged as one of the most important developments in financial theory over the past decade, with far-reaching implications for strategy analysis. The technical details of valuing real options are complex. However, the underlying principles are intuitive. Let me outline the basic ideas of real options theory and what they mean for strategy analysis.

Consider the investments that Royal Dutch Shell is making in joint-venture development projects to produce hydrogen for use in fuel cells. The large-scale use of fuel cells in transportation vehicles or for power generation seems unlikely within the foreseeable future. Shell's expenditure on these projects is small, but almost certainly these funds would generate a higher return if they were used in Shell's core oil and gas business. So, how can these investments—indeed, all of Shell's investments in renewable energy—be consistent with shareholder interests?

The answer lies in the option value of these investments. Shell is not developing a full-scale fuel cell business, and nor is it developing commercial-scale hydrogen production plants: it is developing technologies that could be used to produce hydrogen if fuel cells become widely used. By building know-how and intellectual property in this technology, Shell has created an *option*. If economic, environmental, or political factors restrict hydrocarbon use and if fuel cells advance to the point of technical and commercial viability, then Shell could exercise that option by investing much larger amounts in commercial-scale hydrogen production.

In a world of uncertainty, where investments, once made, are irreversible, flexibility is valuable. Instead of committing to an entire project, there is virtue in breaking the project into a number of phases, where the decision of whether and how to embark on the next phase can be made in the light of prevailing circumstances and the learning gained from the previous stage of the project. Most large companies have a "phases and gates" approach to product development in which the development process is split into distinct "phases," at the end of which the project is reassessed before being allowed through the "gate." Such a phased approach creates the options to continue the project, to abandon it, to amend it, or to wait. Venture capitalists clearly recognize the value of growth options. In November 2014, Kik, a Toronto-based start-up, received $38.3 million in venture capital financing. Kik is a free mobile chat service that targets 13- to 15-year-olds and has 200 million users, but almost no revenues. For its investors, Kik offers an option. Their funding is just to take Kik to its next level of development where it can add a browser and links to other mobile applications which can make Kik into a broader-based user platform together with the potential to carry paid advertising.[33] The emphasis that venture capitalists place on *scalability*—the potential to scale up or replicate a business should the initial launch be successful—similarly acknowledges the value of growth options. Strategy Capsule 2.6 addresses the calculation of real option values.

Strategy as Options Management

For strategy formulation, our primary interest is how we can use the principles of option valuation to create shareholder value. There are two types of real option: growth options and flexibility options. *Growth options* allow a firm to make small initial investments in a number of future business opportunities but without committing to them. *Flexibility options* relate to the design of projects and plants that permit adaptation to different circumstances—flexible manufacturing systems allow different product models to be manufactured on a single production line. Individual projects can be designed to introduce both growth options and flexibility options. This means avoiding commitment to the complete project and introducing decision points at multiple stages, where the main options are to delay, modify, scale up, or abandon the project. Merck, an early adopter of option pricing, notes, "When you make an initial investment in a research project, you are paying an entry fee for a right, but you are not obligated to continue that research at a later stage."[34]

Calculating Real Option Value

Application of real option value to investment projects and strategies has been limited by the complexity of the valuation techniques. Yet, even without getting into the mathematics needed to quantify option values, we can use the basic principles involved to understand the factors that determine option values and to recognize how projects and strategies can be designed in order to maximize their option values.

The early work on real option valuation adapted the Black–Scholes option-pricing formula developed for valuing financial options to the valuation of real investment projects.[a] Black–Scholes comprises six determinants of option value, each of which has an analogy in the valuation of a real option:

1   Stock price: The NPV of the project: a higher NPV increases option value.

2   Exercise price: Investment cost: the higher the cost, the lower the option value.

3   Uncertainty: for both financial and real options, uncertainty increases option value.

4   Time to expiry: for both financial and real options, the longer the option lasts, the greater its value.

5   Dividends: Decrease in the value of the investment over the option period: lowers option value.

6   Interest rate: a higher interest rate increases option value by making deferral more valuable.[b]

However, the dominant methodology used for real option valuation is the binomial options pricing model. By allowing the sources of uncertainty and key decision points in a project to be modeled explicitly, the technique offers a more intuitive appreciation of the sources of option value. The analysis involves two main stages:

1   Create an event tree that shows the value of the project at each development period under two different scenarios.

2   Convert the event tree into a decision tree by identifying the key decision points on the event tree, typically the points where commitments of new funds to the project are required or where there is the option to defer development. Incremental project values at each stage can then be calculated for each decision point by working back from the final nodes of the decision tree (using a discount factor based upon the replicating portfolio technique). If the incremental project value at the initial stage exceeds the initial investment, proceed with the first phase, and similarly for each subsequent phase.[c]

Notes:

[a]See: F. Black and M. Scholes, "The Pricing of Options and Corporate Liabilities," *Journal of Political Economy* 81 (1993): 637–54.

[b]See: K. J. Leslie and M. P. Michaels, "The Real Power of Real Options," *McKinsey Quarterly Anthology: On Strategy* (Boston: McKinsey & Company, 2000). See also A. Dixit and R. Pindyck, "The Options Approach to Capital Investment," *Harvard Business Review* (May/June 1995): 105–15.

[c]This approach is developed in T. Copeland and P. Tufano, "A Real-world Way to Manage Real Options," *Harvard Business Review* (March 2004). See also T. Copeland, Developing Strategy Using Real Options (Monitor Company, October 2003).

In developing strategy, our main concern is with growth options. These might include:

- Platform investments. These are investments in core products or technologies that create a stream of additional business opportunities.[35] 3M's investment in nanotechnology offers the opportunity to create new products across a wide range of its businesses, from dental restoratives and drug-delivery systems to adhesives and protective coatings. Google's search engine and the huge internet traffic it draws has offered a platform for a large number of initiatives—not just search products but also a wide array of other software products and internet services (e.g., Gmail, Chrome, Android, Google+).[36]

- Strategic alliances and joint ventures, which are limited investments that offer options for the creation of whole new strategies.[37] Virgin Group has used joint ventures as the basis for creating a number of new businesses: with Stagecoach to create Virgin Rail, with AMP to create Virgin Money (financial services), with Deutsche Telecom to form Virgin Mobile. Shell has used joint ventures and alliances as a means of making initial investments in wind power, biodiesel fuel, solar power, and other forms of renewable energy.

- Organizational capabilities can also be viewed as options that offer the potential to create competitive advantage across multiple products and businesses.[38] Apple's capability in combining hardware, software, aesthetics, and ergonomics to create products of exceptional user-friendliness has given it the option to expand from PCs into several new product areas: MP3 audio players, smartphones, tablet computers, and interactive TV.

Summary

Chapter 1 introduced a framework for strategy analysis that provides the structure for Part II of this book. This chapter has explored the first component of that framework—the goals, values, and performance of the firm.

We have explored in some depth the difficult, and still contentious, issue of the appropriate goals for the firm. While each firm has a specific business purpose, common to all firms is the desire, and the necessity, to create value. How that value is defined and measured distinguishes those who argue that the firms should operate primarily in the interests of owners (shareholders) from those who argue for a stakeholder approach. Our approach is pragmatic: shareholder and stakeholder interests tend to converge and, where they diverge, the pressure of competition limits the scope for pursuing stakeholder interests at the expense of profit, hence my conclusion that long-run profit—or its equivalent, enterprise value—is appropriate both as an indicator of firm performance and as a guide to strategy formulation. We explored the relationships between value, profit, and cash flow and saw how the failings of shareholder value maximization resulted more from its misapplication than from any inherent flaw.

The application of financial analysis to the assessment of firm performance is an essential component of strategic analysis. Financial analysis creates a basis for strategy formulation, first, by appraising overall firm performance and, second, by diagnosing the sources of unsatisfactory performance. Combining financial analysis and strategic analysis allows us to establish performance targets for companies and their business units.

Finally, we looked beyond the limits of our useful, yet simplistic, profit-oriented approach to firm performance and business strategy. We looked, first, at how the principles of corporate social responsibility can be incorporated within a firm's strategy to enhance its creation of both social and shareholder value. Second, we extended our analysis of value maximization to take account of the fact that strategy creates enterprise value not only by generating profit but also by creating real options.

Self-Study Questions

1. Table 2.1 compares companies according to different profitability measures.

    a. Which two of the six performance measures do you think are the most useful indicators of how well a company is being managed?
    b. Is return on sales or return on equity a better basis on which to compare the performance of the companies listed?
    c. Several companies are highly profitable yet delivered very low returns to their shareholders during 2014. How is this possible?

2. India's Tata Group is a diversified group. Some of its largest companies are: Tata Steel, Tata Motors, Tata Consultancy Services (IT), Tata Power (electricity generation), Tata Chemicals, Tata Tea, Indian Hotels, and Tata Communications. How do you think Tata Group's recent adoption of EVA as a performance management tool is likely to influence the way in which it allocates investment among the companies listed above?

3. With regard to Strategy Capsule 2.2, what additional data would you seek and what additional analysis would you undertake to investigate further the reasons for UPS's superior profitability to FedEx?

4. The CEO of a chain of pizza restaurants wishes to initiate a program of CSR to be funded by a 5% levy on the company's operating profit. The board of directors, fearing a negative shareholder reaction, is opposed to the plan. What arguments might the CEO use to persuade the board that CSR might be in the interests of shareholders, and what types of CSR initiatives might the program include to ensure that this was the case?

5. Nike, a supplier of sports footwear and apparel, is interested in the idea that it could increase its stock market value by creating options for itself. What actions might Nike take that might generate option value?

Notes

1. A. P. Sloan, *My Years at General Motors* (New York: Doubleday, 1963).
2. J. A. Schumpeter, *The Theory of Economic Development* (Cambridge, MA: Harvard University Press 1934).
3. "Henry Ford: The Man Who Taught America to Drive," *Entrepreneur* (October 8, 2008), www.entrepreneur.com/article/197524, accessed July 20, 2015.
4. C. A. Montgomery, "Putting Leadership Back into Strategy," *Harvard Business Review* (January 2008): 54–60.
5. In this chapter, I use the term *value* in two distinct senses. Here I am referring to *economic value*, which is worth as measured in monetary units. I shall also be discussing values as moral principles or standards of behavior.
6. T. Donaldson and L. E. Preston, "The stakeholder theory of the corporation," *Academy of Management Review* 20 (1995): 65–91.
7. In several countries, company law has been amended to allow companies to pursue explicit social goals. In the US, these "benefit corporations" (or B-corporations) include the outdoor apparel company, Patagonia. See J. Surowiecki, "Companies with Benefits," *The New Yorker*, August 4, 2014.
8. See M. B. Lieberman, N. Balasubramanian, and R. García-Castro "Value Creation and Appropriation in Firms: Conceptual Review and a Method for Measurement," (June 10, 2013, available at SSRN: http://ssrn.com/abstract=2381801) for an approach to estimating.
9. M. C. Jensen, "Value Maximization, Stakeholder Theory, and the Corporate Objective Function," *Journal of Applied Corporate Finance* 22 (Winter 2010): 34.
10. J. Helwege, V. Intintoli, and A. Zhang, "Voting with Their Feet or Activism? Institutional Investors' Impact on CEO Turnover," *Journal of Corporate Finance* Vol. 18 (2012): 22–37.
11. T. M. Jones, "Instrumental Stakeholder Theory: A Synthesis of Ethics and Economics," *Academy of Management Review* 20 (1995): 404–37.
12. M. Orlitzky, F. L. Schmidt, and S. L. Rynes, "Corporate Social and Financial Performance: A Meta-Analysis," *Organization Studies* 24 (Summer 2003): 403–441.
13. See www.sternstewart.com. See also J. L. Grant, *Foundations of Economic Value Added*, 2nd edn (New York: John Wiley & Sons, Ltd, 2003).
14. The cost of equity capital is calculated using the capital asset pricing model: Firm X's cost of equity · the risk-free rate of interest + a risk premium. The risk premium is the excess of the stock market rate of return over the risk-free rate multiplied by Firm X's beta coefficient (its measure of systematic risk). See T. Koller, M. Goedhart, and D. Wessels, *Valuation: Measuring and Managing the Value of Companies*, 5th edn (Hoboken, NJ: John Wiley & Sons, Inc., 2010), Chapter 11.
15. T. Koller, M. Goedhart, D. Wessels, *Valuation: Measuring and Managing the Value of Companies*, 5th edn (Hoboken, NJ: John Wiley & Sons, Inc., 2010).
16. F. Modigliani and M. H. Miller, "The Cost of Capital, Corporation Finance, and the Theory of Investments," *American Economic Review* 48 (1958): 261–297.
17. Some calculations of enterprise value deduct the balance sheet value of a firm's cash and marketable securities from the market value of its equity and debt in order to value only the business itself.
18. J. A. Kay and C. Meyer, "On the Application of Accounting Rates of Return," *Economic Journal* 96 (1986): 199–207.
19. R. S. Kaplan and D. P. Norton, "The Balanced Scorecard: Measures that Drive Performance," *Harvard Business Review* (January/February 1992): 71–9; R. S. Kaplan and D. P. Norton, "Using the Balanced Scorecard as a Strategic Management System," *Harvard Business Review* (January/February 1996): 75–85.
20. S. Chatterjee, "Enron's Incremental Descent into Bankruptcy: A Strategic and Organizational Analysis," *Long Range Planning* 36 (2003): 133–149.
21. The general principle here is that of *obliquity*: it is often better to pursue our goals indirectly rather than directly. See: J. Kay, *Obliquity* (London: Profile Books, 2010).
22. P. C. Roberts and K. LaFollett *Meltdown: Inside the Soviet Economy* (Washington, DC: Cato Institut, 1990).
23. G. Bevan and C. Hood, "What's Measured Is What Matters: Targets and Gaming in the English Public Health Care System," *Public Administration* 84 (2006): 517–538.
24. M. Friedman, *Capitalism and Freedom* (Chicago: University of Chicago Press, 1963).
25. L. Bryan, "Enduring Ideas: The 7-S Framework," *McKinsey Quarterly* (March 2008).
26. J. Collins and J. Porras, "Building Your Company's Vision," *Harvard Business Review* (September/October 1996): 65–77.
27. W. T. Allen, "Our Schizophrenic Conception of the Business Corporation," *Cardozo Law Review* 14 (1992): 261–281.
28. A. Smith, *An Inquiry into the Nature and Causes of the Wealth of Nations*, 5th edn (London: Methuen & Co., 1905), Chapter 2.
29. A. de Geus, "The Living Company," *Harvard Business Review* (March/April 1997): 51–59.
30. M. E. Porter and M. R. Kramer, "Strategy and Society: The Link between Competitive Advantage and Corporate Social Responsibility," *Harvard Business Review* (December 2006): 78–92.
31. M. E. Porter and M. R. Kramer, "Creating Shared Value," *Harvard Business Review* (January 2011): 62–77.
32. C. K. Prahalad and S. L. Hart, "The Fortune at the Bottom of the Pyramid," *strategy + business* 26 (2002): 54–67;

T. London and S. L. Hart, "Reinventing Strategies for Emerging Markets: Beyond the Transnational Model," *Journal of International Business Studies* 35 (2004): 350–370.

33. "Kik Teen Chat App Draws Venture Capital," *Financial Times* (November 19, 2014).

34. N. Nichols, "Scientific Management at Merck: An Interview with CFO Judy Lewent," *Harvard Business Review* (January/February 1994): 89–105.

35. B. Kogut and N. Kulatilaka, "Options Thinking and Platform Investments: Investing in Opportunity," *California Management Review* (Winter 1994): 52–69.

36. A. Gower and M. A. Cusamano, "How Companies Become Platform Leaders," *Sloan Management Review* (Winter 2008): 28–35.

37. T. Chi, "Option to Acquire or Divest a Joint Venture," *Strategic Management Journal* 21 (2000) 665–687.

38. B. Kogut and N. Kulatilaka, "Capabilities as Real Options," *Organization Science* 12 (2001) 744–758; R. G. McGrath, W. Furrier, and A. Mendel, "Real Options as Engines of Choice and Heterogeneity," *Academy of Management Review* 29 (2004): 86–101.

3 Industry Analysis: The Fundamentals

> When a management with a reputation for brilliance tackles a business with a reputation for poor fundamental economics, it is the reputation of the business that remains intact.
>
> —WARREN BUFFETT, CHAIRMAN, BERKSHIRE HATHAWAY

> The reinsurance business has the defect of being too attractive-looking to new entrants for its own good and will therefore always tend to be the opposite of, say, the old business of gathering and rendering dead horses that always tended to contain few and prosperous participants.
>
> —CHARLES T. MUNGER, CHAIRMAN, WESCO FINANCIAL CORP

OUTLINE

Introduction and Objectives

In this chapter and the next we explore the external environment of the firm. In Chapter 1 we observed that profound understanding of the competitive environment is a critical ingredient of a successful strategy. We also noted that business strategy is essentially a quest for profit. The primary task for this chapter is to identify the sources of profit in the external environment. The firm's proximate environment is its industry environment; hence our environmental analysis will focus on the firm's industry surroundings.

Industry analysis is relevant both to corporate-level and business-level strategy.

- Corporate strategy is concerned with deciding which industries the firm should be engaged in and how it should allocate its resources among them. Such decisions require assessment of the attractiveness of different industries in terms of their profit potential. The main objective of this chapter is to understand how the competitive structure of an industry determines its profitability.
- Business strategy is concerned with establishing competitive advantage. By analyzing customer needs and preferences and the ways in which firms compete to serve customers, we identify the general sources of competitive advantage in an industry—what we call *key success factors*.

By the time you have completed this chapter, you will be able to:

- Appreciate that the firm's industry forms the core of its external environment and understand that its characteristics and dynamics are essential components of strategy analysis.
- Recognize the main structural features of an industry and understand how they impact the intensity of competition and overall level of profitability in the industry.
- Apply industry analysis to explain the level of profitability in an industry and predict how profitability is likely to change in the future.
- Develop strategies that (a) position the firm most favorably in relation to competition and (b) influence industry structure in order to enhance industry attractiveness.
- Define the boundaries of the industry within which a firm is located.
- Identify opportunities for competitive advantage within an industry (key success factors).

From Environmental Analysis to Industry Analysis

The business environment of the firm consists of all the external influences that impact its decisions and its performance. Given the vast number of external influences, how can managers hope to monitor, let alone analyze, environmental conditions? The starting point is some kind of system or framework for organizing information. Environmental influences can be classified by source, for example, into political, economic, social, and technological factors—what is known as *PEST analysis*. PEST analysis and similar approaches to macro-level environmental scanning can be useful in keeping a firm alert to what is happening in the world. The danger, however, is that continuous, systematic scanning and analysis of such a wide range of external influences is costly and may result in information overload.

The prerequisite for effective environmental analysis is to distinguish the vital from the merely important. To do this let us return to first principles in order to establish what features of a firm's external environment are relevant to its decisions. For the firm to make a profit it must create value for customers. Hence, it must understand its customers. Second, in creating value, the firm acquires goods and services from suppliers. Hence, it must understand its suppliers and manage relationships with them. Third, the ability to generate profitability depends on the intensity of competition among firms that vie for the same value-creating opportunities. Hence, the firm must understand competition. Thus, *the core of the firm's business environment is formed by its relationships with three sets of players: customers, suppliers, and competitors*. This is its industry environment.

This is not to say that macro-level factors such as general economic trends, changes in demographic structure, or social and political trends are unimportant for strategy analysis. They may be critical determinants of the threats and opportunities a company will face in the future. The key issue is how these more general environmental factors affect the firm's industry environment (Figure 3.1). Consider the threat of global warming. For most companies this is not a core strategic issue (at least, not within their normal planning horizons). However, for those businesses most directly affected by changing weather patterns—farmers and ski resorts—and those subject to carbon taxes and environmental regulations—electricity generators and automobile producers—global warming is a vital issue. For these businesses, the key is to analyze the strategic implications of global warming for their particular industry. In the case of the automobile makers: will it cause consumers to switch to electric cars, will it cause governments to favor public over private transportation, will it encourage new entrants into the auto industry?

If strategy is about identifying and exploiting sources of profit, then the starting point for industry analysis is the simple question "What determines the level of profit in an industry?"

In the last chapter we learned that for a firm to make profit it must create value for the customer. Value is created when the price the customer is willing to pay for a product exceeds the costs incurred by the firm. But creating customer value

FIGURE 3.1   From environmental analysis to industry analysis

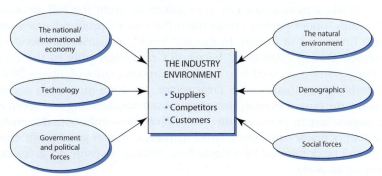

does not necessarily yield profit. The value created is distributed between customers and producers by the forces of competition. The stronger competition is among producers, the more value is received by customers as *consumer surplus* (the difference between the price they actually pay and the maximum price they would have been willing to pay) and the less is received by producers (as *producer surplus* or *economic rent*). A single supplier of umbrellas outside the Gare de Lyon on a wet Parisian morning can charge a price that fully exploits commuters' desire to keep dry. As more and more umbrella sellers arrive, so the price of umbrellas will be pushed closer to the wholesale cost.

However, the profit earned by Parisian umbrella sellers, or any other industry, does not just depend on the competition between them. It also depends upon their suppliers. If an industry has a powerful supplier—a single wholesaler of cheap, imported umbrellas—that supplier may be able to capture a major part of the value created in the local umbrella market.

Hence, the profits earned by the firms in an industry are determined by three factors:

- the value of the product to customers
- the intensity of competition
- the bargaining power of industry members relative to their suppliers and buyers.

Industry analysis brings all three factors into a single analytic framework.

Analyzing Industry Attractiveness

Table 3.1 shows the profitability of different US industries. Some industries consistently earn high rates of profit; others fail to cover their cost of capital. The basic premise that underlies industry analysis is that the level of industry profitability is neither random nor the result of entirely industry-specific influences: it is determined by the systematic influences of the industry's structure.

The underlying theory of how industry structure drives competitive behavior and determines industry profitability is provided by industrial organization (IO) economics. The two reference points are the theory of monopoly and the theory of perfect competition. In a monopoly a single firm is protected by high **barriers to entry**. In perfect competition many firms supply a homogeneous product and there are no entry barriers; these form end points of the spectrum of industry structures. While a monopolist can appropriate in profit the full amount of the value it creates, under perfect competition the rate of profit falls to a level that just covers firms' cost of capital. In the real world, industries fall between these two extremes. During 1996–2002, Microsoft's near monopoly of the market for PC operating systems allowed it to earn a return on equity of almost 30%. In the close-to-perfectly competitive, US farm sector, the long-run return on equity is 3.0%—below the cost of capital. However, most manufacturing and service industries are somewhere in between: they are *oligopolies*—industries dominated by a small number of major companies. Small markets can offer good profit opportunities if they can be dominated by a single firm. Strategy Capsule 3.1 gives examples of such niche markets.

TABLE 3.1 The profitability of US industries, 2000–2013

Industry[a]	Median ROE (%)[b]	Leading companies
Tobacco	36.2	Philip Morris Intl., Altria, Reynolds American
Household and Personal Products	27.0	Procter & Gamble, Kimberly-Clark, Colgate-Palmolive
Food Consumer Products	21.7	PepsiCo, Kraft Foods, General Mills
Food Services	21.7	McDonald's, Yum! Brands, Starbucks
Pharmaceuticals	20.5	Pfizer, Johnson & Johnson, Merck
Medical Products and Equipment	18.0	Medtronic, Baxter International, Boston Scientific
Petroleum Refining	17.9	ExxonMobil, Chevron, ConocoPhillips
Aerospace and Defense	16.5	Boeing, United Technologies, Lockheed Martin
Chemicals	16.4	Dow Chemical, DuPont, PPG Industries
Construction and Farm Equipment	15.9	Caterpillar, Deere, Cummins
Securities	15.2	BlackRock, KKR, Franklin Resources
Mining, Crude Oil Production	15.0	Conoco Phillips, Occidental Petroleum, Freeport-McMoRan
IT Services	14.9	IBM, Xerox, Computer Sciences
Specialty Retailers	14.6	Home Depot, Costco, Lowe's
Healthcare Insurance and Managed Care	13.0	United Health Group, WellPoint, Aetna
General Merchandisers	12.9	Wal-Mart, Target, Sears Holdings
Communications Equipment	12.2	Cisco Systems, Motorola, Qualcomm
Pipelines	12.0	Plains All American, Enterprise Products, ONEOK
Engineering, Construction	11.9	Fluor, Jacobs Engineering, KBR
Commercial Banks	11.5	Bank of America, JPMorgan Chase, Wells Fargo
Automotive Retailing and Services	10.8	AutoNation, Penske, Hertz
Computers, Office Equipment	10.8	Apple, Hewlett-Packard, Dell Computer
Food and Drug Stores	10.2	CVS, Kroger, Walgreens
Utilities: Gas and Electric	9.6	Execon, Duke Energy, Southern
Packaging and Containers	9.6	Rock-Ten, Ball, Crown Holdings
Insurance: Property and Casualty	9.0	Berkshire Hathaway, AIG, Allstate
Semiconductors and Electronic Components	8.6	Intel, Texas Instruments, Jabil Circuit
Hotels, Casinos, Resorts	8.1	Marriott International, Las Vegas Sands, MGM Resorts
Insurance: Life and Health	7.9	MetLife, Prudential, Aflac
Metals	7.7	Alcoa, US Steel, Nucor
Forest and Paper Products	7.1	International Paper, Weyerhaeuser, Domtar
Telecommunications	7.0	Verizon, AT&T, Comcast
Motor Vehicles and Parts	6.4	GM, Ford, Johnson Controls
Entertainment	6.1	Time Warner, Walt Disney, News Corp.
Food Production	5.9	Archer Daniels Midland, Tyson Foods, Smithfield Foods
Airlines	−7.1	United Continental, Delta Air Lines, American Airlines

Notes:
[a]Industries with fewer than five firms were excluded (with the exception of tobacco). Also omitted were industries that were substantially redefined during the period.
[b]Median return on equity for each industry averaged across the 14 years (2000–2013). For those firms with negative shareholders' equity, return on assets was substituted for ROE.
Source: Data from Fortune 500.

STRATEGY CAPSULE 3.1
Chewing Tobacco, Sausage Skins, and Slot Machines: The Joys of Niche Markets

US Smokeless Tobacco Company earned an operating margin of 55% during 2011–2013, making a major contribution to the 102% return on equity earned by its parent, Altria Inc., over the same period. What's the secret of USSTC's profitability? It accounts for 55% of the US market for smokeless tobacco, and its long-established brands (including Skoal, Copenhagen, and Red Seal), its distribution through thousands of small retail outlets, and government restrictions on advertising tobacco products create formidable barriers to entry to would-be competitors.

Devro plc, based in the Scottish village of Moodiesburn, is the world's leading supplier of collagen sausage skins ("casings"). "From the British 'Banger' to the Chinese Lap Cheong, from the French Merguez to the South American Chorizo, Devro has a

casing to suit all product types." Its overall world market share is around 60%. During 2010–2013, it earned a return on equity of 25%—about three times its cost of equity.

International Game Technology (IGT) based in Reno, Nevada is the world's dominant manufacturer of slot machines for casinos. IGT maintains its 70% US market share through close relations with casino operators and a continuous flow of new products. With heavy investment in R & D (it holds over 6,000 patents), and a policy of leasing rather than selling machines, IGT limits rivals' market opportunities. Despite heavy investment in new technologies and new products, IGT earned an ROE of 21% from 2011 to 2013.

Sources: www.altria.com, www.devro.com, and www.igt.com.

Porter's Five Forces of Competition Framework

The most widely used framework for analyzing competition within industries was developed by Michael Porter of Harvard Business School.[1] Porter's five forces of competition framework views the profitability of an industry (as indicated by its rate of return on capital relative to its cost of capital) as determined by five sources of competitive pressure. These five forces of competition include three sources of "horizontal" competition: competition from substitutes, competition from entrants, and competition from established rivals; and two sources of "vertical" competition: the power of suppliers and the power of buyers (Figure 3.2).

The strength of each of these competitive forces is determined by a number of key structural variables, as shown in Figure 3.3.

Competition from Substitutes

The price that customers are willing to pay for a product depends, in part, on the availability of substitute products. The absence of close substitutes for a product, as in the case of gasoline or cigarettes, means that consumers are comparatively insensitive to price (demand is inelastic with respect to price). The existence of close substitutes means that customers will switch to substitutes in response to price increases for the product (demand is elastic with respect to price). The internet has

FIGURE 3.2   Porter's five forces of competition framework

FIGURE 3.3   The structural determinants of the five forces of competition provided a new source of substitute competition that has proved devastating for a number of established industries. Travel agencies, newspapers, and telecommunication providers have all suffered severe competition from internet-based substitutes.

The extent to which substitutes depress prices and profits depends on the propensity of buyers to substitute between alternatives. This, in turn, depends on their price-performance characteristics. If city-center to city-center travel between Washington and New York is 50 minutes quicker by air than by train and the average traveler values time at $30 an hour, the implication is that the train will be competitive at fares of $25 below those charged by the airlines. The more complex a product and the more differentiated are buyers' preferences, the lower the extent of substitution by customers on the basis of price differences.

Threat of Entry

If an industry earns a return on capital in excess of its cost of capital, it will attract entry from new firms and firms diversifying from other industries. If entry is unrestricted, profitability will fall toward its competitive level. In both the UK and the US, the popularity of craft beers and the low capital cost of small-batch beer production have meant a flood of new entrants into the beer markets of both countries. Between 1990 and 2014, the number of breweries increased from 284 to 2822 in the US and from 241 to 1285 in the UK, despite the fact that overall beer production declined in both countries.[2] Wage differences between occupations are also influenced by entry barriers. Why is it that my wife, a psychotherapist, earns much less than our niece, a recently qualified medical doctor? In psychotherapy there are multiple accrediting bodies and less restrictive government licensing than in medicine, hence there are much lower barriers to entry.

Threat of entry rather than actual entry may be sufficient to ensure that established firms constrain their prices to the competitive level. An industry where no barriers to entry or exit exist is *contestable*: prices and profits tend toward the competitive level, regardless of the number of firms within the industry.[3] Contestability depends on the absence of sunk costs—investments whose value cannot be recovered on exit. With no sunk costs, an industry is vulnerable to "hit and run" entry whenever established firms raise their prices above the competitive level.

In most industries, however, new entrants cannot enter on equal terms with those of established firms. A *barrier to entry* is any disadvantage that new entrants face relative to established firms. The size of this disadvantage determines the height of a barrier to entry. The principal sources of barriers to entry are as follows.

Capital Requirements   The capital costs of becoming established in an industry can be so large as to discourage all but the largest companies. The duopoly of Boeing and Airbus in large passenger jets is protected by the huge investments needed to develop, build, and service big jet planes. In other industries, entry costs can be modest. Intense competition in the market for smartphone apps reflects the low cost of developing most applications. Across the service sector, start-up costs tend to be low: the start-up cost for a franchised pizza outlet starts at $118,500 for Domino's and $129,910 for Papa John's.[4]

Economies of Scale   Industries with high capital requirements for new entrants are also subject to **economies of scale**. Thus, large, indivisible investments in production facilities or technology or research or marketing, cost efficiency require amortizing these indivisible costs over a large volume of output. The problem for new entrants is that they typically enter with a low market share and, hence, are forced to accept high unit costs. A major source of scale economies is new product development costs. Airbus's A380 superjumbo cost about $18 billion to develop. Airbus must sell about 400 planes to break even. Once Airbus had committed to the project, then Boeing was effectively excluded from the superjumbo segment of the market: global demand was insufficient to make two superjumbos viable. In automobiles, Fiat CEO, Sergio Marchionne, argues that financial viability requires producing at least six million vehicles a year.

Absolute Cost Advantages Established firms may have a unit cost advantage over entrants, irrespective of scale. Absolute cost advantages often result from the ownership of low-cost sources of raw materials. Established oil and gas producers, such as Saudi Aramco and Gazprom, which have access to the world's biggest and most accessible reserves, have an unassailable cost advantage over more recent entrants such as Cairn Energy and BG Group. Absolute cost advantages may also result from economies of learning. Intel's dominance of the market for advanced microprocessors arises in part from the efficiency benefits it derives from its wealth of experience.

Product Differentiation In an industry where products are differentiated, established firms possess the advantages of brand recognition and customer loyalty. Products with very high levels of brand loyalty include cosmetics, disposable diapers, coffee, toothpaste, and pet food.[5] New entrants to such markets must spend disproportionately heavily on advertising and promotion to establish brand awareness. One study found that, compared to early entrants, late entrants into consumer goods markets incurred additional advertising and promotional costs amounting to 2.12% of sales revenue.[6]

Access to Channels of Distribution For many new suppliers of consumer goods, the principal barrier to entry is gaining distribution. Limited capacity within distribution channels (e.g., shelf space), risk aversion by retailers, and the fixed costs associated with carrying an additional product result in retailers being reluctant to carry a new manufacturer's product. The battle for supermarket shelf space between the major food processors (typically involving "slotting fees" to reserve shelf space) further disadvantages new entrants. An important competitive impact of the internet has been allowing new businesses to circumvent barriers to distribution.

Governmental and Legal Barriers Some economists claim that the only truly effective barriers to entry are those created by government. In taxicabs, banking, telecommunications, and broadcasting, entry usually requires a license from a public authority. Since medieval times favored businesses have benefitted from governments granting them an exclusive right to ply a particular trade. Today, patents, copyrights, and trademarks protect the creators of intellectual property from imitators. Regulatory requirements and environmental and safety standards often put new entrants at a disadvantage in comparison with established firms because compliance costs tend to weigh more heavily on newcomers.

Retaliation   Barriers to entry also depend on the entrants' expectations as to possible retaliation by established firms. Retaliation against a new entrant may take the form of aggressive price-cutting, increased advertising, sales promotion, or litigation. The major airlines have a long history of retaliation against low-cost entrants. Southwest and other budget airlines have alleged that selective price cuts by American and other major airlines amounted to predatory pricing designed to prevent its entry into new routes.[7] To avoid retaliation by incumbents, new entrants may initiate small-scale entry into marginal market segments. When Toyota, Nissan, and Honda first entered the US auto market, they targeted the small-car segments, partly because this was a segment that had been written off by the Detroit Big Three as inherently unprofitable.[8]

The Effectiveness of Barriers to Entry   Industries protected by high entry barriers tend to earn above-average rates of profit.[9] Capital requirements and advertising appear to be particularly effective impediments to entry.[10] The effectiveness of barriers to entry depends on the resources and capabilities that potential entrants possess. Barriers that are effective against new companies may be ineffective against established firms that are diversifying from other industries.[11] Google's massive web presence has allowed it to challenge the seemingly impregnable market positions of several other firms, notably Microsoft in web browsers and Apple in smartphones.

Rivalry between Established Competitors

In most industries, the major determinant of the overall state of competition and the general level of profitability is rivalry among the firms within the industry. In some industries, firms compete aggressively—sometimes to the extent that prices are pushed below the level of costs and industry-wide losses are incurred. In other industries, price competition is muted and rivalry focuses on advertising, innovation, and other non-price dimensions. The intensity of competition between established firms is the result of interactions between six factors. Let us look at each of them.

Concentration   **Seller concentration** refers to the number and size distribution of firms competing within a market. It is most commonly measured by the *concentration ratio*: the combined market share of the leading producers. For example, the four-firm concentration ratio (CR4) is the market share of the four largest producers. In markets dominated by a single firm (for example P&G's Gillette in razor blades, Apple in MP3 players, or Altria in the US smokeless tobacco market), the dominant firm can exercise considerable discretion over the prices it charges. Where a market comprises a small group of leading companies (an oligopoly), price competition may also be restrained, either by outright collusion or, more commonly, by "parallelism" of pricing decisions. Thus, in markets dominated by two companies, such as soft drinks (Coca-Cola and Pepsi), news weeklies (*Time* and *Newsweek*), and financial intelligence (Bloomberg and Reuters), prices tend to be similar and competition focuses on advertising, promotion, and product development. As the number of firms supplying a market increases, coordination of prices becomes more difficult and the likelihood that one firm will initiate price-cutting increases. In wireless telecommunications, regulators in the US and Europe have favored four operators in each national market. To limit price competition and improve margins, the operators favor mergers that would reduce the number of competitors to three in each market.[12] However, despite the frequent observation that the exit of a competitor reduces price competition, while the entry of a new competitor stimulates it, there is little systematic evidence that seller concentration increases profitability. "The relation, if any, between seller concentration and profitability is weak statistically and the estimated effect is usually small."[13]

Diversity of Competitors   The ability of rival firms to avoid price competition in favor of collusive pricing practices depends on how similar they are in their origins, objectives, costs, and strategies. The cozy atmosphere of the US auto industry prior to the advent of import competition was greatly assisted by the similarities of the companies in terms of cost structures, strategies, and top management mindsets. Conversely, the difficulties that OPEC experiences in agreeing and enforcing output quotas among its member countries are exacerbated by their differences in terms of objectives, production costs, politics, and religion.

Product Differentiation   The more similar the offerings among rival firms, the more willing are customers to switch between them and the greater is the inducement for firms to cut prices to boost sales. Where the products of rival firms are virtually indistinguishable, the product is a commodity and price is the sole basis for competition. By contrast, in industries where products are highly differentiated (perfumes, pharmaceuticals, restaurants, management consulting services), competition tends to focus on quality, brand promotion, and customer service rather than price.

Excess Capacity and Exit Barriers   Why, especially in commodity industries, does industry profitability tend to fall so drastically during periods of recession? The key is the balance between demand and capacity. Unused capacity encourages firms to offer price cuts to attract new business. Excess capacity may be cyclical (e.g., the boom–bust cycle in the semiconductor industry); it may also be part of a structural problem resulting from overinvestment and declining demand. In this latter situation, the key issue is whether excess capacity will leave the industry. **Barriers to exit** are costs associated with capacity leaving an industry. Where resources are durable and specialized, and where employees are entitled to job protection, barriers to exit may be substantial.[14] In the European auto industry, excess capacity together with high exit barriers have devastated industry profitability. Conversely, demand growth creates capacity shortages that boost margins. Rising production of shale oil in North America during 2012–2015 created an acute shortage of pipeline capacity, greatly increasing the profitability of the pipeline companies. On average, companies in growing industries earn higher profits than companies in slow-growing or declining industries (Figure 3.4).

Cost Conditions: Scale Economies and the Ratio of Fixed to Variable Costs   When excess capacity causes price competition, how low will prices go? The key factor is cost structure. Where fixed costs are high relative to variable costs, firms will take on marginal business at any price that covers variable costs. The incredible volatility of bulk shipping rates reflects the fact that almost all the costs of operating bulk carriers are fixed. The daily charter rates for "capesize" bulk carriers fell from $233,998 on June 5, 2008 to $2773 25 weeks later in response to a sudden contraction in world trade.[15] Similarly, in the airline industry the emergence of excess capacity almost invariably leads to price wars and industry-wide losses. The willingness of

FIGURE 3.4   The impact of growth on profitability

Source: Based upon the PIMS multiple regression equation. See R.M. Grant *Contemporary Strategy Analysis*, 5th edition (Blackwell, 2005): 491.

airlines to offer heavily discounted tickets on flights with low bookings reflects the very low variable costs of filling empty seats. "Cyclical" stocks are characterized not only by cyclical demand but also by a high ratio of fixed to variable costs, which means that fluctuations in revenues are amplified into much bigger fluctuations in profits.

Scale economies may also encourage companies to compete aggressively on price in order to gain the cost benefits of greater volume. If scale efficiency in the auto industry means producing six million cars a year, a level that is currently achieved by only seven companies, the outcome is a battle for market share as each firm tries to achieve critical mass.

Bargaining Power of Buyers

The firms in an industry compete in two types of markets: in the markets for inputs and the markets for outputs. In input markets firms purchase raw materials, components, services, and labor. In the markets for outputs, firms sell their goods and services to customers (who may be distributors, consumers, or other manufacturers). The ability of buyers to drive down the prices they pay depends upon two factors: their price sensitivity and their bargaining power relative to the firms within the industry.

Buyers' Price Sensitivity   The extent to which buyers are sensitive to the prices charged by the firms in an industry depends on the following.

- The greater the importance of an item as a proportion of total cost, the more sensitive buyers will be about the price they pay. Beverage manufacturers are highly sensitive to the costs of aluminum cans because this is one of their largest single cost items. Conversely, most companies are not sensitive to the fees charged by their auditors, since auditing costs are a tiny fraction of total company expenses.
- The less differentiated the products of the supplying industry, the more willing the buyer is to switch suppliers on the basis of price. The manufacturers

of T-shirts and light bulbs have much more to fear from Walmart's buying power than have the suppliers of cosmetics.

● The more intense the competition among buyers, the greater their eagerness for price reductions from their sellers. As competition in the world automobile industry has intensified, so component suppliers face greater pressures for lower prices.

● The more critical an industry's product to the quality of the buyer's product or service, the less sensitive are buyers to the prices they are charged. The buying power of personal computer manufacturers relative to the manufacturers of microprocessors (Intel and AMD) is limited by the vital importance of these components to the functionality of PCs.

Relative Bargaining Power   Bargaining power rests, ultimately, on the refusal to deal with the other party. The balance of power between the two parties to a transaction depends on the credibility and effectiveness with which each makes this threat. The key issue is the relative cost that each party would incur in the event of a hold-out by the counterparty, together with the relative bargaining skills of each party. Several factors influence the bargaining power of buyers relative to that of sellers:

● Size and concentration of buyers relative to suppliers. The smaller the number of buyers and the bigger their purchases, the greater the cost of losing one. Because of their size, health maintenance organizations can purchase healthcare from hospitals and doctors at much lower costs than can individual patients. Empirical studies show that buyer concentration lowers prices and profits in the supplying industry.[16]

● Buyers' information. The better-informed buyers are about suppliers and their prices and costs, the better they are able to bargain. Doctors and lawyers do not normally display the prices they charge, nor do traders in the bazaars of Marrakesh or Chennai. Keeping customers ignorant of relative prices is an effective constraint on their buying power. But knowing prices is of little value if the quality of the product is unknown. In the markets for haircuts, interior design, and management consulting, the ability of buyers to bargain over price is limited by uncertainty over the precise attributes of the product they are buying.

● Capacity for **vertical integration**. In refusing to deal with the other party, the alternative to finding another supplier or buyer is to do it yourself. Large beer companies have reduced their dependence on the manufacturers of aluminum cans by manufacturing their own. Large retail chains introduce their own label brands to compete with those of their suppliers. Backward integration need not necessarily occur—a credible threat may suffice.

Bargaining Power of Suppliers

Analysis of the determinants of relative power between the producers in an industry and their suppliers is precisely analogous to analysis of the relationship between producers and their buyers. The only difference is that it is now the firms in the industry that are the buyers and the producers of inputs that are the suppliers. Again, the relevant factors are the ease with which the firms in the industry can switch between different input suppliers and the relative bargaining power of each party.

The suppliers of commodities tend to lack bargaining power relative to their customers, hence they may use cartels to boost their influence over prices (e.g., OPEC, the International Coffee Organization, and farmers' marketing cooperatives). Conversely, the suppliers of complex, technically sophisticated components may be able to exert considerable bargaining power. The dismal profitability of the personal computer industry may be attributed to the power exercised by the suppliers of key components (processors, disk drives, LCD screens) and the dominant supplier of operating systems (Microsoft). The profitability of the wireless telecommunications carriers also suffers from the presence of a powerful supplier: the monopoly position of national governments which auction spectrum licenses.

Labor unions are important sources of supplier power. US industries where over 60% of employees are unionized (such as automobiles, steel, and airlines) earned a return on investment that was five percentage points lower than industries where less than 35% of employees were unionized.[17]

Applying Industry Analysis to Forecasting Industry Profitability

Once we understand how industry structure drives competition, which, in turn, determines industry profitability, we can apply this analysis to forecast industry profitability in the future.

Identifying Industry Structure

The first stage of any industry analysis is to identify the key elements of the industry's structure. In principle, this is a simple task. It requires identifying who are the main players—the producers, the customers, the input suppliers, and the producers of substitute goods—then examining some of the key structural characteristics of each of these groups that will determine competition and bargaining power.

In most manufacturing industries identifying the main groups of players is straightforward; in other industries, particularly in service industries, mapping the industry can be more difficult. Consider the television industry. It comprises production companies that produce content in the form of TV shows; network broadcasters and cable channels that commission the TV shows and create program schedules; distributors in the form of local TV stations, cable providers, satellite TV providers, and online video streaming companies; and customers in the form of viewers and advertisers. Additional complexity is created by the fact that some companies occupy multiple roles within the industry. For example, Time Warner is a content producer (Warner Brothers), a broadcast network (CW), a cable channel (CNN, HBO), a local TV broadcaster, and a cable provider. Such complexity raises issues of industry definition which we shall return to later in this chapter.

Forecasting Industry Profitability

We can use industry analysis to understand why profitability has been low in some industries and high in others but, ultimately, our interest is not to explain the past but to predict the future. Investment decisions made today will commit resources to an industry for years—often for a decade or more—hence, it is critical that we are able to predict what level of returns the industry is likely to offer in the future. Current profitability is a poor indicator of future profitability—industries such as newspapers, solar (photovoltaic) panels, and investment banking have suffered massive declines in profitability; in other industries such as chemicals and food processing—profitability has revived. However, if an industry's profitability is determined by the structure of that industry then we can use observations of the structural trends in an industry to forecast likely changes in competition and profitability. Changes in industry structure typically result from fundamental shifts in customer buying behavior, technology, and firm strategies which can be anticipated well in advance of their impacts on competition and profitability.

To predict the future profitability of an industry, our analysis proceeds in three stages:

1 Examine how the industry's current and recent levels of competition and profitability are a consequence of its present structure.

2 Identify the trends that are changing the industry's structure. Is the industry consolidating? Are new players seeking to enter? Are the industry's products becoming more differentiated or more commoditized? Will additions to industry capacity outstrip growth of demand? Is technological innovation causing new substitutes to appear?

3 Identify how these structural changes will affect the five forces of competition and resulting profitability of the industry. Will the changes in industry structure cause competition to intensify or to weaken? Rarely do all the structural changes move competition in a consistent direction, typically some will exacerbate competitive intensity; others will cause it to abate. Hence, determining the overall impact on profitability tends to be a matter of judgment.

Strategy Capsule 3.2 discusses the outlook for profitability in the wireless handset industry.

Using Industry Analysis to Develop Strategy

Once we understand how industry structure influences competition, which in turn determines industry profitability, we can use this knowledge to develop firm strategies. First, we can develop strategies that influence industry structure in order to moderate competition; second, we can position the firm to shelter it from the ravages of competition.

The Future of the Wireless Handset Industry

Wireless telephony has been one of the greatest growth industries of the past two decades—and almost as lucrative for the handset makers as for the service providers. During the 1990s, growth of handset sales in North America, Europe, and Japan averaged close to 50% each year and generated massive profits and shareholder value for the early leaders, Motorola and Nokia.

During 2005–2015, there have been profound changes in competition and margins. Despite continued demand growth (especially in emerging markets), profitability has fallen. During 2000–2005, the industry leaders—Nokia, Motorola, Sony-Ericsson, Samsung, LG, and Siemens—earned an average operating margin of 23% on their sales of mobile devices. By 2014, the top seven suppliers (Samsung, Apple, Lenovo, Huawei, Nokia, LG, and Xiaomi) were earning an average operating margin of 4% (with Apple and Samsung accounting for almost all the combined profit).

The structural changes undermining industry profitability included new entry; several Chinese and Taiwanese contact manufacturers—including HTC, Huawei, and Xiaomi—introduced branded phones. As mature markets became saturated, so excess capacity emerged throughout the industry, which, in turn, reinforced the buying power of the major distributors of phones, the wireless service companies.

During 2016–2020, competition and profitability will be affected by several factors:

- New entry seems likely to continue. In the smartphone market, the availability of the Android platform making it easy for contract manufacturers to design and brand their own phones will increase the number of firms competing in this segment.
- Most emerging markets, including China and India, are likely to become saturated.
- Product differentiation will decline. In smartphones, the Apple and Android platforms offer increasingly similar functionality and most of the same apps.
- Mergers among telecom service providers will increase their buying power.

Strategies to Alter Industry Structure

Understanding how the structural characteristics of an industry determine the intensity of competition and the level of profitability provides a basis for identifying opportunities for changing industry structure to alleviate competitive pressures. The first issue is to identify the key structural features of an industry that are responsible for depressing profitability. The second is to consider which of these structural features are amenable to change through appropriate strategic initiatives. For example:

- Between 2000 and 2006, a wave of mergers and acquisitions among the world's iron ore miners resulted in three companies—Vale, Rio Tinto, and BHP Billiton—controlling 75% of global iron ore exports. The growing power of the iron ore producers relative to their customers, the steel makers, contributed to the 400% rise in iron ore prices between 2004 and 2010.[18]

- Excess capacity was a major problem in the European petrochemicals industry during the 1970s and 1980s. Through a series of bilateral plant exchanges, each company built a leading position within a particular product area.[19]
- In the US airline industry, the major airlines have struggled to change an unfavorable industry structure resulting in a dismal record of profitability. In the absence of significant product differentiation, the airlines have used frequent-flyer schemes to build customer loyalty. Through hub-and-spoke route systems, the companies have achieved dominance of particular airports: American at Miami and Dallas/Fort Worth, Delta at Atlanta, and Southwest at Baltimore. Mergers and alliances have reduced the numbers of competitors on most routes.[20]
- Building entry barriers is a vital strategy for preserving high profitability in the long run. A primary goal of the American Medical Association has been to maintain the incomes of its members by controlling the numbers of doctors trained in the US and imposing barriers to the entry of doctors from overseas.

The idea of firms reshaping their industries to their own advantage has been developed by Michael Jacobides. He begins with the premise that industries are in a state of continual evolution and that all firms, even quite small ones, have the potential to influence the development of industry structure to suit their own interests—thereby achieving what he calls *architectural advantage.* Jacobides encourages firms to look broadly at their industry—to see their entire value chain and links with firms producing complementary goods and services. The key is then to identify "bottlenecks"—activities where scarcity and the potential for control offer superior opportunities for profit.[21] Architectural advantages results from three sources:

- Creating one's own bottleneck: Apple's dominance of the music download market through iTunes is achieved through a digital rights management (DRM) strategy that effectively locks in consumers' through the incompatibility of its music files with other MP3 formats.
- Relieving bottlenecks in other parts of the value chain: Google developed Android to prevent other firms from gaining a bottleneck in operating systems for mobile devices which might have threatened Google's ability to transfer its dominance of search services from fixed to mobile devices.
- Redefining roles and responsibilities in the industries: IKEA's ability to become the world's biggest and most successful supplier of furniture was based upon a strategy which required a transfer of furniture assembly from furniture manufacturers to consumers.

Positioning the Company

Recognizing and understanding the competitive forces that a firm faces within its industry allows managers to position the firm where competitive forces are weakest. The recorded music industry, once reliant on sales of CDs, has been devastated by the substitute competition in the form of digital downloads, piracy, file sharing, and streaming. Yet not all segments of the recorded music business have been equally affected. The old are less inclined to new technology than younger listeners are, hence classical music, country, and golden oldies have become comparatively more attractive than pop and hip hop genres.

Porter describes the success of US truck-maker Paccar in sheltering itself from the bargaining power of fleet buyers. By focusing on the preferences of independent owner-operators (e.g., by providing superior sleeping cabins, higher-specification seats, a roadside assistance program) Paccar has consistently been able to earn the highest rate of return in the industry.[22]

Effective positioning requires the firm to anticipate changes in the competitive forces likely to affect the industry. Traditional book retailing has been devastated by online retailers such as Amazon and e-books. The survivors are those that have positioned themselves to avoid these powerful competitive forces, for example by creating new revenue sources such as cafes and events for which admission is charged.

Defining Industries: Where to Draw the Boundaries

In our earlier discussion of the structure of the television broadcasting industry, I noted that a key challenge in industry analysis is defining the relevant industry. The Standard Industrial Classification (SIC) offers an official guide, but this provides limited practical assistance. Suppose Ferrari is analyzing its industry environment. Should it consider itself part of the "motor vehicles and equipment" industry (SIC 371), the automobile industry (SIC 3712), or the performance car industry? Should it see itself as part of the Italian, European, or global auto industry?

Industries and Markets

The first issue is clarifying what we mean by the term *industry*. Economists define an industry as a group of firms that supplies a market. Hence, a close correspondence exists between markets and industries. So, what's the difference between analyzing industry structure and analyzing market structure? The principal difference is that industry analysis, notably five forces analysis, looks at industry profitability being determined by competition in two markets: product markets and input markets.

Everyday usage draws a clearer distinction between industries and markets. Typically, *industries* are identified with relatively broad sectors, whereas *markets* relate to specific products. Thus, the firms within the packaging industry compete in many distinct product markets—glass containers, steel cans, aluminum cans, paper cartons, plastic containers, and so on.

Similar issues arise in relation to geographical boundaries. From an economist's viewpoint, the US automobile industry would denote all companies supplying the US auto market, irrespective of their location. In everyday usage, the US auto industry usually refers to auto manufacturers located within the US.

To define an industry, it makes sense to start by identifying the firms that compete to supply a particular market. At the outset, this approach may lead us to question conventional concepts of industry boundaries. For example, what is the industry commonly referred to as *banking*? Institutions called *banks* supply a number of different products and services each comprising different sets of competitors. The most basic distinction is between retail banking, corporate/ wholesale banking, and investment banking. Each of these can be disaggregated into several different product markets. Retail banking comprises deposit taking, transaction services, credit cards, and mortgage lending. Investment banking includes corporate finance and underwriting, trading, and advisory services (such as mergers and acquisitions).

Defining Industries and Markets: Substitution in Demand and Supply

The central issue in defining industries and markets is to establish who is competing with whom. To do this we need to draw upon the principle of *substitutability*. There are two dimensions to this: substitutability on the demand side and substitutability on the supply side.

Let us consider once more the industry within which Ferrari competes. Starting with the demand side, if customers are willing to substitute only between Ferraris and other sports-car brands brands on the basis of price differentials, then Ferrari is part of the performance car industry. If, on the other hand, customers are willing to substitute Ferraris for other mass-market brands, then Ferrari is part of the broader automobile industry.

But this fails to take account of substitutability on the supply side. If volume car producers such as Ford and Hyundai are able to apply their production facilities and distribution networks to supply sports cars, then, on the basis of supply-side substitutability, we could regard Ferrari as part of the broader automobile industry. The same logic can be used to define the major domestic appliances as an industry. Although consumers are unwilling to substitute between refrigerators and dishwashers, manufacturers can use the same plants and distribution channels for different appliances.

Similar considerations apply to geographical boundaries. Should Ferrari view itself as competing in a single global market or in a series of separate national or regional markets? The criterion here again is substitutability. If customers are willing and able to substitute cars available on different national markets, or if manufacturers are willing and able to divert their output among different countries to take account of differences in margins, then a market is global. The key test of the geographical boundaries of a market is price: if price differences for the same product between different locations tend to be eroded by demand-side and supply-side substitution, then these locations lie within a single market.

In practice, drawing the boundaries of markets and industries is a matter of judgment that depends on the purposes and context of the analysis. Decisions regarding pricing and market positioning will require a micro-level approach to market and industry definition. Decisions over investments in technology, new plants, and new products require a wider view of the relevant market and industry.

The boundaries of a market or industry are seldom clear-cut. A firm's competitive environment is a continuum rather than a bounded space. Thus, we may view the competitive market of Disneyland, Hong Kong as a set of concentric circles.

The closest competitors are nearby theme parks Ocean Park and Ma Wan Park. Slightly more distant are Shenzhen Happy Valley, Shenzhen Window of the World, and Splendid China. Further still are Disneyland parks in Tokyo and Shanghai and alternative forms of entertainment, e.g., a trip to Macau or to a beach resort such as Sanya on Hainan Island.

For the purposes of applying the five forces framework, industry definition is seldom critical. Thus, we may define the "box" within which industry rivals compete quite narrowly, but because we take account of competitive forces outside the industry box, we can view nearby competitors as the suppliers of substitutes and potential entrants. Hence, the precise boundaries of the industry box are not greatly important.[23]

From Industry Attractiveness to Competitive Advantage: Identifying Key Success Factors

The five forces framework allows us to determine an industry's potential for profit. But how is industry profit shared between the different firms competing in that industry? Let us look explicitly at the sources of competitive advantage within an industry. In subsequent chapters I shall develop a more comprehensive analysis of competitive advantage. My goal in this chapter is simply to identify an industry's **key success factors**: those factors within an industry that influence a firm's ability to outperform rivals.[24] In Strategy Capsule 3.3, Kenichi Ohmae, former head of McKinsey's Tokyo office, discusses key success factors in forestry.

Like Ohmae, our approach to identifying key success factors is straightforward and commonsense. To survive and prosper in an industry, a firm must meet two criteria: first, it must supply what customers want to buy; second, it must survive competition. Hence, we may start by asking two questions:

- What do our customers want?
- What does the firm need to do to survive competition?

To answer the first question we need to look more closely at customers of the industry and to view them not as a source of buying power and a threat to profitability but as the *raison d'être* of the industry and its underlying source of profit. This requires that we inquire: Who are our customers? What are their needs? How do they choose between competing offerings? Once we recognize the basis upon which customers' choose between rival offerings, we can identify the factors that confer success upon the individual firm. For example, if travelers choose airlines primarily on price, then cost efficiency is the primary basis for competitive advantage in the airline industry and the key success factors are the determinants of relative cost.

The second question requires that we examine the nature of competition in the industry. How intense is competition and what are its key dimensions? Thus, in airlines, it is not enough to offer low fares. To survive intense competition during

STRATEGY CAPSULE 3.3

Probing for Key Success Factors

As a consultant faced with an unfamiliar business or industry, I make a point of first asking the specialists in the business, "What is the secret of success in this industry?" Needless to say, I seldom get an immediate answer and so I pursue the inquiry by asking other questions from a variety of angles in order to establish as quickly as possible some reasonable hypotheses as to key factors for success. In the course of these interviews it usually becomes quite obvious what analyses will be required in order to prove or disprove these hypotheses. By first identifying the probable key factors for success and then screening them by proof or disproof, it is often possible for the strategist to penetrate very quickly to the core of a problem.

Traveling in the US last year, I found myself on one occasion sitting in a plane next to a director of one of the biggest lumber companies in the country. Thinking I might learn something useful in the course of the five-hour flight, I asked him, "What are the key factors for success in the lumber industry?" To my surprise, his reply was immediate: "Owning large forests and maximizing the yield from them." The first of these key factors is a relatively simple matter: purchase of forestland. But his second point required further explanation. Accordingly, my next question was: "What variable or variables do you control in order to maximize the yield from a given tract?"

He replied: "The rate of tree growth is the key variable. As a rule, two factors promote growth: the amount of sunshine and the amount of water. Our company doesn't have many forests with enough of both. In Arizona and Utah, for example, we get more than enough sunshine but too little water and so tree growth is very low. Now, if we could give the trees in those states enough water, they'd be ready in less than 15 years instead of the 30 it takes now. The most important project we have in hand at the moment is aimed at finding out how to do this."

Impressed that this director knew how to work out a key factor strategy for his business, I offered my own contribution: "Then under the opposite conditions, where there is plenty of water but too little sunshine—for example, around the lower reaches of the Columbia River—the key factors should be fertilizers to speed up the growth and the choice of tree varieties that don't need so much sunshine."

Having established in a few minutes the general framework of what we were going to talk about, I spent the rest of the long flight very profitably hearing from him in detail how each of these factors was being applied.

Source: Kenichi Ohmae, *The Mind of the Strategist* (New York: McGraw-Hill, 1982): 85 © The McGraw-Hill Companies Inc., reproduced with permission.

recessionary periods an airline requires financial strength; it may also require good relations with regulators and suppliers.

A basic framework for identifying key success factors is presented in Figure 3.5. Application of the framework to identify key success factors in three industries is outlined in Table 3.2.

Key success factors can also be identified through the direct modeling of profitability. In the same way that the five forces analysis models the determinants of

FIGURE 3.5 Identifying key success factors

TABLE 3.2 Identifying key success factors: Steel, fashion clothing, and supermarkets

	What do customers want? (Analysis of demand)	How do firms survive competition? (Analysis of competition)	Key success factors
Steel	Low price Product consistency Reliability of supply Technical specifications (for special steels)	Intense price competition results from undifferentiated products, excess capacity, exit barriers, and high fixed costs. Hence, cost efficiency and financial strength are essential	Cost efficiency requires: large-scale plants, availability of low-cost raw materials, rapid capacity adjustment Also, high-technology, small-scale plants can achieve low costs through flexibility and high productivity High technical specifications, quality, and service can yield a price premium
Fashion clothing	Diversity of customer preferences Customers willing to pay premium for brand, style, exclusivity, and quality Mass market is highly price sensitive	Low barriers to entry and exit, low seller concentration, and buying power of retail chains imply intense competition Differentiation offers price premium, but imitation is rapid	Combining differentiation with low costs Differentiation based upon style, reputation, quality, and speed of response to changing fashions Cost efficiency requires manufacture in low-wage countries
Supermarkets	Low prices Convenient location Wide product range adapted to local preferences Fresh/quality produce, good service, ease of parking, pleasant ambience	Intensity competition depends on number and proximity of competitors Bargaining power a key determinant of cost of bought-in goods	Low costs require operational efficiency, large-scale purchases, low wages Differentiation requires large stores (to allow wide product range), convenient location, familiarity with local customer preferences

industry-level profitability, we can also model firm-level profitability by identifying the drivers of a firm's relative profitability within an industry. Using the same approach as in Chapter 2 (Figure 2.1), we can disaggregate return on capital employed into component ratios, which then point to the main drivers of superior profitability. In some industries, there are well-known formulae that link operating ratios to overall profitability. Strategy Capsule 3.4 uses such a formula used in the airline industry to identify key success factors.

In their battle for survival, the airlines have sought to optimize as many of these factors as possible in order to improve their profitability. To enhance revenue, several airlines have withdrawn from their most intensely competitive routes; others have sought to achieve a fare premium over the cut-price airlines through superior punctuality, convenience, comfort, and services. To improve load factors, companies have become more flexible in their pricing and in allocating different planes to different routes. Most notably, companies have sought to cut costs by increasing employee productivity, reducing overheads, sharing services with other airlines, and reducing salaries and benefits.

STRATEGY CAPSULE 3.4

Identifying Key Success Factors by Profitability Modeling: Airlines

Profitability, as measured by operating income per available seat-mile (ASM), is determined by three factors: yield, which is total operating revenues divided by the number of revenue passenger miles (RPMs); load factor, which is the ratio of RPMs to ASMs; and unit cost, which is total operating expenses divided by ASMs. Thus:

$$\frac{\text{Profit}}{\text{ASMs}} = \frac{\text{Revenue}}{\text{RPMs}} \times \frac{\text{RPMs}}{\text{ASMs}} - \frac{\text{Expenses}}{\text{ASMs}}$$

Some of the main determinants of each of these component ratios are the following:

◆ Revenue/RPMs
  • intensity of competition on routes flown
  • effective yield management to permit quick price adjustment to changing market conditions
  • ability to attract business customers
  • superior customer service.

◆ Load factor (RPMs/ASMs)
  • competitiveness of prices
  • efficiency of route planning (e.g., through hub-and-spoke systems)
  • building customer loyalty through quality of service, frequent-flier programs
  • matching airplane size to demand for individual flights.

◆ Expenses/ASMs
  • wage rates and benefit levels
  • fuel efficiency of aircraft
  • productivity of employees (determined partly by their job flexibility)
  • load factors
  • level of administrative cost.

The usefulness of industry-level success factors in formulating strategy has been scorned by some strategy scholars. Pankaj Ghemawat observes that the "whole idea of identifying a success factor and then chasing it seems to have something in common with the ill-considered medieval hunt for the philosopher's stone, a substance that would transmute everything it touched into gold."[25] However, the existence of common success factors in an industry does not imply that firms should adopt similar strategies. In the fashion clothing business we identified a number of key success factors (Table 3.2), yet all the leading companies—Inditex (Zara), H&M, Diesel, and Mango—have adopted unique strategies to exploit these key success factors.

Summary

In Chapter 1 we established that a profound understanding of the competitive environment is a critical ingredient of a successful strategy. Despite the vast number of external influences that affect every business enterprise, our focus is the firm's industry environment which we analyze in order to evaluate the industry's profit potential and to identify the sources of competitive advantage.

The centerpiece of our approach is Porter's five forces of competition framework, which links the structure of an industry to the competitive intensity within it and to the profitability that it realizes. The Porter framework offers a simple yet powerful organizing framework for identifying the relevant features of an industry's structure and predicting their implications for competitive behavior.

The primary application for the Porter five forces framework is in predicting how changes in an industry's structure are likely to affect its profitability. Once we understand the drivers of industry profitability, we can identify strategies through which a firm can improve industry attractiveness and position itself in relation to these different competitive forces.

As with most of the tools for strategy analysis that we shall consider in this book, the Porter five forces framework is easy to comprehend. However, real learning about industry analysis and about the Porter framework in particular derives from its application. It is only when we apply the Porter framework to analyzing competition and diagnosing the causes of high or low profitability in an industry that we are forced to confront the complexities and subtleties of the model. A key issue is identifying the industry within which a firm competes and recognizing its boundaries. By employing the principles of substitutability and relevance, we can delineate meaningful industry boundaries.

Finally, our industry analysis allows us to make a first approach at identifying the sources of competitive advantage through recognizing key success factors in an industry.

I urge you to put the tools of industry analysis to work—not just in your strategic management coursework but also in interpreting everyday business events. The value of the Porter framework is as a practical tool—in helping us to understand the disparities in profitability between industries, whether an industry will sustain its profitability into the future, and which start-up companies have the best potential for making money. Through practical applications, you will also become aware of the limitations of the Porter framework. In the next chapter we will see how we can extend our analysis of industry and competition.

Self-Study Questions

1. From Table 3.1, select a high-profit industry and a low-profit industry. From what you know of the structure of your selected industry, use the five forces framework to explain why profitability has been high in one industry and low in the other.

2. With reference to Strategy Capsule 3.1, use the five forces framework to explain why profitability has been so high in the US market for smokeless tobacco.

3. The major forces shaping the business environment of the fixed-line telecom industry are technology and government policy. The industry has been influenced by fiber optics (greatly increasing transmission capacity), new modes of telecommunication (wireless and internet telephony), the convergence of telecom and cable TV, and regulatory change (including the opening of fixed-line infrastructures to "virtual operators"). Using the five forces of competition framework, show how each of these developments has influenced competition and profitability in the fixed-line telecom industry.

4. By March 2015, the online travel agency industry had consolidated around two leaders: Expedia (which had acquired Travelocity, Lastminute.com, and Orbitz) and Priceline (which owned booking.com, Kayak and OpenTable). These two market leaders competed with numerous smaller online travel agents (e.g., TripAdvisor, Travelzoo), with traditional travel agencies (e.g., Carlson Wagonlit, TUI, American Express—all of which had adopted a "bricks 'n' clicks" business model), and with direct online sales by airlines, hotel chains, and car rental companies. Amazon and Google were both viewed as likely entrants to the market. The online travel agents are dependent upon computerized airline reservation systems such as Sabre, Amadeus, and Travelport. Use Porter's five forces framework to predict the likely profitability of the online travel agency industry over the next ten years.

5. Walmart (like Carrefour, Ahold, and Tesco) competes in several countries of the world, yet most shoppers choose between retailers within a radius of a few miles. For the purposes of analyzing profitability and competitive strategy, should Walmart consider the discount retailing industry to be global, national, or local?

6. What do you think are key success factors in:
   a. the pizza delivery industry?
   b. the credit card industry (where the world's biggest issuers are: Bank of America, JPMorgan Chase, Citigroup, American Express, Capital One, HSBC, and Discover)?

Notes

1. M. E. Porter, "The Five Competitive Forces that Shape Strategy," *Harvard Business Review* 57 (January 2008): 57–71.
2. Brewers Association, "Historical U.S. Brewery Count," http://www.brewersassociation.org/statistics/number-of-breweries/; "Good Beer Guide 2015 Shows UK has Most Breweries," *Guardian* (September 11, 2014).
3. W. J. Baumol, J. C. Panzar, and R. D. Willig, *Contestable Markets and the Theory of Industry Structure* (New York: Harcourt Brace Jovanovich, 1982). See also M. Spence, "Contestable Markets and the Theory of Industry Structure: A Review Article," *Journal of Economic Literature* 21 (1983): 981–990.
4. "Annual Franchise 500," *Entrepreneur* (January 2014).
5. "Brand Keys Customer Loyalty 2013," http://brandkeys.com/wp-content/uploads/2013/02/2013-CLEI-Press-Release-FINAL-Overall.pdf, accessed July 20, 2015.

6. R. D. Buzzell and P. W. Farris, "Marketing Costs in Consumer Goods Industries," in H. Thorelli (ed.), *Strategy + Structure = Performance* (Bloomington, IN: Indiana University Press, 1977): 128–129.

7. In October 1999, the Department of Justice alleged that American Airlines was using unfair means in attempting to monopolize air traffic out of Dallas/Fort Worth, http://openjurist.org/743/f2d/1114/united-states-v-american-airlines-inc-l, accessed July 20, 2015.

8. M. Lieberman ("Excess Capacity as a Barrier to Entry," *Journal of Industrial Economics* 35, 1987: 607–627) argues that, to be credible, the threat of retaliation needs to be supported by incumbents investing in excess capacity so that they have the potential to flood the market.

9. See, for example, J. S. Bain, *Barriers to New Competition* (Cambridge, MA: Harvard University Press, 1956); and H. M. Mann, "Seller Concentration, Entry Barriers, and Rates of Return in Thirty Industries," *Review of Economics and Statistics* 48 (1966): 296–307.

10. J. L. Siegfried and L. B. Evans, "Empirical Studies of Entry and Exit: A Survey of the Evidence," *Review of Industrial Organization* 9 (1994): 121–155.

11. G. S. Yip, "Gateways to Entry," *Harvard Business Review* 60 (September/October 1982): 85–93.

12. "Mobile Telecoms: Four is a Magic Number," *Economist* (March 15, 2014): 64.

13. R. Schmalensee, "Inter-Industry Studies of Structure and Performance," in R. Schmalensee and R. D. Willig (eds), *Handbook of Industrial Organization*, 2nd edn (Amsterdam: North Holland, 1988): 976.

14. C. Baden-Fuller (ed.), *Strategic Management of Excess Capacity* (Oxford: Basil Blackwell, 1990).

15. "Dry bulk shipping rates approach all-time low," *Financial Times* (November 27, 2008).

16. T. Kelly and M. L. Gosman, "Increased Buyer Concentration and its Effects on Profitability in the Manufacturing Sector," *Review of Industrial Organization* 17 (2000): 41–59.

17. R. D. Buzzell and B. T. Gale, *The PIMS Principles* (New York: Free Press, 1987): 67.

18. "Iron Ore Companies Consolidated," *International Resource Journal* (October 2014).

19. J. Bower, *When Markets Quake* (Boston: Harvard Business School Press, 1986).

20. M. Carnall, S. Berry, and P. Spiller, "Airline Hubbing, Costs and Demand," in D. Lee (ed.), *Advances in Airline Economics*, vol. 1 (Amsterdam: Elsevier, 2006).

21. M. G. Jacobides, "Strategy Bottlenecks: How TME Players Can Shape and Win Control of Their Industry Architecture," *Insights*, 9 (2011): 84–91; M. G. Jacobides and J. P. MacDuffie, "How to Drive Value Your Way," *Harvard Business Review*, 91 (July/August 2013): 92–100.

22. M. E. Porter, "The Five Competitive Forces that Shape Strategy," *Harvard Business Review* 57 (January 2008): 57–71.

23. For a concise discussion of market definition see Office of Fair Trading, *Market Definition* (London: December 2004), especially pp. 7–17.

24. The term was coined by Chuck Hofer and Dan Schendel (*Strategy Formulation: Analytical Concepts*, St Paul: West Publishing, 1977: 77). They define key success factors as "those variables that management can influence through its decisions and that can affect significantly the overall competitive positions of the firms in an industry."

25. P. Ghemawat, *Commitment: The Dynamic of Strategy* (New York: Free Press, 1991): 11.

4 Further Topics in Industry and Competitive Analysis

Economic progress, in capitalist society, means turmoil.

—JOSEPH A. SCHUMPETER, AUSTRIAN ECONOMIST, 1883–1950

OUTLINE

Introduction and Objectives

Last chapter was concerned with outlining Porter's five forces framework and showing how it can be applied to analyzing competition, predicting industry profitability, and developing strategy. The Porter framework is one of the most useful and widely applied tools of strategic analysis. It also has its limitations. In this chapter, we shall extend our analysis of industry and competition beyond the limits of the Porter framework.

By the time you have completed this chapter, you will be able to:

♦ Recognize the limits of the Porter five forces framework, and extend the framework to include the role of complements as well as substitutes.

♦ Acknowledge competition as a dynamic process that changes industry structures, appreciate the insights that game theory offers into the dynamics of rivalry, and use competitor analysis to predict the competitive moves by rivals.

♦ Segment an industry into its constituent markets, appraise the relative attractiveness of different segments and apply strategic group analysis to classify firms according to their strategic types.

Extending the Five Forces Framework

Does Industry Matter?

Porter's five forces of competition framework has been subject to two main attacks. Some have criticized its theoretical foundations, arguing that the "structure–conduct–performance" approach to industrial organization that underlies it lacks rigor (especially when compared with the logical robustness of game theory). Others have noted its empirical weaknesses. It appears that industry environment is a relatively minor determinant of a firm's profitability. Studies of the sources of interfirm differences in profitability have produced very different results (Figure 4.1), but all acknowledge that industry factors account for a minor part (less than 20%) of variation in return on assets among firms.

Do these findings imply that industry doesn't matter and we relegate the analysis of industry and competition to a minor role in our strategic analysis? Let me offer a few thoughts.

We need to acknowledge that profitability differences within industries are greater than profitability differences between industries. In Table 3.1, the difference in return on equity (ROE) between the most and least profitable industries was 43 percentage points; yet, in personal care products the spread in ROE between Colgate-Palmolive and Avon Products was 102 percentage points, while in general retailing Walmart's ROE exceeded that of J. C. Penney by 66 percentage points.[1]

FIGURE 4.1 How much does industry matter?

Percentage of variance in firms' return on assets explained by:

■ Industry effects ■ Firm effects ■ Other and unexplained

Sources: R. Schmalensee, "Do markets differ much?" *American Economic Review* 75 (1985): 341–51; R. P. Rumelt, "How much does industry matter?" *Strategic Management Journal* 12 (1991): 167–85; A. M. McGahan and M. E. Porter, "How much does industry matter, really?" *Strategic Management Journal* 18 (1997): 15–30; G. Hawawini, V. Subramanian, and P. Verdin, "Is Performance Driven by Industry or Firm-Specific Factors? A New Look at the Evidence," *Strategic Management Journal* 24 (2003): 1–16; J. A. Roquebert, R. L. Phillips, and P. A. Westfall, "Markets vs. Management: What 'Drives' Profitability?" *Strategic Management Journal* 17 (1996): 653–64; V. F. Misangyi, H. Elms, T. Greckhamer, and J. A. Lepine, "A New Perspective on a Fundamental Debate: A Multilevel Approach to Industry, Corporate and Business Unit Effects," *Strategic Management Journal* 27 (2006): 571–90.

However, the usefulness of industry analysis is not conditional upon the relative importance of inter-industry and intra-industry profitability differences. Industry analysis is important because, without a deep understanding of their competitive environment, firms cannot make sound strategic decisions. Industry analysis is not relevant just to choosing which industries to locate within, it is also important for identifying attractive segments and the sources of competitive advantage within an industry.

If our industry analysis is to fulfill its potential, it needs to go beyond the confines of the Porter five forces framework. We need to go further in understanding the determinants of competitive behavior between companies, in particular using more rigorous approaches to analyze the relationship between market structure and competition. We need to disaggregate broad industry sectors to examine competition within particular segments and among particular groups of firms. But let's begin by considering the potential to extend the Porter framework.

Complements: A Missing Force in the Porter Model?

The Porter framework identifies the suppliers of substitute goods and services as one of the forces of competition that reduces the profit available to firms within an

FIGURE 4.2   Five forces, or six?

industry. However, economic theory identifies two types of relationship between different products: *substitutes* and *complements*. While the presence of substitutes reduces the value of a product, complements increase its value: without ink cartridges my printer is useless.

Given the importance of complements to most products—the value of my car depends on the availability of gasoline, insurance, and repair services; the value of my razor depends upon the supply of blades and shaving foam—our analysis of the competitive environment needs to take them into account. The simplest way is to add a sixth force to Porter's framework (Figure 4.2).[2]

Complements have the opposite effect to substitutes. While substitutes reduce the value of an industry's product, complements increase it. Indeed, where products are close complements (as with my printer and ink cartridges), they have little or no value in isolation: customers value the whole system. But how is the value shared between the producers of the different complementary products? Bargaining power, and its deployment, is the key. During the 1990s, Nintendo earned huge profits from its video game consoles. Although most of the revenue and consumer value was in the software, mostly supplied by independent developers, Nintendo was able to appropriate most of the profits of the entire system through establishing dominance over the games developers. Nintendo used its leadership in the console market and ownership of the console operating system to enforce restrictive developer licenses and maintained tight control over the manufacture and distribution of games cartridges (from which Nintendo earned a hefty royalty).[3]

A similar hardware/software complementarity exists in personal computers— but here power has lain with the software suppliers—Microsoft in particular. IBM's adoption of open architecture meant that Microsoft Windows became a proprietary standard, while PCs were gradually reduced to commodity status. This is a very different situation from video games, where hardware suppliers keep propri-etary control over their operating systems.

Where two products complement one another, profit will accrue to the supplier that builds the stronger market position and reduces the value contributed by the other. How is this done? The key is to achieve monopolization, differentiation, and shortage of supply in one's own product, while encouraging competition, com-moditization, and excess capacity in the production of the complementary product. This is the same principle of creating a *bottleneck* that we discussed in the last chap-ter. Google has pioneered Android and Chrome as open-source operating systems in order to counter Apple's dominance of mobile devices and Microsoft's dominance of personal computers systems.

As the above examples suggest, products based on digital technologies present some interesting issues in relation to competition and the quest for profit. In digital markets users typically require systems that comprise hardware, an operating sys-tem, application software, and probably internet connection as well. In these mar-kets, competition tends to be among rival **platforms**—the interfaces that link the component parts of the system. Both the users and the suppliers of applications tend to congregate around the market-leading platform—a phenomenon we call *network externality*. The result is the creation of **winner-takes-all markets** where a mar-ket share leader accounts for most industry sales and scoops most, if not all, of the industry's profit pool. Strategy Capsule 4.1 discusses competition between different smartphone platforms.

In winner-takes-all markets, the whole notion of industry attractiveness becomes meaningless: the industry is only attractive to the firm that attains market leader-ship. In smartphones the situation is slightly different because the leading platform, Android, is open source. It is the #2 platform owner, Apple, that scoops most of the industry's profit—in 2014 the other leading suppliers (Samsung, Sony, LG, Lenovo, and HTC) either made losses or earned a thin margin.[4] We return to the role of network externalities in Chapter 9, when we discuss strategy in technology-based industries.

Dynamic Competition: Hypercompetition, Game Theory, and Competitor Analysis

Hypercompetition

The Porter five forces framework is based upon the assumption that industry struc-ture determines competitive behavior, which in turn determines industry profitabil-ity. But competition also unleashes the forces of innovation and entrepreneurship that transform industry structures. Joseph Schumpeter viewed competition as a "perennial gale of creative destruction" in which market-dominating incumbents are challenged, and often unseated, by rivals' innovations.[5]

This view of Schumpeter (and the "Austrian school" of economics) that com-petition is a dynamic process in which industry structure is constantly changing raises the issue of whether competitive behavior should be seen as an outcome of industry structure or a determinant of industry structure.[6] The issue is the speed of structural change in the industry—if structural transformation is rapid, then the

STRATEGY CAPSULE 4.1
Platform-based Competition in Smartphones

A key feature of the relationship between complementary products in digital markets is that they tend to be *co-specialized*. Video games are adapted to play on a specific video game console; video game consoles need to be designed to accommodate the characteristics of the games they will play. This is different from the relationship between automobiles and gasoline: Shell gasoline will power any gasoline-fueled internal combustion engine; a Ford Focus will run on any brand of gasoline.

Co-specialization creates *network externalities*. Network externalities arise when the value of a product to a user depends upon the number of other users of the product. The availability of complementary products is a major source of network externalities in digital markets—the outcome tends to be *winner-takes-all* markets.

Consider the market for smartphones. The attractiveness of a particular smartphone to a user depends upon the number and quality of applications ("apps") available. App developers will target those platforms with the greatest number of users. Migration by users and developers from platforms with a low market share to those with a high market share creates the "winner-takes-all" effect.

Like many other digital markets, the market for smartphones is a *two-sided market* where the platform—the operating system—forms an interface between the two sides. The two sides are the two types of customer for operating systems: the consumers who buy smartphones and the developers who develop applications and pay for access.

The early market leader in smartphone operating systems was Symbian, which was jointly owned by Nokia, Sony-Ericsson, and Motorola. However, the launch of Apple's iPhone in 2007 with its proprietary iOS system, quickly displaced Symbian. While the iOS was exclusive to Apple, apps could be created by third-party developers who purchased Apple's software development kit and offered their apps through Apple's App Store. Revenues were split 30% for Apple and 70% for the developer.

The introduction of Google's Android OS proved to be a game-changer. Android was not only available to any manufacturer, it was also open-source, which meant that it was free. The first Android smartphone was launched by HTC in October 2008. At the end of 2014, there were more than 50 firms supplying Android smartphones. Moreover, there were 1.43 million apps on offer at Google Play—the app store for Android applications—compared with 1.21 million at Apple's App Store.

The operation of network externalities in the market is evident in the growing dominance of Android and Apple's iOS in smartphones. Between 2011 and 2014, the combined market share of Microsoft Phone, Blackberry OS, and Symbian declined from 46 to 4%. By contrast, Android rose from 37 to 84%, while Apple iOS declined from 18 to 12%.

Sources: C. Cennamo and J. Santalo, "Platform Competition: Strategic Trade-offs in Platform Markets." *Strategic Management Journal*, 34 (2013): 1331–1350; GSMA Intelligence, *Analysis: Mobile Platform Wars* (London: February 2014).

five forces framework does not offer a stable basis on which to predict competition and profitability.

In most industries, Schumpeter's process of "creative destruction" tends to be more of a breeze than a gale. In established industries entry occurs so slowly that profits are undermined only gradually,[7] while changes in industrial concentration tend to be slow.[8] One survey observed: "the picture of the competitive process … is, to say the least, sluggish in the extreme."[9] As a result, both at the firm and the industry level, profits tend to be highly persistent in the long run.[10]

But what about recent trends? Has accelerating technological change and intensifying international competition reinforced the processes of "creative destruction"? Rich D'Aveni argues that a general feature of industries today is **hypercompetition**: "intense and rapid competitive moves, in which competitors must move quickly to build [new] advantages and erode the advantages of their rivals."[11] If industries are hypercompetitive, their structures are likely to be less stable than in the past, and competitive advantage will be temporary.[12] According to Rita McGrath, "Transient advantage is the new normal."[13]

Despite everyday observations that markets are becoming more volatile and market leadership more tenuous, research findings are inconsistent. One large-scale statistical study conclude: "The heterogeneity and volatility of competitive advantage in US manufacturing industries has steadily and astonishingly increased since 1950. These results suggest that a shift toward hypercompetition has indeed occurred."[14] Another study found that this increased volatility extended well beyond technology-intensive industries but also extended beyond manufacturing industries.[15] However, another study found a "lack of widespread evidence … that markets are more unstable now than in the recent past."[16]

The Contribution of Game Theory

Central to the criticisms of Porter's five forces as a static framework is its failure to take full account of competitive interactions among firms. In Chapter 1, we noted that the essence of strategic competition is the interaction among players, such that the decisions made by any one player are dependent on the actual and anticipated decisions of the other players. By relegating competition to a mediating variable that links industry structure with profitability, the five forces analysis offers little insight into competition as a process of interactive decision making by rival firms. Game theory allows us to model this competitive interaction. In particular, it offers two especially valuable contributions to strategic management:

- It permits the framing of strategic decisions. Apart from its predictive value, game theory provides a structure, a set of concepts, and a terminology that allows us to describe and structure a competitive situation in terms of:
  - identity of the players;
  - specification of each player's options;
  - specification of the payoffs from every combination of options;
  - the sequencing of decisions.
- It can predict the outcome of competitive situations and identify optimal strategic choices. Through the insight that it offers into situations of competition and bargaining, game theory can predict the equilibrium outcomes of

competitive interaction and the consequences of strategic moves by any one player. Game theory provides penetrating insights into central issues of strategy that go well beyond pure intuition. Simple models (e.g., the **prisoners' dilemma**) predict whether outcomes will be competitive or cooperative, whereas more complex games permit analysis of the effects of reputation,[17] deterrence,[18] information,[19] and commitment,[20] especially within the context of multi-period games. Particularly important for practicing managers, game theory can indicate strategies for improving the structure and outcome of the game through manipulating the payoffs to the different players.[21]

Game theory has been used to analyze a wide variety of competitive situations. These include the Cuban missile crisis of 1962,[22] rivalry between Boeing and Airbus,[23] NASCAR race tactics,[24] auctions of airwave spectrum,[25] the 2008 financial crisis,[26] and the reasons why evolution has conferred such magnificent tails upon male peacocks.[27] In terms of applications to competition among business enterprises, game theory points to five aspects of strategic behavior through which a firm can influence competitive outcomes: *cooperation, deterrence, commitment, changing the structure of the game being played,* and *signaling*.

Cooperation   One of the key merits of game theory is its ability to encompass both competition and cooperation. A key deficiency of the five forces framework is in viewing interfirm relations as exclusively competitive in nature. Central to Adam Brandenburger and Barry Nalebuff's concept of *co-opetition* is recognition of the competitive/cooperative duality of business relationships.[28] While some relationships are predominantly competitive (Coca-Cola and Pepsi) and others are predominantly cooperative (Intel and Microsoft), there is no simple dichotomy between competition and cooperation: all business relationships combine elements of both. For all their intense rivalry, Coca-Cola and Pepsi cooperate on multiple fronts, including common policies on sales of soda drinks within schools, environmental issues, and health concerns. They may also coordinate their pricing and product introductions.[29] Exxon and Shell have competed for leadership of the world's petroleum industry for over a century; at the same time they cooperate in a number of joint ventures. The desire of competitors to cluster together—antique dealers in London's Bermondsey Market or movie studios in Hollywood—points to the common interests of competing firms in growing the size of their market and developing its infrastructure. Typically, competition results in inferior outcomes for participants than cooperation. The prisoners' dilemma game analyzes this predicament, but also points to the strategic initiatives through which a player can transform the game in order to reach a cooperative outcome (Strategy Capsule 4.2).

Deterrence   As we see in Strategy Capsule 4.2, one way of changing a game's equilibrium is through *deterrence*. The principle behind deterrence is to impose costs on the other players for actions deemed to be undesirable. By establishing the certainty that deserters would be shot, the British army provided a strong incentive to its troops to participate in advances on heavily fortified German trenches during the First World War.

The key to the effectiveness of any deterrent is that it must be credible. The problem here is that, if administering the deterrent is costly or unpleasant for the threatening party, the deterrent is not credible. If an incumbent firm threatens a

STRATEGY CAPSULE 4.2
The Prisoners' Dilemma

The classic prisoners' dilemma game involves a pair of crime suspects who are arrested and interrogated separately. The dilemma is that each will rat on the other with the result that both end up in jail despite the fact that if both had remained silent they would have been released for lack of evidence.

The dilemma arises in almost all competitive situations—everyone could be better off with collusion. Consider competition between Coca-Cola and Pepsi in Ecuador, where each has the choice of spending big or small on advertising. Figure 4.3 shows the payoffs to each firm.

Clearly, the best solution for both firms is for them to each restrain their advertising expenditure (the upper left cell). However, in the absence of cooperation, the outcome for both firms is to adopt big budgets (the lower right cell)—the reason being that each will fear that any restraint will be countered by the rival seeking advantage by shifting to a big advertising budget. The resulting maxi-min choice of strategies (each company chooses the strategy that maximizes the minimum payoff) is a Nash equilibrium: no player can increase his/her payoff by a unilateral change in strategy. Even if collusion can be achieved, it will be unstable because

of the incentives for cheating—a constant problem for OPEC, where the member countries agree quotas but then cheat on them.

How can a firm escape from such prisoners' dilemmas? One answer is to change a one-period game (single transaction) into a repeated game. In the above example of competition in advertising, a multi-period perspective allows the companies to recognize the futility of advertising campaigns that merely cancel one another out. In the case of supplier–buyer relations, where the typical equilibrium is a low-quality product at a low price, moving from a spot-transaction to a long-term vendor relationship gives the supplier the incentive to offer a better-quality product and the buyer to offer a price that reflects the preferred quality.

A second solution is to change the payoffs through deterrence. In the classic prisoners' dilemma, the Mafia shifts the equilibrium from the suspects both confessing to their both remaining silent by using draconian reprisals to enforce its "code of silence." Similarly, if both Coca-Cola and Pepsi were to threaten one another with aggressive price cuts should the other seek advantage through a big advertising budget, this could shift the equilibrium to the top-left cell.

FIGURE 4.3   Coca-Cola's and Pepsi's advertising budget: The prisoners' dilemma potential new entrant with a price war, such a threat will lack credibility if such a price war would inflict more damage on the incumbent than on the new entrant. Investing in excess capacity can be an effective means of discouraging entry. Prior to the expiration of its NutraSweet patents, Monsanto invested heavily in unneeded plant capacity to deter manufacturers of generic aspartame.[30] Conversely, in compact disks, the reluctance of the dominant firm (Philips) to invest heavily in new capacity to meet growing demand encouraged a wave of new entrants.[31]

However, deterrence only works when the adversaries can be deterred. A central weakness of President George W. Bush's "war on terror" was that ideologically motivated terrorists are not susceptible to deterrence.[32]

Commitment   For deterrence to be credible, it must be backed by commitment. Commitment involves the elimination of strategic options: "binding an organization to a future course of action."[33] When Hernán Cortés destroyed his ships on arrival in Mexico in 1519, he communicated, both to Montezuma and his people, that there was no alternative to conquest of the Aztec empire. Once Airbus had decided to build its A380 superjumbo, it was critical to signal its commitment to the project. During 2000–2002, Airbus spent heavily on advertising the plane, even before completing the design phase, in order to encourage airlines to place orders and discourage Boeing from developing a rival plane.

These commitments to aggressive competition can be described as *hard commitments*. A company may also make commitments that moderate competition; these are called *soft commitments*. For example, if a company committed to achieving certain target profit levels in the coming year, this would be a soft commitment: it would signal its desire to avoid aggressive competitive initiatives or reactions.

How different types of commitment affect a firm's profitability depends upon the mode of competition. Where companies compete on price, game theory shows that they tend to match one another's price changes.[34] Hence, under price adjustments, hard commitments (such as a commitment to cut price) tend to have a negative profit impact and soft commitments (such as a commitment to raise prices) have a positive impact. Conversely, where companies compete by changing their levels of output, game theory shows that increases in output by one firm result in output reductions by the other.[35] In this situation, a hard commitment (e.g., a commitment to build new plants) will tend to have a positive effect on the committing firm's profitability because it will tend to be met by other firms reducing their output.[36]

Changing the Structure of the Game   Creative strategies can change the structure of the competitive game. A company may seek to change the structure of the industry within which it is competing in order to increase the profit potential of the industry or to appropriate a greater share of the available profit. Thus, establishing alliances and agreements with competitors can increase the value of the game by increasing the size of the market and building joint strength against possible entrants. There may be many opportunities for converting win–lose (or even lose–lose) games into win–win games by rivals designing cooperative solutions.

In some cases, it may be advantageous for a firm to assist its competitors. When in June 2014, Tesla Motors offered to make available its patents to competitors, it was betting that any loss in its own competitive advantage would be offset by the benefits of expanding the market for electric vehicles and encouraging the wider adoption of its own technologies with regard to battery design and battery recharging systems. As we shall see in Chapter 9, standards battles often involve the deliberate sacrificing of potential monopoly positions by the main contestants.[37]

Signaling   Competitive reactions depend on how the competitor perceives its rival's initiative. The term *signaling* is used to describe the selective communication of information to competitors (or customers) designed to influence their perceptions and hence provoke or suppress certain types of reaction.[38] The use of misinformation is well developed in military intelligence. Ben McIntyre's book *Operation Mincemeat* describes how British military intelligence used a corpse dressed as a marine officer and carrying fake secret documents to convince German high command that the Allied landings would be in Greece, not Sicily.[39]

The credibility of threats is critically dependent on reputation.[40] Even though carrying out threats against rivals is costly and depresses short-term profitability, exercising such threats can build a reputation for aggressiveness that deters competitors in the future. The benefits of building a reputation for aggressiveness may be particularly great for diversified companies where reputation can be transferred from one market to another.[41] Hence, Procter & Gamble's protracted market share wars in disposable diapers and household detergents have established a reputation for toughness that protects it from competitive attacks in other markets.

Signaling may also be used to communicate a desire to cooperate: pre-announced price changes can facilitate collusive pricing among firms.[42]

Is Game Theory Useful?

How useful is game theory to strategic management? The great virtue of game theory is its rigor: it has established the analysis of competition on a much more secure theoretical foundation.

However, the price of mathematical rigor has been limited applicability to real-world situations. Game theory provides clear predictions in highly stylized situations involving few external variables and restrictive assumptions. The result is a mathematically sophisticated body of theory that suffers from unrealistic assumptions and lack of generality. When applied to more complex (and more realistic) situations, game theory frequently results in either no equilibria or multiple equilibria, and outcomes that are highly sensitive to small changes in initial assumptions. Overall, game theory has not developed to the point where it permits us to model real business situations in a level of detail that can generate precise predictions.[43]

In its empirical applications, game theory does a better job of explaining the past than of predicting the future. In diagnosing Nintendo's domination of the video games industry in the 1980s, Monsanto's efforts to prolong NutraSweet's market leadership beyond the expiration of its patents, or Airbus's wresting of market leadership from Boeing, game theory provides penetrating insight into the competitive situation and deep understanding of the rationale behind the strategies deployed. However, in predicting outcomes and designing strategies, game theory has been much less impressive—the application of game theory by US and European governments to design auctions for wireless spectrum has produced some undesirable and unforeseen results.[44]

So, where can game theory assist us in designing successful strategies? As with all our theories and frameworks, game theory is useful not because it gives us answers but because it can help us understand business situations. Game theory provides a set of tools that allows us to structure our view of competitive interaction. By identifying the players in a game, the decision choices available to each, and the implications of each combination of decisions, we have a systematic framework for exploring the dynamics of competition. Most importantly, by describing the structure of the game we are playing, we have a basis for suggesting ways of changing the game and thinking through the likely outcomes of such changes.

Game theory continues its rapid development and, although it is still a long way from providing the central theoretical foundation for strategic management, we draw upon it in several places in this book, especially in exploring competitive dynamics in highly concentrated markets. However, our emphasis in strategy formulation will be less on achieving advantage through influencing the behavior of competitors and much more on transforming competitive games through building positions of unilateral competitive advantage. The competitive market situations with which we shall be dealing will, for the most part, be different from those considered by game theory. Game theory typically deals with competitive situations with closely matched players where each has a similar range of strategic options (typically relating to price changes, advertising budgets, capacity decisions, and new product introductions). The outcome of these games is highly dependent on the order of moves, signals, bluffs, and threats. Our emphasis will be less on managing competitive interactions and more on establishing competitive advantage through exploiting uniqueness.

Competitor Analysis and Competitive Intelligence

In highly concentrated industries, the dominant feature of a company's competitive environment is likely to be the behavior of its closest rivals. In household detergents, Unilever's industry environment is dominated by the strategy of Procter & Gamble. The same is true in soft drinks (Coca-Cola and Pepsi), jet engines (GE, United Technologies, and Rolls-Royce), and financial information (Bloomberg and Reuters). Similarly in local markets: the competitive environment of my local Costa coffee shop is dominated by the presence of Starbucks across the road. While game theory provides a theoretical apparatus for analyzing competitive interaction between small numbers of rivals, for everyday business situations, a less formal and more empirically based approach to predicting competitors' behavior may be more useful. Let us examine how information about competitors can be used to predict their behavior.

Competitive Intelligence   Competitive intelligence involves the systematic collection and analysis of information about rivals for informing decision making. It has three main purposes:

- to forecast competitors' future strategies and decisions;
- to predict competitors' likely reactions to a firm's strategic initiatives;
- to determine how competitors' behavior can be influenced to make it more favorable.

For all three purposes, the key requirement is to understand competitors in order to predict their responses to environmental changes and our own competitive moves. To understand competitors, it is important to be informed about them. Competitive intelligence is a growth field, with specialist consulting firms,

FIGURE 4.4   A framework for competitor analysis

professional associations,[45] and a flood of recent books.[46] About one-quarter of large US corporations have specialist competitive intelligence units.

The boundary between legitimate competitive intelligence and illegal industrial espionage is not always clear. The distinction between public and private information is uncertain and the law relating to trade secrets is much less precise than that which covers patents and copyrights. Well-publicized cases of information theft include the $100 million fine levied on the McLaren Mercedes Formula 1 team for possessing confidential technical information belonging to Ferrari and the theft by Kolon Industries of South Korea of trade secrets concerning the production of DuPont's Kevlar fiber.[47] More generally, the US National Counterintelligence Executive has alleged systematic industrial espionage by the China and Russia.[48]

A Framework for Predicting Competitor Behavior   Competitive intelligence is not simply about collecting information. The problem is likely to be too much rather than too little information. The key is a systematic approach that makes it clear what information is required and for what purposes it will be used. The objective is to understand one's rival. A characteristic of great generals from Hannibal to Patton has been their ability to go beyond military intelligence and to "get inside the heads" of their opposing commanders. Michael Porter proposes a four-part framework for predicting competitor behavior (Figure 4.4).

- *Competitor's current strategy*: To predict how a rival will behave in the future, we must understand how that rival is competing at present. As we noted in Chapter 1, identifying a firm's strategy requires looking at what the company says and what it does (see "Where Do We Find Strategy?" in Chapter 1). The key is to link the content of top management communication (with investors, the media, and financial analysts) with the evidence of strategic actions, particularly those that involve a commitment of resources. For both sources of information, company websites are invaluable.

- *Competitor's objectives*: To forecast how a competitor might change its strategy, we must identify its goals. A key issue is whether a company is driven by financial goals or market goals. A company whose primary goal is attaining market share is likely to be much more aggressive a competitor than one that is mainly interested in profitability. The willingness of the US automobile and consumer electronics producers to cede market share to Japanese competitors was partly a result of their preoccupation with short-term profitability. By comparison, companies like Procter & Gamble and Coca-Cola are obsessed with market share and tend to react aggressively when rivals step on their turf. The most difficult competitors can be those that are not subject to profit disciplines at all—state-owned enterprises in particular. The level of current performance in relation to the competitor's objectives determines the likelihood of strategy change. The more a company is satisfied with present performance, the more likely it is to continue with its present strategy. But if performance is falling well short of target, radical strategic change, possibly accompanied by a change in top management, is likely.

- *Competitor's assumptions about the industry*: A competitor's strategic decisions are conditioned by its perceptions of itself and its environment. These perceptions are guided by the beliefs that senior managers hold about their industry and the success factors within it. These beliefs tend to be stable over time and also converge among the firms within an industry: what J.-C. Spender refers to as "industry recipes."[49] Industry recipes may engender "blindspots" that limit the capacity of a firm—even an entire industry—to respond to an external threat. During the 1960s, the Big Three US automobile manufacturers believed that small cars were unprofitable (which was partly a consequence of how they allocated their overheads). The result was a willingness to yield the fast-growing small car segment of the market to imports. The complacency with which British and US motorcycle manufacturers viewed Japanese competition reflected similar beliefs (Strategy Capsule 4.3).

- *Competitor's resources and capabilities*: Evaluating the likelihood and seriousness of a competitor's potential challenge requires assessing the strength of that competitor's resources and capabilities. If our rival has a massive cash pile, we would be unwise to unleash a price war. Conversely, if we direct our competitive initiatives toward our rivals' weaknesses, it may be difficult for them to respond. Richard Branson's Virgin Group has launched a host of entrepreneurial new ventures, typically in markets dominated by a powerful incumbent—British Airways in airlines, EMI in music, Vodafone in wireless telecommunications. Branson's strategy has been to adopt innovative forms of differentiation that are difficult for established incumbents to respond to.

Segmentation and Strategic Groups

Segmentation Analysis[50]

In Chapter 3 we noted the difficulty of drawing industry boundaries and the need to define industries both broadly and narrowly according to the types of question we are seeking to answer. Initially, it may be convenient to define industries broadly,

STRATEGY CAPSULE 4.3

Motorcycle Myopia

During the 1960s, lightweight Japanese motorcycles began to flood Britain and North America. The chairman of BSA, Eric Turner, was dismissive of this competitive challenge to the dominant position of his Triumph and BSA brands:

> The success of Honda, Suzuki, and Yamaha has been jolly good for us. People start out by buying one of the low-priced Japanese jobs. They get to enjoy the fun and exhilaration of the open road and they frequently end up buying one of our more powerful and expensive machines.

(Advertising Age, December 27, 1965)

Similar complacency was expressed by William Davidson, president of Harley-Davidson:

Basically, we do not believe in the lightweight market. We believe that motorcycles are sports vehicles, not transportation vehicles. Even if a man says he bought a motorcycle for transportation, it's generally for leisure time use. The lightweight motorcycle is only supplemental. Back around World War I, a number of companies came out with lightweight bikes. We came out with one ourselves. We came out with another in 1947 and it just didn't go anywhere. We have seen what happens to these small sizes.

(American Motor Cycle, September 15, 1966)

By 1980, BSA and Triumph had ceased production and Harley-Davidson was struggling for survival. The world motorcycle industry, including the heavyweight segment, was dominated by the Japanese.

but for a more detailed analysis of competition we need to focus on markets that are drawn more narrowly in terms of both products and geography. This process of disaggregating industries into specific markets we call **segmentation**.

Segmentation is particularly important if competition varies across the different submarkets within an industry such that some are more attractive than others. While Sony and Microsoft battled for dominance for leadership among so-called hard-core gamers with their technologically advanced PS3 and Xbox 360 consoles, Nintendo's Wii became a surprise market share leader by focusing on a large and underserved market segment: casual and older video game players. In the cutthroat tire industry, Pirelli has achieved superior margins by investing heavily in technology and focusing on high-performance tires for sports and luxury cars.[51]

The purpose of segmentation analysis is to identify attractive segments, to select strategies for different segments, and to determine how many segments to serve. The analysis proceeds in five stages (see Strategy Capsule 4.4 for an application; Strategy Capsule 4.5 looks at vertical segmentation).

1 *Identify key segmentation variables*: Our starting point is to determine the basis of segmentation. Segmentation decisions are essentially choices about

FIGURE 4.5   The basis for segmentation: The characteristics of buyers and products

which customers to serve and what to offer them: hence segmentation variables relate to the characteristics of customers and the product (Figure 4.5). The most appropriate segmentation variables are those that partition the market most distinctly in terms of limits to substitution by customers (demand-side substitutability) and by producers (supply-side substitutability). Price differentials are good indicators of market segments: distinct market segments tend to display sustained price differentials. Typically, segmentation analysis generates far too many segmentation variables and too many categories for each variable. For our analysis to be manageable and useful, we need to reduce these to two or three. To do this we need to (a) identify the most strategically significant segmentation variables and (b) combine segmentation variables that are closely correlated. For example, in the restaurant industry, price level, service level (waiter service/self-service), cuisine (fast-food/full meals), and alcohol license (wine served/soft drinks only) are likely to be closely related. We could use a single variable, restaurant type, with three categories—full-service restaurants, cafés, and fast-food outlets—as a proxy for all of these variables.

2 *Construct a Segmentation Matrix*: Once the segmentation variables have been selected and discrete categories determined for each, the individual

segments may be identified using a two- or three-dimensional matrix. Strategy Capsule 4.4 shows a two-dimensional segmentation matrix for the world automobile industry.

3 *Analyze segment attractiveness*: Profitability within an industry segment is determined by the same structural forces that determine profitability within an industry as a whole. As a result, Porter's five forces of competition framework is equally effective in relation to a segment as to an entire industry. There are, however, a few differences. First, when analyzing the pressure of competition from substitute products, we are concerned not only with substitutes from other industries but also, more importantly, with substitutes from other segments within the same industry. Second, when considering entry into the segment, the main source of entrants is likely to be producers established in other segments within the same industry. The barriers that protect a segment from firms located in other segments are called *barriers to mobility* to distinguish them from the *barriers to entry*, which protect the industry as a whole.[52] When barriers to mobility are low, then the superior returns of high-profit segments tend to be quickly eroded. As Strategy Capsule 4.4 suggests, differences in competitive conditions between segments can make some much more profitable than others; however, these profit differentials are unlikely to be sustained over the long term.

Segmentation analysis can also be useful in identifying unexploited opportunities in an industry. Companies that have built successful strategies by concentrating on unoccupied segments include Walmart (discount stores in small towns), Enterprise Rent-A-Car (suburban locations), and Edward Jones (full-service brokerage for small investors in smaller cities). This identification of unoccupied market segments is one dimension of what Kim and Mauborgne refer to as **blue-ocean strategy**: the quest for uncontested market space.[53]

4 *Identify the segment's key success factors (KSFs)*: Differences in competitive structure and in customer preferences between segments result in different KSFs. By analyzing buyers' purchasing criteria and the basis of competition within individual segments, we can identify KSFs for individual segments. For example, we can segment the US bicycle market into high-price enthusiasts' bikes sold through specialist bike stores and economy bikes sold through discount stores. KSFs in the enthusiast segment are technology, reputation, and dealer relations. In the economy segment, KSFs are low-cost manufacture (most likely in China) and a supply contract with a leading retail chain.

5 *Select segment scope*: Finally, a firm needs to decide whether it wishes to be a segment specialist or to compete across multiple segments. The advantages of a broad over a narrow segment focus depend on two main factors: similarity of KSFs and the presence of shared costs. If KSFs are different across segments, a firm will need to deploy distinct strategies which may require different capabilities for different segments. Harley-Davidson has found it difficult to expand from its core segments of heavyweight cruiser and touring bikes into other segments of the motorcycle industry. Conversely, in automobiles, segment specialists have found it difficult to survive competition from broad-scope, volume producers.

STRATEGY CAPSULE 4.4
Segmenting the World Automobile Industry

1 Identify key segmentation variables and categories. Possible segmentation variables include: price, size, engine power, body style, buyer type (retail versus fleet), and geographical market. We can reduce the number of segmentation variables—in particular, price, size, and engine power tend to be closely correlated. Other variables clearly define distinct markets (e.g., geographical regions and individual national markets).

2 Construct a segmentation matrix. The segmentation matrix in Figure 4.6 shows geographical regions (columns) and product types (rows). These product types combine multiple segmentation variables: price, size, design, and fuel type.

3 Analyze segment attractiveness. Applying five forces analysis to individual segments points to the attractiveness of the growth markets of Asia and Latin America (especially for luxury cars) as compared with the saturated, excess capacity laden markets of Europe and North America. In these mature markets, the hybrid and electric car segments may be attractive due to fewer competitors and lack of excess capacity.

4 Identify KSFs in each segment. In sports cars, technology and design aesthetics are likely to be key differentiators. In luxury cars, quality and interior design are likely to be essential. In family compact and mini-cars, low cost is the primary basis for competitive advantage.

5 Analyze attractions of broad versus narrow segment scope. Because of the potential to share technology, design, and components across models, all product segments are dominated by full-range mass-manufactures. In terms of geographical segments, only in the biggest markets (primarily China) have nationally focused producers survived.

FIGURE 4.6 A segmentation matrix of the World Automobile Market

	REGIONS						
PRODUCTS	North America	Western Europe	Eastern Europe	Asia	Latin America	Australia & NZ	Africa
Luxury cars							
Full-size cars							
Mid-size cars							
Small cars							
Station wagons							
Minivans							
Sports cars							
Sport utility							
Pickup trucks							
Hybrids							

STRATEGY CAPSULE 4.5

Vertical Segmentation: Profitability along the Value Chain

Segmentation is usually horizontal: markets are dis-aggregated according to products, geography, and customer groups. We can also segment an industry vertically by identifying different value chain activities. Bain & Company's profit pool analysis offers one approach to mapping profitability differences between different vertical activities. Bain's *profit pool mapping* involves, first, estimating the industry's total profit by applying the average margin earned by a sample of companies in the industry to an estimate of the industry's total revenues and, second,

using company financial data to estimate the profit at each stage of the value chain. Figure 4.7 shows the distribution of value in the US automobile sector. The area of each segment's rectangle corresponds to the total profit for that activity. Alternatively, stock market capitalization can be used to identify which groups of firms within a sector are most successful at appropriating value. In the computer sector, the market value of hardware companies has declined sharply in relation to that of software and semiconductor companies.

FIGURE 4.7   The US auto industry profit pool

FIGURE 4.8   Strategic groups within the world petroleum industry

Strategic Groups

Whereas segmentation analysis concentrates on the characteristics of markets as the basis for disaggregating industries, strategic group analysis segments an industry on the basis of the strategies of the member firms. A **strategic group** is "the group of firms in an industry following the same or a similar strategy along the strategic dimensions."[54] These strategic dimensions might include product range, geographical breadth, choice of distribution channels, level of product quality, degree of vertical integration, choice of technology, and so on. By selecting the most important strategic dimensions and locating each firm in the industry along them, it is possible to identify groups of companies that have adopted more or less similar approaches to competing within the industry. In some industries strategic groups are readily observable, for example airlines fall into two broad strategic groups: "legacy carriers" (such as American, JAL, and British Airways) and "low-cost carriers" (such as Ryanair, Easyjet, and Southwest). Other industries are more complex: Figure 4.8 shows strategic groups within the petroleum industry.[55]

Most of the empirical research into strategic groups has been concerned with competition and profitability between groups—the basic argument being that mobility barriers between strategic groups permit some groups of firms to be persistently more profitable than other groups.[56] In general, the proposition that profitability differences within strategic groups are less than differences between strategic groups has not received robust empirical support.[57] This may reflect the fact that the members of a strategic group, although pursuing similar strategies, are not necessarily in competition with one another. For example, within the European airline industry, the low-cost carriers pursue similar strategies, but do not, for the most part, compete on the same routes. Hence, the main usefulness of strategic group analysis is in understanding strategic positioning, recognizing patterns of competition, and identifying strategic niches; it is less useful as a tool for analyzing interfirm profitability differences.[58]

Summary

The purpose of this chapter has been to go beyond the basic analysis of industry structure, competition, and profitability presented in Chapter 3 to consider the dynamics of competitive rivalry and the internal complexities of industries.

In terms of industry and competitive analysis, we have extended our strategy toolkit in several directions:

◆ We have recognized the potential for complementary products to add value and noted the importance of strategies that can exploit this source of value. Such complementary relationships are especially important in industries based upon digital technologies. Here complementarities between hardware and software and between operating systems and applications have given rise to *platform-based competition* and *winner-takes-all markets*. We shall explore these competitive dynamics further in Chapter 9.

◆ We have noted the importance of competitive interactions between close rivals and learned a structured approach to analyzing competitors and predicting their behavior. At a more sophisticated theoretical level, we have recognized how game theory offers insights into competition, bargaining, and the design of winning strategies.

◆ We examined the microstructure of industries and markets and the value of segmentation analysis and strategic group analysis in understanding industries at a more detailed level and in selecting an advantageous strategic position within an industry.

Self-Study Questions

1. HP, Canon, Epson, and other manufacturers of inkjet printers make most of their profits from their ink cartridges. Why are cartridges more profitable than printers? Would the situation be different:

   a. if cartridges were manufactured by different firms from those which make printers?
   b. if cartridges were interchangeable between different printers?
   c. if patent and copyright restrictions did not prevent other firms from supplying ink cartridges that could be used in the leading brands of printer?

2. In July 2015, Microsoft announced its write-off of its Nokia handset business (acquired a year earlier) and its withdrawal from the smartphone market. Its Windows Phone operating system had a 1% share of the smartphone market and there were about 290,000 Windows Phone apps (compared to 1.6 million for Android and 1.3 million for the Apple iPhone). How do the dynamics of platform-based competition (see Strategy Capsule 4.1) help explain Microsoft's failure in the market for smartphones?

3. In November 2005, six of Paris's most luxurious hotels—including George V, Le Bristol, the Ritz, and Hotel de Crillon—were fined for colluding on room rates. Regular guests showed little concern—noting that, whatever the listed rack rate, it was always possible

to negotiate substantial discounts. Using the prisoners' dilemma model, can you explain why the hotels were able to collude over their listed rates but not over discounts?

4. During 2015, Netflix and Amazon were battling for leadership in the video streaming markets of North America and Europe. Both offered a fixed-price subscription, the main difference being that Amazon Prime's annual subscription bundled video streaming of movies and TV shows with the free delivery of goods from amazon.com. Netflix's apprehension about Amazon stemmed from Amazon's huge revenue stream (16 times that of Netflix), its willingness to diversify into related businesses (Amazon supplied its own hardware for viewing video, the Kindle Fire, and was producing its own original video content) and its willingness to endure losses in the quest for market leadership through aggressive price cutting. How might Netflix use the competitor analysis framework outlined in Figure 4.4 to predict Amazon's competitive strategy in the market for streamed video content?

5. How would you segment the restaurant market in your hometown? How would you advise someone thinking of starting a new restaurant which segments might be most attractive in terms of profit potential?

6. Consider either the North American or European markets for air travel. Can these markets be segmented? If so, by what variables and into which categories? Can an airline be financially viable by specializing in certain segments or must airlines seek to compete across all (or most) segments?

Notes

1. Data from http://fortune.com/fortune500/2014/
2. A. Brandenburger and B. Nalebuff (*Co-opetition*, New York: Doubleday, 1996) propose an alternative framework, the *value net*, for analyzing the impact of complements.
3. See A. Brandenburger and B. Nalebuff, "The Right Game: Use Game Theory to Shape Strategy," *Harvard Business Review* (July/August 1995): 63–64; and A. Brandenburger, J. Kou, and M. Burnett, *Power Play (A): Nintendo in 8-bit Video Games* (Harvard Business School Case No. 9-795-103, 1995).
4. A. Orlowski, "The Great Smartphone Massacre: Android Bloodbath Gathers Pace," *The Register* (November 4, 2014). www.theregister.co.uk/2014/11/04/android_bloodbath_gathers_pace, accessed November 30, 2014.
5. J. A. Schumpeter, *The Theory of Economic Development* (Cambridge, MA: Harvard University Press, 1934).
6. See R. Jacobson, "The Austrian School of Strategy," *Academy of Management Review* 17 (1992): 782–807; and G. Young, K. Smith, and C. Grimm, "Austrian and Industrial Organization Perspectives on Firm-Level

Competitive Activity and Performance," *Organization Science* 7 (May/June 1996): 243–254.
7. R. T. Masson and J. Shaanan, "Stochastic Dynamic Limit Pricing: An Empirical Test," *Review of Economics and Statistics* 64 (1982): 413–422; R. T. Masson and J. Shaanan, "Optimal Pricing and Threat of Entry: Canadian Evidence," *International Journal of Industrial Organization* 5 (1987): 520–535.
8. R. Caves and M. E. Porter, "The Dynamics of Changing Seller Concentration," *Journal of Industrial Economics* 19 (1980): 1–15; P. Hart and R. Clarke, *Concentration in British Industry* (Cambridge: Cambridge University Press, 1980).
9. P. A. Geroski and R. T. Masson, "Dynamic Market Models in Industrial Organization," *International Journal of Industrial Organization* 5 (1987): 1–13.
10. D. C. Mueller, *Profits in the Long Run* (Cambridge: Cambridge University Press, 1986).
11. R. D'Aveni, *Hypercompetition: Managing the Dynamics of Strategic Maneuvering* (New York: Free Press, 1994): 217–218.

12. R. A. D'Aveni, G. B. Dagnino, and K. G. Smith, "The Age of Temporary Advantage," *Strategic Management Journal* 31 (2010): 1371–1385.

13. R. G. McGrath, "Transient Advantage," *Harvard Business Review* 91 (June 2013).

14. L. G. Thomas and R. D'Aveni, "The Rise of Hypercompetition in the US Manufacturing Sector, 1950–2002." Tuck School of Business, Dartmouth College, Working Paper No. 2004-11 (2004).

15. R. R. Wiggins and T. W. Ruefli, "Schumpeter's Ghost: Is Hypercompetition Making the Best of Times Shorter?" *Strategic Management Journal* 26 (2005): 887–911.

16. G. McNamara, P. M. Vaaler, and C. Devers, "Same As It Ever Was: The Search for Evidence of Increasing Hypercompetition," *Strategic Management Journal* 24 (2003): 261–278.

17. K. Weigelt and C. F. Camerer, "Reputation and Corporate Strategy: A Review of Recent Theory and Applications," *Strategic Management Journal* 9 (1988): 137–142.

18. A. K. Dixit, "The Role of Investment in Entry Deterrence," *Economic Journal* 90 (1980): 95–106; P. Milgrom and J. Roberts, "Informational Asymmetries, Strategic Behavior and Industrial Organization," *American Economic Review* 77, no. 2 (May 1987): 184–189.

19. P. Milgrom and J. Roberts, "Informational Asymmetries, Strategic Behavior and Industrial Organization," *American Economic Review* 77, no. 2 (May 1987): 184–9.

20. P. Ghemawat, *Commitment: The Dynamic of Strategy* (New York: Free Press, 1991).

21. See, for example: A. K. Dixit and B. J. Nalebuff, *Thinking Strategically: The Competitive Edge in Business, Politics, and Everyday Life* (New York: W. W. Norton, 1991); and J. McMillan, *Games, Strategies, and Managers* (New York: Oxford University Press, 1992).

22. G. T. Allison and P. Zelikow, *Essence of Decision: Explaining the Cuban Missile Crisis*, 2nd edn (Boston: Little, Brown and Company, 1999).

23. B. C. Esty and P. Ghemawat, "Airbus vs. Boeing in Superjumbos: A Case of Failed Preemption," Harvard Business School Working Paper No. 02-061 (2002).

24. D. Ronfelt, "Social Science at 190 mph on NASCAR's Biggest Superspeedways," *First Monday* 5 (February 7, 2000).

25. July 17, 2014 202-408-7500, barry.toiv@aau.edu "Economists Behind the FCC's Spectrum Auctions to Receive Golden Goose Award" (July 17, 2014), http://www.goldengooseaward.org/wp-content/uploads/2014/07/Wilson-Milgrom-McAfee-to-Receive-Golden-Goose-Awards-7-17-14.pdf, accessed November 15, 2014.

26. John Cassidy "Rational Irrationality," *New Yorker* (October 5, 2009).

27. J. Maynard Smith, "Sexual Selection and the Handicap Principle," *Journal of Theoretical Biology* 57 (1976): 239–242.

28. A. Brandenburger and B. Nalebuff, *Co-opetition* (New York: Doubleday, 1996).

29. T. Dhar, J.-P. Chatas, R. W. Collerill, and B. W. Gould, "Strategic Pricing between Coca-Cola Company and PepsiCo," *Journal of Economics and Management Strategy* 14 (2005): 905–931.

30. *Bitter Competition: Holland Sweetener vs. NutraSweet (A)* (Harvard Business School Case No. 9-794-079, 1994).

31. A. M. McGahan, "The Incentive not to Invest: Capacity Commitments in the Compact Disk Introduction," in R. A. Burgelman and R. S. Rosenbloom (eds), *Research on Technological Innovation Management and Policy*, vol. 5 (Greenwich, CT: JAI Press, 1994).

32. D. K. Levine and R. A. Levine, "Deterrence in the Cold War and the War on Terror," *Defence and Peace Economics* 17 (2006): 605–617.

33. D. N. Sull, "Managing by Commitments," *Harvard Business Review* (June 2003): 82–91.

34. Games where price is the primary decision variable are called *Bertrand models* after the 19th century French economist Joseph Bertrand.

35. Games where quantity is the primary decision variable are called *Cournot models* after the 19th century French economist Antoine Augustin Cournot.

36. F. Scott Morton, "Strategic Complements and Substitutes," *Financial Times Mastering Strategy Supplement* (November 8, 1999): 10–13.

37. R.M. Grant, "Tesla Motors: Disrupting the Auto Industry," in *Contemporary Strategy Analysis: Text and Cases*, 9th edn. (Wiley, 2016).

38. For a review of research on competitive signaling, see O. Heil and T. S. Robertson, "Toward a Theory of Competitive Market Signaling: A Research Agenda," *Strategic Management Journal* 12 (1991): 403–418.

39. B. Macintyre, *Operation Mincemeat: The True Spy Story that Changed the Course of World War II* (London: Bloomsbury, 2010).

40. For a survey of the strategic role of reputation, see K. Weigelt and C. Camerer, "Reputation and Corporate Strategy: A Review of Recent Theory and Applications," *Strategic Management Journal* 9 (1988): 443–454.

41. P. Milgrom and J. Roberts, "Predation, Reputation, and Entry Deterrence," *Journal of Economic Theory* 27 (1982): 280–312.

42. R. M. Grant, "Pricing Behavior in the UK Wholesale Market for Petrol," *Journal of Industrial Economics* 30 (1982): 271–292; L. Miller, "The Provocative Practice of Price Signaling: Collusion versus Cooperation," *Business Horizons* (July/August 1993).

43. On the ability of game theory to predict almost any equilibrium solution (the Pandora's Box Problem) see C. F. Camerer, "Does Strategy Research Need Game Theory?" *Strategic Management Journal*, Special Issue 12 (Winter 1991): 137–152; F. M. Fisher, "The Games Economists Play: A Noncooperative View," *Rand Journal of Economics* 20 (Spring 1989): 113–124; and Steve Postrel illustrates the point with a game, S. Postrel, "Burning Your Britches behind You: Can Policy Scholars Bank on Game Theory?" *Strategic Management Journal*, Special Issue 12 (Winter 1991): 153–155.

44. G. F. Rose and M. Lloyd, "The Failure of FCC Spectrum Auctions," (Washington DC: Center for American Progress, May 2006); P. Klemperer, "How not to Run Auctions: The European 3G Mobile Telecom Auctions. *European Economic Review* 46 (2002): 829–845.

45. Strategic and Competitive Intelligence Professionals; the Institute for Competitive Intelligence.

46. For example, J. D. Underwood, *Competitive Intelligence For Dummies* (Chichester: John Wiley & Sons, Ltd, 2014); L. M. Fuld, *The Secret Language of Competitive Intelligence* (Indianapolis: Dog Ear Publishing, 2010); M. Ioia, *The New Rules of Competitive Intelligence* (Bloomington, IN: Xlibris, 2014).

47. "McLaren Docked F1 Points for Spying," *Financial Times* (September 14, 2007); "Kolon Loses $920 Million Verdict to DuPont in Trial Over Kevlar," *Washington Post* (September 15, 2011).

48. Office of the National Counterintelligence Executive, *Foreign Spies Stealing US Economic Secrets in Cyberspace: Report to Congress on Foreign Economic Collection and Industrial Espionage, 2009–2011* (October 2011).

49. J.-C. Spender, *Industry Recipes: The Nature and Sources of Managerial Judgment* (Oxford: Blackwell, 1989). How social interaction promotes convergence of perceptions and beliefs is discussed by Anne Huff in "Industry Influences on Strategy Reformulation," *Strategic Management Journal* 3 (1982): 119–131.

50. This section draws heavily on M. E. Porter, *Competitive Advantage* (New York: Free Press, 1985): Chapter 7.

51. "Pirelli's Bet on High-performance Tires," *International Herald Tribune* (April 2, 2005).

52. R. E. Caves and M. E. Porter, "From Entry Barriers to Mobility Barriers: Conjectural Decisions and Contrived Deterrence to New Competition," *Quarterly Journal of Economics* 91 (1977): 241–262.

53. W. C. Kim and R. Mauborgne, "Blue Ocean Strategy: From Theory to Practice," *California Management Review* 47 (Spring 2005): 105–121.

54. M. E. Porter, *Competitive Strategy* (New York: Free Press, 1980): 129.

55. For more on strategic groups, see J. McGee and H. Thomas, "Strategic Groups: Theory, Research, and Taxonomy," *Strategic Management Journal* 7 (1986): 141–160.

56. A. Feigenbaum and H. Thomas, "Strategic Groups and Performance: The US Insurance Industry," *Strategic Management Journal* 11 (1990): 197–215.

57. K. Cool and I. Dierickx, "Rivalry, Strategic Groups, and Firm Profitability," *Strategic Management Journal* 14 (1993): 47–59.

58. K. Smith, C. Grimm, and S. Wally, "Strategic Groups and Rivalrous Firm Behavior: Toward a Reconciliation," *Strategic Management Journal* 18 (1997): 149–157.

5 Analyzing Resources and Capabilities

One gets paid only for strengths; one does not get paid for weaknesses. The question, therefore, is first: What are our specific strengths? And then: Are they the right strengths? Are they the strengths that fit the opportunities of tomorrow, or are they the strengths that fitted those of yesterday? Are we deploying our strengths where the opportunities no longer are, or perhaps never were? And finally, what additional strengths do we have to acquire?

— PETER DRUCKER[1]

You've gotta do what you do well.

—LUCINO NOTO, FORMER VICE CHAIRMAN, EXXONMOBIL

OUTLINE

Introduction and Objectives

In Chapter 1, I noted that the focus of strategy thinking has been shifted from the external environment of the firm toward its internal environment. In this chapter, we will make the same transition. Looking within the firm, we will concentrate our attention on the resources and capabilities that firms possess. In doing so, we shall build the foundations for our analysis of competitive advantage (which began in Chapter 3 with the discussion of key success factors).

By the time you have completed this chapter, you will be able to:

◆ Appreciate the role of a firm's resources and capabilities as a basis for formulating strategy.

◆ Identify the resources and capabilities of a firm.

◆ Evaluate the potential for a firm's resources and capabilities to confer sustainable competitive advantage.

◆ Formulate strategies that exploit internal strengths while defending against internal weaknesses.

We begin by explaining why a company's resources and capabilities are so important to its strategy.

The Role of Resources and Capabilities in Strategy Formulation

Strategy is concerned with matching a firm's resources and capabilities to the opportunities that arise in the external environment. So far, the emphasis of the book has been on the identification of profit opportunities in the external environment of the firm. In this chapter, our emphasis shifts from the interface between strategy and the external environment toward the interface between strategy and the internal environment of the firm—more specifically, with the resources and capabilities of the firm (Figure 5.1).

There is nothing new in the idea that strategy should exploit the resource and capability strengths of a person or an organization. The biblical tale of David and Goliath can be interpreted from this perspective (Strategy Capsule 5.1). The growing emphasis on the role of resources and capabilities as the basis for strategy is the result of two factors. First, as firms' industry environments have become more unstable, so internal resources and capabilities rather than external market focus have been viewed as comprising a more secure base for formulating strategy. Second, it has become increasingly apparent that competitive advantage rather than industry attractiveness is the primary source of superior profitability. Let us consider each of these factors.

Basing Strategy on Resources and Capabilities

During the 1990s, ideas concerning the role of resources and capabilities as the principal basis for firm strategy and the primary source of profitability coalesced into what has become known as the *resource-based view of the firm*.[2]

FIGURE 5.1   Analyzing resources and capabilities: The interface between strategy and the firm

To understand why the resource-based view has had a major impact on strategy thinking, let us go back to the starting point for strategy formulation: the underlying purpose of the firm which can be answered by posing the question: "What is our business?" Conventionally, this question has been answered in terms of the market being served: "Who are our customers?" and "Which of their needs are we seeking to serve?" However, in a world where customer preferences are volatile and the identity of customers and the technologies for serving them are changing, a market-focused strategy may not provide the stability and constancy of direction needed to guide strategy over the long term. When the external environment is in a state of flux, the

---

STRATEGY CAPSULE 5.1
David and Goliath

In about 1000 BC, David, an Israeli shepherd boy, took up the challenge of meeting Goliath, the champion of the Philistines in single combat. Goliath's "height was six cubits and a span [three meters]. He had a bronze helmet on his head and wore a coat of scale armor of bronze weighing five thousand shekels [58 kg]; on his legs he wore bronze greaves, and a bronze javelin was slung on his back." King Saul of the Israelites offered David armor and a helmet, but David discarded them: "'I cannot go in these,' he said to Saul, 'because I am not used to them.' … Then he took his staff in his hand, chose five smooth stones from the stream, put them in the pouch of his shepherd's bag and, with his sling in his hand, approached the Philistine… As the Philistine moved closer to attack him, David ran quickly toward

the battle line to meet him. Reaching into his bag and taking out a stone, he slung it and struck the Philistine on the forehead. The stone sank into his forehead, and he fell facedown on the ground."

David's victory over Goliath reflects a strategy based upon exploiting three core strengths: David's courage and self-confidence, his speed and mobility, and his expertise with a sling. This strategy allowed him to negate Goliath's core strengths: his size, his advanced offensive and defensive equipment, and his combat experience. Had he followed King Saul's advice and adopted a conventional strategy for armed single combat, the outcome would almost certainly have been very different.

Source: *Holy Bible* (New International Version): 1 Samuel 17: 39–49.

firm itself, in terms of the bundle of resources and capabilities it possesses, may be a much more stable basis on which to define its identity.

This emphasis on resources and capabilities as the foundation of firm strategy was popularized by C. K. Prahalad and Gary Hamel in their 1990 landmark paper "The Core Competence of the Corporation."[3] The potential for capabilities to be the "roots of competitiveness," the sources of new products, and the foundation for strategy is exemplified by Honda and 3M, among other companies (Strategy Capsule 5.2).

In general, the greater the rate of change in a firm's external environment, the more likely it is that internal resources and capabilities rather than external market focus will provide a secure foundation for long-term strategy. In fast-moving, technology-based industries, basing strategy upon capabilities can help firms to outlive the life-cycles of their initial products. Microsoft's initial success was the result of its MS-DOS operating system for the IBM PC. However, by building its software development, marketing, and partnering capabilities Microsoft has successfully expanded from other operating systems to applications software (e.g., Office), internet services (e.g., Xbox Live), and cloud-based computing services. Similarly, Apple's ability to combine hardware, software, ergonomics, and aesthetics to create products with superior functionality, design, and ease of use has allowed it to expand beyond desktop and notebook computers into MP3 players (iPod), smartphones (iPhone), tablet computers (iPad), and watches.

Conversely, those companies that attempted to maintain their market focus in the face of radical technological change have often experienced huge difficulties in building the new technological capabilities needed to serve their customers.

The saga of Eastman Kodak is a classic example. Its dominance of the world market for photographic products was threatened by digital imaging. Kodak invested billions of dollars developing digital technologies and digital imaging products. Yet, in January 2012, Kodak was forced into bankruptcy. Might Kodak have been better off by sticking with its chemical know-how, allowing its photographic business to decline while developing its interests in specialty chemicals, pharmaceuticals, and healthcare?[4]

Typewriter and office equipment makers Olivetti and Smith Corona offer similar cautionary tales. Despite their investments in microelectronics, both failed as suppliers of personal computers. Might Olivetti and Smith Corona have been better advised to deploy their existing electrical and precision engineering know-how in other products?[5] This pattern of established firms failing to adjust to disruptive technological change within their own industries is well documented—in typesetting and in disk drive manufacturing, successive technological waves have caused market leaders to falter and have allowed new entrants to prosper.[6]

Resources and Capabilities as Sources of Profit

In Chapter 1, we identified two major sources of superior profitability: industry attractiveness and competitive advantage. Of these, competitive advantage is the more important. Internationalization and deregulation have increased competitive pressure within most sectors; as a result, few industries (or segments) offer cozy refuges from vigorous competition. As we observed in the previous chapter (Figure 4.1), industry factors account for only a small proportion of interfirm profit differentials. Hence, establishing competitive advantage through the development and deployment of resources and capabilities, rather than seeking shelter from the storm of competition, has become the primary goal of strategy.

The distinction between industry attractiveness and competitive advantage (based on superior resources) as sources of a firm's profitability corresponds to economists'

STRATEGY CAPSULE 5.2

Basing Strategy upon Resources and Capabilities: Honda and 3M

Honda Motor Company has never defined itself either as a motorcycle or an automobile company. As Figure 5.2 shows, since its founding in 1948, its development of expertise in designing and manufacturing engines has taken it from motorcycles to a wide range of internal engine products.

3M Corporation (originally Minnesota Mining and Manufacturing) has expanded from sandpaper into over 55,000 industrial, office, medical, and household products. Is it a conglomerate?

Certainly not, claims 3M. Its vast product range rests on a cluster of technological capabilities that it has systematically developed for over more than a century (Figure 5.3).

FIGURE 5.2 Key initiatives at Honda Motor Company

FIGURE 5.3 The evolution of products and technical capabilities at 3M distinctions between different types of profit (or *rent*). The profits arising from market power are referred to as *monopoly rents*; those arising from superior resources are *Ricardian rents*, after the 19th century British economist David Ricardo. Ricardo showed that, in a competitive wheat market, when land at the margin of cultivation earned a negligible return, fertile land would yield high returns. Ricardian rent is the return earned by a scarce resource over and above the cost of using the resource.[7] Most of the $879 million of royalties earned in 2014 by Dolby Laboratories from licensing its sound reduction technologies comprises Ricardian rents, as does most of the $56.2 million earned in 2014 by tennis player Roger Federer.

Distinguishing between profit arising from market power and profit arising from resource superiority is less clear in practice than in principle. A closer look at Porter's five forces framework suggests that industry attractiveness often derives from the ownership of strategic resources. Barriers to entry, for example, are typically the result of patents, brands, know-how, or distribution channels, learning, or some other resource possessed by incumbent firms. Monopoly is usually based on the ownership of a key resource such as a technical standard or government license.

The resource-based approach has profound implications for companies' strategy formulation. When the primary concern of strategy was industry selection and positioning, companies tended to adopt similar strategies. The resource-based view, by contrast, recognizes that each company possesses a unique collection of resources and capabilities; the key to profitability is not doing the same as other firms but rather exploiting differences. Establishing competitive advantage involves formulating and implementing a strategy that exploits a firm's unique strengths.

The remainder of this chapter outlines a resource-based approach to strategy formulation. Fundamental to this approach is a thorough and profound understanding of the resources and capabilities of a firm. Such understanding provides a basis for selecting a strategy that exploits the key resource and capabilities of an organization.

While our emphasis is on firm strategy, the same principles can be applied to guiding our own careers. A sound career strategy is one that, like David against Goliath, recognizes and exploits one's strengths while minimizing vulnerability to one's weaknesses—see Strategy Capsule 5.3 for an example. For both individuals and organizations the starting point is to identify the available resources and capabilities.

Identifying Resources and Capabilities

 Let us begin by distinguishing between the **resources** and the **capabilities** of the firm. Resources are the productive assets owned by the firm; capabilities are what the firm can do. On their own, individual resources do not confer competitive advantage; they must work together to create organizational capability. Organizational capability, when applied through an appropriate strategy, provides the foundation for competitive advantage. Figure 5.4 shows the relationships between resources, capabilities, and competitive advantage.

Identifying Resources

Drawing up an inventory of a firm's resources can be surprisingly difficult. No such document exists within the accounting or management information systems of most organizations. The balance sheet provides only a partial view of a firm's resources—it comprises mainly financial and physical resources. Our broader view

STRATEGY CAPSULE 5.3

Capability-based Strategy: Lyor Cohen on Mariah Carey

The year 2001 was disastrous for Mariah Carey. Her first movie, *Glitter*, was a flop, the soundtrack was Carey's worst selling album in years, she was dropped by EMI, and suffered a nervous breakdown.

Lyor Cohen, the workaholic chief executive of Island Def Jam records was quick to spot an opportunity: "I cold-called her on the day of her release from EMI and I said, I think you are an unbelievable artist and you should hold your head up high. What I said stuck on her and she ended up signing with us."

His strategic analysis of Carey's situation was concise: "I said to her, what's your competitive advantage? A great voice, of course. And what else? You write every one of your songs—you're a great writer. So why did you stray from your competitive advantage? If you

have this magnificent voice and you write such compelling songs, why are you dressing like that, why are you using all these collaborations [with other artists and other songwriters]? Why? It's like driving a Ferrari in first—you won't see what that Ferrari will do until you get into sixth gear."

Cohen signed Carey in May 2002. Under Universal Music's Island Def Jam Records, Carey returned to her versatile voice, song-writing talents, and ballad style. Her next album, *The Emancipation of Mimi*, was the biggest-selling album of 2005, and in 2006 she won a Grammy award.

Source: "Rap's Unlikely Mogul," *Financial Times* (August 5, 2002). © The Financial Times, reproduced with permission.

FIGURE 5.4 The links between resources, capabilities, and competitive advantage

STRATEGY CAPSULE 5.4
Resource Utilization: Revival at Walt Disney

In 1984, Michael Eisner became CEO of the Walt Disney Company. Between 1984 and 1988, Disney's net income increased from $98 million to $570 million, and its stock market valuation from $1.8 billion to $10.3 billion.

The key to the Disney turnaround was the mobilization of Disney's considerable resource base. With the acquisition of Arvida, a real estate development company, Disney's land holdings in Florida were developed into hotels, convention facilities, residential housing, and a new theme park, the Disney-MGM Studio Tour.

To exploit its huge film library, Disney began selling the Disney classics on videocassette and licensing packages of movies to TV networks. To put Disney's underutilized movie studios to work, Eisner doubled the number of movies in production and made Disney a major producer of TV programs.

Supporting the exploitation of these tangible resources was Disney's critically important intangible resource: the enduring affection of millions of people across generations and throughout the world for Disney and its characters. As a result, Disney's new management was able to boost theme park admission charges, launch a chain of Disney Stores to push sales of Disney merchandise, and replicate Disney theme parks in Europe and Asia.

of a firm's resources, encompasses three main types of resource: tangible, intangible, and human.

Tangible Resources   Tangible resources are the easiest to identify and value: financial resources and physical assets are valued in the firm's balance sheet. Yet, accounting conventions—especially historic cost valuation—typically result in tangible resources being misvalued. The Walt Disney Company's annual accounts for 2014 valued its entire movie library—based on production cost less amortization—at a mere $1.4 billion and its total land assets (including its 28,000 acres in Florida) at a paltry $1.2 billion.[8]

However, the primary goal of resource analysis is not to value a company's tangible resources but to understand their potential for generating profit. This requires not just balance sheet valuation but information on their composition and characteristics. With that information we can explore two main routes to create additional value from a firm's tangible resources:

- What opportunities exist for economizing on their use? Can we use fewer resources to support the same level of business or use the existing resources to support a larger volume of business?
- Can existing assets be deployed more profitably?

Strategy Capsule 5.4 discusses how Michael Eisner's turnaround of Walt Disney during the mid-1980s used both these approaches.

Intangible Resources   For most companies, intangible resources are more valuable than tangible resources. Yet, in companies' balance sheets, intangible resources tend to be either undervalued or omitted altogether. The exclusion or undervaluation of intangible resources is a major reason for the large and growing

TABLE 5.1   Large companies with the highest valuation ratios, December 12, 2014

Company	Ratio	Nationality
Alibaba	40.25	China
Altria	23.11	USA
Colgate-Palmolive	21.96	USA
AbbVie	21.81	USA
Amazon	15.18	USA
Roche	14.24	Switz.
Celgene Corporation	13.50	USA
Gilead Sciences	11.61	USA
Facebook	11.24	USA
Starbucks	10.92	USA
GlaxoSmithKline	10.87	UK
Tata Consultancy Services	10.07	India
Accenture	9.15	USA
British American Tobacco	8.09	UK
Inditex	7.57	Spain
Nike	7.54	USA
Diageo	6.89	UK
Unilever	6.84	Neth./UK
IBM	6.40	USA
PepsiCo	6.24	USA
Boeing	6.07	USA

Note:
The table shows companies with market capitalizations exceeding $50 billion with the highest ratios of market capitalization to balance-sheet net asset value.
Sources: Yahoo! Finance, Financial Times.

divergence between companies' balance-sheet valuations (or book values) and their stock-market valuations (Table 5.1). Among the most important of these undervalued or unvalued intangible resources are brands (Table 5.2). Interbrand values the Walt Disney brand at $32 billion; yet in Disney's balance sheet, all its trademarks are valued at $1.2 billion.

Trademarks provide the legal basis for brand ownership. Trademarks are one type of intellectual property. Other types of intellectual property are patents, copyrights, and trade secrets which form the proprietary knowledge assets of the firm. The growing importance of proprietary technology as a strategic resource is apparent from the efforts companies make to protect their innovations with patents and enforce their patents through litigation. As the economy becomes increasingly knowledge-based, so patents and copyrights become increasingly important resources. For companies such as Qualcomm, a leader in CDMA digital wireless telephony, ARM, the world's leading designer of microprocessors for mobile devices, and W. L. Gore Associates, the manufacturer of Gore-Tex and other high-tech fabrics, patents are their most valuable resources.

A firm's relationships can also be considered resources. They provide a firm with access to information, know-how, inputs, and a wide range of other resources that lie beyond the firm's boundaries. Being embedded within an inter-firm network also conveys legitimacy upon a firm, which can enhance its survival capacity. These inter-firm relationships have been referred to as "network resources."[9]

TABLE 5.2   The world's 20 most valuable brands, 2014

Rank	Brand	Value, 2014 ($ bn)	Change from 2013
1	Apple	118.9	+21%
2	Google	107.4	+15%
3	Coca-Cola	81.6	+3%
4	IBM	72.2	−8%
5	Microsoft	61.2	+3%
6	General Electric	45.5	−3%
7	Samsung	45.5	+15%
8	Toyota	42.4	+20%
9	McDonald's	42.3	+1%
10	Mercedes-Benz	34.3	+8%
11	BMW	34.2	+7%
12	Intel	34.2	−8%
13	Disney	32.2	+14%
14	Cisco	30.9	+6%
15	Amazon	25.5	+25%
16	Oracle	26.0	+8%
17	Hewlett-Packard	23.8	−8%
18	Gillette	22.9	−8%
19	Louis Vuitton	22.6	−9%
20	Honda	21.7	+17%

Note:
Brand values are calculated as the net present value of forecasted future earnings generated by the brand.
Source: Interbrand, http://www.bestglobalbrands.com/2014/ranking/.

Finally, organizational culture may also be considered an intangible resource. Organizational culture is "an amalgam of shared beliefs, values, assumptions, significant meanings, myths, rituals, and symbols that are held to be distinctive."[10] Although difficult to identify and describe, it is clear that **organizational culture** is a critically important resource in most firms: it exerts a strong influence on the capabilities an organization develops and the effectiveness with which they are exercised.[11]

Human Resources   Human resources comprise the skills and productive effort offered by an organization's employees. Human resources do not appear on the firm's balance sheet—the firm does not own its employees; it purchases their services under employment contacts. However, the stability of employment relationships allows us to consider human resources as part of the resources of the firm. In the US the average length of time an employee stays with an employer is 4.6 years, in Europe it is longer—9.5 years in Great Britain, 12.3 in France and 11.7 in Germany; in Japan it is 16.2 years.[12]

Organizations devote considerable effort to analyzing their human resources: both in hiring new employees and in appraising their performance and planning their development. Human resource appraisal has become far more systematic and sophisticated. Many organizations have established assessment centers to measure employees' skills and attributes using indicators that research has identified as predictors of superior job performance. *Competency modeling* involves identifying the set of skills, content knowledge, attitudes, and values associated with superior performers within a particular job category, then assessing each employee against that profile.[13] A key research finding is the importance of psychological and social aptitudes in determining superior work performance—recent interest in *emotional* and *social intelligence* reflects this.[14] These findings explain the growing trend among companies to "hire for attitude; train for skills."

Identifying Organizational Capabilities

Resources are not productive on their own. A brain surgeon is close to useless without a radiologist, anesthetist, nurses, surgical instruments, imaging equipment, and a host of other resources. To perform a task, resources must work together. An organizational capability is a "firm's capacity to deploy resources for a desired end result."[15] Just as an individual may be capable of playing the violin, ice-skating, and speaking Mandarin, so an organization may possess the capabilities needed to manufacture widgets, distribute them globally, and hedge the resulting foreign-exchange exposure.

Although the idea that organizations possess *distinctive competences* is long established,[16] it was not until Prahalad and Hamel introduced the term *core competences* to describe those capabilities fundamental to a firm's strategy and performance that organizational capabilities became a central concept in strategy analysis.[17] The resulting flood of literature has created considerable confusion over terminology: I shall use the terms *capability* and *competence* interchangeably.[18]

Classifying Capabilities   Before deciding which organizational capabilities are "distinctive" or "core," the firms needs to take a systematic view of its capabilities. To identify a firm's organizational capabilities, we need to have some basis for classifying and disaggregating the firm's activities. Two approaches are commonly used:

- A *functional analysis* identifies organizational capabilities within each of the firm's functional areas: A firm's functions would typically include: operations, purchasing, logistics/supply chain management, design, engineering, new product development, marketing, sales and distribution, customer service, finance, human resource management, legal, information systems, government relations, communication and public relations, and HSE (health, safety, and environment).
- A *value chain analysis* identifies a sequential chain of the main activities that the firm undertakes. Michael Porter's generic **value chain** distinguishes between primary activities (those involved with the transformation of inputs and interface with the customer) and support activities (Figure 5.5).[19] Porter's broadly defined value chain activities can be disaggregated to provide a more detailed identification of the firm's activities (and the capabilities that correspond to each activity). Thus, marketing might include market research, test marketing, advertising, promotion, pricing, and dealer relations.

The problem of both approaches is that, despite providing a comprehensive view of an organization's capabilities, they may fail to identify those idiosyncratic capabilities that are truly distinctive and critical to an organization's competitive advantage. In the case of Apple we observed earlier how its remarkable ability to create

FIGURE 5.5   Porter's value chain

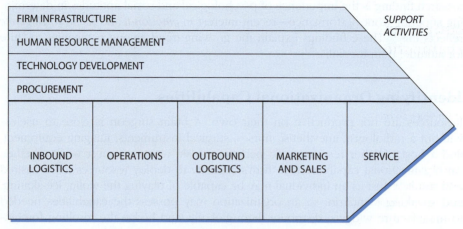

products of unrivaled ease of use and customer appeal results from its combining technical capability with penetrating market insight. This capability is not readily apparent from either a functional or a value chain analysis. To look beyond generic capabilities to uncover those that are unique requires insight and judgment. A careful examination of an organization's history can be especially revealing. In reviewing an organization's successes and failures over time, do patterns emerge and what do these patterns tell us about the capabilities that the organization possesses?

At the basis of every organizational capability is coordinated behavior among organizational members. This is what distinguishes an organizational capability from an individual skill. Routines and processes play a critical role in integrating individual actions to create organizational capabilities (see Strategy Capsule 5.5). Integration is also important among organizational capabilities. The capabilities of an organization may be viewed as a hierarchical system in which lower-level capabilities are integrated to form higher-level capabilities. For oil and gas companies, a key requirement for success is the ability to find oil and gas. Figure 5.6 shows that exploration capability comprises a number of component capabilities, which, in turn, can be further disaggregated into even more specialized capabilities.

For most companies it is these higher-level capabilities that constitute the "core competences" described by Prahalad and Hamel. Thus, Toyota's "lean production" capability integrates multiple capabilities that relate to just-in-time scheduling, total quality management, statistical process control, flexible manufacturing, and continuous improvement.

These higher-level capabilities tend to be cross-functional. For example, new product development capability is an upper-level capability that integrates technological development, marketing, design, product engineering, process engineering, and finance.

Some writers have proposed that at the highest level of the capability hierarchy are **dynamic capabilities**—capabilities that allow the modification and adaptation of lower-level operational and functional capabilities.[20] We shall look more closely at dynamic capabilities in Chapter 8.

STRATEGY CAPSULE 5.5

Routines and Processes: The Foundations of Organizational Capability

Resources are combined to create organizational capabilities; however, an organization's capabilities are not simply an outcome of the resources upon which they are based.

In sport, resource-rich teams are often outplayed by teams that create strong capabilities from modest resources. In European soccer, star-studded teams (e.g., Chelsea, Real Madrid, and Manchester City) are frequently humbled by those built from limited means (e.g., Borussia Dortmund, Arsenal, and Athletico Madrid). In business too we see upstarts with modest resources outcompeting established giants: Dyson against Electrolux in domestic appliances, Hyundai against Toyota in automobiles, Cisco Systems against Ericsson in telecom equipment, ARM against Intel in microprocessors. Clearly, there is more to organizational capability than just resources.

The academic literature views organizational capability as based upon organizational routines. These "regular and predictable behavioral patterns [comprising] repetitive patterns of activity"[a] are viewed by evolutionary economists as determining what firms do, who they are, and how they develop and grow. Like individual skills, organizational routines develop through learning by doing—and, if not used, they wither. Hence, there is a tradeoff between efficiency and flexibility. A limited repertoire of routines can be performed highly efficiently with near-perfect coordination. The same organization may find it difficult to respond to novel situations.

Organizational capabilities do not simply emerge: they must be created through management action: hence in this book we shall focus on processes rather than routines. Processes are coordinated sequences of actions through which specific productive tasks are performed. Not only is the term *process* well understood by managers, the tools for designing, mapping, and improving business processes are well developed.[b]

However, creating and developing organizational capabilities is not only about putting in place processes. Processes need to be located within appropriately designed organizational units, the individuals involved need to motivated, and the resources, processes, structures, and management systems need to be aligned with one another.[c] In Chapter 8 we shall address in greater detail the challenge that companies face in developing organizational capabilities.

Notes:

[a] R. R. Nelson and S. G. Winter, *An Evolutionary Theory of Economic Change* (Cambridge, MA: Belknap, 1982).

[b] T. W. Malone, K. Crowston, J. Lee, and B. Pentland, "Tools for Inventing Organizations: Toward a Handbook of Organizational Processes," *Management Science* 45 (1999): 425–43.

[c] T. Felin, N. J. Foss, K. H. Heimeriks, and T. L. Madsen, "Microfoundations of Routines and Capabilities: Individuals, Processes, and Structure," *Journal of Management Studies*, 49 (2012): 1351–1374.

Whatever the hierarchical structure of a company's capabilities, their effectiveness depends upon the extent to which they are mutually reinforcing in delivering the firm's value proposition. This complementary relationship among a company's principal capabilities is the basis for "corporate coherence." Thus, Walmart's competitive advantage rests upon four mutually reinforcing capabilities: aggressive vendor management, point-of-sale data analysis, superior logistics, and rigorous working capital management.[21]

FIGURE 5.6   Organization capabilities as a hierarchy of integration: the case of oil and gas exploration

Appraising Resources and Capabilities

Having identified the principle resources and capabilities of an organization, how do we appraise their potential for value creation? There are two fundamental issues: first, how *strategically important* are the different resources and capabilities of the firm and, second, how *strong* are the firm's resources and capabilities relative to those of its competitors'. Let us begin by considering how to appraise the strategic importance of a firm's resources and capabilities.

Appraising the Strategic Importance of Resources and Capabilities

Strategically important resources and capabilities are those with the potential to generate substantial streams of profit for the firm that owns them. This depends on three factors: their potential to establish a competitive advantage, to sustain that competitive advantage, and to appropriate the returns from the competitive advantage. Each of these is determined by a number of resource characteristics. Figure 5.7 summarizes the key relationships.

Establishing Competitive Advantage   For a resource or capability to establish a competitive advantage, two conditions must be present:

- *Relevance*: A resource or capability must be relevant to the key success factors in the market—in particular, it must be capable of creating value for customers. British coal mines produced some wonderful brass bands, but these musical capabilities did little to assist the mines in meeting competition from cheap imported coal and North Sea gas. As retail banking shifts toward automated teller machines and online transactions, so the retail branch networks of the banks have become less relevant for customer service.
- *Scarcity*: If a resource or capability is widely available within the industry, it may be necessary in order to compete but it will not be an adequate basis for competitive advantage. In oil and gas exploration, technologies such as directional drilling and 3-D seismic analysis are widely available—hence they are "needed to play" but they are not "sufficient to win."

FIGURE 5.7 Appraising the strategic importance of resources and capabilities

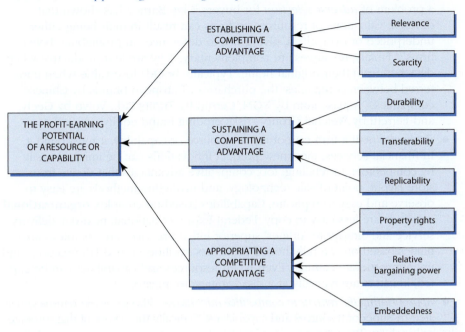

Sustaining Competitive Advantage   Once established, competitive advantage tends to erode; three characteristics of resources and capabilities determine the sustainability of the competitive advantage they offer:

- *Durability*: The more durable a resource, the greater its ability to support a competitive advantage over the long term. For most resources, including capital equipment and proprietary technology, the quickening pace of technological innovation is shortening their life spans. Brands, on the other hand, can show remarkable resilience to time. Heinz sauces, Kellogg's cereals, Guinness stout, Burberry raincoats, and Coca-Cola have been market leaders for over a century.

- *Transferability*: Competitive advantage is undermined by competitive imitation. If resources and capabilities are transferable between firms—i.e., if they can be bought and sold—then any competitive advantage that is based upon them will be eroded. Most resources—including most human resources—can be bought and sold with little difficulty. Other resources and most capabilities are immobile and not easily transferred. Some resources are specific to certain locations and cannot be relocated. A competitive advantage of the Laphroaig distillery and its 10-year-old, single malt whiskey is its water spring on the Isle of Islay, which supplies water flavored by peat and sea spray. Capabilities, because they combine multiple resources embedded in an organization's management systems, are also difficult to move from one firm to another. Another barrier to transferability is limited information regarding resource quality. In the case of human resources, hiring decisions are typically based on very little knowledge of how the new employee will perform. Sellers of resources have better information about the performance characteristics of resources than buyers do. This creates a problem of *adverse selection* for buyers.[22] Jay Barney has shown that different valuations of resources by firms can result in their being either underpriced or overpriced, giving rise to differences in profitability between firms.[23] Finally, resources are complementary: they are less productive when detached from their original home. Typically brands lose value when transferred between companies: the purchase of European brands by Chinese companies—Aquascutum by YGM, Cerruti by Trinity Ltd., Volvo by Geely, and Ferretti by Weichai Group—risks eroding brand equity.

● *Replicability*: If a firm cannot buy a resource or capability, it must build it. In financial services, most new product innovations can be imitated easily by competitors. In retailing, too, competitive advantages that derive from store layout, point-of-sale technology, and marketing methods are easy to observe and easy to replicate. Capabilities based on complex **organizational routines** are less easy to copy. Federal Express's national, next-day delivery service and Singapore Airlines' superior inflight services are complex capabilities based on carefully honed processes, well-developed HR practices, and unique corporate cultures. Even when resources and capabilities can be copied, imitators are typically at a disadvantage to initiators.[24]

● *Appropriating the returns to competitive advantage*: Who gains the returns generated by superior resources and capabilities? Typically the owner of that resource or capability. But ownership may not be clear-cut. Are organizational capabilities owned by the employees who provide skills and effort or by the firm which provides the processes and culture? In human-capital-intensive firms, there is an ongoing struggle between employees and shareholders as to the division of the rents arising from superior capabilities. As Strategy Capsule 5.6 describes, bargaining between star employees and owners over the sharing of spoils is a characteristic feature of both investment banking and professional sports. This struggle is reminiscent of Karl Marx's description of the conflict between labor and capital to capture surplus value. The prevalence of partnerships (rather than shareholder-owned companies) in law, accounting, and consulting firms is one solution to the battle for rent appropriation. The less clear are property rights in resources and capabilities, the greater the importance of relative bargaining power in determining the division of returns between the firm and its members. Also, the more deeply embedded are individual skills and knowledge within organizational routines, and the more they depend on corporate systems and reputation, the weaker the employee is relative to the firm.

Strategy Capsule 5.7 compares my approach to appraising the strategic importance of resources and capabilities with that of Jay Barney.

Appraising the Relative Strength of a Firm's Resources and Capabilities

Having established which resources and capabilities are strategically most important, we need to assess how a firm measures up relative to its competitors. Making an objective appraisal of a company's resources and capabilities relative to its competitors' is difficult. Organizations frequently fall victim to past glories, hopes for the

Appropriating Returns from Superior Capabilities: Employees vs. Owners

Investment banks are a fascinating arena to view the conflict between employees and owners to appropriate the returns to organizational capability. Goldman Sachs possesses outstanding capabilities in merger and acquisition services, underwriting and proprietary trading. These capabilities combine employee skills, IT infrastructure, corporate reputation, and the company's systems and culture. All but the first of these are owned by the company. However, the division of returns between employees and owners suggests that employees have the upper hand in appropriating rents (Table 5. 3).

Similarly in professional sport: star players are well positioned to exploit the full value of their contribution to their teams' performance. The $23.5 million salary paid to Kobe Bryant for the 2014/15 NBA season seems likely to fully exploit his value to the Los Angeles Lakers.

So too CEOs: Disney's CEO, Robert Iger, was paid $34.3 million in 2014. But determining how much Iger contributed to Disney's 2013 net income of $7.4 billion as compared with that of Disney's other 180,000 employees is unknown.

The more organizational performance can be identified with the expertise of an individual employee, the more mobile is that employee, and the more likely that the employee's skills can be deployed with another firm, then the stronger is the bargaining position of that employee.

Hence, the emphasis that many investment banks, advertising agencies, and other professional service firms give to team-based rather than individual skills. "We believe our strength lies in . . . our unique team-based approach," declares audit firm Grant Thornton. However, employees can reassert their bargaining power through emphasizing team mobility: in September 2010, most of UBS's energy team moved to Citi.

TABLE 5.3   Profits, dividends, and employee compensation at Goldman Sachs

	2009	2011	2013
Net profits	$13,390m	$4,442m	$8,040m
Dividends to ordinary shareholders	$579m	$780m	$988m
Total employee compensation	$16,190m	$12,200m	$12,613m
Compensation per employee	$498,000	$366,360	$383,374

future, and their own wishful thinking. The tendency toward hubris among companies, and their senior managers, means that business success often sows the seeds of its own destruction.[25] Royal Bank of Scotland's successful acquisition of NatWest Bank was followed by an acquisition binge culminating in the disastrous takeover of ABN Amro in 2007.[26]

Benchmarking—the process of comparing one's processes and performance to those of other companies—offers an objective and quantitative way for a firm to assess its resources and capabilities relative to its competitors'.[27] The results can be salutary: Xerox Corporation, a pioneer of benchmarking during the 1980s, observed the massive superiority of its Japanese competitors in cost efficiency, quality, and

STRATEGY CAPSULE 5.7
Appraising Resources and Capabilities: Grant *versus* Barney

The approach outlined in this chapter for appraising the strategic importance of resources is an
alternative to the more widely used VRIO framework

developed by Jay Barney. Let me compare the two
approaches so that their similarities and differences
are apparent.

GRANT: Strategic Importance Framework	BARNEY: VRIO Framework	Comparison
Establishing competitive advantage		
• Relevance	• Valuable	Similar: both are concerned with creating value for customers
• Scarcity	• Rare	Identical: scarcity = rareness
Sustaining competitive advantage		
• Durability	—	No equivalent criterion in VRIO
• Transferability	• Imitable	Similar: imitating a resource or capability
• Replicability		requires either buying it (i.e. transferring it) or replicating it
Appropriating competitive advantage		
• Appropriability	• Organization	Similar: being organized to capture value implies the ability to appropriate value

Sources: The VRIO Framework is found in J. B. Barney, "Looking Inside for Competitive Advantage," *Academy of Management Executive* 9 (1995): 49–61 and J. B. Barney and W. Hesterly, *Strategic Management and Competitive Advantage* 5th edn. (Pearson, 2014).

new-product development. More recent evidence shows wide gaps in most industries between average practices and best practices.[28]

My own experience with companies points to the need for benchmarking to be
supplemented by more reflective approaches to recognizing strengths and weaknesses. As I indicated in relation to the earlier discussion of "Identifying Organizational
Capabilities," it can be highly instructive to get groups of managers together to ask
them to identify things that the company has done well in recent years and things
that it has done badly, then to ask whether any patterns emerge.

Developing Strategy Implications

Our analysis so far—identifying resources and capabilities and appraising them in
terms of strategic importance and relative strength—can be summarized in the form
of a simple display (Figure 5.8).

FIGURE 5.8   The framework for appraising resources and capabilities

Our key focus is on the two right-hand quadrants of Figure 5.8. How do we exploit our key strengths most effectively? How can we address our key weaknesses in terms of both reducing our vulnerability to them and correcting them? Finally, what about our "inconsequential" strengths: are these really superfluous or are there ways in which we can deploy them to greater effect? Let me offer a few suggestions.

Exploiting Key Strengths

The foremost task is to ensure that the firm's critical strengths are deployed to the greatest effect:

- If some of Walt Disney's key strengths are the Disney brand, the worldwide affection that children and their parents have for Disney characters, and the company's capabilities in the design and operation of theme parks, the implication is that Disney should not limit its themes park activities to six locations (Anaheim, Orlando, Paris, Tokyo, Hong Kong, and Shanghai); it should open theme parks in other locations which have adequate market potential for year-round attendance.

- If a core competence of quality newspapers such as the *New York Times*, the *Guardian* (UK), and *Le Monde* (France) is their ability to interpret events and identify emerging trends, can this capability be used as a basis for establishing new businesses such as customized business intelligence and other types of consulting in order to supplement their declining revenues from newspaper sales?

- If a company has few key strengths, this may suggest adopting a niche strategy. Harley-Davidson's key strength is its brand identity; its strategy has been to focus upon traditionally styled, technologically backward, cruiser motorcycles. British semiconductor company ARM is a technology leader in RISC architecture; its strategy is highly focused: it licenses its microprocessor designs for mobile devices worldwide.

Managing Key Weaknesses

What does a company do about its key weaknesses? It is tempting to counter weaknesses with plans to upgrade existing resources and capabilities. However, converting weakness into strength is likely to be a long-term task for most companies. In the short to medium term, a company is likely to be stuck with the resources and capabilities that it has inherited.

The most decisive, and often most successful, solution to weaknesses in key functions is to *outsource*. Thus, in the automobile industry, companies have become increasingly selective in the activities they perform internally. The trend toward vertical deintegration is the result of companies concentrating on their key strengths and outsourcing other activities. Across a range of activities specialist suppliers have more highly developed capabilities than most companies. Hence the outsourcing of IT (to Accenture, IBM, Capgemini), logistics (to Exel, Kuehne + Nagle, UPS), and food service (to Compass, Sodexo).

Some companies may be present in relatively few activities within their value chains. In athletic shoes and clothing, Nike undertakes product design, marketing, and overall "systems integration," but manufacturing, logistics, and many other functions are contracted out. We shall consider the vertical scope of the firm in greater depth in Chapter 11.

Clever strategy formulation can allow a firm to negate its vulnerability to key weaknesses. Consider once more Harley-Davidson. It cannot compete with Honda, Yamaha, and BMW on technology. The solution? It has made a virtue out of its outmoded technology and traditional designs. Harley-Davidson's old-fashioned, push-rod engines, and recycled designs have become central to its retro-look authenticity.

What about Superfluous Strengths?

What about those resources and capabilities where a company has particular strengths that don't appear to be important sources of sustainable competitive advantage? One response may be selective divestment. If a retail bank has a strong but increasingly underutilized branch network, it may be time to prune its real-estate assets and invest in web-based customer services.

However, in the same way that companies can turn apparent weaknesses into competitive strengths, so it is possible to develop innovative strategies that turn apparently inconsequential strengths into key strategy differentiators. Edward Jones' network of brokerage offices and 8000-strong sales force looked increasingly irrelevant in an era when brokerage transactions were going online. However, by emphasizing personal service, trustworthiness, and its traditional, conservative investment virtues, Edward Jones has built a successful contrarian strategy based on its network of local offices.[29]

In the fiercely competitive MBA market, business schools should also seek to differentiate on the basis of idiosyncratic resources and capabilities. Georgetown's Jesuit heritage is not an obvious source of competitive advantage for its MBA programs. Yet, the Jesuit approach to education is about developing the whole person; this fits well with an emphasis on developing the values, integrity, and emotional intelligence necessary to be a successful business leader. Similarly, Dartmouth College's location in the woods of New Hampshire far from any major business center is not an obvious benefit to its business programs. However, Dartmouth's Tuck Business School has used the isolation and natural beauty of its locale to create an MBA program that features unparalleled community and social involvement that fosters personal development and close network ties.

The Industry Context of Resource Analysis

An important use of resource and capability analysis is in indicating the industry and market segments that are best aligned with a firm's strengths and weaknesses. Appraising resources and capabilities on the basis of strategic importance and relative strength is highly sensitive to how we define the competitive environment of the focal firm. Consider the case of Harley-Davidson: its greatest weakness is in technology. Harley-Davidson would be ill advised to enter the performance motorcycle segment, where technology is a key success factor; its focus on heavyweight cruiser motorcycles makes much more sense: in this segment technology is much less important.

This implies that the results of any resource and capability analysis depend critically upon how broadly or narrowly an industry is defined. In general, it is best to define industries fairly broadly; otherwise, there is a risk our resource/capability analysis will become limited by the focal firm's existing strategy and tend to ignore both threats from distant competitors and opportunities for new strategic departures.

More generally, as with all strategy frameworks, we need to be alert to the limitations of resource and capability analysis. Not only are our criteria of strategic importance and relative strength context-dependent but also individual resources and capabilities are themselves multidimensional aggregations. For example, a firm's manufacturing capability might be assessed in relation to efficiency, quality, and flexibility. Hence, the resource and capability analysis as outlined in this chapter is likely to be a fairly crude tool for appraising a firm's potential for competitive advantage. However, what it does offer is a systematic approach to describe and assess an organization's portfolio of resources and capabilities that can be subsequently refined.

Strategy Capsule 5.8 provides an example of how the approach outlined in this chapter can be applied to identify and appraise the resources and capabilities of the Icelandair Group and indicate the potential to establish a competitive advantage within the airline industry.

STRATEGY CAPSULE 5.8

Resource and Capability Analysis in Action: Icelandair Group

If the key success factor in the airline business is providing safe, reliable transportation between city pairs at a competitive price, we can begin by identifying the resources and capabilities needed to achieve that goal. We can then use the value chain to fill out more systematically this list of resources and capabilities. Table 5.4 and Figure 5.9 show the major resources and capabilities required in the airline business and assess Icelandair's position relative to a peer group of competitors.

In terms of strategy implications, a key resource that distinguishes Icelandair is location: Iceland's population of 326,000 offers a passenger and freight market that Icelandair can easily dominate, but is too small to support an international airline. Hence, to achieve efficient scale, Icelandair must (a) collaborate with other firms and the Icelandic government to develop Iceland

as a tourist destination and (b) compete on North Atlantic routes between European and North American cities. For (b) to be viable, Icelandair needs to make routes that involve a stopover at its Reykjavik hub competitive with the point-to-point routes offered by the major US and European airlines. This requires (a) using Icelandair's operational efficiency to undercut other airlines on price and (b) exploiting Icelandair's operational and customer service capabilities, its human resource strengths, and the appeal of Reykjavik/Iceland as a stopover to establish a differentiation advantage. Icelandair's strategy is encapsulated in its vision statement: "To unlock Iceland's potential as a year-round destination, to strengthen Iceland's position as a connecting hub and to maintain our focus on flexibility and experience."

FIGURE 5.9   Icelandair's resource and capability profile

TABLE 5.4   The resources and capabilities of Icelandair Group

	Strategic importance [1 to 10]	Icelandair's relative strength [1 to 10]
Resources		
Fleet	Planes are transferrable; main differentiator is age of fleet [2]	Above-average age of fleet until new planes are delivered in 2018–2021 [2]
Financial resources	Critical for (a) buying other resources (b) surviving downturns [7]	Strong balance sheet; positive cash flow [8]
Location and route network	Critical to market access and exploiting network economies [9]	Tiny domestic market and inferior North Atlantic routes [3]
Landing slots	Key determinant of access to congested airports [6]	Limited presence at the key capacity-constrained airports of Europe and North America [3]
Brand	Important indicator of quality and reliability [5]	Lacks international prominence and still tainted by former image as a "hippy airline" [4]
Human resources	Human resources critical to most capabilities [8]	Well-educated, well-trained, and well-motivated employees [8]
Capabilities		
Flight operations	Operational capabilities are critical to cost efficiency and user satisfaction [9]	Strong record of operational efficiency, safety, and flexibility; cost per average seat mile below that of US and European legacy carriers [8]
Cabin services	Critically important in business class; less important in economy class [6]	Customer reviews suggest parity in business class and superior quality/price combination in economy [6]
Maintenance	Relevant to reliability and safety, but easily outsourced [3]	Safety record and reliability performance suggest super capability [7]
Marketing	Important for building brand awareness and stimulating demand [5]	A key element in Icelandair's success in expanding tourist traffic and market share of North Atlantic market [8]
General management	Essential for developing and maintaining operational, customer service, marketing, and support capabilities [8]	Icelandair has a dynamic, hands-on senior management team that supports a flexible and committed approach to management [9]

Notes:
This exercise is for illustrative purposes only. The assessments provided are based upon the author's perceptions, not upon objective measurement.
Compared to peer group, comprising Norwegian, SAS, Lufthansa, British Airways, American, EasyJet, and WOW Air.

Summary

We have shifted the focus of our attention from the external environment of the firm to its internal environment. We have observed that internal resources and capabilities offer a sound basis for building strategy. Indeed, when a firm's external environment is in a state of flux, internal strengths are likely to provide the primary basis upon which it can define its identity and its strategy.

In this chapter we have followed a systematic approach to identifying the resources and capabilities that an organization has access to and then have appraised these resources and capabilities in terms of their potential to offer a sustainable competitive advantage and, ultimately, to generate profit.

Having built a picture of an organization's key resources and capabilities and having identified areas of strength and weakness, we can then devise strategies through which the organization can exploit its strengths and minimize its vulnerability to its weaknesses. Figure 5.10 summarizes the main stages of our analysis.

In the course of the chapter, we have encountered a number of theoretical concepts and relationships; however, the basic issues of resource and capability analysis are intensely practical. At its core, resource and capability analysis asks what is distinctive about a firm in terms of what it can do better than its competitors and what it cannot. This involves not only analysis of balance sheets, employee competencies, and benchmarking data, but also insight into the values, ambitions, and traditions of a company that shape its priorities and identity.

FIGURE 5.10 Summary: A framework for analyzing resources and capabilities

Because the resources and capabilities of the firm form the foundation for building competitive advantage, we shall return again and again to the concepts of this chapter. In the next chapter we shall consider the organizational structure and management systems through which resources and capabilities are deployed. In Chapter 7 we shall look more closely at the competitive advantages that arise when resource and capability strengths intersect with key success factors. In Chapter 8 we shall consider how companies build the capabilities needed to deal with the challenges of the future.

Self-Study Questions

1. Since it was founded in 1994, Amazon has expanded its business from online book sales, to online general retailing, to audio and video streaming, to e-readers and tablet computers, to cloud computing. Is Amazon's strategy based primarily upon serving a market need or primarily on exploiting its resources and capabilities?

2. The world's leading typewriter manufacturers in the 1970s included Olivetti, Underwood, IBM, Olympia, Remington, Smith Corona, and Brother Industries. While IBM and Brother adapted to the microelectronics revolution, most of the others failed. What strategies might these companies have pursued rather than entering the personal computer and electronic work processing market?

3. I have argued that the part of discrepancy between firms' stock market value and their book value reflects the fact than intangible resources are typically undervalued or not valued at all in their balance sheets. For the companies listed in Table 5.1, which types of resource are likely to be absent or undervalued in the firms' balance sheets?

4. Many companies announce in their corporate communications: "Our people are our greatest resource." In terms of the criteria listed in Figure 5.7, can employees be considered of the utmost strategic importance? For Walmart, McDonald's, and McKinsey & Company, how important are employees to their competitive advantages?

5. The chapter argues that Apple's key capabilities are product design and product development which combine hardware technology, software engineering, aesthetics, ergonomics, and cognitive awareness to create products with a superior user interface and unrivalled market appeal. How easy would it be for Samsung to replicate these capabilities of Apple?

6. Given the profile of Icelandair's resources and capabilities outlined in Strategic Capsule 5.8, how might Icelandair best exploit its resources and capabilities to (a) expand passenger numbers traveling to and from Iceland and (b) profitably grow its share of the North Atlantic market?

7. Apply resource and capability analysis to your own business school. Begin by identifying the resources and capabilities relevant to success in the market for business education, appraise the resources and capabilities of your school, and then make strategy recommendations regarding such matters as the programs to be offered and the overall positioning and differentiation of the school and its offerings.

Notes

1. P. F. Drucker, *Managing in Turbulent Times* (New York: Harper & Row, 1990).
2. The resource-based view is described in J. B.Barney, "Firm Resources and Sustained Competitive Advantage," *Journal of Management* 17 (1991): 99–120; J. Mahoney and J. R. Pandian, "The Resource-Based View within the Conversation of Strategic Management," *Strategic Management Journal* 13 (1992): 363–380; M. A. Peterlaf, "The Cornerstones of Competitive Advantage: A Resource-Based View," *Strategic Management Journal* 14 (1993): 179–192; and R. M. Grant, "The Resource-based Theory of Competitive Advantage," *California Management Review* 33 (1991): 114–135.
3. C. K. Prahalad and G. Hamel, "The Core Competence of the Corporation," *Harvard Business Review* (May/June1990): 79–91.
4. "Eastman Kodak: Failing to Meet the Digital Challenge," in R. M. Grant, *Cases to Accompany Contemporary Strategy Analysis* 8th edn (Oxford: Blackwell, 2013).
5. E. Danneels, "Trying to Become a Different Type of Company: Dynamic Capability at Smith Corona", *Strategic Management Journal* 32 (2011): 1–31. E. Danneels, B. Provera, and G. Verona, "(De-)Institutionalizing Organizational Competence: Olivetti's Transition from Mechanical to Electronic Technology", Bocconi University, Milan, 2012.
6. M. Tripsas, "Unraveling the Process of Creative Destruction: Complementary Assets and Incumbent Survival in the Typesetter Industry," *Strategic Management Journal* 18 (Summer 1997): 119–142; J. Bower and C. M. Christensen, "Disruptive Technologies: Catching the Wave," *Harvard Business Review* (January/February 1995): 43–53.
7. A. Madhok, S. Li, and R. L. Priem, "The Resource-Based View Revisited: Comparative Firm Advantage, Willingness-Based Isolating Mechanisms and Competitive Heterogeneity", *European Management Review* 7 (2010): 91–100.
8. Walt Disney Company, 10-K report, 2014.
9. R. Gulati, "Network Location and Learning: The Influence of Network Resources and Firm Capabilities on Alliance Formation," *Strategic Management Journal*, 20 (1999): 397–420.
10. S. Green, "Understanding Corporate Culture and Its Relationship to Strategy," *International Studies of Management and Organization*, 18 (Summer 1988): 6–28.
11. J. Barney, "Organizational Culture: Can It Be a Source of Sustained Competitive Advantage?" *Academy of Management Review*, 11 1986): 656–665.
12. OECD data for 2013. http://stats.oecd.org/Index.aspx?DatasetCode=TENURE_AVE.
13. E. Lawler, "From Job-Based to Competency-Based Organizations," *Journal of Organizational Behavior* 15 (1994): 3–15; L. Spencer and S. Spencer, *Competence at Work: Models for Superior Performance* (New York: John Wiley & Sons, Inc., 1993).
14. D. Goleman, *Emotional Intelligence* (New York: Bantam, 1995); D. Goleman, *Social Intelligence* (New York: Bantam, 2006).
15. C. E. Helfat and M. Lieberman, "The Birth of Capabilities: Market Entry and the Importance of Prehistory," *Industrial and Corporate Change* 12 (2002) 725–760.
16. P. Selznick, *Leadership in Administration: A Sociological Interpretation* (New York: Harper & Row, 1957).
17. C. K. Prahalad and G. Hamel, "The Core Competence of the Corporation," *Harvard Business Review* (May/June 1990): 79–91.
18. G. Hamel and C. K. Prahalad state: "the distinction between competencies and capabilities is purely semantic" (letter, *Harvard Business Review*, May/June 1992: 164–165).
19. M. E. Porter, *Competitive Advantage* (New York: Free Press, 1984).
20. D. J. Teece, G. Pisano, and A. Shuen, "Dynamic Capabilities and Strategic Management," *Strategic Management Journal* 18 (1997): 509–533.
21. P. Leinwand and C. Mainardi, "The Coherence Premium", *Harvard Business Review* 88 (June 2010): 86–92.
22. *Adverse selection* refers to the propensity for a market to be dominated by low-quality or risky offerings as a result of information asymmetry. This is also known as the *lemons problem*. See G. Akerlof, "The Market for Lemons: Qualitative Uncertainty and the Market Mechanism," *Quarterly Journal of Economics* 84 (1970): 488–500.
23. J. B. Barney, "Strategic Factor Markets: Expectations, Luck and Business Strategy," *Management Science* 32 (October 1986): 1231–1241.
24. I. Dierickx and K. Cool ("Asset Stock Accumulation and Sustainability of Competitive Advantage," *Management Science* 35 (1989): 1504–1513) point to two major disadvantages of imitation. They are subject to *asset mass efficiencies* (the incumbent's strong initial resource position facilitates the subsequent accumulation of these resources) and *time compression diseconomies* (additional costs incurred by an imitator when seeking to rapidly accumulate a resource or capability e.g., "crash programs" of R & D and "blitz" advertising campaigns tend to be costly and unproductive).
25. D. Miller, *The Icarus Paradox: How Exceptional Companies Bring About Their Own Downfall* (New York: Harper-Business, 1990).
26. I. Martin, *Making It Happen: Fred Goodwin, RBS and the Men Who Blew up the British Economy* (London: Simon & Schuster, 2013).
27. "What is Benchmarking?" *Benchnet: The Benchmarking Exchange*, www.benchnet.com, accessed July 20, 2015.
28. "N. Nicholas and J. Van Reenen, "Why Do Management Practices Differ across Firms and Countries?" *Journal of Economic Perspectives* 24 (2010): 203–224.
29. C. Markides, *All the Right Moves* (Boston: Harvard Business School Press, 1999).

6 Organization Structure and Management Systems: The Fundamentals of Strategy Implementation

> Ultimately, there may be no long-term sustainable advantage other than the ability to organize and manage.
>
> —JAY GALBRAITH AND ED LAWLER

> I'd rather have first-rate execution and second-rate strategy anytime than brilliant ideas and mediocre management.
>
> —JAMIE DIMON, CEO, JPMORGAN CHASE & CO.

> Many people regard execution as detail work that's beneath the dignity of a business leader. That's wrong. To the contrary, it's a leader's most important job.
>
> —LARRY BOSSIDY, FORMER CEO, HONEYWELL

OUTLINE

Introduction and Objectives

We spend a lot of our time strategizing: figuring out how we can best develop our careers; making plans for a summer vacation; thinking about how to improve our sexual attractiveness. Most of these strategies remain just wishful thinking: if strategy is to yield results, it must be backed by commitment and translated into action.

The challenges of strategy implementation are much greater for organizations than for individuals. Executing strategy requires the combined efforts of all the members of the organization. Many of those implementing strategy will have played no role in its formulation; others will find that the strategy conflicts with their own personal interests; some may not believe in the strategy. Even without these impediments, there is the simple truth that implementation tends to be neglected because it requires commitment, persistence, and hard work. "How many meetings have you attended where people left without firm conclusions about who would do what and when?" asks super-consultant, Ram Charan.[1]

We begin with the management systems through link strategy to action. As we shall see, formal strategic planning systems may not be particularly effective at formulating strategy; their primary value is in creating a mechanism for linking strategy to a system of implementation that involves operational planning, target setting, and resource allocation.

However, the challenge of strategy implementation goes beyond the tasks of operationalizing strategic decisions. The way in which a company organizes itself is fundamental to the effectiveness of its strategic management. Hence, a wider goal of this chapter is to introduce the concepts needed to understand the challenge of organizing and to provide a framework for designing organizational structure. Finally, we shall consider not just the role of organizational structure but also the informal aspects of an organization's social structure, namely its organizational culture.

The broader aim of this chapter is to introduce the fundamentals of strategy implementation: the basic aspects of organizational structure and systems that determine the effectiveness with which strategy is executed. In subsequent chapters we shall consider strategy implementation in particular business contexts. For example, Chapter 8 discusses the management of strategic change; Chapter 9 considers the organizational conditions conducive to innovation; Chapter 10 considers organizing to compete in mature industries; Chapter 12 examines the structure and systems of the multinational corporation; Chapter 14 deals with organizing the multibusiness company; Chapter 15 discusses the role of mergers, acquisitions, and alliances in strategy implementation.

By the time you have completed this chapter, you will be able to:

- ◆ Understand how strategic planning links to operational planning, performance management, and resource allocation in implementing strategy.
- ◆ Appreciate the basic principles that determine the structural characteristics of complex human organizations.
- ◆ Select the organizational structure best suited to a particular business context.
- ◆ Recognize how companies have been changing their organizational structures in recent years and the forces driving these changes.

From Strategy to Execution

Strategic management has conventionally been viewed as a two-stage process: first, formulation, then implementation. As we observed in Chapter 1, the notion of strategic management as a top-down process in which top management formulates then the lower levels of the organization implement has been challenged by Henry Mintzberg. His strategy-as-process view recognized that in the course of implementation the *intended strategy* is reformulated and redirected by the *emergent strategy*.[2]

The notion that strategic management can be separated into self-contained formulation and implementation stages is wrong. The intended strategy of any organization is inevitably incomplete: it comprises goals, directions, and priorities, but it can never be a comprehensive plan. It is during the implementation phase that the gaps are filled in and, because circumstances change and unforeseen issues arise, inevitably the strategy changes. At the same time, strategy formulation must take account of the conditions of implementation. The observation "Great strategy; lousy implementation" is typically a misdiagnosis of strategic failure: a strategy which has been formulated without taking account of its ability to be implemented is a poorly formulated strategy. The conventional formulation–implementation sequence is summed up in the adage "Structure follows strategy." Yet, management guru Tom Peters argues the reverse:[3] for Domino's Pizza, with its global network of 8000 franchised outlets, or Amway, with its pyramid of commission-based, independent distributors, the structure *is* the strategy.

Clearly, strategy formulation and implementation are interdependent. Nevertheless, the fact remains that purposeful behavior requires that action must be preceded by intention. Hence, a feature of all the strategic planning systems that I have encountered is recognition that a strategy cannot be implemented until it has been formulated. In these strategy processes, formulation is linked to implementation by systems of operational planning, performance management, and resource allocation.

The Strategic Planning System: Linking Strategy to Action

Our outline of the development of strategic management in Chapter 1 (see "A Brief History of Business Strategy") indicated that companies adopted corporate planning, not to formulate strategy but to facilitate coordination and control in increasingly large and complex organizations.

Similarly with entrepreneurial start-ups. When Steve Jobs and Steve Wozniak founded Apple Computer at the beginning of 1977, strategy was developed in their heads and through their conversation. A written articulation of Apple's strategy did not appear until they needed to write a business plan in order to attract venture capital funding.[4] However, Apple did not adopt a systematic strategic planning process until several years later when it needed to establish capital expenditure budgets for its different functions and product teams and link strategy to day-to-day decision making.

Thus, Mintzberg's claim that formalized strategic planning is a poor way to make strategy, even if it is right, fails to recognize the real value of strategic planning systems. As we shall see, strategic planning systems play an important role in building consensus, communicating the strategy and its rationale throughout the organization, allocating resources to support the strategy, and establishing performance goals to guide and motivate the individuals and groups responsible for carrying out the strategy.

The Annual Strategic Planning Cycle   Most large companies have a regular (normally annual, sometimes bi-annual) strategic planning process that results in a document that is endorsed by the board of directors and provides a development plan for the company for the next three to five years. The strategic planning process is a systematized approach that assembles information, shares perceptions, conducts analysis, reaches decisions, ensures consistency among those decisions, and commits managers to courses of action and performance targets.

Strategic planning processes vary between organizations. At some it is highly centralized. Even after an entrepreneurial start-up has grown into a large company, strategy making may remain the preserve of the chief executive. At MCI Communications, former CEO Orville Wright observed: "We do it strictly top-down at MCI."[5] However, at most large companies, the strategic planning process involves a combination of top-down direction and bottom-up initiatives.[6]

Figure 6.1 shows a typical strategic planning cycle. The principal stages are:

1. *Setting the context: guidelines, forecasts, assumptions.* The CEO typically initiates the process by indicating strategic priorities—these will be influenced by the outcome of the previous performance reviews. In addition, the strategic planning unit may provide assumptions or forecasts that offer a common basis for strategic planning by different units within the organization. For example, the 2014–2017 strategic plan of the Italian oil and gas company Eni was built upon (a) the goal of increasing free cash flow by expanding petroleum production and rationalizing downstream activities and (b) assumptions that the price of crude would average $90 per barrel and the dollar/euro exchange rate would average 1.3.[7]

FIGURE 6.1   The generic annual strategic planning cycle

2. *Business plans.* On the basis of these priorities and planning assumptions, the different organizational units—product divisions, functional departments, and geographical units—create strategic plans which are then presented for comment and discussion to top management. This dialogue represents a critically important feature of the strategy system: it provides a process for sharing knowledge, communicating ideas, and reaching consensus. This process may be more important than the strategic plans that are created. As General (later President) Dwight Eisenhower observed: "Plans are nothing; planning is everything." At Eni, business plans were created for each of Eni's major divisions: exploration and production, gas and power, and refining and marketing.

3. *The corporate plan.* Once agreed, the business plans are then integrated to create the corporate strategic plan that is then presented to the board for approval.

4. *Capital expenditure budgets.* Capital expenditure budgets link strategy to resource allocation. They are established through both top-down and bottom-up initiatives. When organizational units prepare their business plans, they will indicate the major projects they plan to undertake during the strategic planning period and the capital expenditures involved. When top management aggregates business plans to create the corporate plan, it establishes capital expenditure budgets both for the company as a whole and for the individual businesses. The businesses then submit capital expenditure requests for specific projects that are evaluated through standard appraisal methodologies, typically using risk-adjusted discounted cash flow analysis. Capital expenditure approvals take place at different levels of a company according to their size. Projects of up to $5 million might be approved by a business unit head; projects of up to $25 million might be approved by divisional top management; larger projects might need to be approved by the top management committee; the biggest projects may require approval by the board of directors. Eni's strategic plan for 2014–2017 established a capital expenditure budget of €54 billion, of which €44.4 billion would go to exploration and production.

5. *Operational plans and performance targets.* Implementing strategy requires breaking down strategic plans into a series of shorter-term plans that provide a focus for action and a basis for performance monitoring. At the basis of the annual operating plan are a set of performance targets derived from the strategic plan. These performance targets are both financial (sales growth, margins, return on capital) and operational (inventory turns, defect rates, number of new outlets opened). In the section on "Setting Performance Targets" in Chapter 2, I outlined the basic cascading logic for goal setting: overall goals of the organization are disaggregated into more specific performance goals as we move down the organization. As Chapter 2 shows, this can use either a simple financial disaggregation or the balanced scorecard methodology. There is nothing new about this approach: management by objectives (the process of participative goal setting) was proposed by Peter Drucker in 1954.[8] Performance targets can be built into the annual operating budget. The operating budget is a pro forma profit-and-loss statement for the company as a whole and for individual divisions and business units for the upcoming year. It is usually divided into quarters and months to permit continual monitoring and the early identification of variances. The operating budget is part forecast and part target. Each business typically prepares an operating budget for the

following year that is then discussed with the top management committee and, if acceptable, approved. In some organizations the budgeting process is part of the strategic planning system: the operating budget is the first year of the strategic plans; in others, budgeting follows strategic planning. Operational planning is more than setting performance targets and agreeing budgets; it also involves planning specific activities. As Bossidy and Charan explain: "An operating plan includes the programs your business is going to complete within one year … Among these programs are product launches; the marketing plan; a sales plan that takes advantage of market opportunities; a manufacturing plan that stipulates production outputs; and a productivity plan that improves efficiency."[9]

Organizational Design: The Fundamentals of Organizing

Implementing strategy is not just about strategic planning processes and linking them to goal setting, operational activities, and resource allocation. Strategy implementation encompasses the entire design of the organization. How a firm is organized determines its capacity for action. We saw in the previous chapter that the design of processes and structures is fundamental to organizational capabilities. The same is true in war: from the conquests of the Roman legions, to the one-sided outcome of the Franco-Prussian War (1871) and the Israeli victories in the Six-Day War (1967) and Yom Kippur War (1973), organizational superiority has played a critical role in military success.

Business enterprises come in many shapes and sizes. Samsung Corporation and Louie's Sandwich Bar on 32nd Street, New York share few organizational commonalities. When we include social enterprises, we expand the range of organizations even further. Yet, almost all organizations begin as tiny start-ups that involve merely the ambition and efforts of an individual or a small group of people. Strategy Capsule 6.1 summarizes some of the key developments in the development of the business corporation.

Despite their diversity, all business enterprises face the same challenge of designing structures and systems that match the particular circumstances of their own situation. In the same way that strategic management is a quest for unique solutions to the matching of internal resources and capabilities to external business opportunity, so organizational design is about selecting structures, systems, and management styles that can best implement such strategies. To establish principles, guidelines, and criteria for designing business organizations we need to consider the fundamental challenges of organizing.

To design a firm we must first recognize what it is supposed to do. According to Henry Mintzberg:

Every organized human activity—from making pots to placing a man on the moon—gives rise to two fundamental and opposing requirements: the division of labor into various tasks, and the coordination of these tasks to accomplish the activity. The structure of the organization can be defined simply as the ways in which labor is divided into distinct tasks and coordination is achieved among these tasks.[10]

Specialization and Division of Labor

Firms exist because of their efficiency advantages in producing goods and services. The fundamental source of efficiency is *specialization* through the *division of labor* into separate tasks. Consider Adam Smith's description of pin manufacture:

> One man draws out the wire, another straightens it, a third cuts it, a fourth points it, a fifth grinds it at the top for receiving the head; to make the head requires two or three distinct operations; to put it on is a peculiar business, to whiten the pins is another; it is even a trade by itself to put them into the papers.[11]

Smith's pin makers produced about 4800 pins per person each day. "But if they had all wrought separately and independently, and without any of them having been educated to this peculiar business, they certainly could not each have made 20, perhaps not one pin, in a day." Henry Ford's assembly-line system introduced in 1913 was based on the same principle. Between the end of 1912 and early 1914 the time taken to assemble a Model T fell from 106 hours to six hours.

But specialization comes at a cost. The more a production process is divided between different specialists, the more complex is the challenge of integrating their separate efforts. The more volatile and unstable the external environment, the greater the number of decisions that need to be made and the greater are the coordination costs. Hence, the more stable the environment, the greater the optimal division of labor. This is true both for firms and for entire societies. Civilizations are built on an increased division of labor, which is only possible through stability. As the recent histories of Somalia, Syria, and the Congo have demonstrated so tragically, once chaos reigns, societies regress toward subsistence mode, where each family unit must be self-sufficient.

The Cooperation Problem

Integrating the efforts of specialist individuals involves two organizational problems: first, there is the cooperation problem—that of aligning the interests of individuals who have divergent goals—second, the coordination problem—even in the absence of goal conflict, how do individuals harmonize their different activities?

The economics literature analyzes cooperation problems arising from goal misalignment as the **agency problem**.[12] An agency relationship exists when one party (the principal) contracts with another party (the agent) to act on behalf of the principal. The problem is ensuring that the agent acts in the principal's interest. Within the firm, the major agency problem is between owners (shareholders) and managers. The problem of ensuring that managers operate companies to maximize shareholder wealth is at the center of the corporate governance debate. During the 1990s, changes in top management remuneration—in particular the increasing use of stock options—were intended to align the interests of managers with those of shareholders. However, it seems that bonus and stock option plans offer perverse incentives: encouraging either an emphasis on short-term over long-term profitability or even the manipulation of reported earnings (e.g., Enron, WorldCom).[13]

Agency problems exist throughout the hierarchy. For individual employees, systems of incentives, monitoring, and appraisal encourage them to pursue organizational goals rather than doing their own thing or simply shirking. In addition, the

STRATEGY CAPSULE 6.1
The Emergence of the Modern Corporation

The large corporation, the dominant feature of the advanced capitalist economy, is of recent origin. At the beginning of the 19th century, most production, even in Britain, the most industrially advanced economy of the time, was undertaken by individuals and by families working in their own homes. In the US, the biggest business organizations in the mid-19th century were family-owned farms, especially some of the large plantations of the South.[a] The business corporation, one of the greatest innovations of modern society, resulted from two main sources: legal development and organizational innovation.

A corporation is an enterprise that has a legal identity: it can own property, enter into contracts, sue, and be sued. The first corporations were created by royal decree, notably the colonial trading companies: the British East India Company (1600), the Dutch East India Company (1602), and Hudson's Bay Company (1670). The introduction of limited liability during the mid-19th century, protected shareholders from corporate debts thereby pemitting large-scale equity financing.[b]

During the 19th century, most ideas about organization and management derived from the biggest organizations of that time: European armies. General von Moltke's organization of the Prussian army into divisions and general staff functions during the 1860s provided the basic model for large industrial corporations.[c] However, toward the end of the 19th century organizational developments in the US encouraged new thinking about business administration which would form the basis of "the second industrial revolution":

- *Line-and-Staff Structure*: Lack of transportation and communication meant that most companies operated in just one place. The railroad and the telegraph changed all that. In the US, the railroad companies were the first to create geographically separate operating units managed by an administrative headquarters. "Line" employees were engaged in operational tasks within operating units; "staff" comprised administrators and functional specialists located at head office. These simple line-and-staff structures developed into more complex functional structures; companies such as Sears Roebuck & Co. and Shell Transport and Trading managed numerous operating units with large functionally specialized headquarters.

- *The holding company* was a financial structure created by a parent company acquiring controlling equity stakes in a number of subsidiary companies. Its management structures were simple: the parent appointed the board of directors of the subsidiaries and received dividends, but otherwise there was little integration or overall managerial control. The holding company structure allows entrepreneurs such as Richard Branson and families such as the Tata family of India to control large business empires without the need for either the capital or the management structure required by an integrated corporation.

- *The multidivisional corporation*: During the 1920s, the multidivisional form began to replace both centralized, functional structures and loose-knit holding companies. At DuPont, increasing size and a widening product range strained the functional structure and overloaded top management. The solution devised by Pierre Du Pont was to decentralize: 10 product divisions were created, each with their own sales, R & D, and support activities. The corporate head office headed by an executive committee took responsibility for coordination, strategy, and resource allocation.[d] Soon after, General Motors, a loose holding company built by acquisition, adopted a similar structure to solve its problems of weak financial control and a confused product line.

FIGURE 6.2   General Motors Corporation: Organizational structure, 1921

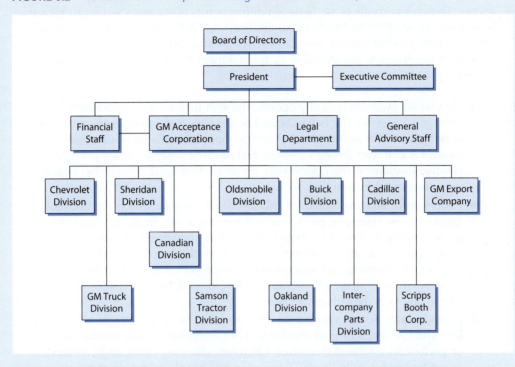

Source: A. P. Sloan, *My Years with General Motors* (Orbit Publishing, 1972): 57. © 1963 by Alfred P. Sloan. © renewed 1991, Alfred P. Sloan Foundation. Reproduced with Permission.

The new structure (shown in Figure 6.2) divided decision making between the division heads, each responsible for their division's operations and performance, and the president, as head of the general office and responsible for the corporation's development and control.[e] During the next 50 years, the multidivisional structure became the dominant organizational form for large corporations.

During recent decades, international expansion has been the dominant source of corporate growth. Industry after industry has been transformed by the emergence of global giants: Arcelor Mittal in steel, AB-Inbev in beer, Toyota in automobiles, McDonald's in fast food. Yet, despite the incredible success of the shareholder-owned corporations, other business forms continue to exist. Some sectors—agriculture, retailing, and many service industries—are dominated by family

firms and individual proprietorships; partnerships predominate in professional service industries such as law; cooperatives are prominent in some sectors, especially agriculture; despite the privatization trend of the 1990s, state-owned enterprises are highly influential. Saudi Aramco, Indian Railways, China Mobile, China National Petroleum, and Royal Bank of Scotland are all industry leaders that are majority state-owned.

Notes:

[a] A. D. Chandler, *The Visible Hand: The Managerial Revolution in American Business* (Cambridge, MA: MIT Press, 1977): Chapter 2.

[b] J. Micklethwait and A. Wooldridge, *The Company: A Short History of a Revolutionary Idea* (New York: Modern Library, 2005).

[c] R. Stark, *Sociology*, 10th edn. (Belmont, CA: Wadsworth, 2006).

[d] A. D. Chandler, *Strategy and Structure* (Cambridge: MIT Press, 1962): 382–3.

[e] A. P. Sloan, *My Years with General Motors* (London: Sidgwick & Jackson, 1963): 42–56.

organization structure may cause organizational goals to fragment. Each department tends to create its own subgoals that conflict with those of other departments. The classic conflicts are between different functions: sales wishes to please customers, production wishes to maximize output, R & D wants to introduce mind-blowing new products, while finance worries about profit and loss.

Several mechanisms are available to management for achieving goal alignment within organizations:

- *Control mechanisms* typically operate through hierarchical supervision. Managers supervise the behavior and performance of subordinates who must seek approval for actions that lie outside their defined area of discretion. Control is enforced through positive and negative incentives: the primary positive incentive is the opportunity for promotion up the hierarchy; negative incentives are dismissal and demotion.

- *Performance incentives* link rewards to output: they include piece rates for production workers and profit bonuses for executives. Such performance-related incentives have two main benefits: first, they are high powered—they relate rewards directly to output—and, second, they economize on the need for costly monitoring and supervision of employees. Pay-for-performance becomes more difficult when employees work in teams or on activities where output is difficult to measure.

- *Shared values*. Some organizations are able to achieve high levels of cooperation and low levels of goal conflict without extensive control mechanisms or performance-related incentives. Churches, charities, clubs, and voluntary organizations typically display a commonality of values among members that supports common purpose. Similarly for business enterprises, as we saw in Chapter 2 (see pp. 52-53), shared values encourage the perceptions and views of organizational members to converge, which facilitates consensus, averts conflict and enhances firm performance.[14] In doing so shared values can act as a control mechanism that is an alternative to bureaucratic control or financial incentives. An organization's values are one component of its culture. Strategy Capsule 6.2 discusses the role of organizational culture for aligning individual actions with company strategy.

- *Persuasion*. Implementing strategy requires leadership and at the heart of leadership is persuasion. For J.-C. Spender, language is central, both to the conceptualization of strategy and to its implementation.[15] The effectiveness of all leaders—political, military, religious, and business—is dependent upon their ability to influence the behavior of others. The use of language for the purposes of persuasion is the art of rhetoric. Management rhetoric is not simply about communicating strategy; it is about changing the perceptions of organizational members, their relationships with the organization, and, ultimately, guiding their actions to actualize the strategy under conditions of uncertainty and ambiguity.

The Coordination Problem

The desire to cooperate is not enough to ensure that organizational members integrate their efforts—it is not a lack of a common goal that causes Olympic relay teams

STRATEGY CAPSULE 6.2
Organizational Culture as an Integrating Device

Corporate culture comprises the beliefs, values, and behavioral norms of the company, which influence how employees think and behave.[a] It is manifest in symbols, ceremonies, social practices, rites, vocabulary, and dress. While shared values are effective in aligning the goals of organizational members, culture as a whole exercises a wider influence on an organization's capacity for purposeful action. Organizational culture is a complex phenomenon. It is influenced by the external environment—in particular the national and ethnic cultures within which the firm is embedded. It may also be influenced by the social and professional cultures of organizational members. Most of all, it is a product of the organization's history: the founder's personality and beliefs tend to be especially influential. For example, the corporate culture of Walt Disney Company continues to reflect the values, aspirations, and personal style of Walt Disney. A corporate culture is seldom homogeneous: different cultures may be evident in the research lab, in sales, and within the accounting department.

Culture can facilitate both cooperation and coordination. In companies such as Starbucks, Shell, Nintendo, and Google, strong corporate cultures create a sense of identity among employees that supports communication and organizational routines. However, culture can also impede strategy implementation. Cultures can also be divisive and dysfunctional. At the British bank NatWest during the 1990s, John Weeks identified a "culture of complaining" which was a barrier to top-down strategy initiatives.[b] A culture is likely to support some types of corporate action but handicap others. Salomon Brothers (now part of Citigroup) was renowned for its individualistic, internally competitive culture that reinforced drive and individual effort but did little to support cooperation. The culture of the British Broadcasting Corporation (BBC) reflects internal politicization, professional values, internal suspicion,

and a dedication to the public good, but without a strong sense of customer focus.[c]

Cultures take a long time to develop and cannot easily be changed. As the external environment changes, a highly effective culture may become dysfunctional. The police forces of many US cities have developed cultures of professionalism and militarism, which increased their effectiveness in fighting crime, but also contributed to problems of isolation and unresponsiveness to community needs.[d]

Culture is probably the single most powerful determinant of how an organization behaves—according to Peter Drucker, "Culture eats strategy for breakfast!"[e] Yet, culture is far from being a flexible management tool at the disposal of chief executives. Culture is a property of the organization as a whole, which is not amenable to top management manipulation. CEOs inherit rather than create the culture of their organizations. The key issue is to recognize the culture of the organization and to ensure that structure and systems work with the culture and not against it. Where organizational culture supports strategy, it can be very valuable. First, it is cheap: as a control device it saves on the costs of monitoring and financial incentives; second, it permits flexibility: when individuals internalize the goals and principles of the organization, they can be allowed to use their initiative and creativity in their work.

Notes:

[a] E. H. Schein, "Organizational Culture," *American Psychologist* 45 (1990): 109–19.

[b] J. Weeks, *Unpopular Culture: The Ritual of Complaint in a British Bank* (Chicago: University of Chicago Press, 2004).

[c] T. Burns, *The BBC: Public Institution and Private World* (London: Macmillan, 1977).

[d] "Policing: Don't Shoot," *Economist* (December 13, 2014): 37.

[e] J. Weeks, "On Management: Culture Eats Strategy," *Management Today* (June 2006).

to drop the baton. Unless individuals can find ways of coordinating their efforts, production doesn't happen. As we have already seen in our discussion of organizational capabilities, the exceptional performance of Walmart, the Cirque du Soleil, and the US Marine Corps Band derives less from the skills of the individual members as from superb coordination between them. Among the mechanism for coordination, the following can be found in all firms:

- *Rules and directives*: A basic feature of the firm is the existence of general employment contracts under which individuals agree to perform a range of duties as required by their employer. This allows managers to exercise authority by means of general rules ("Secret agents on overseas missions will have essential expenses reimbursed only on production of original receipts") and specific directives ("Miss Moneypenny, show Mr Bond his new toothbrush with 4G communication and a concealed death ray").
- *Routines*: Where activities are performed recurrently, coordination based on mutual adjustment and rules becomes institutionalized within organizational routines. As we noted in the previous chapter, these "regular and predictable sequences of coordinated actions by individuals" are fundamental to the operation of organizational processes and provide the foundation of organizational capability. If organizations are to perform complex activities efficiently and reliably, rules, directives, and mutual adjustments are not enough—coordination must become embedded in routines.
- *Mutual adjustment*: The simplest form of coordination involves the mutual adjustment of individuals engaged in related tasks. In soccer or doubles tennis, players coordinate their actions spontaneously without direction or established routines. Such mutual adjustment occurs in leaderless teams and is especially suited to novel tasks where routinization is not feasible.

The relative roles of these different coordination devices depend on the types of activity being performed and the intensity of collaboration required. Rules are highly efficient for activities where standardized outcomes are required—most quality-control procedures involve the application of simple rules. Routines are essential for activities where close interdependence exists between individuals, be the activity a basic production task (supplying customers at Starbucks) or more complex (performing a heart bypass operation). Mutual adjustment works best for non-standardized tasks (such as problem solving) where those involved are well informed of the actions of their co-workers, either because they are in close visual contact (a chef de cuisine and his/her sous chefs) or because of information exchange (designers using interactive CAD software).

Hierarchy in Organizational Design

Hierarchy is the fundamental feature of organizational structure. It is the primary means by which companies achieve specialization, coordination, and cooperation. Despite the negative images that hierarchy often conveys, it is a feature of all complex human organizations and is essential for efficiency and flexibility. The critical issue is not whether to organize by hierarchy—there is little alternative—but how the hierarchy should be structured and how its various parts should be linked. Hierarchy can be viewed both as a system of control based upon relationships of authority and as a system of coordination where hierarchy is a means of achieving efficiency and adaptation.

Hierarchy as Control: Bureaucracy Hierarchy is an organizational system in which individuals are positioned at different vertical levels. At each level, members of the organization report to their superior, and have subordinates to supervise and monitor. Hierarchy offers a solution to the problem of cooperation through the imposition of top-down control.

As a formalized administrative system for exercising centralized power, hierarchy was the basis of the government system of the Ch'in dynasty of China in the late third century BC and, since then, has been a feature of all large organizations in the fields of public administration, religion, and the military. For Max Weber, "the father of organizational theory," hierarchy was the central feature of his system of bureaucracy which involved: "each lower office under the control and supervision of a higher one"; a "systematic division of labor"; formalization in writing of "administrative acts, decisions, and rules"; and work governed by standardized rules and operating procedures, where authority is based on "belief in the legality of enacted rules and the right of those elevated to authority under such rules to issue commands."[16]

Weber's preference for rationality and efficiency over cronyism and personal use of hierarchical authority typical of his time encouraged organizational designs that sought safeguards against human traits such as emotion, creativity, fellowship, and idiosyncrasies of personality. As a result bureaucratic organizations have been referred to as *mechanistic*[17] or as *machine bureaucracies*.[18]

Hierarchy as Coordination: Modularity Almost all complex systems are organized as hierarchies where elements combine to form components which themselves combine to form more complex entities:[19]

- The human body comprises subsystems such as the respiratory system, nervous system, and digestive system, each of which consists of organs, each of which is made up of individual cells.
- The physical universe is hierarchy with galaxies at the top, below them are solar systems and we can continue down all the way to atoms and further to of subatomic particles.
- Social systems comprise individuals, families, communities, and nations.
- A novel is organized by chapters, paragraphs, sentences, words, and letters.

Viewing organizations as natural hierarchies rather than as systems of vertical control points to the advantages of hierarchical structures in coordinating productive activities:

- *Economizing on coordination*: Suppose we launch a consulting firm with five partners. If we structure the firm as a "self-organized team" where coordination is by mutual adjustment (Figure 6.3a), 10 bilateral interactions must be managed. Alternatively, if we appoint the partner with the biggest feet as managing partner (Figure 6.3b), there are only four relationships to be managed. Of course, this says nothing about the quality of the coordination: for routine tasks such as assigning partners to projects, the hierarchical structure is clearly advantageous; for complex problem solving, the partners are better

FIGURE 6.3 How hierarchy economizes on coordination

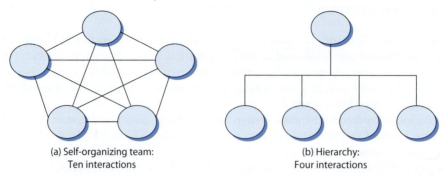

(a) Self-organizing team:
Ten interactions

(b) Hierarchy:
Four interactions

reverting to a self-organizing team to thrash out a solution. The larger the number of organizational members, the greater the efficiency benefits from organizing hierarchically. Microsoft's Windows 8 development team involved about 3200 software development engineers, test engineers, and program managers. These were organized into 35 "feature teams," each of which was divided into a number of component teams. As a result, each engineer needed to coordinate only with the members of his or her immediate team. The modular structure of the Windows 8 development team mirrors the modular structure of the product.

● *Adaptability*: Hierarchical, modular systems can evolve more rapidly than unitary systems. This adaptability requires *decomposability*: the ability of each component subsystem to operate with some measure of independence from the other subsystems. Modular systems that allow significant independence for each module are referred to as *loosely coupled*.[20] The modular structure of Windows 8 enabled a single feature team to introduce innovative product features and innovative software solutions without the need to coordinate with all 34 other teams. The key requirement is that the different modules must fit together—this requires a standardized interface. The multidivisional firm is a modular structure. At Procter & Gamble, decisions about developing new shampoos can be made by the Beauty, Hair and Personal Care sector without involving P&G's other three sectors (Baby, Feminine and Family Care; Fabric and Home Care; and Health and Grooming). A divisional structure also makes it easier for P&G to add new businesses (Gillette, Wella) and to divest them (Folgers Coffee, Pringles, pet foods, Duracell batteries).[21]

Contingency Approaches to Organization Design

Like strategy, organizational design has been afflicted by the quest to find the "best" way of organizing. During the first half of the 20th century, bureaucracy and scientific management were believed to be the best way of organizing. During the 1950s and 1960s, the human relations school recognized that cooperation and coordination within organizations was about social relationships, which bureaucracy stifled through inertia and alienation: "Theory X" had been challenged by "Theory Y."[22]

However, empirical studies pointed to different organizational characteristics being suited to different circumstances. Among Scottish engineering companies, Burns and

TABLE 6.1 Mechanistic versus organic organizational forms

Feature	Mechanistic forms	Organic forms
Task definition	Rigid and highly specialized	Flexible and broadly defined
Coordination and control	Rules and directives vertically imposed	Mutual adjustment, common culture
Communication	Vertical	Vertical and horizontal
Knowledge	Centralized	Dispersed
Commitment and loyalty	To immediate superior	To the organization and its goals
Environmental context	Stable with low technological uncertainty	Dynamic with significant technological uncertainty and ambiguity

Source: Adapted from Richard Butler, *Designing Organizations: A Decision-Making Perspective* (London: Routledge, 1991): 76, by permission of Cengage Learning.

Stalker found that firms in stable environments had *mechanistic forms*, characterized by bureaucracy; those in less stable markets had *organic forms* that were less formal and more flexible.[23] Table 6.1 contrasts key characteristics of the two forms.

By the 1970s, *contingency theory*—the idea there was no one best way to organize; it depended upon the strategy being pursued, the technology employed, and the surrounding environment—had become widely accepted.[24] Although Google and McDonald's are of similar sizes in terms of revenue, their structures and systems are very different. McDonald's is highly bureaucratized: high levels of job specialization, formal systems, and a strong emphasis on rules and procedures. Google emphasizes informality, low job specialization, horizontal communication, and the importance of principles over rules. These differences reflect differences in strategy, technology, human resources, and the dynamism of the business environments that each firm occupies. In general, the more standardized goods or services (beverage cans, blood tests, or haircuts for army inductees) are and the more stable the environment is, the greater are the efficiency advantages of the bureaucratic model with its standard operating procedures and high levels of specialization. Once markets become turbulent, or innovation becomes desirable, or buyers require customized products—then the bureaucratic model breaks down.

These contingency factors also cause functions within companies to be organized differently. Stable, standardized activities such as payroll, treasury, taxation, customer support, and purchasing activities tend to operate well when organized along bureaucratic principles; research, new product development, marketing, and strategic planning require more organic modes of organization.

As the business environment has become increasingly turbulent, the trend has been toward organic approaches to organizing, which have tended to displace more bureaucratic approaches. Since the mid-1980s, almost all large companies have made strenuous efforts to restructure and reorganize in order to achieve greater flexibility and responsiveness. Within their multidivisional structures, companies have decentralized decision making, reduced their number of hierarchical layers, shrunk headquarters staffs, emphasized horizontal rather than vertical communication, and shifted the emphasis of control from supervision to accountability.

However, the trend has not been one way. The financial crisis of 2008 and its aftermath have caused many companies to reimpose top-down control. Greater awareness of the need to manage financial, environmental, and political risks in sectors such as financial services, petroleum, and mining have also reinforced centralized control and reliance on rules. It is possible that the cycles of centralization and decentralization that many companies exhibit are a means by which they balance the tradeoff between integration and flexible responsiveness.[25]

Developments in ICT have worked in different directions. In some cases the automation of processes has permitted their centralization and bureaucratization (think of the customer service activities of your bank or telecom supplier). In other areas, ICT has encouraged informal approaches to coordination. The huge leaps in the availability of information available to organizational members and the ease with which they can communicate with one another has increased vastly the capacity for mutual adjustment without the need for intensive hierarchical guidance and leadership.

Organizational Design: Choosing the Right Structure

We have established that the basic feature of organizations is hierarchy. In order to undertake complex tasks, people need to be grouped into organizational units, and cooperation and coordination need to be established among these units. The key organizational questions are now:

- On what basis should specialized units be defined?
- How should the different organizational units be assembled for the purposes of coordination and control?

In this section we will tackle these two central issues of organizational design. First, on what basis should individuals be grouped into organizational units? Second, how should organizational units be configured into overall organizational structures?

Defining Organizational Units

In creating a hierarchical structure, on what basis are individuals assigned to organizational units within the firm? This issue is fundamental and complex. Multinational, multiproduct companies are continually grappling with the issue of whether they should be structured around product divisions, country subsidiaries, or functional departments, and periodically they undergo the disruption of changing from one to another. Employees can be grouped on the basis of:

- common tasks: cleaners will be assigned to maintenance services and teachers will assigned to a unit called a faculty;
- products: shelf fillers and customer services assistants will be assigned to one of the following departments: kitchen goods, tableware, bedding, or domestic appliances;
- location: the 141,000 associates that work in Starbucks stores are organized by location: each store employs an average of 16 people;
- process: in most production plants, employees are organized by process: assembly, quality control, warehousing, shipping. Processes tend to be grouped into functions.

How do we decide whether to use task, product, geography, or process to define organizational units? The fundamental issue is *intensity of coordination needs*: those individuals who need to interact most closely should be located within the same organizational unit. In the case of Starbucks, the individual stores are the natural units: the manager, the baristas, and the cleaners at a single location need to form a single organizational unit. British Airways needs to be organized by processes and functions: the employees engaged in particular processes—flying, in-flight services, baggage handling, aircraft maintenance, and accounts—need to be working in the same organizational units. These process units then can be combined into broader functional groupings: flight operations, engineering, marketing, sales, customer service, human resources, information, and finance.

This principle of grouping individuals according to the intensity of their coordination needs was developed by James Thompson in his analysis of interdependence within organizations. He distinguished three levels of interdependence: *pooled interdependence* (the loosest), where individuals operate independently but depend on one another's performance; *sequential interdependence*, where the output of one individual is the input of the other; and *reciprocal interdependence* (the most intense), where individuals are mutually dependent. At the first level of organization, priority should be given to creating organizational units for reciprocally interdependent employees (e.g., members of an oilfield drilling team or consultants working on a client assignment).[26]

In general, the priorities for the first level of organization tend to be clear: it is usually fairly obvious whether employees need to be organized by task, process, or location. How the lower-level organizational units should be grouped into broader organizational units tends to be less clear. In 1921 it was far from obvious as to whether DuPont would be better off with its functional structure or reorganized into product divisions. In taking over as Procter & Gamble's CEO in 2000, A. G. Lafley had to decide whether to keep P&G's new-product divisional structure or revert to the previous structure in which the regional organizations were dominant.

In deciding how to organize the upper levels of firm structure the same principle applies: where are the coordination needs the greatest?. At Nestlé, it is more important for the managers of the chocolate plants to coordinate with the marketing and sales executives for chocolate than with the plant manager for Evian bottled water: Nestlé is better organized around product divisions than around functions. Hyundai Motor produces a number of different models of car and is present in many countries of the world; however, given its global strategy and the close linkages between its different models, Hyundai is better organized by function rather than by product or geography.

Over time, the relative importance of these different coordination needs changes, causing firms to change their structures. The process of **globalization** has involved easier trade and communication between countries and growing similarities in consumer preferences. As a result multinational corporations have shifted from geographically based structures to worldwide product divisions.

Alternative Structural Forms: Functional, Multidivisional, Matrix

On the basis of these alternative approaches to grouping tasks and activities we can identify three basic organizational forms for companies: the **functional structure**, the **multidivisional structure**, and the **matrix structure**.

The Functional Structure   Single-business firms tend to be organized along functional lines. Grouping together functionally similar tasks is conducive to exploiting scale economies, promoting learning and capability building, and deploying standardized control systems. Since cross-functional integration occurs at the top of the organization, functional structures are conducive to a high degree of centralized control by the CEO and top management team.

However, even for single-product firms, functional structures are subject to the problems of cooperation and coordination. Different functional departments develop their own goals, values, vocabularies, and behavioral norms, which makes cross-functional integration difficult. As the size of the firm increases, the pressure on top management to achieve effective integration increases. Because the different functions of the firm tend to be tightly coupled rather than loosely coupled, there is limited scope for decentralization. In particular, it is very difficult to operate individual functions as semi-autonomous profit centers.

Hence, even undiversified companies may replace a functional structure with a structure based upon product divisions during their growth phases: this was the case with General Motors during the 1920s.

However, as companies and their industries mature, the need for efficiency, centralized control, and well-developed functional capabilities can cause companies to revert to functional structures. For example:

- When John Scully became CEO of Apple in 1984, the company was organized by product: Apple II, Apple III, Lisa, and Macintosh. Cross-functional coordination within each product was strong, but there was little integration across products: each had a different operating system, applications were incompatible, and scale economies in purchasing, manufacturing, and distributions could not be exploited. Scully's response was to reorganize Apple along functional lines to gain control, reduce costs, and achieve a more coherent product strategy.
- General Motors, a pioneer of the multidivisional structure, moved toward a more functional structure. As cost efficiency became its strategic priority, it maintained its brand names (Cadillac, Chevrolet, Buick) but merged these separate divisions into a more functionally based structure to exploit scale economies and foster the development and transfer of know-how (compare Figure 6.4 with Figure 6.2).

The Multidivisional Structure   We have seen how the product-based, multidivisional structure emerged during the 20th century in response to the coordination problems caused by diversification. The key advantage of divisionalized structures (whether product based or geographically based) is the potential for decentralized decision making. The multidivisional structure is the classic example of a loose-coupled, modular organization where business-level strategies and operating decisions can be made at the divisional level, while the corporate headquarters concentrates on corporate planning, budgeting, and providing common services.

Central to the efficiency advantages of the multidivisional corporation is the ability to apply a common set of corporate management tools to a range of different businesses. At ITT, Harold Geneen's system of "managing by the numbers" allowed him to cope with over 50 divisional heads reporting directly to him. At BP, a system

FIGURE 6.4   General Motors Corporation: Organizational structure, January 2015

of "performance contracts" allowed CEO John Browne to oversee BP's 24 businesses, each of which reported directly to him. Divisional autonomy also fosters the development of leadership capability among divisional heads—an important factor in grooming candidates for CEO succession.

The large, divisionalized corporation is typically organized into three levels: the corporate center, the divisions, and the individual business units, each representing a distinct business for which financial accounts can be drawn up and strategies formulated. Figure 6.5 shows General Electric's organizational structure at the corporate and divisional levels.

In Chapter 14, we shall look in greater detail at the organization of the multibusiness corporation.

Matrix Structures   Whatever the primary basis for grouping, all companies that embrace multiple products, multiple functions, and multiple locations must

FIGURE 6.5   General Electric: Organizational structure, January 2015

Source: Based on information in General Electric's Annual Report, 2014.

coordinate across all three dimensions. Organizational structures that formalize coordination and control across multiple dimensions are called *matrix structures*.

Figure 6.6 shows the Shell management matrix (prior to reorganization in 1996). Within this structure, the general manager of Shell's Berre refinery in France reported to his country manager, the managing director of Shell France, but also to his business sector head, the coordinator of Shell's refining sector, as well as having a functional relationship with Shell's head of manufacturing.

Many diversified, multinational companies, including Philips, Nestlé, and Unilever, adopted matrix structures during the 1960s and 1970s, although in all cases one dimension of the matrix tended to be dominant in terms of authority. Thus, in the old Shell matrix the geographical dimension, as represented by country heads and regional coordinators, had primary responsibility for budgetary control, personnel appraisal, and strategy formulation.

Since the 1980s, most large corporations have dismantled or reorganized their matrix structures. Shell abandoned its matrix during 1995–1996 in favor of a structure based on four business sectors: upstream, downstream, chemicals, and gas and

FIGURE 6.6   Royal Dutch Shell Group: Pre-1996 matrix structure

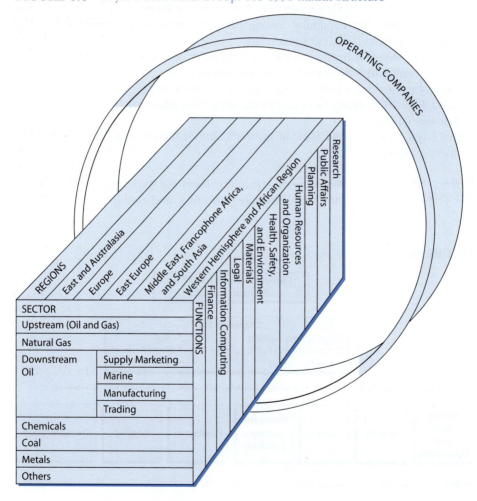

power. During 2001–2002, the Swiss/Swedish engineering giant ABB abandoned its much-lauded matrix structure in the face of plunging profitability and mounting debt. In fast-moving business environments companies have found that the benefits from formally coordinating across multiple dimensions have been outweighed by excessive complexity, larger head-office staffs, slower decision making, and diffused authority. Bartlett and Ghoshal observe that matrix structures "led to conflict and confusion; the proliferation of channels created informational logjams as a proliferation of committees and reports bogged down the organization; and overlapping responsibilities produced turf battles and a loss of accountability."[27]

Yet, all complex organizations that comprise multiple products, multiple functions, and multiple geographical markets need to coordinate within each of these dimensions. The problem of the matrix organization is not attempting to coordinate across multiple dimensions—in complex organizations such coordination is essential. The problem is when this multidimensional coordination is over-formalized, resulting in a top-heavy corporate HQ and over-complex systems that slow decision making and dull entrepreneurial initiative. The trend has been for companies to focus formal systems of coordination and control on one dimension, then allowing the other dimensions of coordination to be mainly informal. Thus, while Shell is organized primarily around four business sectors and these sectors exercise financial and strategic control over the individual operating companies, Shell still has country heads, responsible for coordinating all Shell's activities in relation to legal, taxation, and government relations within each country, and functional heads, responsible for technical matters and best-practice transfer within their particular function, be it manufacturing, marketing, or HR.

Trends in Organizational Design

Consultants and management scholars have proclaimed the death of hierarchical structures and the emergence of new organizational forms. Two decades ago, two of America's most prominent scholars of organization identified a "new organizational revolution" featuring "flatter hierarchies, decentralized decision making, greater tolerance for ambiguity, permeable internal and external boundaries, empowerment of employees, capacity for renewal, self-organizing units, [and] self-integrating coordination mechanisms."[28]

In practice, there has been more organizational evolution than organizational revolution. Certainly major changes have occurred in the structural features and management systems of industrial enterprises, yet there is little that could be described as radical organizational innovation or discontinuities with the past. Hierarchy remains the basic structural form of almost all companies, and the familiar structural configurations—functional, divisional, and matrix—are still evident. Nevertheless, within these familiar structural features, change has occurred:

- *Delayering*: Companies have made their organizational hierarchies flatter. The motive has been to reduce costs and to increase organizational responsiveness. Wider spans of control have also changed the relationships between managers and their subordinates, resulting in less supervision and greater decentralization of initiative. At Tata Steel, the management hierarchy was reduced from 13 layers to five. In briefing the McKinsey lead consultant, the CEO, Dr Irani, observed: "We are over-staffed, no doubt, but more damaging is the lack of responsiveness to fleeting opportunities … Our decision making is not as fast as it should be with everyone looking over their shoulder for approval … The objective is to redesign job content more meaningfully. The purpose is to rejuvenate the organization by defining richer jobs with fewer hierarchical layers of reporting.[29]

- *Adhocracy and team-based organization*: Adhocracies, according to Henry Mintzberg, are organizations that feature shared values, high levels of participation, flexible communication, and spontaneous coordination. Hierarchy, authority, and control mechanisms are largely absent.[30] Adhocracies tend to exist where problem solving and other non-routine activities predominate and where expertise is prized. Individual teams involved in research, consulting, engineering, entertainment, and crisis response tend to be adhocracies. At a larger organizational scale, companies such as Google, W. L. Gore & Associates, and some advertising agencies have adopted team-based structures with many of the features of adhocracies.

- *Project-based organizations*: Closely related to team-based organizations are project-based organizations. A key feature of the project-based organization is recognition that work assignments are for a finite duration, hence the organization structure needs to be dynamically flexible. Project-based organizations are common in sectors such as construction, consulting, oil exploration, and engineering. Because every project is different and involves a sequence of phases, each project needs to be undertaken by a closely interacting team that is able to draw upon the know-how of previous and parallel project teams. As cycle times become compressed across more and more activities, companies are introducing project-based organization into their conventional divisional and functional structures—for example new product development, change management, knowledge management, and research are increasingly organized into projects.

- *Network structures*: A common feature of new approaches to company organization is an emphasis on the informal over formal aspects of organizational structure. The main approach to describing and analyzing this informal structure is from the perspective of a social network—the pattern of interactions among organizational members (which can also be extended to those outside the organization). Social network analysis offers insight into how information and know-how move within organizations, how power and influence are determined, and how organizations adapt. The importance of social networks to the behavior and performance of organizations has led several management thinkers to recommend that these informal social structures be the primary basis for organizational structure and supplant traditional, formal structures. Thus, Gunnar Hedlund and Bartlett and Ghoshal have proposed network-based models of the multinational corporation.[31] This emphasis on patterns of communication and interaction rather than the formal relationships puts emphasis on the informal mechanisms through which coordination occurs and work gets done within organizations. Advances in information and communications technology have greatly increased the scope for coordination to occur outside of the formal structure, leading many observes to advocate the dismantling of much of the formal structures that firms have inherited.

- *Permeable organizational boundaries*: Network relationships exist between firms as well as between individuals. As firms specialize around their core competencies and products become increasingly complex, so these interfirm networks become increasingly important. As we shall see when we look more closely at strategic alliances (Chapter 15), localized networks of closely interdependent firms have been a feature of manufacturing for centuries. Such networks are a traditional feature of the industrial structure of much of northern Italy.[32] Hollywood and Silicon Valley also feature clusters of specialized firms that coordinate to design and produce complex products.[33]

These emerging organizational phenomena share several common characteristics:

- A focus on coordination rather than on control: In contrast to the command-and-control hierarchy, these structures focus almost wholly on achieving coordination. Financial incentives, culture, and social controls take the place of hierarchical control.
- Reliance on informal coordination where mutual adjustment replaces rules and directives: Central to all non-hierarchical structures is their dependence on voluntary coordination through bilateral and multilateral adjustment. The capacity for coordination through mutual adjustment has been greatly enhanced by information technology.
- Individuals in multiple organizational roles: Reconciling complex patterns of coordination with high levels of flexibility and responsiveness is difficult if job designs and organizational structures are rigidly defined. Increasingly, individual employees are required to occupy multiple roles simultaneously. For example, in addition to a primary role as a brand manager for a particular product category, a person might be a member of a committee that monitors community engagement activities, part of a task force to undertake a benchmarking study, and a member of a community of practice in web-based marketing.

Summary

Strategy formulation and strategy implementation are closely interdependent. The formulation of strategy needs to take account of an organization's capacity for implementation; at the same time, the implementation process inevitably involves creating strategy. If an organization's strategic management process is to be effective then its strategic planning system must be linked to actions, commitments and their monitoring, and the allocation of resources. Hence, operational plans and capital expenditure budgets are critical components of a firm's strategic management system.

Strategy implementation involves the entire design of the organization. By understanding the need to reconcile specialization with cooperation and coordination, we are able to appreciate the fundamental principles of organizational design.

Applying these principles, we can determine how best to allocate individuals to organizational units and how to combine these organizational units into broader groupings—in particular the choice between basic organizational forms such as functional, divisional, or matrix organizations.

We have also seen how company's organizational structures have been changing in recent years, influenced both by the demands of their external environments and the opportunities made available by advances in information and communication technologies.

The chapters that follow will have more to say on the organizational structures and management systems appropriate to different strategies and different business contexts. In the final chapter (Chapter 16) we shall explore some of the new trends and new ideas that are reshaping our thinking about organizational design.

Self-Study Questions

1. Jack Dorsey, the CEO of Twitter, Inc., has asked for your help in designing a strategic planning system for the company. Would you recommend a formal strategic planning system with an annual cycle such as that outlined in "The Strategic Planning System: Linking Strategy to Action" and Figure 6.1? (Note: Twitter's strategy is summarized in Strategy Capsule 1.5 in Chapter 1.)

2. Referring to Strategy Capsule 6.1, as DuPont expanded its product range (from explosives into paints, dyes, plastics, and synthetic fibers) why do you think the functional structure (organized around manufacturing plants and other functions such as sales, finance, and R & D) became unwieldy? Why did the multidivisional structure based on product groups improve management effectiveness?

3. Within your own organization (whether a university, company, or not-for-profit organization), which departments or activities are organized mechanistically and which organically? To what extent does the mode of organization fit the different environmental contexts and technologies of the different departments or activities?

4. In 2008, Citigroup announced that its Consumer business would be split into Consumer Banking, which would continue to operate through individual national banks, and Global Cards, which would form a single global business (similar to Citi's Global Wealth Management division). On the basis of the arguments relating to the "Defining Organizational Units" section above, why should credit cards be organized as a global unit and all other consumer banking services as national units?

5. The examples of Apple and General Motors (see "Functional Structure" section above) point to the evolution of organizational structures over the industry life-cycle. During the growth phase, many companies adopt multidivisional structures; during maturity and decline, many companies revert to functional structures. Why might this be? (Note: you may wish to refer to Chapter 8, which outlines the main features of the life-cycle model.)

6. Draw an organizational chart for a business school that you are familiar with. Does the school operate with a matrix structure (for instance, are there functional/discipline-based departments together with units managing individual programs)? Which dimension of the matrix is more powerful, and how effectively do the two dimensions coordinate? How would you reorganize the structure to make the school more efficient and effective?

Notes

1. L. Bossidy and R. Charan, *Execution: The Discipline of Getting Things Done* (New York: Random House, 2002): 71.

2. H. Mintzberg, "Patterns of Strategy Formulation," *Management Science* 24 (1978): 934–48; "Of Strategies: Deliberate and Emergent," *Strategic Management Journal* 6 (1985): 257–272.

3. T. J. Peters, "Strategy Follows Structure: Developing Distinctive Skills," *California Management Review*, 26 (Spring 1984): 111-128.

4. Apple Computer: Preliminary Confidential Offering Memorandum, 1978. http://www.computerhistory.org/collections/catalog/102712693.

5. *MCI Communications: Planning for the 1990s* (Harvard Business School Case No. 9-190-136, 1990): 1.

6. For a description of the strategic planning systems of the world's leading oil and gas majors, see: R. M. Grant, "Strategic Planning in a Turbulent Environment: Evidence from the Oil Majors," *Strategic Management Journal* 24 (2003): 491–518.

7. "Eni 2014–2017 Strategic Plan" (Rome: Eni, February 13, 2014).

8. P. F. Drucker, *The Practice of Management* (New York: Harper, 1954).

9. L. Bossidy and R. Charan, *Execution: The Discipline of Getting Things Done* (New York: Random House, 2002): 227.

10. H. Mintzberg, *Structure in Fives: Designing Effective Organizations* (Englewood Cliffs, NJ: Prentice Hall, 1993): 2.

11. A. Smith, *The Wealth of Nations* (London: Dent, 1910): 5.

12. K. Eisenhardt, "Agency Theory: An Assessment and Reviews," *Academy of Management Review* 14 (1989): 57–74.

13. L. A. Bebchuk and J. M. Fried, "Pay without Performance: Overview of the Issues." *Academy of Management Perspectives* 20 (2006): 5–24.

14. T. Peters and R. Waterman, *In Search of Excellence* (New York: Harper & Row, 1982).

15. J.-C. Spender, *Business Strategy: Managing Uncertainty, Opportunity, and Enterprise* (Oxford: Oxford University Press, 2014).

16. M. Weber, *Economy and Society: An Outline of Interpretive Sociology* (Berkeley, CA: University of California Press, 1968).

17. T. Burns and G. M. Stalker, *The Management of Innovation* (London: Tavistock Institute, 1961).

18. H. Mintzberg, *Structure in Fives: Designing Effective Organizations* (Englewood Cliffs: Prentice Hall, 1993): Chapter 9.

19. H. A. Simon, "The Architecture of Complexity," *Proceedings of the American Philosophical Society* 106 (1962): 467–482.

20. J. D. Orton and K. E. Weick, "Loosely Coupled Systems: A Reconceptualization," *Academy of Management Review* 15 (1990): 203–223.

21. On organizational modularity, see R. Sanchez and J. T. Mahoney, "Modularity, Flexibility, and Knowledge Management in Product and Organizational Design," *Strategic Management Journal* 17 (Winter 1996): 63–76; C. Baldwin and K. Clark, "Managing in an Age of Modularity," *Harvard Business Review* (September/October 1997): 84–93.

22. "Idea: Theories X and Y," *The Economist* online extra (October 6, 2008), www.economist.com/node/12370445, accessed July 20, 2015.

23. T. Burns and G. M. Stalker, *The Management of Innovation* (London: Tavistock, 1961).

24. L. Donaldson, "Contingency Theory (Structural)," in R. Thorpe and R. Holt (eds.), *The Sage Dictionary of Qualitative Management Research* (London: Sage, 2008).

25. J. Nickerson and T. Zenger refer to this as *structural modulation:* "Being Efficiently Fickle: A Dynamic Theory of Organizational Choice," *Organization Science* 13 (2002): 547–567.

26. J. D. Thompson, *Organizations in Action* (New York: McGraw-Hill, 1967). The nature of interdependence in organizational processes is revisited in T. W. Malone, K. Crowston, J. Lee, and B. Pentland, "Tools for Inventing Organizations: Toward a Handbook of Organizational Processes," *Management Science* 45 (March 1999): 489–504.

27. C. A. Bartlett and S. Ghoshal, "Matrix Management: Not a Structure, a Frame of Mind," *Harvard Business Review* (July/August 1990): 138–145.

28. R. Daft and A. Lewin, "Where are the theories for the new organizational forms?" *Organization Science* 3 (1993): 1–6.

29. R. Kumar, "De-Layering at Tata Steel," *Journal of Organizational Behavior Education* 1 (2006): 37–56.

30. H. Mintzberg, *Structure in Fives: Designing Effective Organizations* (Englewood Cliffs, NJ: Prentice Hall, 1993): Chapter 12.

31. G. Hedlund, "The Hypermodern MNC: A Heterarchy?" *Human Resource Management* 25 (1986): 9–35; C. Bartlett and S. Ghoshal, *Managing across Borders: The Transnational Solution*, 2nd edn (Boston, Harvard Business School, 1998).

32. M. H. Lazerson and G. Lorenzoni, "The Firms that Feed Industrial Districts: A Return to the Italian Source," *Industrial and Corporate Change* 8 (1999): 235–266; A. Grandori, *Interfirm Networks* (London: Routledge, 1999).

33. R. J. DeFilippi and M. B. Arthur, "Paradox in Project-based Enterprise: The Case of Film Making," *California Management Review* 42 (1998): 186–191.

III

BUSINESS STRATEGY AND THE QUEST FOR COMPETITIVE ADVANTAGE

7 The Sources and Dimensions of Competitive Advantage

SEARS MOTOR BUGGY: $395

For car complete with rubber tires, Timken roller bearing axles, top, storm front, three oil-burning lamps, horn, and one gallon of lubricating oil. Nothing to buy but gasoline.

. . . We found there was a maker of automobile frames that was making 75 percent of all the frames used in automobile construction in the United States. We found on account of the volume of business that this concern could make frames cheaper for automobile manufacturers than the manufacturers could make themselves. We went to this frame maker and asked him to make frames for the Sears Motor Buggy and then to name us prices for those frames in large quantities. And so on throughout the whole construction of the Sears Motor Buggy. You will find every piece and every part has been given the most careful study; you will find that the Sears Motor Buggy is made of the best possible material; it is constructed to take the place of the top buggy; it is built in our own factory, under the direct supervision of our own expert, a man who has had fifteen years of automobile experience, a man who has for the past three years worked with us to develop exactly the right car for the people at a price within the reach of all.

—EXTRACT FROM AN ADVERTISEMENT IN THE SEARS ROEBUCK & CO. CATALOG, 1909: 1150

If the three keys to selling real estate are location, location, location, then the three keys of selling consumer products are differentiation, differentiation, differentiation.

—ROBERT GOIZUETA, FORMER CHAIRMAN, COCA-COLA COMPANY

OUTLINE

Introduction and Objectives

In this chapter, we integrate and develop the elements of competitive advantage that we have analyzed in previous chapters. Chapter 1 noted that a firm can earn superior profitability either by locating in an attractive industry or by establishing a competitive advantage over its rivals. Of these two, competitive advantage is the more important. As competition has intensified across almost all industries, very few industry environments can guarantee secure returns; hence, the primary goal of a strategy is to establish a position of competitive advantage for the firm.

Chapters 3 and 5 provided the two primary components of our analysis of competitive advantage. The last part of Chapter 3 analyzed the external sources of competitive advantage: customer requirements and the nature of competition determine the key success factors within a market. Chapter 5 analyzed the internal sources of competitive advantage: the potential for the firm's resources and capabilities to establish and sustain competitive advantage.

This chapter looks more deeply at competitive advantage. We look first at the dynamics of competitive advantage, examining the processes through which competitive advantage is created and destroyed. This gives us insight into how competitive advantage can be attained and sustained. We then look at the two primary dimensions of competitive advantage: cost advantage and differentiation advantage and develop systematic approaches to their analysis.

By the time you have completed this chapter, you will be able to:

◆ Identify the circumstances in which a firm can create and sustain competitive advantage over a rival and recognize how resource conditions create imperfections in the competitive process that offer opportunities for competitive advantage.

◆ Distinguish the two primary types of competitive advantage: cost advantage and differentiation advantage.

◆ Identify the sources of cost advantage in an industry, apply cost analysis to assess a firm's relative cost position, and recommend strategies to enhance cost competitiveness.

◆ Appreciate the potential for differentiation to create competitive advantage, analyze the sources of differentiation, and formulate strategies that create differentiation advantage.

How Competitive Advantage Is Established and Sustained

To understand how **competitive advantage** emerges, we must first understand what competitive advantage is. Most of us can recognize competitive advantage when we see it: Walmart in discount retailing, Singapore Airlines in long-haul air travel, Google in online search, Embraer in regional jets. Yet, defining competitive advantage is troublesome. At a basic level we can define it as follows: *When two or more* *firms compete within the same market, one firm possesses a competitive advantage over its rivals when it earns (or has the potential to earn) a persistently higher rate of profit.*

The problem here is that if we identify competitive advantage with superior profitability, why do we need the concept of competitive advantage at all? A key distinction is that competitive advantage may not be revealed in higher profitability—a firm may forgo current profit in favor of investing in market share, technology, customer loyalty, or executive perks.[1]

In viewing competitive advantage as the result of matching internal strengths to external success factors, I may have conveyed the notion of competitive advantage as something static and stable. In fact, as we observed in Chapter 4 when discussing competition as a process of "creative destruction," competitive advantage is a disequilibrium phenomenon: it is created by change and, once established, it sets in motion the competitive process that leads to its destruction.

Establishing Competitive Advantage

The changes that generate competitive advantage can be either internal or external. Figure 7.1 depicts the basic relationships.

External Sources of Change   For an external change to create competitive advantage, the change must have differential effects on companies because of their different resources and capabilities or strategic positioning. For example, during 2014, the price of Brent crude declined from $108 to $58 per barrel. As a result, within the automobile industry the competitive position of Daimler, Jaguar Land Rover, and other companies producing large, conventionally powered cars improved relative to Toyota, Honda, Tesla, and other producers of electric and fuel-efficient cars.

The greater the magnitude of the external change and the greater the difference in the strategic positioning of firms, the greater the propensity for external change to generate competitive advantage, as indicated by the dispersion of profitability

FIGURE 7.1   The emergence of competitive advantage

among the firms within an industry. The world's tobacco industry has a relatively stable external environment and the leading firms pursue similar strategies with similar resources and capabilities: differences in profitability among firms tend to be small. The toy industry, on the other hand, comprises a heterogeneous group of firms that experience unpredictable shifts in consumer preferences and technology. As a result, profitability differences are wide and variable.

The competitive advantage that arises from external change also depends on firms' ability to respond to change. Any external change creates entrepreneurial opportunities that will accrue to the firms that exploit these opportunities most effectively. Entrepreneurial responsiveness involves one of two key capabilities:

- The ability to anticipate changes in the external environment. IBM has displayed a remarkable ability to renew its competitive advantage through anticipating, and then taking advantage of, most of the major shifts in the IT sector: the rise of personal computing, the advent of the internet, the shift in value from hardware to software and services, and the development of cloud computing. Conversely, Hewlett-Packard has failed to recognize and respond to these changes.
- Speed. As markets become more turbulent and unpredictable, quick-response capability has become increasingly important as a source of competitive advantage. Quick responses require information. As conventional economic and market forecasting has become less effective, so companies rely increasingly on "early-warning systems" through direct relationships with customers, suppliers, and even competitors. Quick responses also require short cycle times so that information can be acted upon speedily. In fashion retailing, quick response to fashion trends is critical to success. Zara, the retail clothing chain owned by the Spanish company Inditex, has built a vertically integrated supply chain that cuts the time between a garment's design and retail delivery to under three weeks (against an industry norm of three to six months.[2] This emphasis on speed as a source of competitive advantage was popularized by the Boston Consulting Group's concept of *time-based competition*[3] and in the surge of interest by consultants and academics in *strategic agility*.[4] Advances in IT—the internet, real-time electronic data exchange, and wireless communication—have greatly enhanced response capabilities throughout the business sector.

Internal Sources of Change: Competitive Advantage from Innovation

Competitive advantage may also be generated internally through innovation which creates competitive advantage for the innovator while undermining the competitive advantages of previous market leaders—the essence of Schumpeter's process of "creative destruction."[5] Although innovation is typically thought of as new products or processes that embody new technology, a key source of competitive advantage is *strategic innovation*—new approaches to serving customers and competing with rivals.

Strategic innovation typically involves creating value for customers from novel products, experiences, or modes of product delivery. Thus, in the retail sector, competition is driven by a constant quest for new retail concepts and formats. This may take the form of big-box stores with greater variety (Toys "R" Us, Home Depot), augmented customer service (Nordstrom), novel approaches to display and store

STRATEGY CAPSULE 7.1
STRATEGY CAPSULE 7.1
Business Model Innovation

Among business buzzwords, the term *business model* is one of the most loosely defined. According to Joan Magretta, business models are simply "stories that explain how enterprises work." In doing so they address the fundamental questions of "How do we make money in this business?" and "What is the underlying economic logic that explains how we deliver value to customers and at an appropriate cost?"[a] Subsequent definitions have extended the concept of the business model to encompass not only the core logic of how the business creates and captures value but also the broader business system through which that value creation and capture occurs. Thus, Zott *et al.* define the business model as "depicting the content, structure, and governance of transactions designed to create value through the exploitation of business opportunities."[b]

Although the terms *business model* and *strategy* are often used synonymously, if "business model" is to be a useful concept, it needs to be distinguished from "strategy." While "business model" describes the overall configuration of a firm's business system, "strategy" describes the specifics of how that business model fits a firm's particular market context and its resource and capability endowments. Thus, Southwest Airlines developed a new business model involving minimal passenger services and point-to-point routes using a single model of aircraft. This low-cost carrier model has been imitated by start-up airlines throughout the world. Yet, Southwest, Ryanair, EasyJet, and AirAsia each have distinct strategies in terms of the routes they fly and variations in how they apply the basic business model.

Strategic innovation through new business models has the capacity to revolutionize established industries. This was certainly the case with the low-cost carrier model pioneered by Southwest. It is also true of franchising, a business model first adopted by the Singer sewing machine company for its dealers, but perfected and popularized by McDonald's.

Recent interest in business models has been closely associated with the rise of e-commerce, where the strategic challenge for new businesses has been devising business models that permit the monetization of their innovations.[c] Thus, newspapers have adopted a variety of business models in their quest to generate revenues from their online content, these include:

◆ free access with paid third-party advertising;

◆ user subscriptions;

◆ metered access with limited free access;

◆ "freemium" models with some content offered free but more valuable content only available through subscription.

Notes:
[a] J. Magretta, "Why Business Models Matter," *Harvard Business Review* (May 2002): 86–92.
[b] C. Zott, R. Amit, and L. Massa, "The Business Model: Recent Developments and Future Research," *Journal of Management,* 37 (July 2011): 1019–1042.
[c] "The Search for a New Business Model," *Pew Journalism Research Project* (March 4, 2012). http://www.journalism.org/2012/03/05/search-new-business-model/.

layout (Sephora in cosmetics), or new systems of supplying customers that reconfigure the entire value chain (IKEA). Strategic innovations—especially within e-commerce—often take the form of business model innovations. Strategy Capsule 7.1 introduces the concept of a **business model** and provides examples of business model innovations.

STRATEGY CAPSULE 7.2
Blue Ocean Strategy

Kim and Mauborgne argue that the best value-creating opportunities for business lie not in existing industries following conventional approaches to competing (what they refer to as "red oceans") but seeking uncontested market space. These "blue oceans" may be entirely new industries created by technological innovation (such as wireless telephony and biotechnology) but are more likely to be the creation of new market space within existing industries using existing technologies. This may involve:

♦ New customer segments for existing products, e.g., Apple Computer's recognition of the potential of the use of microcomputers in homes and schools.

♦ Reconceptualization of existing products, e.g., Cirque du Soleil's reinvention of the circus as a multimedia, theatrical experience.

♦ Novel recombinations of product attributes and reconfigurations of established value chains that establish new positions of competitive advantage,

e.g., Dell's integrated system for ordering, assembling, and distributing PCs, which permitted unprecedented customer choice and speed of fulfilment.

The *strategy canvas* is a framework for developing blue ocean strategies. The horizontal axis shows the different product characteristics along which the firms in the industry compete; the vertical axis shows the amount of each characteristic a firm offers its customers. Starting with the value line showing the industry's existing offerings, the challenge is to identify a strategy that can provide a novel combination of attributes. This involves four types of choice:

♦ Raise: What factors should be raised well above the industry's standard?

♦ Eliminate: Which factors that the industry has long competed on should be eliminated?

♦ Reduce: Which factors should be reduced well below the industry's standard?

An alternative approach to identifying the potential for strategic innovation is that developed by Insead's Kim Chan and Renee Mauborgne. Their blue ocean strategy represents a quest for "uncontested market space" (Strategy Capsule 7.2).[6] Strategic innovation often involves combining performance attributes that were previously viewed as conflicting. Thus, Virgin America offers the low fares typical of budget airlines together with inflight services that are superior to those of most legacy carriers. Indeed, a common feature of many innovative strategies is the combination of low cost with superior customer value. However, Gary Hamel warns that few strategic innovations offer sustainable competitive advantage: management innovations such as Procter & Gamble's brand management system and Toyota's lean production are likely to offer competitive advantages that endure.[7]

Sustaining Competitive Advantage

Once established, competitive advantage is eroded by competition. The speed with which competitive advantage is undermined depends on the ability of competitors

◆ Create: Which factors should be created that the industry has never offered?

Figure 7.2 compares value lines for Cirque du Soleil and a traditional circus.

Source: Based upon W. C. Kim and R. Mauborgne, *Blue Ocean Strategy: How to Create Uncontested Market Space and Make the Competition Irrelevant* (Boston: Harvard Business School Press, 2005).

FIGURE 7.2   The Strategy Canvas: Value lines for Cirque du Soleil and the traditional circus

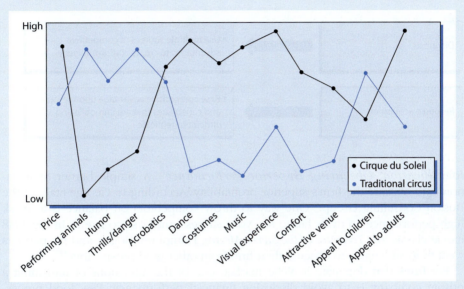

to challenge either by imitation or innovation. Imitation is the most direct form of competition; thus, for competitive advantage to be sustained over time, *barriers to imitation* must exist. Rumelt uses the term **isolating mechanisms** to describe the barriers that prevent the erosion of the superior profitability of individual firms.[8] Past evidence suggests that isolating mechanisms have been effective in sustaining competitive advantage: interfirm profit differentials often persist for periods of a decade or more.[9] However, as discussed in Chapter 4 (see the "Dynamic Competition" section), the advent of hypercompetition may have accelerated the erosion of competitive advantages.

To identify the sources of isolating mechanisms, we need to examine the process of competitive imitation. For one firm to successfully imitate the strategy of another, it must meet four conditions: it must identify the competitive advantage of a rival, it must have an incentive to imitate, it must be able to diagnose the sources of the rival's competitive advantage, and it must be able to acquire the resources and capabilities necessary for imitation. At each stage the incumbent can create isolating mechanisms to impede the would-be imitator (Figure 7.3).

FIGURE 7.3   Sustaining competitive advantage: Types of isolating mechanism

REQUIREMENT FOR IMITATION	ISOLATING MECHANISM
Identification	• Obscure superior performance
Incentives for imitation	• Deterrence: signal aggressive intentions • Pre-emption: exploit all available opportunities
Diagnosis	• Use multiple sources of competitive advantages to create *causal ambiguity*
Resource acquisition	• Base competitive advantage upon resources and capabilities that are immobile and difficult to replicate

Identification: Obscuring Superior Performance   A simple barrier to imitation is to obscure the firm's superior profitability. According to George Stalk of the Boston Consulting Group: "One way to throw competitors off balance is to mask high performance so rivals fail to see your success until it's too late."[10] In the 1948 movie classic *The Treasure of the Sierra Madre*, Humphrey Bogart and his partners went to great lengths to obscure their find from other gold prospectors.[11]

For firms that dominate a niche market, one of the attractions of remaining a private company is to avoid disclosing financial performance. Few food processors realized the profitability of canned cat and dog food until the UK Monopolies Commission revealed that the leading firm, Pedigree Petfoods (a subsidiary of Mars Inc.), earned a return on capital employed of 47%.[12]

In order to discourage the emergence of competitors, companies may forgo maximizing their short-term profits. The *theory of limit pricing*, in its simplest form, postulates that a firm in a strong market position sets prices at a level that just fails to attract entrants.[13]

Deterrence and Preemption   A firm may avoid competition by undermining the incentives for imitation. If a firm can persuade rivals that imitation will be unprofitable, it may be able to avoid competitive challenges. In Chapter 4 we discussed strategies of deterrence and the role of signaling and commitment in supporting them.[14] For deterrence to work, threats must be credible. Following the expiration of its NutraSweet patents in 1987, Monsanto fought an aggressive price war against the Holland Sweetener Company. Although costly, this gave Monsanto a reputation for aggression that deterred other would-be entrants into the aspartame market.[15]

A firm can also deter imitation by *preemption*—occupying existing and potential strategic niches to reduce the range of investment opportunities open to the challenger. Preemption can take many forms:

- Proliferation of product varieties by a market leader can leave new entrants and smaller rivals with few opportunities for establishing a market niche. Between 1950 and 1972, for example, the six leading suppliers of breakfast cereals introduced 80 new brands into the US market.[16]

- Large investments in production capacity ahead of the growth of market demand also preempt market opportunities for rivals. Monsanto's heavy investment in plants for producing NutraSweet ahead of its patent expiration was a clear threat to would-be producers of generic aspartame.

- Patent proliferation can protect technology-based advantage by limiting competitors' technical opportunities. In 1974, Xerox's dominant market position was protected by a wall of over 2000 patents, most of which were not used. When IBM introduced its first copier in 1970, Xerox sued it for infringing 22 of these patents.[17]

Diagnosing Competitive Advantage: Causal Ambiguity and Uncertain Imitability If a firm is to imitate the competitive advantage of another, it must understand the basis of its rival's success. For Kmart or Target to imitate Walmart's success in discount retailing they must first understand what makes Walmart so successful. While it is easy to point to what Walmart does differently, the difficult task is to identify which differences are the critical determinants of superior profitability. Is it Walmart's store locations (typically in small towns with little direct competition)? Its tightly integrated supply chain? Its unique management system? The information system that supports Walmart's logistics and decision-making practices? Or is it a culture built on traditional rural American values of thrift and hard work? Similarly, problems face Sony in seeking to imitate Apple's incredible success in consumer electronics.

Lippman and Rumelt identify this problem as **causal ambiguity**: when a firm's competitive advantage is multidimensional and is based on complex bundles of resources and capabilities, it is difficult for rivals to diagnose the success of the leading firm. The outcome of causal ambiguity is *uncertain imitability*: if the causes of a firm's success cannot be known for sure, successful imitation is uncertain.[18]

Recent research suggests that the problems of strategy imitation may run even deeper. We observed in Chapter 5 that capabilities are the outcome of complex combinations of resources and that multiple capabilities interact to confer competitive advantage. Research into complementarity among an organization's activities suggests that these interactions extend across the whole range of management practices.[19] Strategy Capsule 7.3 describes Urban Outfitters as an example of a unique "activity system." Where activities are tightly linked, complexity theory—NK modeling in particular—predicts that, within a particular competitive environment, a number of *fitness peaks* will appear, each associated with a unique combination of strategic variables.[20] The implications for imitation is that to locate on the same fitness peak as another firm not only requires recreating a complex configuration of strategy, structure, management systems, leadership, and business processes but also means that getting it just a little bit wrong may result in the imitator missing the fitness peak and finding itself in an adjacent valley.[21]

One of the challenges for the would-be imitator is deciding which management practices are generic best practices and which are *contextual*—complementary with

STRATEGY CAPSULE 7.3
Urban Outfitters

Urban Outfitters Inc. was founded in Philadelphia in 1976. By 2014, its three main chains—Urban Outfitters, Anthropologie, and Free People—comprised over 500 stores in ten countries. The company describes itself as targeting well-educated, urban-minded, young adults aged 18 to 30 through its unique merchandise mix and compelling store environment: "We create a unified environment in our stores that establishes an emotional bond with the customer. Every element of the environment is tailored to the aesthetic preferences of our target customers. Through creative design, much of the existing retail space is modified to incorporate a mosaic of fixtures, finishes and revealed architectural details. In our stores, merchandise is integrated into a variety of creative vignettes and displays designed to offer our customers an entire look at a distinct lifestyle."

According to Michael Porter and Nicolaj Siggelkow, Urban Outfitters offers a set of management practices that is both distinctive and highly interdependent. The urban-bohemian-styled product mix, which includes clothing, furnishings, and gift items, is displayed within bazaar-like stores, each of which has a unique design. To encourage frequent customer visits, the layout of each store is changed every two weeks, creating a new shopping experience whenever customers return. Emphasizing community with its customers, it forgoes traditional forms of advertising in favor of blogs and word-of-mouth transmission. Each practice makes little sense on its own, but together they represent a distinctive, integrated strategy. Attempts to imitate Urban Outfitters' competitive advantage would most likely fail because of the difficulty of replicating every aspect of the strategy before integrating them in the right manner.

Source: Urban Outfitters Inc. 10-K Report to January 31, 2014; M. E. Porter and N. Siggelkow, "Contextuality within Activity Systems and Sustainable Competitive Advantage," *Academy of Management Perspectives* 22 (May 2008): 34–56.

other management practices. For example, if we consider Sears Holdings' deliberation of which of Walmart's management practices to imitate in its Kmart stores, some practices (e.g., employees required to smile at customers, point-of-sale data transferred direct to the corporate database) are likely to be generically beneficial. Others, such as Walmart's "everyday low prices" pricing policy, low advertising sales ratio, and hub-and-spoke distribution are likely to be beneficial only when combined with other practices.

Acquiring Resources and Capabilities   Having diagnosed the sources of an incumbent's competitive advantage, the imitator's next challenge is to assemble the necessary resources and capabilities for imitation. As we saw in Chapter 5, a firm can acquire resources and capabilities in two ways: it can buy them or it can build them. The imitation barriers here are limits to the *transferability* and *replicability* of resources and capabilities. (See Chapter 5's "Sustaining Competitive Advantage" section for a discussion of these resource characteristics.) Strategy Capsule 7.4 shows how the resource requirements for competitive advantage differ across different market settings.

STRATEGY CAPSULE 7.4
Competitive Advantage in Different Market Settings

Competitive advantage arises where there are imperfections in the competitive process, which in turn result from the conditions under which essential resources and capabilities are available. Hence, by analyzing imperfections of competition, we can identify the sources of competitive advantage in different types of market. The key distinction is between the two types of value-creating activity: *trading* and *production*.

In trading markets the limiting case is *efficient markets*, which correspond closely to perfectly competitive markets (examples include the markets for securities, foreign exchange, and commodity futures). If prices reflect all available information and adjust instantaneously to newly available information, no market trader can expect to earn more than any other. It is not possible to beat the market on any consistent basis—in other words competitive advantage is absent. This absence of competitive advantage reflects the conditions of resource availability. Both of the resources needed to compete—finance and information—are equally available to all traders.

Competitive advantage in trading markets requires imperfections in the competitive process:

◆ Where there is an imperfect availability of information, competitive advantage results from superior access to information—hence the criminal penalties for insider trading in most advanced economies.

◆ Where transaction costs are present, competitive advantage accrues to the traders with the lowest transaction costs, hence the superior returns to low-cost index mutual funds over professionally managed funds. Vanguard´s S&P 500 Index fund with administrative costs of 0.5% annually has outperformed 90% of US equity mutual funds.

◆ If markets are subject to systematic behavioral trends (e.g., the *small firm effect* or the *January effect*), competitive advantage accrues to traders with superior knowledge of market psychology or of systematic price patterns (chart analysis). If markets are subject to bandwagon effects, competitive advantage can be gained in the short term by following the herd (momentum trading) and longer term by a contrarian strategy. Warren Buffett is a contrarian who is "fearful when others are greedy, and greedy when others are fearful."

In production markets the potential for competitive advantage is much greater because of the complex combinations of the resources and capabilities required, the highly differentiated nature of these resources and capabilities, and the imperfections in their supply. Within an industry, the more heterogeneous are firms' endowments of resources and capabilities, the greater the potential for competitive advantage. In the European electricity-generating industry, the growing diversity of players—utilities (EDF, ENEL), gas distributors (Gaz de France, Centrica), petroleum majors (Shell, ENI), independent power producers (AES, E.ON), and wind generators—has expanded opportunities for competitive advantage and widened the profit differentials between them.

Differences in resource endowments also influence the erosion of competitive advantage: the more similar are competitors' resources and capabilities, the easier is imitation.

Types of Competitive Advantage: Cost and Differentiation

A firm can achieve a higher rate of profit (or potential profit) over a rival in one of two ways: either it can supply an identical product or service at a lower cost or it can supply a product or service that is differentiated in such a way that the customer is willing to pay a price premium that exceeds the additional cost of the differentiation. In the former case, the firm possesses a cost advantage; in the latter, a differentiation advantage. In pursuing cost advantage, the goal of the firm is to become the cost leader in its industry or industry segment. Cost leadership requires the firm to "find and exploit all sources of cost advantage [and] sell a standard, no-frills product."[22] Differentiation by a firm from its competitors is achieved "when it provides something unique that is valuable to buyers beyond simply offering a low price."[23] Figure 7.4 illustrates these two types of advantage. By combining the two types of competitive advantage with the firm's choice of scope—broad market versus narrow segment—Michael Porter has defined three generic strategies: cost leadership, differentiation, and focus (Figure 7.5).

Cost Analysis

Historically, strategic management has emphasized cost advantage as the primary basis for competitive advantage in an industry. This focus on cost reflected the traditional emphasis by economists on price as the principal medium of competition. It also reflected the quest by large industrial corporations during the last century to exploit economies of

FIGURE 7.4   Sources of competitive advantage

FIGURE 7.5   Porter's generic strategies

scale and scope through investments in mass production and mass distribution. During the 1970s and 1980s, this preoccupation with cost advantage was reflected in the widespread interest in the experience curve as a tool of strategy analysis (Strategy Capsule 7.5).

In recent decades, companies have been forced to think more broadly and radically about cost efficiency. Growing competition from emerging market countries has created intense cost pressures for Western and Japanese firms, resulting in novel approaches to cost reduction, including outsourcing, offshoring, process re-engineering, lean production, and organizational delayering.

The Sources of Cost Advantage

There are seven principal determinants of a firm's unit costs (cost per unit of output) relative to its competitors; we refer to these as *cost drivers* (Figure 7.7).

The relative importance of these different cost drivers varies across industries, between firms within an industry, and across the different activities within a firm. By examining each of these different cost drivers in relation to a particular firm, we can analyze a firm's cost position relative to its competitors', diagnose the sources of inefficiency, and make recommendations as to how a firm can improve its cost efficiency.

Economies of Scale   The predominance of large corporations in most manufacturing and service industries is a consequence of economies of scale. Economies of scale exist wherever proportionate increases in the amounts of inputs employed in a production process result in lower unit costs. Economies of scale have been conventionally associated with manufacturing. Figure 7.8 shows a typical relationship between unit cost and plant capacity. The point at which most scale economies are exploited is the *minimum efficient plant size* (MEPS).

Scale economies arise from three principal sources:

- Technical input–output relationships: In many activities, increases in output do not require proportionate increases in input. A 10000-barrel oil storage tank does not cost five times as much as a 2000-barrel tank. Similar volume-related economies exist in ships, trucks, and steel and petrochemical plants.
- Indivisibilities: Many resources and activities are "lumpy"—they are unavailable in small sizes. Hence, they offer economies of scale as firms are able to spread the costs of these items over larger volumes of output. In R & D, new product development and advertising market leaders tend to have much lower costs as a percentage of sales than their smaller rivals.
- Specialization: Increased scale permits greater task specialization. Mass production involves breaking down the production process into separate tasks performed by specialized workers using specialized equipment. Division of labor promotes learning and assists automation. Economies of specialization are especially important in knowledge-intensive industries such as investment banking, management consulting, and software development, where large firms are able to offer specialized expertise across a broad range of know-how.

Scale economies are a key determinant of an industry's level of concentration (the proportion of industry output accounted for by the largest firms). In many consumer goods industries, scale economies in marketing have driven industry consolidation.

STRATEGY CAPSULE 7.5

BCG and the Experience Curve

The experience curve has its basis in the systematic reduction in the time taken to build airplanes and Liberty ships during World War II. In a series of studies, ranging from bottle caps and refrigerators to long-distance calls and insurance policies, the Boston Consulting Group (BCG) observed a remarkable regularity in the reductions in unit costs with increased cumulative output. Its *law of experience* states: the unit cost of value added to a standard product declines by a constant percentage (typically between 15 and 30%) each time cumulative output doubles. (Where "unit cost of value added" is the unit cost of production less the unit cost of bought-in components and materials).[a] Figure 7.6 shows the experience curve for Ford's Model T.

The experience curve has important implications for strategy. If a firm can expand its output faster than its competitors can, it can move down the experience curve more rapidly and open up a widening cost differential. BCG concluded that a firm's primary strategic goal should be driving volume growth through maximizing market share. BCG identified Honda in

motorcycles as an exemplar of this strategy.[b] The quest for market share was supported by numerous studies confirming a positive relationship between profitability and market share.[c] However, association does not imply causation—it seems likely that market share and profitability are both outcomes of some other source of competitive advantage—product innovation, or superior marketing.[d]

The weaknesses of the experience curve as a strategy tool are, first, it fails to distinguish several sources of cost reduction (learning, scale, process innovation); second, it presumes that cost reductions from experience are automatic—the reality is that they must be managed.

Notes:
[a] Boston Consulting Group, *Perspectives on Experience* (Boston: BCG, 1970).
[b] Boston Consulting Group, *Strategy Alternatives for the British Motorcycle Industry* (London: HMSO, 1975).
[c] R. Jacobsen and D. Aaker, "Is Market Share All That It's Cracked Up To Be?" *Journal of Marketing*, 49 (Fall 1985): 11–22.
[d] R. Wensley , "PIMS and BCG: New Horizons or False Dawn?" *Strategic Management Journal*, 3 (1982): 147–58.

FIGURE 7.6 Experience curve for the Ford Model T, 1909–1920

Note: The figure shows an 85% experience curve, i.e., unit costs declined by approximately 15% with each doubling of cumulative volume.

FIGURE 7.7   The drivers of cost advantage

ECONOMIES OF SCALE	• Technical input–output relationships • Indivisibilities • Specialization
ECONOMIES OF LEARNING	• Increased individual skills • Improved organizational routines
PRODUCTION TECHNIQUES	• Process innovation • Re-engineering of business processes
PRODUCT DESIGN	• Standardization of designs and components • Design for manufacture
INPUT COSTS	• Location advantages • Ownership of low-cost inputs • Nonunion labor • Bargaining power
CAPACITY UTILIZATION	• Ratio of fixed to variable costs • Fast and flexible capacity adjustment
RESIDUAL EFFICIENCY	• Organizational slack/X-inefficiency • Motivation and organizational culture • Managerial effectiveness

FIGURE 7.8   The long-run average cost curve for a plant

Figure 7.9 shows how soft drink brands with the greatest sales volume tend to have the lowest unit advertising costs. In other industries—especially aerospace, automobiles, software, and telecommunications—the need to amortize the huge costs of new product development has forced consolidation. Where product development is

very costly, volume is essential to profitability. The Boeing 747 was hugely profitable because 1508 were built between 1970 and 2014. The challenge for the Airbus A380 is whether there is sufficient worldwide demand to cover its $18 billion development cost.

Yet, even in industries where scale economies are important, small and medium-sized companies continue to survive and prosper in competition with much bigger rivals. In automobiles, BMW, Jaguar Land Rover, and Hyundai have been more profitable than Toyota, Ford, and GM. In commercial banking, there is no evidence that big banks outperform smaller players either on profitability or costs.[24] How do small and medium-sized firms offset the disadvantages of small scale? First, by exploiting superior flexibility; second, by outsourcing activities where scale is critical to efficiency (e.g., specialist car makers typically license technologies and designs and buy in engines); third, by avoiding the motivational and coordination problems that often afflict large organizations.[25]

Economies of Learning   The experience curve has its basis in learning-by-doing. Repetition develops both individual skills and organizational routines. In 1943, it took 40,000 labor-hours to build a B-24 Liberator bomber. By 1945, it took only 8000 hours.[26] Intel's dominance of the world microprocessor market owes much to its accumulated learning in the design and manufacture of these incredibly complex products. Learning occurs both at the individual level through improvements in dexterity and problem solving and at the group level through the development and refinement of organizational routines.[27]

Process Technology and Process Design   Superior processes can be a source of huge cost economies. Pilkington's revolutionary float glass process gave it (and its licensees) an unassailable cost advantage in producing flat glass. Ford's moving assembly line reduced the time taken to assemble a Model T from 106 hours in 1912 to six hours in 1914. When process innovation is embodied in new capital equipment, diffusion is likely to be rapid. However, the full benefits of new process technologies typically require system-wide changes in job design, employee incentives, product design, organizational structure, and management controls. Between 1979 and 1986, General Motors spent $40 billion on new process technology with

FIGURE 7.9   Economies of scale in advertising: US soft drinks

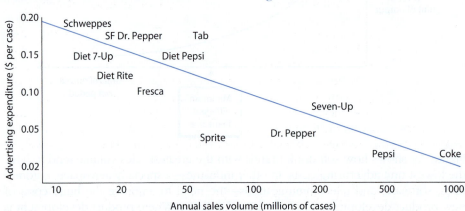

the goal of becoming the world's most efficient manufacturer of automobiles. However, major efficiency gains from improved processes may come from process redesign without significant technological innovation. Dell's cost leadership in personal computers during the 1990s resulted from its reconfiguration of the industry's traditional value chain. Toyota's system of lean production combines several work practices including just-in-time scheduling, total quality management, continuous improvement (kaizen), teamwork, job flexibility, and supplier partnerships.[28]

Business process re-engineering (BPR) is an approach to redesigning operational processes that gained massive popularity during the 1990s. "Re-engineering gurus" Michael Hammer and James Champy define BPR as: "the fundamental rethinking and radical redesign of business processes to achieve dramatic improvements in critical contemporary measures of performance, such as cost, quality, service, and speed."[29] BPR recognizes that operational and commercial processes evolve over time without consistent direction or systematic appraisal. BPR begins with the question: "If we were starting afresh, how would we design this process?"

BPR has led to major gains in efficiency, quality, and speed (Strategy Capsule 7.6), but where business processes are complex and embedded in organizational routines, it is likely that no one in the organization fully understands the operation of existing processes. In such circumstances, Hammer and Champy's recommendation to "obliterate" existing processes and start with a "clean sheet of paper" runs the risk of destroying organizational capabilities that have been nurtured over a long period. In recent years BPR has been partly superceded by *business process management*, where the emphasis has shifted from workflow management to the broader application of information technology (web-based applications in particular) to the redesign and enhancement of organizational processes.[30]

Product Design   *Design-for-manufacture*—designing products for ease of production rather than simply for functionality and esthetics—can offer substantial cost savings, especially when linked to the introduction of new process technology.

- Volkswagen cut product development and component costs by redesigning its 30 different models around just four separate platforms. The VW Beetle, Audi TT, Golf, and Audi A3, together with several Seat and Skoda models, all share a single platform.
- In printed circuit boards (PCBs), design-for-manufacture has resulted in huge productivity gains through increasing yields and facilitating automation.

Service offerings, too, can be designed for ease and efficiency of production. Motel 6, cost leader in US budget motels, carefully designs its product to keep operating costs low. Its motels occupy low-cost, out-of-town locations; it uses standard motel designs; it avoids facilities such as pools and restaurants; and it designs rooms to facilitate easy cleaning and low maintenance. However, efficiency in service design is compromised by the tendency of customers to request deviations from standard offerings ("I'd like my hamburger with the bun toasted on one side only, please"). This requires a clear strategy to manage variability either through accommodation or restriction.[31]

Capacity Utilization   Over the short and medium terms, plant capacity is more or less fixed and variations in output cause capacity utilization to rise or fall. Underutilization raises unit costs because fixed costs must be spread over

STRATEGY CAPSULE 7.6
Process Re-Engineering at IBM Credit

Michel Hammer and James Champy describe how business process re-engineering resulted in IBM reducing the time taken to approve requests by sales personnel for new customer credit approval from six days to four hours. Under the old system, five stages were involved:

1   an IBM salesperson telephoned a request for financing, which was logged on a piece of paper;

2   the request was sent to the credit department, which checked the customer's creditworthiness;

3   the request and credit check were sent to the business practices department where a loan covenant was drawn up;

4   the paperwork was passed to a pricer, who determined the interest rate;

5   the clerical group prepared a quote letter that was sent to the salesperson.

Frustrated by the delays and resulting lost sales, two managers undertook an experiment. They took a financing request and walked it through all five steps. They discovered that all five stages could be completed within 90 minutes!

The problem was that the process had been designed for the most complex credit requests that IBM received, whereas in the vast majority of cases no specialist judgment was called for: all that was needed was to check credit ratings and to plug numbers into standard algorithms. The credit approval process was redesigned by replacing the specialists (credit checkers, pricers, and so on) with generalists who undertook all five processes. Only where the request was non-standard or unusually complex were specialists called in. Not only was processing time reduced by 94%, but the number of employees involved was reduced and the total number of customer approvals greatly increased.

Source: Adapted from M. Hammer and J. Champy, *Re-engineering the Corporation: A Manifesto for Business Revolution* (New York: HarperBusiness, 1993): 36–9.

fewer units of production; pushing output beyond normal full capacity also creates inefficiencies. Boeing's efforts to boost output during 2006–2011 resulted in increased unit costs due to overtime pay, premiums for night and weekend shifts, increased defects, and higher levels of maintenance. Hence, the ability to speedily adjust capacity to downturns in demand can be a major source of cost advantage. During the 2008–2009 recession, survival in hard-hit sectors such as house building, construction equipment, and retailing required fast response to declining demand: Caterpillar announced it was cutting 20,000 jobs on January 28, 2008, the same day it reported a downturn in its quarterly sales.[32]

Input Costs   The firms in an industry do not necessarily pay the same price for identical inputs. There are several sources of lower input costs:

- Locational differences in input prices: The prices of inputs, and wage rates in particular, vary between locations. In the US, software engineers earned an average of $82,000 in 2014. In India, the average was $11,000. In auto assembly the hourly rate in Chinese plants was about $3.50 an hour in 2014 compared with $28 in the US (not including benefits).[33]

● Ownership of low-cost sources of supply: In raw-material-intensive industries, ownership of low-cost sources of material can offer a massive cost advantage. In petroleum, lifting costs for the three "supermajors" (ExxonMobil, Royal Dutch Shell, and BP) were about $18 per barrel in 2013; for Saudi Aramco they were about $5.

● Non-union labor: Labor unions result in higher levels of pay and benefits and work rules that can lower productivity. In the US airline industry, non-union Virgin America had average salary and benefit cost per employee of $79,161 in 2013 compared with $98,300 for United (80% unionized).

● Bargaining power: The ability to negotiate preferential prices and discounts can be a major source of cost advantage for industry leaders, especially in retailing.[34] Amazon's growing dominance of book retailing allows it to demand discounts from publishers of up to 60%.[35]

Residual Efficiency Even after taking account of the basic cost drivers—scale, technology, product and process design, input costs, and capacity utilization—unexplained cost differences between firms typically remain. These residual efficiencies relate to the extent to which the firm approaches its efficiency frontier of optimal operation which depends on the firm's ability to eliminate "organizational slack"[36] or "X-inefficiency."[37] These excess costs have a propensity to accumulate within corporate headquarters—where they become targets for activist investors.[38] Eliminating these excess costs often requires a threat to a company's survival—in his first year as CEO, Carlos Ghosn cut Nissan Motor's operating costs by 20%.[39] At Walmart, Ryanair, and Amazon, high levels of residual efficiency are the result of management systems and company values that are intolerant of unnecessary costs and glorify frugality.

Using the Value Chain to Analyze Costs

To analyze an organization's cost position and seek opportunities for cost reduction, we need to look at individual activities. Chapter 5 introduced the *value chain* as a framework for viewing the sequence of activities that a company or business unit performs. Each activity tends to be subject to a different set of cost drivers, which give it a distinct cost structure. A value chain analysis of a firm's costs seeks to identify:

● the relative importance of each activity with respect to total cost;
● the cost drivers for each activity and the comparative efficiency with which the firm performs each activity;
● how costs in one activity influence costs in another;
● which activities should be undertaken within the firm and which activities should be outsourced.

A value chain analysis of a firm's cost position comprises the following stages:

1 Disaggregate the firm into separate activities: Determining the appropriate value chain activities is a matter of judgment. It requires identifying which activities

are separate from one another, which are most important in terms of cost, and their dissimilarity in terms of cost drivers.

2 Estimate the cost that each activity contributes to total costs. Michael Porter suggests the detailed assignment of operating costs and assets to each value activity; however, even with activity-based costing, detailed cost allocation can be a major exercise.[40]

3 Identify cost drivers: For each activity, what factors determine the level of unit cost relative to other firms? For some activities, cost drivers can be deduced simply from the nature of the activity and the types of cost incurred. For activities with large fixed costs such as new product development or marketing, the principal cost driver is likely to be the ability to amortize costs over a large volume of sales. For labor-intensive activities, key cost drivers tend to be wage rates, process design, and defect rates.

4 Identify linkages: The costs of one activity may be determined, in part, by the way in which other activities are performed. Xerox discovered that its high service costs relative to competitors' reflected the complexity of design of its copiers, which required 30 different interrelated adjustments.

5 Identify opportunities for reducing costs: By identifying areas of comparative inefficiency and the cost drivers for each, opportunities for cost reduction become evident. If scale economies are a key cost driver, can volume be increased? If wage costs are excessive, will employees accept productivity-increasing measures; alternatively, can production be relocated? If an activity cannot be performed efficiently within the firm, can it be outsourced?

Figure 7.10 shows how the application of the value chain to automobile manufacture can identify possible cost reductions.

Differentiation Analysis

A firm differentiates itself from its competitors "when it provides something unique that is valuable to buyers beyond simply offering a lower price."[41] Differentiation advantage occurs when a firm is able to obtain from its differentiation a price premium that exceeds the cost of providing the differentiation.

Every firm has opportunities for differentiating its offering to customers, although the range of differentiation opportunities depends on the characteristics of the product. An automobile or a restaurant offers greater potential for differentiation than cement, wheat, or memory chips. These latter products are called *commodities* precisely because they lack physical differentiation. Yet, according to Tom Peters, "Anything can be turned into a value-added product or service."[42] Consider the following:

- Cement is the ultimate commodity product, yet Cemex, based in Mexico, has become a leading worldwide supplier of cement and ready-mix concrete through emphasizing "building solutions"—one aspect of which is ensuring that 98% of its deliveries are on time (compared to 34% for the industry as a whole).[43]

FIGURE 7.10   Using the value chain in cost analysis: An automobile manufacturer

SEQUENCE OF ANALYSIS	VALUE CHAIN	COST DRIVER
1. IDENTIFY ACTIVITIES Establish the basic framework of the value chain by identifying the principal activities of the firm. **2. ALLOCATE TOTAL COSTS** For a first-stage analysis, a rough estimate of the breakdown of total cost by activity is sufficient to indicate which activities offer the greatest scope for cost reductions. **3. IDENTIFY COST DRIVERS** (See diagram.) **4. IDENTIFY LINKAGES** Examples include: 1. Consolidating purchase orders to increase discounts increases inventories. 2. High-quality parts and materials reduce costs of defects at later stages. 3. Reducing manufacturing defects cuts warranty costs. 4. Designing different models around common components and platforms reduces manufacturing costs. **5. IDENTIFY OPPORTUNITIES** **COST REDUCTION** For example: *Purchasing*: Concentrate purchases on fewer suppliers to maximize purchasing economies. Institute just-in-time component supply to reduce inventories. *R & D/Design/Engineering*: Reduce frequency of model changes. Reduce number of different models (e.g., single range of global models). Design for commonality of components and platforms. *Component manufacture*: Exploit economies of scale through concentrating production of each component on fewer plants. Outsource wherever scale of production or run lengths are suboptimal or where outside suppliers have technology advantages. For labor-intensive components (e.g., seats, dashboards, trim), relocate production in low-wage countries. Improve capacity utilization through plant rationalization or supplying components to other manufacturers.	**PURCHASING COMPONENTS AND MATERIALS** **R & D, DESIGN, AND ENGINEERING** **COMPONENT MANUFACTURE** **ASSEMBLY** **TESTING AND QUALITY CONTROL** **INVENTORIES OF FINISHED PRODUCTS** **SALES AND MARKETING** **DISTRIBUTION AND DEALER SUPPORT**	Prices of bought-in components depend upon: • Order sizes • Average value of purchases per supplier • Location of suppliers Size of R & D commitment Productivity of R & D Number and frequency of new models Sales per model Scale of plants Run length per component Capacity utilization Location of plants Scale of plants Number of models per plant Degree of automation Level of wages Location of plants Level of quality targets Frequency of defects Predictability of sales Flexibility of production Customers' willingness to wait Size of advertising budget Strength of existing reputation Sales volume Number of dealers Sales per dealer Desired level of dealer support Frequency of defects repaired under warranty

● Online bookselling is inherently a commodity business—any online book-
seller has access to the same titles and same modes of distribution. Yet
Amazon has exploited the information generated by its business to offer
a range of value-adding services: best-seller lists, reviews, and customized
recommendations.

The lesson is this: differentiation is not simply about offering different product
features; it is about identifying and understanding every possible interaction between
the firm and its customers and asking how these interactions can be enhanced or
changed in order to deliver additional value to the customer. This requires looking
at both the firm (the supply side) and its customers (the demand side). While *supply-
side analysis* identifies the firm's potential to create uniqueness, the critical issue is
whether such differentiation creates value for customers and whether the value created exceeds the cost of the differentiation. Only by understanding what customers
want, how they choose, and what motivates them can we identify opportunities for
profitable differentiation.

Thus, differentiation strategies are not about pursuing uniqueness for its own sake.
Differentiation is about understanding customers and how to best meet their needs.
To this extent, the quest for differentiation advantage takes us to the heart of business
strategy. The fundamental issues of differentiation are also the fundamental issues of
business strategy: Who are our customers? How do we create value for them? And
how do we do it more effectively and efficiently than anyone else?

Because differentiation is about uniqueness, establishing differentiation advantage
requires creativity: it cannot be achieved simply through applying standardized frameworks and techniques. This is not to say that differentiation advantage is not amenable to systematic analysis. As we have observed, there are two requirements for
creating profitable differentiation. On the supply side, the firm must be aware of the
resources and capabilities through which it can create uniqueness (and do it better
than competitors). On the demand side, the key is insight into customers and their
needs and preferences. These two sides form the major components of our analysis
of differentiation.

The Nature and Significance of Differentiation

The potential for differentiating a product or service is partly determined by its
physical characteristics. For products that are technically simple (a pair of socks, a
brick), that satisfy uncomplicated needs (a corkscrew, a nail), or must meet rigorous
technical standards (a DRAM chip, a thermometer), differentiation opportunities are
constrained by technical and market factors. Products that are technically complex
(an airplane), that satisfy complex needs (an automobile, a vacation), or that do not
need to conform to particular technical standards (wine, toys) offer much greater
scope for differentiation.

Beyond these constraints, the potential in any product or service for differentiation
is limited only by the boundaries of the human imagination. For seemingly simple
products such as shampoo, toilet paper, and bottled water, the proliferation of brands
on any supermarket's shelves is testimony both to the ingenuity of firms and the
complexity of customers' preferences. Differentiation extends beyond the physical
characteristics of the product or service to encompass everything about the product
or service that influences the value that customers derive from it. This means that

differentiation includes every aspect of the way in which a company relates to its customers. Starbucks' ability to charge up to $5 for a cup of coffee (compared to a US average price of $1.38) rests not just on the characteristics of the coffee but also on the overall "Starbucks Experience" which encompasses the retail environment, the sense of community in which customers participate, and the values that Starbucks projects. Differentiation activities are not specific to particular functions such as design and marketing; they infuse all aspects of the relationship between an organization and its customers, including the identity and culture of a company.

Differentiation includes both tangible and intangible dimensions. *Tangible differentiation* is concerned with the observable characteristics of a product or service that are relevant to customers' preferences and choice processes, for example size, shape, color, weight, design, material, and performance attributes such as reliability, consistency, taste, speed, durability, and safety. Tangible differentiation also extends to products and services that complement the product in question: delivery, after-sales services, and accessories.

Opportunities for *intangible differentiation* arise because the value that customers perceive in a product is seldom determined solely by observable product features or objective performance criteria. Social, emotional, psychological, and esthetic considerations are present in most customer choices. For consumer goods and services the desire for status, exclusivity, individuality, security, and community are powerful motivational forces. Where a product or service is meeting complex customer needs, differentiation choices involve the overall image of the firm and its offering. Image differentiation is especially important for those products and services whose qualities and performance are difficult to ascertain at the time of purchase (so-called experience goods). These include cosmetics, medical services, and education.

Differentiation and Segmentation   Differentiation is different from segmentation. Differentiation is concerned with how a firm competes—the ways in which it can offer uniqueness to customers. Such uniqueness might relate to consistency (McDonald's), reliability (Federal Express), status (American Express), quality (BMW), and innovation (Apple). Segmentation is concerned with where a firm competes in terms of customer groups, localities, and product types.

Whereas segmentation is a feature of market structure, differentiation is a strategic choice made by a firm. Differentiation may lead to focusing upon particular market segments, but not necessarily. IKEA, McDonald's, Honda, and Starbucks all pursue differentiation, but position themselves within the mass market spanning multiple demographic and socioeconomic segments.[44]

The Sustainability of Differentiation Advantage   Differentiation offers a more secure basis for competitive advantage than low cost does. A position of cost advantage is vulnerable to the emergence of new competitors from low-cost countries and to adverse movements in exchange rates. Cost advantage can also be overturned by innovation: discount brokerage firms were undercut by internet brokers, discount stores by online retailers. Differentiation advantage would appear to be more sustainable. Large companies that consistently earn above-average returns on capital—such as Colgate-Palmolive, Diageo, Johnson & Johnson, Kellogg's, Procter & Gamble, 3M, and Wyeth—tend to be those that have pursued differentiation through quality, branding, and innovation.

Analyzing Differentiation: The Demand Side

Analyzing customer demand enables us to determine which product characteristics have the potential to create value for customers, customers' willingness to pay for differentiation, and a company's optimal competitive positioning in terms of differentiation variables. Analyzing demand begins with understanding why customers buy a product or service. Market research systematically explores customer preferences and customer perceptions of existing products. However, the key to successful differentiation is to understand customers: a simple, direct inquiry into the purpose of a product and the needs of its customers can often be far more illuminating than statistically validated market research (Strategy Capsule 7.7).

Understanding customer needs requires the analysis of customer preferences in relation to product attributes. Techniques include:

- *Multidimensional scaling* (MDS) permits customers' perceptions of competing products to be represented graphically in terms of key product attributes.[45] For example, a survey of consumer ratings of competing pain relievers resulted in the mapping shown in Figure 7.11. Multidimensional scaling has also been used to classify 109 single-malt Scotch whiskies according to the characteristics of their color, nose, palate, body, and finish.[46]
- *Conjoint analysis* measures the strength of customer preferences for different product attributes. The technique requires, first, an identification of the underlying attributes of a product and, second, market research to rank hypothetical products that contain alternative bundles of attributes. The results can then be used to estimate the proportion of customers who would prefer a hypothetical new product to competing products already available in the market.[47] Conjoint analysis was used by Marriott to design the attributes of its Courtyard hotel chain.
- *Hedonic price analysis* views products as bundles of underlying attributes.[48] It uses regression analysis to estimate the implicit market price for each attribute. For example, price differences among European automatic washing machines can be related to differences in capacity, spin speed, energy consumption, number of programs, and reliability. A machine that spins at 1000 rpm sold at about a $200 price premium to one that spins at 800 rpm.[49] Similarly, price differences between models of personal computer reflect differences in processor speed, memory, and hard drive capacity. The results of this analysis can then be used to make decisions as to what levels of each attribute to include within a new product and the price point for that product.

The Role of Social and Psychological Factors Analyzing product differentiation in terms of measurable performance attributes tends to ignore customers' underlying motivations. Few goods or services only satisfy physical needs: most buying is influenced by social and psychological motivations, such as the desire to find community with others and to reinforce one's own identity. Psychologist Abraham Maslow proposed a hierarchy of human needs that progress from basic survival needs to security needs, to belonging needs, to esteem needs, up to the desire for self-actualization.[50] For most goods, brand equity has more to do with status and identity than with tangible product performance. The disastrous introduction

STRATEGY CAPSULE 7.7
Understanding What a Product Is about

Getting back to strategy means getting back to a deep understanding of what a product is about. Some time ago, for example, a Japanese home appliance company was trying to develop a coffee percolator. Should it be a General Electric-type percolator, executives wondered? Should it be the same drip type that Philips makes? Larger? Smaller? I urged them to ask a different kind of question: Why do people drink coffee? What are they looking for when they do? If your objective is to serve the customer better, then shouldn't you understand why that customer drinks coffee in the first place? Then you would know what kind of percolator to make.

The answer came back: good taste. Then I asked the company's engineers what they were doing to help the consumer enjoy good taste in a cup of coffee. They said they were trying to design a good percolator. I asked them what influences the taste in a cup of coffee. No one knew. That became the next question we had to answer. It turns out that lots of things can affect taste—the beans, the temperature, the water. We did our homework and discovered all the things that affect taste . . .

Of all the factors, water quality, we learned, made the greatest difference. The percolator in design at the time, however, didn't take water quality into account

at all . . . We discovered next that grain distribution and the time between grinding the beans and pouring in the water were crucial. As a result we began to think about the product and its necessary features in a new way. It had to have a built-in dechlorinating function. It had to have a built-in grinder. All the customer should have to do is pour in water and beans . . .

To start you have to ask the right questions and set the right kinds of strategic goals. If your only concern is that General Electric has just brought out a percolator that brews coffee in 10 minutes, you will get your engineers to design one that brews it in seven minutes. And if you stick to that logic, market research will tell you that instant coffee is the way to go . . . Conventional marketing approaches won't solve the problem. If you ask people whether they want their coffee in 10 minutes or seven, they will say seven, of course. But it's still the wrong question. And you end up back where you started, trying to beat the competition at its own game. If your primary focus is on the competition, you will never step back and ask what the customers' inherent needs are, and what the product really is about.

Source: Reprinted by permission of Harvard Business Review. From "Getting Back to Strategy," Kenichi Ohmae, November/December 1988, p. 154, Copyright © 1988 by the Harvard Business School Publishing Corporation; all rights reserved.

of "New Coke" in 1985 was the result of Coca-Cola giving precedence to tangible differentiation (taste preferences) over intangible differentiation (authenticity).[51] Harley-Davidson harbors no such illusions: it recognizes quite clearly that it is in the business of selling lifestyle, not transportation.

If the dominant customer needs that a product satisfies are identity and social affiliation, the implications for differentiation are far reaching. In particular, to identify profitable differentiation opportunities requires that we analyze not only the product and its characteristics but also customers, their lifestyles and aspirations, and the relationship of the product to those lifestyles and aspirations. Market research that focuses upon traditional demographic and socioeconomic factors may be less useful than a deep understanding of consumers' relationships with a product. As consumers

FIGURE 7.11 Consumer perceptions of competing pain relievers: A multidimensional scaling mapping

become increasingly sensitive to the activities of companies that supply their goods and services, so companies are drawn toward corporate social responsibility as a means of protecting and augmenting the value of their brands.[52]

Figure 7.12 summarizes the key points of this discussion by posing some basic questions that explore the potential for demand-side differentiation.

Analyzing Differentiation: The Supply Side

Demand analysis identifies customers' demands for differentiation and their willingness to pay for it, but creating differentiation advantage also depends on a firm's ability to offer differentiation. This in turn depends upon the activities that the firm performs and the resources it has access to.

The Drivers of Uniqueness   Differentiation is concerned with the provision of uniqueness. A firm's opportunities for creating uniqueness in its offerings to customers are not located within a particular function or activity but can arise in virtually everything that it does. Michael Porter identifies several sources of uniqueness:

- product features and product performance;
- complementary services (such as credit, delivery, repair);
- intensity of marketing activities (such as rate of advertising spending);
- technology embodied in design and manufacture;
- quality of purchased inputs;
- procedures that influence the customer experience (such as the rigor of quality control, service procedures, frequency of sales visits);

FIGURE 7.12   Identifying differentiation potential: The demand side

- skill and experience of employees;
- location (such as with retail stores);
- degree of vertical integration (which influences a firm's ability to control inputs and intermediate processes).[53]

Differentiation can also occur through *bundling*—offering a combination of complementary products and services.[54] Such bundling counteracts the normal tendency toward unbundling as markets mature: products become commoditized while complementary services become provided by specialist suppliers. Electronic commerce reinforces the process, enabling customers to assemble their own bundles of goods and services with few **transaction costs**. The business of European tour operators has shrunk as vacationers use online travel and reservations systems to create their own customized vacations.

Rebundling of products and services has become especially important in business-to-business transactions through "providing customer solutions"—combinations of goods and services that are tailored to the needs of each client. This involves a radical rethink of the business models in most companies.[55]

Product Integrity   Differentiation decisions cannot be made on a piecemeal basis. Establishing a coherent and effective differentiation position requires the firm to assemble a complementary package of differentiation attributes. If Burberry, the British fashion house, wants to expand its range of clothing and accessories, it needs to ensure that every new product offering is consistent with its overall image as a quality-focused brand that combines traditional British style with contemporary edginess. *Product integrity* refers to the consistency of a firm's differentiation; it is the extent to which a product achieves:

total balance of numerous product characteristics, including basic functions, esthetics, semantics, reliability, and economy . . . Product integrity has both internal and external dimensions. Internal integrity refers to consistency between the function and structure of the product—e.g., the parts fit well, components match and work well together, layout achieves maximum space efficiency. External integrity is a measure of how well a product's function, structure, and semantics fit the customer's objectives, values, production system, lifestyle, use pattern, and self-identity.[56]

Simultaneously achieving internal and external integrity is a complex organizational challenge: it requires a combination of close cross-functional collaboration and intimate customer contact.[57] This integration of internal and external product integrity is especially important to those supplying "lifestyle" products, where differentiation is based on customers' social and psychological needs. Here, the credibility of the image depends critically on the consistency of the image presented. One element of this integration is a linked identity between customer and company employees. For instance:

- Harley-Davidson's image of ruggedness, independence, individuality, and community is supported by a top management team that dons biking leathers and participates in owners' group rides, and a management system that empowers shop-floor workers and fosters quality, initiative, and responsibility.
- The revival of Starbucks' fortunes after the return of Howard Schultz as CEO in 2008 was the result of a reinvigoration of the "Starbucks Experience" through reconnecting with customers, reemphasizing the mystique of good coffee, and renewing Starbucks' commitment to social and environmental responsibility.

Signaling and Reputation   Differentiation is only effective if it is communicated to customers. But information about the qualities and characteristics of products is not always readily available to potential customers. The economics literature distinguishes between *search goods*, whose qualities and characteristics can be ascertained by inspection, and *experience goods*, whose qualities and characteristics are only recognized after consumption. This latter class of goods includes medical services, baldness treatments, frozen TV dinners, and wine. Even after purchase, performance attributes may be slow in revealing themselves. Bernie Madoff established Bernard L. Madoff Investment Securities LLC in 1960—it took 48 years before the renowned investment house was revealed as a "giant Ponzi scheme."[58]

In the terminology of game theory (see Chapter 4), the market for experience goods corresponds to a classic prisoners' dilemma. A firm can offer a high-quality or a low-quality product. The customer can pay either a high or a low price. If quality cannot be detected, then equilibrium is established, with the customer offering a low price and the supplier offering a low-quality product, even though both would be better off with a high-quality product sold at a high price. The resolution of this dilemma is for producers to find some credible means of signaling quality to the customer. The most effective signals are those that change the payoffs in the prisoners' dilemma. Thus, an extended warranty is effective because providing such a warranty would be more expensive for a low-quality producer than a high-quality producer. Brand names, warranties, expensive packaging, money-back guarantees, sponsorship of sports and cultural events, and a carefully designed retail environment in which the product is sold are all signals of quality. Their effectiveness stems from the fact that they represent significant investments by the manufacturer that will be devalued if the product proves unsatisfactory to customers.

The more difficult it is to ascertain performance prior to purchase, the more important signaling is.

- A perfume can be sampled prior to purchase and its fragrance assessed, but its ability to augment the identity of the wearer and attract attention remains uncertain. Hence, the key role of branding, packaging, advertising, and lavish promotional events in establishing the perfume's identity and performance credentials.

- In financial services, the customer cannot easily assess the honesty, financial security, or competence of the supplier. Hence, financial service companies emphasize symbols of security and stability: imposing head offices, conservative office decor, smartly dressed employees, and trademarks such as Prudential's rock and Travelers' red umbrella. Bernie Madoff's multibillion investment swindle was sustained by his close association with leading figures among New York's Jewish community, his prominent role in cultural and charitable organizations, and the aura of exclusivity around his investment firm.

Brands Brands fulfill multiple roles. At its most basic level, a brand provides a guarantee of the quality of a product simply by identifying the producer of a product, thereby ensuring the producer is legally accountable for the products supplied. Further, the brand represents an investment that provides an incentive to maintain quality and customer satisfaction. It is a credible signal of quality because of the disincentive of its owner to devalue it. As a result, a brand acts as a guarantee to the customer that reduces uncertainty and search costs. The more difficult it is to discern quality on inspection, and the greater the cost to the customer of purchasing a defective product, the greater the value of a brand: a trusted brand name is more important to us when we purchase mountaineering equipment than when we buy a pair of socks.

This role of the brand as a guarantor of reliability is particularly significant in e-commerce. Internet transactions are characterized by the anonymity of buyers and sellers and lack of government regulation. As a result, well-established players in e-commerce—Amazon, Microsoft, eBay, and Yahoo!—can use their brand to reduce consumers' perceived risk.

By contrast, the value conferred by consumer brands such as Red Bull, Harley-Davidson, Mercedes-Benz, Gucci, Virgin, and American Express is less a guarantee of reliability and more an embodiment of identity and lifestyle. Traditionally, advertising has been the primary means of influencing and reinforcing customer perceptions. Increasingly, however, consumer goods companies are seeking new approaches to brand development that focus less on product characteristics and more on "brand experience," "tribal identity," "shared values," and "emotional dialogue." Traditional mass-market advertising is less effective for promoting this type of brand identity as word-of-mouth promotion deploying web-based social networks—what has been referred to as *viral marketing* or *stealth marketing*.[59]

The Costs of Differentiation   Differentiation adds cost: higher-quality inputs, better-trained employees, higher advertising costs, and better after-sales service. If differentiation narrows a firm's market scope, it also limits the potential for exploiting scale economies.

One means of reconciling differentiation with cost efficiency is to postpone differentiation to later stages of the firm's value chain. Modular design with common components permits scale economies while permitting product variety. All the major automakers have standardized platforms, engine types, and components while offering customers multiple models and a wide variety of colors, trim, and accessory options.

Bringing It All Together: The Value Chain in Differentiation Analysis

There is little point in identifying the product attributes that customers value most if the firm is incapable of supplying those attributes. Similarly, there is little purpose in identifying a firm's ability to supply certain elements of uniqueness if these are not valued by customers. The key to successful differentiation is matching the firm's capacity for creating differentiation to the attributes that customers value most. For this purpose, the value chain provides a particularly useful framework. Let's begin with the case of a producer good i.e., one that is supplied by one firm to another.

Value Chain Analysis of Producer Goods   Using the value chain to identify opportunities for differentiation advantage involves three principal stages:

1 Construct a value chain for the firm and its customer. It may be useful to consider not just the immediate customer but also firms further downstream in the value chain. If the firm supplies different types of customers, it's useful to draw separate value chains for each major category of customer.

2 Identify the drivers of uniqueness in each activity of the firm's value chain. Figure 7.13 identifies some possible sources of differentiation within Porter's generic value chain.

3 Locate linkages between the value chain of the firm and that of the buyer. What can the firm do with its own value chain activities that can reduce the cost or enhance the differentiation potential of the customer's value chain activities? The amount of additional value that the firm creates for its customers through exploiting these linkages represents the potential price premium the firm can charge for its differentiation. Strategy Capsule 7.8 demonstrates the identification of differentiation opportunities by lining the value chains of a firm and its customers.

Value Chain Analysis of Consumer Goods   Value chain analysis of differentiation opportunities can also be applied to consumer goods. Few consumer goods

FIGURE 7.13   Using the value chain to identify differentiation potential on the supply side

are consumed directly: typically, consumers engage in a chain of activities that involve search, acquisition, and use of the product. In the case of consumer durables, the value chain may include search, purchase, financing, acquisition of complementary products and services, operation, service and repair, and eventual disposal. Such complex consumer value chains offer many potential linkages with the manufacturer's value chain, with rich opportunities for innovative differentiation. Harley-Davidson has built its strategy around the notion that it is not supplying motorcycles; it is supplying a customer experience. This has encouraged it to expand the scope of its contact with its customers to provide a wider range of services than any other motorcycle company. Even nondurables involve the consumer in a chain of activities. Consider a frozen TV dinner: it must be purchased, taken home, removed from the package, heated, and served before it is consumed. After eating, the consumer must clean any used dishes, cutlery, or other utensils. A value chain analysis by a frozen foods producer would identify ways in which the product could be formulated, packaged, and distributed to assist the consumer in performing this chain of activities.

Implementing Cost and Differentiation Strategies

The two primary sources of competitive advantage define two fundamentally different approaches to business strategy. A firm that is competing on low cost is distinguishable from a firm that competes through differentiation in terms of market positioning, resources and capabilities, and organizational characteristics. Table 7.1 outlines some of the principal features of cost and differentiation strategies.

STRATEGY CAPSULE 7.8

Using the Value Chain to Identify Differentiation Opportunities for a Manufacturer of Metal Containers

The metal container industry is a highly competitive, low-growth, low-profit industry. Cans lack much potential for differentiation, and buyers (especially beverage and food canning companies) are very powerful. Cost efficiency is essential, but can we also identify opportunities for profitable differentiation? Following the procedure outlined above, we can construct a value chain for a firm and its customers, and then identify linkages between the two. Figure 7.14 identifies five such linkages:

1   Distinctive can designs (e.g., Sapporo's beer can) can support the customer's efforts to differentiate its product.

2   Manufacturing cans to high tolerances can minimize breakdowns on customers' canning lines.

3   Reliable, punctual can deliveries allow canners to economize on their can inventories.

4   An efficient order-processing system reduces canners' ordering costs.

5   Speedy, proficient technical support allows customers to operate their canning lines with high-capacity utilization.

FIGURE 7.14   Identifying differentiation opportunities by linking the firm's value chain to that of the customer

Porter views cost leadership and differentiation as mutually exclusive strategies. A firm that attempts to pursue both is "stuck in the middle":

> The firm stuck in the middle is almost guaranteed low profitability. It either loses the high-volume customers who demand low prices or must bid away its profits to get this business from the low-cost firms. Yet it also loses high-margin business—the cream—to the firms who are focused on high-margin targets or have achieved differentiation overall. The firm that is stuck in the middle also probably suffers from a blurred corporate culture and a conflicting set of organizational arrangements and motivation system.[60]

TABLE 7.1   Features of cost leadership and differentiation strategies

Generic strategy	Key strategy elements	Organizational requirements
Cost leadership	Scale-efficient plants	Access to capital
	Maximizing labor productivity	Division of labor with incentives linked to quantitative performance targets
	Design for manufacture	Product design coordinated with manufacture
	Control of overheads	
	Process innovation	Tight cost controls
	Outsourcing	Process engineering skills
	Avoid marginal customering accounts	Benchmarking
		Measuring profit per customer
Differentiation	Emphasis on branding, advertising, design, customer service, quality, and new product development	Marketing abilities
		Product engineering skills
		Cross-functional coordination
		Creativity
		Research capability
		Incentives linked to qualitative performance targets

In practice, few firms are faced with such stark alternatives. Differentiation is not simply an issue of "to differentiate or not to differentiate." All firms must make decisions as to which customer requirements to focus on and where to position their product or service in the market. A cost leadership strategy typically implies limited-feature, standardized offerings, but this does not necessarily imply that the product or service is an undifferentiated commodity. Southwest Airlines and AirAsia are budget airlines with a no-frills offering yet have clear market positions with unique brand images. The VW Beetle shows that a utilitarian, mass-market product can achieve cult status.

In most industries, market leadership is held by a firm that maximizes customer appeal by reconciling effective differentiation with low cost—Toyota in cars, McDonald's in fast food, Nike in athletic shoes. The simultaneous pursuit of cost efficiency, quality, innovation, and brand building was a feature of Japanese suppliers of cars, motorcycles, consumer electronics, and musical instruments during the late 20th century. In many industries, the cost leader is not the market leader but a smaller competitor with minimal overheads, non-union labor and cheaply acquired assets. In oil refining, the cost leaders tend to be independent refining companies rather than integrated giants such as ExxonMobil or Shell. In car rental, the cost leader is more likely to be Rent-A-Wreck (a subsidiary of J. J. F. Management, Inc.) rather than Hertz or Avis. Reconciling cost efficiency with differentiation has been facilitated by new management techniques: total quality management has repudiated perceived tradeoff between quality and cost; flexible manufacturing systems have reconciled scale economies with variety.

Summary

Making money in business requires establishing and sustaining competitive advantage. Identifying opportunities for competitive advantage requires insight into the nature and process of competition within a market. Our analysis of the imperfections of the competitive process takes us back to the resources and capabilities needed to compete in a particular market and conditions under which these are available. Similarly, the isolating mechanisms that sustain competitive advantage are dependent primarily upon the ability of rivals to access the resources and capabilities needed for imitation.

Competitive advantage has two primary dimensions: cost advantage and differentiation advantage. The first of these, cost advantage, is the outcome of seven primary cost drivers. We showed that by applying these cost drivers and by disaggregating the firm into a value chain of linked activities we can appraise a firm's cost position relative to competitors and identify opportunities for cost reduction. The principal message of this section is the need to look behind cost accounting data and beyond simplistic approaches to cost efficiency, and to analyze the factors that drive relative unit costs in each of the firm's activities in a systematic and comprehensive manner.

The appeal of differentiation is that it offers multiple opportunities for competitive advantage with a greater potential for sustainability than does cost advantage. The vast realm of differentiation opportunity extends beyond marketing and design to encompass all aspects of a firm's interactions with its customers. Achieving a differentiation advantage requires the firm match its own capacity for creating uniqueness to the requirements and preferences of customers. The value chain offers firms a useful framework for identifying how they can create value for their customers by combining demand-side and supply-side sources of differentiation.

Finally, the basis of a firm's competitive advantage has important implications not just for the design of its strategy but for the design of its organizational structure and systems. Typically, companies that are focused on cost leadership design their organizations differently from those that pursue differentiation. However, the implications of competitive strategy for organizational design are complicated by the fact that, for most firms, cost efficiency and differentiation are not mutually exclusive—in today's intensely competitive markets, firms have little choice but to pursue both.

Self-Study Questions

1. Figure 7.1 implies that stable industries, where firms have similar resources and capabilities, offer less opportunity for competitive advantage than industries where change is rapid and firms are heterogeneous. On the basis of these considerations, among the following industries, in which do you predict that inter-firm differences in profitability will

be small and in which will they be wide: retail banking, video games, wireless handsets, insurance, supermarkets, and semiconductors?

2. Since 2009, Apple has been the world's most profitable supplier of wireless handsets by a large margin. Can Apple sustain its competitive advantage in this market?

3. Illy, the Italian-based supplier of quality coffee and coffee-making equipment, is launching an international chain of gourmet coffee shops. What advice would you offer Illy for how it can best build competitive advantage in the face of Starbucks' market leadership?

4. Which drivers of cost advantage (Figure 7.7) did Sears exploit in order to offer its Sears Motor Buggy "at a price within the reach of all"? (See quotation that opens this chapter.)

5. Target (the US discount retailer), H&M (the Swedish fashion clothing chain), and Primark (the UK discount clothing chain) have pioneered *cheap chic*—combining discount store prices with fashion appeal. What are the principal challenges of designing and implementing a cheap chic strategy? Design a cheap chic strategy for a company entering another market e.g., restaurants, sports shoes, cosmetics, or office furniture.

6. To what extent are the seven cost drivers shown in Figure 7.7 relevant in analyzing the costs per student at your business school or educational institution? What recommendations would you make to your dean for improving the cost efficiency of your school?

7. Bottled water sells at least 200 times the price of tap water, with substantial price differentials between different brands. What are the key differentiation variables that determine the price premium that can be obtained for bottled water?

8. Advise a chain of movie theaters on a differentiation strategy to restore its flagging profitability. Use the value chain framework outlined in Strategy Capsule 7.8 to identify potential linkages between the company's value chain and that of its customers in order to identify differentiation opportunities.

Notes

1. Richard Rumelt argues that competitive advantage lacks a clear and consistent definition ("What in the World is Competitive Advantage?" Policy Working Paper 2003-105, Anderson School, UCLA, August, 2003).

2. K. Ferdows, M. A. Lewis, and J. Machuca, "Rapid-Fire Fulfillment," *Harvard Business Review* (November 2004): 104–110.

3. G. Stalk Jr., "Time: The Next Source of Competitive Advantage," *Harvard Business Review* (July/August, 1988): 41–51.

4. See, for example: Y. Doz and M. Kosonen, "Embedding Strategic Agility: A Leadership Agenda for Accelerating Business Model Renewal," *Long Range Planning*, 43 (April

2010): 370–382; and S. Fourné, J. Jansen, and T. Mom, "Strategic Agility in MNEs: Managing Tensions to Capture Opportunities across Emerging and Established Markets," *California Management Review*, 56 (Spring 2014)

5. J. A. Schumpeter, *Capitalism, Socialism and Democracy* (London: Routledge, 1994, first published 1942): 82–83.

6. C. Kim and R. Mauborgne, "Blue Ocean Strategy," *Harvard Business Review* (October 2004). A similar approach to analyzing strategic innovation is McKinsey's new game strategies. See: R. Buaron, "New Game Strategies," *McKinsey Quarterly Anthology* (2000): 34–36.

7. G. Hamel, "The Why, What, and How of Management Innovation," *Harvard Business Review* (February 2006).

8. R. P. Rumelt, "Toward a Strategic Theory of the Firm," in R. Lamb (ed.), *Competitive Strategic Management* (Englewood Cliffs, NJ: Prentice Hall, 1984): 556–570.

9. R. Jacobsen, "The Persistence of Abnormal Returns,"*Strategic Management Journal* 9 (1988): 415–430; R. R. Wiggins and T. W. Ruefli, "Schumpeter's Ghost: Is Hypercompetition Making the Best of Times Shorter?" *Strategic Management Journal* 26 (2005): 887–911.

10. G. Stalk, "Curveball: Strategies to Fool the Competition," *Harvard Business Review* (September 2006): 114–122.

11. The film was based on the book by B. Traven, *The Treasure of the Sierra Madre* (New York: Knopf, 1947).

12. Monopolies and Mergers Commission, *Cat and Dog Foods* (London: Her Majesty's Stationery Office, 1977).

13. D. Besanko, D. Dranove, S. Schaefer, and M. Shanley, *Economics of Strategy*, 6th edn. (Hoboken, NJ: John Wiley & Sons, Inc., 2013): section on "Limit Pricing," pp. 207–211.

14. T. C. Schelling, *The Strategy of Conflict*, 2nd edn (Cambridge, MA: Harvard University Press, 1980): 35–41.

15. A. Brandenburger and B. Nalebuff, *Co-opetition* (New York: Doubleday, 1996): 72–80.

16. R. Schmalensee, "Entry Deterrence in the Ready-to-Eat Breakfast Cereal Industry," *Bell Journal of Economics* 9 (1978): 305–327.

17. Monopolies and Mergers Commission, *Indirect Electrostatic Reprographic Equipment* (London: Her Majesty's Stationery Office, 1976): 37, 56.

18. S. A. Lippman and R. P. Rumelt, "Uncertain Imitability: An Analysis of Interfirm Differences in Efficiency under Competition,"*Bell Journal of Economics* 13 (1982): 418–438. See also: R. Reed and R. DeFillippi, "Causal Ambiguity, Barriers to Imitation, and Sustainable Competitive Advantage," *Academy of Management Review* 15 (1990): 88–102.

19. P. R. Milgrom and J. Roberts, "Complementarities and Fit: Strategy, Structure and Organizational Change in Manufacturing," *Journal of Accounting and Economics* 19 (1995): 179–208.

20. J. W. Rivkin, "Imitation of Complex Strategies," *Management Science* 46 (2000): 824–844.

21. M. E. Porter and N. Siggelkow, "Contextuality within Activity Systems and Sustainable Competitive Advantage,"*Academy of Management Perspectives* 22 (May 2008): 34–56.

22. M. E. Porter, *Competitive Advantage* (New York: Free Press, 1985): 13.

23. Ibid.,: 120.

24. M. Venzin, *Building an International Financial Services Firm: How Successful Firms Design and Execute Cross-border Strategies* (Oxford: Oxford University Press, 2009).

25. R. P. McAfee and J. McMillan, "Organizational Diseconomies of Scale," *Journal of Economics and Management Strategy* 4 (1996): 399–426.

26. L. Rapping, "Learning and World War II Production Functions," *Review of Economics and Statistics* (February 1965): 81–86.

27. L. Argote, S. L. Beckman, and D. Epple, "The Persistence and Transfer of Learning in Industrial Settings,"*Management Science* 36 (1990): 140–154; M. Zollo and S. G. Winter, "Deliberate Learning and the Evolution of Dynamic Capabilities," *Organization Science* 13 (2002): 339–351.

28. J. Womack and D. T. Jones, "From Lean Production to Lean Enterprise," *Harvard Business Review* (March/April 1994); J. Womack and D. T. Jones, "Beyond Toyota: How to Root Out Waste and Pursue Perfection," *Harvard Business Review* (September/ October, 1996).

29. M. Hammer and J. Champy, *Re-engineering the Corporation: A Manifesto for Business Revolution* (New York: HarperBusiness, 1993): 32.

30. V. Glover and M. L. Marcus, "Business Process Transformation," *Advances in Management Information Systems* 9 (M. E. Sharpe, March 2008); R. Merrifield, J. Calhoun, and D. Stevens, "The Next Revolution in Productivity," *Harvard Business Review* (November 2006): 72–79.

31 F. X. Frei, "Breaking the Tradeoff between Efficiency and Service," *Harvard Business Review* (November 2006): 92–103.

32. "Caterpillar to Cut 20,000 Jobs as Downturn Worsens," *Wall Street Journal* (January 28, 2009).

33. Bureau of Labor Statistics, http://www.bls.gov/iag/tgs/iagauto.htm, accessed July 20, 2015.

34. "Buying Power of Multiproduct Retailers," *OECD Journal of Competition Law and Policy* 2 (March, 2000).

35. P. Krugman, "Amazon's Monopsony Is Not O.K.," *New York Times* (October 19, 2014).

36. R. Cyert and J. March, *A Behavioral Theory of the Firm* (Englewood Cliffs, NJ: Prentice Hall, 1963).

37. H. Leibenstein, "Allocative Efficiency versus X-Efficiency," *American Economic Review* 54 (June 1966): 392–415.

38. "Fighting the Flab," *Economist* (March 22, 2014).

39. K. Kase, F. J. Saez, and H. Riquelme, *The New Samurais of Japanese Industry* (Cheltenham: Edward Elgar, 2006).

40. M. E. Porter, *Competitive Advantage* (New York: Free Press, 1985): 87; and R. S. Kaplan and S. R. Anderson, "Time-Driven Activity-based Costing," *Harvard Business Review* (November 2004): 131–138.

41. M. E. Porter, *Competitive Advantage* (New York: Free Press, 1985): 120.

42. T. Peters, *Thriving on Chaos* (New York: Knopf, 1987): 56.

43. "Cemex: Cementing a Global Strategy," Insead Case No. 307-233-1 (2007).

44. The distinction between segmentation and differentiation is discussed in P. R. Dickson and J. L. Ginter, "Market Segmentation, Product Differentiation and Marketing Strategy," *Journal of Marketing* 51 (April 1987): 1–10.

45. S. Schiffman, M. Reynolds, and F. Young, *Introduction to Multidimensional Scaling: Theory, Methods, and Applications* (Cambridge, MA: Academic Press, 1981).

46. F.-J. Lapointe and P. Legendre, "A Classification of Pure Malt Scotch Whiskies," *Applied Statistics* 43 (1994): 237–257. On the principles of MDS, see I. Borg and

P. Groenen, *Modern Multidimensional Scaling: Theory and Application* (New York: Springer-Verlag, 1997).

47. P. Cattin and D. R. Wittink, "Commercial Use of Conjoint Analysis: A Survey," *Journal of Marketing* 46 (Summer 1982): 44–53.

48. K. Lancaster, *Consumer Demand: A New Approach* (New York: Columbia University Press, 1971).

49. P. Nicolaides and C. Baden-Fuller, *Price Discrimination and Product Differentiation in the European Domestic Appliance Market* (London: Center for Business Strategy, London Business School, 1987).

50. A. Maslow, "A Theory of Human Motivation," *Psychological Review* 50 (1943): 370–396.

51. "Coke Lore: The Real Story of New Coke," www.thecocacolacompany.com/heritage/cokelore_newcoke.html, accessed July 20, 2015.

52. S. Zadek, "The Path to Corporate Responsibility," *Harvard Business Review*, 82 (December, 2004): 125–129.

53. Porter, *Competitive Advantage*, op. cit.,124–125.

54. S. Mathur, "Competitive Industrial Marketing Strategies," *Long Range Planning* 17 (1984): 102–109.

55. K. R. Tuli, A. K. Kohli, and S. G. Bharadwaj, "Rethinking Customer Solutions: From Product Bundles to Relational Processes," *Journal of Marketing* 71, (2007): 1–17.

56. K. Clark and T. Fujimoto, *Product Development Performance* (Boston: Harvard Business School Press, 1991): 29–30.

57. K. B. Clark and T. Fujimoto, "The Power of Product Integrity," *Harvard Business Review* (November/December, 1990): 107–118.

58. "The Madoff Affair: Going Down Quietly," *Economist* (March 14, 2009).

59. D. J. Watts and J. Peretti, "Viral Marketing for the Real World," *Harvard Business Review* (May 2007): 22–23.

60. M. E. Porter, *Competitive Strategy* (New York: Free Press, 1980): 42.

8 Industry Evolution and Strategic Change

No company ever stops changing . . . Each new generation must meet changes—in the automotive market, in the general administration of the enterprise, and in the involvement of the corporation in a changing world. The work of creating goes on.

—ALFRED P. SLOAN JR., PRESIDENT OF GENERAL
MOTORS 1923–37, CHAIRMAN 1937–56

It is not the strongest of the species that survive, nor the most intelligent, but the one that is most responsive to change.

—CHARLES DARWIN

You keep same-ing when you ought to be changing.

—LEE HAZLEWOOD, THESE BOOTS ARE MADE FOR WALKING,
RECORDED BY NANCY SINATRA, 1966

OUTLINE

Introduction and Objectives

Everything is in a state of constant change—the business environment especially. One of the greatest challenges of strategic management is to ensure that the firm keeps pace with changes occurring within its environment.

Change in the industry environment is driven by the forces of technology, consumer needs, politics, economic development, and a host of other influences. In some industries, these forces for change combine to create massive, unpredictable changes. In telecommunications new digital and wireless technologies combined with regulatory changes have resulted in an industry which in 2015 is almost unrecognizable from that which existed 25 years ago. In other industries—food processing, railroads, and car rental—change is more gradual and more predictable. Change is not just the result of external forces: the competitive strategies of firms are key drivers of change—industries are being continually recreated by competition.

The purpose of this chapter is to help us to understand and manage change. To do this we shall explore the forces that drive change and look for patterns that can help us to predict how industries are likely to evolve over time. While each industry follows a unique development path, there are common drivers of change that give rise to similar patterns of change, thereby allowing us to identify opportunities for competitive advantage.

Understanding, even predicting, change in an industry's environment is difficult. But an even greater challenge is adapting to change. For individuals change is disruptive, costly, and uncomfortable. For organizations the forces of inertia are even stronger. As a result, the life cycles of firms tend to be much shorter than the life cycles of industries: changes at the industry level tend to occur through the death of existing firms and the birth of new firms rather than through continuous adaptation by a constant population of firms. We need to understand these sources of inertia in organizations in order to overcome them. We also need to look beyond adaptation to see the potential for a firm to initiate change. What determines the ability of some firms to become game-changers in their industries?

Whether adapting to or initiating change, competing in a changing world requires the development of new capabilities. How difficult can this be? The short answer is "Very." We will look not just at the challenges of building new capabilities but also at the approaches that organizations can take to overcome these difficulties.

By the time you have completed this chapter, you will be able to:

◆ Recognize the different stages of industry development and understand the factors that drive the process of industry evolution.

◆ Identify the key success factors associated with industries at different stages of their development and recommend strategies, organizational structures, and management systems appropriate to these stages.

◆ Appreciate the sources of organizational inertia, the challenges of managing strategic change, and be familiar with different approaches to strategic change—including the use of scenario analysis and the quest for ambidexterity.

♦ Become familiar with the different approaches that firms have taken in developing organizational capabilities—and the merits and pitfalls of each.

♦ Recognize the principal tools of knowledge management and the roles they can play in developing organizational capability.

The Industry Life Cycle

One of the best-known and most enduring marketing concepts is the *product life cycle*.[1] Products are born, their sales grow, they reach maturity, they go into decline, and they ultimately die. If products have life cycles, so the industries that produce them experience an **industry life cycle**. To the extent that an industry produces multiple generations of a product, the industry life cycle is likely to be of longer duration than that of a single product.

The life cycle comprises four phases: *introduction* (or *emergence*), *growth*, *maturity*, and *decline* (Figure 8.1). Let us first examine the forces that drive industry evolution, and then look at the features of each of these stages. Two forces are fundamental: demand growth and the production and diffusion of knowledge.

Demand Growth

The life cycle and the stages within it are defined primarily by changes in an industry's growth rate over time. The characteristic profile is an S-shaped growth curve.

● In the *introduction stage*, sales are small and the rate of market penetration is low because the industry's products are little known and customers are few. The novelty of the technology, small scale of production, and lack of experience mean high costs and low quality. Customers for new products tend to be affluent, innovation-oriented, and risk-tolerant.

FIGURE 8.1   The industry life cycle

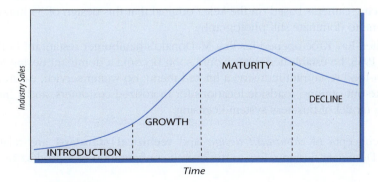

- The *growth stage* is characterized by accelerating market penetration as technical improvements and increased efficiency open up the mass market.
- Increasing market saturation causes the onset of the *maturity stage*. Once saturation is reached, demand is wholly for replacement.
- Finally, as the industry becomes challenged by new industries that produce technologically superior substitute products, the industry enters its *decline stage*.

Creation and Diffusion of Knowledge

The second driver of the industry life cycle is knowledge. New knowledge in the form of product innovation is responsible for an industry's birth, and the dual processes of knowledge creation and knowledge diffusion exert a major influence on industry evolution.

In the introduction stage, product technology advances rapidly. There is no dominant product technology, and rival technologies compete for attention. Competition is primarily between alternative technologies and design configurations:

- The first 30 years of steam ships featured competition between paddles and propellers, wooden hulls and iron hulls, and, eventually, between coal and oil.
- The beginnings of the home computer industry during 1978–1982 saw competition between different data storage systems (audiotapes versus floppy disks), visual displays (TV receivers versus dedicated monitors), operating systems (CPM versus DOS versus Apple II), and microprocessors.

Dominant Designs and Technical Standards   The outcome of competition between rival designs and technologies is usually convergence by the industry around a **dominant design**—a product architecture that defines the look, functionality, and production method for the product and becomes accepted by the industry as a whole. Dominant designs have included:

- The Underwood Model 5 introduced in 1899 established the basic architecture and main features of typewriters for the 20th century: a moving carriage, the ability to see the characters being typed, a shift function for upper-case characters, and a replaceable inked ribbon.[2]
- Leica's Ur-Leica camera launched in Germany in 1924 established key features of the 35 mm camera, though it was not until Canon began mass-producing cameras based on the Leica original that this design of 35 mm camera came to dominate still photography.
- When Ray Kroc opened his first McDonald's hamburger restaurant in Illinois in 1955, he established what would soon become a dominant design for the fast-food restaurant industry: a limited menu, no waiter service, eat-in and take-out options, roadside locations for motorized customers, and a franchising model of business system licensing.

The concepts of *dominant design* and **technical standard** are related but distinct. Dominant design refers to the overall configuration of a product or system.

A technical standard is a technology or specification that is important for compatibility. While technical standards typically embody intellectual property in the form of patents or copyright, dominant designs usually do not. A dominant design may or may not embody a technical standard. IBM's PC established both a dominant design for personal computers and the "Wintel" standard. Conversely, the Boeing 707 was a dominant design for large passenger jets but did not set industry standards in aerospace technology that would dominate subsequent generations of airplanes. Technical standards emerge where there are **network effects**—the need for users to connect in some way with one another. Network effects cause each customer to choose the same technology as everyone else to avoid being stranded. Unlike a proprietary technical standard, which is typically embodied in patents or copyrights, a firm that sets a dominant design does not normally own intellectual property in that design. Hence, except for some early-mover advantage, there is not necessarily any profit advantage from setting a dominant design.

Dominant designs also exist in processes. In the flat glass industry there has been a succession of dominant process designs from glass cylinder blowing to continuous ribbon drawing to float glass.[3] Dominant designs are present, too, in business models. In many new markets, competition is between rival *business models*. In home grocery delivery, e-commerce start-ups such as Webvan and Peapod soon succumbed to competition from "bricks and clicks" retailers such as Giant, and Walmart (and Tesco in the UK).

From Product to Process Innovation The emergence of a dominant design marks a critical juncture in an industry's evolution. Once the industry coalesces around a leading product design, there's a shift from radical to incremental product innovation. This transition helps inaugurate the industry's growth phase: greater standardization reduces risks to customers and encourages firms to invest in production capacity. The shift in emphasis from design to manufacture triggers process innovation as firms seek to reduce costs and increase product reliability through large-scale production methods (Figure 8.2). The combination of process improvements, design modifications, and scale economies results in falling costs and greater availability, which in turn drive rapidly increasing market penetration.

FIGURE 8.2 Product and process innovation over time

Strategy Capsule 8.1 uses the history of the automobile industry to illustrate these patterns of development.

Knowledge diffusion is also important on the customer side. Over the course of the life cycle, customers become increasingly informed. As they become more knowledgeable about the performance attributes of rival manufacturers' products, so they are better able to judge value for money and become more price sensitive.

STRATEGY CAPSULE 8.1
Evolution of the Automobile Industry

The period 1890–1912 was one of rapid product innovation in the auto industry. After 1886, when Karl Benz received a patent on his three-wheel motor carriage, a flurry of technical advances occurred in Germany, France, the US, and the UK. Developments included:

♦ the first four-cylinder four-stroke engine (by Karl Benz in 1890);

♦ the honeycomb radiator (by Daimler in 1890);

♦ the manual gearbox (Panhard and Levassor in 1895);

♦ automatic transmission (by Packard in 1904);

♦ electric headlamps (by General Motors in 1908);

♦ the all-steel body (adopted by General Motors in 1912).

Ford's Model T, introduced in 1908, with its front-mounted, water-cooled engine and transmission with a gearbox, wet clutch, and rear-wheel drive, acted as a dominant design for the industry. During the remainder of the 20th century, automotive technology and design converged. A key indicator of this was the gradual elimination of alternative technologies and designs. Volkswagen's Beetle was the last mass-produced car with a rear-mounted, air-cooled engine. Citroen abandoned its distinctive suspension and braking systems. Four-stroke engines with four or six inline cylinders became dominant. Distinctive national differences eroded as American cars became smaller and Japanese and Italian cars became bigger. The fall of the Iron Curtain extinguished the last outposts of nonconformity: by the mid-1990s, East German two-stroke Wartburgs and Trabants were collectors' items.

As product innovation slowed, so process innovation took off. In October 1913, Ford opened its Highland Park Assembly Plant, with its revolutionary production methods based on interchangeable parts and a moving assembly line. Radical productivity improvement resulted in the price of the Model T falling from $628 in 1908 to $260 in 1924. By 1927, 15 million Model T's had been produced.

The second major process innovation in automobiles was Toyota's system of *lean production*, involving a tightly integrated "pull" system of production embodying just-in-time scheduling, team-based production, flexible manufacturing, and total quality management. During the 1970s and 1980s, lean production diffused throughout the world's vehicle industry in the same way that Ford's mass-production system had transformed the industry half a century before.

However, by 2015 this period of technological stability was threatened by two developments: electric cars and driverless cars.

Sources: www.ford.com; http://en.wikipedia.org/wiki/History_of_the_automobile.

How General Is the Life-Cycle Pattern?

To what extent do industries conform to this life-cycle pattern? To begin with, the duration of the life cycle varies greatly from industry to industry:

- The hotel industry has its origins over two millennia ago. In year 1 AD, the baby Jesus was born in a stable in Bethlehem because, according to Luke's Gospel, "there was no room at the inn." In the US, hotels (as distinct from inns) were established in the late 18th century. After World War II, the industry grew rapidly with expanding tourism and business travel. However, during the 21st century the industry began making the transition from maturity to decline with the growth of videoconferencing and advent of residential sharing services such as Airbnb.

- The introduction phase of the US railroad industry extended from the building of the first railroad, the Baltimore and Ohio in 1827, to the growth phase of the 1870s. With the growth of road transport, the industry entered its decline phase during the late 1950s.

- In personal computers, the introduction phase lasted a mere four years before growth took off in 1978. Between 1978 and 1983, a flood of new and established firms entered the industry. During the 1990s, growth slowed, excess capacity emerged, and the industry began to consolidate around fewer companies. In 2011, global sales of PCs peaked and the industry entered its decline phase.

- Digital audio players (MP3 players) were first introduced by Seehan Information Systems and Diamond Multimedia in 1997. With the launch of Apple's iPod in 2001, the industry entered its growth phase. After reaching a peak in 2009, global sales of MP3 players, including the iPod, went into steep decline. By 2015, dedicated MP3 players were widely viewed as obsolete.

Over time, industry life cycles have become increasingly compressed. This is especially evident in e-commerce. The speed of diffusion of online gambling, online taxi services, and social networking have reduced the time from initial introduction to maturity to a few years. The implication is that "competing on internet time" requires a radical rethink of strategies and management processes.[4]

Patterns of evolution also differ. Industries supplying basic necessities such as residential construction, food processing and clothing may never enter a decline phase because obsolescence is unlikely for such needs. Some industries may experience a rejuvenation of their life cycle. The market for TV receivers has experienced multiple revivals: color TVs, portable TVs, flat-screen TVs, and HDTVs. Similar waves of innovation have revitalized retailing (Figure 8.3).

An industry is likely to be at different stages of its life cycle in different countries. Although the automobile markets of the EU, Japan, and the US are in their decline phase, those of Asia and Latin America are in their growth phase. Multinational companies can exploit such differences: developing new products and introducing them into the advanced industrial countries, then shifting attention to other growth markets once maturity sets in.

A further feature of industry evolution is shifting industry boundaries—some industries converge (cell phones, portable game players, cameras, and calculators);

FIGURE 8.3 Innovation and renewal in the industry life cycle: Retailing

other industries, (banking, medical services) fragment. To understand the dynamics of industry change, we may need to look at clusters of related industries.[5]

Implications of the Life Cycle for Competition and Strategy

Changes in demand growth and technology over the cycle have implications for industry structure, the population of firms, and competition. Table 8.1 summarizes the principal features of each stage of the industry life cycle.

Product Differentiation The introduction stage typically features a wide variety of product types that reflect the diversity of technologies and designs—and the lack of consensus over customer requirements. Convergence around a dominant design is often followed by commoditization during the mature phase unless producers develop new dimensions for differentiation. Personal computers, credit cards, online financial services, wireless communication services, and internet access have all become commodity items which buyers select primarily on price. However, the trend toward commoditization also creates incentives for firms to create novel approaches to differentiation.

Organizational Demographics and Industry Structure The number of firms in an industry changes substantially over the life cycle. The field of **organizational ecology**, founded by Michael Hannan, John Freeman, and Glen Carroll, analyzes the population of industries and the processes of founding and selection that determine entry and exit.[6] Some of the main findings of the organizational ecologists in relation to industry evolution are:

- The number of firms in an industry increases rapidly during the early stages of an industry's life. Initially, an industry may be pioneered by a few firms. However, as the industry gains legitimacy, failure rates decline and the rate of new firm foundings increases. The US automobile industry comprised 272 manufacturers in 1909,[7] while in TV receivers there were 92 companies in

TABLE 8.1   The evolution of industry structure and competition over the life cycle

	Introduction	Growth	Maturity	Decline
Demand	Limited to early adopters: high-income, avant-garde	Rapidly increasing market penetration	Mass market, replacement/repeat buying. Customers knowledgeable and price sensitive	Obsolescence
Technology	Competing technologies, rapid product innovation	Standardization around dominant technology, rapid process innovation	Well-diffused technical know-how: quest for technological improvements.	Little product or process innovation
Products	Poor quality, wide variety of features and technologies, frequent design changes	Design and quality improve, emergence of dominant design	Trend to commoditization. Attempts to differentiate by branding, quality, and bundling	Commodities the norm: differentiation difficult and unprofitable
Manufacturing and distribution	Short production runs, high-skilled labor content, specialized distribution channels	Capacity shortages, mass production, competition for distribution	Emergence of overcapacity, deskilling of production, long production runs, distributors carry fewer lines	Chronic overcapacity, reemergence of specialty channels
Trade	Producers and consumers in advanced countries	Exports from advanced countries to rest of world	Production shifts to newly industrializing then developing countries	Exports from countries with lowest labor costs
Competition	Few companies	Entry, mergers, and exits	Shakeout, price competition increases	Price wars, exits
Key success factors	Product innovation, establishing credible image of firm and product	Design for manufacture, access to distribution, brand building, fast product development, process innovation	Cost efficiency through capital intensity, scale efficiency, and low input costs	Low overheads, buyer selection, signaling commitment, rationalizing capacity

1951.[8] New entrants have very different origins. Some are start-up companies (*de novo* entrants); others are established firms diversifying from related industries (*de alio* entrants).

- With the onset of maturity, the number of firms begins to fall. Very often, industries go through one or more *shakeout* phases during which the rate of firm failure increases sharply. After this point, rates of entry and exit decline and the survival rate for incumbents increases substantially.[9] The shakeout phase of intensive acquisition, merger, and exit occurs, on average, 29 years into the life cycle and results in the number of producers being halved.[10] In the US tire industry, the number of firms grew from one (Goodrich) in 1896 to 274 in 1922 before shakeout reduced the industry to 49 firms in 1936.[11]

- As industries become increasingly concentrated and the leading firms focus on the mass market, so a new phase of entry may take place as new firms create niche positions in the market. An example of this *resource partitioning* is the US brewing industry: as the mass market became dominated by a handful of national brewers, so opportunities arose for new types of brewing companies—microbreweries and brew pubs—to establish themselves in specialist niches.[12]

However, in different industries structural change follows very different paths. In most industries maturity is associated with increasing concentration, but where scale economies are unimportant and entry barriers are low, maturity and commoditization may cause concentration to decline (as in credit cards, television broadcasting, and processed foods).

Location and International Trade   Industries migrate internationally during their life cycles. New industries begin in the advanced industrial countries because of the presence of affluent consumers and the availability of technical and scientific resources. As demand grows in other countries, they are serviced initially by exports, but a reduced need for sophisticated labor skills makes production attractive in newly industrialized countries. The advanced industrialized countries begin to import. With maturity, commoditization, and deskilling of production processes, production eventually shifts to developing countries where labor costs are lowest.

At the beginning of the 1990s, the production of wireless handsets was concentrated in the US, Japan, Finland, and Germany. By the end of the 1990s, South Korea had joined this leading group. In 2014, almost 75% of the world's mobile phones were produced in China.

The Nature and Intensity of Competition   These changes in industry structure over the life cycle—commoditization, new entry, and international diffusion of production—have implications for competition: first, a shift from non-price competition to price competition; second, margins shrink as the intensity of competition grows.

During the introduction stage, the battle for technological leadership means that price competition may be weak, but heavy investments in innovation and market development depress profitability. The growth phase is more conducive to profitability as market demand outstrips industry capacity, especially if incumbents are protected by barriers to entry. With the onset of maturity, increased product standardization and excess capacity stimulate price competition, especially during shakeout. How intense this is depends a great deal on the balance between capacity and demand and the extent of international competition. In food retailing, airlines, motor vehicles, metals, and insurance, maturity was associated with strong price competition and slender profitability. In household detergents, breakfast cereals, cosmetics, and cigarettes, high seller concentration and strong brands have limited price rivalry and supported high margins. The decline phase is almost always associated with strong price competition (often degenerating into destructive price wars) and dismal profit performance.

Key Success Factors and Industry Evolution   These same changes in structure together with changes in demand and technology over the industry life cycle also have important implications for the sources of competitive advantage at each stage of industry evolution:

FIGURE 8.4 Differences in strategy and performance between businesses at different stages of the industry life cycle

Note: The figure shows standardized means for each variable for businesses at each stage of the life cycle.
Source: C. Anderson and C. Zeithaml, "Stage of the Product Life Cycle, Business Strategy and Business Performance," *Academy of Management Journal* 27 (1984): 5–24.

1 During the introductory stage, product innovation is the basis for initial entry and for subsequent success. Soon, other requirements for success emerge: growing investment requirements necessitate increased financial resources; product development needs to be supported by capabilities in manufacturing, marketing, and distribution.

2 Once the growth stage is reached, the key challenge is scaling up. As the market expands, product design and manufacturing must adapt to the needs of large-scale production. As Figure 8.4 shows, investment in R & D, plant and equipment, and sales tends to be high during the growth phase. Increased manufacturing must be matched by widening distribution.

3 With the maturity stage, competitive advantage is increasingly a quest for efficiency, particularly in industries that tend toward commoditization. Cost efficiency through scale economies, low wages, and low overheads becomes the key success factor. Figure 8.4 shows that R & D, capital investment, and marketing are lower in maturity than during the growth phase.

4 The transition to decline intensifies pressures for cost cutting. It also requires maintaining stability by encouraging the orderly exit of industry capacity and capturing residual market demand. We consider the strategic issues presented by mature and declining industries more fully in Chapter 10.

The Challenge of Organizational Adaptation and Strategic Change

We have established that industries change. But what about the companies within them? Let us turn our attention to business enterprises and consider both the impediments to change and the means by which change takes place.

Why is Change so Difficult? The Sources of Organizational Inertia

At the heart of all approaches to change management is the recognition that organizations find change difficult. Why is this so? Different theories of organizational and industrial change emphasize different barriers to change:

- *Organizational routines*: Evolutionary economists emphasize the fact that capabilities are based on organizational routines—patterns of coordinated interaction among organizational members that develop through continual repetition. The more highly developed are an organization's routines, the more difficult it is to develop new routines. Hence, organizations get caught in **competency traps**[13] where "core capabilities become core rigidities."[14]

- *Social and political structures*: Organizations are both social systems and political systems. As social systems, organizations develop patterns of interaction that make organizational change stressful and disruptive.[15] As political systems, organizations develop stable distributions of power; change represents a threat to the power of those in positions of authority. Hence, both as social systems and political systems, organizations tend to resist change.

- *Conformity*: Institutional sociologists emphasize the propensity of firms to imitate one another in order to gain legitimacy. The process of **institutional isomorphism** locks organizations into common structures and strategies that make it difficult for them to adapt to change.[16] The pressures for conformity can be external—governments, investment analysts, banks, and other resource providers encourage the adoption of similar strategies and structures. Isomorphism also results from voluntary imitation—risk aversion encourages companies to adopt similar strategies and structures to their peers.[17]

- *Limited search*: The Carnegie School of organizational theory (associated with Herbert Simon, Jim March, and Richard Cyert) views *search* as the primary driver of organizational change. Organizations tend to limit search to areas close to their existing activities—they prefer *exploitation* of existing knowledge over *exploration* for new opportunities.[18] Limited search is reinforced, first, by **bounded rationality**—human beings have limited information processing capacity, which constrains the set of choices they can consider and, second, by *satisficing*—the propensity for individuals (and organizations) to terminate the search for better solutions when they reach a satisfactory level of performance rather than to pursue optimal performance. The implication is that organizational change is triggered by declining performance.

- *Complementarities between strategy, structure, and systems*: The notion of *fit* is a core principle of management. Chapter 1 discussed the need for strategy to fit with the firm's external environment and its internal resources and capabilities, and observed that strategy is manifest as an *activity system*. Chapter 6 referred to *contingency theory*: the idea that an organization's optimal design is determined by its environment and strategy. Ultimately, all the features of an organization—strategy, structure, systems, culture, goals, and employee skills—are complementary.[19] Organizations establish complex, idiosyncratic combinations of multiple characteristics during their early phases of development in order to match the conditions of their business environment. However, once established, this complex configuration becomes a barrier to change. To respond to a change in its external environment, it is not enough to make incremental changes in a few dimensions of strategy—it is likely that the firm will need to find a new configuration that involves a comprehensive set of changes (Strategy Capsule 8.2).[20] The implication is that organizations

---

STRATEGY CAPSULE 8.2

A Tight-Fitting Business System Makes Change Perilous: The Liz Claiborne Story

During the 1980s, Liz Claiborne became a highly successful designer, manufacturer, and retailer of clothes for professional women. Liz Claiborne's success was based upon a strategy that combined a number of closely linked choices concerning functions and activities.

◆ Design was based around a "color by numbers" approach involving "concept groups" of different garments that could be mixed and matched.

◆ Department stores were encouraged to provide dedicated space to present Liz Claiborne's concept collections. Liz Claiborne consultants visited department stores to train their sales staff and to ensure that the collections were being displayed correctly.

◆ Retailers could not purchase individual garment lines; they were required to purchase the entire concept group and had to submit a single order for each season—they could not reorder.

◆ Most manufacturing was contracted out to garment makers in SE Asia.

◆ To create close contact with customers, Liz Claiborne offered fashion shows at department stores, "breakfast clinics" where potential customers could see the latest collection, and tracked customer preferences through point-of-sale data collection.

◆ Rather than the conventional four-season product cycle, Liz Claiborne operated a six-season cycle.

During the 1990s, Liz Claiborne's performance went into a sharp decline. The key problem was the trend toward more casual clothes in the workplace. Moreover, financial pressures on department stores made them less willing to buy complete collections. As a result Liz Claiborne allowed reordering by retailers. However, once retailers could split orders into smaller, more frequent orders, the entire Liz Claiborne system began to break down: it could not adapt to the quick-response, fast-cycle model that was increasingly dominant within the garment trade. In 1994, Liz Claiborne appointed a new CEO who systematically rebuilt the business around a more casual look more flexibility within its collections (although still with a common "color card"), and a shorter supply chain, with most production in North and Central America.

Source: N. Siggelkow, "Change in the Presence of Fit: The Rise, the Fall, and the Renaissance of Liz Claiborne," *Academy of Management Journal* 44 (2001): 838–57.

tend to evolve through a process of *punctuated equilibrium*, involving long periods of stability during which the widening misalignment between the organization and its environment ultimately forces radical and comprehensive change on the company.[21] This typically requires a change in leadership.

Organizational Adaptation and Industry Evolution

Thinking about industrial and organizational change has been strongly influenced by ideas from evolutionary biology. Evolutionary change is viewed as an adaptive process that involves *variation, selection,* and *retention.*[22] The key issue is the level at which these evolutionary processes occur:

- *Organizational ecology* has been discussed in relation to changes in the number of firms in an industry over time. However, organizational ecology is a broader theory of economic change based on the assumption of organizational inertia. As a result, industry evolution occurs through changes in the population of firms rather than by adaptation of firms themselves. Industries develop and grow through new entry spurred by the imitation of initial successful entrants. The competitive process is a *selection mechanism*, in which organizations whose characteristics match the requirements of their environment can attract resources; those that do not are eliminated.[23]

- *Evolutionary economics* focuses upon individual organizations as the primary agents of change. The process of variation, selection, and retention takes place at the level of the *organizational routine*—unsuccessful routines are abandoned; successful routines are retained and replicated within the organization.[24] As we discussed in Chapter 5, these patterns of coordinated activity are the basis for organizational capability. While evolutionary theorists view firms as adapting to external change through the search for new routines, replication of successful routines, and abandonment of unsuccessful routines, such adaptation is neither fast nor costless.

Empirical evidence points to the importance of both processes. The ability of some companies to adapt is indicated by the fact that many have been leaders in their industries for a century or more—BASF, the world's largest chemical company, has been a leader in chemicals since it was founded in 1865 as a producer of synthetic dyes. Exxon and Shell have led the world's petroleum industry since the late 19th century.[25] Budweiser Budvar, the Czech beer company (that has a long-running trademark dispute with Anheuser-Busch) traces its origins to 1785. Mitsui Group, a Japanese conglomerate, is even older—its first business, a retail store, was established in 1673.

Yet these companies are exceptions. Among the companies forming the original Dow Jones Industrial Average in 1896, only General Electric remains in the index today. Of the world's 12 biggest companies in 1912, just two were in the top 12 by 2015 (Table 8.2). And life spans are shortening: the average period in which companies remained in the S&P 500 was 90 years in 1935; in 1958 it was 61 years; by 2011 it was down to 18 years.

The demise of great companies partly reflects the rise of new industries—notably the information and communications technology (ICT) sector, but also the failure of established firms to adapt successfully to the life cycles of their own industries.

TABLE 8.2 World's biggest companies in terms of market capitalization, 1912 and 2015

1912	$billion	2015	$billion
US Steel	0.74	Apple	637
Standard Oil NJ (Exxon)	0.39	ExxonMobil	393
J&P Coates	0.29	Microsoft	385
Pullman	0.20	Johnson & Johnson	292
Royal Dutch Shell	0.19	Wells Fargo	282
Anaconda	0.18	Walmart	277
General Electric	0.17	Novartis	252
Singer	0.17	General Electric	249
American Brands	0.17	China Mobile	240
Navistar	0.16	Nestlé	237
British American Tobacco	0.16	Chevron	213
De Beers	0.16	China Construction Bank	201

Sources: L. Hannah "Marshall's 'Trees' and the Global 'Forest': Were 'Giant Redwoods' Different?" in N. Lamoreaux, D. Raff, and P. Temin (eds), *Learning by Doing in Markets, Firms and Nations*, Chicago: University of Chicago Press, 1999: 253–94; *Financial Times* (January 3, 2015).

Even though the industry life cycle involves changes that are largely predictable, changing key success factors implies that the different stages of the life cycle require different resources and capabilities. The innovators that pioneer the creation of a new industry are typically different companies from the "consolidators" that develop it:

> The fact that the firms that create new product and service markets are rarely the ones that scale them into mass markets has serious implications for the modern corporation. Our research points to a simple reason for this phenomenon: the skills, mind-sets, and competences needed for discovery and invention are not only different from those needed for commercialization; they conflict with the needed characteristics. This means that the firms good at invention are unlikely to be good at commercialization and vice versa.[26]

The typical pattern is that technology-based start-ups that pioneer new areas of business are acquired by companies that are well established in closely related industries, and these established incumbents offer the financial resources and functional capabilities needed to grow the start-up. In plant biotechnology, the pioneers were start-ups such as Calgene, Cetus Corporation, DNA Plant Technologies, and Mycogen; by 2015, the leading suppliers of genetically modified seeds were DuPont, Monsanto, Syngenta, and Dow Chemical—all long-established chemical firms. Of course, some start-ups do survive industry shakeouts and acquisition to become industry leaders: Google, Cisco Systems, and Facebook are examples. Geoffrey Moore describes the transition from a start-up serving early adopters to an established business serving mainstream customers as "crossing the chasm."[27]

In most new industries we find a mixture of start-up companies (*de novo* entrants) and established companies that have diversified from other sectors (*de alio* entrants). Which are likely to be more successful? The basic issue is whether the flexibility and entrepreneurial advantages of start-ups outweigh the superior resources and capabilities of established firms. This further depends upon whether the resources and capabilities required in the new industry are similar to those present in an existing industry. Where these linkages are close, *de alio* entrants are at an advantage: in automobiles, former bicycle, carriage, and engine manufacturers tended to be the best performers;[28] television production was dominated by former producers of radios.[29]

Many start-up ventures also draw resources and capabilities from established firms. A high proportion of new ventures are established by former employees of existing firms within that sector. In Silicon Valley most of the leading semiconductor firms, including Intel, trace their origins to Shockley Semiconductor Laboratories, the pioneer of integrated circuits.[30] Established companies are often important investors in new ventures. Investors in Uber include the Chinese internet giant Baidu and the founders of Amazon, Napster, and Yelp.

Coping with Technological Change

Competition between new start-ups and established firms is not just a feature of the early phases of an industry's life cycle: it is ongoing. The greatest threat that newcomers pose to established firms is during periods of technological change. New technology is especially challenging to incumbents when it is "competence destroying," when it is "architectural," and when it is "disruptive."

Competence enhancing and competence destroying technological change Some technological changes undermine the resources and capabilities of established firms—according to Tushman and Anderson, they are "competence destroying." Other changes are "competence enhancing"—they preserve, even strengthen, the resources add capabilities of incumbent firms.[31] The quartz watch radically undermined the competence base of mechanical watchmakers. Conversely, the turbofan, a major advance in jet engine technology, reinforced the capability base of existing aero engine manufacturers. The key issue is how the new technology influences the strategic importance of resources and capabilities possessed by established firms. In the typesetting industry, the ability of incumbent firms to withstand the transition to radically new technologies rested upon the continuing importance of certain key resources: customer relationships, sales and service networks, and font libraries.[32]

Architectural and Component Innovation The ease with which established firms adapt to technological change depends upon whether the innovation occurs at the *component* or the *architectural* level. Henderson and Clark argue that innovations which change the overall architecture of a product create great difficulties for established firms because an architectural innovation requires a major reconfiguration of a company's strategy and activity system.[33] In automobiles, the hybrid engine was an important innovation but did not require a major reconfiguration of car design and engineering. The battery-powered electric motor is an architectural innovation—it requires redesign of the entire car and involves carmakers in creating systems for recharging. In many sectors of e-commerce—online grocery purchases and online banking—the internet involved innovation at the component level (it provided a new channel of distribution for existing products). Hence, existing supermarket chains and established retail banks with their clicks and bricks business models have dominated online groceries and online financial services. The rise of Boeing during the 1960s to become the world's leading producer of passenger aircraft was primarily because of its recognition that the jet engine was an architectural innovation that necessitated a major redesign of airplanes.[34]

Disruptive Technologies   Clay Christiansen distinguishes between new technology that is *sustaining*—it augments existing performance attributes—and new technology that is *disruptive*—it incorporates different performance attributes than the existing technology.[35]

Steam-powered ships were initially slower, more expensive, and less reliable than sailing ships. The leading shipbuilders failed to make the transition to steam power because their leading customers, the transoceanic shipping companies, remained loyal to sail until after the turn of the 20th century. Steam power was used mainly for inland waters, which lacked constant winds. After several decades of gradual development for these niche markets, stream-powered ships were able to outperform sailing ships on ocean routes.

In the disk-drive industry, some technological innovations—such as thin-film heads and more finely dispersed ferrous oxide coatings—enhanced the dominant performance criterion, recording density, reinforcing the market positions of established industry leaders. Other disk-drive technologies, notably new product generations with smaller diameters, were disruptive: established companies lagged behind newcomers in launching the new disk sizes and typically lost their industry leadership.[36] They stored less data and were resisted by major customers. Thus, the 3.5-inch disk was introduced by Connor Peripherals (mainly for use in laptop computers), but was initially rejected by industry leader, Seagate. Within three years the rapid development of the 3.5-inch disk had rendered the 5.25-inch disk obsolete.[37]

Managing Strategic Change

Given the many barriers to organizational change and the difficulties that companies experience in coping with disruptive technologies and architectural innovation, how can companies adapt to changes in their environment?

Just as the sources of organizational inertia are many, so too are the theories and methods of organizational change. Until the 1980s, most approaches to organizational change were based upon the behavioral sciences and emphasized bottom-up, decentralized initiatives. Socio-technical systems emphasized the need for social systems to adapt to the requirements of new technologies,[38] while organizational development (OD) emphasized group dynamics and the role of "change agents."[39]

More recently, managing change has become a central topic within strategic management practice and research. In this section we review four approaches to managing strategic change. We begin with the dual challenge of managing for today while preparing for tomorrow and discuss the potential for **organizational ambidexterity**. Second, we examine management tools for counteracting organizational inertia. Third, we explore the means by which companies develop new capabilities. Finally, we address the role and nature of **dynamic capabilities**.

Dual Strategies and Organizational Ambidexterity

In Chapter 1 we learned that strategy has two major dimensions: positioning for the present and adapting to the future. As we observed then, reconciling the two is difficult. Derek Abell argued that "managing with dual strategies" is the most challenging dilemma that senior managers face:

> Running a successful business requires a clear strategy in terms of defining target markets and lavishing attention on those factors which are critical to success; changing a business in anticipation of the future requires a vision of how the future will look and a strategy for how the organization will have to adapt to meet future challenges.[40]

Abell argues that dual strategies require dual planning systems: short-term planning that focuses on strategic fit and performance over a one- or two-year period; and longer-term planning to develop vision, reshape the corporate portfolio, redefine and reposition individual businesses, develop new capabilities, and redesign organizational structures over periods of five years or more. This challenge of reconciling "competing for today" with "preparing for tomorrow" is closely related to the tradeoff between exploitation and exploration that we discussed in relation to organizational inertia. The observation we made then, concerning the propensity of organizations to favor exploitation over exploration, applies equally to strategy: competing for the present tends to take precedence over preparing for the future.

The capacity to reconcile the two is what Charles O'Reilly and Michael Tushman refer to as "organizational ambidexterity." The ambidextrous firm is "capable of simultaneously exploiting existing competences and exploring new opportunities."[41] Two types of organizational ambidexterity have been identified: *structural* and *contextual*.

Structural Ambidexterity is where exploration and exploitation are undertaken in separate organizational units, on the basis that it is usually easier to foster change initiatives in new organizational units rather in existing ones. For example, faced with the challenge of disruptive technologies, Christensen and Overdorf suggest that established companies develop products and businesses that embody the new technologies in organizationally separate units.[42] For example:

- IBM developed its PC in a separate unit in Florida—far from IBM's corporate headquarters in New York. Its leader, Bill Lowe, claimed that this separation was critical to creating a business system that was radically different from IBM's core mainframe business.[43]
- Shell's GameChanger program was established to develop new avenues for future growth by exploiting innovations and entrepreneurial initiatives that would otherwise be stifled by Shell's financial system and organizational structure.[44] The key challenge is whether the initiatives fostered within the "exploration" unit will lead change within the organization as a whole. Xerox's Palo Alto Research Center developed many of the innovations that drove the microcomputer revolution of the 1980s and 1990s, but few of these innovations were exploited by Xerox itself. Similarly, the innovative business system established by General Motors' Saturn division did little to turn GM into "a new kind of car company."[45]

Contextual ambidexterity involves the same organizational units and the same organizational members pursuing both exploratory and exploitative activities. At Oticon, the Danish hearing aid company, employees were encouraged to sustain existing products while pursuing innovation and creativity.[46] Under the slogan "Innovation from Everyone, Everywhere" Whirlpool sought to embed innovation throughout its existing organization: "Innovation had been the responsibility of a couple of groups, engineering and marketing. Now, you have thousands of people involved."[47] The problem of contextual ambidexterity is that the management systems and the individual behaviors required for efficient exploitation are incompatible with these needed for exploration.

Combatting Organizational Inertia

If organizational change follows a process of punctuated equilibrium in which periods of stability are interspersed by periods of intense upheaval, what precipitates these episodes of transformational change? Most large companies exhibit periodic restructuring, involving simultaneous changes in strategy, structure, management systems, and top management personnel. Such restructuring typically follows declining performance caused either by a major external shock or by a growing misalignment between the firm and its external environment. For example, the oil and gas majors underwent far-reaching restructuring during 1986–1992 following the oil price decline of 1986.[48] If sustained, the oil price decline of 2014 may also trigger far-reaching strategic changes. A challenge for top management is to undertake large-scale change before being pressured by declining performance. This may require managers to let go of the beliefs that wed them to the prevailing strategy. Polaroid's failure to adapt to digital imaging despite developing leading-edge digital-imaging capabilities can be attributed to top management's unchanging system of beliefs regarding the company and its strategy.[49]

Creating Perceptions of Crisis Crises create the conditions for strategic change by loosening the organization's attachment to the status quo. The problem is that by the time the organization is engulfed in crisis it may already be too late. Hence, a useful tool for leaders of change is to create the perception of impending crisis so that necessary changes can be implemented well before a real crisis emerges. At General Electric, even when the company was reporting record profits, Jack Welch was able to convince employees of the need for change in order to defend against emerging threats. Andy Grove's dictum "Only the paranoid survive" helped Intel to maintain a continual striving for improvement and development despite its dominance of the market for PC microprocessors.

Establishing Stretch Targets Another approach to weakening the powers of organizational inertia is to continually pressure the organizations by means of ambitious performance targets. The idea is that performance targets that are achievable but only with an extension of employee effort can motivate creativity and initiative while attacking complacency. Stretch targets are normally associated with short- and medium-term performance goals for individuals and organizational units. However, they also relate to long-term strategic goals. A key role of vision statements and ambitious strategic intent is to create a sustained sense of ambition and organizational purpose. These ideas are exemplified by Collins and Porras' notion of "Big Hairy Ambitious Goals" that I discussed in Chapter 1. Apple's success in introducing "insanely great" new products owes much to Steve Jobs imposing seemingly impossible goals on his product development teams. For the iPod he insisted that it should store thousands of songs, have a battery life exceeding four hours, and be smaller and thinner than any existing mp3 player.[50]

Organizational Initiatives as Catalysts of Change   Chief executives are limited in their ability to initiate and implement organization-wide change. However, by a combination of authoritative and charismatic leadership, they may be able to pioneer specific initiatives with a surprisingly extensive impact. Corporate initiatives sponsored by the CEO are effective for disseminating strategic changes, best practices, and management innovations. At General Electric Jack Welch was an especially effective exponent of using corporate initiatives to drive organizational change. These were built around communicable and compelling slogans such as "Be number 1 or number 2 in your industry," "GE's growth engine," "boundarylessness," "six-sigma quality," and "destroy-your-business-dot-com." Leaders can also have a profound impact through symbolic actions. A key incident in the transformation of the Qingdao Refrigerator Plant into Haier, one of the world's biggest appliance companies, was when the CEO, Zhang Ruimin, took a sledgehammer to defective refrigerators in front of the assembled workforce.[51]

Reorganizing Company Structure   By reorganizing the structure top management can redistribute power, reshuffle top management, and introduce new blood. One of the last major actions of CEO Steve Ballmer before retiring in August 2013 was to reorganize Microsoft's divisional structure in order to break down established power centers and facilitate the transition to a more integrated company. At General Electric, Jeff Immelt's quest for a more flexible, collaborative company was supported by five major divisional reorganizations between 2002 and 2014. Periodic changes in organizational structure can stimulate decentralized search and local initiatives while encouraging more effective exploitation of the outcomes of such search.[52] Reconciling the benefits of integration and flexibility may require organizations to oscillate between periods of decentralization and periods of centralization.[53]

New Leadership   If strategic change is hampered by management's adherence to outmoded beliefs or if the existing team lacks the diversity of opinion and outlook for new strategic thinking then an outsider may be needed to lead change. Evidence of the relative performance of internal and external CEOs is mixed. However, if an organization is performing poorly, an external CEO tends to be more effective at leading change than an internal appointment.[54] Certainly, this was the case of IBM under Lou Gerstner and 3M under Jim McNerney. Organizational change is also stimulated by recruiting new managers from outside the organization.

Scenario Analysis   Adapting to change requires anticipating change. Yet predicting the future is hazardous, if not impossible. "Only a fool would make predictions especially about the future," remarked movie mogul Samuel Goldwyn. But the inability to predict does not preclude preparing for change. **Scenario analysis** is a systematic way of thinking about how the future might unfold. Scenario analysis is not a forecasting technique, but a process for thinking about and analyzing the future by drawing upon a broad range of information and expertise.

Herman Kahn, who pioneered their use first at the Rand Corporation, defined scenarios as "hypothetical sequences of events constructed for the purpose of focusing attention on causal process and decision points."[55] The multiple-scenario approach constructs several distinct, internally consistent views of how the future may look five to 50 years ahead. Its key value is in combining the interrelated impacts of a wide range of economic, technological, demographic, and political factors into a few distinct alternative stories of how the future might unfold. Scenario analysis can be either qualitative or quantitative or a combination of the two. Quantitative scenario analysis builds simulation models to identify likely outcomes. Qualitative scenarios typically take the form of narratives and can be particularly useful in engaging the insight and imagination of decision makers.

Scenario analysis is used to explore paths of industry evolution, the development of particular countries, and the impact of new technology. However, as with most strategy techniques, the value of scenario analysis is not in the results but in the process. Scenario analysis is a powerful tool for communicating different ideas and insights, surfacing deeply held beliefs and assumptions, identifying possible threats and opportunities, generating and evaluating alternative strategies, encouraging more flexible thinking, and building consensus. Evaluating different strategies under different scenarios can help identify which strategies are most robust and force managers to address "what if?" questions. Strategy Capsule 8.3 outlines the use of scenarios at Shell.

Developing New Capabilities

Ultimately, adapting to a changing world requires developing the capabilities needed to renew competitive advantage. To recognize the challenges this presents, we need to ask, Where do capabilities come from?

The Origins of Organizational Capability: Early Experiences and Path Dependency Distinctive capabilities can often be traced back to the circumstances which prevailed during companies' founding and early development. They are subject to **path dependency**—a company's capabilities today are the result of its history.[56] For example:

- How did Walmart, develop its outstanding capability in supply chain logistics? This super-efficient system of warehousing, distribution, and vendor relationships was not the result of careful planning and design; it evolved from the circumstances that Walmart faced during its early years of existence. Its small-town locations in Arkansas and Oklahoma resulted in unreliable delivery from its suppliers; consequently, Walmart established its own distribution system. What about the other capabilities that contribute to Walmart's remarkable cost efficiency? These too can be traced back to Walmart's origins in rural Arkansas and the values of its founder, Sam Walton.

- Despite a common competitive environment and similar strategies, the world's leading oil and gas majors display very different capability profiles (Table 8.3). Industry leaders ExxonMobil and Royal Dutch Shell exemplify these differences. ExxonMobil is known for its outstanding financial management which can be traced back to its role (as Standard Oil New Jersey) in providing overall financial management for Rockefeller's Standard Oil Trust.

STRATEGY CAPSULE 8.3
Multiple-Scenario Development at Shell

Royal Dutch Shell has used scenarios as a basis for long-term strategic planning since 1967, Mike Pocock, Shell's former chairman, observed: "We believe in basing planning not on single forecasts, but on deep thought that identifies a coherent pattern of economic, political, and social development."

Shell's scenarios are critical to the transition of its planning function from producing plans to leading a process of dialogue and learning, the outcome of which is improved decision making by managers. This involves continually challenging current thinking within the group, encouraging a wider look at external influences on the business, and forging coordination among Shell's 200-odd subsidiaries.

Shell's global scenarios are prepared every four or five years by a team comprising corporate planning staff, executives, and outside experts. Economic, political, technological, and demographic trends are analyzed up to 50 years into the future. In 2014, Shell identified two global scenarios for the period to 2060:

- *Mountains:* A world where current elites retain their power, manage for stability, and "unlock resources steadily and cautiously, not solely dictated by immediate market forces. The resulting rigidity within the system dampens economic dynamism and stifles social mobility."

- *Oceans:* A world of devolved power where "competing interests are accommodated and compromise is king. Economic productivity surges on a huge wave of reforms, yet social cohesion is sometimes eroded and politics destabilized … giving immediate market forces greater prominence."

Once approved by top management, the scenarios are disseminated by reports, presentations, and workshops, where they form the basis for long-term strategy discussion by business sectors and operating companies.

Shell is adamant that its scenarios are not forecasts. They represent carefully thought-out stories of how the various forces shaping the global energy environment of the future might play out. Their value is in stimulating the social and cognitive processes through which managers envisage the future "They are designed to stretch management to consider even events that may be only remotely possible.". According to former CEO Jeroen van der Veer: "the imperative is to use this tool to gain deeper insights into our global business environment and to achieve the cultural change that is at the heart of our group strategy."

Sources: A. de Geus, "Planning as Learning," *Harvard Business Review* (March/April 1988): 70–4; P. Schoemacher, "Multiple Scenario Development: Its Conceptual and Behavioral Foundation," *Strategic Management Journal* 14 (1993): 193–214; Royal Dutch Shell, *New Lens Scenarios: A Shift in Perspective for a World in Transition* (2014).

Royal Dutch Shell is known for its decentralized, international management capability, which allows it to become an "insider" wherever it does business. Shell was established to ship Russian oil in China while Royal Dutch was created to exploit Indonesian oil reserves. With head offices thousands of miles away in Europe, both parts of the group developed a decentralized, adaptable management style.

These observations are troubling for managers in established companies: if a firm's capabilities are determined during the early stages of its life, is it really possible to

TABLE 8.3   Distinctive capabilities as a consequence of childhood experiences: The oil majors

Company	Distinctive capability	Early history
ExxonMobil	Financial management	ExxonMobil's predecessor, Standard Oil (NJ), was the holding company for Rockefeller's Standard Oil Trust
Royal Dutch Shell	Coordinating a decentralized global network of 200 operating companies	Shell Transport & Trading headquartered in London and founded to sell Russian oil in China and the Far East Royal Dutch Petroleum headquartered in The Hague; founded to exploit Indonesian reserves
BP	Elephant hunting	Discovered huge Persian reserves, went on to find Forties field (North Sea) and Prudhoe Bay (Alaska)
ENI	Deal making in politicized environments	The Enrico Mattei legacy; the challenge of managing government relations in post-war Italy
Mobil	Lubricants	Vacuum Oil Co. founded in 1866 to supply patented petroleum lubricants

develop the new capabilities needed to adapt to changes? Established capabilities embedded within organizational structure and culture present formidable barriers to building new capabilities. Indeed, the more highly developed a firm's organizational capabilities, the greater the barrier they create. Because Dell Computer's direct sales model was so highly developed, Dell found it difficult to adapt to selling through retail outlets as well. Hence the argument that core capabilities are simultaneously core rigidities.[57]

Integrating Resources to Create Capability   To understand how to develop new capabilities let us look once more at the structure of organizational capability. In Chapter 5 (Strategy Capsule 5.5) we observed that organizational capability results from the combination of different resources, particularly the skills of different organizational members. This integration requires suitable processes, an appropriate organizational structure, motivation, and overall organizational alignment, especially with the organization's culture.

These components form the building blocks for new capabilities:

● *Processes*: Without processes, organizational capability will be completely dependent on individual skills. With processes (or *organizational routines*) we can ensure that task performance is efficient, repeatable, and reliable. When Whirlpool launched its innovation drive, the emphasis was on creating processes: processes for training employees in the tools of innovation, processes for idea generation, and processes for idea selection and development.[58] Once processes are in place they are developed through routinization and learning—essential to capability development is the creation of mechanisms that facilitate learning-by-doing and ensure the retention and sharing of learning.

- *Structure*: The people and processes that contribute to an organizational capability need to be located within the same organizational unit if they are to achieve the coordination needed to ensure a high performance capability. When McKinsey & Company wanted to develop specialized consulting capabilities in relation to different sectors and different management functions, it created a matrix structure comprising industry practices and functional practices. The need for the organizational structure to be aligned with capabilities means capabilities that span different organizational units tend to be underdeveloped. When European and US automakers adopted cross-functional product development teams to replace the previous sequential system that spanned multiple functions, their product development became faster and smoother.[59]

- *Motivation*: Without motivation not only will individuals give less than their best but equally important, they will not set aside their personal preferences and prejudices to integrate as a team. Creating the motivation that drives outstanding team capabilities—be it Bayern Munich football team, the Royal Air Force's aerobatic team (the Red Arrows), or the Simon Bolivar Youth Orchestra—involves a combination of leadership skills that, as yet, are poorly understood. Which is why outstanding former sports coaches are able to command huge fees on the corporate lecture circuit.

- *Organizational alignment*: Finally, there is the issue of fit. Exceptional performance requires that all the components of a capability fit with one another and with the broader organizational context. Following the 1989 Exxon Valdez oil spill, safety became a priority for ExxonMobil. The development of ExxonMobil's HSE (health, safety, and environment) capability has been the result of a multifaceted program of training, process redesign, incentives, and penalties that are articulated in its Operations Integrity Management System. A safety-first culture was inculcated by an obsession with accident prevention that required the reporting of paper cuts and other trivial injuries, strict rules on parking practices in company car parks, and the requirement that all meetings begin with a "safety minute."[60] Conversely, BP's dismal safety record during 2000–2010 reflects weaknesses in safety processes, a lack of accountability by middle managers for safety performance, and a management system dominated by short- and medium-term financial targets.[61]

Developing Capabilities Sequentially   Developing new capabilities requires a systematic and long-term process of development that integrates the four components described above. For most organizations, the key challenge is not obtaining the underlying resources—indeed, many examples of outstanding capabilities have resulted from the pressures of resource shortage. Toyota's lean production capability was born during a period of acute resource shortage in Japan.

If the key challenge is integrating resources through establishing and developing processes through routinization and learning, building structure, motivating the people involved, and aligning the new capability with other aspects of the organization, the demands upon management are considerable. Hence, an organization must limit the number and scope of the capabilities that it is attempting to create at any point in time. This implies that capabilities need to be developed sequentially rather than all at once.

The task is further complicated by the fact that we have limited knowledge about how to manage capability development. Hence, it may be helpful to focus not on the organizational capabilities themselves but on developing and supplying the products that use those capabilities. A trajectory through time of related, increasingly sophisticated products allows a firm to develop the "integrative knowledge" that is at the heart of organizational capability.[62] Consider Panasonic's approach to developing manufacturing capabilities in new markets:

> In every country batteries are a necessity, so they sell well. As long as we bring a few advanced automated pieces of equipment for the processes vital to final product quality, even unskilled labor can produce good products. As they work on this rather simple product, the workers get trained, and this increased skill level then permits us to gradually expand production to items with increasingly higher technology levels, first radios, then televisions.[63]

The key to such a sequential approach is for each stage of development to be linked not just to a specific product (or part of a product) but also to a clearly defined set of capabilities. Strategy Capsule 8.4 outlines Hyundai's sequential approach to capability development.

Dynamic Capabilities

The ability of some firms (e.g., IBM, General Electric, 3M, Toyota, and Tata Group) to repeatedly adapt to new circumstances while others stagnate and die suggests that the capacity for change is itself an organizational capability. David Teece and his colleagues introduced the term *dynamic capabilities* to refer to a "firm's ability to integrate, build, and reconfigure internal and external competences to address rapidly changing environments."[64]

Despite a lack of consensus over definition, common to almost all conceptions of dynamic capabilities is that they are "higher order" capabilities that orchestrate change among lower-level "ordinary" or "operational" capabilities. However, specifying, in precise terms, the definition and nature of dynamic capabilities has proved elusive. Teece proposes that "dynamic capabilities can be disaggregated into the capacity (1) to sense and shape opportunities and threats, (2) to seize opportunities, and (3) to maintain competitiveness through enhancing, combining, protecting, and, when necessary, reconfiguring the business enterprise's intangible and tangible assets."[65] However, this does not help us much when trying to identify the dynamic capabilities a company possesses or in distinguishing dynamic from ordinary capabilities. To facilitate the identification of dynamic capabilities, it is therefore useful to equate dynamic capabilities with "specific and identifiable processes"[66] and "patterned and routine"[67] behavior (as opposed to ad hoc problem solving).

IBM offers an example of how management processes can build higher-level dynamic capabilities. Under the leadership of three CEOs—Lou Gerstner, Sam Palmisano, and Ginni Rometty—IBM's Strategic Leadership Model comprised a number of processes designed to sense new business opportunities and then fund their development into new business initiatives. Strategy Capsule 14.3 in Chapter 14 outlines IBM's strategic management system.[68]

STRATEGY CAPSULE 8.4

Hyundai Motor: Developing Capabilities through Product Sequencing

Hyundai's emergence as a world-class automobile producer is a remarkable example of capability development over a sequence of compressed phases (Figure 8.5). Each phase of the development process was characterized by a clear objective in terms of product outcome, a tight time deadline, an empowered development team, a clear recognition of the capabilities that needed to be developed in each phase, and an atmosphere of

impending crisis should the project not succeed. The first phase was the construction of an assembly plant in the unprecedented time of 18 months in order to build Hyundai's first car—a Ford Cortina imported in semi-knocked down (SKD) form. Subsequent phases involved products of increasing sophistication and the development of more advanced capabilities.

FIGURE 8.5   Phased development at Hyundai Motor, 1968–1995

Source: Draws upon L. Kim, "Crisis construction and organizational learning: Capability building and catching up at Hyundai Motor," *Organizational Science* 9 (1998): 506–21.

Gary Hamel and Management Revolution   For Gary Hamel the idea that dynamic capability can be built on processes and routines is anathema. Change requires breaking away from existing management practice: "escaping the gravitational pull of the current paradigm."[69] According to Gary Hamel, in an era of nonlinear change, "the company that is evolving slowly is already on its way to extinction."[70] Revolution must be met by revolution. In books, articles, talks, and blogs over two decades, Hamel has expounded the kinds of changes needed for managers to cast off the status quo and reconceptualize the structural, psychological, and sociological norms of organizations. The Management Innovation Exchange (MIX) cofounded by Hamel has the premise: "To thrive in the 21st century, organizations must be adaptable, innovative, inspiring and socially accountable. That will require a genuine revolution in management principles and practice" and that "while modern management is one of humankind's most important inventions, it is now a mature technology that must be reinvented for a new age."[71]

Despite the enthusiasm for dynamic capabilities, new business models, management reinvention, and new organizational forms, the fact remains that successful transformations by large, established organizations are few—and those that undergo multiple transformations are exceedingly rare. The risks inherent in radical transformation are evident in the demise of several of the most prominent exponents of strategic metamorphosis and innovative business models:

- Enron's transformation from a utility and pipeline company to a trader and market-maker in energy futures and derivatives ended in its demise in 2001;
- Vivendi's transformation from a French water and waste utility into a leading global multimedia empire fell apart in 2002;
- Skandia, the Swedish insurance company, pioneered knowledge-based innovation but was overtaken by management scandal and was acquired by Old Mutual.

Using Knowledge Management to Develop Organizational Capability

Since the early 1990s, the development of capabilities by organizations has been profoundly influenced by a set of concepts and practices referred to as *knowledge management*. Knowledge management comprises a range of management organizational processes and practices whose common feature is their goal of generating value from knowledge.[72] Knowledge management includes many long-established organizational functions such as R & D, management information systems, employee training, and managing intellectual property, even strategic planning; however, at its core it comprises:

- The application of information technology to management processes—especially the use of databases, intranets, expert systems, and groupware for storing, analyzing, and disseminating information.
- The promotion of organizational learning—including best practices transfer, "lessons learned" from ongoing activities, and processes for sharing know-how.

These two areas of knowledge management correspond to the two principal types of knowledge—knowing *about* and knowing *how*:[73]

- *Knowing about* is explicit: it comprises facts, theories, and sets of instructions. *Explicit knowledge* can be communicated at negligible marginal cost between individuals and across space and time. This ability to disseminate knowledge such that any one person's use does not limit anyone else's access to the same knowledge means that explicit knowledge has the characteristic of a public good: once created, it can be replicated among innumerable users at low cost. Information and communication technologies play a major role in storing, analyzing, and disseminating explicit knowledge.

- *Know-how* is tacit in nature: it involves skills that are expressed through their performance (riding a bicycle, playing the piano). Such *tacit knowledge* cannot be directly articulated or codified. It can only be observed through its application and acquired through practice. Its management requires socially embedded person-to-person processes.

If explicit knowledge can be transferred so easily, it is seldom the foundation of sustainable competitive advantage. It is only secure from rivals when it is protected, either by intellectual property rights (patents, copyrights, trade secrets) or by secrecy ("The formula for Coca-Cola will be kept in a safe in the vault of our Atlanta headquarters guarded by heavily-armed Coca-Cola personnel."). The challenge of tacit knowledge is the opposite. The Roca brothers' Catalan restaurant, El Celler de Can Roca, has been declared the world's best restaurant. If their culinary skills have been acquired through intuition and learning-by-doing, how do they transfer this know-how to the chefs and managers of their new restaurant in Barcelona's Hotel Omm? To build organizational capability, individual know-how must be shared within the organization. Replicating knowledge in a new location requires making know-how explicit. This systematization is the basis of McDonald's incredible growth, but is more difficult for a Michelin three-starred restaurant. Moreover, while systematization permits internal replication, it also facilitates imitation by rivals. For consulting companies, the distinction between tacit (personalized) and explicit (systematized) knowledge defines their business model and is a central determinant of their strategy.[74] The result is a "paradox of replication." In order to utilize knowledge to build organizational capability we need to replicate it; and replication is much easier if the knowledge is in explicit form.[75]

Knowledge Management Activities that Contribute to Capability Development   Knowledge management can be represented as a series of activities that contribute to capability development by building, retaining, accessing, transferring, and integrating knowledge. Table 8.4 lists several knowledge-management practices.

However, the contribution of knowledge management to capability development in organizations may be less about specific techniques and more about the insight that the **knowledge-based view of the firm** has given to organizational performance and the role of management. For example, Ikujiro Nonaka's model of knowledge creation offers penetrating insights into the organizational processes through which knowledge is created and value is created from knowledge (Strategy Capsule 8.5).

TABLE 8.4   Knowledge-management practices

Knowledge process	Contributing activities	Explanation and examples
Knowledge identification	Intellectual property management	Firms are devoting increased effort to identifying and protecting their intellectual property, and patents especially
	Corporate yellow pages	BP's Connect comprises personnel data that allows each employee to identify the skills and experience of other employees in the organization
Knowledge measurement	Intellectual capital accounting	Skandia's intellectual capital accounting system pioneered the measurement and valuation of a firm's stock of knowledge. Dow Chemical uses intellectual capital metrics to link its patent portfolio to shareholder value
Knowledge retention	Lessons learned	The US Army's Center for Lessons Learned distils the results of maneuvers, simulated battles, and actual operations into tactical guidelines and recommended procedures. Most consulting firms have post-project reviews to capture the knowledge gained from each project
Knowledge transfer and sharing	Databases	Project-based organizations typically store knowledge generated by client assignments in searchable databases
	Communities-of-practice	Communities of practice are informal, self-organizing networks for transferring experiential knowledge among employees who share the same professional interests
	Best practice transfer	Where operations are geographically dispersed, different units are likely to develop local innovations and improvements. Best practice methodology aims to identify then transfer superior practices
Data analysis	Big data	"Big data" refers to the collation and analysis of huge data sets such as Walmart's more than one million customer transactions each hour and UPS's tracking of its 16.3 million packages per day and telematic data for its 46,000 vehicles.

STRATEGY CAPSULE 8.5

Knowledge Conversion and Knowledge Replication

Ikujiro Nonaka's theory of knowledge creation argues that knowledge conversion between tacit and explicit forms and between individual and organizational levels produces a "knowledge spiral" in which the organization's stock of knowledge broadens and deepens. For example, explicit knowledge is internalized into tacit knowledge in the form of intuition, know-how, and routines, while tacit knowledge is externalized into explicit knowledge through articulation and codification. Knowledge also moves between levels: individual knowledge is combined into organizational knowledge; individual knowledge is socialized into organizational knowledge.

Knowledge conversion lies at the heart of a key stage of business development: the transition from the *craft enterprise* based upon individual, tacit knowledge, to the *industrial enterprise* based upon explicit, organizational knowledge. This transition is depicted in Figure 8.6 and is illustrated by the following examples:

◆ Henry Ford's Model T was initially produced on a small scale by skilled workers. Ford's assembly line mass-production technology systematized that individual, tacit knowledge and built it into machines and processes. Ford's industrial system was no longer dependent upon skilled craftsmen: the assembly lines could be operated by former farm workers and new immigrants.

◆ When Ray Kroc discovered the McDonald brothers' hamburger stand in Riversdale, California, he recognized the potential for systematizing and replicating their process. McDonald's business model was replicated through operating manuals and training programs. Now 400,000 employees, most of whom lack the most rudimentary culinary skills, serve 68 million customers daily. The relevant knowledge is embedded within McDonald's business system.

This systematization of knowledge offers massive potential for value creation through replication and deskilling. This systematization has transformed the service sector: with the replacement of individual proprietorships by international chains in hotels (Marriott), car rental (Hertz), coffee shops (Starbucks), and tax preparation (H&R Block).

FIGURE 8.6 Knowledge conversion

Source: Based upon I. Nonaka, "A Dynamic Theory of Organizational Knowledge Creation," *Organization Science* 5 (1994): 14–37.

Summary

A vital task of strategic management is to navigate the crosscurrents of change. But predicting and adapting to change are huge challenges for businesses and their leaders.

The life-cycle model allows us to understand the forces driving industry evolution and to anticipate their impact on industry structure and the basis of competitive advantage.

But, identifying regularities in the patterns of industry evolution is of little use if firms are unable to adapt to these changes. The challenge of adaptation is huge: the presence of organizational inertia means that industry evolution occurs more through the birth of new firms and the death of old ones rather than through adaptation by established firms. Even flexible, innovative companies experience problems in coping with new technologies—especially those that are "competence destroying," "disruptive," or embody "architectural innovation."

Managing change requires managers to operate in two time zones: they must optimize for today while preparing the organization for the future. The concept of the ambidextrous organization is an approach to resolving this dilemma. Other tools for managing strategic change include: creating perceptions of crisis, establishing stretch targets, corporate-wide initiatives, recruiting external managerial talent, dynamic capabilities, and scenario planning.

Whatever approach or tools are adopted to manage change, strategic change requires building new capabilities. To the extent that an organization's capabilities are a product of its entire history, building new capabilities is a formidable challenge. To understand how organizations build capability we need to understand how resources are integrated into capability—in particular, the role of processes, structure, motivation, and alignment. The complexities of capability development and our limited understanding of how capabilities are built point to the advantages of sequential approaches to developing capabilities.

Ultimately, capability building is about harnessing the knowledge which exists within the organization. For this purpose knowledge management offers considerable potential for increasing the effectiveness of capability development. In addition to specific techniques for identifying, retaining, sharing, and replicating knowledge, the knowledge-based view of the firm offers penetrating insights into the challenges of and potential for the creation and exploitation of knowledge by firms.

In the next two chapters, we discuss strategy formulation and strategy implementation in industries at different stages of their development: *emerging industries*, which are characterized by rapid change and technology-based competition, and *mature industries*.

Self-Study Questions

1. Consider the changes that have occurred in a comparatively new industry (e.g., wireless telecommunications, smartphones, video game consoles, online brokerage services, fitness clubs). To what extent has the evolution of the industry followed the pattern predicted by the industry life-cycle model? What are the features of the industry that have influenced its pattern of evolution? At what stage of development is the industry today? How is the industry likely to evolve in the future?

2. Select a product that has become a *dominant design* for its industry (e.g., the IBM PC in personal computers, McDonald's in fast food, Harvard Business School in MBA education, Southwest in budget airlines). What factors caused one firm's product architecture to become dominant? Why did other firms imitate this dominant design? How did the emergence of the dominant design influence the evolution of the industry?

3. The *resource partitioning* model argues that as industries become dominated by a few major companies with similar strategies and products so opportunities open for new entrants to build specialist niches. Identify an opportunity for establishing a specialist new business in an industry currently dominated by mass-market giants.

4. Choose an industry that faces significant change over the next ten years. Identify the main drivers of change and construct two scenarios of how these changes might play out. In relation to one of the leading firms in the industry, what are the implications of the two scenarios, and what strategy options should the firm consider?

5. Identify two sports teams: one that is rich in resources (such as talented players) but whose capabilities (as indicated by performance) have been poor; one that is resource-poor but has displayed strong team capabilities. What clues can you offer as to the determinants of capabilities among sports teams?

6. The market leaders in video games for mobile devices during 2012–14 were start-up companies such as DeNA, GungHo Online, Supercell, King, and Rovio. Why have start-ups outperformed established video game giants such as Electronic Arts, Rock Star Games, and Activision Blizzard in this market?

7. The dean of your business school wishes to upgrade the school's educational capabilities in order to better equip its graduates for success in their careers and in their lives. Advise your dean on what tools and systems of knowledge management might be deployed in order to support these goals.

Notes

1. T. Levitt, "Exploit the Product Life Cycle," *Harvard Business Review* (November/December 1965): 81–94; G. Day, "The Product Life Cycle: Analysis and Applications," *Journal of Marketing* 45 (Autumn 1981): 60–67.

2. F. F. Suárez and J. M. Utterback, "Dominant Designs and the Survival of Firms," *Strategic Management Journal* 16 (1995): 415–430.

3. P. Anderson and M. L. Tushman, "Technological Discontinuities and Dominant Designs," *Administrative Science Quarterly* 35 (1990): 604–633.

4. M. A. Cusumano and D. B. Yoffie, *Competing on Internet Time: Lessons from Netscape and Its Battle with Microsoft* (New York: Free Press, 1998).

5. M. G. Jacobides, "Industry Change through Vertical Disintegration: How and Why Markets Emerged in Mortgage Banking," *Academy of Management Journal* 48 (2005): 465–498; M. G. Jacobides, C. Y. Baldwin, and R. Dizaji, "From the Structure of the Value Chain to the Strategic Dynamics of Industry Sectors," Academy of Management Presentation (Philadelphia, August 7, 2007).

6. G. Carroll and M. Hannan, *The Demography of Corporations and Industries* (Princeton, MA: Princeton University Press, 2000). For a survey see J. Baum, "Organizational Ecology," in S. R. Clegg, C. Hardy, and W. R. Nord (eds), *The SAGE Handbook of Organizational Studies* (Thousand Oaks, CA: SAGE Publications, 1996); and D. Barron, "Evolutionary Theory," in D. O. Faulkner and A. Campbell (eds), *The Oxford Handbook of Strategy* (Oxford: Oxford University Press, 2003), vol. 1: 74–97.

7. G. R. Carroll, L. S. Bigelow, M.-D. Seidel, and B. Tsai, "The Fates of de novo and de alio Producers in the American Automobile Industry, 1885–1981," *Strategic Management Journal* 17 (Summer 1996): 117–137.

8. S. Klepper and K. L. Simons, "Dominance by Birthright: Entry of Prior Radio Producers and Competitive Ramifications in the US Television Receiver Industry," *Strategic Management Journal* 21 (2000): 997–1016.

9. High rates of entry and exit may continue well into maturity. See T. Dunne, M. J. Roberts, and L. Samuelson, "Patterns of Firm Entry and Exit in US Manufacturing Industries," *Rand Journal of Economics* 19 (1988): 495–515.

10. S. Klepper and E. Grady, "The Evolution of New Industries and the Determinants of Industry Structure," *Rand Journal of Economics* 21 (1990): 27–44.

11. S. Klepper and K. Simons, "The Making of an Oligopoly: Firm Survival and Technological Change in the Evolution of the US Tire Industry," *Journal of Political Economy* 108 (2000): 728–760.

12. G. Carroll and A. Swaminathan, "Why the Microbrewery Movement? Organizational Dynamics of Resource Partitioning in the American Brewing Industry," *American Journal of Sociology* 106 (2000): 715–762.

13. B. Levitt and J. G. March, "Organizational Learning," *Annual Review of Sociology* 14 (1988): 319–340.

14. D. Leonard-Barton, "Core Capabilities and Core Rigidities: A Paradox in Managing New Product Development," *Strategic Management Journal* 13 (Summer 1992): 111–125.

15. M. T. Hannan, L. Polos, and G. R. Carroll, "Structural Inertia and Organizational Change Revisited III: The Evolution of Organizational Inertia," *Stanford GSB Research Paper* 1734 (April 2002).

16. P. J. DiMaggio and W. Powell, "The Iron Cage Revisited: Institutional Isomorphism and Collective Rationality in Organizational Fields," *American Sociological Review* 48 (1983): 147–160.

17. J.-C. Spender, *Industry Recipes* (Oxford: Blackwell Publishing, 1989).

18. J. G. March, "Exploration and Exploitation in Organizational Learning," *Organizational Science* 2 (1991): 71–87.

19. The concept of fit is common to several disciplines within management including: organizational economics (e.g., P. R. Milgrom and J. Roberts, "Complementarities and Fit: Strategy, Structure, and Organizational Change in Manufacturing," *Journal of Accounting and Economics* 19 (1995): 179–208); socio-technical systems (e.g., E. Trist, "The Sociotechnical Perspective," in A. H. Van de Ven and W. H. Joyce (eds), *Perspectives on Organization Design and Behavior* (New York: John Wiley & Sons, Inc., 1984); and complexity theory (e.g. J. W. Rivkin, "Imitation of Complex Strategies," *Management Science* 46 (2000): 824–844).

20. M. E. Porter and N. Siggelkow, "Contextual Interactions within Activity Systems," *Academy of Management Perspectives* 22 (May 2008): 34–56.

21. E. Romanelli and M. L. Tushman, "Organizational Transformation as Punctuated Equilibrium: An Empirical Test," *Academy of Management Journal* 37 (1994): 1141–1166.

22. H. E. Aldrich, *Organizations and Environments* (Stanford, CA: Stanford University Press, 2007).

23. For an introduction to organizational ecology, see M. T. Hannan and G. R. Carroll, "An introduction to organizational ecology," in G. R. Carroll and M. T. Hannan (eds), *Organizations in Industry* (Oxford: Oxford University Press, 1995): 17–31.

24. For a survey of evolutionary approaches, see R. R. Nelson, "Recent Evolutionary Theorizing about Economic Change," *Journal of Economic Literature* 33 (March 1995): 48–90.

25. R. Foster, "Creative Destruction Whips through Corporate America," *Innosight Executive Briefing* (Winter 2012).

26. C. Markides and P. Geroski, "Colonizers and Consolidators: The Two Cultures of Corporate Strategy," *Strategy and Business* 32 (Fall 2003).

27. G. A. Moore, *Crossing the Chasm* (New York: HarperCollins, 1991).

28. S. Klepper, "The Capabilities of New Firms and the Evolution of the US Automobile Industry," *Industrial and Corporate Change* 11 (2002): 645–666.

29. S. Klepper and K. L. Simons, "Dominance by Birthright: Entry of Prior Radio Producers and Competitive Ramifications in the US Television Receiver Industry," *Strategic Management Journal* 21 (2000): 997–1016.

30. D. A. Kaplan, *The Silicon Boys and Their Valley of Dreams* (New York: Morrow, 1999).

31. M. L. Tushman and P. Anderson, "Technological Discontinuities and Organizational Environments," *Administrative Science Quarterly* 31 (1986): 439–465.

32. M. Tripsas, "Unravelling the Process of Creative Destruction: Complementary Assets and Incumbent Survival in the Typesetter Industry," *Strategic Management Journal* 18 (Summer 1997): 119–142.

33. R. M. Henderson and K. B. Clark, "Architectural Innovation: The Reconfiguration of Existing Systems and the Failure of Established Firms," *Administrative Science Quarterly* (1990): 9–30.

34. Ibid, page 17.

35. J. Bower and C. M. Christensen, "Disruptive Technologies: Catching the Wave," *Harvard Business Review* (January/February 1995): 43–53.

36. C. M. Christensen, *The Innovator's Dilemma* (Boston: Harvard Business School Press, 1997).

37. Ibid.

38. W. A. Pasmore, *Designing Effective Organizations: The Sociotechnical Systems Perspective* (New York: John Wiley & Sons, Inc., 1988).

39. W. G. Bennis, *Organization Development: Its Nature, Origins, and Prospects* (New York: Addison-Wesley, 1969).

40. D. F. Abell, *Managing with Dual Strategies* (New York: Free Press, 1993): 3.

41. C. A. O'Reilly and M. L. Tushman, "The Ambidextrous Organization," *Harvard Business Review* (April 2004): 74–81.

42. C. M. Christensen and M. Overdorf, "Meeting the Challenge of Disruptive Change," *Harvard Business Review* (March/April 2000): 66–76.

43. T. Elder, "Lessons from Xerox and IBM," *Harvard Business Review* (July/August 1989): 66–71.

44. "Shell GameChanger: A Safe Place to Get Crazy Ideas Started," http://www.managementexchange.com, Management Innovation eXchange (January 7, 2013), www.managementexchange.com/story/shell-game-changer, accessed July 20, 2015.

45. See "Lab Inventors: Xerox PARC and its Innovation Machine," in A. Rao and P. Scaruffi, *A History of Silicon Valley,* 2nd edn (Omniware, 2013); and "Saturn: Why One of Detroit's Brightest Hopes Failed," *Christian Science Monitor* (October 1, 2009).

46. G. Verona and D. Ravasi, "Unbundling dynamic capabilities: An exploratory study of continuous product innovation," *Industrial and Corporate Change* 12 (2002): 577–606.

47. Interview with Nancy Snyder, Whirlpool's vice-president of leadership and strategic competency development, *Business Week* (March 6, 2006), http://www.businessweek.com/innovate/content/mar2006/id20060306_287425.htm?.

48. R. Cibin and R. M. Grant, "Restructuring among the World's Leading Oil Companies," *British Journal of Management* 7 (1996): 283–308.

49. M. Tripsas and G. Gavetti, "Capabilities, Cognition and Inertia: Evidence from Digital Imaging," *Strategic Management Journal* 21 (2000): 1147–1161.

50. H. Y. Howard, "Decoding Leadership: How Steve Jobs Transformed Apple to Spearhead a Technological Informal Economy," *Journal of Business and Management* 19 (2013): 33–44.

51. "Haier: Taking a Chinese Company Global in 2011," Harvard Business School Case No. 712408-PDF-ENG (August 2011).

52. N. Siggelkow and D. A. Levinthal, "Escaping Real (Non-benign) Competency Traps: Linking the Dynamics of Organizational Structure to the Dynamics of Search," *Strategic Organization* 3 (2005): 85–115.

53. J. Nickerson and T. Zenger, "Being Efficiently Fickle: A Dynamic Theory of Organizational Choice," *Organization Science* 13 (September/October 2002): 547–567.

54. A. Karaevli and E. Zajac, "When is an Outsider CEO a Good Choice?" *MIT Sloan Management Review* (Summer 2013); A. Falato and D. Kadyrzhanova, "CEO Successions and Firm Performance in the US Financial Industry," *Finance and Economics Discussion Series* (Federal Reserve Board, 2012).

55. H. Kahn, *The Next 200 Years: A Scenario for America and the World* (New York: William Morrow, 1976). For a guide to the use of scenarios in strategy making, see K. van der Heijden, *Scenarios: The Art of Strategic Conversation* (Chichester: John Wiley & Sons, Ltd, 2005).

56. B. Wernerfelt, "Why Do Firms Tend to Become Different?" in C. E. Helfat (ed.), *Handbook of Organizational Capabilities* (Oxford: Blackwell, 2006): 121–133.

57. D. Leonard-Barton, "Core Capabilities and Core Rigidities," *Strategic Management Journal* 13 (Summer 1992): 111–126.

58. N. T. Snyder and D. L. Duarte, *Unleashing Innovation: How Whirlpool Transformed an Industry* (San Francisco: Jossey-Bass, 2008).

59. K. B. Clark and T. Fujimoto, *Product Development Performance: Strategy, Organization, and Management in the World Auto Industry* (Boston: HBS Press, 1991).

60. S Coll, *Private Empire: ExxonMobil and American Power* (New York: Penguin, 2012).

61. *The Report of the BP U.S. Refineries Independent Safety Review Panel* (January 2007).

62. C. E. Helfat and R. S. Raubitschek, "Product Sequencing: Co-evolution of Knowledge, Capabilities and Products," *Strategic Management Journal* 21 (2000): 961–979. The parallel development of capabilities and products has also been referred to as "dynamic resource fit." See: H. Itami, *Mobilizing Invisible Assets* (Boston: Harvard University Press, 1987): 125.

63. A. Takahashi, *What I Learned from Konosuke Matsushita* (Tokyo: Jitsugyo no Nihonsha, 1980); in Japanese, quoted by H. Itami, *Mobilizing Invisible Assets* (Boston: Harvard University Press, 1987): 25.

64. D. J. Teece, G. Pisano, and A. Shuen, "Dynamic Capabilities and Strategic Management," *Strategic Management Journal* 18 (1997): 509–533.

65. D. J. Teece, "Explicating Dynamic Capabilities: The Nature and Microfoundations of (Sustainable) Enterprise Performance," *Strategic Management Journal* 28 (2007): 1319.

66. K. M. Eisenhardt and J. Martin, "Dynamic Capabilities: What Are They?" *Strategic Management Journal* 21 (2000): 1105–1121.

67. S. G. Winter, "Understanding Dynamic Capabilities," *Strategic Management Journal* 24 (2003): 991–995.

68. J. B. Harreld, C. A. O'Reilly and M. L. Tushman, "Dynamic Capabilities at IBM: Driving Strategy into Action," *California Management Review* 49 (2007): 21–43.

69. http://www.strategos.com/category-creators-reach-escape-velocity/, accessed July 20, 2015.

70. G. Hamel, *Leading the Revolution* (Boston: Harvard Business School Press, 2000): 5.

71. http://www.managementexchange.com/about-the-mix, accessed July 20, 2015.

72. K. Dalkir, *Knowledge Management in Theory and Practice*, 2nd edn (Cambridge, MA: MIT Press, 2011).

73. R. M. Grant, "Toward a Knowledge-Based Theory of the Firm," Strategic Management Journal 17 (Winter Special Issue, 1996): 109-122.

74. M. Hansen, N. Nohria, and T. Tierney, "What's Your Strategy for Managing Knowledge?" *Harvard Business Review* (March 1999): 106–116.

75. J. Rivkin, "Reproducing Knowledge: Replication without Imitation at Moderate Complexity," *Organization Science* 12 (2001): 274–293.

9 Technology-based Industries and the Management of Innovation

Whereas a calculator on the ENIAC is equipped with 18,000 vacuum tubes and weighs 30 tons, computers in the future may have only 1000 vacuum tubes and perhaps weigh only 1.5 tons.

—POPULAR MECHANICS, MARCH 1949

There's no chance that the iPhone is going to get any significant market share.

—STEVE BALLMER, CEO, MICROSOFT, APRIL 30, 2007

OUTLINE

Introduction and Objectives

In the previous chapter we saw that technology is the primary force that creates new industries and transforms existing ones. New industries include wireless telephony, biotechnology, photovoltaic power, fiber optics, robotics, and social networking. Industries transformed by new technologies include photography, recorded music, pharmaceuticals, and securities trading. New technology is a source of opportunity, especially for new businesses but, as we saw in the previous chapter, it presents major problems for many established companies.

This chapter focuses on business environments where technology is a key driver of change and an important source of competitive advantage. These technology-intensive industries include both emerging industries (those in the introductory and growth phases of their life cycle) and established industries where technology continues to drive competition. The issues we examine, however, are also relevant to all industries where technology has the potential to create competitive advantage including those which may be revolutionized by new technology such as healthcare and education .

In the last chapter, we viewed technology as an external driver of industrial change. In this chapter our primary concern will be the use of technology as a tool of competitive strategy. How can an enterprise best exploit technology to establish a competitive advantage?

The chapter is organized around these four learning objectives. First, we examine the links between technology and competition and the potential for innovation to establish sustainable competitive advantage. Second, we discuss key issues in the design of technology strategies, including alternative strategies for exploiting an innovation, timing, and managing risk. Third, we discuss network externalities and setting industry standards. Fourth, we look at how firms are extending their innovation processes beyond their organizational boundaries. Finally, we examine how technology-based strategies can best be implemented.

By the time you have completed this chapter, you will be able to:

- Identify the factors that determine the returns to innovation, and evaluate the potential for an innovation to establish competitive advantage.
- Formulate strategies for exploiting innovation and managing technology, including:
  - identifying and evaluating strategic options for exploiting innovation;
  - assessing the relative advantages of being a leader or a follower in innovation;
  - managing risk;
  - Formulate strategies to exploit network effects and win standards wars.
- Understand why companies are widening their quest for innovation, including the adoption of *open innovation*.
- Implement strategies in technology-based industries by designing the organizational structures and systems that foster innovation and new product development.

Competitive Advantage in Technology-intensive Industries

Innovation forms the key link between technology and competitive advantage. The quest for competitive advantage stimulates the search for innovation and successful innovations allow some firms to dominate their industries. To explore the conditions under which innovation creates competitive advantage, let us begin by examining the innovation process.

The Innovation Process

Invention is the creation of new products and processes through the development of new knowledge or from new combinations of existing knowledge. Most inventions are the result of novel applications of existing knowledge. Samuel Morse's telegraph, patented in 1840, was based on several decades of research into electromagnetism from Ben Franklin to Ørsted, Ampère, and Sturgeon. The compact disk embodies knowledge about lasers developed several decades previously.

√ **Innovation** is the initial commercialization of invention by producing and marketing a new good or service or by using a new method of production. Once introduced, innovation diffuses: on the demand side, through customers purchasing the good or service; on the supply side, through imitation by competitors. An innovation may be the result of a single invention (most product innovations in chemicals and pharmaceuticals involve discoveries of new chemical compounds) or it may combine many inventions. The first automobile, introduced by Karl Benz in 1885, embodied a multitude of inventions, from the wheel, invented some 5000 years previously, to the internal combustion engine, invented nine years earlier. Not all invention progresses into innovation: among the patent portfolios of most technology-intensive firms are inventions that have yet to find a viable commercial application. Conversely, innovations may involve little or no new technology: the personal computer was a new configuration of existing technologies; most new types of packaging, including the vast array of tamper-proof packages, involve novel designs but no new technology.

Figure 9.1 shows the pattern of development from knowledge creation to invention and innovation. Historically, the lags between knowledge creation and innovation have been long:

- Chester F. Carlson invented xerography in 1938 by combining established knowledge about electrostatics and printing. The first patents were awarded in 1940. Xerox purchased the patent rights and launched its first office copier in 1958. By 1974, the first competitive machines were introduced by IBM, Kodak, Ricoh, and Canon.

- The jet engine, employing Newtonian principles, was patented by Frank Whittle in 1930. The first commercial jet airliner, the De Havilland Comet, flew in 1957, followed two years later by the Boeing 707.

Recently, the innovation cycle has speeded up:

- The use of satellite radio signals for global positioning was developed by physicists at Johns Hopkins University in late 1950s. An experimental GPS satellite was launched by the US Air Force in 1978 and the GPS system was

FIGURE 9.1   The development of technology: From knowledge creation to diffusion

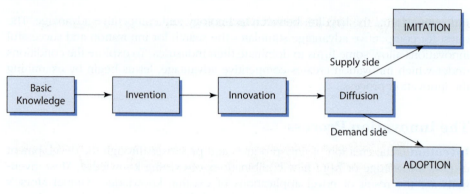

fully operational by 1995. Commercial applications began in the 1990s: Garmin launched its car sat-nav system in 1998 followed by TomTom in 2002.

- MP3, the audio file compression software, was developed at the Fraunhofer Institute in Germany in 1987; by the mid-1990s, the swapping of MP3 music files had taken off in US college campuses, and in 1998 the first MP3 player, Diamond Multimedia's *Rio*, was launched. Apple's iPod was introduced in 2001.

The lag between new knowledge and its commercial application depends on the motivation behind the initial research. A key distinction is between basic research motivated by pure science (e.g., Niels Bohr's research into atomic physics) and basic research motivated by practical needs (e.g., Louis Pasteur's research into microbiology.)[1] The huge, and rapid, commercial impact of the research undertaken by the US Department of Defense's Advanced Research Projects Agency—GPS satellites, the internet, RISC computing, motion-sensing devices—underlines the potential of basic research inspired by practical needs.[2]

Capturing Value from Innovation

"If a man can . . . make a better mousetrap than his neighbor, though he build his house in the woods, the world will make a beaten path to his door," claimed Emerson. Yet the inventors of new mousetraps, and other gadgets too, are more likely to be found at the bankruptcy courts than in the millionaires' playgrounds of the Caribbean. Certainly, innovation is no guarantor of fame and fortune, either for individuals or for companies. There is no consistent evidence that either R & D intensity or frequency of new-product introductions is positively associated with profitability.[3]

The profitability of an innovation to the innovator depends on the value created by the innovation and the share of that value that the innovator is able to capture. As Strategy Capsule 9.1 shows, different innovations result in very different distributions of value. In the case of aspartame, the innovator G. D. Searle with NutraSweet was the primary beneficiary. In the case of the personal computer, suppliers and consumers were the primary beneficiaries. In the case of smartphones, followers have appropriated most of the value.

STRATEGY CAPSULE 9.1
How the Returns on Innovation Are Shared

The value created by an innovation is distributed among a number of different parties (Figure 9.2).

◆ *Aspartame*: Aspartame, the artificial sweetener, was discovered in 1965 by the drug company G. D. Searle & Co. (later acquired by Monsanto) and launched in 1981 as NutraSweet. The patent on aspartame expired in 1992, after which competition grew. However, Searle/Monsanto, successfully appropriated a major part of the value created.

◆ *Personal computers*: The innovators—MITS, Tandy, Apple, and Xerox—earned modest profits from their innovation. The followers— IBM, Dell, Compaq, Acer, Toshiba, and a host of later entrants—did somewhat better, but their returns were overshadowed by the huge profits

earned by the suppliers to the industry, especially: Intel in microprocessors and Microsoft in operating systems Complementors, notably the suppliers of applications software, also did well. However, intense price competition meant that the primary beneficiaries from the PC were consumers, who typically paid prices for their PCs that were a fraction of the value they derived.

◆ *Smartphones*: The first were the IBM Simon (1993) and the Nokia 9000 series (1996). Followers— notably RIM, Apple, and Samsung—have earned huge profits from smartphones. Several suppliers have also been big winners (e.g., microprocessor supplier, ARM); also complementors, notably app suppliers.

FIGURE 9.2   Appropriating of value: Who gets the benefits from innovation?

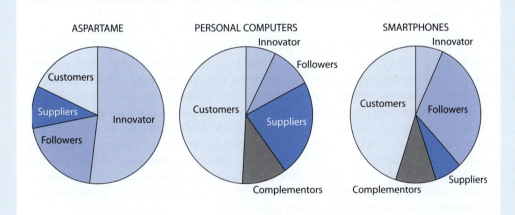

The term **regime of appropriability** is used to describe the conditions that influence the distribution of the value created by innovation. In a strong regime of appropriability, the innovator is able to capture a substantial share of that value: Pilkington's float glass process, Pfizer's Viagra, and Dyson's dual-cyclone vacuum cleaner—like Searle's NutraSweet—all generated huge profits for their owners. In a weak regime of appropriability, other parties derive most of the value. E-book readers, and online brokerage services, are similar to personal computers: a lack of proprietary technology results in fierce price competition and most of the value created goes to consumers.

The regime of appropriability comprises four key components which determine the innovator's ability to profit from innovation: property rights, the tacitness and complexity of the technology, lead time, and complementary resources.

Property Rights in Innovation   Capturing the returns to innovation depends, to a great extent, on the ability to establish property rights in the innovation. It was the desire to protect the returns to inventors that prompted the English Parliament to pass the 1623 Statute of Monopolies, which established the basis of patent law. Since then, the law has been extended to several areas of **intellectual property**, including:

- *Patents*: Exclusive rights to a new and useful product, process, substance, or design. Obtaining a patent requires that the invention is novel, useful, and not excessively obvious. Patent law varies from country to country. In the US, a patent is valid for 17 years (14 for a design).
- *Copyrights*: Exclusive production, publication, or sales rights to the creators of artistic, literary, dramatic, or musical works. Examples include articles, books, drawings, maps, photographs, and musical compositions.
- *Trademarks*: Words, symbols, or other marks used to distinguish the goods or services supplied by a firm. In the US and the UK, they are registered with the Patent Office. Trademarks provide the basis for brand identification.
- *Trade secrets*: Offer a modest degree of legal protection for recipes, formulae, industrial processes, customer lists, and other knowledge acquired in the course of business.

The effectiveness of intellectual property law depends on the type of innovation being protected. For new chemical products (a new drug or plastic), patents can provide effective protection. For products that involve new configurations of existing components or new manufacturing processes, patents may fail to prevent rivals from innovating around them. The scope of the patent law has been extended to include computer software, business methods, and genetically engineered life forms. Business method patents have generated considerable controversy, especially Amazon's patent on "one-click-to-buy" internet purchasing.[4] While patents and copyright establish property rights, their disadvantage (from the inventor's viewpoint) is that they make information public. Hence, companies often prefer secrecy to patenting as a means of protecting innovations.

In recent decades, companies have devoted increasing attention to protecting and exploiting the economic value of their intellectual property. When Texas Instruments began exploiting its patent portfolio as a revenue source during the 1980s, the technology sector as a whole woke up to the value of its knowledge assets. During the 1990s, TI's royalty income exceeded its operating income from other sources. One outcome has been an upsurge in patenting. The US Patent and Trademark Office granted 302,948 patents in 2013; during 1980–1985 it averaged 67,000 annually.

Tacitness and Complexity of the Technology   In the absence of effective legal protection the extent to which an innovation can be imitated by a competitor depends on the ease with which the technology can be comprehended and replicated. This depends, first, on the extent to which the technical knowledge is codifiable. Codifiable knowledge, by definition, is that which can be written down. Hence, if it is not effectively protected by patents or copyright, diffusion is likely to be rapid and the competitive advantage not sustainable. Financial innovations such as mortgage-backed securities and credit default swaps embody readily codifiable knowledge that can be copied very quickly. Similarly, Coca-Cola's recipe is codifiable and, in the absence of trade-secret protection, is easily copied. Intel's designs for advanced microprocessors are codified and can be copied; however, the processes for manufacturing these integrated circuits are based on deeply tacit knowledge.

The second key factor is *complexity*. Every new fashion, from the Mary Quant miniskirt of 1962 to Burberry's blanket coat of fall 2014 involves simple, easy-to-copy ideas. Conversely, Airbus's A380 and Intel's Core M processor based upon its 14-nanometer technology present entirely different challenges for the would-be imitator.

Lead Time   Tacitness and complexity do not provide lasting barriers to imitation, but they do offer the innovator *time*. Innovation creates a temporary competitive advantage that offers a window of opportunity for the innovator to build on the initial advantage.

The innovator's *lead time* is the time it will take followers to catch up. The challenge for the innovator is to use initial lead-time advantages to build the capabilities and market position to entrench industry leadership. Intel in microprocessors, Cisco Systems in routers, and Canon in inkjet printers were brilliant at exploiting lead time to build advantages in efficient manufacture, quality, and market presence. Conversely, innovative British companies are notorious for having squandered their lead-time advantage in jet planes, radars, CT scanners, and genomics.

Lead time allows a firm to move down its learning curve ahead of followers. In new generations of microprocessors, Intel has traditionally been first to market, allowing it to move quickly down its experience curve, cut prices, and so pressuring the profit margins of its rival, AMD.

Complementary Resources   Bringing new products and processes to market requires not just invention; it also requires the diverse resources and capabilities needed to finance, produce, and market the innovation. These are referred to as *complementary resources* (Figure 9.3). Chester Carlson invented xerography but was unable for many years to bring his product to market because he lacked the complementary resources needed to develop, manufacture, market, distribute, and service his invention. Conversely, Searle (and its later parent, Monsanto) was able to provide almost all the development, manufacturing, marketing, and distribution resources needed to exploit its NutraSweet innovation. As a result, Carlson was able to appropriate only a tiny part of the value created by his invention of the plain-paper Xerox copier, whereas Searle/Monsanto was successful in appropriating a major part of the value created by its new artificial sweetener.

FIGURE 9.3   Complementary resources

Complementary resources may be accessed through alliances with other firms, for example biotech firms ally with large pharmaceutical companies for clinical trials, manufacture, and marketing.[5] When an innovation and the complementary resources that support it are supplied by different firms, the division of value between them depends on their relative power. A key determinant of this is whether the complementary resources are *specialized* or *unspecialized*. Fuel cells may eventually displace both internal combustion engines and battery-powered electric motors in most of the world's automobiles. However, the problem for the developers of fuel cells is that their success depends on automobile manufacturers making specialized investments in designing a whole new range of cars, service station owners providing specialized refueling facilities, and repair firms investing in training and new equipment. For fuel cells to be widely adopted will require that the benefits of the innovation are shared widely with the different providers of these complementary resources. Where complementary resources are generic, the innovator is in a much stronger position to capture value. Because Adobe Systems' Acrobat Portable Document Format (PDF) works with files created in almost any software application, Adobe is well positioned to capture most of the value created by its innovatory software product. However, one advantage of co-specialized complementary resources is that they raise barriers to imitation. Consider the threat that Linux presents to Microsoft Window's dominance of PC operating systems. Intel has adapted its microprocessors to the needs of Windows and most applications software is written to run on Windows, so the challenge for the Linux community is not just to develop a workable operating system but also to encourage the development of applications software and hardware that are compatible with the Linux operating system.

Which Mechanisms Are Effective at Protecting Innovation?

How effective are these different mechanisms in protecting innovations? Table 9.1 shows that, despite considerable variation across industries, patent protection is of limited effectiveness as compared with lead time, secrecy, and complementary manufacturing and sales/service resources. Indeed, since the late 1980s, the effectiveness of patents appeared to have declined despite the strengthening of patent law. Although patents are effective in increasing the lead time before competitors are able to bring imitative products to market, these gains tend to be small. The great majority of patented products and processes are duplicated within three years.[6]

Given the limited effectiveness of patents, why do firms continue to engage in patenting? Figure 9.4 shows that, while protection from imitation is the principal motive, several others are also very important. In particular, much patenting activity appears to be strategic; it is directed toward blocking the innovation efforts of other companies and establishing property rights in technologies that can then be used in bargaining with other companies for access to their proprietary technologies. In semiconductors and electronics, cross-licensing arrangements—where one company gives access to its patents across a field of technology in exchange for access to another company's patents—are critical in permitting "freedom to design": the ability to design products that draw on technologies owned by different companies.[7]

TABLE 9.1 The effectiveness of different mechanisms for protecting innovation

	Secrecy (%)	Patents (%)	Lead-time (%)	Sales/service (%)	Manufacturing (%)
Product innovations					
Food	59	18	53	40	51
Drugs	54	50	50	33	49
Electronic components	34	21	46	50	51
Telecom equipment	47	26	66	42	41
Medical equipment	51	55	58	52	49
All industries	51	35	53	43	46
Process innovations					
Food	56	16	42	30	47
Drugs	68	36	36	25	44
Electronic components	47	15	43	42	56
Telecom equipment	35	15	43	34	41
Medical equipment	49	34	45	32	50
All industries	51	23	38	31	43

Note:
These data show the percentage of companies reporting that the particular mechanism, their sales and service, and their manufacturing capabilities were effective in protecting their innovations.
Source: W. M. Cohen, R. R. Nelson, and J. P. Walsh, "Protecting Their Intellectual Assets: Appropriability Conditions and Why US Manufacturing Firms Patent (Or Not)," NBER Working Paper No. W7552 (February 2000). © 2000. Reprinted by permission of the authors.

FIGURE 9.4   Why do companies patent? (Responses by 674 US companies)

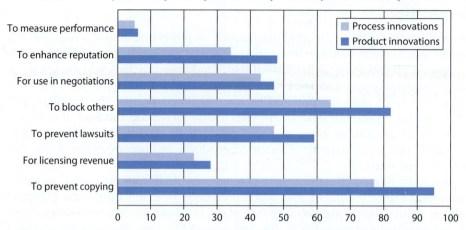

Source: W. M. Cohen, R. R. Nelson, and J. P. Walsh, "Protecting Their Intellectual Assets: Appropriability Conditions and Why US Manufacturing Firms Patent (Or Not)," NBER Working Paper No. W7552 (February 2000). © 2000. Reprinted by permission of the authors.

Strategies to Exploit Innovation: How and When to Enter

Having established some of the key factors that determine the returns to innovation, let us consider some of the main questions concerning the formulation of strategies to manage technology and exploit innovation.

Alternative Strategies to Exploit Innovation

How should a firm maximize the returns to its innovation? A number of alternative strategies are available. Figure 9.5 orders them according to the size of the commitment of resources that each requires. Thus, licensing requires little involvement by the innovator in subsequent commercialization, hence is a limited investment. Internal commercialization, possibly through creating a new enterprise or business unit, involves a much greater investment of resources and capabilities. In between there are various opportunities for collaboration with other companies—joint ventures, strategic alliances, and outsourcing that allow resource sharing between companies.

A firm's choice of exploitation mode depends on two sets of factors: the characteristics of the innovation and the resources and capabilities of the firm.

Characteristics of the Innovation   The extent to which a firm can establish clear property rights in an innovation is a critical determinant of its innovation strategy. Licensing is only viable where ownership in the innovation is protected by patent or copyrights. Thus, in pharmaceuticals, licensing is widespread because patents are clear and defensible. Many biotech companies engage only in R & D and license their drug discoveries to large pharmaceutical companies that possess the necessary

FIGURE 9.5   Alternative strategies for exploiting innovation

Low —— High

	Licensing	Outsourcing certain functions	Strategic alliance	Joint venture	Internal commercialization
Risk and return	Little investment risk but returns also limited. Risk that the licensee either lacks motivation or steals the innovation	Limits capital investment, but may create dependence on suppliers/partners	Benefits of flexibility. Risks of informal structure	Shares investment and risk. Risk of partner disagreement and culture clash	Biggest investment requirement and corresponding risks. Benefits of control
Resource requirements	Legal protection	Capability in managing outsourced activities	Pooling of the resources and capabilities of multiple firms requires collaborative capability		Full set of complementary resources and capabilities
Examples	ARM plc licenses its microprocessor technology to over 200 semiconductor companies; Stanford University earns over $100m annually from licensing its inventions	Apple designs its iPhones and Nvidia designs its graphics processing units, but both outsource manufacturing	Nike and Apple's alliance to develop wearable devices was followed in 2014 by Samsung and Under Armour forming a similar alliance	Panasonic and Tesla Motors formed a joint venture in 2014 to develop a gigafactory to produce lithium ion batteries	Larry Page and Sergey Brin established Google Inc. to develop and market their internet search technology

complementary resources. Royalties from licensing its sound-reduction technologies accounted for 82% of Dolby Laboratories' 2014 revenues. Conversely, when Steve Jobs and Steve Wozniak developed their Apple I and Apple II computers, they had little option other than to go into business themselves: the absence of proprietary technology ruled out licensing as an option.

The advantages of licensing are, first, that it relieves the company of the need to acquire the complementary resources and capabilities needed for commercialization and, second, that it can allow the innovation to be commercialized quickly. If the lead time offered by the innovation is short, multiple licensing can allow for a fast global rollout. The problem, however, is that the success of the innovation in the market is totally dependent on the commitment and effectiveness of the licensees. James Dyson, the British inventor of the dual cyclone vacuum cleaner, created his own company to manufacture and market his vacuum cleaners after failing to interest any major appliance company in licensing his technology.

Resources and Capabilities of the Firm   As Figure 9.5 shows, different strategies require very different resources and capabilities. Hence, the choice of how to exploit an innovation depends critically upon the resources and capabilities that the innovator brings to the party. Start-up firms possess few of the complementary resources and capabilities needed to commercialize their innovations. Inevitably, they will be attracted to licensing or to accessing the resources of larger firms through outsourcing, alliances, or joint ventures. As we noted in the previous chapter, new industries often follow a two-stage evolution where "innovators" do the pioneering and "consolidators" with their complementary resources do the developing.

Certain large, resource-rich corporations such as DuPont, Siemens, Hitachi, and IBM have strong traditions of pursuing basic research, then internally developing the innovations that arise. However, even these companies have been forced into more technological collaborations with other companies. Ron Adner observes that innovation increasingly requires coordinated responses by multiple companies. Innovating firms need to identify and map their *innovation ecosystem*, then manage the interdependencies within it. The long delay in the introduction of HDTV can be attributed to inadequate coordination among TV manufacturers, production studios, and broadcasters.[8] We shall return to the challenges of managing innovation ecosystems when we look closer at platform-based competition.

Timing Innovation: To Lead or to Follow?

To gain competitive advantage in emerging and technologically intensive industries, is it better to be a leader or a follower in innovation? As Table 9.2 shows, the evidence is mixed: in some products the leader has been the first to grab the prize; in others, the leader has succumbed to the risks and costs of pioneering. Optimal timing of entry into an emerging industry and the introduction of new technology are complex issues. The advantage of being an early mover depends on the following factors:

- *The extent to which innovation can be protected by property rights or lead-time advantages:* If an innovation is appropriable through a patent, copyright, or lead-time advantage, there is advantage in being an early mover. This is especially the case where patent protection is important, as in

TABLE 9.2   Leaders, followers, and success in emerging industries

Product	Innovator	Follower	The winner
Jet airliner	De Havilland (Comet)	Boeing (707)	Follower
Float glass	Pilkington	Corning	Leader
X-ray scanner	EMI	General Electric	Follower
Office PC	Xerox	IBM	Follower
VCRs	Ampex/Sony	Matsushita	Follower
Instant camera	Polaroid	Kodak	Leader
Microwave oven	Raytheon	Samsung	Follower
Video games player	Atari	Nintendo/Sony	Followers
Disposable diaper	Procter & Gamble	Kimberley-Clark	Leader
Compact disk	Sony/Philips	Matsushita, Pioneer	Leader
Web browser	Netscape	Microsoft	Follower
Web search engine	Lycos	Google	Follower
MP3 music players	Diamond Multimedia	Apple (iPod)	Follower
Operating systems for mobile devices	Symbian, Palm OS	Microsoft, Apple, Google	Followers
Laser printer	Xerox, IBM	Canon	Follower
Flash memory	Toshiba	Samsung, Intel	Followers
E-book reader	Sony (Digital Reader)	Amazon (Kindle)	Follower
Social networking	SixDegrees.com	Facebook	Follower

Source: Updated from D. Teece, *The Competitive Challenge: Strategies for Industrial Innovation and Renewal* (Cambridge: Ballinger, 1987): 186–8.

pharmaceuticals. Notable patent races include that between Alexander Bell and Elisha Gray to patent the telephone (Bell got to the Patent Office a few hours before Gray),[9] and between Celera Inc. and the National Institutes of Health to patent the sequence of the human genome.[10]

- *The importance of complementary resources*: The more important complementary resources are in exploiting an innovation, the greater the costs and risks of pioneering. Prior to Tesla Motors, just abut every company that tried to pioneer an all-electric car failed miserably. The problem for the pioneer is that the development costs are huge because of the need, not just to orchestrate multiple technologies but also to establish an entire infrastructure for distribution, service, and recharging. Where the need for complementary resources is great, followers are also favored by the fact that, as an industry develops, specialist firms emerge to supply complements. Thus, in pioneering electric cars, a key challenge for Tesla Motors—especially in major overseas markets such as China—is establishing chains of charging stations. Later entrants into electric cars will be able to rely upon an established infrastructure.

- *The potential to establish a standard*: As we shall see later in this chapter, some markets converge toward a technical standard. The greater the importance of technical standards, the greater the advantages of being an early mover in order to influence those standards and gain the market momentum needed to establish leadership. Once a standard has been set, displacing it becomes exceptionally difficult. IBM was responsible for establishing Microsoft's MS-DOS as the dominant operating system for personal computers. However, when in 1987 IBM launched its OS/2 operating system, it had little success against the entrenched position of Microsoft. Only by offering their products for free have Linux and Google's Chrome been able to take market share from Microsoft's Windows.

The implication is that optimal timing depends on the resources and capabilities that a firm has at its disposal. Hence, different firms have different *strategic windows*—periods in time when their resources and capabilities are aligned with the opportunities available in the market. A small, technology-based firm may have no choice but to pioneer innovation: its opportunity is to grab **first-mover advantage** and then develop the necessary complementary resources before more powerful rivals appear. For the large, established firm with financial resources and strong production, marketing, and distribution capabilities, the strategic window is likely to be both longer and later. The risks of pioneering are greater for an established firm with a reputation and brands to protect, while to exploit its complementary resources effectively typically requires a more developed market. Consider the following examples:

- In the early days of personal computers, Apple was a pioneer, IBM a follower. The timing of entry was probably optimal for each. Apple's resources comprised the vision of Steve Jobs and the technical genius of Steve Wozniak; only by pioneering could it hope to be successful. IBM had enormous strengths in manufacturing, distribution, and reputation. It could build competitive advantage even without technological leadership. The key for IBM was to delay its entry until the time when the market had developed to the point where IBM's strengths could have their maximum impact.

- In the browser war between Netscape and Microsoft, Microsoft had the luxury of being able to follow the pioneer, Netscape. Microsoft's huge product development, marketing, and distribution capabilities, and, most important, its vast installed base of the Windows operating system allowed it to overhaul Netscape's initial lead.

- EMI, the British music and electronics company, introduced the world's first CT scanner in 1972. Despite a four-year lead, General Electric's vast technological and commercial capabilities within medical electronics allowed it to drive EMI out of the market.[11]

Followers are especially effective in initiating a new product's transition from niche market to mass market. According to Markides and Geroski, successful first movers pioneer new products that embody new technologies and new functionality.[12] The opportunity for the fast-second entrant is to grow the niche market into a mass market by lowering cost and increasing quality. Timing is critical. Don Sull argues that a successful follower strategy requires "active waiting": a company needs to monitor market developments and assemble resources and capabilities while it prepares for large-scale market entry.[13]

Managing Risks

Emerging industries are risky. There are two main sources of uncertainty:

- *Technological uncertainty* arises from the unpredictability of technological evolution and the complex dynamics through which technical standards and dominant designs are selected. Hindsight is always 20/20, but *ex ante* it is difficult to predict how technologies and the industries that deploy them will evolve.

- *Market uncertainty* relates to the size and growth rates of the markets for new products. When Xerox introduced its first plain-paper copier in 1959, Apple its first personal computer in 1977, or Sony its Walkman in 1979, none had any idea of the size of the potential market. Similarly with Facebook: when Mark Zuckerberg launched it from his Harvard dorm in February 2004, there was little indication that it would grow from a college website into a global social network with over one billion active users. Forecasting demand for new products is hazardous—most forecasting techniques are based on past data. Demand forecasts for new products tend to rely either on analogies[14] or expert opinion— e.g., combining expert insight and experience using the *Delphi technique*.[15]

If managers are unable to forecast technology and demand, then to manage risk they must be alert to emerging trends while limiting their exposure to risk through avoiding large-scale commitments. Useful strategies for limiting risk include:

- *Cooperating with lead users*: During the early phases of industry development, careful monitoring of and response to market trends and customer requirements is essential to avoid major errors in technology and design. Von Hippel argues that lead users provide a source of leading market indicators, can assist in developing new products and processes, and offer an early cash flow to fund development expenditures.[16] In computer software, *beta versions* are released to computer enthusiasts for testing. Nike has two sets of lead users: professional athletes who are trendsetters for athletic footwear and hip-hop artists who are at the leading edge of urban fashion trends. In communications and aerospace, government defense contracts play a crucial role in developing new technologies.[17]

- *Limiting risk exposure*: The financial risks of emerging industries can be mitigated by financial and operational practices that minimize a firm's exposure to adversity. By avoiding debt and keeping fixed costs low, a firm can lower its financial and operational gearing. Outsourcing and strategic alliance can also hold down capital investment and fixed costs.

- *Flexibility*: Uncertainty necessitates rapid responses to unpredicted events. Achieving such flexibility means keeping options open and delaying commitment to a specific technology until its potential becomes clear. Twitter—originally Odeo—was founded to develop a podcasting platform. Once Apple added a podcasting facility to iTunes, Odeo redirected itself toward a platform for internet-hosted text messages.

- *Multiple strategies*: Eric Beinhocker of McKinsey & Company argues that uncertainty favors multiple strategies over a single focused strategy—what he refers to as "robust, adaptive strategies." Faced with technological uncertainty, well-resourced companies—such as IBM, Microsoft, and Google—have the luxury of simultaneously investing in a variety of technological options. For Microsoft this has meant a number of prominent failures—MP3 players (Zune), smartphones (Kin), tablet computers (Surface), and social networking (Yammer). Nevertheless, Microsoft's multiplicity of investments has allowed it to build leadership positions in several new fields, including online gaming and cloud computing.[18] Large, well-resourced companies have the luxury of pursuing multiple strategic options.

Standards, Platforms, and Network Externalities

In the previous chapter, we noted that the establishment of a standard can be a key event in an industry's development and growth. In the digital, networked economy, more and more markets are subject to standards which play a vital role in ensuring compatibility between users. For companies, owning a standard can be an important source of competitive advantage with the potential to offer returns that are unmatched by any other type of competitive advantage. Table 9.3 lists several companies which own key technical standards within a particular product category. A characteristic of most of these companies is the fact that these standards have generated considerable profits and shareholder value.

Types of Standard

A *standard* is a format, an interface, or a system that allows interoperability. Adhering to standards allows us to browse millions of different web pages, ensures the light bulbs made by any manufacturer will fit any manufacturer's lamps, and keeps the traffic moving in Los Angeles (most of the time). Standards can be *public* or *private*.

- Public (or *open*) standards are those that are available to all either free or for a nominal charge. Typically, they do not involve any privately owned

TABLE 9.3 Examples of companies that own de facto industry standards

Company	Product category	Standard
Microsoft	PC operating systems	Windows
Intel	PC microprocessors	x86 series
Sony/Philips	Compact disks	CD-ROM format
ARM (Holdings)	Microprocessors for mobile devices	ARM architecture
Oracle Corporation	Programming language for web apps	Java
Qualcomm	Digital cellular wireless communication	CDMA
Adobe Systems	Common file format for creating and viewing documents	Acrobat Portable Document Format
Adobe Systems	Web page animation	Adobe Flash
Adobe Systems	Page description language for document printing	Post Script
Bosch	Antilock braking systems	ABS and TCS (Traction Control System)
IMAX Corporation	Motion picture filming and projection system	IMAX
Apple	Music downloading system	iTunes/iPod
Sony	High definition DVD	Blu-ray
NTT DOCOMO	Mobile phone payment system in Japan	Osaifu-Keitai

intellectual property, or the intellectual-property owners make access free (such as Linux). Public standards may be *mandatory standards* set by government and backed by the force of law (these relate mainly to safety, environmental, and consumer protection standards) or they are voluntary standards set by industry associations of standards bodies such as the International Organization for Standardization (ISO), the American National Standards Institute, or the British Standards Institute. Thus, the GSM mobile phone standard was set by the European Telecom Standards Institute. Internet protocols (standards governing internet addressing and routing) are mostly public. They are governed by several international bodies, including the Internet Engineering Task Force.

- Private (*proprietary*) standards are those where the technologies and designs are owned by companies or individuals. If I own the technology that becomes a standard, I can embody the technology in a product that others buy or license the technology to others who wish to use it. Thus, in smartphones the major rival standards are Apple's iOS and Google's Android. Apple's iOS is used only in Apple's mobile devices; Android is licensed widely. Android also represents another variant on technical standards: it is *open source*; it is freely available; and it can be used, adapted, and developed by anyone. Most private standards are de facto standards: they emerge through voluntary adoption by producers and consumers. Table 9.3 gives examples.

A problem with *de facto* standards is that they may take a long time to emerge, resulting in a duplication of investments and delaying the development of the market. It was 40 years before a standard railroad gauge was agreed in the US.[19] A mandated, public standard can avoid much of this uncertainty. Europe's mandating of standards for wireless telephony as compared with the US's market-based approach resulted in Europe making the transition to 2G much quicker than the US. However, with 4G the situation has reversed: it is Europe that is the laggard.[20] Delayed emergence of a standard may kill the technology altogether. The failure of quadraphonic sound to displace stereophonic sound during the 1970s resulted from incompatible technical standards, which inhibited audio manufacturers, record companies, and consumers from investing in the technology.[21]

The Role of Network Externalities

Standards emerge in markets that are subject to **network externalities**. A network externality exists whenever the value of a product to an individual customer depends on the number of other users of that product. The classic example of network externality is the telephone. Since there is little satisfaction to be gained from talking to oneself on the telephone, the value of a telephone to each user depends on the number of other users connected to the same network. This is different from most products. When I pour myself a glass of Glenlivet after a couple of exhausting MBA classes, my enjoyment is independent of how many other people in the world are drinking whiskey. Indeed, some products may have *negative* network externalities—the value of the product is less if many other people purchase the same product. If I spend $3000 on an Armani silver lamé tuxedo and find that half my colleagues at the faculty Christmas party are wearing the same jacket, my satisfaction is lessened.

Networks require technical standards to ensure connection to the network. This does not require everyone to use the same product or even the same technology, but rather that the different products are *compatible* with one another through some form of common interface. In the case of wireless telephone service, it doesn't matter (as far as network access is concerned) whether I purchase service from AT&T, Verizon, or T-Mobile: technical standards ensure compatibility between each network which allows connectivity. Similarly with railroads: if I am transporting coal from Wyoming to Boston, my choice of railroad company is not critical. Unlike in the 1870s, every railroad company now uses a standard gauge and is required to give "common carrier" access to other companies' rolling stock.

Network externalities arise from several sources:

- *Products where users are linked to a network*: Telephones, railroad systems, and email instant messaging groups are networks where users are linked together. Applications software, whether spreadsheet programs or video games, also links users—they can share files and play games interactively. User-level externalities may also arise through social identification. I watch *Game of Thrones* and the Hollywood Oscar presentations on TV not because I enjoy them but so that I have something to talk to my colleagues about in the faculty common room.[22]
- *Availability of complementary products and services*: Where products are consumed as systems, the availability of complementary products and services depends on the number of customers for that system. Microsoft's key problem in the smartphone market is that Windows' 3% market share results in an acute shortage of third-party apps for the Windows Phone. Similarly, I choose to own a Ford Focus rather than a Ferrari Testarossa, not only because I'm a lousy driver but also because I know that, should I break

down 200 miles from Bismarck, North Dakota, spare parts and a repair service will be more readily available.

- *Economizing on switching costs*: By purchasing the product or system that is most widely used, there is less chance that I shall have to bear the costs of switching. By using Microsoft PowerPoint rather than an alternative presentation software such as SlideRocket or Prezi, it is more likely that I will avoid the costs of retraining and file conversion when I become a visiting professor at another university.

Network externalities create *positive feedback*. Once a technology or system gains market leadership, it attracts more and more users. Conversely, once market leadership is lost, a downward spiral is likely. This process is called *tipping*: once a certain threshold is reached, cumulative forces become unstoppable—the result is a *winner-takes-all* market.[23] Those markets subject to significant network externalities tend to be dominated by a single supplier (e.g., Microsoft in PC operating systems and office applications, eBay in internet auctions, and Airbnb in residential accommodation sharing).

Once established, technical and design standards tend to be highly resilient. Standards are difficult to displace due to learning effects and collective lock-in. Learning effects cause the dominant technology and design to be continually improved and refined. Even where the existing standard is inherently inferior, switching to a superior technology may not occur because of collective lock in. The classic case is the QWERTY typewriter layout. Its 1873 design was based on the need to *slow* the speed of typing to prevent typewriter keys from jamming. Although the jamming problem was soon solved, the QWERTY layout has persisted, despite the availability of the faster Dvorak Simplified Keyboard (DSK).[24]

Platform-based Markets

Digital technologies together with internet or wireless connectivity have created markets where network externalities arise both from user connections and from the availability of complements. These platform-based markets are also referred to as *two-sided* (or even *multi-sided*) markets because they form an interface between two groups of users: customers and the suppliers of complementary products.

Operating systems are the quintessential platforms: Microsoft's Windows, Apple's iOS, and Google's Android create network externalities among users (*direct* externalities) and among the suppliers of applications (*indirect* externalities). Each of these platforms is central to an ecosystem comprising thousands of interdependent companies that coevolve. Thus, the Android ecosystem comprises over 100 smartphone manufacturers, thousands of app developers, suppliers of hardware components, accessory providers, and many other types of player. As Strategy Capsule 4.1 in Chapter 4 describes in relation to smartphones, competition between rival platforms for market dominance is often intense.

However, platforms are not restricted to digital markets, and nor do the networks necessarily require technical standards. A shopping mall is a platform: the mall developer creates a two-sided market comprising the retailers who lease the individual stores and the customers who do the shopping—network externalities operate on both sides.

Deciding whether to pursue a product strategy or a platform strategy is a key strategic issue. Google and Facebook both began with product strategies but soon recognized the potential for their products—Google's search engine and Facebook's social network—to become platforms. Many department stores have undertaken a similar transition: abandoning retailing in favor of managing an infrastructure that hosts multiple concession stores. The success of the Apple Macintosh between 1984 and 2004 was limited by Apple's pursuit of a product rather than a platform strategy. We look further at platform strategies in Strategy Capsule 9.2.

Competing for Standards

In markets subject to network externalities, control over standards is the primary basis for competitive advantage. Owning a proprietary standard can be the basis for market domination—and, as in the case of the Wintel standard for personal computers—a source of massive profits. What do we know about designing winning strategies in markets subject to network externalities?

The first key issue is to determine whether we are competing in a market that will converge around a single technical standard. This requires a careful analysis of the presence and sources of network externalities.

The second strategic issue in standards setting is recognizing the role of positive feedback: the technology that can establish early leadership will rapidly gain momentum. Building a "bigger bandwagon" according to Shapiro and Varian[25] requires the following:

- *Before you go to war, assemble allies*: You'll need the support of consumers, suppliers of complements, even your competitors. Not even the strongest companies can afford to go it alone in a standards war.

- *Preempt the market*: Enter early, achieve fast-cycle product development, make early deals with key customers, and adopt penetration pricing.

- *Manage expectations*: The key to managing positive feedback is to convince customers, suppliers, and the producers of complementary goods that you will emerge as the victor. These expectations become a self-fulfilling prophecy. The massive pre-launch promotion and publicity built up by Sony prior to the American and European launch of PlayStation 2 in October 2000 was an effort to convince consumers, retailers, and game developers that the product would be the blockbuster consumer electronics product of the new decade, thereby stymieing Sega's and Nintendo's efforts to establish their rival systems.

A great deal has been learned from the standards battles of the past four decades, particularly those involving competing platforms. Strategy Capsule 9.2 outlines the lessons from past platform wars. If a company attempts to appropriate too great a share of the value created, it may well fail to build a big enough bandwagon to gain market leadership. Thus, most recent standards battles have involved broad alliances, which comprise multiple ecosystem members. In the 2006–2008 struggle between Sony (Blu-ray) and Toshiba (HD-DVD), each camp recruited movie studios, software firms, and producers of computers and consumer electronics using various inducements, including direct cash payments. The defection of Warner Brothers to the Sony camp was critical to the market tipping suddenly in Sony's favor. However, it appears that all the financial gains from owning the winning standard were dissipated by the costs of the war.[26]

STRATEGY CAPSULE 9.2
Winning Platform Wars

Past competitive battles between rival platforms have exercised a powerful influence over current thinking about designing strategies for markets subject to network externalities. None has been more influential than the competitive battles of the late 1970 and 1980s in video-cassette recorders (VCRs) and personal computers (PCs).

In neither case was technical superiority the key—indeed, in both instances it could be argued that the superior technology lost. The key factor was managing the dynamics of market penetration in order to build market leadership:

◆ In VCRs, Sony kept tight proprietary control of its Betamax system; JVC licensed its VHS system to Sharp, Philips, GE, RCA, and others, fueling market penetration.

◆ In computers, IBM's PC platform became dominant because access to its product specifications and the availability of the core technologies—notably Microsoft's operating system and Intel's microprocessors—allowed a multitude of "clone makers" to enter the market. The problem for IBM was that it established the dominant platform

but Intel and Microsoft appropriated most of the value. For Apple, the situation was the reverse: by keeping tight control over its Macintosh operating system and product architecture, it earned high margins, but it forfeited the opportunity for market dominance.

This tradeoff between penetrating the market and appropriating the returns to platform ownership is shown in Figure 9.6. Learning from these two epic contests, platform owners have relinquished more and more value to complementors, competitors, and customers in order to build a bigger bandwagon than their rivals. In some cases this has meant foregoing all possible profits. In the browser war of 1995–1998, both Netscape (Navigator) and Microsoft (Explorer) ended up giving away their products.

Finding a better balance between market penetration and value appropriation has resulted in new pricing models. Adobe (and many other software suppliers) follows a "freemium" model—Acrobat Reader is available free of charge, but to create or convert PDF files, the necessary Acrobat software must be purchased.

Achieving compatibility with existing products is a critical issue in standards battles. Advantage typically goes to the competitor that adopts an *evolutionary strategy* (i.e., offers backward compatibility) rather than one that adopts a *revolutionary strategy*.[27] A key advantage of the Sony PlayStation 2 over Microsoft Xbox and Nintendo Cube was its compatibility with the PlayStation 1. However, the limited compatibility of PlayStation 3 with PlayStation 2 was one of the many problems that limited the success of PlayStation 3.

What are the key resources needed to win a standards war? Shapiro and Varian emphasize the following:

● control over an installed base of customers;
● owning intellectual property rights in the new technology;

Other platform battles have indicated that winning platform wars is not only about building market momentum through maximizing the numbers of complementors and customers. Customers are, typically, not buying a platform; they are buying a system, and the attractiveness of that system is not determined exclusively by the number of users and the number of complements available. Consider two exceptionally profitable platform owners: Nintendo in video game consoles during 1988–1996 and Apple in smartphones during 2008–2015. In both cases the success of the platforms—the Nintendo

Entertainment System (NES) and the iPhone—was determined by the overall quality of the system, not just the hardware but the applications software as well. Both Nintendo and Apple exercised tight control over application developers imposing quality standards and ensuring overall system integration.

Sources: A. Gawer and M. A. Cusumano, "How Companies Become Platform Leaders," *MIT Sloan Management Review* 49 (2008): 28–35; C. Cennamo and J. Santal, "Platform Competition: Strategic Trade-offs in Platform Markets," *Strategic Management Journal* 34 (2013): 133150.

FIGURE 9.6   Platform wars in videocassette recorders and personal computers

- the ability to innovate in order to extend and adapt the initial technological advance;
- early-mover advantage;
- strength in complements (e.g., Intel has preserved its standard in microprocessors by promoting standards in buses, chipsets, graphics controllers, and interfaces between motherboards and CPUs);
- reputation and brand name.[28]

However, the dynamics of standards wars are complex and we are far from being able to propose general strategy principles. As Strategy Capsule 9.2 shows, in platform-based competition it is not always the case that "the biggest bandwagon wins"—issues of quality and brand differentiation are also important. Nor does platform leadership necessarily translate into the platform owner's ability to capture value. Finally, it is often unclear whether a market will converge around a single platform (e.g., eBay in online auctions) or multiple platforms (e.g., video game consoles and smartphones.)[29]

Implementing Technology Strategies: Creating the Conditions for Innovation

As we have noted previously, strategy formulation cannot be separated from its implementation. Nowhere is this more evident than in technology-intensive businesses.

Our analysis so far has taught us about the potential for generating competitive advantage from innovation and about the design of technology-based strategies but has said little about the conditions under which innovation is achieved. Incisive strategic analysis of how to make money out of innovation is of little use if we cannot generate innovation in the first place. We know that innovation requires certain resources—people, facilities, information, and time—but, like other capabilities, the relationship between R & D input and innovation output is weak—indeed under some circumstances lack of resources may act as a spur to innovation.[30] The productivity of R & D depends critically on the organizational conditions that foster innovation. What are these conditions and how do we create them?

Let's begin with the critical distinction between invention and innovation. While these activities are complementary, they require different resources and different organizational conditions. While invention depends on creativity, innovation requires collaboration and cross-functional integration.

Fostering Creativity

The Conditions for Creativity   Invention is an act of creativity requiring knowledge and imagination. The creativity that drives invention is typically an individual act that establishes a meaningful relationship between concepts or objects that had not previously been related. This reconceptualization can be triggered by accidents: an apple falling on Isaac Newton's head or James Watt observing a kettle boiling. Creativity is associated with particular personality traits. Creative people tend to be curious, imaginative, adventurous, assertive, playful, self-confident, risk taking, reflective, and uninhibited.[31]

Individual creativity also depends on the organizational environment in which they work—this is as true for the researchers and engineers at Amgen and Google as it was for the painters and sculptors of the Florentine and Venetian schools. Few great works of art or outstanding inventions are the products of solitary geniuses. Creativity is stimulated by human interaction: the productivity of R & D laboratories depends critically on the communication networks that the engineers and scientists establish.[32] An important catalyst of interaction is *play*, which creates an environment of inquiry, liberates thought from conventional constraints, and provides the opportunity to establish new relationships by rearranging ideas and structures at a safe distance from reality. The essence of play is that it permits unconstrained forms of experimentation.[33] The potential for low-cost experimentation has expanded vastly thanks to advances in computer modeling and simulation that permit prototyping and market research to be undertaken speedily and virtually.[34]

Organizing for Creativity   Creativity requires management systems that are quite different from those that are appropriate for efficiency—we observed in Chapter 8, when discussing the challenge of *ambidexterity,* exploration needs to be managed very differently from exploitation. In particular, creatively oriented people tend to be responsive to distinctive types of incentive. They desire to work in an egalitarian culture with enough space and resources to provide the opportunity to be spontaneous, experience freedom, and have fun in the performance of a task that, they feel, makes a difference to the performance of their organization (and, possibly, to the world as a whole). Praise, recognition, and opportunities for education and professional growth are also more important than assuming managerial responsibilities.[35] Evidence from open-source projects shows that people will devote time and effort to creative activities even in the absence of financial rewards.[36] Nurturing the drive to create may require a degree of freedom and flexibility that conflicts with conventional HR practices. At many technology-based companies, including Google and W. L. Gore & Associates, engineers choose which projects they wish to join.

Organizational environments conducive to creativity tend to be both nurturing and competitive. Creativity requires a work context that is secure but not cozy. Dorothy Leonard points to the merits of *creative abrasion* within innovative teams—fostering innovation through the interaction of different personalities and perspectives. Managers must resist the temptation to clone in favor of embracing diversity of cognitive and behavioral characteristics within work groups—creating *whole brain teams.*[37] Exploiting diversity may require constructive conflict. Microsoft's development team meetings are renowned for open criticism and intense disagreement. Such conflict can spur progress toward better solutions.

Table 9.4 contrasts some characteristics of innovative organizations compared with those designed for operational efficiency.

Accessing External Sources of Innovation

Internal creativity is not the sole source of innovation: innovation can be accessed beyond an organization's boundaries. A major trend in innovation management has been a shift in focus away from firms' internal R & D toward accessing ideas and knowledge from the wider world. New tools of information and communications technology have reinforced this trend.

Customers as Sources of Innovation

We observed earlier in this chapter that research directed toward practical needs is more likely to lead to innovation than that motivated toward scientific discovery. Few important inventions have been spontaneous creations by technologists—most have resulted from grappling with practical problems. The invention of the Xerox

TABLE 9.4 The characteristics of "operating" and "innovating" organizations

	Operating organization	Innovating organization
Structure	Bureaucratic Specialization and division of labor Hierarchical control Defined organizational boundaries	Flat organization without hierarchical control Task-oriented project teams Fuzzy organizational boundaries
Processes	Emphasis on eliminating variation (e.g., six-sigma) Top-down control Tight financial controls	Emphasis on enhancing variation Loose controls to foster idea generation Flexible strategic planning and financial control
Reward systems	Financial compensation Promotion up the hierarchy Power and status symbols	Autonomy Recognition Equity participation in new ventures
People	Recruitment and selection based on the needs of the organization structure for specific skills: functional and staff specialists, general managers, and operatives	Key need is for idea generators who combine required technical knowledge with creative personality traits Managers must act as sponsors and orchestrators.

Source: Adapted from J. K. Galbraith and R. K. Kazanjian, *Strategy Implementation: Structure, Systems and Processes,* 2nd edn (St. Paul, MN: West, 1986).

copying process (xerography) by Chester Carlson, a patent attorney, was inspired by his frustration with the tedious task of making multiple copies of patent applications. Joseph Lister, a British surgeon, developed sterile surgery in response to the appalling fatality rate from surgery in the Victorian era.

The old adage that "necessity is the mother of invention" explains why customers are such fertile sources of innovation—they are most acutely involved with matching existing products and services to their needs. However, listening to customers is typically a weak inspiration and guide for innovation. As Henry Ford remarked: "If I had asked people what they wanted, they would have said faster horses!" Moreover, as studies of disruptive innovation have shown, major customers are likely to be dismissive of radical innovation.

According to Adrian Slywotzky, the key is "Creating What People Love Before They Know They Want It." This requires focusing not on what customers want but on their sources of dissatisfaction. He advocates creating a "hassle map": a sequence of customers' frustrations and negative emotions that can guide new approaches to creating customer value.[38]

Eric von Hippel advocates making customers part of the innovation process.[39] Companies can induce and exploit customer initiated innovation by identifying leading-edge customers, supplying them with easy-to-use design tools, and ensuring flexibility in production processes so that customers' innovations can be effectively exploited.[40]

Open Innovation

Involving customers (and suppliers, too) in innovation may be seen as an intermediate stage in opening the innovation processes. As innovation increasingly requires integrating multiple technologies—often from traditionally separate scientific areas—so firms have been forced to look more widely in sourcing technology and sharing know-how. The evidence that interpersonal interaction stimulates innovation is overwhelming. This is true whether we are considering R & D teams within organizations, inter-firm alliances, interpersonal networks, or clusters of firms concentrated within industrial districts.[41] Building on the principle that the gains to collaborative knowledge sharing outweigh the risks of one's proprietary knowledge being expropriated, an increasing number of firms are adopting **open innovation**—an approach to innovation that seeks, exploits, and applies knowledge both from inside and outside the organization. According to Henry Chesbrough: "Open innovation is fundamentally about operating in a world of abundant knowledge, where not all the smart people work for you, so you'd better go find them, connect to them, and build upon what they can do."[42] While the pioneers of open innovation have been open-source software communities and networks of small and medium-sized firms, some of its leading exponents are giant corporations (Strategy Capsule 9.3).

Buying Innovation

For all the exhortations by business leaders and management consultants to cultivate innovation, the fact remains that small, technology-intensive start-ups have advantages over large corporations in the early stages of the innovation process. Hence, the major source of innovation for many large companies is to buy it through licensing, outright purchase of patents, or acquiring young, technology-based companies. Pharmaceutical companies have been especially prominent in this outsourcing of innovation, especially within biotechnology. In addition to licensing drug patents and signing collaborative agreements, outright acquisitions of specialist biotech firms (these include Alios BioPharma by Johnson & Johnson in 2014, Genentech by Roche in 2009, ICOS by Eli Lily in 2007, and Chiron by Novartis in 2006).[43] We shall look more closely at mergers, acquisitions, and alliances in Chapter 15.

Organizing for Innovation

For creativity to create value, both for the company and for society, it must be directed and harnessed. Balancing creative freedom with commercial discipline is a challenge for all innovative companies. The problem is not restricted to technology-based companies but also affects fashion and media companies: "The two cultures—of the ponytail and the suit—are a world apart, and combustible together."[44] Many innovative companies have been formed by frustrated inventors leaving established companies. The success of Google in internet-based software, Apple in digital mobile devices, Disney in animated movies, and HBO with its succession of award-winning TV series reveals a remarkable ability to mesh creativity with commercial acuity.

Reconciling creativity with commercial effectiveness is a major challenge for organizational design—as Table 9.4 shows, the organizational requirements of the two are very different. The organizational solution (as we explored in Chapter 6) comes from reconciling *differentiation* and *integration*. The creative and operational functions of the organization need different structures and systems. Yet, the

STRATEGY CAPSULE 9.3

Open Innovation at Procter & Gamble and IBM

PROCTER & GAMBLE'S CONNECT AND DEVELOP

P&G's *Connect and Develop* innovation process seeks to "identify promising ideas throughout the world and apply our own R & D, manufacturing, marketing, and purchasing capabilities to them to create better and cheaper products, faster." The program was a response to the realization that, despite a research staff of 7500, P&G was not generating the new products needed to meet its growth targets. For each of its own research scientists, P&G estimated there were at least 200 outside the company with the potential to contribute to its development efforts. To focus its search, each business was asked to identify its top ten customer needs (e.g., reduce wrinkles, improve skin texture, softer paper products with higher wet strength) which were translated into specific technical requirements (e.g., biotechnology solutions that permit detergents to perform well at low temperatures). The initiatives were prioritized according to

their fit with P&G's existing areas of brand and technological strength.

The Connect and Develop process involved:

◆ Seventy technology entrepreneurs within P&G responsible for developing external contacts and exploring for innovation in particular localities and with a focus around particular product or technology areas.

◆ Suppliers with whom P&G shared technology briefs and engaged in regular meetings with senior P&G executives to explore mutual development opportunities.

◆ Technology brokering networks such as *NineSigma* linking companies with universities, government bodies, consultants, and other solutions providers; *Innocentive*, which brokers solutions to science-based problems; *YourEncore*, a network of retired scientists and engineers; and Yet2.com, an online marketplace for intellectual capital.

key to successful innovation is in integrating creativity and technological expertise with capabilities in production, marketing, finance, distribution, and customer support. Achieving such integration is difficult. Tension between the operating and the innovating parts of organizations is inevitable. Innovation upsets established routines and threatens the status quo. The more stable the operating and administrative side of the organization, the greater the resistance to innovation. The opposition of the US naval establishment to continuous-aim firing, an innovation offering huge improvements in gunnery accuracy, illuminates this resistance to innovation.[45]

As innovation has become an increasing priority for established corporations, so chief executives have sought to emulate the flexibility, creativity, and entrepreneurial spirit of technology-based start-ups. Organizational initiatives aimed at stimulating new product development and the exploitation of new technologies include the following:

● *Cross-functional Product Development Teams*: These have proven highly effective mechanisms for integrating creativity with functional effectiveness. Conventional approaches to new product development involved

The resulting flow of suggestions and proposals are screened and disseminated through P&G's *Eureka* online catalog. It is then up to executives within the business groups to identify interesting proposals, to pursue these with the external provider through P&G's External Business Development group, and to then move the initiative into their own product development process.

By 2005, 35% of P&G's new product launches had their origins outside the company. These included Swiffer cleaning cloths, Olay Regeneration, and Crest Spinbrush.

IBM'S INNOVATION JAM

IBM's *Innovation Jam* is one element of IBM's extensive collaborative innovation network. It is a massive online brainstorming process to generate, select, and develop new business ideas. The 2006 Jam was based upon an initial identification of 25 technology clusters grouped into six broad categories. Websites were built for each technology cluster and, for a 72-hour period, IBM employees, their families and friends, suppliers, customers, and individual scientists and engineers from all around the world were invited to contribute ideas for innovations based on these technologies. The 150,000 participants generated vast and diverse suggestions that were subject to text mining software and review by 50 senior executives and technical specialists who worked in nine separate teams to identify promising ideas. The next phase of the Jam subjected the selected innovation ideas to comments and review by the online community. This was followed by a further review process in which the ten best proposals were selected and a budget of $100 million was allocated to their development. The selected business ideas included a real-time foreign language translation service, smart healthcare payment systems, IT applications to environmental projects, and 3-D internet. The new businesses were begun as incubator projects and were then transferred to one or other of IBM's business groups. As well as divisional links, the new ventures were also subject to monthly review by IBM's corporate top management. IBM has since extended its jam methodology to address a widening array of issues.

Sources: www.pgconnectdevelop.com; L. Huston and N. Sakkab, "Connect and Develop: Inside Procter & Gamble's New Model for Innovation," *Harvard Business Review* (March 2006): 58–66; www.collaborationjam.com; O. M. Bjelland and R. C. Wood, "An Inside View of IBM's Innovation Jam," *MIT Sloan Management Review* (Fall 2008): 32–43.

a sequential process that began in the corporate research lab then went "over the wall" to engineering, manufacturing, finance, and so on. Japanese companies pioneered autonomous product development teams staffed by specialists seconded from different departments with leadership from a "heavyweight" team manager who was able to protect the team from undue corporate influence.[46] Such teams have proven effective in deploying a broad range of specialist knowledge and, most importantly, integrating that knowledge flexibility and quickly, for example through rapid prototyping and concurrent engineering.[47]

● *Product champions*: These provide a means, first, for incorporating individual creativity within organizational processes and, second, for linking invention to subsequent commercialization. The key is to permit the individuals who are sources of creative ideas to lead the teams which develop those ideas—but also to allow this leadership to continue through into the commercialization phases. Companies that are consistently successful in innovation have the ability to design organizational processes that capture, direct, and exploit individuals' drive for achievement and success and their commitment to their innovations. The rationale for creating product champions is that these committed individuals can overcome resistance to change within the organization and generate the enthusiasm that attracts the involvement of others and forges cross-functional integration. Schön's study of 15 major innovations concludes that: "the new idea either finds a champion or dies."[48] A British study of 43 matched pairs of successful and unsuccessful innovations similarly concluded that a key factor distinguishing successful innovation was the presence of a "business innovator" to exert entrepreneurial leadership.[49] 3M Corporation has a long tradition of using product champions to develop new product ideas and grow them into new businesses (Strategy Capsule 9.4).

- *Corporate incubators*: These are business development units that fund and nurture new businesses based upon technologies that have been developed internally but have limited applications within a company's established businesses. Corporate incubators became very popular during the IT boom at the end of the 1990s, when companies saw the potential to generate substantial value from establishing then spinning off new tech-based ventures.[50] Despite a sound strategic and organizational logic, few major companies have achieved sustained success from the incubator units that they established and among the successful ones many have been sold to venture capital firms. A key problem, according to Hamel and Prahalad, is that: "Many corporate incubators became orphanages for unloved ideas that had no internal support or in-house sponsorship."[51] Despite their uneven track record, several leading companies have experienced considerable success in introducing company-wide processes for developing new businesses based upon internally generated innovations. Cisco Systems created its Emerging Technology Business Group (EMTG) in 2006 to detect emerging market trends, conceive of opportunities to exploit them, and organically grow new ventures inside the company. Within 18 months, 400 ideas for new businesses had been posted on the Cisco wiki and several were under development, including TelePresence, a video surveillance security system that later became a business unit. A key feature of Cisco's incubator is its close linkage with the rest of the company—especially with senior management.[52]

STRATEGY CAPSULE 9.4
Innovation at 3M: The Role of the Product Champion

START LITTLE AND BUILD

We don't look to the president or the vice-president for R & D to say, all right, on Monday morning 3M is going to get into such-and-such a business. Rather, we prefer to see someone in one of our laboratories, or marketing, or manufacturing units bring forward a new idea that he's been thinking about. Then, when he can convince people around him, including his supervisor, that he's got something interesting, we'll make him what we call a "project manager" with a small budget of money and talent, and let him run with it. Throughout all our 60 years of history here, that has been the mark of success. Did you develop a new business? (Bob Adams, Vice-President for R & D, 3M Corporation)

SCOTCHLITE

Someone asked the question, "Why didn't 3M make glass beads, because glass beads were going to find increasing use on the highways?" . . . I had done a little work on trying to color glass beads and had learned a little about their reflecting properties. And, as a little extra-curricular activity, I'd been trying to make luminous house numbers.

Well, this question and my free-time lab project combined to stimulate me to search out where glass beads were being used on the highway. We found a place where beads had been sprinkled on the highway and we saw that they did provide a more visible line at night . . . From there, it was only natural for us

to conclude that, since we were a coating company, and probably knew more than anyone else about putting particles onto a web, we ought to be able to coat glass beads very accurately on a piece of paper.

So, that's what we did. The first reflective tape we made was simply a double-coated tape—glass beads sprinkled on one side and an adhesive on the other. We took some out here in St. Paul and, with the cooperation of the highway department, put some down. After the first frost came, and then a thaw, we found we didn't know as much about adhesives under all weather conditions as we thought . . .

We looked around inside the company for skills in related areas. We tapped knowledge that existed in our sandpaper business on how to make waterproof sandpaper. We drew on the expertise of our roofing people who knew something about exposure. We reached into our adhesive and tape division to see how we could make the tape stick to the highway better.

The resulting product became known as "Scotchlite." Its principal application was in reflective signs; only later did 3M develop the market for highway marking. The originator of the product, Harry Heltzer, interested the head of the New Products Division in the product, and he encouraged Heltzer to go out and sell it. Scotchlite was a success and Heltzer became the general manager of the division set up to produce and market it.

Source: "The Technical Strategy of 3M: Start More Little Businesses and More Little Businesses," *Innovation* 5 (1969).

Summary

In emerging and technology-based industries, nurturing and exploiting innovation is the fundamental source of competitive advantage and the focus of strategy formulation. Yet the fundamental strategic issues in these industries—the dynamics of competition, the role of the resources and capabilities in establishing competitive advantage, and the design of structures and systems to implement strategy—are ones we have already encountered and require us to apply our basic strategy toolkit.

Yet, the unpredictability and instability of these industries mean that strategic decisions in technology-driven industries have a very special character. The remarkable dynamics of these industries mean that the difference between massive value creation and total failure may be the result of small differences in timing or technological choices.

The speed and unpredictability of change in these markets means that sound strategic decision making can never guarantee success. Yet, managing effectively amidst such uncertainty is only possible with a strategy based upon understanding technological change and its implications for competitive advantage.

In this chapter I have distilled what we have learned in recent decades—about strategies to successfully manage innovation and technological change. The key lessons learned relate to:

♦ how the value created by innovation is shared among the different players in a market, including the roles of intellectual property, tacitness and complexity of the technology, lead time, and complementary resources;

♦ the design of innovation strategies, including whether to be an early mover or a follower; whether to exploit an innovation through licensing, an alliance, a joint venture, or internal development; and how to manage risk;

♦ competing for standards and platform leadership in markets subject to network externalities;

♦ how to implement strategies for innovation, including organizing to stimulate creativity, access innovation from outside, and developing new products.

Many of the themes we have dealt with—such as appropriating value from innovation and reconciling creativity with commercial discipline—are general issues in the strategic management of technology. Ultimately, however, the design and implementation of strategies in industries where innovation is a key success factor requires strategy to be closely tailored to the characteristics of technology, market demand, and industry structure. BCG's list of the world's most innovative companies includes among its top ten Apple, Samsung, Amazon, Toyota, and Facebook. While all these companies have been highly successful in using innovation to build competitive advantage, the strategies each has deployed have been closely tailored to their individual circumstances.

Self-Study Questions

1. Trevor Baylis, a British inventor, submitted a patent application in November 1992 for a wind-up radio for use in Africa in areas where there was no electricity supply and people were too poor to afford batteries. He was excited by the prospects for radio broadcasts as a means of disseminating health education in areas of Africa devastated by AIDS. After appearances on British and South African TV, Baylis attracted a number of entrepreneurs and companies interested in manufacturing and marketing his clockwork radio. However, Baylis was concerned by the fact that his patent provided only limited protection for his invention: most of the main components—a clockwork generator and transistor radio—were long-established technologies. What advice would you offer Baylis as to how he can best exploit his invention?

2. Table 9.1 shows that:

a. patents have been more effective in protecting product innovations in drugs and medical equipment than in food or electronic components;

b. patents are more effective in protecting product innovations than process innovations.

Can you suggest reasons why?

3. Page 251 refers to James Dyson's difficulties in licensing his innovative vacuum cleaner (see http://www.cdf.org/issue_journal/dyson_fills_a_vacuum.html for further information). What lessons would you draw from Dyson's experience concerning the use of licensing by small firms to exploit innovation?

4. From the evidence presented in Table 9.2, what conclusions can you draw regarding the factors that determine whether leaders or followers win out in the markets for new products?

5. In the market for ride sharing services, Uber is the market leader, followed by Lyft, Curb, and Sidecar. In each overseas country where Uber operates, it faces local competitors: UK rivals include BlaBlaCar, Carpooling.com, and Hailo. What are the sources of network externalities in this market? Do they operate at the city, national, or global level? Does the strength of these network effects mean that Uber's competitors are doomed to failure?

Notes

1. D. Stokes, *Pasteur's Quadrant: Basic Science and Technological Innovation* (Washington, DC: Brookings Institution Press, 1997).

2. R. E. Dugan and K. J. Gabriel, "Special Forces Innovation: How DARPA Attacks Problems," *Harvard Business Review* (October 2013).

3. In the US, the return on R & D spending was estimated at between 3.7% and 5.5%. See M. Warusawitharana, "Research and Development, Profits and Firm Value: A Structural Estimation," Discussion Paper (Washington, DC: Federal Reserve Board, September, 2008). See also: K. W. Artz, P. M. Norman, D. E. Hatfield, and L. B. Cardinal, "A Longitudinal Study of the Impact of R&D, Patents, and Product Innovation on Firm Performance." *Journal of Product Innovation Management* 27 (2010): 725–740.

4. "Amazon Loses 1-Click Patent," *Forbes* (July 7, 2011); "Justices Deny Patent to Business Methods," *New York Times* (June 19, 2014).

5. F. T. Rothermael, "Incumbent Advantage through Exploiting Complementary Assets via Interfirm Cooperation," *Strategic Management Journal* 22 (2001): 687–699.

6. R. C. Levin, A. K. Klevorick, R. R. Nelson, and S. G. Winter, "Appropriating the Returns from Industrial Research and Development," *Brookings Papers on Economic Activity* 18, no. 3 (1987): 783–832.

7. P. Grindley and D. J. Teece, "Managing Intellectual Capital: Licensing and Cross-Licensing in Semiconductors and Electronics," *California Management Review* 39 (Winter 1997): 8–41.

8. R. Adner, "Match your Innovation Strategy to your Innovation Ecosystem," *Harvard Business Review* (April 2006): 17–37.

9. S. Shulman, *The Telephone Gambit* (New York: Norton, 2008).

10. "The Human Genome Race," *Scientific American* (April 24, 2000).

11. "EMI and the CT Scanner," Harvard Business School Case No. 383-194 (June 1983).

12. C. Markides and P. A. Geroski, *Fast Second* (San Francisco: Jossey-Bass, 2005).

13. D. Sull, "Strategy as Active Waiting," *Harvard Business Review* (September 2005): 120–129.

14. For example, data on penetration rates for electric toothbrushes and CD players were used to forecast the market demand for HDTVs in the United States (B. L. Bayus, "High-Definition Television: Assessing Demand Forecasts for the Next Generation Consumer Durable," *Management Science* 39 (1993): 1319–1333).

15. G. Rowe and G. Wright "The Delphi Technique as a Forecasting Tool: Issues and Analysis," *International Journal of Forecasting* 15 (1999) 353–375.

16. E. Von Hippel, "Lead Users: A Source of Novel Product Concepts," *Management Science* 32 (July, 1986).

17. In electronic instruments, customers' ideas initiated most of the successful new products introduced by manufacturers. See E. Von Hippel, "Users as Innovators," *Technology Review* 5 (1976): 212–239.

18. E. D. Beinhocker, "Robust Adaptive Strategies," *Sloan Management Review* (Spring 1999): 95–106; E. D. Beinhocker, "Strategy at the Edge of Chaos," *McKinsey Quarterly* (Winter 1997).

19. A. Friedlander, *The Growth of Railroads* (Arlington, VA: CNRI, 1995).

20. "Europe Is Losing the 4G Race," *Wall Street Journal* (June 3, 2013).

21. S. Postrel, "Competing Networks and Proprietary Standards: The Case of Quadraphonic Sound," *Journal of Industrial Economics* 24 (December 1990): 169–186.

22. S. J. Liebowitz and S. E. Margolis ("Network Externality: An Uncommon Tragedy," *Journal of Economic Perspectives* 8 (Spring 1994): 133–150) refer to these user-to-user externalities as *direct externalities*.

23. M. Gladwell, *The Tipping Point* (Boston: Little, Brown and Company, 2000).

24. P. David, "Clio and the Economics of QWERTY," *American Economic Review* 75 (May 1985): 332–337; S. J. Gould, "The Panda's Thumb of Technology," *Natural History* 96, no. 1 (1986): 14–23. For an alternative view see S. J. Liebowitz and S. Margolis, "The Fable of the Keys," *Journal of Law and Economics* 33 (1990): 1–26.

25. C. Shapiro and H. R. Varian, "The Art of Standards Wars," *California Management Review* 41 (Winter 1999): 8–32.

26. R. M. Grant "The DVD War of 2006–8: Blu-Ray vs. HD-DVD," *Cases to Accompany Contemporary Strategy Analysis*, 7th edn (Chichester: John Wiley & Sons, Ltd, 2010).

27. C. Shapiro and H. R. Varian, "The Art of Standards Wars," *California Management Review* 41 (Winter 1999): 15–16.

28. C. Shapiro and H. R. Varian, "The Art of Standards Wars," *California Management Review* 41 (Winter 1999): 16–18.

29. For recent research into competitive advantage and network effects see: D. P. McIntyre and M. Subramaniam, "Strategy in Network Industries: A Review and Research Agenda," *Journal of Management* 35 (2009): 1494–1517; A. Afuah, "Are Network Effects Really About Size? The Role of Structure and Conduct," *Strategic Management Journal* 34 (2013): 257–273; K. J. Boudreau and L. B. Jeppesen, "Unpaid Crowd Complementors: The Platform Network Effect Mirage," *Strategic Management Journal* 36 (2015) forthcoming.

30. R. Katila and S. Shane, "When Does Lack of Resources Make New Firms Innovative?" *Academy of Management Journal* 48 (2005): 814–829.

31. J. M. George, "Creativity in Organizations," *Academy of Management Annals* 1 (2007): 439–477.

32. M. L. Tushman, "Managing Communication Networks in R & D Laboratories," *Sloan Management Review* 20 (Winter 1979): 37–49.

33. D. Dougherty and C. H. Takacs, "Team Play: Heedful Interrelating as the Boundary for Innovation," *Long Range Planning* 37 (December 2004): 569–590.

34. S. Thomke, "Enlightened Experimentation: The New Imperative for Innovation," *Harvard Business Review* (February 2001): 66–75.

35. R. Florida and J. Goodnight, "Managing for Creativity," *Harvard Business Review* (July/August 2005): 124–131.

36. G. von Krogh, S. Haefliger, S. Spaeth, M. W. Wallin, "Carrots and Rainbows: Motivation and Social Practice in Open Source Software Development," *MIS Quarterly* 36 (2012): 649–676.

37. D. Leonard and S. Straus, "Putting Your Company's Whole Brain to Work," *Harvard Business Review* (August 1997): 111–121; D. Leonard and P. Swap, *When Sparks Fly: Igniting Creativity in Groups* (Boston: Harvard Business School Press, 1999).

38. A. J. Slywotzky, *Demand: Creating What People Love Before They Know They Want It* (Paris: Hachette, 2012).

39. E. Von Hippel (*The Sources of Innovation*, New York: Oxford University Press, 1988).

40. S. Thomke and E. von Hippel, "Customers as Innovators: A New Way to Create Value," *Harvard Business Review* (April 2002).

41. M. Dodgson, "Technological Collaboration and Innovation," in M. Dodgson and R. Rothwell (eds.), *The Handbook of Industrial Innovation* (Cheltenham: Edward Elgar, 1994); A. Arora, A. Fosfur, and A. Gambardella, *Markets for Technology* (Cambridge, MA: MIT Press, 2001); S. Breschi and F. Malerba, Clusters, Networks and Innovation (Oxford: Oxford University Press, 2005).

42. H. Chesbrough, *Open Innovation: The New Imperative for Creating and Profiting from Technology* (Boston: Harvard Business School Press, 2003). See also, B. Cassiman and G. Valentini, "What is Open Innovation, Really?" Bocconi University working paper (2014).

43. P. M. Danzon, A. Epstein, and S. Nicholson, "Mergers and Acquisitions in the Pharmaceutical and Biotech Industries," NBER Working Paper No. 10536 (Washington DC, June 2004).

44. "How to Manage a Dream Factory," *Economist* (January 16, 2003).

45. E. Morrison, "Gunfire at Sea: A Case Study of Innovation," in M. Tushman and W. L. Moore (eds), *Readings in the Management of Innovation* (Cambridge, MA: Ballinger, 1988): 165–178.

46. K. Clark and T. Fujimoto, *Product Development Performance: Strategy, Organization, and Management in the World Auto Industry* (Boston: Harvard Business School Press, 1991).

47. K. Imai, I. Nonaka, and H. Takeuchi, "Managing the New Product Development Process: How Japanese Companies Learn and Unlearn," in K. Clark, R. Hayes, and C. Lorenz (eds), *The Uneasy Alliance* (Boston: Harvard Business School Press, 1985).

48. D. A. Schön, "Champions for Radical New Inventions," *Harvard Business Review* (March/April, 1963): 84.

49. R. Rothwell, C. Freeman, A. Horlsey, V. T. Jervis, A. B. Robertson, and J. Townsend, "SAPPHO Updated: Project SAPPHO Phase II," *Research Policy* 3 (1974): 258–291.

50. M. T. Hansen, H. W. Chesborough, N. Nohria and D. N. Sull, "Networked Incubators: Hothouse of the New Economy," *Harvard Business Review* (September/October 2000): 74–88; "How to Make the Most of a Brilliant Idea," *Financial Times* (December 6, 2000): 21.

51. G. Hamel and C. K. Prahalad, "Nurturing Creativity: Putting Passions to Work," *Shell World* (Royal Dutch Shell, September 14, 2007): 1–12.

52. "Cisco: Emerging Markets technology Group," www.benzinga.com/life/entrepreneurship/10/12/656767/cisco-emerging-markets-technology-group, accessed July 20, 2015.

10 Competitive Advantage in Mature Industries

We are a true "penny profit" business. That means that it takes hard work and attention to detail to be financially successful—it is far from being a sure thing. Our store managers must do two things well: control costs and increase sales. Cost control cannot be done by compromising product quality, customer service, or restaurant cleanliness, but rather by consistent monitoring of the "vital signs" of the business through observation, reports, and analysis. Portion control is a critical part of our business. For example, each Filet-O-Fish sandwich receives 1 fluid ounce of tartar sauce and 0.5 ounces of cheese. Our raw materials are fabricated to exacting tolerances, and our managers check them on an ongoing basis. Our written specification for lettuce is over two typewritten pages long. Our French fries must meet standards for potato type, solid and moisture content, and distribution of strand lengths.

—EDWARD H. RENSI, PRESIDENT AND CHIEF OPERATING OFFICER, MCDONALD'S USA[1]

OUTLINE

Introduction and Objectives

Despite the infatuation of both the media and the stock market with technology-based companies such as Google, Facebook, and Twitter, the fact remains that industries where most of us earn our living and spend most of our income are comparatively mature. Of the world's 20 biggest companies (in terms of sales), 18 are in petroleum, retailing, automobiles, financial services, mining, and electricity: industries that have existed for more than a century. (The other two, Apple and Samsung Electronics, represent new, technology-based industries.)[2]

Despite their heterogeneity—they range from beauty parlors to steel—mature industries present several similarities from a strategic perspective. The purpose of this chapter is to explore these characteristics of mature industries, identify strategies through which competitive advantage can be established within them, and recognize the implications of these strategies for structure, systems, and leadership style. As we shall see, maturity does not imply lack of opportunity. Companies such as H&M (fashion clothing), AirAsia (airlines), Starbucks (coffee shops), and Nucor (steel) have successfully deployed innovative strategies within mature sectors. Neither does maturity imply sluggish performance: Coca-Cola, ExxonMobil, and Daimler were founded in the 19th century, yet, over the past two decades, have achieved combinations of profitability and growth that would make most high-tech companies envious. Nor does maturity mean lack of innovation: as we shall see, many mature industries have been transformed by new technologies and new strategies.

By the time you have completed this chapter, you will be able to:

- ◆ Recognize the principal strategic characteristics of mature industries.
- ◆ Identify key success factors within mature industries and formulate strategies directed toward their exploitation.
- ◆ Design organizational structures and management systems that can effectively implement such strategies.
- ◆ Recognize the characteristics of declining industries, the opportunities for profit they may offer, and the strategy options available to firms.

Competitive Advantage in Mature Industries

Our analysis of the industry life cycle (Chapter 8) suggests that maturity undermines profitability in two ways. First, overcapacity and commoditization increase competitive pressure. Second, competitive advantage is more difficult to establish and sustain as a result of:

- Less scope for differentiation advantage resulting from better informed buyers, product standardization, and lack of technological change.
- Diffusion of process technology means that cost advantages are difficult to obtain and sustain. Once a cost advantage is established, it is vulnerable

to exchange rate movements and the emergence of low-cost overseas competitors.

- A highly developed industry infrastructure together with the presence of powerful distributors makes it easier for new entrants to attack established firms.

Warren Buffett, The Sage of Omaha, uses different words to convey a similar idea. He categorizes businesses into "franchises" and "businesses" and views maturity as a process of value destruction in which franchises degenerate into businesses:

An economic franchise arises from a product or service that (1) is needed or desired; (2) is thought by customers to have no close substitute; and (3) is not subject to price regulation. Franchises earn high rates of return on capital . . . [and] can tolerate mismanagement . . . In contrast, "a business" earns exceptional profits only if it is a low-cost operator or if supply of its product or service is tight. And a business, unlike a franchise, can be killed by poor management.[3]

Cost Advantage

Commoditization implies that cost efficiency is the primary basis for competitive advantage in many mature industries. Three cost drivers tend to be especially important:

- *Economies of scale*: In capital-intensive industries, or where advertising, distribution, or new product development is an important element of total cost, economies of scale are important sources of interfirm cost differences. The increased standardization that accompanies maturity greatly assists the exploitation of such scale economies. In automobiles, as with many other manufacturing industries, industry evolution has been driven by the quest for scale economies. The significance of scale economies in mature industries is indicated by the fact that the association between return on investment and market share is stronger in mature industries than in emerging industries.[4]
- *Low-cost inputs*: The quest for low-cost inputs explains the migration of maturing industries from the advanced to the newly industrializing countries of the world. But accessing low-cost inputs does not necessarily mean establishing operations in India or Vietnam. Established firms can become locked into high salaries and benefits, inefficient working practices, and bloated overheads inherited from more prosperous times. New entrants into mature industries may gain cost advantages by acquiring plant and equipment at bargain-basement levels and by cutting labor costs. Valero Energy Corporation is the largest oil refiner in the US: it acquired loss-making refineries from the majors at below-book prices then operated them with rigorous cost efficiency. Convenience stores throughout North America and Western Europe are increasingly owned and operated by immigrants whose family-based operation offers cost and flexibility advantages.
- *Low overheads*: Some of the most profitable companies in mature industries are those able to minimize overhead costs. In discount retailing, Walmart is famous for its parsimonious approach to costs. Among the oil majors, Exxon

is known for its rigorous control of overhead costs. Exxon's headquarters cost (relative to netassets) was about one-quarter that of Mobil's.[5] When Exxon merged with Mobil, it was able to extract huge cost savings from Mobil.

In newspaper and magazine publishing, newcomers such as EMAP in the UK and Media News Group in the US (run by "Lean" Dean Singleton) have deployed a strategy of acquiring titles then pruning overheads.

As cost inefficiencies tend to become institutionalized within mature enterprises, cost reduction may require drastic interventions. **Corporate restructuring**—intensive periods of structural and strategic change—typically involves cost reduction through outsourcing, headcount reduction, and downsizing, especially at corporate headquarters.[6] Successful turnaround strategies in mature industries typically involve aggressive cost cutting together with measures to boost productivity and prune assets.[7]

Segment and Customer Selection

Sluggish demand growth, lack of product differentiation, and international competition tend to depress the profitability of mature industries. Yet, even unattractive industries may offer attractive niche markets with strong growth of demand, few competitors, and abundant potential for differentiation. As a result, segment selection can be a key determinant of differences in the performance of companies within the same industry. Walmart's profitability was boosted by locating its stores in small and medium-sized towns where it faced little competition. In the auto industry, there is a constant quest to escape the intense competition of most market segments with "crossover" vehicles that span existing segments. The propensity for market leaders to focus on the mass market, creates opportunities for smaller players to carve out new market niches by supplying underserved customer needs—what Chapter 8 refers to as "resource partitioning."[8]

The logic of segment focus implies further disaggregation of markets—down to the level of the individual customer. Information technology permits new approaches to **customer relationship management** (CRM), making it possible to analyze individual characteristics and preferences, identify individual customers' profit contribution to the firm, and organize marketing around individualized, integrated approaches to customers. In the same way that Las Vegas casinos have long recognized that the major part of their profits derives from a tiny minority of customers—the "high rollers"—so banks, supermarkets, credit card companies, and hotels increasingly use transaction data to identify their most attractive customers, and those that are a drag on profitability.

The next stage in this process is to go beyond customer selection to actively target more attractive customers and transform less valuable customers into more valuable customers. For example, credit card issuer Capital One uses data warehousing, experimentation, simulation, and sophisticated statistical modeling to estimate the lifetime profitability of each customer and adjust the terms and features of its credit card offers to the preferences, characteristics, and profit potential of individual customers. "Big data" is transforming companies' ability to individualize marketing. McKinsey & Company points to the potential for big data and other information and communications technologies to usher in an era of "on-demand marketing."[9]

The Quest for Differentiation

Cost leadership, as we noted in Chapter 7, is difficult to sustain, particularly in the face of international competition. Hence, differentiating to attain some insulation from the rigors of price competition is particularly attractive in mature industries. The problem is that the trend toward commoditization narrows the scope for differentiation and reduces customer willingness to pay a premium for differentiation:

- In tires and domestic appliances, companies' investments in differentiation through product innovation, quality, and brand reputation have generated disappointing returns. Vigorous competition, price-sensitive customers, and strong, aggressive retailers have limited the price premium that differentiation will support.
- Attempts by airlines to gain competitive advantage through offering more legroom, providing superior in-flight entertainment, and achieving superior punctuality have met little market response from consumers. The only effective differentiators appear to be frequent-flier programs and services offered to first- and business-class travelers.

Standardization of the physical attributes of a product and convergence of consumer preferences constrains, but does not eliminate, opportunities for meaningful and profitable differentiation. Product standardization is frequently accompanied by increased differentiation of complementary services—financing terms, leasing arrangements, warranties, after-sales services and the like. In consumer goods, maturity often means a shift from physical differentiation to image differentiation. Entrenched consumer loyalties to specific brands of cola or cigarettes are a tribute to the capacity of brand promotion over long periods to create distinct images among near-identical products.

The intensely competitive retail sector produces particularly interesting examples of differentiation strategies. The dismal profitability earned by many retail chains (Toys "R" Us, Foot Locker, Radio Shack, and J. C. Penny in the US; Carrefour, Metro, and Dixons in Europe) contrasts sharply with the sales growth and profitability of stores that have established clear differentiation through variety, style, and ambiance (Wholefoods, TJX, Limited Brands, and Bed, Bath & Beyond in the US; Inditex, H&M, Sephora, and IKEA from Europe). A further lesson from highly competitive mature sectors such as retailing is that competitive advantage is difficult to sustain. Most of the outstandingly successful retailers of the previous decade—Best Buy, Body Shop, Tesco, and Marks & Spencer—have slipped into mediocrity.

Innovation

We have characterized mature industries as industries where the pace of technical change is slow. In many mature industries—steel, textiles, food processing, insurance, and hotels—R & D expenditure is below 1% of sales revenue, while in US manufacturing as a whole just three sectors—computers and electronics, pharmaceuticals, and aerospace—account for 65% of R & D spending.[10] Yet, measured by patenting activity, some mature industries are as innovative as emerging industries.[11] Among BCG's list of the world's 50 most innovative companies, three are consumer goods companies (Procter & Gamble, Nestlé, and Unilever), two are conglomerates

STRATEGY CAPSULE 10.1

Innovation in Mature Industries: Brassiere Technology

Women have used fabric to bind and support their breasts for at least two millennia, but it was not until the late 19th century that the term *brassiere* was used to refer to such undergarments. In 1913, the first US patent for a brassiere was issued to Mary Phelps Jacob. Since then, the technological quest for a better bra has continued—between 2005 and 2014 228 US patents relating to brassieres were issued. Design innovations include:

- Wonderbra (owned by Sara Lee) introduced a "variable cleavage" bra equipped with a system of pulleys;

- the Airotic bra designed by Gossard (also owned by Sara Lee) featured "twin air bags as standard";

- Charnos's Bioform bra replaced underwiring with soft molded polypropylene around a rigid ring—a design inspired by the Frisbee and engineered by Ove Arup (who also engineered London's Millennium Bridge which had to be closed because of excessive wobbling);

- Japan's Triumph lingerie company introduced a "Close Sister Bra": inspired by Disney's *Frozen* movie, the matched bras change color simultaneously;

- Recent "smart bras" include University of Wollongong's sports bra that adjusts for breast movement during exercise and Microsoft's bra that embodies sensors that collect EKG activity and sends messages concerning the wearer's emotional state to a smartphone.

Source: "Bra Wars," *Economist* (December 2, 2000): 112; USTPO Patent Database; "The Physics of Bras," *Discover Magazine* (November 2005) ; "Microsoft Developed a 'Smart' Bra," *CNN* (December 4, 2013).

(GE and Tata Group), and six are automobile producers.[12] Even in mature low-tech products such as tires, brassieres, and fishing rods, continuing inventiveness is indicated by a steady flow of new patents (Strategy Capsule 10.1).

Despite an increased pace of technological change in many mature industries, most opportunities for establishing competitive advantage are likely to arise from *strategic innovation*—including *new game strategies* and *blue-ocean strategies* that we discussed in Chapter 7. Indeed, as identified in Chapter 8, it may be that strategic innovation constitutes a third phase of innovation that becomes prominent once product and process innovation slacken. In addition to the *value chain reconfiguration* approach discussed in Chapter 7,[13] firms can seek strategic innovation by redefining markets and market segments. This may involve:

- *Embracing new customer groups*: Harley-Davidson has created a market for expensive motorcycles among the middle-aged, while in the maturing market for video game consoles Nintendo achieved remarkable success with its Wii by appealing to consumers outside the core market of young males. The most rapidly growing churches—for example Jehovah's Witnesses in Russia and Amway Christian Fellowship in America—tend to be those that recruit among non-church-going social and demographic groups.

- *Augmenting, bundling, and theming*: Some of the most successful approaches to differentiation in mature industries involve bundling additional products or services with the core offering. In book retailing, Barnes & Noble offers not only a wide range of titles but also Starbucks coffee shops within its stores. Neighborhood bookstores that have survived competition from the megastores and Amazon.com are often those that have added poetry readings, live music, and other recreational services. This augmenting and bundling of the product offering may extend to involve the customer in an entire experience. Theming by retail stores (such as Disney Stores and American Girl) and restaurants (such as Hard Rock Café and Rainforest Café) reflects the desire to involve customers in an experience that goes beyond the products being sold.[14]

- *Customer solutions*: Another approach to differentiation through bundling products and services is to offer *customer solutions*—an integrated bundle of products and support services that are offered as a customized package. For example, Alstom's rail transport division has transitioned from "being a supplier of goods to a system and service provider": rather than supplying locomotives, rolling stock, and signaling systems as standalone items, it offers "complete transport solutions for train availability during the life cycle of the product."[15] However, as a senior manager from the Italian engineering firm, Bonfiglioli, explained to me: "Supplying customer solutions is an appealing strategy, but execution is far from easy. Once we had sales representatives who visited customers carrying a product directory. Now the sales representative has to visit the customer with a team comprising product and maintenance engineers and a financial analyst."

- *Liberation from the maturity mindset*: The ability to create competitive advantage requires managers to free themselves from the cognitive limits associated with notions of maturity. Baden-Fuller and Stopford argue that maturity is a state of mind, not a state of the business—every enterprise has the potential for rejuvenation. The key to strategic innovation is for managers to prevent industry conventions from imprisoning their companies into conventional thinking about strategy. This means cultivating an entrepreneurial organization where middle managers are encouraged to experiment and learn.[16]

Costas Markides identifies several firms that have successfully broken away from conventional wisdom to establish a unique positioning within mature industries:

- Edward Jones, with 2000 offices, mostly in the US but also in Canada and the UK, has rejected the conventional wisdom that successful brokerage firms require scale economies, product diversification, e-commerce, and integration with investment banks. Each Edward Jones' office has just one investment adviser who is motivated to grow local business through face-to-face relationships; there are no proprietary investment products and no online investing.

- Enterprise Rent-A-Car has adopted a location strategy that is quite different from its major competitors, Hertz and Avis. Rather than concentrate on serving the business traveler through locating at airports and downtown, Enterprise concentrates on suburban locations, where it caters primarily to the consumer market.[17]

How do companies break away from the pack and achieve strategic innovation? The problem is that breaking with industry conventions requires confronting industry-wide systems of belief—what J.-C. Spender refers to as *industry recipes*."[18] This is likely to require that managers find ways of altering their *cognitive maps*— the mental frameworks through which they perceive and understand their industry environments.[19] This may explain why strategic innovation in mature industries is so often associated with firms that are either outsiders or peripheral players.

Gary Hamel proposes fostering strategic innovation through reorganizing the strategy-making process. This means breaking top management's monopoly over strategy formulation, bringing in younger people from further down the organization, and gaining involvement from those on the periphery of the organization.[20]

Strategy Implementation in Mature Industries: Structure, Systems, and Style

Across most mature industries, the primary basis for competitive advantage is operational efficiency; however, as we have seen, cost efficiency must be reconciled with innovation and customer responsiveness. What kinds of organizational structures, management systems, and leadership styles do mature businesses need to adopt in order to achieve these multiple performance goals?

Efficiency through Bureaucracy

As we observed in Chapter 6, the conventional prescription for stable environments was *mechanistic* organizations characterized by centralization, precisely defined roles, and predominantly vertical communication.[21] Henry Mintzberg describes this formalized type of organization dedicated to the pursuit of efficiency as the *machine bureaucracy*.[22] Efficiency is achieved through standardized routines, division of labor, and close management control based on bureaucratic principles. Division of labor extends to management as well as operatives—high levels of vertical and horizontal specialization are typical among managers. Vertical specialization is evident in the concentration of strategy formulation at the apex of the hierarchy, while middle and junior management supervise and administer through the application of standardized rules and procedures. Horizontal specialization takes the form of functional structures.

The machine bureaucracy as described by Mintzberg is a caricature of actual organizations—probably the closest approximations are found in government departments performing highly routine administrative duties (e.g., the Internal Revenue Service or departments of motor vehicle licensing). However, in most mature industries, the features of mechanistic organizations are evident in highly routinized operations controlled by detailed rules and procedures. McDonald's is far from being a typical bureaucracy—in particular, the majority of outlets are franchises operated by independent companies—however, the cost efficiency and consistency that characterizes its performance is achieved through highly standardized and detailed operating procedures that govern virtually every aspect of how it does business (see the quotation that introduces this chapter). Similarly, in Marriott Hotels, HSBC, Toyota Motor Company, and Walmart the ability of these huge organizations to achieve efficiency and consistent high quality is the result of management

TABLE 10.1 Strategy implementation in mature industries: The conventional model

STRATEGY	The primary goal is cost advantage through economies of scale and capital-intensive production of standardized products/services
	Strategy formulation primarily the realm of top managers
	Middle managers responsible for strategy implementation
STRUCTURE	Functional departments (e.g., production, marketing, customer service, distribution)
	Distinction between line and staff
	Clearly defined job roles with strong vertical reporting/delegation relationships
CONTROLS	Performance targets are primarily quantitative and short term and are specified for all members of the organization
	Performance is closely monitored by well-established, centralized management information systems and formalized reporting requirements
	Financial controls through budgets and profit targets particularly important
INCENTIVES	Incentives are based on achievement of individual targets and take the form of financial rewards and promotion up the hierarchy
	Penalties exist for failure to attain quantitative targets, for failure to adhere to the rules, and for lack of conformity to company norms
COMMUNICATION	Primarily vertical for the purposes of delegation and reporting
	Lateral communication limited, often achieved through interdepartmental committees
LEADERSHIP	Primary functions of top management: control and strategic direction
	Typical CEO profiles include the *administrator*, who guides the organization through establishing and operating organizational systems and principles and building consensus (e.g., Alfred Sloan Jr. of General Motors); the *autocrat*, who uses top-down decision making and leads through centralization of power and force of personality (Lee Iacocca of Chrysler and Steve Jobs at Apple); and the *strategic leader*, who combines clear strategic direction with considerable decentralization of decision making (Sam Palmisano at IBM, Carlos Ghosn at Renault-Nissan, Jeff Immelt at GE).

systems that draw heavily upon the principles of bureaucracy. The key features of these mature organizations are summarized in Table 10.1.

Trends in Strategy Implementation among Mature Businesses

When competitive advantage in mature industries was all about cost advantage through scale and division of labor, management practices based upon standardized processes, elaborately defined rules, hierarchical control, quantitative performance targets, and incentives closely linked to individual performance work well. However, as we have discussed, the requirements for success in mature industries and the strategies needed to achieve success given these requirements have become much more complex. In terms of cost efficiency, scale advantages have become less important than the flexibility to exploit low-cost inputs and to outsource to low-cost specialists, and creating an organizational environment that constantly strives to eliminate waste and discover new sources of efficiency.

The efficiency leaders in mature industries are not necessarily the biggest firms that are able to exploit scale benefits to the maximum: they are more likely to be companies that have dedicated themselves to efficiency through implementing performance-oriented management systems. Top-performing companies in mature businesses—UPS in delivery services, Walmart in discount retailing, Nucor in steel, ExxonMobil in petroleum—have integrated management systems where performance goals are the centerpiece of strategy and these goals are implemented through financial controls, HR policies, and operating practices which are closely tailored to these goals.

Unifying an organization around the pursuit of efficiency requires management systems that allow disaggregation of company-wide goals into specific performance targets for departments and individuals—the *balanced scorecard* is one of the most widely used techniques for achieving this (see Chapter 2). Most important, however, is embedding performance goals within the company's organizational culture:

- Central to UPS's performance-driven management style is a corporate culture that simultaneously embraces high levels of employee autonomy and the company's "obsessive-compulsive personality."[23]
- Walmart's culture of frugality reflects the values of founder Sam Walton. According to Walmart executive Ron Loveless: "Sam valued every penny. People say that Walmart is making $10 billion a year, or whatever. But that's not how people within the company think of it. If you spent a dollar, the question was: 'How many dollars of merchandise would you need to sell to make that dollar?'"[24]
- Ryanair has mastered the art of managing for cost efficiency. From a simple strategic goal of being Europe's lowest-cost airline, Ryanair's route structure, choice of airports, fleet, ticketing system, and HR practices are meticulously aligned to cost minimization. Ryanair's obsession with cost cutting is reflected in the large proportion of employees that are on temporary contracts, the requirement that crews pay for their own uniforms and training, and a heavy emphasis on incentive pay (cabin crew receive a commission on inflight sales).[25]

Reconciling differentiation and innovation with a relentless drive for cost efficiency creates difficult challenges for designing management systems that promote these goals without blunting the imperatives for cost minimization. The conventional model for reconciling efficiency with innovation in mature companies is *internal differentiation*: innovation and entrepreneurship are the responsibility of specialist R & D, new product development, and business development units. However, some established companies in mature industries, including Toyota and Whirlpool, have embraced dispersed innovation, encouraging initiative and ideas from all employees.[26]

Strategies for Declining Industries

The transition from maturity to decline can be a result of technological substitution (typewriters, photographic film), changes in consumer preferences (canned food, men's suits), demographic shifts (children's toys in Europe), or foreign competition (textiles in the advanced industrialized countries). Shrinking market demand gives rise to acute strategic issues. Among the key features of declining industries are:

- excess capacity;
- lack of technical change (reflected in a lack of new product introduction and stability of process technology);
- a declining number of competitors, but some entry as new firms acquire the assets of exiting firms cheaply;
- high average age of both physical and human resources;
- aggressive price competition.

Despite the inhospitable environment offered by declining industries, research by Kathryn Harrigan has uncovered declining industries where at least some participants earned surprisingly high profits. These included electronic vacuum tubes, cigars, and leather tanning. However, elsewhere—notably in prepared baby foods, rayon, and meat processing—decline was accompanied by aggressive price competition, company failures, and instability.[27]

What determines whether or not a declining industry becomes a competitive bloodbath? Two factors are critical: the balance between capacity and output, and the nature of the demand for the product.

Adjusting Capacity to Declining Demand

The smooth adjustment of industry capacity to declining demand is the key to stability and profitability during the decline phase. In industries where capacity exits from the industry in an orderly fashion, decline can occur without trauma. Where substantial excess capacity persists, as has occurred among the oil refineries of America and Europe, in the bakery industry, in coal mining, and in long-haul bus transportation, the potential exists for destructive competition. The ease with which capacity adjusts to declining demand depends on the following factors:

- *The predictability of decline*: If decline can be forecast, it is more likely that firms can plan for it. The decline of traditional photography with the advent of digital imaging was anticipated and planned for. Conversely, the decline in sales of personal computers which began in 2011 was largely unexpected. The more cyclical and volatile the demand, the more difficult it is for firms to perceive the trend of demand, even after the onset of decline.
- *Barriers to exit*: Barriers to exit impede the exit of capacity from an industry. The major barriers are:
  - Durable and specialized assets. Just as capital requirements impose a barrier to entry into an industry, those same investments also discourage exit. The longer they last and the fewer the opportunities for using those assets in another industry are, the more companies are tied to that particular industry.
  - Costs incurred in plant closure. Apart from the accounting costs of writing off assets, substantial cash costs may be incurred in redundancy payments to employees, compensation for broken contacts with

customers and suppliers, decommissioning the plant, and environmental cleanup.

- ○ *Managerial commitment.* In addition to financial considerations, firms may be reluctant to close plants for a variety of emotional and moral reasons. Resistance to plant closure and divestment arises from pride in company traditions and reputation, managers' unwillingness to accept failure, and loyalties to employees and the local community.

- *The strategies of the surviving firms*: Smooth exit of capacity ultimately depends on the willingness of the industry players to close plants and divest assets. The sooner companies recognize and address the problem, the more likely it is that independent and collective action can achieve capacity reduction. In European gasoline retailing, for example, the problem of excess capacity was partially solved by bilateral exchanges of service stations among the major oil companies. Stronger firms in the industry can facilitate the exit of weaker firms by offering to acquire their plants and take over their after-sales service commitments. A key strategy among private equity firms has been initiating *roll-ups* in declining industries—consolidating multiple acquisitions. Clear Channel Communications rolled up the US market for radio stations, eventually owning more than 900. Felix Salmon argues that the financial news industry is also ripe for a roll up: merging Forbes Media with online financial news sites The Street, Business Insider, and Seeking Alpha to create a major rival to Bloomberg and Reuters.[28]

Strategy Alternatives for Declining Industries

Conventional strategy recommendations for declining industries are either to divest or to harvest (i.e., to generate the maximum cash flow from existing investments without reinvesting). However, these strategies assume that declining industries are inherently unprofitable. If profit potential exists, then other strategies may be attractive. Harrigan and Porter identify four strategies that can profitably be pursued either individually or sequentially in declining industries:[29]

- *Leadership*: By gaining leadership, a firm is well placed to outstay competitors and play a dominant role in the final stages of an industry's life cycle. Once leadership is attained, the firm is in a good position to switch to a harvest strategy and enjoy a strong profit stream from its market position. Establishing leadership can be done by acquiring competitors, but a cheaper way is to encourage competitors to exit (and then acquire their plants). Inducements to competitors to exit may include showing commitment to the industry, helping to lower their exit costs, releasing pessimistic forecasts of the industry's future, and raising the stakes, for example by supporting more stringent environmental controls that make it costly for them to stay in business.

- *Niche*: Identify a segment that is likely to maintain a stable demand and that other firms are unlikely to invade, then pursue a leadership strategy to establish dominance within the segment. The most attractive niches are those that offer the greatest prospects for stability and where demand is most inelastic. In products facing technological obsolescence, established firms have often been successful in cultivating a lucrative high-price, high-quality segment. For example, Richemont has created a very profitable business based upon mechanical watches (Lange & Söhne, Baume et Mercier, Cartier, Piaget, Vacheron Constantin) and luxury fountain pens (Montblanc).

- *Harvest*: By harvesting, a firm maximizes its cash flow from existing assets, while avoiding further investment. A harvesting strategy seeks to boost margins wherever possible through raising prices and cutting costs by rationalizing the number of models, number of channels, and number of customers. Note, however, that a harvest strategy can be difficult to implement. In the face of strong competition, harvesting may accelerate decline, particularly if employee morale is adversely affected by a strategy that offers no long-term future for the business.

- *Divest*: If the future looks bleak, the best strategy may be to divest the business in the early stages of decline before a consensus has developed as to the inevitability of decline. Once industry decline is well established, it may be extremely difficult to find buyers.

Choosing the most appropriate strategy requires a careful assessment both of the profit potential of the industry and the competitive position of the firm. Harrigan and Porter pose four key questions:

- Can the structure of the industry support a hospitable, potentially profitable decline phase?
- What are the exit barriers that each significant competitor faces?
- Do your company strengths fit the remaining pockets of demand?
- What are your competitors' strengths in these pockets? How can their exit barriers be overcome?

Selecting an appropriate strategy requires matching the opportunities remaining in the industry to the company's competitive position. Figure 10.1 shows a simple framework for strategy choice.

FIGURE 10.1 Strategic alternatives for declining industries

		COMPANY'S COMPETITIVE POSITION	
		Strengths in remaining demand pockets	Lacks strength in remaining demand pockets
INDUSTRY STRUCTURE	Favorable to decline	LEADERSHIP or NICHE	HARVEST or DIVEST
	Unfavorable to decline	NICHE or HARVEST	DIVEST QUICKLY

Summary

Mature industries present challenging environments for the formulation and implementation of business strategies. Competition—price competition in particular—is usually strong, and competitive advantage is often difficult to build and sustain: cost advantages are vulnerable to imitation; differentiation opportunities are limited by the trend to standardization.

Stable positions of competitive advantage in mature industries are traditionally associated with cost advantage from economies of scale or experience, with selecting the most attractive market segments and customers to serve, with creating differentiation advantage, and with pursuing technological and strategic innovation.

Implementing these strategies, especially those associated with rigorous cost efficiency, typically requires management systems based upon standardized processes and relentless performance management. However, as mature industries become increasingly complex and turbulent, so the pursuit of cost efficiency needs to be matched with flexibility, responsiveness, and innovation. Companies such as Walmart, Coca-Cola, McDonald's, Hyundai and UPS show remarkable capacity to reconcile vigorous cost efficiency with adaptability.

Declining industries present special challenges to companies: typically, they are associated with intense competition and low margins. However, such environments also present profitable opportunities for those firms that can orchestrate orderly decline from a position of leadership, establish a niche, or generate cash from harvesting assets.

Self-Study Questions

1. Consider Table 3.1 in Chapter 3. Most of the least profitable US industries are mature industries. Yet at the top of the table are tobacco, personal and household products, and food consumer products, all mature industries. What is it about this latter group of industries that has allowed them to escape the intense price competition and low profitability often associated with mature sectors?

2. Established airlines are cutting costs to compete with the increasing number of budget airlines. Yet, it is unlikely that they will ever match the costs of Southwest, Ryanair, or AirAsia. Which, if any, of the strategies outlined in this chapter offers the best opportunity for the established airlines to improve their competitive position vis-à-vis the budget airlines?

3. Department stores (e.g., Macy's and Sears in the US, Selfridges and House of Fraser in the UK) face increasing competition from specialized chain retailers and discount stores. What innovative strategies might department stores adopt to revitalize their competitiveness?

4. Book retailing is in decline. From the strategy options identified in the section "Strategy Alternatives for Declining Industries," what recommendations would you offer to (a) Barnes & Noble and (b) an independent book retailer located in your vicinity?

Notes

1. E. H. Rensi, "Computers at McDonald's," in J. F. McLimore and L. Larwood (eds), *Strategies, Successes: Senior Executives Speak Out* (New York: Harper & Row, 1988): 159–160.

2. *Fortune Global 500*, 2014.

3. Letter to Shareholders, Annual Report of Berkshire Hathaway Inc., 1991.

4. R. D. Buzzell and B. T. Gale, *The PIMS Principles* (New York: Free Press, 1987): 279.

5. T. Copeland, T. Koller, and J. Murrin, *Valuation: Measuring and Managing the Value of Companies*, 3rd edn (New York: John Wiley & Sons, Inc., 2000): 305.

6. R. Cibin and R. M. Grant, "Restructuring among the World's Leading Oil Companies," *British Journal of Management* 7 (December 1996): 283–308.

7. D. C. Hambrick and S. M. Schecter, "Turnaround Strategies for Mature Industrial-Product Business Units," *Academy of Management Journal* 26 (1983): 231–248; J. L. Morrow, Jr., Richard A. Johnson and Lowell W. Busenitz, "The Effects of Cost and Asset Retrenchment on Firm Performance: The Overlooked Role of a Firm's Competitive Environment," *Journal of Management* 30 (2004): 189.

8. G. R. Carroll and A. Swaminathan, "Why the Microbrewery Movement? Organizational Dynamics of Resource Partitioning in the American Brewing Industry," *American Journal of Sociology* 106 (2000): 715–762; C. Boone, G. R. Carroll, and A. van Witteloostuijn, "Resource Distributions and Market Partitioning: Dutch Daily Newspapers 1964–1994," *American Sociological Review* 67 (2002): 408–431.

9. *Capital One Financial Corporation*, Harvard Business School Case No. 9-700-124 (2000).

10. National Science Foundation, *Research and Development in Industry*: 2002 (www.nsf.gov/statistics/industry).

11. A. M. McGahan and B. S. Silverman, "How Does Innovative Activity Change as Industries Mature?" *International Journal of Industrial Organization* 19 (2001): 1141–1160.

12. "Innovation in 2014," *BCG Perspectives* (October 28, 2014).

13. See section entitled: "Internal Sources of Change: Competitive Advantage from Innovation," Chapter 7.

14. B. J. Pine and J. Gilmore, "Welcome to the Experience Economy," *Harvard Business Review* (July/August 1998): 97–105.

15. A. Davies, T. Brady, and M. Hobday, "Organizing for Solutions: System Seller vs. System Integrator," *Industrial Marketing Management* 36 (2007): 183–193.

16. C. Baden-Fuller and J. Stopford, *Rejuvenating the Mature Business* (Boston: HBS Press, 1994): especially Chapters 3 and 4.

17. C. C. Markides, *All the Right Moves* (Boston: Harvard Business School Press, 1999).

18. J.-C. Spender, *Industry Recipes: The Nature and Sources of Managerial Judgment* (Oxford: Blackwell Publishing, 1989). On a similar theme, see also A. S. Huff, "Industry Influences on Strategy Reformulation," *Strategic Management Journal* 3 (1982): 119–131.

19. P. S. Barr, J. L. Stimpert, and A. S. Huff, "Cognitive Change, Strategic Action, and Organizational Renewal," *Strategic Management Journal* 13 (Summer 1992): 15–36.

20. G. Hamel, "Strategy as Revolution," *Harvard Business Review* 96 (July/August 1996): 69–82.

21. T. Burns and G. M. Stalker, *The Management of Innovation* (London: Tavistock Institute, 1961).

22. H. Mintzberg, *Structure in Fives: Designing Effective Organizations* (Englewood Cliffs, NJ: Prentice Hall, 1983): Chapter 9.

23. G. Nieman, *Big Brown: The Untold Story of UPS* (Chichester: John Wiley & Sons, Ltd, 2007): 70.

24. C. Fishman, *The Wal-Mart Effect: The High Cost of Everyday Low Prices* (Harmondsworth: Penguin, 2006).

25. *Ryanair: Defying Gravity*, IMD Case No. 3-1633 (2007). Available from www.ecch.com.

26. "How Whirlpool Defines Innovation," *Business Week* (March 6, 2006).

27. K. R. Harrigan, *Strategies for Declining Businesses* (Lexington, MA: D. C. Heath, 1980).

28. F. Salmon, "The Financial Media Rollup Strategy," (November 15, 2013), http://blogs.reuters.com/felix-salmon/2013/11/15/the-financial-media-rollup-strategy/, accessed July 20, 2015.

29. K. R. Harrigan and M. E. Porter, "End-Game Strategies for Declining Industries," *Harvard Business Review* (July/August 1983): 111–120.

IV

CORPORATE STRATEGY

11 Vertical Integration and the Scope of the Firm

The idea of vertical integration is anathema to an increasing number of companies. Most of yesterday's highly integrated giants are working overtime at splitting into more manageable, more energetic units—i.e., de-integrating. Then they are turning around and re-integrating—not by acquisitions but via alliances with all sorts of partners of all shapes and sizes.

—TOM PETERS, *LIBERATION MANAGEMENT*

Bath Fitter has control of the product from raw material to installation. This control allows them to better guarantee the quality by knowing exactly how it is made, not outsourcing it to someone that could take shortcuts to manufacture the product without Bath Fitter knowing. Also, they control the measuring, installation, and customer facing representative. By doing this, Bath Fitter would be able to get accurate and fast feedback about how the product is being used, quality issues, or the ease of installation.

—"BATH FITTER HAS VERTICAL INTEGRATION," HTTP://BEYONDLEAN.WORDPRESS.COM/2011/08/29/

OUTLINE

Introduction and Objectives

Chapter 1 introduced the distinction between corporate strategy and business strategy. Corporate strategy is concerned with decisions over the scope of the firm's activities, including:

◆ *Product scope*: How specialized should the firm be in terms of the range of products it supplies? Coca-Cola (soft drinks), SABMiller (beer), Gap (fashion retailing), and SAP (software) are engaged in a single industry sector; Sony, Berkshire Hathaway, and Tata Group are diversified across multiple industries.

◆ *Geographical scope*: What is the optimal geographical spread of activities for the firm? In the chocolate industry Hershey are heavily focused on North America; Nestlé operates globally.

◆ *Vertical scope*: What range of vertically linked activities should the firm encompass? Walt Disney is vertically integrated from the production of movies and TV shows, through movie distribution and TV networks (ABC, Disney Channel, ESPN), to exploiting its movies' characters in its Disney stores and theme parks. Nike is more vertically specialized: it designs and markets footwear and apparel but outsources most activities in its value chain, including manufacturing, distribution, and retailing.

The distinction between corporate and business strategy may be summarized as follows: *corporate strategy* is concerned with *where* a firm competes; *business strategy* is concerned with *how* a firm competes within a particular area of business.[1] So far, the primary focus of the book has been business strategy. In this final part, we shift our attention to corporate strategy: decisions that define the scope of the firm. I devote separate chapters to the different dimensions of scope—vertical scope (*vertical integration*), geographical scope (*multinationality*), and product scope (*diversification*). However, as we shall discover, the key underlying concepts for analyzing these different dimensions—economies of scope in resources and capabilities, transaction costs, and costs of corporate complexity—are common to all three.

In this chapter we begin by considering the overall scope of the firm. We then focus specifically on vertical integration. This takes us to the core factors that determine firm boundaries, in particular, the role of *transaction costs*. As we shall discover, vertical integration has been a hot topic in corporate strategy. Opportunities for outsourcing, alliances, and electronic commerce have caused companies to rethink which of their activities should remain within their organizational boundaries.

By the time you have completed this chapter, you will be able to:

◆ Appreciate the role of firms and markets in organizing economic activity and apply the principles of *transaction cost economics* to explain why boundaries between firms and markets shift over time.

◆ Understand the relative advantages of vertical integration and outsourcing in organizing vertically related activities, and apply this understanding to decisions over whether a particular activity should be undertaken internally or outsourced.

◆ Identify alternative ways of organizing vertical transactions and, given the characteristics and circumstances of a transaction, recommend the most suitable transaction mode.

Transaction Costs and the Scope of the Firm

In Chapter 6 (Strategy Capsule 6.1), we traced the development of the business corporation. Firms came into existence because of their efficiency advantages in organizing production. Let us explore this issue further and clarify its implications for the boundaries of the firm.

Although the capitalist economy is frequently referred to as a "market economy," it actually comprises two forms of economic organization. One is the *market mechanism*, where individuals and firms, guided by market prices, make independent decisions to buy and sell goods and services. The other is the *administrative mechanism* of firms, where decisions concerning production and resource allocation are made by managers and carried out through hierarchies. The market mechanism was characterized by Adam Smith as the "invisible hand" because its coordinating role does not require conscious planning. Alfred Chandler referred to the administrative mechanism of firms as the "visible hand" because it involves active planning and direction.[2]

Firms and markets may be viewed as alternative institutions for organizing production. Firms are distinguished by the fact they comprise a number of individuals bound by employment contracts with a central contracting authority. But production can also be organized through market transactions. When I remodeled my basement, I contracted a self-employed builder to undertake the work. He in turn subcontracted parts of the work to a plumber, an electrician, a joiner, a drywall installer, and a painter. Although the job involved the coordinated activity of several individuals, these self-employed specialists were not linked by employment relations but by market contracts ("$4000 to install wiring, lights, and power outlets").

The relative roles of firms and markets vary in different areas of business. Compare the supply of mainframe computers with that of personal computers. IBM's System z mainframe computers are assembled by IBM using IBM microprocessors and IBM's z/OS operating system, and run IBM applications software. IBM also undertakes distribution, marketing, and customer support. HP's laptop computers are manufactured by Flextronics, Quanta, and other companies using components produced by firms such as Intel, Seagate, Nvidia, and Samsung. Customer support is also outsourced to companies located in India and South-East Asia.

What determines which activities are undertaken within a firm and which through market contracts? Ronald Coase's answer was the *relative cost* of organizing within firms as compared to organizing across markets.[3] Markets are not costless: the *transaction costs* of markets include the costs of search, negotiation, drawing up contracts, and monitoring and enforcing contracts (including the costs of litigation should a dispute arise). Conversely, if an activity is internalized within a firm, then the firm incurs certain *administrative costs*. If the transaction costs of organizing an activity through the market are more than the administrative costs of organizing it within a firm, we can expect that activity to be encompassed within a firm.

Consider the packaging business (Figure 11.1). With regard to vertical scope, which is more efficient: three independent companies—one producing raw materials (e.g., bauxite), the next producing semi-finished packaging materials (e.g., aluminum foil), and the third producing finished packaging (e.g., aluminum cans)—or having all three stages undertaken by a single company? In the case of product scope, should aluminum cans, plastic containers, and paper cartons be produced by three separate companies or are there efficiencies from merging all

FIGURE 11.1 The scope of the firm: Specialization versus integration in the packaging industry

three into a single company? In the case of geographical scope, which is more efficient: three independent companies producing cans in the US, Brazil, and the European Union, or a single multinational company owning can-making plants in all three countries?

The relative roles of firms and markets in organizing production have experienced major shifts over the past 200 years. As Figure 11.2 shows, these shifts can be

FIGURE 11.2 The shifting roles of firms and markets in the US economy, 1800 to 2010

Source: Author's estimates based upon various sources including: L. J. White, "Trends in Aggregate Concentration in the United States," *Journal of Economic Perspectives* 16 (Fall 2002): 137–60; A. Chandler Jr., *The Visible Hand* (Cambridge, MA: MIT Press, 1977); S. Kim "The Growth of Modern Business Enterprises in the Twentieth Century," *Research in Economic History* 19 (1999): 75–110.

linked to technological changes, including innovation in management and organization favored large firms. Around the mid-1970s, the trend toward growing corporate size and scope went into reverse: a more turbulent business environment and new information and communications technologies favored more focused enterprises coordinated through markets.

The Benefits and Costs of Vertical Integration

So far we have considered the overall scope of the firm. Let us focus now on just one dimension of corporate scope: vertical integration. The question we seek to answer is this: *Is it better to be vertically integrated or vertically specialized?* With regard to a specific activity, this translates into: *To make or to buy?* First, we must be clear what we mean by vertical integration.

Vertical integration is a firm's ownership and control of multiple vertical stages in the supply of a product. The extent of a firm's vertical integration is indicated by the number of stages of the industry's value chain that it spans, and can be measured by the ratio of its value added to sales revenue.[4]

Vertical integration can be either *backward* (or upstream) into its suppliers' activities or *forward* (or downstream) into its customers' activities. Vertical integration may also be *full* or *partial.* Some California wineries are fully integrated: they produce wine only from the grapes they grow, and sell it all through direct distribution. Most are partially integrated: their homegrown grapes are supplemented with purchased grapes; they sell some wine through their own tasting rooms but most through independent distributors.

Strategies toward vertical integration have been subject to shifting fashions. For most of the 20th century the prevailing wisdom was that vertical integration was beneficial because it allowed superior coordination and reduced risk. In the 1960s, J. K. Galbraith predicted the triumph of corporate capitalism: only huge, integrated companies offered the security needed to develop and commercialize new technologies.[5] Yet, the past 30 years have witnessed a profound change of opinion: outsourcing, it is claimed, enhances flexibility and allows firms to concentrate on those activities where they possess superior capabilities. Moreover, many of the coordination benefits associated with vertical integration can be achieved through collaboration between vertically related companies.

However, as in other areas of management, fashion is fickle. Strategy Capsule 11.1 describes vertical integration in the entertainment and media sector, where integration between content producers and distribution allows the coordinated development and distribution of new content (e.g., Disney's *Frozen*), yet multichannel commercial exploitation can also be achieved through licensing contracts with multiple firms (e.g., J. K. Rowling's *Harry Potter*).

Our task is to go beyond fads and fashions to uncover the factors that determine whether vertical integration enhances or weakens performance.

STRATEGY CAPSULE 11.1

Vertical Integration in the Entertainment Industry: *Frozen* versus *Harry Potter*

Over the past two decades integration between *content* producers (film studios, music publishing) and distribution companies (theaters, TV broadcasting, cable companies, satellite TV, digital streaming) has reshaped the entertainment industry. Key players include:

- Time Warner Inc. (Warner Bros. Studios, New Line Cinema, Castle Rock, *Time* magazines, Warner Cable, HBO, Turner Broadcasting, Cartoon Network, CNN)

- 21st Century Fox (20th Century Fox, Fox Broadcasting, Sky TV, MySpace)

- Comcast Corp. (Universal Pictures, NBC, Telemundo, Comcast Cable, Universal Parks and Resorts)

- Viacom (Paramount Pictures, MTV, BET, Nickelodeon, Comedy Central)

- Walt Disney (Walt Disney Studios, Pixar, Disney Theatrical Productions, Walt Disney Records, Walt Disney Pictures, ABC, ESPN, Disney Channel, Disney Online).

The mergers creating these integrated production and distribution companies have not all been successful: AOL's 2000 merger with Time Warner and the acquisition spree that transformed Compagnie Générale des Eaux into Vivendi Universal were disasters.

To illustrate the relative merits of vertical integration and market-based contracts, consider the commercial exploitation of the fictional characters from *Harry Potter* with those of *Frozen*.

HARRY POTTER

- Seven *Harry Potter* novels written by J. K. Rowling were published by Bloomsbury in the UK and Scholastic Press in the US between 1997 and 2007 with total sales of 240 million (to 2014).

- Film rights were acquired by Warner Bros., which produced eight movies generating $7.7 billion in box office receipts.

- 11 *Harry Potter* video games were produced by Electronic Arts.

- A *Harry Potter* attraction opened at Comcast's Universal Orlando Resort in 2010, while a Warner Bros. *Harry Potter* studio tour opened in the UK in 2012.

- *Harry Potter* copyrights and trademarks have been licensed to Mattel, Coca-Cola, Lego, Hasbro, Gund, Tonner Doll Company, Whirlwood Magic Wands, and other companies for the production of toys, clothing, and other products.

FROZEN

Frozen is a computer-animated film inspired by Hans Christian Andersen's *The Snow Queen*, produced by Walt Disney Animation Studios, and released by Walt Disney Pictures in 2013. Within eight months it generated $1.2 billion in worldwide box office revenue. Prior to release, *Frozen* was promoted heavily at Disney theme parks. Commercial spinoffs from the movie and its lead characters, Elsa and Anna, include:

- a range of merchandise including dolls, costumes and "home décor, bath, textile, footwear, sporting goods, consumer electronics, and pool and summer toys" developed by Disney Consumer Products and sold through Disney Stores and independent channels;

- DVD and Blu-ray releases by Walt Disney Studios Home Entertainment;

- a video game launched by Disney Mobile for handheld devices;

- a Broadway stage musical adaptation by Disney Theatrical (under development in 2014);

- temporary Anna and Elsa attractions introduced in Disney theme parks during 2014; a larger scale *Frozen* ride was under consideration.

The Benefits from Vertical Integration

Technical Economies from the Physical Integration of Processes

Proponents of vertical integration have often emphasized the *technical economies* it offers: cost savings that arise from the physical integration of processes. Thus, most steel sheet is produced by integrated producers in plants that first produce steel and then roll hot steel into sheet. Linking the two stages of production at a single location reduces transportation and energy costs. Similar technical economies arise in integrating pulp and paper production and from linking oil refining with petrochemical production.

However, although these considerations explain the need for the co-location of plants, they do not explain why vertical integration in terms of *common ownership* is necessary. Why can't steel and steel strip production or pulp and paper production be undertaken by separate firms that own facilities which are physically integrated with one another? To answer this question, we must look beyond technical economies and consider the implications of linked processes for *transaction costs.*[6]

Avoiding Transaction Costs in Vertical Exchanges

Consider the value chain for steel cans which extends from mining iron ore to the use of cans by food-processing companies (Figure 11.3). There is vertical integration between some stages; other stages are linked by market contracts between specialist firms. In the final linkage—between can producing and canning—most cans are produced by specialist packaging companies (such as Crown Holdings and Ball Corporation).[7] An analysis of transaction costs can explain these different arrangements.

The predominance of market contracts between the producers of steel strip and the producers of cans reflects low transaction costs in the market for steel strip: there are many buyers and sellers, information is readily available, and the switching costs for buyers and suppliers are low. The same is true for many other commodity products: few jewelry companies own gold mines; flour-milling companies seldom own wheat farms.

FIGURE 11.3 The value chain for steel cans

To understand why vertical integration predominates across steel production and steel strip production, let us see what would happen if the two stages were owned by separate companies. Because there are technical economies from hot-rolling steel as soon as it is poured from the furnace, steel makers and strip producers must invest in integrated facilities. A competitive market between the two stages is impossible; each steel strip producer is tied to its adjacent steel producer. In other words, the market becomes a series of *bilateral monopolies*.

The reason these relationships between steel producers and strip producers are problematic in that each steel supplier negotiates with a single buyer; there is no market price: it all depends on relative bargaining power. Such bargaining is costly: the mutual dependency of the two parties encourages *opportunism* and *strategic misrepresentation* as each company seeks to enhance and exploit its bargaining power at the expense of the other. Thus, once we move from a competitive market situation to one where individual buyers and sellers are locked together in close bilateral relationships, the efficiencies of competitive markets are lost.

The culprits in this situation are *transaction-specific investments*. When a can-maker buys steel strip, neither the steel strip producer nor the can-maker needs to invest in equipment or technology that is specific to the needs of the other party. In the case of the steel producer and the steel roller, each company's plant is built to match the other party's plant. Once built, the plant's value depends upon the availability of the other party's complementary facilities—each seller is tied to a single buyer, which gives each the potential to *hold up* the other (i.e., each party can threaten the other with withholding business).

If the future were predictable, these issues could be resolved in advance. However, in an uncertain world it is impossible to write a complete contract that covers every possible eventuality over the entire life span of the capital investments being made.

Empirical research confirms the tendency for transaction-specific investments to encourage vertical integration:[8]

- Among automakers, specialized components are more likely to be manufactured in-house than commodity items such as tires and spark plugs.[9] Similarly, in aerospace, company-specific components are more likely to be produced in-house rather than purchased externally.[10]

- In semiconductors, integration across design and fabrication is more likely for the technically complex integrated circuits (such as those produced by Intel and STMicroelectronics) than for simpler chips. The more complex the chip, the greater the need for the designer and fabricator to invest in close technical collaboration.[11]

The Costs of Vertical Integration

The presence of transaction costs in intermediate markets is not sufficient justification for vertical integration. While vertical integration avoids the transaction costs of using the market, it imposes an administrative cost. The extent of these costs depends on several factors.

Differences in Optimal Scale between Different Stages of Production

UPS's delivery vans are manufactured to its own specifications by Morgan Olson in Sturgis, Michigan. Should UPS build its own vans and trucks? Almost certainly not: the transaction costs avoided by UPS will be trivial compared with the inefficiencies incurred in manufacturing its own vans: the 20,000 vans UPS purchases each year are well below the minimum efficient scale of an assembly plant. Similarly, specialist brewers such as Anchor Brewing of San Francisco or Adnams of Suffolk, England do not make their own containers (as do Anheuser-Busch InBev and SABMiller). Small brewers simply lack the scale needed for the low-cost manufacture of cans and bottles.

The Need to Develop Distinctive Capabilities

Another reason for UPS not making its own vans is that it is likely to be a poor vehicle manufacturer. A key advantage of a company specializing in a few activities is its ability to develop distinctive capabilities in those activities. Even large, technology-based companies such as Xerox, Sony, and Philips cannot maintain IT capabilities that match those of IT services specialists such as IBM, TCS, and Accenture. A major advantage of these IT specialists is the learning they gain from working with multiple clients. If Sony's IT department only serves the in-house needs of Sony, this limits the development of its IT capabilities.

However, this assumes that capabilities in different vertical activities are independent of one another and the required capabilities are generic rather than highly customized. Where one capability is closely integrated with capabilities in adjacent activities, vertical integration may help develop these integrated, system-wide capabilities. Thus, Walmart keeps its IT in-house. The reason is that real-time information is central to Walmart's supply chain management, in-store operations, and upper-level managerial decision making. Walmart's need for tightly integrated information and communication services customized to meet its unique business systems inclines it toward in-sourcing.

Problems of Managing Strategically Different Businesses

These problems of differences in optimal scale and developing distinctive capabilities may be viewed as part of a wider set of problems—that of managing vertically related businesses that are strategically very different. A major disadvantage of UPS owning a truck-manufacturing company is that the management systems and organizational capabilities required for truck manufacturing are very different from those required for express delivery. These considerations explain the lack of vertical integration between manufacturing and retailing. Firms that are integrated across design, manufacturing, and retailing, such as Zara (Inditex S.A.) and Gucci (Kering S.A.), are unusual. Most of the world's leading retailers—Walmart, Gap, Carrefour—do not manufacture. Similarly, few manufacturing companies retail their own products. Not only do manufacturing and retailing require very different organizational capabilities, they also require different strategic planning systems, different approaches to control and human resource management, and different top-management styles and skills.

These strategic dissimilarities are a key factor in the trend to vertically de-integrate. Marriott's split into two separate companies, Marriott International and Host Marriott, was influenced by the belief that *owning* hotels is a strategically different business from *operating* hotels. Similarly, the Coca-Cola Company spun off its bottling activities as Coca-Cola Enterprises Inc. partly because managing local bottling and distribution operations is very different from managing the global Coca-Cola brand and producing and distributing concentrates.

Incentive Problems

Vertical integration changes the incentives between vertically related businesses. Where a market interface exists between a buyer and a seller, profit incentives ensure that the buyer is motivated to secure the best possible deal and the seller is motivated to pursue efficiency and service in order to attract and retain the buyer—these are termed *high-powered incentives*. With vertical integration, internal supplier–customer relationships are subject to *low-powered incentives*. When my office computer malfunctions, I call the university's IT department. The incentives for the in-house technicians to respond promptly to my email and voice messages are weak. If I were free to use an outside IT specialist, that specialist would only get the business if they were able to offer same-day service and would only get paid once the problem was resolved.

One approach to creating stronger performance incentives within vertically integrated companies is to open internal divisions to external competition. As we shall examine more fully in Chapter 14, many large corporations have created *shared service organizations*, where internal suppliers of corporate services—such as IT, training, and engineering—compete with external suppliers of the same services to serve internal operating divisions.

Competitive Effects

For a monopolist, one of the supposed benefits of vertical integration is to extend a monopoly position at one stage of an industry's value chain to adjacent stages. Classic cases of this are Standard Oil and Alcoa. However, economists have shown that there is no additional monopoly profit to be extracted by extending a monopoly to adjacent stages of the value chain.[12]

For a firm that is not monopolist, vertical integration risks damaging its competitive position in its core business. If it forward integrates it becomes a competitor of its customers (or, if it backwards integrates, a competitor of its suppliers), potentially damaging its attractiveness as a business partner. When Google acquired Motorola, a major risk was that other handset makers that were customers for its Android operating system (Samsung in particular) might regard Google as a less reliable supplier and be inclined to find an alternative operating system to Android.[13]

Flexibility

Both vertical integration and market transactions can claim advantage with regard to different types of flexibility. Where the required flexibility is rapid responsiveness to uncertain demand, there may be advantages in market transactions. The lack of vertical integration in the construction industry reflects, in part, the need for flexibility in adjusting both to cyclical patterns of demand and to the different requirements of each project.[14] Vertical integration may also be disadvantageous in responding quickly to new product development opportunities that require new combinations of technical capabilities. Some of the most successful new electronic products of recent years—Apple's iPod, Microsoft's Xbox, Dell's range of notebook computers— have been produced by contract manufacturers. Extensive outsourcing has been a key feature of fast-cycle product development throughout the electronics sector.

Yet, where system-wide flexibility is required, vertical integration may allow for speed and coordination in achieving simultaneous adjustment throughout the vertical chain. American Apparel is a rare example of a successful US *manufacturer* of apparel. Its tightly coordinated vertical integration from its Los Angeles design and manufacturing base to its 160 retail stores across ten countries allows a super-fast design-to-distribution cycle. Figure 11.4 shows an advertisement for American Apparel.

FIGURE 11.4   An American Apparel advertisement

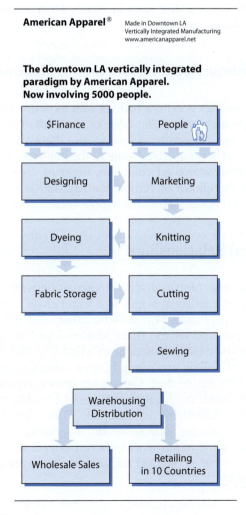

Source: American Apparel Inc.

Investing in an Unattractive Business

Finally, one of the biggest disadvantages of vertical integration is that it may involve investing in an inherently unattractive industry. Irrespective of transaction costs and coordination benefits, McDonald's chooses not to backward integrate into beef raising and potato growing, because agriculture is a low-margin industry.

Compounding Risk

To the extent that it ties a company to its internal suppliers and internal customers, vertical integration represents a compounding of risk: problems at any one stage of production threaten production and profitability at all other stages. When union workers at a General Motors brake plant went on strike in 1998, GM's 24 US assembly plants were soon brought to a halt. If Disney animation studios fail to produce blockbuster animation movies that introduce new characters, then the knock-on effects are felt through plummeting DVD sales, lack of spin-off shows on the Disney Channel, reduction of merchandise sales in Disney Stores, and a shortage of new attractions at Disney theme parks.

Applying the Criteria: Deciding Whether to Make or Buy

Vertical integration is neither good nor bad. As with most questions of strategy, it all depends upon the specific context. The value of our analysis is that we can identify the factors that determine the relative advantages of the market transactions versus internalization. Figure 11.5 summarizes some of the key criteria.

However, our analysis is not yet complete; we must consider some additional factors that influence the choice of vertical strategy, and in particular the fact that vertical relationships are not limited to the simple choice of make or buy.

Designing Vertical Relationships

Our discussion so far has compared vertical integration with arm's-length market contracts. In practice, the adjacent stages in a value chain can be linked through a variety of relationships. Figure 11.6 shows a number of different types of relationship between buyers and sellers. These relationships may be classified in relation to two characteristics. First, the extent to which the buyer and seller commit resources to the relationship: arm's-length, spot contracts involve no resource commitment beyond the single deal; vertical integration typically involves a substantial investment. Second, the formality of the relationship: long-term contracts and franchises are formalized by the complex written agreements they entail; spot contracts typically involve little or no documentation and are governed by common law; collaborative agreements between buyers and sellers are usually informal—they are trust based; vertical integration allows management discretion to replace legal formality.

FIGURE 11.5 Vertical integration (VI) versus outsourcing: Key considerations

FIGURE 11.6   Different types of vertical relationship

Different Types of Vertical Relationship

Different vertical relationships offer different combinations of advantages and disadvantages. For example:

- *Long-term contracts*: Market transactions can be either *spot contracts*—buying a cargo of crude oil on the Rotterdam petroleum market—or *long-term contracts*—a series of transactions over a period of time that specify the terms of sales and the responsibilities of each party. Spot transactions work well under competitive conditions (many buyers and sellers and a standard product) where there is no need for transaction-specific investments by either party. Where closer supplier–customer ties are needed, particularly when one or both parties need to make transaction-specific investments, a longer-term contract can help avoid opportunism and provide the security needed to make the necessary investment. However, long-term contracts face the problem of anticipating the circumstances that may arise during the life of the contract: either they are too restrictive or so loose that they give rise to opportunism and conflicting interpretation. Long-term contracts often include provisions for the arbitration of contract disputes.

- *Vertical partnerships*: The greater the difficulties of specifying complete contracts for long-term supplier–customer deals, the greater the advantage of vertical relationships based on trust and mutual understanding. Such relationships can provide the security needed to support transaction-specific investments, the flexibility to meet changing circumstances, and the incentives to avoid opportunism. Such arrangements may be entirely *relational contracts*, with no written contract at all. The model for vendor partnerships has been the close collaborative relationships that many Japanese companies have with their suppliers. Japanese automakers have been much less backward integrated than their US or European counterparts but have also achieved close collaboration with component makers in technology, design, quality, and production scheduling.[15]

● *Franchising*: A franchise is a contractual agreement between the owner of a business system and trademark (the franchiser) that permits the franchisee to produce and market the franchiser's product or service in a specified area. Franchising brings together the brand, marketing capabilities, and business systems of the large corporation with the entrepreneurship and local knowledge of small firms. The franchising systems of companies such as McDonald's, Century 21 real estate, Hilton Hotels, and 7-Eleven convenience stores combine the advantages of vertical integration in terms of coordination and investment in transaction-specific assets with advantages of market contracts in terms of high-powered incentives, flexibility, and separate ownership of strategically dissimilar businesses.

Choosing Among Alternative Vertical Relationships

The criteria listed in Figure 11.5 establish the basic features of the vertical relation that favor either market transactions or vertical integration. However, the availability of other types of vertical relationships, such as vendor partnerships and franchises, mean that vertical integration is not the sole solution to problems of transaction costs. Moreover, many of these relational contracts and hybrid arrangements have the capacity to combine the advantages of both vertical integration and market contracts.

Choosing the optimal vertical relationships needs to take account of additional factors to those listed in Figure 11.5. In particular:

● *Resources, capabilities, and strategy:* Within the same industry, different companies will choose different vertical arrangements according to their reactive resource and capability strengths and the strategies they pursue. Thus, in fashion clothing, Zara's high level of vertical integration compared to H&M's or Gap's reflects strategy based upon fast-cycle new-product development and tight integration between its retail stores, designers, and manufacturers. While most fast-food chains have expanded through franchising, California-based In-N-Out Burger seeks to maintain its unique culture and distinctive business practices by directly owning and managing its restaurants. While most banks have been outsourcing IT to companies such as IBM and EDS, US credit card group Capital One sees IT as a key source of competitive advantage: "IT is our central nervous system … if we outsourced tomorrow we might save a dollar or two on each account, but we would lose flexibility and value and service levels."[16]

● *Allocation of risk*: Any arrangement beyond a spot contract must cope with uncertainties over the course of the contract. A key feature of any contract is that its terms allocate (often implicitly) risks between the parties. How risk is shared is dependent partly on bargaining power and partly on efficiency considerations. In franchise agreements, the franchisee (as the weaker partner) bears most of the risk—it is the franchisee's capital that is at risk and the franchisee pays the franchiser a flat royalty based on sale revenues. In oil exploration, outsourcing agreements between the national oil companies (e.g.,

PDVSA, Petronas, and Statoil) and drilling companies (e.g., Schlumberger or Halliburton) have moved from fee-for-service contracts to risk service contracts where the drilling company bears much more of the risk.

- *Incentive structures*: Incentives are central to the design of vertical rela-tionships. Incentives for opportunistic behavior are the bugbear of market contracts, while weak performance incentives are a key problem of vertical integration. It seems possible that hybrid and intermediate governance modes offer the best solutions to the design of incentives. Toyota, Benetton, Boeing, and Marks & Spencer have relationships with their vendors that may involve formal contracts, but their essence is that they are long-term and trust based. The key to these relationships is that the promise of a long-term, mutually beneficial relationship trumps short-term opportunism.

Recent Trends

The main feature of recent years has been a growing diversity of hybrid vertical relationships that have attempted to combine the flexibility and incentives of market transactions with the close collaboration provided by vertical integration. These col-laborative vertical arrangements we have described as "vertical partnerships" have also been denoted "virtual vertical integration" and "value-adding partnerships." Leading models have included Toyota's supply chain with its three tiers of suppliers,[17] Dell's build-to-order, direct sales model involving close coordination among a small group of suppliers, and Apple's "ecosystem" in which Apple leads product devel-opment and tightly controls its intellectual property but integrates the capabilities and innovations of a broad network of firms that include component suppliers and contract assemblers and a developer community responsible for over one million applications for the OS X and iOS platforms.

Although these collaborative vertical relationships are viewed as a recent phenomenon—associated with microelectronics, biotechnology, and other hi-tech sectors—local clusters of vertically collaborating firms have long been a feature of European industries—in northern Italy, the localized firm networks in traditional industries such as clothing, footwear, and furniture are also apparent in newer sec-tors such as packaging equipment[18] and motorcycles.[19]

Collaborative vertical partnerships have encouraged the scope of outsourcing to extend from raw materials and basic components to more complex products and business services that represent whole chunks of the value chain. In electronics, contract manufacturers, such as Flextronics and Foxconn (a subsidiary of Hon Hai Precision Industry Co.) design and manufacture entire products. Business services and corporate functions such as payroll, IT, training, customer service and support, and external communications are often outsourced to specialist providers.

However, there seem to be limits to the extent to which a firm can outsource activities while still retaining the capabilities needed to develop and evolve. The *virtual corporation*, a firm whose sole function is to coordinate the activities of a network of suppliers and partners, remains an abstract concept rather than a tan-gible reality.[20] The viability of a firm whose role is as a *systems integrator* depends upon a clear separation between the *component capabilities* of the various partners and contractors and the *architectural capabilities* needed to manage integration. Brusoni *et al.* point to the complementarity between architectural capabilities and component capabilities: even when the aero engine manufacturers outsource key components, they continue R & D into those component technologies.[21] More generally, managing a network of suppliers during a period of rapid technological change is highly complex—as indicated by Boeing's difficulties in managing the development of its 787 Dreamliner.[22]

Summary

The size and scope of firms reflects the relative efficiencies of markets and firms in organizing production. Over the past 200 years, the trend has been for firms to grow in size and scope as a result of technology and advances in management, causing the administrative costs of firms to fall relative to the transaction costs of markets.

In relation to vertical integration, the transaction costs of markets relative to the administrative costs of firms determine whether a vertically integrated firm is more efficient than specialist firms linked by market contracts. By considering the factors which determine the transaction costs of markets and the administrative costs of firms, we can determine whether a particular activity should be internalized within the firm or outsourced.

The dominant trend of the past three decades is for firms to outsource more and more of their activities and in the process become more vertically specialized. The dominant consideration has been to concentrate upon those activities where the firm possesses distinctive capabilities. However, this trend has involved the replacement of vertical integration, not by arm's-length market contracts but by collaborative arrangements which combine the specialization benefits of outsourcing with the coordination and knowledge-sharing benefits of vertical integration.

In subsequent chapters we shall return to issues of vertical integration. In the next chapter we shall consider the offshoring phenomenon: firms seeking the optimal international location for different value chain activities. In Chapter 15 we shall look more closely at alliances—the collaborative relationships between firms that have become so typical of modern supply chains.

Self-Study Questions

1. Figure 11.2 and the section on "Transaction Costs and the Scope of the Firm" argues that developments in information and communication technology (e.g., regarding telephones and computers) during the 20th century tended to lower the costs of administration within the firm relative to the costs of market transactions, thereby increasing the size and scope of firms. What about the internet? How has this influenced the efficiency of large, integrated firms relative to small, specialized firms coordinated by markets?

2. Figure 11.2 shows that during 1980–2014 large US companies accounted for a smaller percentage of total employment—a development that is attributed to a more turbulent business environment. Explain why external turbulence causes firms to reduce their size and scope.

3. A large proportion of major corporations outsource their IT functions to specialist suppliers of IT services such as IBM, EDS (now owned by Hewlett-Packard), Accenture, and Capgemini. What benefits do corporations derive from outsourcing their IT requirements? What transaction costs arise from these arrangements?

4. Strategy Capsule 11.1 compares alternative strategies for exploiting children's characters. Hello Kitty is owned by the Japanese company Sanrio Co. Ltd. and is exploited throughout the world through licensing contracts with toy makers, jewelry companies, fashion companies, restaurants, theme parks, retail stores, and many other types of businesses. Could Hello Kitty be exploited more effectively by a vertically integrated entertainment company, such as Disney?

5. For its Zara brand, Inditex manufactures the majority of the garments it sells and undertakes all of its own distribution from manufacturing plants to its directly managed retail outlets. The Gap outsources its production and focuses upon design, marketing, and retail distribution. Applying the considerations listed in Figure 11.5, should Gap backward integrate into manufacture?

Notes

1. M. J. Piskorski ("A Note on Corporate Strategy," *Harvard Business School* 9-705-449, 2005) defines *corporate strategy* as: "a set of choices that a corporation makes to create value through configuration and coordination of its multimarket activities." In practice, determining the boundary between business strategy and corporate strategy depends on where we draw the boundaries of industries and markets.
2. A. Chandler Jr., *The Visible Hand: The Managerial Revolution in American Business* (Cambridge, MA: MIT Press, 1977).
3. R. H. Coase, "The Nature of the Firm," *Economica* 4 (1937): 386–405.
4. The more of its inputs a firm makes rather than buys, the greater is its value added relative to its sales revenue. Ruth Maddigan discusses "The Measurement of Vertical Integration," *Review of Economics and Statistics* 63 (August, 1981).
5. J. K. Galbraith, *The New Industrial State* (Harmondsworth: Penguin, 1969).
6. O. E. Williamson, *Markets and Hierarchies: Analysis and Antitrust Implications* (New York: Free Press, 1975); O. E. Williamson, *The Economic Institutions of Capitalism: Firms, Markets and Relational Contracting* (New York: Free Press, 1985).

7. Some large food processors, such as Campbell Soup and H. J. Heinz, have backward integrated into can production.
8. For a review of empirical evidence on transaction costs and vertical integration see J. T. Macher and B. D. Richman, "Transaction Cost Economics: An Assessment of Empirical Research in the Social Sciences," *Business and Politics* 10 (2008): Article 1; and M. D, Whinston, "On the Transaction Cost Determinants of Vertical Integration," *Journal of Law, Economics & Organization* 19 (2003): 1–23.
9. K. Monteverde and J. J. Teece, "Supplier Switching Costs and Vertical Integration in the Automobile Industry," *Bell Journal of Economics* 13 (Spring 1982): 206–213.
10. S. Masten, "The Organization of Production: Evidence from the Aerospace Industry," *Journal of Law and Economics* 27 (October 1984): 403–417.
11. J. T. Macher, "Technological Development and the Boundaries of the Firm: A Knowledge-based Examination in Semiconductor Manufacturing," *Management Science* 52 (2006): 826–843; K. Monteverde, "Technical Dialogue as an Incentive for Vertical Integration in the Semiconductor Industry," *Management Science* 41 (1995): 1624–1638.

12. R. Rey and J. Tirole, "A Primer on Foreclosure," Chapter 33 in M. Armstrong and R. H. Porter (eds), *Handbook of Industrial Organization: Vol. 3* (Amsterdam: Elsevier, 2007).

13. "Would Samsung ever leave Android? New CEO drops hints," CNET (June 16, 2012), http://www.cnet.com/uk/news/would-samsung-ever-leave-android-new-ceo-drops-hints/, accessed July 20, 2015.

14. However, E. Cacciatori and M. G. Jacobides ("The Dynamic Limits of Specialization: Vertical Integration Reconsidered," *Organization Studies* 26 (2005): 1851–1883) point to changes in construction that are causing reintegration.

15. J. H. Dyer, "Effective Interfirm Collaboration: How Firms Minimize Transaction Costs and Maximize Transaction Value," *Strategic Management Journal* 18 (1997): 535–556; J. H. Dyer, "Specialized Supplier Networks as a Source of Competitive Advantage: Evidence from the Auto Industry," *Strategic Management Journal* 17 (1996): 271–292.

16. L. Willcocks and C. Sauer, "High Risks and Hidden Costs in IT Outsourcing," *Financial Times* (May 23, 2000): 3.

17. J. H. Dyer and K. Nobeoka, "Creating and Managing a High-performance Knowledge-sharing Network: The Toyota Case," *Strategic Management Journal* 21 (2000): 345–368.

18. G. Lorenzoni and A. Lipparini, "The Leveraging of Interfirm Relationships as Distinctive Organizational Capabilities: A Longitudinal Study," *Strategic Management Journal* 20 (1999): 317–338.

19. A. Lipparini, G. Lorenzoni, and S. Ferriani, "From Core to Periphery and Back: A Study on the Deliberate Shaping of Knowledge Flows in Interfirm Dyads and Networks," *Strategic Management Journal* 35 (2014): 578–595.

20. H. W. Chesborough and D. J. Teece, "When is Virtual Virtuous? Organizing for Innovation," *Harvard Business Review* (May/June 1996): 68–79.

21. S. Brusoni, A. Prencipe, and K. Pavitt, "Knowledge Specialization, Organizational Coupling and the Boundaries of the Firm: Why Do Firms Know More than They Make?" *Administrative Science Quarterly* 46 (2001): 597–621.

22. "Boeing 787's Problems Blamed on Outsourcing, Lack of Oversight," *Seattle Times* (February 3, 2013).

12 Global Strategy and the Multinational Corporation

Uber to Deliver Ice Creams Tomorrow in Over 38 Countries Including India
In India, Uber will be delivering ice creams in Delhi, Mumbai, Chennai, Bangalore, Pune and Hyderabad, tomorrow between 11AM and 5PM. All you have to do is order ice cream from the Uber app, and an ice cream car will arrive at your doorstep. In Delhi, Mumbai, Chennai and Bangalore, you will need to pay Rs 700 for Haagen-Dazs Belgian Chocolate and Strawberry sundaes. Uber users in Hyderabad and Pune, on the other hand, will pay Rs 450 for two cookies and cream and strawberry ice creams.

—BGR INDIA, JULY 17, 2014 (HTTP://WWW.BGR.IN/NEWS/
UBER-TO-DELIVER-ICE-CREAMS-TOMORROW-IN-OVER-38-COUNTRIES-INCLUDING-INDIA/)

OUTLINE

Introduction and Objectives

There have been two primary forces driving change in the business environment during the past half century. One is technology; the other is internationalization. Internationalization is a source of huge opportunity. In 1994, Embraer was a struggling, state-owned Brazilian aircraft manufacturer. By 2015, it was the world's third-biggest plane maker (after Boeing and Airbus) and global market leader in 70- to 130-seater commercial jets with 85% of its revenues generated outside of Brazil.

Internationalization is also a potent destroyer. For centuries, Sheffield, England was the world's leading center of cutlery manufacture. By 2015, only a few hundred people were employed making cutlery in Sheffield. The industry had been devastated by low-cost competition first from South Korea and then from China. Nor is it just the industries in the mature industrial nations that have been ravaged by imports. Bulk imports of second-hand clothing from Europe and North America (much of it from charities and churches) have been ruinous for Kenya's textile and apparel sector.

Internationalization occurs through two mechanisms: trade and direct investment. Both are the result of the strategic decisions of individual businesses to exploit either market opportunities outside their national boundaries or resources and capabilities located in other countries. The resulting "globalization of business" has created massive flows of international transactions comprising payments for trade and services, payments to factors of production (interest, profits, and licensing fees), and flows of capital.

What does the internationalization mean for our strategy analysis? As we have noted, internationalization is both a threat and an opportunity. However, in terms of our strategic analysis, the primary implication of introducing the international dimension is that it adds considerable complexity—not just in broadening the scope of markets (and competition) but also in complicating the analysis of competitive advantage.

By the time you have completed this chapter, you will be able to:

- Use the tools of industry analysis to examine the impact of internationalization on industry structure and competition.

- Analyze the implications of a firm's national environment for its competitive advantage.

- Formulate strategies for exploiting overseas business opportunities, including overseas market entry strategies and overseas production strategies.

- Formulate international strategies that achieve an optimal balance between global integration and national differentiation.

- Design organizational structures and management systems appropriate to the pursuit of international strategies.

We begin by exploring the implications of international competition, first for industry analysis and then for the analysis of competitive advantage.

Implications of International Competition for Industry Analysis

Patterns of Internationalization

Internationalization occurs through trade—supplying goods and services from one country to another—and direct investment—building or acquiring productive assets in another country.[1] On this basis we can identify different types of industry according to the extent and mode of their internationalization (Figure 12.1):

- *Sheltered industries* are shielded from both imports and inward direct investment by regulation, trade barriers, or because of the localized nature of the goods and services they offer. Hence, they are served by indigenous firms. Growing internationalization has made this category progressively smaller over time. The remaining sheltered industries tend to be fragmented service industries (dry cleaning, hairdressing, auto repair), some small-scale production industries (handicrafts, residential construction), and industries producing products that are non-tradable because they are perishable (fresh milk, bread) or difficult to move (beds, garden sheds). *Little*

- *Trading industries* are those where internationalization occurs primarily through imports and exports. If a product is transportable, if it is not nationally differentiated, and if it is subject to substantial scale economies, exporting from a single location is the most efficient means to exploit overseas markets. This is the case with commercial aircraft, shipbuilding, and defense equipment. Trading industries also include products whose inputs are available only in a few locations (rare earths from China, caviar from Iran and Azerbaijan). *A lot*

FIGURE 12.1   Patterns of industry internationalization

- *Multidomestic industries* are those that internationalize through direct invest-ment—either because trade is not feasible (e.g., service industries such as banking, consulting, hotels) or because products are nationally differentiated (e.g., frozen ready meals, book publishing).
- *Global industries* are those that feature high levels of both trade and direct investment. These include most major manufacturing and extractive indus-tries that are populated by multinational corporations.

By which route does internationalization typically occur? The Uppsala Model pre-dicts that firms internationalize in a sequential pattern, first exporting to countries with the least "psychic distance" from their home markets (i.e., geographically or culturally close), then broadening and deepening their engagement, and eventually establishing manufacturing subsidiaries in foreign markets.[2] In service industries, exporting is not usually feasible, hence internationalization involves either direct investment ("green-field entry," acquisition, or joint venture) or licensing (including franchising).

Implications for Competition

Internationalization usually means more competition and lower industry profitabil-ity. In 1976, the US automobile market was dominated by GM, Ford, and Chrysler, with 84% of the market. By 2014, there were 13 companies with auto plants within the US; GM and Ford were the remaining indigenous producers accounting for 33.2% of auto sales.

We can use Porter's five forces of competition framework to analyze the impact of internationalization on competition and industry profitability. If we define an inter-national industry in terms of a number of different national markets, in each national market internationalization directly influences three of the five forces of competition:

- *Competition from potential entrants*: Internationalization is both a cause and a consequence of falling barriers to entry into most national markets. Tariff reductions, declining real costs of transportation, foreign-exchange convert-ibility, internationalization of standards, and converging customer preferences make it much easier for producers in one country to supply customers in another. Entry barriers that are effective against domestic entrants may be ineffective against established producers in other countries.
- *Rivalry among existing firms*: Internationalization increases internal rivalry primarily because it increases the number of firms competing within each national market—it *lowers seller concentration*. The western European market for motor scooters was once dominated by Piaggio (Vespa) and Innocenti (Lambretta). There are now over 25 suppliers of scooters to the European market, including BMW from Germany; Honda, Yamaha, and Suzuki from Japan; Kwang Yang Motor Co (KYMCO) from Taiwan; Baotian, Qingqi, and Znen from China; Bajaj from India; and Tomos from Slovenia. Although internationalization typically triggers a wave of mergers and acquisitions that reduce the global population of firms in the industry, because each firm competes in multiple national markets, the number of competitors in each national market increases.[3] In addition, internationalization stimulates

competition by increasing investments in capacity and increasing the diversity of competitors within each national market.

- *Increasing the bargaining power of buyers*: The option of sourcing from overseas greatly enhances the power of industrial buyers. It also allows distributors to engage in international arbitrage: pharmaceutical distributors have become adept at searching the world for low-price pharmaceuticals and then importing them for their domestic markets.

Analyzing Competitive Advantage in an International Context

Growing international competition has been associated with some stunning reversals in the competitive positions of different companies. In 1989, US Steel was the world's biggest steel company; in 2014, ArcelorMittal based in Luxemburg and India was the new leader. In 2000, all the world's top-20 airlines (in terms of passenger kilometers flown) were US or European based. By 2014, one half were based in Asia, with Emirates the world leader in terms of international passengers.

To understand how internationalization impacts a firm's competitive position, we need to extend our framework for analyzing competitive advantage to include the influence of firms' national environments. Competitive advantage, we have noted, is achieved when a firm matches its internal strengths in resources and capabilities to the key success factors within its industry. When competing firms are based in different countries, competitive advantage depends not just on their internal resources and capabilities but on the availability of resources within those countries. Figure 12.2 summarizes the implications of internationalization for our basic strategy model in terms of the impact both on industry conditions and firms' access to resources and capabilities.

National Influences on Competitiveness: Comparative Advantage

The effect of national resource availability on international competitiveness is the subject of the *theory of comparative advantage*. The theory states that a country has a comparative advantage in those products which make intensive use of those resources available in abundance within that country. Thus, Bangladesh has an abundant supply of unskilled labor. Its comparative advantage lies in labor-intensive

FIGURE 12.2   Competitive advantage in an international context products such as clothing, handicrafts, leather goods, and assembly of consumer electronic products. The US has an abundant supply of technological resources: trained scientists and engineers, research facilities, and universities. Its comparative advantage lies in technology-intensive products such as microprocessors, computer software, pharmaceuticals, medical diagnostic equipment, and management consulting services.

The term **comparative advantage** refers to the *relative* efficiencies of producing different products. So long as exchange rates are well behaved (i.e. they do not deviate far from their purchasing power parity levels), then comparative advantage translates into competitive advantage. Comparative advantages are revealed in trade performance. Table 12.1 shows revealed comparative advantages for several product categories and several countries.[4]

Trade theory initially looked to natural resource endowments, labor supply, and capital stock as the main determinants of comparative advantage. Emphasis has shifted to the central role of knowledge (including technology, human skills, and management capability) and the resources needed to commercialize that knowledge (capital markets, communications facilities, and legal systems).[5] For industries where scale economies are important, a large home market is an additional source of comparative advantage (e.g., the US in aerospace).[6]

Porter's National Diamond

Michael Porter has extended the traditional theory of comparative advantage by proposing that the key role of the national environment upon a firm's potential for international competitive advantage is its impact upon the dynamics through which resources and capabilities are developed.[7] Porter's *national diamond* framework identifies four key factors that determine whether firms from a particular country can establish competitive advantage within their industry sector (Figure 12.3).[8]

TABLE 12.1 Indexes of revealed comparative advantage for selected product categories, 2013

	US	UK	Japan	Switzerland	Germany	Australia	China	India
Cereals	1.91	0.13	0.00	0.00	0.44	4.78	0.03	5.33
Beverages	0.72	3.30	0.09	1.38	0.75	1.28	0.10	0.06
Mineral fuels	0.55	0.68	0.14	0.04	0.17	1.49	0.09	1.23
Pharmaceuticals	0.94	2.19	0.15	9.14	1.90	0.00	0.10	1.34
Vehicles	1.15	1.27	2.79	0.14	2.25	0.16	0.36	0.56
Aerospace	4.32	1.96	0.33	0.50	1.78	0.30	0.05	0.71
Electrical and electronic equipment	0.91	0.49	1.29	0.51	0.84	0.10	2.18	0.29
Optical, medical, and scientific equipment	1.76	1.16	1.83	2.25	1.53	0.35	1.12	0.23
Clocks and watches	0.30	0.58	0.60	40.13	0.64	0.16	0.99	0.04
Apparel (knitted)	0.15	0.45	0.02	0.03	0.50	0.06	3.52	1.72

Note:
Country X's revealed comparative advantage within product category A is measured as: Country X's share of world exports in product category A / Country X's share of world exports in all products.
Source: International Trade Center.

FIGURE 12.3 Porter's national diamond framework

1 *Factor conditions*: Whereas the conventional analysis of comparative advantage focuses on endowments of broad categories of resource, Porter emphasizes the role of highly specialized resources, many of which are "home grown" rather than "endowed." For example, the US's preeminence in producing movies and TV shows is based upon the concentration in Los Angeles of highly skilled labor and supporting institutions including financiers and film schools. These specialized resources and capabilities may develop in response to resource constraints: Japan's "lean manufacturing" capabilities were developed during acute raw material shortages after the Second World War.

2 *Related and supporting industries*: One of Porter's most striking empirical findings is that national competitive strengths tend to be associated with "clusters" of industries. Silicon Valley's cluster comprises semiconductor, computer, software, and venture capital firms. For each industry, closely related industries are sources of critical resources and capabilities. Denmark's global leadership in wind power is based upon a cluster comprising wind turbine manufacturers, offshore wind farm developers and operators, and utilities.

3 *Demand conditions*: In the domestic market these provide the primary driver of innovation and quality improvement. For example:

   ● Switzerland's preeminence in watches is supported by the obsessive punctuality of the Swiss.

   ● Japan's dominant share of the world market for cameras by companies owes much to the Japanese enthusiasm for amateur photography and customers' eager adoption of innovation in cameras.

   ● German dominance of high-performance automobiles (Daimler, BMW, Porsche, VW-Audi) reflects German motorists' love of quality engineering and their irrepressible urge to drive on autobahns at terrifying speeds.

4 *Strategy, structure, and rivalry*: International competitive advantage depends upon how firms within a particular sector interact within their domestic markets. Porter proposes that intense competition within the domestic market drives innovation, quality, and efficiency. The global success of Japanese companies in cars, cameras, consumer electronics, and office equipment during the last

two decades of the 20th century was based upon domestic industries where five or more major producers competed strongly with one another. Conversely, European failure in many hi-tech industries may be a result of European governments' propensity to kill domestic competition by creating national champions.

Consistency between Strategy and National Conditions

Establishing competitive advantage in global industries requires congruence between business strategy and the pattern of the country's comparative advantage. In semiconductors, US companies such as Intel, Texas Instruments, Nvidia, and Broadcom tend to focus upon sophisticated microprocessors, digital signal processing chips, graphics chips, and application-specific integrated circuits, and emphasize design rather than manufacture. Chinese semiconductor producers tend to focus upon less sophisticated memory and logic chips, on older generations of analog integrated circuits and microcontrollers, and emphasize fabrication rather than design.

Similarly in footwear. The world's three leading exporters, after China, are Italy, Vietnam, and Germany. Each country's shoe producers exploit the resource strengths of their home country. Italian shoe producers such as Tod's, Fratelli Rosetti, and Santoni emphasize style and craftsmanship; Germany's shoe companies such as Adidas, Puma, and Brütting emphasize technology; Vietnam's shoe industry uses low-cost labor to produce vast numbers of cheap casual shoes.

Achieving congruence between firm strategy and national conditions also extends to the embodiment of national culture within strategy and management systems. The success of US companies in many areas of high technology, including computer software and biotechnology, owes much to a business system of entrepreneurial capitalism which exploits a national culture that emphasizes individuality, opportunity, and wealth acquisition. The global success of Korean corporate giants such as Samsung and LG reflects organizational structures and management systems that embody Korean cultural characteristics such as loyalty, respect for authority, conformity to group norms, commitment to organizational goals, and a strong work ethic.[9]

Internationalization Decisions: Locating Production

To examine how national resource conditions influence company strategies, we will look at two types of strategic decision making in international business: first, where to locate production activities and, second, how to enter a foreign market. Let us begin with the first of these.

Firms move beyond their national borders not only to seek foreign markets but also to access the resources and capabilities available in other countries. Traditionally, multinationals established plants to serve local markets. Increasingly, decisions concerning where to produce are being separated from decisions over where to sell. For example, ST Microelectronics, the world leader in application-specific integrated circuits (ASICs), is headquartered in Switzerland; production is mainly in France, Italy, and Singapore; R & D is conducted mainly in France, Italy, and the US; and the biggest markets are the US, Japan, Netherlands, and Singapore.

Determinants of Geographical Location

Figure 12.2 identified two types of resources and capabilities as relevant to a firm's ability to establish a competitive advantage in internationally competitive markets. Both are important in determining where a firm locates its production:

- *Country-based resources*: Firms should produce where they can benefit from favorable supplies of resources. For the petroleum industry this means exploring where the prospects of finding hydrocarbons are high. In assembly-based manufacturing it is often a quest for low-cost labor. Table 12.2 shows differences in employment costs between countries. For technology-intensive industries it means access to specialist technical know-how.
- *Firm-based resources and capabilities*: For firms whose competitive advantage is based on internal resources and capabilities, optimal location depends on where those resources and capabilities are situated and how mobile they are. Walmart has experienced difficulty replicating its US-based capabilities outside of North America. Conversely, Toyota and IKEA have been highly successful in transferring their operational capabilities to their overseas subsidiaries.

However, these considerations presume that the firm has the flexibility to choose where it locates its production. Most services—hairdressing, restaurant meals, banking, and the like—are not tradable: they need to be produced in close proximity to where they are consumed. Similarly for goods: the more difficult it is to transport a product and the more it is subject to trade barriers (such as tariffs and quotas), the more production will need to take place within each national market.

Location and the Value Chain

The production of most goods and services comprises a vertical chain of activities where the input requirements of each stage vary considerably. Hence, different

TABLE 12.2   Hourly compensation costs for production workers in manufacturing ($)

	1975	2000	2012
Switzerland	6.09	21.24	57.79
Australia	5.62	14.47	47.68
Germany	6.31	24.42	45.79
France	4.52	15.70	39.81
US	6.36	19.76	35.67
Japan	3.00	22.27	35.34
Italy	4.67	14.01	34.18
UK	3.37	16.45	31.23
Spain	2.53	10.78	26.83
Korea	0.32	8.19	20.72
Taiwan	0.40	5.85	9.46
Mexico	1.47	2.08	6.36
Philippines	0.62	1.30	2.10

Source: US Department of Labor, Bureau of Labor Statistics. Reproduced with permission.

TABLE 12.3 Comparative advantages along the value chain for knitted apparel

	Raw cotton	Spun cotton yarn	Knitted fabric	Knitted apparel
US	+0.68	+0.85	+0.03	−0.89
Germany	−1.00	−0.18	+0.30	−0.18
Korea	−1.00	−0.28	+0.94	−0.34
China	−0.99	−0.54	+0.70	+0.97
Bangladesh	−0.98	−0.95	−0.96	+0.98

Note: A country's revealed comparative advantage in particular product is measured as (exports − imports)/ (exports + imports). The scale ranges from −1 to +1.
Source: International Trade Commission.

countries offer advantages at different stages of the value chain. Table 12.3 shows the pattern of international specialization for the different stages of production for knitted clothing (T-shirts, sweaters, etc.). Similarly with consumer electronics: component production is research- and capital-intensive and is concentrated in the US, Japan, Korea, and Taiwan; assembly is labor-intensive and is concentrated in South-East Asia and Latin America.

A key feature of recent internationalization has been the international fragmentation of value chains as firms seek to locate countries whose resource availability and cost best match each stage of the value chain.[10] Table 12.4 shows the international composition of Apple's iPhone; Figure 12.4 shows a similar breakdown of the Boeing 787 Dreamliner.

However, cost is just one factor in offshoring decisions. Moreover, cost advantages are vulnerable to exchange rate changes and inflation. As the iPhone and Boeing Dreamliner indicate, in the case of technologically advanced goods and services, global sourcing is not just about saving cost: the location of sophisticated know-how

TABLE 12.4 Where does the iPhone4 come from?

Item	Supplier	Location
Design and operating system	Apple	US
Flash memory	Samsung Electronics	S. Korea
DRAM memory	Samsung Electronics	S. Korea
	Micron Technology	US
Application processor	Murata	Japan/Taiwan
Baseband	Infineon	Taiwan
	Skyworks	US
	TriQuint	
Power management	Dialog Semiconductor	Taiwan
Audio	Texas Instruments	US
Touchscreen control	Cirrus Logic	US
Accel and gyroscope	STMicroelectronics	Italy
E-compass	AKM Semiconductor	Japan
Assembly	Foxconn	China

Source: "Slicing an Apple," *Economist* (August 10, 2011), http://www.economist.com/node/21525685.

is more important. As the emerging-market countries develop their human and technological resources, so their appeal to Western companies shifts from low labor costs to the availability of technical skills. The quest for scarce scientific and engineering talent is a major factor encouraging US companies to conduct innovation outside their home country.[11] Jim Breyer of Accel Partners, a Silicon Valley venture capital firm, observed: "Taiwan and China have some of the world's best designers of wireless chips and wireless software." In various types of precision manufacturing, companies such as Waffer of Taiwan are world leaders. Most leading Indian IT service companies operate at level 5 (the highest level of expertise) of the Capability Maturity Model (CMM), compared to level 2 or 3 for the internal IT departments of many Western companies.

The benefits from fragmenting the value chain must be traded off against the added costs of coordinating globally dispersed activities. Apart from costs of transportation and higher inventories, a key cost of dispersed activities is time. Just-in-time scheduling often necessitates that production activities are carried out in close proximity to one another. Companies that compete on speed and reliability of

FIGURE 12.4 The globally dispersed production of the Boeing 787 Dreamliner

Source: Boeing Images, © 2015 Boeing Inc. Reprinted with permission.

FIGURE 12.5   Determining the optimal location of value chain activities

delivery (e.g., Inditex) may forsake the cost advantages of a globally dispersed value chain in favor of integrated operations with fast access to the final market. The trend toward US corporations "reshoring" manufacturing activities is partly a result of the narrowing cost gap between the US and China but also because of the flexibility benefits of shorter supply chains.[12] Figure 12.5 summarizes the relevant criteria in location decisions.

Internationalization Decisions: Entering a Foreign Market

Firms enter foreign markets in pursuit of revenue and, ultimately, profitability. A firm's success in generating sales and profits in a foreign market depends on its ability to establish a competitive advantage relative to competitors and other multinationals competing in that market. How a firm can best establish a competitive advantage will determine how it chooses to enter a foreign market.

There are two basic modes of entry into a foreign market: *transactions* or *direct investment*. Figure 12.6 further divides these into a spectrum of market entry types involving progressively higher degrees of resource commitment. Thus, at one extreme, there is exporting through individual export sales market transactions; at the other, there is the establishment of a wholly owned, fully integrated subsidiary.

How does a firm weigh the merits of different market entry modes? Five key factors are relevant:

- *Is the firm's competitive advantage based on firm-specific or country-specific resources?* If the firm's competitive advantage is country-based, the firm must exploit an overseas market by exporting. If Shanghai Auto's competitive advantage in Western car markets is its low domestic cost base, it must produce in China and export to foreign markets. If Toyota's competitive

FIGURE 12.6 Alternative modes of overseas market entry

advantage is its production and management capabilities then, as long as it can transfer these capabilities, it can exploit foreign markets either by exports or by direct investment.[13]

● *Is the product tradable?* If the product is not tradable because of transportation constraints or import restrictions then accessing that market requires entry either by direct inward investment or by licensing the use of key resources to a local company in the overseas market.

● *Does the firm possess the full range of resources and capabilities needed for success in the overseas market?* Competing in an overseas market is likely to require resources and capabilities that the firm does not possess—particularly those needed to market and distribute in an unfamiliar territory. Accessing such country-specific resources is most easily achieved by collaborating with a firm in the overseas market. The form of the collaboration depends, in part, on the resources and capabilities required. If a firm needs marketing and distribution capabilities, it might appoint a distributor or agent with exclusive territorial rights. If a wide range of manufacturing and marketing capabilities is needed, the firm might license its product and/or its technology to a local manufacturer. In technology-based industries, licensing technology to local companies is common. In marketing-intensive industries, firms with strong brands can license their trademarks to local companies. Alternatively, a joint venture might be sought with a local manufacturing company. Danone, the French dairy products company, operates joint ventures in Russia, China, Indonesia, Iran, Mexico, Argentina, Saudi Arabia, and South Africa.

● *Can the firm directly appropriate the returns to its resources?* Whether a firm licenses the use of its resources or chooses to exploit them directly (either through exporting or direct investment) depends partly on appropriability considerations. In chemicals and pharmaceuticals, the patents protecting product innovations tend to offer strong legal protection; in which case, offering licenses to local producers can be an effective means of appropriating their returns. In computer software and computer equipment the protection offered by patents and copyrights is looser, which encourages exporting rather than licensing as a means of exploiting overseas markets.

With all licensing arrangements, the key considerations are the capabilities and reliability of the local licensee. This is particularly important in licensing brand names, where the licenser must carefully protect the brand's reputation. Cadbury (now owned by Mondelēz International, formerly Kraft Foods) licenses its trademarks and product recipes to Hershey for the production and sale of its Cadbury chocolate bars in the US. This arrangement reflects the fact that Hershey has production and distribution facilities in the US that Cadbury cannot match, and that Cadbury views Hershey as a reliable business partner.

● *What transaction costs are involved?* Transaction costs are fundamental to the choice between alternative market entry modes. Barriers to exports in the form of transport costs and tariffs constitute transaction costs that may encourage direct investment. The choice between licensing and direct investment also depends upon the transaction costs of negotiating, monitoring, and enforcing licensing agreements. In the UK, Starbucks owns and operates its coffee shops, while McDonald's franchises its burger restaurants. McDonald's competitive advantage depends primarily upon the franchisee faithfully replicating the McDonald's system. This can be enforced effectively by means of franchise contracts. Starbucks believes that its success is achieved through creating the "Starbucks experience," which is as much about ambiance as it is about coffee. It is difficult to articulate the ingredients of this experience, let alone write it into a contract.

Transaction costs play a central role in the theory of the multinational corporation. In the absence of transaction costs in the markets for both goods and resources, companies will exploit overseas markets either by exporting or by selling the use of their resources to local firms in overseas markets.[14] Hence, multinationals tend to predominate in industries where:

● exports are subject to transaction costs in the form of tariffs or import restrictions;
● firm-specific intangible resources such as brands and technology are important and licensing the use of these resources incurs transaction costs;
● customer preferences are reasonably similar between countries.

Multinational Strategies: Global Integration versus National Differentiation

So far, we have viewed international expansion, whether by export or by direct investment, as a means by which a company can extend its competitive advantages from its home market into foreign markets. However, international scope may itself be a source of competitive advantage over geographically focused competitors. In this section, we explore whether, and under what conditions, firms that operate on an international basis are able to gain a competitive advantage over nationally focused firms. What is the potential for such "global strategies" to create competitive advantage? In what types of industry are they likely to be most effective? And how should they be designed and deployed in order to maximize their potential?

The Benefits of a Global Strategy[15]

A **global strategy** is one that views the world as a single, if segmented, market. There are five major sources of value from operating internationally.

Cost Benefits of Scale and Replication   The primary advantage of companies that compete globally over their local rivals is their access to scale economies in purchasing, manufacturing, marketing, and new product development.[16] Ghemawat refers to these as benefits from cross-border aggregation.[17] Exploiting these scale economies has been facilitated by the growing convergence of customer preferences: "Everywhere everything gets more and more like everything else as the world's preference structure is relentlessly homogenized," observed Ted Levitt.[18] In many industries—commercial aircraft, semiconductors, consumer electronics, video games—firms have no choice: they must market globally to amortize the huge costs of product development. In service industries, the cost efficiencies from multinational operation derive primarily from economies of replication. Once a company has created a knowledge-based asset or product—be it a recipe, a piece of software, or an organizational system—it can be replicated in additional national markets at a fraction of the cost of creating the original.[19] Disneyland theme parks in Tokyo, Paris, Hong Kong, and Shanghai replicate the rides and management systems that Disney develops for its parks in Anaheim and Orlando. This is the appeal of franchising: if I create a brilliantly innovative facial massage system that allows elderly people to maintain the complexion of a 20-year-old, why limit myself to a single outlet in Beverly Hills, California? Why not try to emulate Domino's Pizza with its 11,000 outlets across 71 countries of the world?

Serving Global Customers   In several industries (e.g., investment banking, audit services, and advertising) the primary driver of globalization has been the need to service global customers.[20] Hence, auto-parts manufacturers have internationalized as they follow the global spread of the major automobile producers. Law firms such as Baker & McKenzie, Clifford Chance, and Linklaters have internationalized mainly to better serve their multinational clients.

Exploiting National Resources: Arbitrage Benefits   As we have already seen, firms internationalize not only to expand into new markets but also to access resources outside their home countries.

Traditionally, this has meant a quest for raw materials and low-cost labor. Standard Oil's initial internationalization during 1917–1923 followed its quest for crude oil reserves in Mexico, Colombia, Venezuela, and the Dutch East Indies. Nike's pursuit of low-cost manufacturing facilities has taken it from Japan, to Taiwan and South Korea, to China, and, most recently, to Vietnam, Indonesia, and Bangladesh. Pankaj Ghemawat refers to this exploitation of differences between countries as *arbitrage*.[21] Arbitrage strategies are conventionally associated with exploiting wage differentials by offshoring production to low-wage locations; increasingly arbitrage is about exploiting the distinctive knowledge available in different locations. For example, among semiconductor firms, a critical factor determining the location of overseas subsidiaries is the desire to access knowledge within the host country.[22]

Learning Benefits   The learning benefits of multinational companies are not simply accessing the knowledge available in different locations but also transferring and integrating that knowledge and using the exposure to different national environments to create new knowledge. IKEA's success is based not only on replicating its unique business system but also on its ability to learn from each country where it does business and then transfer that learning to its global network. In Japan, IKEA had to adjust to Japanese style and design preferences, Japanese modes of living, and Japanese consumers' acute quality-consciousness. IKEA was then able to transfer the quality and design capabilities it developed in Japan to its global activities. According to the CEO of IKEA Japan, "One reason for us to enter the Japanese market, apart from hopefully doing very good business, is to expose ourselves to the toughest competition in the world. By doing so, we feel that we are expanding the quality issues for IKEA all over the world."[23]

Recent contributions to the international business literature suggest that this ability of multinational corporations to develop knowledge in multiple locations, to synthesize that knowledge, and to transfer it across national borders may be their greatest advantage over nationally focused companies.[24] The critical requirement for exploiting these learning benefits is that the company possesses some form of global infrastructure for managing knowledge that permits new experiences, new ideas, and new practices to be diffused and integrated.

Competing Strategically   A major advantage of the Romans over the Gauls, Goths, and other barbarian tribes was their ability to draw upon the military and economic resources of the Roman Empire to fight local wars. Similarly, multinational companies possess a key strategic advantage over their nationally focused rivals when engaging in competitive battles in individual national markets: they can use resources from other national markets. At its most simple, this *cross-subsidization* of competitive initiatives in one market using profits from other markets involves *predatory pricing*—cutting prices to a level that drives competitors out of business. Such pricing practices are likely to contravene both the World Trade Organization's anti-dumping rules and national antitrust laws. More usually, cross-subsidization involves using cash flows from other markets to finance aggressive sales and marketing campaigns.[25] Evidence of firms charging lower prices in overseas than in domestic markets and lower export prices to overseas subsidiaries than those charged to third parties supports the argument that firms use domestic profits to subsidize price competition in overseas markets.[26]

Strategic competition between multinational corporations can result in complex patterns of attack, retaliation, and containment.[27] Fujifilm's sponsorship of the 1984 Olympic Games in Los Angeles was seen by Kodak as an aggressive incursion into its backyard; it responded by expanding its marketing efforts in Japan.[28]

The Need for National Differentiation

For all the advantages of global strategy, national market differences persist: with a few notable exceptions (e.g., Apple's iPod and iPad), most products designed to meet the needs of the "global customer" have lacked global appeal. Ford has struggled in its efforts to introduce a standardized global car: after a series of disappointments, its 2012 Focus, produced at five plants throughout the world, was its first truly successful global model. The experience of most auto firms is that their global models become differentiated to meet the needs and preferences of different national markets.[29]

In some industries efforts toward globalization have met with little success. In washing machines, national preferences have shown remarkable resilience: French and US washing machines are primarily top loading—elsewhere in Europe they are mainly front loading; the Germans prefer higher spin speeds than the Italians do; US machines feature agitators rather than revolving drums; and Japanese machines are small. The pioneers of globalization in domestic appliances—Electrolux and Whirlpool—struggle to outperform national and regional specialists.[30] Similarly in retail banking, despite some examples of successful internationalization (Banco Santander, HSBC), most of the evidence points to few economies from cross-border integration and the importance of adapting to local market conditions.[31]

Every nation presents a unique combination of a multitude of distinctive characteristics. How can we recognize and assess the extent of similarities and differences between countries for the purposes of international strategy formulation? Pankaj Ghemawat proposes four key components of *distance* between countries: *cultural, administrative and political, geographical,* and *economic*—Table 12.5 outlines his "CAGE" framework.

Ghemawat's broad categories are only a starting point for exploring the national idiosyncrasies that make international expansion such a minefield. For consumer products firms, the structures of national distribution channels are critical. Procter & Gamble must adapt its marketing, promotion, and distribution of toiletries and household products to take account of the fact that, in the US, a few chains account for a major share of its US sales; in southern Europe, most sales are through small, independent retailers, while in Japan, P&G must sell through a multi-tiered hierarchy

TABLE 12.5   Ghemawat's CAGE framework for assessing country differences

	Cultural distance	Administrative and political distance	Geographical distance	Economic differences
Distance between two countries increases with	Different languages, ethnicities, religions, social norms. Lack of connective ethnic or social networks	Absence of shared political or monetary association. Political hostility. Weak legal and financial institutions	Lack of common border, water-way access, adequate transportation or communication links. Physical remoteness	Different consumer incomes. Different costs and quality of natural, financial, and human resources. Different information or knowledge
Industries most affected by source of distance	Industries with high linguistic content (TV, publishing) and cultural content (food, wine, music)	Industries viewed by government as strategically important (e.g., energy, defense, telecoms)	Products with low value-to-weight (cement), are fragile or perishable (glass, milk), or dependent upon communications (financial services)	Products whose demand is sensitive to consumer income levels (luxury goods). Labor-intensive products (clothing)

of distributors. The closer an industry is to the final consumer, the more important cultural factors are likely to be. Strategy Capsule 12.1 considers some dimensions of national culture. It is notable that so few retailers have been successful outside their domestic markets. Walmart, IKEA, H&M, and Gap are among the few retailers that are truly global. Even fewer have been as successful overseas as at home. For many, franchising has provided a lower-risk internationalization strategy.

Reconciling Global Integration with National Differentiation

Choices about internationalization strategy have been viewed as a tradeoff between the benefits of global integration and those of national adaptation (Figure 12.7).

STRATEGY CAPSULE 12.1
How Do National Cultures Differ?

Do people differ between countries with regard to beliefs, norms, and value systems? The answer from a series of research studies is *yes*.

The best-known study of national cultural differences is by Geert Hofstede. The principal dimensions of national values he identified were:

- *Power distance:* The extent to which inequality, and decision-making power in particular, is accepted within organizations and within society was high in Malaysia, and most Latin American and Arab countries; low in Austria and Scandinavia.

- *Uncertainty avoidance:* Preference for certainty and established norms was high in most southern European and Latin American countries; tolerance for uncertainty and ambiguity was high in Singapore, Sweden, the UK, the US, and India.

- *Individualism:* Concern for individual over group interests was highest in the US, the UK, Canada, and Australia. Identification with groups and the collective interest was strongest in Latin America and Asia (especially Indonesia, Pakistan, Taiwan, and South Korea).

- *Masculinity/femininity:* Hofstede identifies emphasis on work and material goals and demarcation of gender roles as *masculine;* emphasis on personal relationships rather than efficiency and belief in gender equality were viewed as *feminine*. Japan, Austria, Venezuela, and Italy scored high on masculinity; Scandinavia and the Netherlands scored very low.

Other scholars emphasize different dimensions of national cultures. Fons Trompenaars (another Dutchman) identifies the US, Australia, Germany, Sweden and the UK as *universalist societies*—relationships are governed by standard rules—Brazil, Italy, Japan, and Mexico are *particularist societies*—social relationships are strongly influenced by contextual and personal factors. In *affective cultures*, such as Mexico and the Netherlands, people display their emotions; in *neutral cultures*, such as Japan and the UK, people hide their emotions.

Sources: G. Hofstede, *Culture's Consequences: International Differences in Work-related Values* (Thousand Oaks, CA: SAGE Publications, 1984); F. Trompenaars, *Riding the Waves of Culture* (London: Economist Books, 1993).

FIGURE 12.7   Benefits of global integration versus national differentiation

Industries where scale economies are huge and customer preferences homogeneous call for a global strategy (e.g., jet engines). Industries where national preferences are pronounced and meeting them does not impose prohibitive costs favor multidomestic strategies (e.g., retail banking). Indeed, in industries where there are few benefits from global integration, multinational firms may be absent (as in funeral services and laundries). Some industries may be low on both dimensions—car repair and office maintenance services are fairly homogeneous worldwide but lack significant benefits from global integration. Conversely, other industries offer substantial benefits from operating on a global scale, but national preferences and standards may also necessitate considerable adaptation to the needs of specific national markets (telecommunications equipment, military hardware, cosmetics, and toiletries).

Reconciling conflicting forces for global efficiency and national differentiation represents one of the greatest strategic challenges facing multinational corporations. Achieving global localization involves standardizing product features and company activities where scale economies are substantial, and differentiating where national preferences are strongest and where achieving them is not overly costly. Thus, a global car such as the Honda Civic (introduced in 1972 and sold in 110 countries) now embodies considerable local adaptations, to meet not just national safety and environmental standards but also local preferences for legroom, seat specifications, accessories, color, and trim. McDonald's, too, meshes global standardization with local adaptation (Strategy Capsule 12.2).

Reconciling global efficiency with national adaptation requires disaggregating the company by product and function. In retail banking, different products and services have different potential for globalization. Credit cards and basic savings products

STRATEGY CAPSULE 12.2
McDonald's Goes "Glocal"

McDonald's has long been demonized by anti-globalization activists: it crushes national cuisines and independent, family-run restaurants with the juggernaut of US fast-food, corporate imperialism. In reality, its global strategy is a careful blend of global standardization and local adaptation.

McDonald's menus include a number of globally standardized items—the Big Mac and potato fries are international features—however, in most countries McDonald's menus feature an increasing number of locally developed items. These include:

♦ Australia: A range of wraps including Seared Chicken, Tandoori Chicken, and Chicken and Aioli McWrap;

♦ France: Croque McDo (a toasted ham and cheese sandwich);

♦ Hong Kong: Grilled Pork Twisty Pasta and Fresh Corn Cup;

♦ India: McSpicy Paneer and McAloo Tikki

♦ Saudi Arabia: McArabia Kofta, McArabia Chicken;

♦ Switzerland: Shrimp Cocktail, Royal Jalapeno;

♦ UK: Oatso Simple Porridge, Spicy Veggie Wrap, Peri Peri Snack Wrap, Cadbury Creme Egg McFlurry;

♦ US: Sausage Burrito, BBQ Ranch Burger, McRib, Fruit and Yogurt Parfait.

There are differences too in restaurant decor, service offerings (e.g., home delivery in India), and market positioning (outside the US McDonald's is more upmarket). In Israel, most McDonald's are kosher: there are no dairy products and it is closed on Saturdays. In India, neither beef nor pork is served. In Germany, France, and Spain, McDonald's serves beer. A key reason that most non-US outlets are franchised is to facilitate adaptation to national environments and access to local know-how.

Yet, the core features of the McDonald's strategy are identical throughout the world. McDonald's values and business principles are seen as universal and invariant. Its emphasis on families and children is intended to identify McDonald's with fun and family life wherever it does business. Community involvement and the Ronald McDonald children's charity are also worldwide. Corporate trademarks and brands are mostly globally uniform, including the golden arches logo and "I'm lovin' it" tag line. The business system itself—franchising arrangements, training, restaurant operations, and supplier relations—is also highly standardized.

McDonald's international strategy was about adapting its US model to local conditions. Now, as new menu items and business concepts are transferred between countries, it is using local differentiation to drive worldwide adaptation and innovation. McCafés, gourmet coffeehouses within McDonald's restaurants, were first developed in Australia, but by 2013, McCafés were operating in 30 countries. In responding to growing concern over nutrition and obesity McDonald's has drawn upon country initiatives with regard to ingredients, menus, and information labeling to support global learning.

Has McDonald's got the balance right between global standardization and local adaptation? Simon Anholt, a British marketing expert, argues: "By putting local food on the menu, all you are doing is removing the logic of the brand, because this is an American brand. If McDonald's serves what you think is a poor imitation of your local cuisine, it's going to be an insult." But according to McDonald's CEO Jim Skinner: "We don't run our business from Oak Brook. We are a local business with a local face in each country we operate in." His chief marketing manager, Mary Dillon, adds: "McDonald's is much more about local relevance than a global archetype. Globally we think of ourselves as the custodian of the brand, but it's all about local relevance."

Source: www.mcdonalds.com.

such as certificates of deposit tend to be globally standardized; checking accounts and mortgage lending are much more nationally differentiated. Similarly with business functions: R & D, purchasing, IT, and manufacturing have strong globalization potential; sales, marketing, customer service, and human resource management need to be much more nationally differentiated. These differences have important implications for how the multinational corporation is organized.

Implementing International Strategy: Organizing the Multinational Corporation

These same forces that determine international strategies—exploiting global integration while adapting to national conditions—also have critical implications for the design of organizational structures and management systems to implement these strategies. As we shall see, one of the greatest challenges facing the senior managers of multinational corporations is aligning organizational structures and management systems to fit with the strategies being pursued.

The Evolution of Multinational Strategies and Structures

Over the past hundred years, the forces driving internationalization strategies have changed considerably. Yet, the structural configurations of multinational corporations have tended to persist. We discussed organizational inertia in Chapter 8: because of their complexity, multinational corporations face particular difficulties in adapting their structures and systems to change. Chris Bartlett and Sumantra Ghoshal view multinational corporations as captives of their history: their strategy-structure configurations bear the imprint of choices they made at the time of their international expansion. Radical changes in strategy and structure are difficult: once an international distribution of functions, operations, and decision-making authority has been determined, reorganization is slow, difficult, and costly, particularly when host governments become involved. This *administrative heritage* of an multinational corporation—its configuration of assets and capabilities, distribution of managerial responsibilities, and network of relationships—is a critical determinant of its current capabilities and a key constraint upon its ability to build new strategic capabilities.[32]

Bartlett and Ghoshal identify three eras in the development of the multinational corporation (Figure 12.8):

- *The early 20th century: era of the European multinationals.* Companies such as Unilever, Shell, ICI, and Philips were pioneers of multinational expansion. Because of the conditions at the time of internationalization—poor transportation and communications, highly differentiated national markets—the companies created *multinational federations*: each national subsidiary was operationally autonomous and undertook the full range of functions, including product development, manufacturing, and marketing.

- *Post-Second World War: era of the American multinationals.* US dominance of the world economy was reflected in the pre-eminence of US multinationals such as GM, Ford, IBM, Coca-Cola, Caterpillar, and Procter & Gamble. While their overseas subsidiaries were allowed considerable autonomy, this

FIGURE 12.8 The development of the multinational corporation: Alternative parent–subsidiaries relations

The Europeans:
Decentralized
Federations

The Americans:
Coordinated
Federations

The Japanese:
Centralized
Hubs

Note:
The density of shading indicates the concentration of decision making.
Source: C. A. Bartlett and S. Ghoshal, *Managing across Borders: The Transnational Solution* (Boston: Harvard Business School Press, 1998). Copyright © 1989 by the Harvard Business School Publishing Corporation, all rights reserved.

was within the context of the dominant position of their US parent in terms of finance, technology, and management. These US-based resources and capabilities provided the foundation for their international competitive advantages.

- *The 1970s and 1980s: the Japanese challenge.* Honda, Toyota, Matsushita, NEC, and YKK pursued global strategies from centralized domestic bases. R & D and manufacturing were concentrated in Japan; overseas subsidiaries undertook sales and distribution. Globally standardized products manufactured in large-scale plants provided the basis for unrivalled cost and quality advantages. Over time, manufacturing and R & D were dispersed, initially because of trade protection by consumer countries and the rising value of the yen against other currencies.

These different administrative heritages have continued to shape the strategies and capabilities of the different groups of multinational corporations. The strength of European multinationals is adaptation to the conditions and requirements of individual national markets. Their challenge has been to achieve greater integration of their sprawling international empires. For Shell and Philips this has involved periodic reorganization over the past three decades. The strength of the US multinationals is their ability to transfer technology and proven new products from their domestic strongholds to their national subsidiaries. The challenge for companies such as Ford, IBM, and Procter & Gamble has been dispersing technology, design, and product development while achieving a high level of global integration. Japanese multinational corporations exemplified the efficiency benefits of global standardization. Since the 1990s, Japanese multinational corporations such as Sony, Panasonic, Nomura, Hitachi, and NEC have taken major strides to becoming true insiders in the many countries where they do business yet have struggled to sustain leadership in product and process innovation.

Reconfiguring the Multinational Corporation

According to Bartlett and Ghoshal, despite the different heritages of the different groups of multinationals, their key strategic and organizational challenge is the same: reconciling global integration with national differentiation and responsiveness. Escalating costs of research and new product development have made global strategies with global product platforms essential. At the same time, meeting consumer needs in each national market and responding swiftly to changing local circumstances requires greater decentralization. Accelerating technological change further exacerbates these contradictory forces: innovation needs to take place at multiple locations rather than at a centralized R & D facility.

Pankaj Ghemawat views the challenge for multinationals in reconciling the conflicting strategic goals as even more complex.[33] He argues that, in addition to exploiting scale economies from global integration (what he calls "aggregation opportunities") and adapting to meet the different local demands, multinational corporations also need to pursue "arbitrage"—exploiting differences between national markets, particularly with regard to the availability of particular resources in different locations (see the earlier discussion of arbitrage in the section discussing "The Benefits of a Global Strategy"). Strategy Capsule 12.3 outlines the implications of these two analyses for the design of the multinational corporation.

Changing Organization Structure   Over the past three decades the pressure of competition has required multinational corporations to exploit multiple sources of value (see Strategy Capsule 12.3). For North American and European multinational corporations, this has required a shift from a multidomestic approach organized around national subsidiaries and regional groupings to increased global integration involving the creation of worldwide product divisions. Thus, Hewlett-Packard, the world's biggest IT company, conducts its business through four global product groups: Enterprise Services, HP Enterprise Group, Printing and Personal Systems, and Software. In addition HP has functions which include Finance, Strategy, HP Labs, Communications and Marketing, Legal, Technology and Operations, and HR. Each product group and function has activities in multiple countries. For example, HP Labs are in Palo Alto, California; Singapore; Bristol, UK; Haifa, Israel; St Petersburg, Russia; Bangalore, India; and Beijing, China. To assist geographical coordination, HP has regional headquarters for the Americas (in Houston), for Europe, the Middle East, and Africa (in Geneva), and for Asia Pacific (in Singapore); the regional HQs coordinate 41 national offices. Because of the strategic importance of China, this country occupies a special role within HP's organizations. Todd Bradley, executive head of strategic growth initiatives, has special responsibility for HP China's business, reporting directly to CEO Meg Whitman.

Balancing global integration and national adaptation requires a company to adapt to the differential requirements of different products, different functions, and different countries. Procter & Gamble adopts global standardization for some of its products (e.g., Pringles potato chips and high-end perfumes); for others (e.g., hair care products and laundry detergent), it allows significant national differentiation. Across countries, P&G organizes global product divisions to serve most of the industrialized world because of the similarities between their markets, while for emerging-market countries (such as China and India) it operates through country subsidiaries in order to adapt to the distinctive features of these markets. Among functions, R & D is globally integrated, while sales are organized by national units that are differentiated to meet local market characteristics.

The transnational firm is a concept and direction of development rather than a distinct organizational archetype. It involves convergence of the different strategy

STRATEGY CAPSULE 12.3

Designing the Multinational Corporation: Bartlett and Ghoshal's "Transnational" and Ghemawat's "AAA Triangle"

Christopher Bartlett describes the organizational challenges of reconciling global integration and national differentiation as "the corporate equivalent of being able to walk, chew gum, and whistle at the same time … It requires a very different kind of internal management process than existed in the relatively simple multinational or global organizations." Bartlett gives the name *transnational organization* to this emerging form of multinational company (Figure 12.9).[34] Its distinctive characteristic is that it operates as an integrated network of distributed and interdependent resources and capabilities in which:

◆ Each national unit is a source of ideas, skills, and capabilities that can be harnessed for the benefit of the total organization.

◆ National units access global scale economies by designating them worldwide responsibility for a particular product, component, or activity.

◆ The corporate center must establish a new, highly complex managing role that coordinates relationships among units but in a highly flexible way. The key is to focus less on managing activities directly and more on creating an organizational context that is conducive to the coordination and resolution of differences. This context involves "establishing clear corporate objectives, developing managers with broadly based perspectives and relationships, and fostering supportive organizational norms and values."[35]

FIGURE 12.9 Bartlett and Ghoshal's transnational corporation

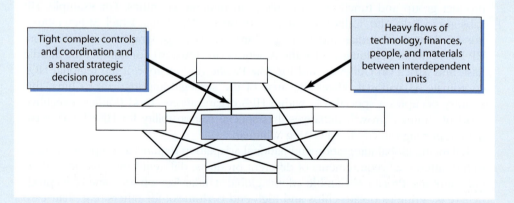

Ghemawat proposes that a multinational corporation's strategy may be represented by its positioning along the three dimensions of aggregation, adaptation, and arbitrage—his "AAA triangle" (Figure 12.10). A firm can be positioned by using proxy variables. Each strategic direction has different organizational implications: aggregation requites strong cross-border integration, e.g., global product divisions and global functions; adaptation requires country-based units with high levels of autonomy; arbitrage requires activities to be located according to the availability of resources and capabilities. However, the managerial challenge of reconciling these different organizational

requirements means that most firms are able to able to pursue two out the three As. For example, among Indian IT service companies, TCS has emphasized arbitrage and aggregation, while Cognizant is oriented toward arbitrage and adaptation. In medical diagnostics, General Electric Healthcare is unusual in terms of its ability to achieve high levels along all three dimensions: it achieves aggregation economies through the highest R & D budget in the industry, arbitrage through locating global production centers in low cost countries, and adaptation by developing country-focused marketing units and offering customer-focused solutions that combine hardware with a range of services.

FIGURE 12.10   Ghemawat's AAA Triangle

Source: P. Ghemawat, "Managing Differences: The Central Challenge of Global Strategy," *Harvard Business Review* 85 (March 2007).

configurations of multinational corporations. Thus, companies such as Philips, Unilever, and Siemens have reassigned roles and responsibilities to achieve greater integration within their traditional "decentralized federations" of national subsidiaries. Japanese global corporations such as Toyota and Panasonic have drastically reduced the roles of their Japanese headquarters. American multinationals such as Citigroup and IBM are moving in two directions: reducing the role of their US bases while increasing integration among their different national subsidiaries.

Multinational corporations are increasingly locating management control of their global product divisions outside their home countries. When Philips adopted a product division structure, it located responsibility for medical electronics in its US subsidiary and leadership in consumer electronics in Japan. Nexans, the world's biggest manufacturer of electric cables, has moved the head office of five of its 20 product divisions outside of France.[36] Exploiting arbitrage opportunities of particular national locations may even require moving entire corporate head offices. Burger King's $11 billion acquisition of the Canadian chain Tim Hortons was motivated in part by the tax advantages of shifting Burger King's headquarters to Canada.[37]

A recent McKinsey study discovered that successful multinationals underperformed successful "national champions." The study identified a "globalization penalty" reflecting the difficulties which multinational corporations experienced in:

- setting a shared vision and engaging employees around it;
- maintaining professional standards and encouraging innovation;
- building government and community relationships and business partnerships.

The interviews conducted for the study highlighted the challenges that multinational corporations faced in reconciling the challenges of local differentiation and global integration:

> Almost everyone we interviewed seemed to struggle with this tension, which often plays out in heated internal debates. Which organizational elements should be standardized? To what extent does managing high-potential emerging markets on a country-by-country basis make sense? When is it better, in those markets, to leverage scale and synergies across business units in managing governments, regulators, partners, and talent?[38]

Organizing R & D and New Product Development   Organizing for innovation represents one of the greatest challenges in reconciling local initiative with global integration. The traditional European decentralized model is conducive to local initiatives, but not to their global exploitation. Philips had an outstanding record of innovation from its different subsidiaries yet lacked the global integration needed for outstanding international success in consumer electronics. Conversely, the centralized model once associated with many Japanese and Korean multinational corporations and with some US companies (Boeing, Caterpillar) failed to access the creativity and know-how available in different locations.

The transnational networked approach in which research and product development is distributed to take advantage of local expertise while collaborating across national boundaries and exploiting globally promising initiatives has become the dominant model of organizing for innovation within the multinational corporation.[39] For example,

P&G, recognizing Japanese obsessiveness over cleanliness, assigned increasing responsibility to its Japanese subsidiary for developing household cleaning products. Its Swiffer dust-collecting products were developed in Japan then introduced into other markets. McKinsey & Company found that 80% of the 1283 executives it surveyed believed that R & D goals were best served by establishing satellite units that operated and collaborated as a network. Yet, 37% of these executives reported that their current R & D organizations consisted of a central function in a single location.[40] The challenge of reconciling autonomy with collaboration and integration in multinational corporations has attracted considerable interest from international management scholars.[41]

Summary

Moving from a national to an international business environment represents a quantum leap in complexity. In an international environment, a firm's potential for competitive advantage is determined not just by its own resources and capabilities but also by the conditions of the national environment in which it operates: including input prices, exchange rates, and institutional and cultural factors. The extent to which a firm is positioned across multiple national markets also influences its economic power.

Our approach in this chapter has been to simplify the complexities of international strategy by applying the same basic tools of strategy analysis that we developed in earlier chapters. For example, to determine whether a firm should enter an overseas market, our focus has been on the profit implications of such an entry. This requires an analysis of (a) the attractiveness of the overseas market using the familiar tools of industry analysis and (b) the potential of the firm to establish competitive advantage in that overseas market, which depends on the firm's ability to transfer its resources and capabilities to the new location and their effectiveness in conferring competitive advantage.

However, establishing the potential for a firm to create value from internationalization is only a beginning. Subsequent analysis needs to design an international strategy: do we enter an overseas market by exporting, licensing, or direct investment? If the latter, should we set up a wholly owned subsidiary or a joint venture? Once the strategy has been established, a suitable organizational structure needs to be designed.

That so many companies that have been outstandingly successful in their home market have failed so miserably in their overseas expansion demonstrates the complexity of international management. In some cases, companies have failed to recognize that the resources and capabilities that underpinned their competitive advantage in their home market could not be readily transferred or replicated in overseas markets. In others, the problems were in designing the structures and systems that could effectively implement the international strategy.

As the lessons of success and failure from international business become recognized and distilled into better theories and analytical frameworks, so we advance our understanding of how to design and implement strategies for competing globally. We are at the stage where we recognize the issues and the key determinants of competitive advantage in an international environment. However, there is much that we do not fully understand. Designing strategies and organizational structures that can reconcile critical tradeoffs between global scale economies versus local differentiation, decentralized learning and innovation versus worldwide diffusion and replication, and localized flexibilities versus international standardization remains a key challenge for senior managers.

Self-Study Questions

1. With reference to Figure 12.1, choose a *sheltered industry*—one that has been subject to little penetration either by imports or foreign direct investment. Explain why the industry has escaped internationalization. Explore whether there are opportunities for profitable internationalization within the industry and, if so, the strategy that would offer the best chance of success.

2. With reference to Table 12.1, what characteristics of national resources explain the different patterns of comparative advantage for the US and Japan?

3. According to Michael Porter's *Competitive Advantage of Nations*, some of the industries where British companies have an international advantage are: advertising, auctioneering of antiques and artwork, distilled alcoholic beverages, hand tools, and chemical preparations for gardening and horticulture. Some of the industries where US companies have an international competitive advantage are: aircraft and helicopters, computer software, oilfield services, management consulting, cinema films and TV programs, healthcare products and services, and financial services. For either the UK or the US, use Porter's national diamond framework (Figure 12.3) to explain the observed pattern of international competitive advantage.

4. When Porsche decided to enter the SUV market with its luxury Cayenne model, it surprised the auto industry by locating its new assembly plant in Leipzig in eastern Germany. Many observers believed that Porsche should have located the plant either in central or eastern Europe where labor costs were very low or (like Mercedes and BMW) in the US where it would be close to its major market. Using the criteria outlined in Figure 12.5, can you explain Porsche's decision?

5. British expatriates living in the US frequently ask friends and relatives visiting from the UK to bring with them bars of Cadbury chocolate on the basis that the Cadbury chocolate available in the US (manufactured under license by Hershey's) is inferior to "the real thing." Should Mondelēz International (formerly Kraft Foods, which acquired Cadbury in 2010) continue Cadbury's licensing agreement with Hershey or should it seek to supply the US market itself, either by export from the UK or by establishing manufacturing facilities in the US?

6. During 2014, McDonald's experienced declining sales. Has it got the balance right between global standardization and national differentiation (Strategy Capsule 12.2)? How much flexibility should it offer its overseas franchisees with regard to new menu items, store layout, operating practices, and marketing? Which aspects of the McDonald's system should McDonald's top management insist on keeping globally standardized?

Notes

1. For the OECD countries (the developed, industrialized nations) the ratio of total trade (imports + exports) to GDP grew from 11% in 1960 to 57% in 2012 (*OECD Factbook*, 2014).

2. J. Johanson and J.-E. Vahlne, "The Uppsala Internationalization Process Model Revisited: From Liability of Foreignness to Liability of Outsidership," *Journal of International Business Studies* 40 (2009): 1411–1431.

3. P. Ghemawat and F. Ghadar, "Global Integration: Global Concentration," *Industrial and Corporate Change* 15 (2006): 595–624.

4. As Tables 12.1 and 12.3 show, revealed comparative advantage can be measured in different ways.

5. A key finding was that human capital (knowledge and skills) was more important than physical capital (plant and equipment) in explaining US comparative advantage. See W. W. Leontief, "Domestic Production and Foreign Trade," in R. E. Caves and H. Johnson (eds), *Readings in International Economics* (Homewood, IL: Irwin, 1968).

6. P. Krugman, "Increasing Returns, Monopolistic Competition, and International Trade," *Journal of International Economics* (November 1979): 469–79.

7. M. E. Porter, *The Competitive Advantage of Nations* (New York: Free Press, 1990).

8. For a review of the Porter analysis, see R. M. Grant, "Porter's Competitive Advantage of Nations: An Assessment," *Strategic Management Journal* 12 (1991): 535–548.

9. Korean business culture has been described as "dynamic collectivism." See: Y.-H. Cho and J. Yoon, "The Origin and Function of Dynamic Collectivism: An Analysis of Korean Corporate Culture," *Asia Pacific Business Review* 7 (2001): 70–88.

10. The linking of value-added chains to national comparative advantages is explained in B. Kogut, "Designing Global Strategies and Competitive Value-Added Chains," *Sloan Management Review* (Summer 1985): 15–38.

11. A. Y. Lewin, S. Massini, and C. Peeters, "Why are companies offshoring innovation? The emerging global race for talent," *Journal of International Business Studies* 40 (2009): 901–925.

12. W. L. Tate, L. M. Ellram, T. Schoenherr, and K. J. Petersen, "Global Competitive Conditions Driving the Manufacturing Location Decisions," *Business Horizons* 57 (May–June 2014): 381–390; "Reshoring driven by quality, not costs, say UK manufacturers," *Financial Times* March 3, 2014.

13. The role of firm-specific assets in explaining the multinational expansion is analyzed in R. Caves, "International Corporations: The Industrial Economics of Foreign Investment," *Economica* 38 (1971): 127.

14. D. J. Teece, "Transactions Cost Economics and Multinational Enterprise," *Journal of Economic Behavior and Organization* 7 (1986): 21–45.

15. This section draws heavily upon G. S. Yip and G. T. M. Hult, *Total Global Strategy* 3rd edn. (Upper Saddle River, NJ: Prentice Hall, 2012).

16. T. Levitt, "The Globalization of Markets," *Harvard Business Review* (May/June 1983): 92–102.

17. P. Ghemawat, *Redefining Global Strategy: Crossing Borders in a World Where Differences Still Matter* (Boston: Harvard Business School, 2007).

18. Levitt, op. cit., 94.

19. S. G. Winter and G. Szulanski, "Replication as Strategy," *Organization Science* 12 (2001): 730–743.

20. G. S. Yip and A. Bink, "Managing Global Account," *Harvard Business Review* 85 (September 2007): 102–111.

21. P. Ghemawat, "The Forgotten Strategy," *Harvard Business Review* (November 2003): 76–84.

22. P. Almeida, "Knowledge Sourcing by Foreign Multinationals: Patent Citation Analysis in the US Semiconductor Industry," *Strategic Management Journal* 17 (Winter 1996): 155–165.

23. Comments by Tommy Kullberg (IKEA Japan) in "The Japan Paradox," conference organized by the European Commission, Director General for External Affairs (December 2003): 62–3, http://www.deljpn.ec.europa.eu/data/current/japan-paradox.pdf, accessed July 20, 2015. See also: A. Jonsson and N. J. Foss, "International Expansion through Flexible Replication: Learning from the Internationalization Experience of IKEA," *Journal of International Business Studies* 42 (2011): 1079–1102.

24. A. K. Gupta and P. Govindarajan, "Knowledge Flows within Multinational Corporations," *Strategic Management Journal* 21 (April 2000): 473–496; P. Almeida, J. Song, and R. M. Grant, "Are Firms Superior to Alliances and Markets? An Empirical Test of Cross-Border Knowledge Building," *Organization Science* 13 (March/April 2002): 147–161.

25. G. Hamel and C. K. Prahalad, "Do You Really Have a Global Strategy?" *Harvard Business Review* (July/August 1985): 139–148.

26. B. Y. Aw, G. Batra, and M. J. Roberts, "Firm Heterogeneity and Export: Domestic Price Differentials: A Study of Taiwanese Electrical Products," *Journal of International Economics* 54 (2001): 149–169; A. Bernard, J. B. Jensen, and P. Schott, "Transfer Pricing by US Based Multinational Firms," Working Papers 08-29, Center for Economic Studies, US Census Bureau, (2008).

27. I. C. Macmillan, A. van Ritten, and R. G. McGrath, "Global Gamesmanship," *Harvard Business Review* (May 2003): 62–71.

28. R. C. Christopher, *Second to None: American Companies in Japan* (New York: Crown, 1986).

29. The Ford Mondeo/Contour is a classic example of a global product that failed to appeal strongly to any national market. See M. J. Moi, "Ford Mondeo: A Model T World Car?" Working Paper, Rotterdam School of Management, Erasmus University (2001); C. Chandler, "Globalization: The Automotive Industry's Quest for a World Car," *globalEDGE Working Paper*, Michigan State University (1997).

30. C. Baden-Fuller and J. Stopford, "Globalization Frustrated," *Strategic Management Journal* 12 (1991): 493–507.

31. R. M. Grant and M. Venzin, "Strategic and Organizational Challenges of Internationalization in Financial Services," *Long Range Planning* 42 (October 2009).

32. C. A. Bartlett and S. Ghoshal, *Managing across Borders: The Transnational Solution*, 2nd edn (Boston: Harvard Business School Press, 1998): 34.

33. P. Ghemawat—"Managing Differences: The Central Challenge of Global Strategy," *Harvard Business Review* 85 (March 2007)—proposes a three-way rather than a two-way analysis. In his Adaptation–Aggregation–Arbitrage (AAA) Triangle he divides integration into aggregation and arbitrage.

34. C. Bartlett, "Building and Managing the Transnational: The New Organizational Challenge," in M. E. Porter (ed.), *Competition in Global Industries* (Boston: Harvard Business School Press, 1986): 377.

35. Ibid., 388.

36. "The Country Prince Comes of Age," *Financial Times* (August 9, 2005).

37. "Burger King Defends Plan to Buy Tim Hortons," *Wall Street Journal* (August 26, 2014); J. Birkinshaw, P. Braunerhjelm, U. Holm, and S. Terjesen, "Why Do Some Multinational Corporations Relocate Their Headquarters Overseas?" *Strategic Management Journal* 27 (2006): 681–700.

38. M. Dewhurst, J. Harris, and S. Heywood, "Understanding your globalization penalty," *McKinsey Quarterly* (June 2011).

39. J. Birkinshaw, N. Hood, and S. Jonsson, "Building Firm-specific Advantages in Multinational Corporations: The Role of Subsidiary Initiative," *Strategic Management Journal* 19 (1998): 221–242.

40. M. M. Capozzi, P. Van Biljon, and J. Williams, "Organizing R&D for the Future," *MIT Sloan Management Review* (Spring 2013).

41. B. Ambos, K. Asakawa, and T. C. Ambos, "A dynamic perspective on subsidiary autonomy," *Global Strategy Journal* 1 (2011): 301–316; T. S. Frost, J. M. Birkinshaw, and P. C. Ensign, "Centers of Excellence in Multinational Corporations," *Strategic Management Journal* 23 (2002): 997–1018.

13 Diversification Strategy

Telephones, hotels, insurance—it's all the same. If you know the numbers inside out, you know the company inside out.

—HAROLD SYDNEY GENEEN, CHAIRMAN OF ITT, 1959–1978, AND INSTIGATOR OF 275 CORPORATE ACQUISITIONS

Creating three independent, public companies is the next logical step for Tyco … the new standalone companies will have greater flexibility to pursue their own focused strategies for growth than they would under Tyco's current corporate structure. This will allow all three companies to create significant value for shareholders.

—ED BREEN, CHAIRMAN AND CEO, TYCO INTERNATIONAL LTD, ANNOUNCING THE COMPANY'S BREAKUP, SEPTEMBER 19, 2011

OUTLINE

Introduction and Objectives

Answering the question *What business are we in?* is the starting point of strategy and the basis for establishing a firm's identity. In their statements of vision and mission, some companies define their businesses broadly. Shell's objective is "to engage efficiently, responsibly, and profitably in oil, oil products, gas, chemicals, and other selected businesses." Other companies define themselves in terms of a particular sector or product type: McDonald's vision is "to be the world's best quick-service restaurant chain"; Caterpillar will "be the leader in providing the best value in machines, engines, and support services for companies dedicated to building the world's infrastructure and developing and transporting its resources."

The dominant trend of the past two decades has been "refocusing on core businesses." Companies such as Philip Morris (now Altria Group, Inc.), Philips (the Netherlands-based electrical and electronics company), and General Mills (once a diversified consumer products company) have each divested a host of different businesses. The tendency for diversified companies to split up altogether has extended from conglomerates—ITT, Hanson, Gulf & Western, Cendant, Vivendi Universal, and Tyco have each split into multiple separate companies—to more integrated companies such as Hewlett-Packard, Kraft Foods, and Fiat Group.

Yet, diversification continues among many technology-based companies—such as Amazon, Apple, and Google—while the emerging economies of Asia and Latin America are dominated by highly diversified business groups.

Diversification remains a conundrum. It liberates firms from the constraints of a single industry yet it has caused more value destruction than almost any other type of strategic initiative.

Our goal in this chapter is to resolve this conundrum. Is it better to be specialized or diversified? Under what conditions does diversification create rather than destroy value? Is there an optimal degree of diversification? What types of diversification are most likely to create value?

We make diversification decisions every day in our personal lives. If my car doesn't start in the morning, should I try to fix it myself or have it towed directly to the garage? There are two considerations. First, is repairing a car an attractive activity to undertake? If the garage charges $85 an hour but I can earn $500 an hour consulting, then car repair is not attractive to me. Second, am I any good at car repair? If I am likely to take twice as long as a skilled mechanic then I possess no competitive advantage in car repair.

Diversification decisions by firms involve the same two issues:

◆ How attractive is the industry to be entered?

◆ Can the firm establish a competitive advantage?

These are the very same factors we identified in Chapter 1 (Figure 1.5) as determining a firm's profit potential. Hence, no new analytic framework is needed for appraising diversification decisions: we may draw upon the industry analysis developed in Chapter 3 and the analysis of competitive advantage developed in Chapters 5 and 7.

Our primary focus will be the latter question: under what conditions does operating multiple businesses assist a firm in gaining a competitive advantage in each? This leads into exploring linkages between different businesses within the diversified firm—a phenomenon often referred to as *synergy*.

By the time you have completed this chapter, you will be able to:

◆ Recognize the corporate goals that have motivated diversification and how these have influenced the diversification trends of the past six decades.

◆ Understand the conditions under which diversification creates value for shareholders, and assess the potential for value creation from economies of scope, internalizing transactions, and corporate parenting.

◆ Comprehend the empirical evidence on the performance outcomes of diversification.

◆ Identify the implications of different types of business relatedness for the success of diversification and the management of diversification.

Motives for Diversification

Changing corporate goals have been the primary driver of trends in diversification. Strategy Capsule 13.1 provides a brief summary of the history of diversification. Diversification by large companies during most of the 20th century was driven by two objectives: *growth* and *risk reduction*. The shift from diversification to refocusing during the last two decades of the 20th century was an outcome of the growing commitment of corporate managers to the goal of *creating shareholder value*.

Growth

In the absence of diversification, firms are prisoners of their industry. For firms in stagnant or declining industries this is a daunting prospect, especially for top management. The urge to achieve corporate growth that outstrips that of a firm's primary industry is an appealing prospect for managers. Companies in low-growth, cash flow-rich industries such as tobacco and oil have been especially susceptible to the temptations of diversification. During the 1980s, Exxon diversified into copper and coal mining, electric motors, and computers and office equipment; RJR Nabisco transformed itself from a tobacco company into a diversified consumer products company. In both cases diversification destroyed shareholder value. The leveraged buyout of RJR Nabisco by Kohlberg Kravis Roberts was followed by its breakup. Reynolds American, Inc. is now a specialist tobacco company.

Diversification is typically very successful in generating revenue growth—especially when it is achieved through acquisition. The critical issue is what are its consequences for profitability? If diversification efforts become a cash drain for companies in declining industries—as they did for Eastman Kodak and Blockbuster—then diversification may well hasten rather than stave off bankruptcy.

Trends in Corporate Diversification over Time

Diversification has followed the same trend as that of corporate scope more generally (see Chapter 11, Figure 11.2). For most of the 20th century—and especially during the 1960s and 1970s—large companies in all the advanced industrial nations diversified into a wider range of product markets.[1] The 1960s also saw the emergence of a new corporate form, the conglomerate: a highly diversified company assembled from multiple, unrelated acquisitions. These included ITT, Textron, and Allied Signal in the US and Hanson, Slater Walker, and BTR in the UK. Their existence reflected the view that senior management no longer needed industry-specific experience: corporate management simply needed to deploy the new techniques of financial and strategic management.[2] Figure 13.1 shows the growing number of highly diversified US and UK firms (both "related business" and "unrelated business") during the decades that followed the Second World War.

After 1980, the diversification trend went into reverse. Between 1980 and 1990, the average index of diversification for Fortune 500 companies declined from 1.00 to 0.67 as "noncore" businesses were divested and diversified companies restructured.[3]

The main driver of this trend was a reordering of corporate goals from growth to profitability. Initially, the key focus was improving the performance of diversified companies through drawing upon new corporate strategy techniques, such as portfolio analysis, and emphasizing related over unrelated diversification.

Evidence of "conglomerate discounts"—that the stock market was valuing diversified companies at less than the sum of their parts—resulted in diversification in general becoming viewed as the enemy of shareholder interests.[4] CEOs came under increasing pressure from both institutional shareholders, including pension

FIGURE 13.1 Diversification strategies of large US and UK companies during the late 20th century

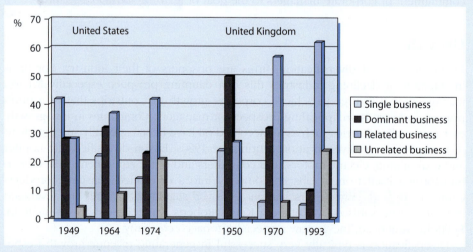

Sources: R. P. Rumelt, "Diversification strategy and profitability," *Strategic Management Journal* 3 (1982): 359-70; R. Whittington, M. Mayer, and F. Curto, "Chandlerism in Post-war Europe: Strategic and Structural Change in France, Germany and the UK, 1950-1993," *Industrial and Corporate Change* 8 (1999): 519-50; D. Channon, *The Strategy and Structure of British Enterprise* (Cambridge: Harvard University Press, 1973).

funds such as California's Public Employees' Retirement System, and hostile takeovers launched by private equity groups. Kohlberg Kravis Roberts' $31 billion takeover of the tobacco and food giant RJR Nabisco in 1989 demonstrated that even the largest US companies were vulnerable to attack from corporate raiders.[5]

In Chapter 11, we observed that volatile, uncertain conditions increase the decision-making burden on top management, making large, complex companies less agile than specialized companies. At the same time, external markets for resources—especially capital markets—have become increasingly efficient at encouraging many diversified companies to spin off their growth businesses in order to tap funding from external capital markets.

Evidence from the US suggests that the pendulum may be swinging back once more with an increasing number of firms viewing diversification as a source of opportunity for value creation. Among technology-based firms the tendency for digital technologies to erode market boundaries and hardware/software complementarities giving rise to "platform-based competition" has encouraged companies such as Microsoft, Cisco Systems, Google, Amazon, and Facebook to continuously expand their product ranges. In more mature sectors, an emphasis on providing "customer solutions" is similarly encouraging firms to offer customizable systems of products and services. A key feature of recent diversification initiative is that they are as likely to occur through inter-firm alliances as conventional diversification.

In the emerging markets of Asia and Latin America the situation is very different. Highly diversified (often family controlled) companies typically dominate the local economy. Examples include: Tata and Reliance in India, Charoen Pokphand (CP) in Thailand, Astra International in Indonesia, Sime Darby in Malaysia, and Grupo Alfa and Grupo Carso in Mexico.[6] We shall consider the reasons for these differences in diversification patterns between mature and emerging countries later in the chapter.

Figure 13.2 summarizes the trends in diversification strategy since the middle of the last century and points to the influence of corporate goals and developments in strategic management concepts and tools on these trends.

FIGURE 13.2 The evolution of diversification strategies, 1960–2015

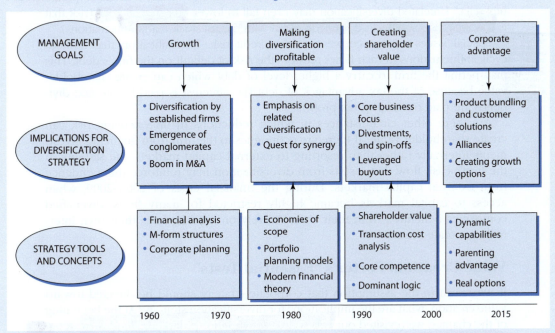

Risk Reduction

The notion that risk spreading is a legitimate goal for the value-creating firm has become a casualty of modern financial theory. If the cash flows of two different businesses are imperfectly correlated then bringing them together under common ownership certainly reduces the variance of the combined cash flow. Such risk reduction is certainly appealing to whoever can enjoy the benefits of managing a more stable enterprise. But what about owners? Shareholders can diversify risk by holding diversified portfolios. Hence, what advantage can there be in companies diversifying for them? The only possible advantage could be if firms can diversify at a lower cost than individual investors. In fact, the reverse is true: the transaction costs to shareholders of diversifying their portfolios are far less than the transaction costs to firms diversifying through acquisition. Not only do acquiring firms incur the heavy costs of using investment banks and legal advisers, they must also pay an acquisition premium to gain control of an independent company.

The *capital asset pricing model* (CAPM) formalizes this argument. The theory states that the risk that is relevant to determining the price of a security is not the overall risk (variance) of the security's return but the *systematic risk*—that part of the variance of the return that is correlated with overall stock market returns. This is measured by the security's *beta coefficient*. Corporate diversification does not reduce systematic risk: if two separate companies are brought under common ownership, and their individual cash flow streams are unchanged, the beta coefficient of the combined company is simply the weighted average of the beta coefficients of the constituent companies. Hence, the simple act of bringing different businesses under common ownership does not create shareholder value through risk reduction.[7]

Empirical studies are generally supportive of the absence of shareholder benefit from diversification that simply combines independent businesses under a single corporate umbrella.[8] Unrelated diversification may even fail to lower unsystematic risk (risk that is specific to a company and is uncorrelated with overall stock market fluctuations).[9]

Special issues arise once we consider credit risk. Diversification that reduces cyclical fluctuations in cash flows reduces the risk of default on the firm's debt. This may permit the firm to carry a higher level of debt which can create shareholder value because of the tax advantages of debt (i.e., interest is paid before tax; dividends are paid out of post-tax profit).[10]

Are there other circumstances in which reductions in unsystematic risk can create shareholder value? If there are economies to the firm from financing investments internally rather than resorting to external capital markets, the stability in the firm's cash flow that results from diversification may reinforce independence from external capital markets. During the financial crisis of 2008–2009, when access to capital markets became highly restricted for many firms, diversified companies benefitted from their ability to rely on funding from their own internally generated funds.[11]

Value Creation: Porter's "Essential Tests"

If we return to the assumption that corporate strategy should be directed toward value creation, what are the implications for diversification strategy? At the beginning of the chapter, we revisited our two sources of superior profitability: industry attractiveness and competitive advantage. In establishing the conditions for profitable diversification, Michael Porter refines these into "three essential tests" that determine whether diversification will truly create shareholder value:

- *The attractiveness test*: The industries chosen for diversification must be structurally attractive or capable of being made attractive.
- *The cost-of-entry test*: The cost of entry must not capitalize all the future profits.
- *The better-off test*: Either the new unit must gain competitive advantage from its link with the corporation or vice versa.[12]

The Attractiveness and Cost-of-Entry Tests   A critical realization in Porter's "essential tests" is that *industry attractiveness* on its own is insufficient to justify diversifying into another industry. Diversification may allow a firm access to more attractive investment opportunities than are available in its own industry, yet it faces the challenge of entering a new industry. The second test, *cost of entry*, recognizes that for outsiders the cost of entry may counteract the attractiveness of the industry. Pharmaceuticals, corporate legal services, and defense contracting offer above-average profitability precisely because they are protected by barriers to entry. Firms seeking to enter these industries may either acquire an established player—in which case the acquisition cost is likely to fully capitalize the target firm's profit prospects (not to mention the need to pay an acquisition premium)[13]—or establish a new corporate venture—in which case the diversifying firm must directly confront the barriers to entry to that industry.[14]

Hewlett-Packard offers a salutary example. It diversified into IT services because of its greater attractiveness than IT hardware. However, its $13.9 billion acquisition of EDS in 2008 was at a 30% premium over EDS's market value and its $10.3 billion acquisition of Autonomy in 2011 involved a 60% premium. HP subsequently took write-offs of $16 billion against the balance sheet values of these two companies.

The Better-Off Test   Porter's third criterion for value creation from diversification—*the better-off test*—addresses the issue of competitive advantage. If two different businesses are brought together under the ownership and control of a single enterprise, is there any reason why they should become any more profitable? The issue here is one of *synergy*: what is the potential for interactions between the two businesses that can enhance the competitive advantage of the new business, the old business, or both?

In most diversification decisions, it is the better-off test that takes center stage. In the first place, industry attractiveness is rarely a source of value from diversification—in most cases, cost-of-entry cancels out advantages of industry attractiveness. Second, the better-off test can work as well in unattractive as in attractive industries. If a diversifying company can establish a strong competitive advantage in an industry, the fact that the industry as a whole generates low profits may be immaterial. Most of Virgin Group's diversification has been into industries where average profitability has been low (or non-existent: airlines, wireless telecommunications, gym clubs, music retailing, and retail financial services). However, through cost efficiency and innovative differentiation, it created considerable value from these ventures. Sony Corporation's acquisition of CBS Records, Bertelsmann Music Group (BMG), and EMI Records took it into the spectacularly unattractive recorded music industry—however, for Sony, music forms a key component of building an integrated presence in home entertainment.

Let us now explore how the better-off test can be applied through analyzing the relationship between diversification and competitive advantage.

Competitive Advantage from Diversification

If the primary source of value creation from diversification is exploiting linkages between different businesses, what are these linkages and how are they exploited? The key linkages are those that permit the sharing of resources and capabilities across different businesses.

Economies of Scope

The most general argument concerning the benefits of diversification focuses on the presence of **economies of scope** in common resources: "Economies of scope exist when using a resource across multiple activities uses less of that resource than when the activities are carried out independently."[15]

Economies of scope exist for similar reasons as economies of scale. The key difference is that economies of scale relate to cost economies from increasing output of a *single product*; economies of scope are cost economies from increasing the output of *multiple products*. The nature of economies of scope varies between different types of resources and capabilities.

Tangible Resources   Tangible resources—such as distribution networks, information technology systems, sales forces, and research laboratories—confer economies of scope by eliminating duplication—a single facility can be shared among several businesses. The greater the fixed costs of these items, the greater the associated economies of scope are likely to be. Diversification by cable TV companies into telecoms and broadband and telephone companies into TV, broadband, and music streaming are motivated by the desire to spread the costs of networks and billing systems over as many services as possible. Common resources such as customer databases, customer service centers, and billing systems have encouraged Centrica, Britain's biggest gas utility, to diversify into supplying electricity, fixed-line and mobile telephony, broadband access, home security, insurance, and home-appliance repair.

Economies of scope also arise from the centralized provision of administrative and support services to the different businesses of the corporation. Accounting, legal services, government relations, and information technology tend to be centralized at the corporate headquarters (or through a *shared service organization*).

Intangible Resources   Intangible resources—such as brands, corporate reputation, and technology—offer economies of scope from the ability to extend them to additional businesses at a low marginal cost. Exploiting a strong brand across additional products is called *brand extension*. Starbucks has extended its brand to ice cream, packaged cold drinks, home espresso machines, audio CDs, and books. Similarly with technology: Fujifilm has extended its proprietary coatings technology from photographic film to cosmetics, pharmaceuticals, and industrial coatings.

Organizational Capabilities   Organizational capabilities can also be transferred within a diversified company. For example:

- LVMH is the world's biggest and most diversified supplier of branded luxury goods. Its distinctive capability is the management of luxury brands. This capability comprises market analysis, advertising, promotion, retail management, and quality assurance. These capabilities are deployed across Louis Vuitton (accessories and leather goods); Hennessey (cognac); Moët & Chandon, Dom Pérignon, Veuve Clicquot, and Krug (champagne); Céline, Givenchy, Kenzo, Christian Dior, Guerlain, and Donna Karan (fashion clothing and perfumes); TAG Heuer and Chaumet (watches); Sephora and La Samaritaine (retailing); Bulgari (jewelry); and some 25 other branded businesses.
- Sharp Corporation's distinctive capability is in the miniaturization of electronic products. This capability has been applied to a stream of innovative products: the world's first transistor calculator (1964), the first LCD pocket calculator (1973), LCD color TVs, PDAs, internet viewcams, ultraportable notebook computers, cell phones, and photovoltaic cells.

Some of the most important capabilities in influencing the performance of diversified corporations are *general management capabilities*. General Electric possesses strong technological and operational capabilities that reside in particular functions within individual divisions and it is good at sharing these capabilities between divisions (e.g., turbine know-how between jet engines and electrical generating equipment). However, GE's core capabilities are in general management and these reside both at the corporate and divisional levels. They include its ability to motivate and develop its managers; its outstanding strategic and financial management, which reconciles decentralized decision making with strong centralized control; and its international management capability.[16]

Similar observations could be made about ExxonMobil. ExxonMobil possesses outstanding technical capabilities in its individual businesses. However, the primary source of its superior financial performance in the oil and gas sectors over the past three decades lies in its management capabilities, which combine rigorous cost control, astute capital allocation, meticulous risk management, and effective strategic planning.[17]

Demand-side Economies of Scope   So far, we have looked only at supply-side economies of scope: cost savings from producers sharing resources and capabilities across different businesses. Economies of scope also arise for customers when they buy multiple products: Walmart's vast array of products offers consumers the convenience of one-stop shopping. General Electric's bundling of goods and services in order to offer "integrated solutions" to customers has extended to "enterprise selling," where a single salesperson represents GE's entire range of offering to a customer.[18]

Economies from Internalizing Transactions

Economies of scope provide cost savings from sharing and transferring resources and capabilities among different businesses, but does a firm have to diversify across these businesses to exploit economies of scope? The answer is *no*. Economies of scope in resources and capabilities can be exploited simply by selling or licensing the use of the resource or capability to another company. In Chapter 9, we observed that a firm can exploit proprietary technology by licensing it to other firms. In Chapter 12, we noted how technology and trademarks are licensed across national frontiers as an alternative to direct investment. Similarly across industries: Starbucks' diversification into the grocery trade was initially through licensing: Unilever and PepsiCo produced Tazo tea beverages, Nestlé produced Starbucks' ice cream, and Kraft distributed Starbucks' packaged coffee. Walt Disney exploits its trademarks, copyrights, and characters directly through diversification into theme parks, live theater, cruise ships, and hotels; but it also earned $2.4 billion in 2013 from licensing its intellectual property to producers of clothing, toys, music, comics, food and drink, and other products.

Even tangible resources can be shared across different businesses through market transactions. Airport and railroad station operators exploit economies of scope in their facilities not by diversifying into catering and retailing but by leasing space to specialist retailers and restaurants.

Is it better to exploit economies of scope in resources and capabilities internally within the firm through diversification or externally through contracts with independent companies? There are two major issues here:

- Can licensing exploit the full value of the resource or capability? This depends, to a great extent, on the transaction costs involved. The transaction costs of licensing include the costs incurred in drafting, negotiating, monitoring, and enforcing a contract. Where property rights are clearly defined—as with trademarks and many types of patents—licensing may be highly effective; for organizational capabilities and know-how more generally, writing and enforcing licensing contracts is problematic. Fujifilm's diversification into cosmetics, pharmaceuticals, and industrial coatings reflects the fact that, despite owning patents, the commercial exploitation of its coatings technology depends critically upon the capabilities of Fujifilm in applying this technology.[19]
- Does the firm have the other resources and capabilities required for successful diversification? For fragrances, Dolce & Gabbana, the Italian fashion house, licenses its brand to Procter & Gamble, which produces and markets Dolce & Gabbana fragrances (along with other licensed brands such as Gucci, Hugo Boss, Rochas, and Dunhill). Dolce & Gabbana lacks the resources and capabilities needed to design, produce, and globally distribute fragrances. Conversely, Starbucks' decision to terminate its licensing agreement with Kraft reflected Starbucks' belief that it could build the resources and capabilities needed to market and distribute packaged coffee to supermarkets.

Parenting Advantage

Michael Goold, Andrew Campbell, and colleagues propose an even more stringent test for assessing diversification (and divestment) opportunities. So far, our case for diversification has rested upon its potential to create value for the firm.[20] Goold, Campbell, and colleagues argue that this is an insufficient justification for diversification. If a parent company is to own a particular business, not only must it be able to add value to that business but also it should be capable of *adding more value than any other potential parent.* Otherwise, it would be better off selling the business to the company that can add the most value. Consider General Electric's sale of NBC Universal to Comcast in 2011. Irrespective of GE's capacity to add value to NBC Universal, the sale was justified because Comcast (as a result of its other media interests) could add more value to NBC Universal than could GE.

The concept of *parenting value* offers a different perspective on diversification from Porter's better-off test. Parenting value comes from applying the management capabilities of the parent company to a business. While Porter's better-off test focuses on the potential to share resources, Goold and colleagues concentrate on the value-adding role of the corporate center. They argue that successful diversification is more about the relationship between corporate management and the new business rather than about sharing resources and transferring capabilities between the different businesses within the diversified firm. We shall return to this concept of the parenting advantage in the next chapter.

The Diversified Firm as an Internal Market

We have seen that economies of scope on their own do not provide an adequate rationale for diversification: we also need to ascertain that the presence of transaction costs makes diversification preferable to licensing contracts. We can go further: the potential for the internal allocation of common resources to economize on transaction costs offers a rationale for diversification even when no economies of scope are present.

Internal Capital Markets   Consider the case of financial capital. The diversified firm possesses an internal capital market in which the different businesses compete for investment funds. Which is more efficient, the internal capital market of diversified companies or the external capital market? Diversified companies have two key advantages:

- By maintaining a balanced portfolio of cash-generating and cash-using businesses, diversified firms can avoid the costs of using the external capital market, including the margin between borrowing and lending rates and the heavy costs of issuing new debt and equity.
- Diversified companies have better access to information on the financial prospects of their different businesses than that typically available to external financiers.[21]

Against these advantages is the critical disadvantage that investment allocation within the diversified company is a politicized process in which strategic and financial considerations are subordinated to turf battles and ego building. Evidence suggests that diversified firms' internal capital markets tend to cross-subsidize poorly performing divisions and are reluctant to transfer cash flows to the divisions with the best prospects.[22] According to McKinsey & Company, high-performing conglomerates—including GE, Berkshire Hathaway, and Danaher of the US; Hutchison Whampoa of Hong Kong; Bouygues and Lagardère of France; Wesfarmers of Australia; ITC of India; and Grupo Carso of Mexico—are those with strict financial discipline, a refusal to overpay for acquisitions, rigorous and flexible capital allocation, lean corporate centers, and a willingness to close or sell underperforming businesses."[23]

Private equity firms also operate efficient internal capital markets that avoid the transaction costs of external capital markets. Firms such as the Blackstone Group, Carlyle Group, and Kohlberg Kravis Roberts each manage multiple funds. Each fund is created with finance from individual and institutional investors and is then used to acquire equity in companies. Funds typically have lives of 10–15 years. Acquisitions by private equity companies include both private and public companies and typically involve creating value through increasing financial leverage, cost cutting, divesting poorly performing assets, and replacing and incentivizing top management.[24]

Internal Labor Markets Efficiencies also arise from the ability of diversified companies to transfer employees, especially managers and technical specialists, between their divisions, and to rely less on hiring and firing. As companies develop and encounter new circumstances, so different management skills are required. The costs associated with hiring include advertising, time spent in interviewing and selection, and the costs of head-hunting agencies. The costs of dismissing employees can be very high where severance payments must be offered. A diversified corporation has a pool of employees and can respond to the specific needs of any one business through transfer from elsewhere within the corporation.

The broader set of career opportunities available in the diversified corporation may also attract a higher caliber of employee. Graduating students compete intensely for entry-level positions in diversified corporations such as Canon, General Electric, Unilever, and Nestlé in the belief that these companies can offer richer career development than more specialized companies.

Most important are informational advantages of diversified firms in relation to internal labor markets. A key problem of hiring from the external labor market is limited information. A résumé, references, and a day of interviews are poor indicators of how a new hire will perform in a particular job. The diversified firm that is engaged in transferring employees between different positions and different internal units can build detailed information on the competencies and characteristics of its employees. This informational advantage exists not only for individual employees but also for groups of individuals working together as teams. Hence, in exploiting a new business opportunity, an established firm is at an advantage over the new firm, which must assemble its team from scratch.

These advantages of internal markets for capital and labor may explain the continued success of highly diversified business groups in emerging economies (Strategy Capsule 13.2).

Diversification and Performance

Where diversification exploits economies of scope in resources and capabilities in the presence of transaction costs, it has the potential to create value for shareholders. Diversification that seeks only growth or risk reduction is likely to destroy value. How do these predictions work in practice?

STRATEGY CAPSULE 13.2
Emerging-market Conglomerates

Highly diversified groups of closely connected companies—*chaebols* in South Korea, *business houses* in India, *holding companies* in Turkey, *grupos económicos* in Latin America, the Hong Kong trading companies that developed from the original British *hongs*—dominate the economies of many Asian and Latin American countries.

The conventional argument for the success of these conglomerates—in contrast to the near disappearance of US and European conglomerates—has been the advantages of this corporate form in countries with poorly developed capital and labor markets. Inefficient capital markets offer a huge advantage to groups, such as Tata of India and Koç of Turkey, in using internally generated cash flows to fund growing businesses and establish new ventures. Similarly with managerial resources, where managerial talent is rare, companies such as Koç or LG of Korea are able to attract exceptionally talented graduates then develop them into highly capable managers.

However, the performance advantages of emerging market conglomerates shows no sign of abating, despite increasingly efficient capital and labor markets in their home countries. South Korean conglomerates have been growing their revenues by 11% a year; Indian business groups by 23% a year.

It seems likely that, especially in growing economies, the management model of the emerging market business groups may offer some advantages over the more integrated multidivisional corporations typical of North America, Europe, and Japan. Business groups such as Tata, Sabancı Holding (Turkey), and SK (Korea) are able to combine high levels of autonomy for their member companies with strong parental leadership that emphasizes identity and values and offers strategic guidance and consultancy.

Sources: "From Dodo to Phoenix," *The Economist* (January 11, 2014): 58; J. Ramachandran, K. S. Manikandan, and A. Pant, "Why Conglomerates Thrive (Outside the US)," *Harvard Business Review* 91 (December 2013): 110–119.

The Findings of Empirical Research

Empirical research into diversification has concentrated on two major issues: first, how do diversified firms perform relative to specialized firms and, second, does related diversification outperform unrelated diversification?

The Performance of Diversified and Specialized Firms   Despite hundreds of empirical studies over the past 50 years, there is no consistent evidence of a systematic relationship between diversification and profitability or firm value. Evidence of a conglomerate discount—of the stock market undervaluing diversified firms relative to specialized firms—seems to be the result of measurement and sampling errors.[25]

Interpreting apparent links between diversification and profitability comes up against the problem of distinguishing *association* from *causation*. Not only does diversification impact profitability, but also profitability influences diversification decisions: highly profitable firms may seek to channel their cash flows into diversification; conversely, unprofitable firms may have an incentive to diversify.

Several studies have detected a curvilinear relationship between diversification and profitability: diversification enhances profitability up to a point, after which further diversification reduces profitability due to increasing costs of complexity.[26] McKinsey & Company also point to the benefits of moderate diversification—"a strategic sweet spot between focus and broader diversification"—which is beneficial when a company has exhausted growth opportunities in its existing markets and can match its existing capabilities to emerging external opportunities.[27]

More consistent evidence concerns the performance results of refocusing initiatives by North American and European companies: when companies divest diversified businesses and concentrate more on their core businesses, the result is, typically, increased profitability and higher stock-market valuation.[28]

Related and Unrelated Diversification Given the importance of economies of scope in shared resources and capabilities, it seems likely that diversification into *related* industries should be more profitable than diversification into *unrelated* industries. Empirical research initially supported this prediction. Rumelt discovered that companies that diversified into businesses closely related to their core activities were significantly more profitable than those that pursued unrelated diversification.[29] By 1982, Tom Peters and Robert Waterman were able to conclude: "virtually every academic study has concluded that unchanneled diversification is a losing proposition."[30] This observation supported one of their "golden rules of excellence":

> *Stick to the Knitting.* Our principal finding is clear and simple. Organizations that do branch out but stick very close to their knitting outperform the others. The most successful are those diversified around a single skill, the coating and bonding technology at 3M for example. The second group in descending order, comprise those companies that branch out into related fields, the leap from electric power generation turbines to jet engines from GE for example. Least successful are those companies that diversify into a wide variety of fields. Acquisitions especially among this group tend to wither on the vine.[31]

Subsequent studies have clouded the picture: once risk and industry influences are taken into account, the superiority of related diversification is less apparent;[32] some studies even point to unrelated diversification outperforming related diversification.[33]

From this confusing body of evidence, several conclusions can be drawn. First, the relationship between diversification strategy and firm performance is complex. It is motivated by different goals, there are very different types of relationships between different businesses, and it is managed with different degrees of effectiveness. Second, the data we have on diversification by firms and its performance consequences is crude. In particular, the reporting by firms of their financial performance by business segment is limited and inconsistent. Third, the performance outcomes of diversification depend not only on the benefits of diversification but also on the management costs that diversification imposes. These costs include the costs of coordinating across businesses, the disproportionate top management attention that a single poorly performing business receives, and the politicization of decision making in a complex corporate structure. These costs of coordination and complexity are likely to be especially great for related diversification—especially when it involves sharing resources across businesses.[34] Finally, the distinction between "related" and "unrelated" diversification is far from clear: it may depend upon the strategy and characteristics of individual firms. Champagne and luggage are not obviously related products, but LVMH applies similar brand management capabilities to both Moët and Louis Vuitton. Let us consider more carefully what we mean by related diversification.

The Meaning of Relatedness in Diversification

If *relatedness* refers to the potential for sharing and transferring resources and capabilities between businesses, there are no unambiguous criteria to determine whether two industries are related; it all depends on the company undertaking the diversification. Empirical studies have defined relatedness in terms of similarities between industries in technologies and markets. These similarities emphasize relatedness at the *operational* level—in manufacturing, marketing, and distribution—typically activities where economies from resource sharing are small and achieving them is costly in management terms. Conversely, one of the most important sources of value creation within the diversified firm is the ability to apply common general management capabilities, strategic management systems, and resource allocation processes to different businesses. Such economies depend on the existence of *strategic* rather than *operational* commonalities among different businesses within the diversified corporation.[35]

- Berkshire Hathaway is involved in insurance, candy stores, furniture, kitchen knives, jewelry, and footwear. Despite this diversity, all these businesses have been selected on the basis of their ability to benefit from the unique style of corporate management established by its chairman and CEO, Warren Buffett, and vice-chairman, Charles Munger.
- Richard Branson's Virgin Group covers a huge array of businesses from airlines to health clubs. Yet they share certain strategic similarities: almost all are start-up companies that benefit from Branson's entrepreneurial zeal and expertise; almost all sell to final consumers and are in sectors that offer opportunities for innovative approaches to differentiation.

The essence of such strategic-level linkages is the ability to apply similar strategies, resource allocation procedures, and control systems across the different businesses within the corporate portfolio.[36] Table 13.1 lists some of the strategic factors that determine similarities among businesses in relation to corporate management activities.

Unlike operational relatedness, where the opportunities for exploiting economies of scope in joint inputs are comparatively easy to identify—even to quantify—strategic relatedness is more elusive. It necessitates an understanding of the overall strategic approach of the company and recognition of its corporate-level management capabilities.

Ultimately, the linkage between the different businesses within a company may depend upon the strategic rationale of the company. Prahalad and Bettis use the term *dominant logic* to refer to managers' cognition of the rationale that unifies the different parts of the company.[37] Such a common view of a company's identity and raison d'être is a critical precondition for effective integration across its different

TABLE 13.1 The determinants of strategic relatedness between businesses

Corporate Management Tasks	Determinants of Strategic Similarity
Resource allocation	Similar sizes of capital investment projects Similar time spans of investment projects Similar sources of risk Similar general management skills required for business unit managers
Strategy formulation	Similar key success factors Similar stages of the industry life cycle Similar competitive positions occupied by each business within its industry
Performance management and control variables	Similar indicators for performance targets Similar time horizons for performance targets

Source: R. M. Grant, "On Dominant Logic, Relatedness, and the Link between Diversity and Performance," *Strategic Management Journal* 9 (1988): 641. Reused by permission of John Wiley & Sons, Ltd.

businesses. For example, the dominant logic of luxury goods giant LVMH extends beyond its brand management capabilities deployed in the marketing of luxury goods into a corporate identity formed by a: "common cultural trunk based on the permanent search for quality of the products and the management, human relations based on responsibility and initiative, and rewarding competences and services."[38]

Summary

Diversification is like sex: its attractions are obvious, often irresistible, yet the experience is often disappointing. For top management, it is a minefield. The diversification experiences of large corporations are littered with expensive mistakes: Exxon's attempt to build Exxon Office Systems as a rival to Xerox and IBM; Vivendi's diversification from water and environmental services into media, entertainment, and telecoms; Royal Bank of Scotland's quest to transform itself from a retail bank into a financial services giant. Despite so many costly failures, the urge to diversify continues to captivate senior managers. Part of the problem is the divergence between managerial and shareholder goals. While diversification has offered meager rewards to shareholders, it is the fastest route to building vast corporate empires. A further problem is hubris. A company's success in one line of business tends to result in the top management team becoming overly confident of its ability to achieve similar success in other businesses.

Nevertheless, for companies to survive and prosper over the long term, they must change; inevitably, this involves redefining the businesses in which they operate. The world's two largest IT companies—IBM and Hewlett-Packard—are both over six decades old. Their longevity is based on their ability to adapt their product lines to changing market opportunities. Essentially, they have applied existing capabilities to developing new products, which have provided new growth trajectories.

Similarly with most other long-established companies: for 3M, Canon, Samsung, and DuPont, diversification has been central to the process of evolution. In most cases, this diversification was not a major discontinuity but an initial incremental step in which existing resources and capabilities were deployed to exploit a perceived opportunity.

If companies are to use diversification as part of their long-term adaptation and avoid the many errors that corporate executives have made in the past then better strategic analysis of diversification decisions is essential. The objectives of diversification need to be clear and explicit. Shareholder value creation has provided a demanding and illuminating criterion with which to appraise investment in new business opportunities. Rigorous analysis also counters the tendency for diversification to be a diversion—corporate escapism resulting from the unwillingness of top management to come to terms with difficult conditions within the core business.

The analytic tools at our disposal for evaluating diversification decisions have developed greatly in recent years. In the late 1980s, diversification decisions were based on vague concepts of synergy that involved identifying linkages between different industries. We are now able to be much more precise about the need for economies of scope in resources and capabilities *and* the economies of internalization that are prerequisites for diversification to create shareholder value. Recognizing the role of these economies of internalization has directed attention to the role of top management capabilities and effective corporate management systems in determining the success of diversification.

Self-Study Questions

1. An ice-cream manufacturer is proposing to acquire a soup manufacturer on the basis that, first, its sales and profits will be more seasonally balanced and, second, from year to year, sales and profits will be less affected by variations in weather. Will this risk spreading create value for shareholders? Under what circumstances could this acquisition create value for shareholders?

2. Tata Group is one of India's largest companies, employing 424,000 people in many different industries, including steel, motor vehicles, watches and jewelry, telecommunications, financial services, management consulting, food products, tea, chemicals and fertilizers, satellite TV, hotels, motor vehicles, energy, IT, and construction. Such diversity far exceeds that of any North American or Western European company. What are the conditions in India that might make such broad-based diversification both feasible and profitable?

3. Giorgio Armani SpA is an Italian private company owned mainly by the Armani family. Most of its clothing and accessories are produced and marketed by the company (some are manufactured by outside contractors). For other products, notably fragrances, cosmetics, and eyewear, Armani licenses its brand names to other companies. Armani is considering expanding into athletic clothing, hotels, and bridal shops. Advise Armani on whether these new businesses should be developed in-house, by joint ventures, or by licensing the Armani brands to specialist companies already within these fields.

4. General Electric, Berkshire Hathaway, and Richard Branson's Virgin Group each comprise a wide range of different businesses that appear to have few close technical or customer linkages? Are these examples of unrelated diversification? For each of the three companies, can you identify linkages among their businesses such that bringing them under common ownership creates value?

5. Assess Amazon's decisions to diversify into (a) e-readers (Kindle), (b) tablet computers (Kindle Fire), and (c) smartphones (Fire Phone).

Notes

1. A. D. Chandler Jr., *Strategy and Structure: Chapters in the History of the Industrial Enterprise* (Cambridge, MA: MIT Press, 1962); R. P. Rumelt, *Strategy, Structure and Economic Performance* (Cambridge, MA: Harvard University Press, 1974); H. Itami, T. Kagono, H. Yoshihara, and S. Sakuma, "Diversification Strategies and Economic Performance," *Japanese Economic Studies* 11 (1982): 78–110.

2. M. Goold and K. Luchs, "Why Diversify? Four Decades of Management Thinking," *Academy of Management Executive* 7 (August 1993): 7–25.

3. G. F. Davis, K. A. Diekman, and C. F. Tinsley, "The Decline and Fall of the Conglomerate Firm in the 1980s: A Study in the De-Institutionalization of an Organizational Form," *American Sociological Review* 49 (1994): 547–570; R. E. Hoskisson and M. A. Hitt, *Downscoping: How to Tame the Diversified Firm* (New York: Oxford University Press, 1994).

4. L. Laeven and R. Levine, "Is there a Diversification Discount in Financial Conglomerates?" *Journal of Financial Economics* 82 (2006): 331–367.

5. B. Burrough, *Barbarians at the Gate: The Fall of RJR Nabisco* (New York: Harper & Row, 1990).

6. T. Khanna and K. Palepu, "Why Focused Strategies May Be Wrong for Emerging Markets," *Harvard Business Review* (July/August, 1997): 41–51; D. Kim, D. Kandemir, and S. T. Cavusgil, "The Role of Family Conglomerates in Emerging Markets," *Thunderbird International Business Review* 46 (January 2004): 7–20.

7. See any standard corporate finance text, for example R. A. Brealey and S. Myers, *Principles of Corporate Finance*, 11th edn (New York: McGraw-Hill, 2013): Chapter 8.

8. See, for example, H. Levy and M. Sarnat, "Diversification, Portfolio Analysis and the Uneasy Case for Conglomerate Mergers," *Journal of Finance* 25 (1970): 795–802; R. H. Mason and M. B. Goudzwaard, "Performance of Conglomerate Firms: A Portfolio Approach," *Journal of Finance* 31 (1976): 39–48; J. F. Weston, K. V. Smith, and R. E. Shrieves, "Conglomerate Performance Using the Capital Asset Pricing Model," *Review of Economics and Statistics* 54 (1972): 357–363.

9. M. Lubatkin and S. Chetterjee, "Extending Modern Portfolio Theory into the Domain of Corporate Strategy: Does It Apply?" *Academy of Management Journal* 37 (1994): 109–136.

10. The reduction in risk that bondholders derive from diversification is termed the *coinsurance effect*. See L. W. Lee, "Coinsurance and the Conglomerate Merger," *Journal of Finance* 32 (1977): 1527–1537; and F. Franco, O. Urcan, and F. P. Vasvari, "Debt Market Benefits of Corporate Diversification and Segment Disclosures" (January 31, 2013). Available at SSRN: http://ssrn.com/abstract=1710562 or http://dx.doi.org/10.2139/ssrn.1710562.

11. V. Kuppuswamy and B. Villalonga, "Does Diversification Create Value in the Presence of External Financing Constraints? Evidence from the 2007–2009 Financial Crisis," Harvard Business School Working Paper (2010).

12. M. E. Porter, "From Competitive Advantage to Corporate Strategy," *Harvard Business Review* (May/June 1987): 46.

13. M. Hayward and D. C. Hambrick, "Explaining the Premiums Paid for Large Acquisitions," *Administrative Science Quarterly* 42 (1997): 103–127.

14. A study of 68 diversifying ventures by established companies found that, on average, breakeven was not attained until the seventh or eighth years of operation; see R. Biggadike, "The Risky Business of Diversification," *Harvard Business Review* (May/June 1979): 103–111.

15. The formal definition of *economies of scope* is in terms of "subadditivity." Economies of scope exist in the production of goods $x_1, x_2, ..., x_n$, if $C(X) < \Sigma_i C_i(x_i)$ where: $X < \Sigma_i(x_i)$
$C(X)$ is the cost of producing all n goods within a single firm
$\Sigma_i C_i(x_i)$ is the cost of producing the goods in n specialized firms.
See W. J. Baumol, J. C. Panzar, and R. D. Willig, *Contestable Markets and the Theory of Industry Structure* (New York: Harcourt Brace Jovanovich, 1982): 71–72.

16. Hay Group, "Best Companies for Leadership: General Electric," http://executiveimpactonline.com/portfolio/the-leadership-edge/, accessed July 20, 2015.

17. The role of capabilities in diversification is discussed in C. C. Markides and P. J. Williamson, "Related Diversification, Core Competencies and Corporate Performance," *Strategic Management Journal* 15 (Special Issue, 1994): 149–165.

18. Demand-side synergies are discussed in G. Ye, R. L. Priem, and A. A. Alshwer, "Achieving Demand-side Synergy from Strategic Diversification: How Combining Mundane Assets can Leverage Consumer Utilities. *Organization Science*, (2011); J. Schmidt, R. Makadok, and T. Keil, "Firm Scope Advantages and the Demand Side," Working Paper (2012).

19. This issue is examined more fully in D. J. Teece, "Towards an Economic Theory of the Multiproduct Firm," *Journal of Economic Behavior and Organization* 3 (1982): 39–63.

20. A. Campbell, J. Whitehead, M. Alexander, and M. Goold, *Strategy for the Corporate-Level: Where to Invest, What to Cut Back and How to Grow Organisations with Multiple Divisions* (New York: John Wiley & Sons, Inc., 2014).

21. J. P. Liebeskind, "Internal Capital Markets: Benefits, Costs and Organizational Arrangements," *Organization Science* 11 (2000): 58–76.

22. D. Scharfstein and J. Stein, "The Dark Side of Internal Capital Markets: Divisional Rent Seeking and Inefficient Investment," *Journal of Finance* 55 (2000): 2537–2564; D. Bardolet, C. Fox, and D. Lovallo, "Corporate Capital Allocation: A Behavioral Perspective", *Strategic Management Journal* 32 (2011): 1465–1483.

23. C. Kaye and J. Yuwono, "Conglomerate Discount or Premium? How Some Diversified Companies Create Exceptional Value," Marakon Associates (2003), http://www.nd.edu/~cba/cc/pdf/Doyle_Portfolio%20decision%20making.pdf, accessed July 20, 2015.

24. J. Kelly *The New Tycoons: Inside the Trillion Dollar Private Equity Industry that Owns Everything* (Hoboken, NJ: John Wiley & Sons, Inc., 2012).

25. S. Erdorf, T. Hartmann-Wendels, N. Heinrichs, and M. Matz, "Corporate Diversification and Firm Value: A Survey of Recent Literature," Cologne Graduate School Working Paper (January 2012); J. D. Martin and A. Sayrak, "Corporate Diversification and Shareholder Value: A Survey of Recent Literature," *Journal of Corporate Finance* 9 (2003): 37–57.

26. L. E. Palich, L. B. Cardinal, and C. C. Miller, "Curvilinearity in the Diversification–Performance Linkage: An Examination of over Three Decades of Research," *Strategic Management Journal* 22 (2000): 155–174.

27. N. Harper and S. P. Viguerie, "Are You Too Focused?" *McKinsey Quarterly* (Special Edition, 2002): 29–37; J. Cyriac, T. Koller, and J. Thomsen, "Testing the Limits of Diversification," *McKinsey Quarterly* (February 2012).

28. C. C. Markides, "Consequences of Corporate Refocusing: Ex Ante Evidence," *Academy of Management Journal* 35 (1992): 398–412; C. C. Markides, "Diversification, Restructuring and Economic Performance," *Strategic Management Journal* 16 (1995): 101–118.

29. R. P. Rumelt, *Strategy, Structure and Economic Performance* (Cambridge, MA: Harvard University Press, 1974).

30. T. Peters and R. Waterman, *In Search of Excellence* (New York: Harper & Row, 1982).

31. Ibid., 294.

32. H. K. Christensen and C. A. Montgomery, "Corporate Economic Performance: Diversification Strategy versus Market Structure," *Strategic Management Journal* 2 (1981): 327–343; R. A. Bettis, "Performance Differences in Related and Unrelated Diversified Firms," *Strategic Management Journal* 2 (1981): 379–383.

33. See, for example, A. Michel and I. Shaked, "Does Business Diversification Affect Performance?" *Financial Management* 13 (1984): 18–24; G. A. Luffman and R. Reed, *The Strategy and Performance of British Industry: 1970–1980* (London: Macmillan, 1984).

34. Y. M. Zhou, "Synergy, Coordination Costs, and Diversification Choices," *Strategic Management Journal* 32 (2011): 624–639.

35. For a discussion of relatedness in diversification, see J. Robins and M. F. Wiersema, "A Resource-Based Approach to the Multibusiness Firm: Empirical Analysis of Portfolio Interrelationships and Corporate Financial Performance," *Strategic Management Journal* 16 (1995): 277–300; and J. Robins and M. F. Wiersema, "The Measurement of Corporate Portfolio Strategy: Analysis of the Content Validity of Related Diversification Indexes," *Strategic Management Journal* 24 (2002): 39–59.

36. R. M. Grant, "On Dominant Logic, Relatedness, and the Link between Diversity and Performance," *Strategic Management Journal* 9 (1988): 639–642.

37. C. K. Prahalad and R. A. Bettis, "The Dominant Logic: A New Linkage between Diversity and Performance," *Strategic Management Journal* 7 (1986): 485–502.

38. R. Calori, "How Successful Companies Manage Diverse Businesses," *Long Range Planning* 21 (June 1988): 85.

14 Implementing Corporate Strategy: Managing the Multibusiness Firm

Some have argued that single-product businesses have a focus that gives them an advantage over multibusiness companies like our own—and perhaps they would have, but only if we neglect our own overriding advantage: the ability to share the ideas that are the result of wide and rich input from a multitude of global sources. GE businesses share technology, design, compensation and personnel evaluation systems, manufacturing practices, and customer and country knowledge.

—JACK WELCH, CHAIRMAN AND CEO, GENERAL ELECTRIC COMPANY, 1981–2001

OUTLINE

Introduction and Objectives

The key feature of the multibusiness firm is that—whether organized as business units, divisions, or subsidiaries—they comprise a number of separate businesses that are coordinated and controlled by a corporate headquarters. These businesses may be organized around different products (e.g., Samsung Electronics), different geographical markets (e.g., McDonald's), or different vertical stages (e.g., Royal Dutch Shell). While the individual businesses are responsible for most business-level decisions, both strategic and operational, the headquarters is responsible for corporate strategy and issues that affect the company as a whole.

The three previous chapters have addressed the three key dimensions of corporate scope: vertical integration, international expansion, and diversification. In relation to all three, the critical issue has been whether the diversified company can create value by operating across multiple businesses. However, value is only realized if these strategies are implemented effectively. This raises multiple issues: how should corporate strategy be formulated and linked to resource allocation? How should the corporate headquarters exercise coordination and control over the businesses? What roles and leadership styles should corporate managers adopt? And, given the critical role of corporate management, what kind of governance structure should corporate managers operate under? To answer these questions we must look closely at the activities of the corporate headquarters and its relationships with the businesses.

By the time you have completed this chapter, you will be able to:

- ◆ Comprehend the basic strategic role of corporate managers: creating value within the businesses owned by the company.
- ◆ Apply the techniques of portfolio analysis to corporate strategy decisions.
- ◆ Understand how the corporate headquarters manages the linkages among the different business units within the company.
- ◆ Appreciate the tools and processes by which the corporate headquarters influences the strategy and performance of its individual businesses.
- ◆ Understand how corporate managers can stimulate and guide strategic change.
- ◆ Recognize the governance issues that impact the work of managers within the multibusiness corporation.

The Role of Corporate Management

Common to decisions over vertical integration, international expansion, and diversification is the basic criterion that the benefits from extending the scope of the firm vertically, geographically, or horizontally should exceed the administrative costs of a larger, more complex corporate entity. Hence, the formulation and implementation of corporate strategy are inseparable: decisions over corporate scope must take account of the costs and benefits from extending or contracting corporate scope which depend upon how corporate strategy is implemented. This requires us to direct our attention to the mechanisms through which multibusiness corporations create value for the businesses they own.

The basic guideline for corporate strategy decisions, that the benefits from a company owning a particular business should exceed the costs of administering that business, has been questioned by Michael Goold and Andrew Campbell. They propose a higher performance hurdle for corporate managers: a company should only own a business if it possesses **parenting advantage**—the surplus of value added over cost should not only be positive, it should be greater than that which could be achieved by any other company. Otherwise the business in question could be profitably sold to that other company.[1]

In this chapter we shall focus on four activities through which corporate management adds value to its businesses:

- managing the corporate portfolio
- managing linkages across businesses
- managing individual businesses
- managing change in the multibusiness corporation.

The four sections that follow consider each of these activities and establish the conditions under which they create value.

Managing the Corporate Portfolio

In order for the multibusiness firm to achieve efficiency in administering a number of different businesses, it must develop common management systems it can apply to its different businesses. At the most basic level, creating value within a multibusiness firm requires operating an effective system of resource allocation: ensuring the firm invests in those businesses which offer the greatest potential for profitability. For some multibusiness firms, portfolio management is their primary source of value creation and the basis of their strategy. Berkshire Hathaway is a conglomerate comprising unrelated acquisitions overseen by a minuscule corporate headquarters whose role is to make acquisitions, allocate capital, and monitor performance.

Portfolio planning matrices are the main strategy tool for facilitating portfolio management in the multibusiness firm. They show the positioning of a firm's different businesses that can be used to analyze their value-creating prospects.

Portfolio planning techniques were an outcome of the pioneering work in corporate strategy initiated by General Electric at the end of the 1960s when GE was a sprawling industrial empire comprising 46 divisions and 190 businesses. GE worked with the Boston Consulting Group, McKinsey & Company, and Arthur D. Little to develop portfolio planning matrices.

Portfolio Planning: The GE/McKinsey Matrix

The basic idea of a portfolio planning model is to represent graphically the individual businesses of a multibusiness company in terms of key strategic variables that determine their potential for profit. These variables typically comprise two dimensions: *market attractiveness* and *competitive advantage* within that market—the same basic drivers of profitability that were identified in Chapter 1 (see Figure 1.5).

In the GE/McKinsey matrix (Figure 14.1), the industry attractiveness axis combines market size, market growth rate, market profitability (return on sales over three years), cyclicality, inflation recovery (potential to increase productivity and product prices), and international potential (ratio of foreign to domestic sales). Business unit competitive advantage combines market share, return on sales relative to competitors, and relative position with regard to quality, technology, manufacturing, distribution, marketing, and cost.[2] The basic strategy implications—concerning the allocation of capital to each business and recommendations for divestment—are shown by three regions of Figure 14.1.

Portfolio Planning: BCG's Growth–Share Matrix

The Boston Consulting Group's *growth–share matrix* also uses the same two dimensions—industry attractiveness and competitive position—to compare the strategic positions of different businesses. However, it uses a single indicator as a proxy for each of these dimensions: industry attractiveness is measured by *rate of market growth* and competitive advantage by *relative market share* (the business unit's market share relative to that of its largest competitor). The four quadrants of the BCG matrix predict patterns of profits and cash flow and indicate strategies to be adopted (Figure 14.2).[3]

The simplicity of the BCG matrix is both its usefulness and its limitation. It can be prepared very easily and offers a clear picture of a firm's business portfolio in relation to some important strategic characteristics. Moreover, the analysis is versatile: it can be applied not only to business units but also to products, geographical

FIGURE 14.1   The GE/McKinsey portfolio planning matrix

Business Unit Competitive Advantage

FIGURE 14.2   The BCG growth–share matrix

markets, brands, and customers. Though simplistic, it can be valuable in providing a preliminary view before embarking upon a more detailed and rigorous analysis.

However, the limitations of both the BCG and McKinsey business portfolio matrices have resulted in both losing their popularity as strategy tools. There are three main problems with these matrices:

- They are simplistic indicators of industry attractiveness and competitive advantage.
- There are problems of definition. For example, in the BCG matrix, is BMW's auto business a "dog" because it holds less than 2% of the world auto market or a "cash cow" because it is the market leader in the luxury car segment?
- They fail to take into account linkages between businesses. The implicit assumption that every business in the portfolio is independent rejects the basic rational for the multibusiness corporation: the presence of synergy.[4]

Portfolio Planning: The Ashridge Portfolio Display

The Ashridge Portfolio Display is based upon the concept of *parenting advantage*.[5] It takes account of the fact that the value-creating potential of a business within a company's business portfolio depends not just on the characteristics of the business (as assumed by the McKinsey and BCG matrices) but also on the characteristics of the parent. The focus, therefore, is on the *fit* between a business and its parent company. The positioning of a business along the horizontal axis of Figure 14.3 depends upon the parent's potential to create profit for the business by, for example, applying its corporate-level management capabilities, sharing resources and capabilities with other businesses, or economizing on transaction costs. The vertical axis measures the potential for value destruction by the parent. This can be caused by the costs of corporate overhead or a mismatch between the management needs of the business

FIGURE 14.3 Ashridge portfolio display: The potential for parenting advantage

LOW

BALLAST
- typical core business position: fit high, but limited potential to add more value

EDGE OF HEARTLAND
- businesses where value-adding potential is lower or risks of value destruction higher

HEARTLAND
- businesses with high potential for adding value

Potential for value destruction from misfit between needs of the business and parent's corporate management style

ALIEN TERRITORY
- exit: no potential for value creation

VALUE TRAP
- potential for adding value is seldom realized because of problems of management fit

HIGH

LOW ⟶ HIGH

Potential for the parent to add value to the business

Source: Ashridge Strategic Management Centre.

and the management systems and style of the parent (this may arise from bureaucratic rigidity, incompatibility with top management's mindset, or politicization of decision making).

In recognizing that businesses are not independent entities and introducing the role of strategic fit in influencing the potential for value creation and value destruction, the Ashridge matrix introduces the key issues of synergy that are ignored by other portfolio-planning matrices. The problem is complexity: both dimensions of the Ashridge matrix require difficult subjective evaluations that do not lend themselves to quantification.

Managing Linkages across Businesses

The chapters on vertical integration, international strategy, and diversification (Chapters 11, 12, and 13) established that the main opportunities for corporate strategy to create value arise from exploiting the linkages between businesses. These include the benefits from accessing, sharing, and transferring resources and capabilities and the ability to avoid the transaction costs of markets. Most multibusiness firms are organized to exploit resource and capability linkages in two areas: first, through the centralization of common services at the corporate level and, second, through managing direct linkages among the businesses.

Common Corporate Services

The simplest form of resource sharing in the multidivisional company is the centralized provision of corporate functions and common services. These include corporate management functions such as strategic planning, financial control, treasury, risk management, internal audit, taxation, government relations, and shareholder relations. They also include business services that are more efficiently provided on a centralized basis, such as research, engineering, human resources management, legal services, management development, purchasing, and any other administrative services subject to economies of scale or learning.[6]

In practice, the benefits of the centralized provision of common services may be smaller than corporate managers anticipate. Centralized provision avoids costs of duplication but there can be little incentive among headquarters staff and specialized corporate units to meet the needs of their business-level customers. The experience of many companies is that economies from centralizing services are offset by the propensity for corporate staffs to grow under their own momentum. PepsiCo's recently renovated corporate headquarters set on 100 acres in Westchester County, New York with a staff of 1100 is a particular target for activist shareholders.[7]

A growing trend has been for companies to separate their corporate headquarters into a *corporate management unit*—responsible for supporting the corporate management team in core activities such as strategic planning, finance, and communication—and a *shared services organization*—responsible for supplying common services such as research, recruitment, training, and information technology to the businesses. Among a sample of 86 large European companies, one-half had established shared services organizations by 2013, with IT being the most commonly shared function.[8] To encourage efficiency and customer-orientation among these shared service organizations, some companies have operated them as profit centers supplying services on an arm's-length basis to internal operating units—sometimes in competition with external suppliers.

Procter & Gamble's Global Business Services organization employs 7000 people in six "global hubs": Cincinnati (US), San Jose (Puerto Rico), Newcastle (UK), Brussels (Belgium), Singapore, and Manila (Philippines). Through scale economies and standardizing systems, it has cut costs by over $800 million. Its innovations include virtualization (e.g., replacing physical product mock-ups with virtual reality applications), internal collaboration tools, decision support (e.g., its "Decision Cockpits"), and real-time digital capabilities.[9]

Deloitte's 2013 survey of global shared services found that:

- Fifty-eight percent of companies had multiple shared service centers, often with centers located in different countries.
- As a result US- and EU-based companies were increasingly locating service units in Asia, Latin America, and Eastern Europe. The location of shared service units is determined primarily by the cost and skills of human resources.
- Shared service centers were expanding the range of services they offered to include traditional corporate functions, such as tax, real estate/facilities, and legal services.
- Companies are increasingly blending shared services with the outsourcing of services.

- The benefits realized from the shared services model include both reduced cost and enhanced quality.[10]

Transferring Skills and Sharing Activities among Businesses

Exploiting economies of scope doesn't necessarily mean centralizing resources and capabilities at the corporate level. There is considerable scope for sharing resources and transferring capabilities between businesses. Michael Porter views these linkages as the powerful means by which corporate strategy can create shareholder value. By contrast, "the days when portfolio management was a valid concept of corporate strategy are past": increasingly efficient capital markets limit the potential for the multibusiness firm to create value simply by allocating capital.[11] However, he also warns that "imagined synergy" can be mistaken for "real synergy" and points to the need for meticulous analysis of the opportunities to transfer skills and share activities. In order to identify real synergies, Porter advocates a careful analysis of the value chains of the different businesses in order to pinpoint commonalities in activities, resources, and capabilities. Porter distinguishes two types of synergy:

- *Transferring skills*: Organizational capabilities can be transferred between business units. LVMH transfers brand management and distribution capabilities among its different luxury-brand businesses. At Procter & Gamble, Gillette draws upon Olay's skincare know-how in designing razors for women. Creating value by sharing skills requires that the same capabilities are applicable to the different businesses and that mechanisms are established to transfer these skills through personnel exchange and best practice transfer. As the opening quotation to this chapter indicates, sharing know-how and capabilities is at the heart of value creation at General Electric.

- *Sharing resources and activities*: Shared resources are most likely to include intangible resources such as brands and proprietary technology, but may also include physical resources such as plant, buildings, and finance. Opportunities for sharing activities can be identified from a detailed comparison of the value chains of different businesses to determine the compatibility of similar activities and potential for combination. Activities that are often shared across business include R & D, purchasing, distribution, and sales. These shared activities correspond closely to the common corporate services discussed in the previous section. The difference is that while common corporate services include corporate and support services, the shared activities we are discussing here form the core operational functions of the businesses. Procter & Gamble's market development organizations, which provide marketing and distribution for all P&G products in each county and region, are one example of such sharing. Another is Samsung Electronics' design centers in London, Tokyo, San Francisco, and Seoul which undertake design for all Samsung's different business units.[12]

Transferring skills and sharing activities both require careful and sustained corporate involvement. In the case of sharing skills, Porter notes that this is "an active process ... that does not happen by accident or by osmosis. It typically involves reassigning critical personnel and participation and support from top management."[13] Even seemingly simple linkages, such as transferring best practices, may be difficult to achieve in practice. A study of 122 best-practice transfers within eight companies found that the barriers to transfer were not primarily motivational (e.g., "knowledge hoarding" by the source or "not-invented-here" resistance by the recipient)—the key barriers were a poor relationship between the source and the recipient of the best practice.[14]

Implications for the Corporate Headquarters

The more closely related are a company's businesses, the greater are potential gains from managing the linkages among those businesses and the greater the need for an active role by the corporate center. Thus, in vertically integrated petroleum companies (such as Royal Dutch Shell or Eni) or companies with close market or technological links (such as IBM, Procter & Gamble, and Sony) corporate staffs tend to be much larger than at companies with few linkages among their businesses. Berkshire Hathaway, which has almost no linkages among its businesses, has a corporate staff of about 50. Hewlett-Packard, with about the same sales but much closer linkages between its divisions, has over 2000 employees at its Palo Alto head office. Where business units share common resources or capabilities, the corporate headquarters is likely to be closely involved developing and deploying those resources and capabilities. For example, both Pfizer and Corning Inc. have strong corporate R & D departments, Dow has a strong corporate manufacturing function, and Virgin's corporate team are heavily involved in managing the Virgin brand.[15]

Developing and sharing organizational capabilities implies an important role for knowledge management. In industries such as beer, cement, food processing, and telecommunication services, internationalization offers few economies of scope in shared resources but does offer important opportunities for transferring innovation and know-how among national subsidiaries.

Exploiting linkages between businesses imposes costs which can easily outweigh the benefits generated. Even straightforward collaborations, such as cross-selling between different businesses, have yielded disappointing results, especially in financial services.[16] Lorsch and Allen's comparison of three US conglomerates with three vertically integrated paper companies found that the heavier coordination requirements of the paper companies resulted in greater involvement of head office staff in divisional operations, larger head office staffs, more complex planning and control devices, and a lower responsiveness to change in the external environment. By contrast, the conglomerates made little attempt to exploit operating synergies even if they were present.[17]

Managing Individual Businesses

In the portfolio management approach to corporate strategy, the corporate headquarters' primary role is as an investor: making acquisitions and divestments and allocating investment funds among the different businesses. In managing linkages among the businesses the essential role of the corporate headquarters is as a coordinator and orchestrator of the synergies between businesses. However, the corporate headquarters may be involved more directly in adding value to its individual businesses by improving the management of those businesses. Andrew Campbell and his associates refer to this direct influence of corporate headquarters on the individual businesses as "vertical value-added" achieved through "stand-alone influence" (i.e., it is not dependent upon exploiting synergistic links between the businesses). The interventions through which corporate management can enhance business-level performance include: appointing (and dismissing) the senior managers of the businesses; approving or rejecting budgets, strategic plans, and capital expenditure proposals; imposing performance targets; making available relationships with governments and other influential stakeholders; providing advice and guidance through meetings and personal interactions; and through managing the corporate culture.[18]

We focus upon just three mechanisms through which the corporate headquarters can impact the performance of its individual businesses: direct corporate involvement in business level management, strategic planning, and performance management and financial control.

Direct Corporate Involvement in Business-level Management

Writing in the late 1980s, Porter characterized the direct involvement of the corporate HQ in the individual businesses as *restructuring*.[19] A restructuring strategy seeks to acquire under-managed or mismanaged companies then intervene to install new managers, change strategy, sell off surplus assets, and possibly make further acquisitions in order to achieve scale and market presence. For the strategy to create value requires that management is able to spot companies that are undervalued or offer turnaround potential to then make strategic and operational interventions to boost their performance. A further requirement, observes Porter, is the willingness to recognize when the work has been done and then dispose of the restructured business.

McKinsey & Company offers a systematic approach to analyzing the potential for creating shareholder value through corporate restructuring and guiding the management actions that need to be undertaken.[20] The McKinsey pentagon framework comprises five stages of analysis which correspond to the five nodes of Figure 14.4:

FIGURE 14.4   The McKinsey restructuring pentagon

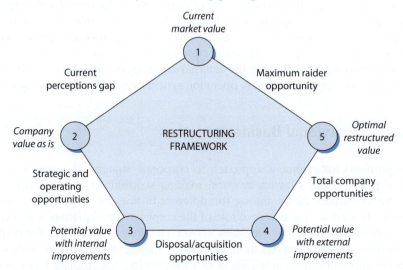

Source: T. E. Copeland, T. Koller, and J. Murrin, *Valuation* (New York: John Wiley & Sons, Inc. 1990).

1 *The current market value of the company*: The starting point of the analysis is current enterprise value, which comprises the value of equity plus the value of debt. (As we know from Chapter 2, if securities markets are efficient, this equals the net present value of anticipated cash flow over the life of the company.)

2 *The value of the company as is*: Even without any changes to strategy or operations, it may be possible to value simply by managing external perceptions of a company's future prospects. Over the past two decades, companies have devoted increasing attention to managing investor expectations by increasing the quantity and quality of information flow to shareholders and investment analysts and establishing departments of investor relations for this purpose.

3 *The potential value of the company with internal improvements*: As we have seen, corporate management has opportunities for increasing the overall value of the company by making strategic and operational improvements to individual businesses that increase their cash flows. These might include exploiting global expansion opportunities, outsourcing certain activities, and cost-cutting opportunities.

4 *The potential value of the company with external improvements*: Having determined the potential value of its constituent businesses, corporate management needs to determine whether changes in the business portfolio can increase overall company value. The key is to apply the principle of parenting advantage: even after strategic and operating improvements have been made, can a business be sold for a price greater than its value to the company?

5 *The optimum restructured value of the company*: The previous four steps establish the maximum value potential of a company. Assuming that these changes could also be undertaken by an alternative owner of the company, the difference between the maximum restructured value and the current market value represents the profit potential available to a corporate raider.

Restructuring was once associated with the strategies of conglomerate companies, most of which have now disappeared from the corporate sectors of North America and Europe. However, restructuring has remained a prominent corporate strategy—especially in industries undergoing radical strategic change. In the beer industry, Anheuser-Busch InBev and SABMiller have led global consolidation. In metals, Rio Tinto, BHP Billiton, and Glencore Xstrata have been front-runners. In many cases, restructuring has involved obsessive attention to cost cutting and divestment—as indicated by the nicknames given to some of its prominent exponents: "Chainsaw Al" Dunlap (at Scott Paper and Sunbeam), "Neutron Jack" Welch (at General Electric), and "Fred-the Shred" Goodwin (at Royal Bank of Scotland).

However, the primary inheritors of the conglomerates' role as restructurers have passed to private equity groups. Firms such as Carlyle Group, Kohlberg Kravis Roberts, Blackstone, and Apollo Global Management in the US and CVC Capital Partners and Cinven in the UK create investment funds organized as limited partnerships that acquire full or partial ownership of private and public companies. Value is created through financial restructuring (primarily increasing leverage), management changes, and making strategic and operational changes. On average, private equity funds have generated returns that exceeded those of the stockmarket.[21]

For most multibusiness companies, involvement by corporate-level management in the strategic and operational decisions at the business level is less intrusive than that implied by a restructuring approach. A feature of multibusiness companies that have a history of superior financial performance is close communication and collaboration between the business level and corporate executives. For example:

- Exxon Mobil Corporation has been consistently the most profitable petroleum major and, after Apple, the world's most valuable company. At the core of ExxonMobil's renowned financial discipline, strategic acuity, and operational effectiveness is the close relationship between its six-person corporate management committee and the subsidiary companies, where the president of each operating subsidiary has a direct link to one of the management committee members. The relationship between corporate and divisional management is embedded in its doctrine of *stewardship*—a system of accountability where each executive is personally responsible to the corporation and its shareholders.[22]

- Wesfarmers Ltd. is a former Australian farmers' cooperative which, since becoming a public company in 1984, has diversified a range of mature industries, including discount stores, supermarkets, office supplies, coal mining, chemicals, and insurance. Wesfarmers near-continuous growth in profits and strong shareholder returns (by 2015 it had become Australia's tenth biggest company by market capitalization) can be attributed to a corporate management style that establishes a close relationship between the corporate executive team and subsidiary management and subjects subsidiary management plans and performance to intense corporate scrutiny.[23]

However, direct corporate involvement in business-level decisions has a serious downside: it undermines the autonomy and motivation of the general managers of those businesses. Authoritarian, highly interventionist CEOs can be highly successful (as in the case of Steve Jobs at Apple) or highly unsuccessful (as in the case of Carly Fiorina at Hewlett-Packard). Universally true, however, is their propensity to centralize initiative and decision-making authority, and this can have an adverse effect on the responsiveness and adaptability of the organization as a whole.[24] A key challenge of managing the multibusiness firm is to design a management system that allows business-level managers to benefit from the expertise and perspective of corporate managers while not undermining their initiative and motivation. Two management systems can assist in this task: strategic planning systems and performance management and financial control systems.

The Strategic Planning System

In most diversified companies, business strategies are initiated by divisional managers (within certain guidelines), and the role of corporate managers is to appraise, amend, approve, and then integrate business-level strategies. The goal is to create a strategy-making process that reconciles the decentralized decision making essential to fostering flexibility, responsiveness, and a sense of ownership at the business level with corporate management's ability to bring to bear its knowledge, perspective, and responsibility for shareholders' interests. Common to the success of General Electric, ExxonMobil, Samsung, and Unilever is a strategic planning system that supports a high level of decision-making autonomy at the business level, motivates business leaders toward high performance, shares knowledge between corporate and business levels, and reconciles business initiative with overall corporate control. The typical strategic planning cycle is outlined in Chapter 6 ("The Strategic Planning System: Linking Strategy to Action").

Rethinking Strategic Planning   Since the early 1980s, the strategic planning systems of large firms have been bombarded by criticism from academics and consultants. Two features of strategic planning have attracted particular scorn:

- *Strategic planning systems don't make strategy.* Ever since Henry Mintzberg attacked the "rational design" school of strategy (see Chapter 1), strategic planning systems have been castigated as ineffective for formulating strategy. In particular, formalized strategic planning has been viewed as the enemy of flexibility, creativity, and entrepreneurship. Marakon consultants Mankins and Steele observe that "strategic planning doesn't really influence most companies' strategy." The rigidities of formal planning cycles mean that "senior executives … make the decisions that really shape their companies' strategies … outside the planning process typically in an ad hoc fashion without rigorous analysis or productive debate."[25] They advocate "continuous, decision-oriented planning" of the kind they identify at Microsoft, Boeing, and Textron, where the top management team accepts responsibility for analyzing the critical issues that face the company and then takes strategic decisions.

- *Weak strategy execution.* A widespread criticism of strategic planning systems is that they place insufficient emphasis on executing strategies once they have been agreed. Part of the problem is: "Strategy execution takes longer, involves more people, demands the integration of many activities, and requires an effective feedback or control system to keep a focus on the execution process over time."[26] To link strategic planning more closely to operational management, Larry Bossidy and Ram Charan recommend using *milestones*—specific actions or intermediate performance goals to be achieved at specified dates—can "bring reality to a strategic plan."[27] As we noted in Chapter 2, the *balanced scorecard* offers another approach to cascading high-level strategic plans into specific functional and operational targets for different parts of the organization. Building on their balanced scorecard approach, Kaplan and Norton propose that *strategy maps* be used to plot the relationships between strategic actions and overall goals.[28] Linking strategic planning more closely to its implementation requires a broader role for strategic planning units. Kaplan and Norton recommend upgrading strategic planning units into *offices of strategy management* that not only manage the annual strategic planning cycle but also oversee the execution of strategic plans.[29]

Performance Management and Financial Control

Most multibusiness companies have a dual planning process: strategic planning is concerned with the medium and long term; financial planning and control typically concentrate upon a two-year horizon. Typically, the first year of the strategic plan includes the performance plan for the upcoming year in terms of an operating budget, a capital expenditure budget, and strategy targets that relate to variables such as market share, output growth, new product introductions, and employment levels which are often expressed as specific strategic milestones. Annual performance plans are agreed between senior business-level managers and corporate-level managers. They are monitored on a monthly and quarterly basis. At the end of each financial year, they are probed and evaluated in performance review meetings held between business and corporate management.

Performance targets emphasize financial indicators (return on invested capital, gross margin, growth of sales revenue) and include strategic goals (market share, new product introductions, market penetration, quality) and operational performance (output, productivity). Performance targets are usually specified in detail for the next year, with less detailed performance targets set for subsequent years. Monthly and quarterly monitoring focuses on the early detection of deviations from targets.

Performance targets are supported by management incentives and sanctions. Companies whose management systems are heavily orientated toward demanding profit targets typically use powerful individual incentives to create an intensely motivating environment for divisional managers. At ITT, Geneen's obsession with highly detailed performance monitoring, a ruthless interrogation of divisional executives, and generous rewards for success developed an intensely competitive cadre of executives. They worked relentless, long hours and applied the same performance demands on their subordinates as Geneen did of them.[30] Creating a performance-driven culture requires unremitting focus on a few quantitative performance targets that can be monitored on a short-term basis. PepsiCo's obsession with monthly market share nourishes an intense, marketing-oriented culture. Chief executive Indra Nooyi observed: "We are a very objective-driven company. We spend a lot of time up front setting objectives and our guys rise to the challenge of meeting those objectives. When they don't meet the objectives, we don't have to flog them because they do it themselves."[31] One executive put it more bluntly: "The place is full of guys with sparks coming out of their asses."[32]

Even in businesses where interdependence is high and investment gestation periods are long, as in petroleum, short- and medium-term performance targets can be highly effective in driving efficiency and profitability. The performance management system of BP, the UK-based petroleum company, is described in Strategy Capsule 14.1. However, BP's performance-oriented culture was also identified as a factor in several tragic accidents involving BP including explosions at its Texas City refinery (in 2005) and Deepwater Horizon drilling platform (in 2010).

Strategic Planning and Financial Control: Alternative Approaches to Corporate Management

The approaches to managing the individual business of the multibusiness company outlined in the two previous sections—strategic planning and performance

STRATEGY CAPSULE 14.1
Performance Management at BP

Under the leadership of John Browne (CEO 1995–2007), BP became the most decentralized, entrepreneurial, and performance focused of the petroleum majors. Brown's management philosophy emphasized three principles:

♦ BP operates in a decentralized manner, with individual business unit leaders (such as refinery managers) given broad latitude for running the business and direct responsibility for delivering performance.

♦ The corporate organization provides support and assistance to the business units through a variety of functions, networks, and peer groups.

♦ BP relies upon individual performance contracts to motivate people.

The CEO was responsible for presenting the five-year and annual corporate plans to the board for approval. The goals, metrics, and milestones in corporate plans were cascaded down in the plans for each segment, function, and region. These same goals and metrics were reflected in individual performance contracts. A performance contract outlined the key results and milestones an employee was expected to achieve that year. Progress against targets and milestones in an employee's performance contract were a key determinant of annual bonuses. Performance contracts were the key mechanism for delegating annual plans into commitments by individual leaders. The performance contracts set goals for financial, operational, strategic, and HSSE (health, safety, security, and environmental) performance that were high, but not so high that they couldn't be reached.

Source: Adapted from *The Report of the BP US Refineries Independent Safety Review Panel*, January 2007, with permission from BP International.

management and financial control—represent alternative mechanisms of corporate control. Strategic planning is a process for exerting corporate control over the strategic decisions made by the business units. Performance management, on the other hand, involves establishing performance targets for its businesses, then backing them up with incentives and penalties to motivate their attainment.

The distinction between these two approaches is between *input* and *output* control. A company can control the inputs into strategy (the decisions) or the output from strategy (the performance). Although most companies use a combination of input and output controls, there is a tradeoff between the two: more of one implies less of the other. If the corporate HQ micromanages divisional decisions, it must accept the performance outcomes that will result from this. If the corporate HQ imposes rigorous performance targets, it must give divisional managers the freedom to make the decisions necessary to achieve those targets.

One implication of the tradeoff between *input control* (controlling decisions) and *output control* (controlling performance) is that, in designing their corporate control systems, companies must emphasize either strategic planning or financial control. This is precisely what Michael Goold and Andrew Campbell found among the corporate management systems of British multibusiness companies emphasized

TABLE 14.1 Characteristics of different corporate management styles

	Strategic planning	Financial control
Business strategy formulation	Businesses and corporate HQ jointly formulate strategy	Strategy formulated at business unit level
	The HQ coordinates strategies of businesses	Corporate HQ largely reactive, offering little coordination
Controlling performance	Primarily strategic goals with medium- to long-term horizon	Financial budgets set annual targets for ROI and other financial variables with monthly and quarterly monitoring
Advantages	Effective for exploiting (a) linkages among businesses, (b) innovation, (c) long-term competitive positioning	Business unit autonomy supports initiative, responsiveness, efficiency, and development of business leaders
Disadvantages	Loss of divisional autonomy and initiative Conducive to unitary strategic view Tendency to persist with failing strategies	Short-term focus discourages innovation and long-term development Limited sharing of resources and capabilities among businesses
Style suited to	Companies with few closely related businesses	Highly diversified companies with low relatedness among businesses
	Works best in highly competitive, technology-intensive sectors where investment projects are large and long term	Works best in mature, low-tech sectors where investment projects are relatively small and short term

Source: Based on M. Goold and A. Campbell, *Strategies and Styles* (Oxford: Blackwell Publishing, 1987) with permission of John Wiley & Sons, Ltd.

one or the other.[33] The *strategic planning companies* emphasized the longer-term development of their businesses and had corporate HQs that were heavily involved in business-level planning. The *financial control companies* had corporate HQs that emphasized short-term budgetary control and rigorously monitored financial performance against ambitious targets, but had limited involvement in business strategy formulation—this was left to divisional and business unit managers. Table 14.1 summarizes the key features of the two styles.

Over time, the trend has been for companies to make increasing use of financial control in managing their businesses. This has occurred even in capital-intensive sectors with long time horizons, such as petroleum, where strategic planning has become increasingly oriented toward short- and medium-term financial targets.[34] However, since the financial crisis of 2008–2009, increasing criticism has been levied against short-term focused shareholder value maximization. Whether this will lead to an increasing emphasis on medium- and long-term strategic planning remains to be seen.

Managing Change in the Multibusiness Corporation

The priorities of the corporate managers of large companies have shifted over time. Until the early 1980s, the dominant concern was growth—influenced in part by the belief that the new tools of strategic and financial management would allow companies to transcend industry and national boundaries. From the mid-1980s until the end of the 20th century, the dominant theme was restructuring diversified corporate empires through outsourcing and refocusing in order to create shareholder value. During the present century, especially since the financial crisis of 2008–2009, the greatest challenge has been increasing responsiveness to external change and accelerating the pace of organizational evolution.

Disillusion with the shareholder value maximization model, diminishing returns to cost cutting, and the need to create new sources of value have resulted in profound shifts in the corporate strategies of multibusiness companies. Increasingly, large multibusiness companies have sought to identify opportunities for innovation, for new product development, and for creating value from exploiting linkages both internally between their businesses and externally with other companies. Corporate headquarters are concerned less with the problem of control and more with the problem of identifying and implementing the means for creating value within and between their individual businesses. The use of the term *parenting* to describe the corporate role reflects this growing emphasis on corporate development and the quest for new sources of value. To get a clearer idea of how this has happened let us look at three examples: GE under Jack Welch, IBM, and Samsung Electronics (Strategy Capsules 14.2, 14.3, and 14.4). These examples point to three approaches to stimulating corporate adaptation:

- *Counteracting inertia:* As we noted in Chapter 8 ("The Challenge of Organizational Adaptation and Strategic Change"), organizations resist change. Multibusiness corporations, because of their greater complexity, are especially subject to organizational inertia. One aspect of this is the difficulty that companies experience in reallocating resources among their existing businesses in response to external change and internal performance differences. Not only do multibusiness companies tend to maintain the same allocation of capital expenditures to their individual businesses from year to year, but there is also a bias toward equalizing capital expenditures to each business.[35] This is despite the fact that those companies that did achieve higher levels of capital reallocation outperformed those which did not.[36]

- *Adaptive tension*: At General Electric, Jack Welch, CEO from 1981 until 2001, created a corporate management system that decentralized decision making to business-level managers but created a level of internal stress that counteracted complacency and fostered responsiveness to external change and a constant striving for performance improvement. While GE's "pressure cooker" atmosphere stimulated incremental change, Welch led systemic change through periodic corporate initiatives (such as his "boundarylessness," "six-sigma," and "be #1 or #2 in your industry" initiatives).

- *Institutionalizing strategic change*: As we have already noted, companies' strategic planning systems are seldom sources of major strategic initiatives: the impetus for major strategy redirection usually comes from outside formal strategy processes. The IBM case example shows that strategic planning systems can be redesigned as systems for sensing external changes and responding to the opportunities these changes offer, in other words to build *dynamic capability* at the corporate level.

STRATEGY CAPSULE 14.2
Jack Welch's Reinventing of Corporate Management

Jack Welch's 20-year tenure as chairman and CEO of General Electric began with aggressive cost cutting and an intensive restructuring of the business portfolio, followed by a systematic rebuilding of GE's management systems in which bureaucratic processes were replaced by rigorous performance management. Welch's initiatives included:

◆ *Delayering*: GE's layers of hierarchy were cut from nine or ten to four or five. The resulting broadening of spans of control meant that each executive was managing more direct reports, forcing executives to delegate decision making.

◆ *Changing the strategic planning system*: Welch replaced the staff-led, document-driven process with more personal, less formal, and more intensive face-to-face discussions. Data-heavy business plans were replaced by slim "play-books" that summarized key strategic issues and proposed actions. Half-day review sessions involved open dialogue between divisional heads and Welch and his top-management team.[a]

◆ *Redefining the role of headquarters*: Welch's objective for the corporate HQ was to "turn their role 180 degrees from checker, inquisitor, and authority figure to facilitator, helper, and supporter … Our job is to help, it's to assist, it's to make these businesses stronger, to help them grow and be more powerful."[b] The businesses were also expected to support one another: the "boundaryless company" had permeable internal boundaries allowing "integrated diversity"—the transfer of ideas, business practices, and people freely and easily. "Boundaryless behavior combines 12 huge global businesses—each number one or number two in its markets—into a vast laboratory whose principal product is new ideas, coupled with a common commitment to spread them throughout the company."[c]

◆ *Work-out*: Welch believed that managers should be pressured from both above and below. Work-out meetings were offsite meetings where business unit and departmental heads were required to respond to criticisms and suggestions from subordinates.

Notes:
[a]*General Electric: Jack Welch's Second Wave (A)*, Case No. 9–391–248 (Boston: Harvard Business School, 1991).
[b]Jack Welch, "GE Growth Engine," speech to employees, 1988.
[c]"Letter to Share Owners," General Electric Company 1993 Annual Report (Fairfield, CT, 1994): 2.

● *New business development*: The compression of industry lifecycles means that multibusiness companies are under increasing pressure to revamp their business portfolios. The barriers to releasing mature and declining businesses lie principally in management psychological and organizational politics: once a company has decided to exit a sector, the divestment is typically applauded by the stock market (e.g., GE's sale of its domestic appliance business or HP's decision to spin off its PC and printer business). Developing new businesses represents a bigger challenge. A few companies are able to build whole new businesses on internally developed new products (e.g., 3M), new technology (e.g., Google, Amazon), or new entrepreneurial initiatives (e.g., the Virgin Group). Mature companies sometimes establish *corporate incubators*

STRATEGY CAPSULE 14.3
Reformulating Strategic Planning at IBM

IBM is an evolutionary wonder. It has successfully transitioned from tabulating machines to mainframe computers, to personal computers, to networked information technology, to cloud computing. During the past two decades it has also changed from a hardware to a software and services company. Under its past three CEOs, IBM's pace of evolution accelerated, assisted by IBM's processes for making and implementing strategy.

Under transformational CEO's Lou Gerstner and Sam Palmisano, IBM recreated its strategic planning system around processes for identifying and responding to emerging opportunities and threats. This IBM Strategic Leadership Model includes systems for sensing new opportunities:

- The technology team meets monthly to assess emerging technologies and their market potential.
- The strategy team comprising a cross section of general managers, strategy executives, and functional managers meets monthly to review business unit strategies and recommend new initiatives.
- The integration and values team comprises 300 key leaders selected by top management. The team is responsible for companywide initiatives called "winning plays" that cut across IBM's divisional boundaries.
- "Deep dives" are conducted by ad hoc teams to explore specific opportunities or issues and may

result in recommendations to enter a new area of business or to exit from a particular technology or product market.

The initiatives arising from these processes are then acted on by the three main executing vehicles:

- *Emerging business opportunities (EBOs)* are business development processes that protect new business initiatives from the financial rigor applied to more conventional projects. EBOs were established to develop Linux applications, autonomic computing, blade servers, digital media, network processing, and life sciences.
- *Strategic leadership forums* are three- to five-day workshops facilitated by IBM's Global Executive and Organizational Capability Group. Their purpose is to transform strategic initiatives into action plans and to address pressing strategic issues, such as poor performance, in specific business areas. They are initiated by a senior manager and overseen by the strategy team.
- *The Corporate Investment Fund* finances new initiatives identified by the integration and values team or by EBOs.

Source: J. B. Harreld, C. A. O'Reilly, and M. L. Tushman, "Dynamic Capabilities at IBM: Driving Strategy into Action," *California Management Review* 49 (Summer 2007): 21–43.

for nurturing new startups: Royal Dutch Shell's GameChanger initiative and Nike's Nike+ Accelerator are examples.[37]

- *Top-down, large-scale development initiatives*: Throughout this book, we have pointed to the key role of strategic intent—top-down strategic goals—in unifying and motivating organizational members. In some companies, linking such strategic intent to specific projects and programs has been an especially powerful vehicle for corporate development. The rise of Samsung Electronics to become the world's largest electronics company has been on the basis of

STRATEGY CAPSULE 14.4

Samsung Electronics: Top-down Initiatives that Drive Corporate Development

Samsung is the biggest of South Korea's *chaebols*—groups of companies linked by cross-shareholdings and controlled by a founding family. The Samsung group comprises 83 companies and is dominated by the founding Lee family. The biggest company is Samsung Electronics, the world's largest electronics company in terms of sales. The head of the Samsung group, and chairman of Samsung Electronics, is Lee Kun-hee, son of the founder Lee Byung-chull and father of Jay Y. Lee, president of Samsung Electronics.

The rise of Samsung Electronics is the result of a series of corporate initiatives that were ambitious, focused, long-term, and driven by intense top-down commitment—and capital investment. In 1982, Samsung Electronics resolved to become world leader in memory devices—it achieved this in DRAM chips in 1992. In 2004, its semiconductor investments began focusing on flash memories, where it also established global leadership. Between 2000 and 2009, it established itself as the world's biggest producer of batteries for mobile digital devices, similarly with flat-panel televisions.

These successes involved massive commitments of resources to technology (Samsung receives more US patents than any other company except IBM), manufacturing (for semiconductor production Samsung built the world's biggest fabrication complex), design (with the creation of design centers in five cities of the world), and the Samsung brand. The effectiveness of this resource mobilization has been supported by a culture and working practices that support high levels of coordination and commitment. Samsung's culture is supported by many tales of outstanding endeavor, including constructing a four-kilometer paved road in a single day to ensure that Samsung's first integrated circuit plant could open on time.

Central to Samsung's success in implementing these ambitious corporate initiatives is a new product development process supported by a knowledge management process that allows product development teams to exploit the expertise of the entire company. In April 2009, the Visual Display Division of Samsung Electronics' Digital Media Business had just completed work on a high-resolution LED TV when it was required to roll out a high-definition, 3-D television within a year. Within a week, the two task forces assigned to the project were scouring Samsung Electronics' Test and Error Management System (TEMS). It contained detailed information on every product development project undertaken at the company to identify know-how within Samsung that might assist the new project.

Recent years show no slackening of Samsung Electronics' top-down drive. In 2010–2011, CEO Lee Kun-hee announced 10-year plans to build five major new businesses in solar panels, LED lighting, electric vehicle batteries, biotechnology, and medical devices. By 2014, he was announcing new strategic priorities: Samsung would transition from a hardware to a software and services company.

Source: "Samsung: The Next Big Bet," *Economist* (October 1, 2011); *Samsung Electronics*, HBS Case 9–705–508 (revised 2009); "Samsung Electronics' Knowledge Management System," *Korea Times* (October 6, 2010).

a small number of hugely ambitious development projects that have involved massive commitments of finance, human ingenuity, and effort.

Adaptation to changing circumstances also requires timing. Intel's former CEO, Andy Grove, emphasizes the importance of CEOs identifying *strategic inflection points*—instances where seismic shifts in a firm's competitive environment require a fundamental redirection of strategy. Grove identifies three such key inflection points at Intel: the transition from DRAM chips to microprocessors as its core business, the choice of its x86 series of microprocessors in preference to a RISC architecture, and its decision to replace its faulty Pentium chips.[38]

Finally, managing change in large organizations also requires providing people with the security and certainty to allow them to leap into the unknown. Some of the companies that have been most effective in adapting to change—IBM, Philips, General Electric, and HSBC—have done so while emphasizing the continuity of their heritage and identity. Creating a sense of identity is more challenging for a company that spans several businesses than for one whose identity is determined by the products it offers (McDonald's or De Beers). It goes beyond "strategic relatedness" and "dominant logic" and embraces vision, mission, values, and principles. For example, the French-based multinational Danone has gone through multiple transitions before emerging as primarily a dairy products and baby foods company in the 21st century. Yet throughout jettisoning its glass, beer, and biscuits businesses, the continuity of the father-and-son top management team and a set of business principles relating to employee welfare and corporate social responsibility have provided stability in the face of transformation.[39]

Governance of Multibusiness Corporations

So far, our discussion of the multibusiness corporation has focused on the means by which the corporate headquarters can create value. What we have not discussed is: value for whom? This takes us to the issue of *corporate governance*—the system by which companies are directed and controlled—or more formally:

> Procedures and processes according to which an organization is directed and controlled. The corporate governance structure specifies the distribution of rights and responsibilities among the different participants in the organization – such as the board, managers, shareholders and other stakeholders – and lays down the rules and procedures for decision-making.[40]

The reason corporate governance is an important issue is because of the separation of ownership from control in large companies, which gives rise to the *agency problem:* the propensity for managers (the agents) to operate companies in their own interests rather than in the interests of the owners (see the discussion of "The Cooperation Problem" in Chapter 6). Although corporate governance is an issue for all companies whose owners are not directly engaged in managing the company, it is especially acute in large public corporations, almost all of which comprise multiple businesses. Indeed, in the multibusiness company the problem of agency is compounded by the separation not only of the shareholders from corporate management but also of corporate management from business-level management.

Let us examine three key issues of corporate governance in relation to large, multibusiness firms: the rights of shareholders, the responsibilities of boards of directors, and the role of corporate management.

The Rights of Shareholders

The tendency for companies to be operating in the interests of their senior managers—whose personal goals tend to be the aggrandizement of their wealth, power, influence, and status—rather than in the interests of their owners is primarily a problem for public companies where, typically, ownership is dispersed among thousands of shareholders. Hence, in most countries company law seeks to protect shareholders' interests through establishing their rights to elect and remove members of the board of directors, to share in the profits of the company, to receive company information (including audited financial statements), and to sell their shares.

However, even with these protections, shareholders' incentives to exercise their governance rights are weak: if each shareholder owns only a small fraction of a company and if that company's shares only account for a small fraction of the shareholder's total wealth then the costs of active engagement are high relative to the likely returns. Disgruntled shareholders typically sell their shares rather than oppose the incumbent management team. The short-term orientation of most shareholders further discourages activism: over the past 40 years the average holding period for US equities has fallen from seven years to seven months.[41] At the time of Kraft's highly contentious takeover of British chocolate maker Cadbury, about 30% of Cadbury's shares were owned by hedge funds.[42]

Mechanisms to limit shareholder power typically involve issuing shares with differential voting rights. This allows the founders of companies and their families to exercise effective control while owning a minority of their companies. At News International, Rupert Murdoch and family owned 12% of the company but controlled 40% of the votes. After Facebook's IPO, Mark Zuckerberg owned 18% of the company but controlled 57% of the votes. Shares with differential voting rights are primarily a defense against hostile takeover. Managers as well as founders tend to oppose takeovers, since they are likely to lose their jobs. Hence the use of "poison pill" defenses. For example, Yahoo! defended against a 2008 takeover bid from Microsoft, first, through a provision that any hostile bid would trigger the creation of a rights issue to existing shareholders and, second, by offering a generous severance package to all its employees that would take effect post-merger.

The Responsibilities of Boards of Directors

The board of directors, according to *OECD Principles of Corporate Governance*, has the responsibility to "ensure the strategic guidance of the company, the effective monitoring of management by the board, and the board's accountability to the company and the shareholders."[43] This requires that:

- board members act in good faith, with due diligence and care, in the best interest of the company and its shareholders;
- board members review and guide corporate strategy, major plans of action, risk policy, annual budgets, and business plans; set and monitor performance

objectives; oversee major capital expenditures; select, monitor, and compensate key executives; ensure the integrity of the corporation's accounting and financial reporting systems; and oversee the process of disclosure and communication.

However, there are several impediments to the effectiveness of boards of directors in exercising oversight and strategic guidance:

- The dominance of the board by executive directors. Among many companies (including many US and UK corporations), the top management team are also board members, hence limiting the board's role in providing independent oversight of management. Such overlap also occurs when the roles of board chair and CEO are held by a single person—a feature of one-half of Fortune 500 corporations in the US, though less common in Europe. The weight of evidence points to the advantages of splitting the roles; however, in general it is the competence of the individuals who do the job that is more important than the structural arrangements.[44]
- Boards have become increasingly preoccupied with compliance issues with the result that their role in guiding corporate strategy has shrunk.

Dominic Barton, global managing director of McKinsey & Company, argues that if boards are to become effective agents of long-term value creation they must devote much more time to their roles and need to have more relevant industry experience, and they need a small analytical staff to support their work.[45]

The harshest criticisms of board oversight have been in relation to management compensation. From 1978 to 2013, the compensation of US CEOs, inflation-adjusted, increased 937% compared to 10.2% for the average worker compensation over the same period.[46] The paradox is that the massive payouts to CEOs have been the result of compensation systems designed to align management goals with those of shareholders', especially through the grant of stock options and emphasis on performance-related bonuses. As Table 14.2 shows, the highest-paid CEOs were not always those who delivered exceptional returns to their shareholders. Poor alignment between executive compensation and shareholder value is often the result of linking bonuses to short-term performance, failing to correct for overall stock market movements, and incentives for creating shareholder value not being matched by penalties for its destruction.[47]

Governance Implications of Multibusiness Structures

In the multibusiness corporation, decision-making responsibilities are divided between a corporate headquarters and the individual businesses—typically through a multidivisional structure. As we saw in Chapter 6 (Strategy Capsule 6.1), the multidivisional form was a key development in the emergence of the modern corporation. What are the implications of this structure for corporate governance?

For organizational economist Oliver Williamson, the widespread adoption of the multidivisional structure (or "M-form") was a result of its advantages both in combining centralized direction and localized adaptation and in overcoming the problems

TABLE 14.2 The highest-paid CEOs of 2013

Rank	CEO	Company	Direct compensation 2013 ($m)	Shareholder return in excess of return on S&P 500 (2010–2013)
1	Larry Ellison	Oracle	76.9	−12%
2	Leslie Moonves	CBS	65.4	+351%
3	Michael Fries	Liberty Global	45.5	+147%
4	Richard C. Adkerson	Freeport-McMoRan	38.9	−66%
5	Phillipe Dauman	Viacom	36.8	+101%
6	Robert A. Iger	Walt Disney	33.4	+53%
7	Jeffrey L. Bewkes	Time Warner	32.6	+51%
8	Mark Bertolini	Aetna	31.4	+36%
9	Fabrizio Freda	Estée Lauder	30.9	+46%
10	Jeffrey Immelt	General Electric	28.2	−2%

Source: Hay Group, Financial Times.

of corporate governance that affect large public companies.[48] The multidivisional form facilitates corporate governance in two ways:

- *Allocation of resources*: Resource allocation within any administrative structure is a political process in which power, status, and influence can triumph over purely commercial considerations.[49] To the extent that the multidivisional company can create a competitive internal capital market in which capital is allocated according to past and projected divisional profitability and projects are subjected to a standardized appraisal process, it can avoid much of this politicization.

- *Agency problems*: Given the limited power of shareholders to discipline and replace managers and the weakness of boards to control management, the corporate head office of a multidivisional firm can act as an interface between shareholders and the divisional managers and enforce adherence to profit goals. With divisions designated as profit centers, financial performance can readily be monitored by the head office and divisional managers can be held responsible for performance failures. Hence, multibusiness companies can be more effective profit maximizers than specialist companies.

Empirical evidence offers limited support for Williamson's "theory of the M-form." At some divisionalized companies—General Electric, ExxonMobil, Wesfarmers—corporate management is highly effective at implementing long-term shareholder value maximization. Other multibusiness companies—Enron, WorldCom, Royal Bank of Scotland, and Kaupthing Bank of Iceland—have provided some of the most notorious examples of corporate headquarters becoming vehicles for CEO ambition resulting in the destruction of shareholder value on a massive scale.

Multidivisional companies may also lack the flexibility and responsiveness that their modular should, in principle, be capable of. Henry Mintzberg points to two key rigidities: first, highly centralized decision making within each division as a result of divisional presidents' personal accountability to the corporate head office; second, standardization of management systems and styles across the different businesses of the multidivisional corporation.[50] As already noted, the rigidities of multidivisional companies' allocation of their capital expenditures is indicative of a lack of performance orientation.[51]

The governance issues that multibusiness companies face are highly dependent upon their structures and ownership patterns. As Strategy Capsule 14.5 shows, the other major type of multibusiness company—the holding company—gives rise to different governance issues from the multidivisional corporation.

STRATEGY CAPSULE 14.5
Governance in Holding Companies

A holding company owns a controlling interest in a number of subsidiary companies. The term *holding company* is used to refer both to the parent company and to the group as a whole. Holding companies are common in Japan (notably the traditional *zaibatsu* such as Mitsubishi and Mitsui), in Korea (*chaebols* such as LG, Hyundai, and SK) and the Hong Kong trading houses (Swire, Jardine Matheson, and Hutchison Whampoa). In the US, holding companies own the majority of US banking assets.

Within holding companies, the parent exercises control over the subsidiary through appointing its board of directors. The individual subsidiaries typically retain high levels of strategic and operational autonomy. Unlike the multidivisional corporation, the holding company lacks financial integration: there is no centralized treasury, profits accrue to the individual operating companies, and there is no centralized budgeting function—each subsidiary is a separate financial entity. The parent company provides equity and debt capital and receives dividends from the subsidiary.

Although the potential for exploiting synergies between businesses is more limited in the holding company than in the divisionalized corporation, the holding company structure has important advantages for large family-owned companies. The attractiveness of holding companies is that they allow family dynasties to retain ownership and control of business empires that diversify family wealth across multiple sectors. At the same time, their decentralization allows

effective management of the group without the need for the parent company to develop a tremendous depth of management capability.

Thus, the Tata Group, India's biggest business concern with over $60 billion in revenue and 424,000 employees, is controlled by the Tata family through Tata Sons Ltd, parent company of the group. Among the many hundreds of subsidiaries, several are leading companies within their industries, including Tata Steel, Tata Motors (owner of Jaguar and Land Rover), Tata Tea (owner of the Tetley brand), and Tata Consulting Services. Twenty-seven Tata companies are publicly listed.

In contrast to the public corporations where the key governance problem is the conflicting interests of owners and managers, the governance problems of holding companies relate to the conflicting interests of different shareholders: especially between the founding family and other shareholders. Through its investment company Exor, the Agnelli family controls a business empire that comprises Fiat Chrysler, Ferrari, CNH Industrial, and Juventus Football Club, despite minority ownership of these enterprises. Similarly with the Tata family: cross-shareholdings and shares with differential voting rights allow family control despite minority ownership.

Sources: M. Granovetter, "Business Groups and Social Organization," in N. J. Smelser and R. Swedberg, *Handbook of Economic Sociology* (Princeton: Princeton University Press, 2005): 429–50; F. Amatori and A. Colli, "Corporate Governance: The Italian Story," Bocconi University, Milan (December 2000).

Summary

While corporate strategies in the form of vertical integration, multinational expansion, and diversification have the potential to create value, ultimately, their success in doing so depends upon the effectiveness with which corporate strategy is implemented. This in turn depends upon the role of the corporate headquarters in managing companies that comprise multiple business units. We have identified four principal types of activity through which corporate management creates value within these companies:

♦ *Managing the business portfolio*: deciding which businesses and geographical markets the company should serve and allocating resources among these different businesses and markets.

♦ *Managing linkages among businesses*: exploiting opportunities for sharing resources and transferring capabilities comprises multiple activities ranging from the centralized provision of functions to best practices transfer. The key is to ensure that the potential gains from exploiting such economies of scope are not outweighed by the costs of managing the added complexity.

♦ *Managing individual businesses*: increasing the performance of individual businesses by enhancing the quality of their decision making, installing better managers, and creating incentives that drive superior performance.

♦ *Managing change and development*: although multibusinesses have the key advantage of not being captives of a single industry, exploiting this advantage means the processes, structures, and attitudes that foster new initiatives and create a willingness to let go of the past.

Finally, there is the contentious and perplexing issue of corporate governance. While broad agreement exists over the goal of corporate governance—ensuring that companies pursue long-term value maximization while taking account of the interest of multiple stakeholders—putting in place a system that achieves this goal remains elusive. Establishing corporate systems that are invulnerable to self-serving managers, short-term orientated shareholders, human greed and stupidity, and bureaucratic inertia represents a design challenge that is unlikely to be realized.

Self-Study Questions

1. Unilever—one of the world's leading consumer goods companies—is reviewing its business portfolio in order to address the problems of unsatisfactory growth and profitability. The head of group planning has asked for your advice on the use of portfolio matrices as an initial screen of Unilever's portfolio of businesses. Should Unilever use portfolio analysis and, if so, which portfolio matrix would you recommend: the McKinsey, BCG, or Ashridge matrix?

2. Apply the BCG matrix to the different programs that your institution offers. (You will need to make some informed guesses about market growth rates and relative market share.) Does this analysis offer useful implications for strategy and resource allocation?

3. The discussion of "performance management and financial control" identified two companies where the corporate HQ imposes a strong performance management system on its business units, PepsiCo and BP. To which company do you think a performance management system using financial targets is better suited?

4. Amazon.com, Inc. is under pressure to improve its profitability (in 2014 it earned a net loss of $241m on revenues of $89bn). Amazon is a highly diversified company engaged in online retailing in 14 different countries, audio and video streaming, the production and sale of mobile electronic devices, web hosting and other cloud computing services, and numerous other activities. Of the four main corporate management roles discussed in this chapter—managing the corporate portfolio, managing linkages among businesses, managing individual businesses, and managing change and development—which offers the greatest opportunities for Amazon's corporate headquarters to create value?

5. Would holding companies (such as Tata Group, Samsung Group, the Virgin Group, and Berkshire Hathaway) be more successful if they were converted into multidivisional corporations (such as General Electric, Philips, and Unilever)?

Notes

1. A. Campbell, M. Goold, and M. Alexander. "Corporate Strategy: The Quest for Parenting Advantage," *Harvard Business Review* (April-May 1995): 120–132.
2. For a fuller discussion of the GE/McKinsey matrix, see "Enduring Ideas: The GE–McKinsey Nine-box Matrix," *McKinsey Quarterly* (September 2008).
3. For a fuller discussion of the BCG matrix, see B. Henderson, *The Experience Curve Reviewed: IV: The Growth Share Matrix or Product Portfolio* (Boston: Boston Consulting Group, 1973).
4. In addition, the core predictions of the model have been criticized. Booz Allen Hamilton claims that "dog" businesses can offer good prospects: H. Quarls, T. Pernsteiner, and K. Rangan, "Love Your Dogs," *strategy+business* (March 15, 2005).
5. A. Campbell, J. Whitehead, M. Alexander, and M. Goold, *Strategy for the Corporate-Level* (San Francisco: Jossey-Bass, 2014).
6. M. Goold, D. Pettifer, and D. Young, "Redesigning the Corporate Center," *European Management Review* 19 (2001): 83–91.
7. "Fighting the flab," Schumpeter column, *Economist* (March 22, 2014).
8. Roland Berger Strategy Consultants, *Corporate Headquarters: Developing Value Adding Capabilities to Overcome the Parenting Advantage Paradox* (Munich, April 2013).
9. P&G's Global Business Services: Transforming the Way Business Is Done, http://www.pg.com/en_US/downloads/company/PG_GBS_Factsheet.pdf, accessed July 20, 2015.
10. Deloitte Consulting LLP, *2013 Global Shared Services Survey Results: Executive Summary* (February 2013).
11. M. E. Porter, "From Competitive Advantage to Corporate Strategy," *Harvard Business Review* (May/June 1987): 46.
12. "How Samsung Became a Global Champion," *Financial Times* (September 5, 2004).
13. Porter, "From Competitive Advantage to Corporate Strategy," op. cit.
14. C. S. O'Dell and N. Essaides, *If Only We Knew What We Know: The Transfer of Internal Knowledge and Best Practice* (New York: Simon & Schuster, 1999).
15. A. Campbell, J. Whitehead, M. Alexander, and M. Goold, *Strategy for the Corporate-level* (San Francisco: Jossey-Bass, 2014).
16. D. Shah and V. Kumar, "The Dark Side of Cross-Selling," *Harvard Business Review* (December 2012).
17. J. W. Lorsch and S. A. Allen III, *Managing Diversity and Interdependence: An Organizational Study of Multidivisional Firms* (Boston: Harvard Business School Press, 1973).
18. Campbell et al, *Strategy for the Corporate-level* op. cit.
19. Porter, "From Competitive Advantage to Corporate Strategy," op. cit.
20. T. Copeland, T. Koller, and J. Murrin, *Valuation: Measuring and Managing the Value of Companies*, (New York: John Wiley & Sons, Inc., 1990).
21. R. S. Harris, T. Jenkinson, and S. N. Kaplan, "Private Equity Performance: What Do We Know?" *Journal of Finance* 69 (October 2014): 1851–1882; S. Ghai, C. Kehoe, and G. Pinkus, "Private Equity: Changing Perceptions and New Realities," *McKinsey Quarterly* (April 2014).

22. S. Coll, *Private Empire: ExxonMobil and American Power* (New York: Penguin, 2012).

23. I am grateful to Professor Peter Murmann for information on Wesfarmers.

24. One study found that powerful CEOs have no significant effect on the level of company performance, but are associated with greater variability in company performance. See: R. B. Adams, H. Almeida, and D. Ferrera, "Powerful CEOs and their Impact on Corporate Performance," *Review of Financial Studies* 18 (2005): 1403–1432.

25. M. C. Mankins and R. Steele, "Stop Making Plans; Start Making Decisions," *Harvard Business Review* (January 2006): 76–84.

26. L. Hrebiniak, *Making Strategy Work*, 2nd edn. (London: Pearson, 2013).

27. L. Bossidy and R. Charan, *Execution: The Discipline of Getting Things Done* (New York: Crown Business, 2002): 197–201.

28. R. S. Kaplan and D. P. Norton, "Having Trouble with Your Strategy? Then Map It," *Harvard Business Review* (September/October 2000): 67–76.

29. R. S. Kaplan and D. P. Norton, "The Office of Strategy Management," *Harvard Business Review* (October 2005): 72–80.

30. Geneen's style of management is discussed in Chapter 3 of R. T. Pascale and A. G. Athos, *The Art of Japanese Management* (New York: Warner Books, 1982).

31. Tuck School of Business, CEO Speaker Series, September 23, 2002.

32. "Those Highflying PepsiCo Managers," *Fortune* (April 10, 1989): 79.

33. M. Goold and A. Campbell, *Strategies and Styles* (Oxford: Blackwell Publishing, 1987).

34. R. M. Grant, "Strategic Planning in a Turbulent Environment: Evidence from the Oil and Gas Majors," *Strategic Management Journal* 24 (2003): 491–518.

35. D. Bardolet, C. R. Fox, and D. Lovallo, "Corporate Capital Allocation: A Behavioral Perspective," *Strategic Management Journal* 32 (2011): 1465–1483.

36. S. Hall, D. Lovallo, and R. Musters, "How to Put Your Money Where Your Strategy Is," *McKinsey Quarterly* (March 2012).

37. Shell's GameChanger is a program for developing and commercializing innovative technologies developed both internally and by outside inventors. The program provides funding of about $500,000 per project to 20 to 40 projects annually (www.shell.com/global/future-energy/innovation/innovate-with-shell/shell-gamechanger.html). Nike's start-up accelerator offers seed funding and development support for digital business proposals submitted by external inventors and entrepreneurs (http://www.wired.com/2012/12/nike-accelerator/).

38. R. A. Burgelman and A. Grove, "Strategic Dissonance," *California Management Review* 38 (Winter 1996): 8–28.

39. R. M. Grant and A. Amodio, "Danone: Strategy Implementation in an International Food and Beverage Company," in R. M. Grant *Contemporary Strategy Analysis: Text and Cases*, 8th edn (Chichester: John Wiley & Sons Ltd, 2013).

40. OECD, *Glossary of Statistical Terms* (Paris: OECD, 2012).

41. D. Barton, "Capitalism for the Long Term," *Harvard Business Review* (March/April 2011): 84–92.

42. D. Cadbury, *Chocolate Wars* (New York: Public Affairs, 2010): 304.

43. *OECD Principles of Corporate Governance* (Paris: OECD, 2004).

44. "Should the Chairman be the CEO?" *Fortune* (October 21, 2014).

45. D. Barton, "Capitalism for the Long Term," *Harvard Business Review* (March/April 2011): 84–92.

46. L. Mishel and A. Davis, "CEO Pay Continues to Rise as Typical Workers Are Paid Less," (Washington, DC: Economic Policy Institute, June 12, 2014).

47. P. Bolton, J. Scheinkman, and W. Xiong, "Pay for Short-term Performance: Executive Compensation in Speculative Markets," NBER Working Paper 12107 (March 2006).

48. O. E. Williamson, *Markets and Hierarchies: Analysis and Antitrust Implications* (New York: Free Press, 1975); and O. E. Williamson, "The Modern Corporation: Origins, Evolution, Attributes," *Journal of Economic Literature* 19 (1981): 1537–1568.

49. J. L. Bower, *Managing the Resource Allocation Process* (Boston: Harvard Business School Press, 1986).

50. H. Mintzberg, *Structure in Fives: Designing Effective Organizations* (Englewood Cliffs, NJ: Prentice Hall, 1983): Chapter 11.

51. See notes 35 and 36 above.

15 External Growth Strategies: Mergers, Acquisitions, and Alliances

When it comes to mergers, hope triumphs over experience.

—IRWIN STELZER, US ECONOMIST AND COLUMNIST

OUTLINE

Introduction and Objectives

Mergers, acquisitions, and alliances are important instruments of corporate strategy. They are the principal means by which firms achieve major extensions in the size and scope of their activities—often within a remarkably short period of time. Mergers and acquisitions have created many of the world's leading enterprises:

◆ Anheuser-Busch InBev was once Belgian-based Interbrew. It became the world's largest beer company after a series of acquisitions, including of Labatt (Canada), Bass (UK), Beck's (Germany), AmBev (Brazil), Anheuser-Busch (US), and Modelo (Mexico).

◆ Cable provider Comcast became the biggest US media company through acquiring Metromedia (1992), QVC (1995), AT&T Broadband (2002), Adelphia Communication and MGM (2005), and NBC Universal (2011). In 2015 it was forced to abandon its merger with Time Warner Cable.

Mergers and acquisitions can also have disastrous consequences:

◆ Royal Bank of Scotland's 2007 acquisition of ABN AMRO was a key factor in the bank's near collapse and subsequent rescue by the British government the following year.

◆ The 2006 merger of Alcatel-Lucent created a telecom hardware giant with sales of $25 billion and a market capitalization of $36 billion. By 2015, it had accumulated losses of $5 billion, sales had fallen by 44%, and market capitalization was down by 73%.

Alliances are also important means of corporate development, particularly with international expansion and accessing resources and capabilities—new technology especially. However, they do bear risks: Danone's disastrous relationship with its Chinese partner Wahaha and VW's failed alliance with Suzuki dented both companies' Asian strategies.

If mergers, acquisitions, and alliances are to contribute to firms' strategic objectives, we must recognize that they are not strategies in themselves: they are tools of strategy—the means by which a firm implements its strategy. Hence, in previous chapters, we have already considered the role of acquisitions and alliances in relation to capability building, technology strategy, international expansion, and diversification. In this chapter we draw together these separate strands and consider what we know about managing these modes of external growth.

Given the diversity in their motives, contexts, and outcomes, decisions concerning mergers, acquisitions, and alliances need to be taken after careful attention has been given to their specific strategic goals, the characteristics of the partner firms, and their industry and national environments. We shall develop a structured approach to analyzing the value-creating potential and risks of these arrangements and consider how they can be managed to best achieve a positive outcome.

By the time you have completed this chapter, you will be able to:

◆ Recognize the prevalence and patterns of recent M&A activity.

◆ Appreciate the disappointing outcomes of most mergers and acquisitions, particularly for acquiring firms.

◆ Understand the factors that motivate mergers and acquisitions.

◆ Assess the potential for a merger or acquisition to create value.

◆ Appreciate the challenges of post-merger integration.

◆ Recognize the different motives for strategic alliances and the circumstances in which they can create value for the partners.

Mergers and Acquisitions

The Pattern of M&A Activity

An **acquisition** (or *takeover*) is the purchase of one company by another. This involves the acquiring company (the *acquirer*) making an offer for the common stock of the other company (the *acquiree* or *target company*). Acquisitions can be "friendly," that is when they are supported by the board of the target company, or "unfriendly," when they are opposed by the target company's board—in the latter case they are known as *hostile takeovers*.

A **merger** is where two companies amalgamate to form a new company. This requires agreement by the shareholders of the two companies, who then exchange their shares for shares in the new company. Mergers typically involve companies of similar size (Daimler and Chrysler; Exxon and Mobil), although, as in these two examples, one firm is usually the dominant partner. Mergers and acquisitions may be initiated by the smaller company, especially if it has a higher market capitalization (e.g., AOL and Time Warner). While mergers are less frequent than acquisitions, they are often preferred because of their tax advantages and (for initiating firms) they avoid having to pay an acquisition premium. For cross-border combinations, mergers may be preferred to acquisitions for political reasons (e.g., Alcatel and Lucent, Daimler-Benz and Chrysler, Mittal Steel and Arcelor).

The term *merger* is sometimes used to denote both mergers and acquisitions—I shall follow this popular convention.

Mergers first became prominent in the US during the latter part of the 19th century. To avoid competition, rival firms assigned their companies' shares to a board of trustees which determined prices and marketing policies for all the companies. John D. Rockefeller's Standard Oil was the most prominent of these trusts. Following the Sherman Antitrust Act of 1890, holding companies displaced trusts as the preferred means of consolidating industries. In 1908, General Motors was founded for the sole purpose of taking over Buick Motors; by 1918 it had acquired 22 other automobile companies.[1]

Since the mid-20th century, mergers and acquisitions (M&A) have increased in frequency and have become a generally accepted mode of corporate development—even in Japan, South Korea, and China. M&A activity follows a cyclical pattern, usually correlated with stock market cycles (Figure 15.1). These cycles are also apparent in the types of mergers and acquisitions undertaken. During the 1960s and 1970s, most mergers and acquisitions were directed toward diversification—with conglomerate companies especially active. During 1998–2000, TMT (technology, media, and telecoms) accounted for almost one-half of all mergers and acquisitions. During 2000–2008, emerging markets, financial services, and natural resources were prominent. Table 15.1 shows some of the biggest deals in recent years. During the past two decades, the trend toward consolidation through mergers and acquisitions has been offset by large companies divesting businesses either through spin-offs or sales to private equity groups.

Are Mergers Successful?

The chief attraction of mergers and acquisitions is the speed at which they can achieve major strategic transformations. In addition to Anheuser-Busch InBev and Comcast's acquisition-fueled growth, Fiat's merger with Chrysler allowed it to join the ranks of the world's leading auto makers, and Hewlett-Packard's transformation from hardware toward software and services is based primarily on acquisitions.

Yet these advantages of speed come at a cost. Research into the performance consequences of mergers and acquisitions points to their generally disappointing outcomes. Empirical studies focus upon two main performance measures: shareholder returns and accounting profits.

FIGURE 15.1   Value of M&A deals worldwide, 1995–2014

Sources: Statista; Reuters.

TABLE 15.1 Top-30 mergers and acquisitions of the 21st century

Year	Purchaser	Purchased	Value ($ billion)
2000	Vodafone AirTouch PLC	Mannesmann	183
2000	AOL	Time Warner	165
2013	Verizon Communications	Verizon Wireless[a]	130
2000	Pfizer	Warner-Lambert	90
2015	Royal Dutch Shell	BG Group	81
2000[b]	Exxon	Mobil	85
2007	Royal Bank of Scotland, Banco Santander, Fortis	ABN AMRO	79
2015	Charter Communications	Time Warner Cable	78
2000	Glaxo Wellcome PLC	SmithKline Beecham PLC	76
2004	Royal Dutch Petroleum Co.	Shell Transport & Trading Co	75
2009	Gaz de France	Suez	75
2006	AT&T Inc.	BellSouth Corporation	73
2001	Comcast Corporation	AT&T Broadband	72
2002	Bell Atlantic	GTE	71
2000	SBC Communications	Ameritech	70
2009	Pfizer	Wyeth	68
2014	Actavis	Allergan	66
2004	Sanofi-Synthélabo SA	Aventis SA	60
2002	Pfizer	Pharmacia Corporation	60
2007	Enel SpA	Endesa SA	60
2004	JPMorgan Chase & Co	Banc One Corp.	59
2007	Procter & Gamble	Gillette	57
2015	HJ Heinz	Kraft Foods Group	54
2008	InBev	Anheuser-Busch	52
2008–11	Novartis	Alcon[c]	52
2008	Bank of America	Merrill Lynch	50
2014	AT&T	DirecTV	49
2014	Meditronic Inc.	Covidien PLC	48
2015	Anthem Inc.	Cigna Corp.[d]	48
2012	Glencore	Xstrata	46

Notes:
[a]45% owned by Vodafone.
[b]Announced in 1998; completed in 2000.
[c]Novartis acquired 77% of Alcon from Nestlé in 2008/09, and the remaining 23% in 2010.
[d]Acquisition subject to regulatory approval.
Source: Press reports.

Evidence from Shareholder Returns   The main findings of studies of the impact of merger announcements on the share prices of bidding and acquired companies are that:

- The overall effect of M&A announcements is a small gain in stock market value: typically around 2% of the combined market value of the companies involved.[2] However, these combined returns change over time: data from McKinsey & Company shows that, since 2000, the combined returns to acquiring and acquired firms went from negative to around 12% between 2010 and 2014.[3]

● The gains from acquisition accrue almost exclusively to the shareholders of the acquired firms. Takeover bids must exceed the target company's stock market price: the acquisition premia for US companies averaged around 22% between 2002 and 2013. As a result, the overall returns to the shareholders of acquiring firms averaged –4% between 2000 and 2014.[4]

However, these findings relate only to short-term stock market responses to merger announcements and reflect investors' expectations rather than actual outcomes—which inevitably require several years to materialize.

Evidence from Accounting Profits   To trace the actual outcomes of mergers and acquisitions we need to observe post-merger performance over several years and compare it to the companies' performance prior to merging. The problem here is separating the effects of the merger from the multitude of other factors that influence companies' performance over time. Hence, it is hardly surprising that the many studies that use accounting data to compare post-merger profitability with pre-merger profitability show little consistency in their findings: "the results from these accounting-based studies are all over the map."[5]

The Diversity of Mergers and Acquisitions   The lack of consistent findings regarding the outcomes of mergers and acquisitions is hardly surprising given their diversity. They are motivated by different goals, take place under different circumstances, involve highly complex interactions between the companies involved, and are conducted by management teams of differing competencies. Even when mergers and acquisitions are grouped into different categories, the performance outcomes remain unclear. For example, one might expect that horizontal mergers (which increase market share and offer gains from scale economies) would be more successful than diversifying mergers; among diversifying mergers, it would be expected that the acquisition of firms in related businesses would outperform unrelated acquisitions. Yet both these highly plausible predictions fail to find robust empirical support.

   Even in the case of individual mergers and acquisitions, the outcomes are seldom predictable. Table 15.2 lists mergers and acquisitions from recent decades that the financial press has identified as either successes or failures. Yet, in few cases were the predictions—either of the stock market or by expert commentators—accurate

TABLE 15.2   Success and failure among prominent mergers and acquisitions

Successes	Failures
Exxon–Mobil	Daimler–Chrysler
Procter & Gamble–Gillette	AOL-Time Warner
Verizon Communications	Royal Bank of Scotland–ABN AMRO
Walt Disney Co.–Pixar	Hewlett Packard–Autonomy
Tata Motor–Jaguar Land Rover	Bank of America–Countrywide
Sirius–XM Radio	Alcatel–Lucent
Cemex–RMC	Sprint–Nextel
Bank of America–Merrill Lynch	Sears–K Mart

Source: Based upon lists of "best" and "worst" mergers published by *Forbes*, *Fortune*, CNBC, and Bloomberg.

about the consequences. The disastrous mergers between Daimler and Chrysler and between AOL and Time Warner were much lauded initially. Conversely, the highly successful Exxon–Mobil and Tata–Jaguar Land Rover combinations were greeted with widespread pessimism at the time.

In the absence of clear general findings about the outcomes of mergers, we need to recognize that each combination of companies is a unique event that must be considered on its own merits. This means we must subject M&A decisions to careful strategic appraisal. Let us start by considering the different goals that motivate mergers and acquisitions.

Motives for Mergers and Acquisitions

Managerial motives A major reason why shareholders should view acquisitions with extreme skepticism is that they are so appealing to top management—and to CEOs in particular. Managerial incentives, both financial and psychological, tend to be associated more with a company's size than with its profitability. Acquisition is certainly the fastest way of growing. Even more dangerous is CEOs' quest for celebrity status; again, large-scale acquisitions are the surest way a CEO can gain media coverage while projecting an image of power and influence.

The quest for acquisition may reflect even more primitive biological forces. Anthropologist John Marshall Townsend views the empire-building propensity of male organizational leaders as reflecting the same sexual urges that drive bulls and stags to dominate herds of females and their offspring.[6]

A genetic and hormonal predisposition toward acquisition may be reinforced by psychological factors. The "titans of industry" that built business empires through multiple acquisitions—from railroad magnate E. H. Harriman to Jean-Marie Messier of Vivendi Universal, Fred Goodwin at Royal Bank of Scotland, and Bernie Ebbers at WorldCom—appear to be victims of *hubris*: exaggerated self-confidence that leads to distorted judgment and an ever-growing gap between perception and reality.[7]

The stock market may collude with such behavior. Michael Jensen suggests that CEOs of companies with overvalued equity will make equity-financed acquisitions to help support their share price.[8] AOL's merger with Time Warner was motivated, in part, by its inflated stock market valuation.

A further factor encouraging imprudent mergers and acquisitions is imitation among companies. We have seen that M&A activity is highly cyclical, with a heavy clustering in specific sectors during specific periods: the petroleum mergers of 1998–2002; the telecoms merger waves of 1998–2005 and 2013–2015; and the global consolidation in beer, pharmaceuticals, and metals sectors during the past two decades.[9] This sectoral clustering reflects firms' propensity to follow the leader: if firms resist the urge to merge, they risk being left at the fringes of the dance floor with only unattractive dancing partners left.

Let us ignore for the moment the interests of managers and make the assumption that mergers and acquisitions are directed toward creating shareholder value. We can then distinguish two sources of value creation: *financial* and *strategic*.

Financially Motivated Mergers Mergers and acquisitions can generate shareholder value simply as a result of stock market inefficiencies or through tax benefits or financial engineering.

- Stock market valuations are affected by psychological factors, especially with regard to how risk and opportunity are perceived, resulting in the under- or over-valuation of companies. Better access to information than is available to the stock market, or superior analysis of generally available information, can provide the basis for identifying and acquiring under-valued companies. Under the leadership of Warren Buffett, Berkshire Hathaway has sought well-managed, strategically well-positioned companies whose potential the stock market has not fully recognized.

- Acquisitions can allow a company to reduce its tax bill. For example, a poorly performing company may be an attractive takeover target simply because of the value of its tax credits to the acquirer. Acquisition also provides a mechanism for a company to relocate to a lower-tax jurisdiction. Such "tax inversion" takeovers by US companies attracted critical attention during 2014—for example, Burger King acquired Tim Hortons, the Canadian coffee chain, with the intention of moving its corporate HQ to Canada.[10]

- By changing the capital structure of an acquired company an acquirer may reduce its cost of capital, thereby creating value. Leveraged buyouts (LBOs) are acquisitions of companies (or divisions of companies) that are financed mainly by debt. Such acquisitions can create value as a result of debt being cheaper than equity. Private equity firms—notably Kohlberg Kravis Roberts—have been prominent exponents of LBOs.

Strategically Motivated Mergers   For the most part, value creation from mergers and acquisitions is the result of their potential to increase the underlying profits of the firms involved. On the basis of the major sources of such value creation we can identify several categories of mergers and acquisitions:

- *Horizontal mergers* can increase profitability by means of cost economies and enhanced market power resulting from combining firms that compete within the same market. US airline mergers—including United and Continental Airlines, American and US Airways, and Delta and Northwest—have played a major role in eliminating excess capacity, exploiting scale economies, and moderating price competition in the industry. The proposed acquisition by Staples of Office Depot (just two years after Office Depot acquired OfficeMax) promises similar benefits in the retailing of office supplies.

- *Geographical extension mergers* are the principal means through which companies enter foreign markets. Between 1980 and 2003, HSBC transformed itself from a local Hong Kong bank into one of the world's leading global banks through acquiring 17 different banks across 12 different countries. Similarly, Luxottica has become the world's largest supplier of eyewear through a series of cross-border acquisitions, including Lens Crafters, Ray-Ban, Sunglass Hut, Oakley, and Grupo Tecnol. Acquisition allows a firm to quickly gain critical mass within an overseas market and to overcome the "liabilities of foreignness"—especially lack of brand recognition, lack of local knowledge, lack of local connections, and barriers to distribution. Spurred by the trend toward globalization, cross-border mergers as a proportion of all mergers grew from 23% in 1998 to 45% in 2007.[11]

- *Vertical mergers* involve the acquisition of either a supplier or a customer. In 2013, the world's fourth-biggest mining company, Xstrata, merged with the world's biggest commodities trader, Glencore International, to form a vertically integrated metals supplier. As discussed in Chapter 11 (see Strategy Capsule 11.1), mergers between content producers and distributors have been a major theme in the restructuring of the media sector in recent years.
- *Diversifying mergers.* As we saw in Chapter 13, acquisition is the predominant mode of diversification for firms. The alternative—diversification by means of new business start-up—is too slow for most companies. While internal "business incubators" can successfully develop new business ventures, such start-ups seldom provide the basis for major diversifications. By contrast, acquisition allows firms to quickly establish a major presence in a different sector. Thus, IBM's transition from a hardware to a software and services company involved the acquisition of 115 companies between 2000 and 2011. Diversification may also involve small acquisitions which provide a foundation for internal investment. For example, Microsoft's entry into video games with the launch of Xbox in November 2001 was preceded by the acquisition of several small companies that supplied 3-D graphics hardware, video game controllers, and video games.

Among all these M&A categories, the primary goal may be less to acquire the *business* of the target company as to acquire its *resources and capabilities*. We discovered in Chapter 5 that the most valuable resources and capabilities are those that are not transferable and not easily replicated. Obtaining such resources and capabilities may require acquisition. UK-based Reckitt Benckiser has used acquisition to build a large portfolio of brands: Clearasil skin products, Dettol disinfectant, Durex contraceptives, Finish dishwashing products, Nurofen analgesics, Scholl footcare products, Woolite laundry products, French's mustard and many more. US-based Fortune Brands has followed a similar strategy.

In technology-based industries, established companies regularly acquire small, start-up firms in order to acquire capabilities in emerging areas of technology. During 2010–2014, Google acquired 117 companies to grow its technical capabilities in robotics, imaging, internet security, artificial intelligence, facial recognition, and cloud computing. Each year, Microsoft hosts its VC Summit, where venture capitalists from all over the world are invited to market their companies. Walt Disney's 2006 acquisition of Pixar, the animated movie studio founded by John Lasseter and Steve Jobs, is a classic example of a large established company acquiring a small start-up in order to obtain technical and creative capabilities.

Acquisition can short circuit the tortuous process of developing internally a new organizational capability, but it poses major risks. To begin with, acquisitions are expensive. In addition to the acquisition premium that must be paid, the targeted capability comes with a mass of additional resources and capabilities that are surplus to requirements for the acquiring firm. Most importantly, once the acquisition has been made, the acquiring company must find a way to integrate the acquiree's capabilities with its own. All too often, culture clashes, personality clashes between senior managers, or incompatibilities of management systems can result in the degradation or destruction of the very capabilities the acquiring company was seeking.

Managing Mergers and Acquisitions: Pre-merger Planning

The unsatisfactory performance outcomes of most mergers and acquisitions suggest that M&A decisions need to be based upon a clear understanding by the companies involved of what their strategies are and how the proposed merger or acquisition will contribute to that strategy. This needs to be followed by a detailed and realistic assessment of the likely outcomes of the merger or acquisition. This is easier with some types of mergers and acquisitions than it is with others. In the case of horizontal acquisitions, it is usually possible not just to identify the sources of cost savings from integrating the companies but also to quantify those savings. Other sources of synergy—in particular benefits from revenue enhancement and innovation—are more elusive. In general, acquiring companies overestimate the gains from mergers.

In relation to costs, McKinsey & Company found that 60% of mergers achieved their cost targets, but a quarter of mergers overestimated cost savings by at least 25%. Forecasts of revenue synergies tended to be widely inaccurate: 70% of mergers overestimated revenue synergies. McKinsey suggests that acquiring companies are especially blind to revenue dis-synergies—a major source of which is the tendency for the customers of the acquired firm to defect.[12] In mergers between retail banks, the cost savings from closing overlapping branches can easily be offset by the consequent loss of customers. In the case of many diversifying mergers within financial services, the potential for cross-selling and customers' desire for one-stop shopping have been wildly optimistic. The risk is that acquirers fall victim to their own propaganda: in seeking to persuade the stock market about the benefits of an acquisition, they believe their own inflated estimates of potential synergies.

A realistic assessment of the potential gains from a merger or acquisition requires intimate knowledge of the target company. This is a bigger problem for hostile takeovers than for agreed acquisitions. However, even friendly takeovers are still prone to information asymmetry (the so-called *lemons problem*)—the seller knows much more about the acquisition target than the buyer, so the acquirer can be hoodwinked into overpaying. Hewlett-Packard's disastrous $11 billion takeover of British software firm Autonomy in 2011 is a bitter lesson in the perils of M&A deals.[13]

Managing Mergers and Acquisitions: Post-merger Integration

Even some of the most carefully planned mergers and acquisitions can end up as failures because of the problems of managing post-merger integration. The combination of Daimler-Benz and Chrysler was exemplary in its pre-merger planning; the outcome was disappointing. Not only did Chrysler's problems appear to be intractable but also Chrysler's demands on the group's top management negatively impacted Daimler-Benz's core business.[14]

Frequently, it appears that where the potential benefits of mergers and acquisitions are great so too are the costs and risks of integration. Thus, Capron and Anand argue that cross-border acquisitions typically have the strongest strategic logic.[15] Yet the evidence of DaimlerChrysler, BMW/Rover, and Alcatel-Lucent suggests that when differences in corporate culture are accentuated by differences in national culture the challenge of post-merger integration becomes immense.

It is increasingly being recognized that managing acquisitions is a rare and complex organizational capability that needs to be developed through explicit, experience-based learning. Acquisition performance improves with experience— though not at first. A learning threshold appears, after which subsequent acquisitions add value.[16] However, the learning from acquisitions needs to be explicitly managed, for example the codifying of acquisition processes appears to be conducive to acquisition success.[17]

Ultimately, successful mergers and acquisition require combining pre-acquisition planning with post-acquisition integration. Most case studies of failed mergers identify poor post-acquisition management as the key problem. Yet, in many instances, these integration problems could have been anticipated. Hence, the critical failure was going ahead with the acquisition without adequate assessment of the challenges of post-merger management. In Quaker Oats' acquisition of Snapple ("the billion-dollar blunder"), the critical problem—the impediments to integrating Snapple's distribution system with that of Quaker's Gatorade—was evident to the marketing managers and the franchised distributors of the two companies prior to the takeover.[18] Conversely, Walt Disney's acquisition of Pixar was preceded by an anticipation of the problems that might arise, followed by a careful and sensitive approach to planning, and then implementing, the integration of Pixar (Strategy Capsule 15.1).

Clay Christensen and colleagues argue that acquisition targets need to be carefully selected to match the strategic objective of the acquisition.[19] They distinguish between acquisitions which *leverage a firm's existing business model* from those intended to *reinvent its business model*. Acquisitions that leverage the existing model need to carefully specify the strategic goal—whether it is to cut costs through absorbing a competitor, extend the firm's geographical market, or acquire a new technology. The key is then to determine (a) whether the proposed acquisition will attain the goal in question and (b) whether the resources and processes of the acquired firm are compatible with those of the acquiring firm.

Thus, in assessing whether a proposed acquisition will achieve the goal of reducing cost, Christensen *et al.* pose some basic questions:

- Will the acquisition's products fit into our product catalogue?
- Do its customers buy products like ours, and vice versa?
- Will the acquired company's products fit into our existing supply chain, production facilities, and distribution?
- Can our people readily service the customers of the acquired company?

One of the most important roles that an acquisition can make is in allowing a firm to reinvent its business model. As IBM and Microsoft discovered, such acquisitions can provide a platform for fundamental strategic change. Yet, as HP found with EDS and Autonomy, the risks of this type of acquisitions are high. In terms of post-merger integration, these acquisitions require a distinctive approach. While acquisitions to leverage an existing business model must be integrated within the acquiring firm's business in order to yield their benefits, "if you buy a company for its business model, it's important to keep the model intact, most commonly by operating it separately."[20]

STRATEGY CAPSULE 15.1

Walt Disney Company and Pixar

Most industry observers were pessimistic about Disney's $7.4 billion acquisition of rival animated movie producer Pixar in 2006. Most acquisitions of movie studios had experienced major difficulties: General Electric's NBC acquisition of Universal Studios and Viacom's of DreamWorks. The worries were that Disney's corporate systems would suppress Pixar's creativity and that Pixar's animators would leave. Although the two companies had allied for several years (Disney distributed Pixar movies), the relationship had not been smooth.

Yet the acquisition is generally regarded as being highly successful. Since the acquisition, several Disney/Pixar animated movies, including *Toy Story 3* and *Frozen*, have been massive box office successes as well as generating huge revenues from DVDs, video streaming, and licensing. Disney's CEO, Bob Iger, claims that, compared with the earlier alliance between the two companies, ownership of Pixar has facilitated the closer coordination needed to exploit the synergies between the two companies.

Factors contributing to the success of the merger included:

- A high level of personal and professional respect among the key personnel at Pixar and Disney. In announcing the acquisition, CEO Iger commented: "We also fully recognize that Pixar's extraordinary record of achievement is in large measure due to its vibrant creative culture, which is something we respect and admire and are committed to supporting and fostering in every way possible."

- Rapid and honest communication to Pixar employees about the merger and its implications.

- Careful pre-acquisition planning specifying which elements of Pixar would remain unchanged and which would be adapted to and integrated with Disney's existing activities and practices.

- Appointing Pixar's president, Edwin Catmull, to head Walt Disney Animation Studios.

- Bob Iger's personal experience of working for acquired companies.

- Explicit guidelines designed to protect Pixar's creative culture, including a continuation of Pixar employees' generous fringe benefits and loosely defined employment conditions.

- Honoring commitments: according to Edwin Catmull: "Everything they've said they would do they have lived up to."

In one respect, the Disney–Pixar merger flouted conventional wisdom. According to Bob Iger: "There is an assumption in the corporate world that you need to integrate swiftly. My philosophy is exactly the opposite. You need to be respectful and patient."

Sources: The Walt Disney Company Press Release, "Disney Completes Pixar Acquisition," (Burbank, CA, May 5, 2006); "Disney: Magic Restored," *The Economist* (April 17, 2008); "Disney and Pixar: The Power of the Prenup," www.nytimes.com/2008/06/01/business/media/01pixar.html?pagewanted+all.

Strategic Alliances

A **strategic alliance** is a collaborative arrangement between two or more firms to pursue agreed common goals. *Strategic alliances* take many different forms:

- A strategic alliance may or may not involve equity participation. Most alliances are agreements to pursue particular activities and do not involve any ownership links. The alliance between IBM and Apple announced in July 2014 will develop enterprise mobility apps that draw upon IBM's big data, analytics, and cloud computing capabilities and the supply of iPhones and iPads to IBM's corporate clients.[21] However, equity stakes can reinforce alliance agreements. Google's alliance with Lending Club, the San Francisco-based online platform for making business loans, involved Google taking a minority equity stake in Lending Club.

- A *joint venture* is a particular form of equity alliance where the partners form a new company that they jointly own. CFM International, one of the world's leading suppliers of jet engines, is a 50/50 joint venture between General Electric of the US and Snecma of France. Volkswagen is China's leading automobile brand through its joint ventures with SAIC Motor and FAW Group.

- Alliances are created to fulfill a wide variety of purposes:
  - Star Alliance is an agreement among 25 airlines (including United, Lufthansa, and Air Canada) to code share flights and link frequent-flier programs.
  - Automobili Lamborghini and Callaway Golf Company formed an R & D alliance in 2010 to develop advanced composite materials.
  - GlaxoSmithKline and Dr Reddy's Laboratories (a leading Indian pharma company) formed an alliance in 2009 to market Dr Reddy's products in emerging-market countries through GSK's sales and marketing network.
  - The Rumaila Field Operating Organization is a joint venture among China National Petroleum Company, BP, and South Oil Company to operate Iraq's biggest oilfield.

- Alliances may be purely bilateral arrangements or they may be a part of a network of inter-firm relationships. One form of alliance network is the supplier network, exemplified by Toyota. Toyota's supplier network comprises first-level, second-level, and tertiary suppliers bound by long-term relationships with Toyota and supported by a set of routines that permit knowledge sharing and continuous improvement.[22] Clothing companies Inditex (Zara) and Benetton maintain similar networks. Another type of alliance network is the localized industry cluster that characterizes the industrial districts of Italy (e.g., Prato woolen knitwear cluster, Carrara stonecutting cluster, and Sassuolo ceramic tile cluster). The Hollywood film industry represents another such cluster. Relationships within these localized networks are based upon history and proximity and are informal rather than formal.[23] In sectors affected by technological changes from multiple sources, alliances can play a vital role in innovation and adaptability. Figure 15.2 shows Samsung Electronics' extensive network of alliances.

FIGURE 15.2   The strategic alliances of Samsung Electronics, 2014

Source: Professor Andrew Shipilov, Insead.

Motives for Alliances

Most inter-firm alliances are created to exploit complementarities between the resources and capabilities owned by different companies:

- Bulgari Hotels and Resorts is a joint venture that combines Bulgari's reputation for luxury and quality with Marriott International's capabilities in developing and operating hotels.
- Nike's alliance with Apple links Nike's capabilities with athletic shoes with Apple's microelectronics capabilities to offer real-time biometric data delivered to an iPod or iPhone.
- The world's main airline alliances—Star Alliance, SkyTeam, and oneworld—allow their members access to one another's route networks.
- Sasol Chevron Holdings is a global joint venture that builds synthetic gasoline plants. It combines Sasol's gas-to-liquids technology with Chevron's natural gas reserves and distribution capability.

There has been a debate in the literature as to whether the primary aim of strategic alliances is to *access* the partner's resources and capabilities or to *acquire* them through learning.[24] The strategic alliance between Intel and DreamWorks Animation allows each company to access the other's capabilities in order to jointly develop next-generation 3-D films.[25] Conversely, General Motor's NUMMI joint venture with Toyota was motivated by GM's desire to learn about the Toyota Production System.[26] In most instances alliances are about accessing rather than acquiring capabilities: for most firms the basic rationale of alliances is that they allow the firm to specialize in a limited range of capabilities while enabling the exploitation of specific opportunities that require a wider range of capabilities.[27]

A major advantage of such alliances is the flexibility they offer: they can be created and dissolved fairly easily, their scope and purpose can change according to the changing requirements of the parties, and (for non-equity alliances) they typically involve modest investments. This flexibility and low cost is especially advantageous for making option-type investments.[28] The experimental projects developed by Google within its Google X unit make extensive use of alliances. In developing its driverless car, Google collaborated with Robert Bosch, Nvidia, GM, Ford, Toyota, and Daimler. Google's drone-based delivery system ("Project Wing") is being developed in collaboration with Unmanned Systems Australia Pty.

Alliances also permit risk sharing. In petroleum, most upstream projects are joint ventures. Kazakhstan's Kashagan field, the world's biggest oil discovery of the past 40 years, has required investment of $105 billion, which is spread among a consortium of seven companies including Eni, Shell, and ExxonMobil.

Managing Strategic Alliances

It is tempting to view a strategic alliance as a quick and low-cost means to extend the resources and capabilities available to a firm. However, managing alliance relationships is itself a critically important organizational capability. *Relational capability* comprises building trust, developing inter-firm knowledge sharing routines, and establishing mechanisms for coordination.[29] The more a company outsources its value chain activities to a network of alliance partners, the more it needs to develop the "systems integration capability" to coordinate and integrate the dispersed activities.[30] The delays that plagued the launch of the Boeing 787 Dreamliner are one indicator of the challenges of managing a network of alliances in developing a complex, technologically advanced product.[31]

There is a lack of comprehensive evidence relating to the overall success of strategic alliances. Alliance formations tend to be met with favorable stock market responses,[32] but longer-term data on alliance performance is conspicuously absent. McKinsey observes that even alliance participants lack knowledge of the costs and benefits of their alliances. McKinsey proposes that establishing a system to track alliance performance is a key component of effective alliance management.[33]

Where strategic alliances play a particularly important role and where management problems can be especially acute is in relation to cross-border alliances. When entering an overseas market, the internationalizing firm will typically lack the local knowledge, political connections, and access to distribution channels that a local firm will possess. At the same time acquiring a local firm may not be an attractive option, either because local regulations or ownership patterns make acquisition difficult or because of the large and irreversible financial commitment involved. In such circumstances, alliances—either with or without equity—can be an attractive entry mode. By sharing resources and capabilities, alliances economize on the investment needed for major international initiatives. The FreeMove Alliance formed by Telefonica (Spain), TIM (Italy), T-Mobile (Germany), and Orange (France) created a seamless third-generation, wireless communication network across Europe at a fraction of the cost incurred by Vodafone, allowing each firm access to the mobile network of the leading operator in at least five major European markets.[34]

Some firms have made extensive use of strategic alliances to build their international presence. Figure 15.3 shows General Motors' network of strategic alliances.

FIGURE 15.3 General Motors' network of international alliances

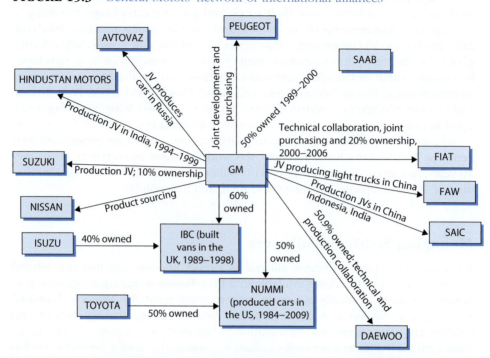

STRATEGY CAPSULE 15.2

Choosing the Right Growth Path: Internal Development *vs.* Contracts, *vs.* Alliances, *vs.* Acquisitions

Choosing the best way to grow requires a careful consideration of a firm's *resource gap*: the resources needed for its strategy relative to the resources it already has.

Capron and Mitchell outline a three-step approach to deciding a firm's growth mode (Figure 15.4).

1. The resources a firm needs for its future development are usually different from those it currently possesses. But how different? The greater the gap, the greater the likelihood it will need to seek these externally rather than develop them internally.

2. If resources are needed from outside the firm, typically the easiest way to obtain them is through a contractual agreement (e.g., licensing a specific technology). But such contracts require agreement over the value of the resources concerned; in the absence of such consensus, a contractual agreement may be impossible.

3. How deeply involved does the firm need to be with its partner in order to effectively transfer and integrate the resources required? If the depth and complexity of involvement is low then an alliance will suffice. However, if closer involvement is needed then the fuller integration potential offered by acquisition is preferable. Researchers at the Wharton School reached a similar conclusion: systemic linkages between the firms—"reciprocal synergies"—favor acquisition; "modular" and "sequential" linkages are better managed through alliances. They also note that choosing whether to ally or acquire depends upon the type of resources involved. Tangible resources such as manufacturing plants or mineral resources are better integrated through mergers and acquisitions; "soft resources" such as people and knowledge can be linked via alliances.

Some of these generated few benefits for GM (e.g., the alliances with Fiat, Isuzu, and Suzuki); others led to full acquisition of the alliance partner (Daewoo, Saab).

For the local partner, an alliance with a foreign firm can also be an attractive means of accessing resources and capabilities. In many emerging-market countries—notably China and India before their accession to the World Trade Organization—governments often oblige foreign companies to take a local partner in order to encourage the flow of technology and management capabilities to the host country.

However, for all their attractions, international alliances are difficult to manage: the usual problems that alliances present—those of communication, agreement, and trust—are exacerbated by differences in language, culture, and greater geographical distance. Danone's joint venture with Wahaha created the largest drinks company in China; however, misunderstanding and misaligned incentives resulted in the joint venture collapsing in 2011.[35]

It is tempting to conclude that international alliances are most difficult where national cultural differences are wide (e.g., between Western and Asian companies). However, some alliances between Western and Asian companies have been highly successful (e.g., Fuji/Xerox and Renault/Nissan). Conversely, many alliances between Western companies have been failures: BT and AT&T's Concert alliance, the GM/Fiat alliance, and Swissair's network of airline alliances. Disagreements over the sharing of the contributions to and returns from an alliance are a frequent source of friction, particularly in alliances between firms that are also competitors. When each partner

FIGURE 15.4 Choosing the right growth path

Sources: L. Capron and W. Mitchell, "Finding the Right Path," *Harvard Business Review*, (September–October 2010): 102–10; J. Dyer, P. Kale, and H. Singh, "When to Ally and When to Acquire?" *Harvard Business Review* (July–Aug 2004): 109–15.

seeks to access the other's capabilities, "competition for competence" results.[36] During the 1980s, Western companies fretted about losing their technological know-how to Japanese alliance partners. In recent years, Western companies have been dismayed by the speed at which their Chinese partners have absorbed their technology and emerged as international competitors. In rail infrastructure, China's state-owned companies have used their partnerships with Germany's Siemens, France's Alstom, Japan's Kawasaki Heavy Industries, and Canada's Bombardier to build homegrown capabilities that are now being exported.[37] The complaints made by Western companies against their Chinese joint-venture partners in 2012 are almost identical to those made against Japanese joint-venture partners in the 1980s.[38]

Firms must also choose which growth mode to follow. Typically, companies have a bias toward either internal or external growth and between either acquisition or alliance without considering carefully enough the relative merits of each. Within the telecom sector, firms that used a combination of growth modes—internal development, alliances, and acquisitions—were more successful than those which stuck to a single mode.[39] Strategy Capsule 15.2 considers the issues involved.

Summary

Mergers and acquisitions can be useful tools of several types of strategy: for acquiring particular resources and capabilities, for reinforcing a firm's position within an industry, and for achieving diversification or horizontal expansion.

However, despite the plausibility of most of the stated goals that underlie mergers and acquisitions, most fail to achieve these goals. Empirical research shows that the gains flow primarily to the shareholders of the acquired companies.

These disappointing outcomes may reflect the tendency for mergers and acquisitions to be motivated by the desire for growth rather than for profitability. The pursuit of growth through merger is sometimes reinforced by CEO hubris, producing a succession of acquisitions that will ultimately lead to the company failing or restructuring.

A second factor in the poor performance consequences of many mergers are the unforeseen difficulties of post-merger integration. However, the diversity of mergers and their outcomes makes it very difficult to generalize about the types of merger or the approaches to integration that are associated with success.

Strategic alliances take many forms. In common is the desire to exploit complementarities between the resources and capabilities of different companies. Like mergers and acquisitions, and like relationships between individuals, they have varying degrees of success. Unlike mergers and acquisitions, the consequences of failure are usually less costly. As the business environment becomes more complex and more turbulent, the advantages of strategic alliances both in offering flexibility and in reconciling specialization with the ability to integrate a broad array of resources and capabilities become increasingly apparent.

Self-Study Questions

1. Most of the mergers and acquisition in Table 15.1 are horizontal (i.e., they are between companies within the same sector). Some of these horizontal mergers and acquisitions are between companies in the same country; some cross national borders. Are there any reasons why horizontal mergers and acquisitions are likely to be more beneficial than other types of mergers and acquisitions (diversifying and vertical) and involve less risk? Among these horizontal mergers and acquisitions, which do you think will be more successful: those between companies in the same country or those that cross borders?

2. All of the CEOs associated with merger-intensive strategies (Jean-Marie Messier at Vivendi Universal, Fred Goodwin at Royal Bank of Scotland, Bernie Ebbers at WorldCom, Steve Case at AOL, Ed Whitacre at AT&T, Jeff Kindler at Pfizer, and Ivan Seidenberg at Verizon) have been male. Does this reflect the predominance of men among the ranks of CEOs, or is there something inherently masculine about the pursuit of growth through merger?

3. Commenting on the Pixar acquisition (Strategy Capsule 15.1), Disney's CEO stated: "You can accomplish a lot more as one company than you can as part of a joint venture." Do you agree? Illustrate your answer by referring to some of the joint ventures (or alliances) referred to in this chapter. Would these have been more successful as mergers?

4. In the motor industry, companies have followed different internationalization paths. Toyota expanded organically, establishing subsidiaries in overseas markets. Ford went on an acquisition spree, buying Volvo, Jaguar, Land Rover, and Mazda. General Motors has made extensive use of strategic alliances (Figure 15.3). Which strategy is best? Which strategy would you recommend to Chinese automobile manufacturers such as SAIC and Dongfeng?

Notes

1. A. P. Sloan, *My Years with General Motors* (Garden City, NY: Doubleday, 1964).
2. S. N. Kaplan, "Mergers and Acquisitions: A Financial Economics Perspective," University of Chicago, Graduate School of Business Working Paper (February, 2006); P. A. Pautler, *Evidence on Mergers and Acquisitions*, Bureau of Economics, Federal Trade Commission (September 25, 2001).
3. "Mergers and Acquisitions: The New Rules of Attraction," *Economist* (November 15, 2014).
4. Ibid.
5. Kaplan, "Mergers and Acquisitions: A Financial Economics Perspective," op. cit., 8.
6. J. M. Townsend, *What Women Want—What Men Want* (New York: Oxford University Press, 1998).
7. R. Roll, "The Hubris Hypothesis of Corporate Takeovers," *Journal of Business* 59 (April 1986): 197–216.
8. M. C. Jensen, "Agency Costs of Overvalued Equity," *Harvard Business School* (May 2004).
9. G. Andrade, M. Mitchell, and E. Stafford, "New Evidence and Perspectives on Mergers," *Journal of Economic Perspectives* 15 (Spring 2001): 103–120.
10. "Warren Buffett Defends Burger King's Tax Deal," *Financial Times* (August 26, 2014).
11. L. Erel, R. C. Liao, and M. S. Weisbach, "Determinants of Cross-Border Mergers and Acquisitions," *Journal of Finance* 67 (2012): 1045–1082.
12. "Where Mergers Go Wrong," *McKinsey Quarterly* (Summer 2004): 92–99.
13. "Hewlett-Packard v Autonomy: Bombshell that Shocked Corporate World," *Financial Times* (August 12, 2014).
14. "DaimlerChrysler: Stalled," *Business Week* (September 10, 2003).
15. L. Capron and J. Anand, "Acquisition-based Dynamic Capabilities," in C. E. Helfat, S. Finkelstein, W. Mitchell, M. A. Peteraf, H. Singh, D. J. Teece, and S. G. Winter, *Dynamic Capabilities* (Malden, MA: Blackwell, 2007): 80–99.

16. S. Finkelstein and J. Haleblian, "Understanding Acquisition Performance: The Role of Transfer Effects," *Organization Science* 13 (2002): 36–47.

17. M. Zollo and H. Singh, "Deliberate Learning in Corporate Acquisitions: Post-acquisition Strategies and Integration Capabilities in US Bank Mergers," *Strategic Management Journal* 24 (2004): 1233–1256.

18. J. Deighton, "How Snapple Got Its Juice Back," *Harvard Business Review* (January 2002).

19. C. M. Christensen, R. Alton, C. Rising, and A. Waldeck, A. "The New M&A Playbook," *Harvard Business Review* (March 2011): 48–57.

20. Ibid, 56.

21. *Apple and IBM Forge Global Partnership to Transform Enterprise Mobility*, http://www.apple.com/pr/library/2014/07/15Apple-and-IBM-Forge-Global-Partnership-to-Transform-Enterprise-Mobility.html, accessed July 20, 2015.

22. J. H. Dyer and K. Nobeoka, "Creating and Managing a High-Performance Knowledge-Sharing Network: The Toyota Case," *Strategic Management Journal* 21 (2000): 345–367.

23. "Local Partnership, Clusters and SME Globalization," *Workshop Paper on Enhancing the Competitiveness of SMEs* (OECD, June 2000).

24. D. C. Mowery, J. E. Oxley, and B. S. Silverman, "Strategic Alliances and Interfirm Knowledge Transfer," *Strategic Management Journal* 17 (Winter 1996): 77–93.

25. "Intel, DreamWorks Animation Form Strategic Alliance to Revolutionize 3-D Filmmaking Technology," (July 8, 2008), www.intel.com/pressroom/archive/releases/2008/20080708corp.htm, accessed July 20, 2012.

26. J. A. Badaracco, *The Knowledge Link: How Firms Compete through Strategic Alliances* (Boston: Harvard Business School Press, 1991).

27. R. M. Grant and C. Baden-Fuller, "A Knowledge Accessing Theory of Strategic Alliances," *Journal of Management Studies* 41 (2004): 61–84.

28. R. S. Vassolo, J. Anand, and T. B Folta, "Non-additivity in Portfolios of Exploration Activities: A Real Options-based Analysis of Equity Alliances in Biotechnology," *Strategic Management Journal* 25 (2004): 1045–1061.

29. P. Kale, J. H. Dyer, and H. Singh, "Alliance Capability, Stock Market Response and Long Term Alliance Success," *Strategic Management Journal* 23 (2002): 747–767.

30. A. Prencipe, "Corporate Strategy and Systems Integration Capabilities," in A. Prencipe, A. Davies, and M. Hobday (eds), *The Business of Systems Integration* (Oxford: Oxford University Press, 2003): 114–132.

31. "Dreamliner Becomes a Nightmare for Boeing," *Der Spiegel* (March 3, 2011), http://www.spiegel.de/international/business/0,1518,753891,00.html, accessed 20 July, 2015.

32. S. H. Chana, J. W. Kensinger, A. J. Keown, and J. D. Martine, "Do strategic alliances create value?" *Journal of Financial Economics* 46 (November 1997): 199–221.

33. J. Bamford and D. Ernst, "Measuring Alliance Performance," *McKinsey Quarterly, Perspectives on Corporate Finance and Strategy* (Autumn 2002): 6–10.

34. Freemove: *Creating Value through Strategic Alliance in the Mobile Telecommunications Industry*, IESE Case 0-305-013 (2004).

35. S. M. Dickinson, "Danone v. Wahaha: Lessons for Joint Ventures in China," www.chinalawblog.com/DanoneWahahaLessons.pdf, accessed July 20, 2015.

36. G. Hamel, "Competition for Competence and Inter-partner Learning within International Strategic Alliances," *Strategic Management Journal* 12 (1991): 83–103.

37. "China: A Future on Track," *Financial Times* (September 24, 2010).

38. R. Reich and E. Mankin, "Joint Ventures with Japan Give Away Our Future," *Harvard Business Review* (March/April 1986).

39. L. Capron and W. Mitchell, "Finding the Right Path," *Harvard Business Review*, (September/October 2010): 102–110.

16 Current Trends in Strategic Management

In any field of human endeavor you reach a point where you can't solve new problems using the old principles. We've reached that point in the evolution of management. When you go back to the principles upon which our modern companies are built—standardization, specialization, hierarchy, and so on—you realize that they are not bad principles, but they are inadequate for the challenges that lie ahead.[1]

—GARY HAMEL, MANAGEMENT THINKER

The truth is you don't know what is going to happen tomorrow. Life is a crazy ride, and nothing is guaranteed.

—EMINEM, HIP-HOP ARTIST AND SONGWRITER

The future ain't what it used to be.

—YOGI BERRA, BASEBALL PLAYER AND COACH

OUTLINE

Introduction

The first two decades of the 20th century were a period of intense turbulence: radical new technologies, the birth of the modern corporation, the beginnings of management, and human slaughter on an unprecedented scale. The first two decades of the 21st century are similar in terms of turbulence and uncertainty. Our challenge in this chapter is to identify the forces that are reshaping the business environment, to assess their implications for strategic management, and to consider what new ideas and tools managers can draw upon to meet the challenges ahead.

We are in poorly charted waters and, unlike the other chapters of this book, this chapter will not equip you with proven tools and frameworks that you can deploy directly in case analysis or in your own companies. Our approach is exploratory. We begin by reviewing the forces that are reshaping the environment of business. We will then draw upon concepts and ideas that are influencing current thinking about strategy and the lessons offered from leading-edge companies about strategies, organizational forms, and management styles that can help us to meet the challenges of this demanding era.

The New Environment of Business

One of most striking parallels between the early 20th and early 21st century concerns the role of technological innovation. In the 20th century, it was electricity, the automobile and the telephone; in the 21st century, digital technologies are the primary source of transformation. Both periods also saw massive political changes: in the early 20th century, the rise of the nation state, the collapse of colonial empires, and the birth of Marxist-Leninism; in the early 21st century, the rise of religious extremism, the decline of liberalism, and discontent with political leaders and political systems. During both periods popular disaffection with big business was a common theme. Let us focus upon four key drivers of change in the 21st century.

Technology

The invention of the integrated circuit in 1958 marked the beginning of the digital era. However, it was not until the advent of the microprocessor (1971), commercial internet (1989), and wireless broadband (2001) that the digital revolution became a truly disruptive force.

On January 27, 2015 (the day on which I am writing these words), two pieces of news confirm the disruptive impact of digital technologies: first, Apple has announced the biggest quarterly profits of any company in history; second, Radio Shack, a pioneer of the microcomputer revolution, is preparing to file for bankruptcy.

Yet a peek into the development projects of Google, Amazon, Apple, and IBM suggests that the full impact of the digital revolution has yet to be felt. The "internet of things"—the connectivity of physical objects such as cars and houses together with sensors, big data analysis, and intelligent systems—promises to affect a wide range of traditional industries. For instance, the impact of driverless vehicles will likely eliminate not only millions of jobs in commercial and personal transportation but also the need for individuals to own cars.

Intelligent systems will inevitably displace many management activities. The economist Brian Arthur refers to the "second economy," where economic activity is coordinated entirely by machines.[2] My visit to the supermarket today was devoid of human contact. I used the self-service checkout. Yet my few purchases set in motion a chain of economic activity most of which is coordinated entirely by machines. The information on my purchases together with those of my fellow shoppers will link with shelf-filling activity within the store. It will also determine deliveries from warehouse to store. Amalgamated with data from other stores, it will automatically adjust manufacturers' production schedules and supply logistics.

Technology is also shifting the boundaries between firms and markets in fundamental ways. The efficiency with which web- and smartphone-based services such as Uber, Handy, and Medicast can link the providers of particular services with their consumers allows freelancers to displace firms across a range of industries.[3] By 2015, Airbnb was offering more rooms than either Hilton or Marriott, while in December 2014, Uber, with only 1,300 employees, had 162,000 drivers in the US alone. Management consulting firms are also threatened by freelancer providers such as Eden McCallum and Business Talent Group.[4]

Competition

Amidst the many uncertainties that firms face when looking into the future, there is one near certainty: economic growth, throughout the world, will remain sluggish for several years to come. In the aftermath of the financial crisis of 2008–2009, most governments continue to run budget deficits and are heavily indebted. Low levels of public sector investment and the absence of fiscal stimuli together with the budgetary caution of both companies and households offers little prospect for robust global growth—especially given the slowing of the Chinese and South American economies. Hence, in most sectors of the world economy, excess capacity is the norm, causing strong price competition and thin profit margins.

As we observed in Chapter 12 ("Implications of International Competition for Industry Analysis"), the entry into world markets by companies from emerging-market countries has added considerably to competitive pressures. In wireless handsets, 67 new companies entered the industry between 2000 and 2009, 34 of them from China and Taiwan. Many of these new suppliers began as OEM suppliers and then went on to develop their own brands thereby competing with their former customers.[5]

The technological trends described in the previous section are also sources of new competition. Most of the companies identified by the *Financial Times* as the "disruptors of 2014" based their disruptive business models on digital technologies (Figure 16.1).

Linked to the increasing intensity of competition in most markets and the challenges that established market leaders face, either from low-cost competitors from emerging markets or new entrants with innovative business models, competitive advantage has become increasingly fleeting. We shall return to the challenges that firms face from the increasing impermanence of competitive advantage when we consider strategies for coping with the new environment of business.

FIGURE 16.1 The "Disruptors of 2014" (as nominated by *Financial Times* journalists)

Technology
- Alibaba (financial services)
- Xiaomi (smartphones)
- Aereo (TV)
- Tinder (dating)
- "Right-to-be-forgotten" activist, Mario Costeja González (Google)

Transport
- Tesla (auto industry)
- Ford F-150 (truck/auto manufacture)
- Embraer (defense aerospace)
- Uber (world taxi industry)

Retail
- Lazada (South-East Asian retailing)
- Aldi (UK supermarkets)
- Just Eat (home-delivered meals)
- Indian e-commerce e.g., Flipkart, Snapdeal (India's traditional retail sector)

Banks
- Lending Club (business loans)
- iMatchative (hedge fund investing)
- Bob Diamond's Mara Group (private investment in Africa)

Telecoms
- Hutchison Whampoa's Three (European wireless telecom)

Real Estate
- Appear Here (retail real estate leasing)
- eMoov (residential real estate)

Media
- Netflix (TV and movie industries)
- SoundCloud (recorded music)

Note: The disrupted sector is shown in parentheses after the name of the disruptor.
Source: Adapted from "Disrupters Bring Destruction and Opportunity," *Financial Times* (December 30, 2014).

Market Volatility

Most of the world's major markets have experienced high levels of volatility during the 21st century. While stock market volatility has not been usual in historical context, in commodity and currency markets volatility has been unprecedented in modern times. The price of Brent crude per barrel increased from $87 to $147 between January and June 2008 before falling to $45 five months later; from September 2014 to January 2015, it again declined sharply—from $100 to $46. Foreign exchange rates experienced similar volatility: in the four months to January 2015, the euro declined by 14% against the US dollar, while the Russian ruble fell by 48%.

This volatility reflects the impact of unexpected events, both political—such as the turmoil across much of the Arab world and Russia's incursion into Ukraine—and economic, such as the financial crisis of 2008–2009. This raises the issue of whether the improbable and unpredicted events that create volatility—what have been called *black swan events*[6]—are random occurrences or whether they reflect systematic factors. The latter seems likely. A feature of the global economy, and human society in general, is increasing interconnectedness through trade, financial flows, markets, and communication. Systems theory predicts that increasing levels of interconnectedness within a complex, nonlinear system increase the tendency for small initial movements to be amplified in unpredictable ways. Global political phenomena—such as the rise of Al Qaeda, the insurrections against autocratic governments throughout

North Africa and the Middle East, and the rise of radical populism throughout much of the West—all suggest systematic forces at work.

Moreover, the eroding political and economic power of the US and Europe limits the capacity of these traditional custodians of the global economic system to control these disruptive forces. The rise of China together with other emerging countries is creating a multipolar world where the mature industrialized nations and the institutions they created—the World Bank, IMF, and OECD—are less able to offer global leadership.[7]

Social Forces and the Crisis of Capitalism

For organizations to survive and prosper requires that they adapt to the values and expectations of society—what organizational sociologists refer to as *legitimacy*.[8] One fall-out from the 2008–2009 financial crisis was the loss of legitimacy that many businesses suffered—banks in particular. This negatively affected their reputations among consumers, the morale of their employees, the willingness of investors and financiers to provide funding, and the government policies toward them. As Chapter 2 ("Beyond Profit: Values and Corporate Social Responsibility") outlined, the loss of social legitimacy that affected many commercial and investment banks was a greater threat to their survival than their weak balance sheets. Similarly with Rupert Murdoch's media empire: its "phone hacking" scandal ultimately triggered the breakup of News Corp.[9]

The notion that the business enterprise is a social institution that must identify with the goals and aspirations of society has been endorsed by many management thinkers, including Peter Drucker, Charles Handy, and Sumantra Ghoshal.[10] The implication is that when the values and attitudes of society are changing so must the strategies and behaviors of companies. While anti-business sentiment has for the most part been restricted to the fringes of the political spectrum—neo-Marxists, environmentalists, and anti-globalization activists—corporate scandals, ranging from Enron in 2001 to Volkswagen in 2015, have moved disdain for business corporations and their leaders into the mainstream of public opinion.

The growing disenchantment with market capitalism is reflected in the unraveling of the *Washington Consensus*—the widely held view that the competitive market economy based on private enterprise, deregulation, flexible labor markets, and liberal economic policies offers the best basis for stability and prosperity and, according to the World Bank and the IMF, the primary foundation for economic development.

Central to the fraying legitimacy of market capitalism has been widespread dismay over changes in the distribution of income and wealth—an issue highlighted by Thomas Piketty's *Capital in the 21st Century*.[11] Figure 16.2 offers one indication of the growing income disparities generated by the modern economy. A popular slogan from the Occupy Wall Street protest of 2008–2010 was, "We are the 99%!"—a reference to the 1% of the population that owns 42% of America's personal wealth.[12] The leaders of banks and other financial institutions have provided lightning rods for popular outrage over the incongruence between their massive financial compensation and the destruction they have brought to the jobs and living standards of the masses.

The rise of China has further undermined confidence in the efficacy of market capitalism. Between 2000 and 2014, the number of Chinese companies among the Global Fortune 500 grew from 10 to 95—most of them state-owned enterprises. In 2014, China overtook the US to become the world's biggest economy.

FIGURE 16.2 Ratio of average CEO compensation to that of average worker, USA, 1965–2013

Source: Institute for Economic Policy

The potential for **state capitalism** to combine the entrepreneurial drive of capitalism with the long-term orientation and coordinated resource deployment of government planning is one aspect of a growing interest in alternative forms of business enterprise.

- *Cooperatives*—businesses that are mutually owned by consumers (e.g., credit unions), employees (e.g., the British retailing giant John Lewis Partnership), or by independent producers (e.g., agricultural marketing cooperatives)— have captured particular attention. Cooperatives account for 21% of total production in Finland, 17.5% in New Zealand, and 16.4% in Switzerland. In Uganda and other African countries, cooperatives are the dominant organizational form in agriculture.[13]
- *Social enterprises* is a term applied to business enterprises directed toward social goals. Social enterprises may be for-profit or not-for-profit companies (and may include both charities and cooperatives). A leading example of a social enterprise is Muhammad Yunus' Grameeen Bank—a for-profit company that encourages business development among poor people through microcredit. The majority of US states now amended their corporate laws to permit *benefit corporations*: companies with explicit goals to pursue social and environmental goals as well as profit.[14]

Adapting to society's growing demands for fairness, ethics, and sustainability presents challenges for business leaders that extend beyond the problems of reconciling societal demands with shareholder interests. Should a company determine unilaterally the values that will govern its behavior or does it seek to reflect those of the society in which it operates? Companies that embrace the values espoused by their founders are secure in their own sense of mission and can ensure a long-term consistency in their strategy and corporate identity (e.g., Walt Disney Company and Walmart with respect to founders Walt Disney and Sam Walton). However, there is a risk that these values become out of step with those of society as a whole or with the requirements for business effectiveness. Thus, at British retailer Marks & Spencer and chocolate maker Cadbury, social responsibility and paternalism toward employees became a source of rigidity rather than a competitive advantage. Other companies have experienced the reverse: by taking account of the interests and needs of different stakeholders and of society at large, some companies report a greater responsiveness to their external environment, greater commitment from employees, and enhanced creativity.

New Directions in Strategic Thinking

These features of the 21st century business environment have created unprecedentedly challenging conditions under which to formulate and implement business strategy. One indicator of the external pressures impacting firms is evident in the rising numbers of company failures in recent years. In the US, business bankruptcy filings grew from 19,695 in 2006 to a peak of 60,837 in 2009 before dropping to 47,806 in 2011. Among these bankruptcies, some companies are victims of intense competition, such as AMR (the parent of American Airlines); others have fallen victim to technological disruption, such as Eastman Kodak, MF Global, Dynegy Holdings, Borders Group, Blockbuster Entertainment, and Radio Shack. The pressures of a more demanding business environment are forcing companies to rethink their strategies.

Reorienting Corporate Objectives

The reaction against shareholder value maximization culminated in one of its leading exponents, former GE chairman Jack Welch, declaring that shareholder value maximization was a "dumb idea." However, the issue of whether companies should be operated in the interests of their owners, in the interests of their stakeholders, or in the interests of society as a whole remains unresolved. Recent efforts to reconcile a broader societal role for firms with shareholder value maximization have emphasized either the need for companies to maintain social legitimacy or the potential for such a broadening of goals to open up new avenues for value creation—the central theme of Porter and Kramer's *shared value* concept.[15] The appeal of this broader concept of the role of the firm is that it maintains the fundamental orientation of the firm toward earning profit or, equivalently, increasing the value of the firm.

The key reorientation of the doctrine of shareholder value creation is away from its 1990s preoccupation with stock market valuation toward a refocusing of top management priorities up on the fundamental drivers of enterprise value. This reflects a recognition that management cannot create stock market value: only the stock market can do that. What management can do is to generate the stream of profits that the stock market capitalizes into its valuation of the firm. Indeed, as I argued in

Chapter 2, the critical focus of top management should not even be profits; it should be the strategic factors that drive profits: operational efficiency, customer satisfaction, innovation, and new product development.

The implication is not that business leaders abandon shareholder value maximization in favor of some impractical goal of reconciling stakeholders' diverse interests or to seek some new model of capitalism, but that they should focus more determinedly on identifying and managing the basic drivers of value creation. Most useful antidote to the threats of corporate empire building, CEO hubris, and blind faith in new business models is likely to be a stronger emphasis on the basic principles of strategy analysis. As Dick Rumelt has pointed out: "Bad strategy abounds!"[16]

Seeking More Complex Sources of Competitive Advantage

Focusing on strategy fundamentals does not necessarily lead to simple strategies. As we have already observed, both in this chapter and in Chapter 7, in today's dynamic business environment competitive advantages are difficult to sustain. According to Rita McGrath, firms need to "constantly start new strategic initiatives, building and exploiting many transient competitive advantages at once. Though individually temporary, these advantages, as a portfolio, can keep companies in the lead over the long run."[17] Complex competitive advantages are more sustainable than simple advantages. A key feature of companies that have maintained both profitability and market share over many years—for example Toyota, Walmart, 3M, Canon, Swatch, and Samsung—is their development of multiple layers of competitive advantage, including cost efficiency, differentiation, innovation, responsiveness, and global learning. As we shall see, reconciling the different requirements of different performance dimensions imposes highly complex organizational challenges that are pushing companies to fundamentally rethink their structures and management systems.

This pursuit of multiple capabilities in contrast to building a single core capability recalls Isaiah Berlin's classification of intellectuals into foxes and hedgehogs: "The fox knows many things; the hedgehog knows one big thing."[18] Despite Jim Collins' praise for companies that have a single penetrating insight into the complexities of their business environments, it appears that companies that have built their strategy on such insight often have difficulty in adapting to subsequent changes in their markets: Toys "R" Us with big-box retailing, Dell with its direct sales model, General Motors with its multi-brand market segmentation strategy, Blockbuster with movie rentals.[19]

The quest for more complex sources of competitive advantage also involves strategies that look beyond industry boundaries to exploit linkages across sectors. The remarkable competitive advantages built by Apple, Google, and Amazon are the result of strategies that coordinate entire ecosystems of linked businesses. Recent interest in business model innovation has been bolstered by the opportunities to exploit sources of value resulting from such linkages.[20] For example, Google's core product, its search engine, generates almost no direct revenue and 24% of its 2014 revenue was from advertising on non-Google websites.

Managing Options

As we observed in the last section of Chapter 2 ("Strategy as Options Management"), the value of the firm derives not only from the present value of its profit stream (cash flows) but also from the value of its options. During turbulent times, real options—growth options, abandonment options, and flexibility options—become increasingly important as sources of value. Taking account of options has typically involved adjustment of investment appraisal methodologies so that option values are incorporated into capital budgeting decisions. However, the implications of option thinking extend to the most fundamental aspects of a firm's strategy—and to the tools employed in analysing strategy. To take just one example of how a failure to take account of option value can lead to a misguided strategy, consider conventional approaches to corporate finance. The attraction of leveraged buyouts is to create shareholder value through substituting low-cost debt (the interest payments on which are tax deductible) for high-cost equity. Yet, such reductions in the cost of capital also destroy option value: highly leveraged firms have fewer opportunities to take advantage of unexpected investment opportunities (including acquisition) and have less flexibility in adjusting to an unexpected downturn.

Viewing strategy as the management of a portfolio of options shifts the emphasis of strategy formulation from making resource commitments to the creation of opportunities. Strategic alliances are especially useful in creating growth options while allowing firms to focus on a narrow set of capabilities.

The adoption of options thinking also has far-reaching implications for our tools and frameworks of strategy analysis. For example:

- Industry analysis has taken the view that decisions about industry attractiveness depend on profit potential. However, if industry structure becomes so unstable that forecasting industry profitability is no longer viable, it is likely that industry attractiveness will depend more on option value. From this perspective, an attractive industry is one that is rich in options. Industries that produce many different products, comprise multiple segments, have many strategic groups, and utilize different technologies—such as consumer electronics, semiconductors, packaging, and investment banking—offer more strategic options than electricity or steel or car rental.

- An options approach also has major implications for the analysis of resources and capabilities. In terms of option value, an attractive resource is one that can be deployed in different businesses and support alternative strategies. A technological breakthrough in nanotechnology is likely to offer greater option value than a new process that increases the energy efficiency of blast furnaces. A relationship with a rising politician is a resource that has more option value than a coalmine. Similarly with capabilities: a highly specialized capability, such as expertise in the design of petrochemical plants, offers fewer options than expertise in the marketing of fast-moving consumer goods. Dynamic capabilities are important because they generate new options: "Dynamic capabilities are the organizational and strategic routines by which firms achieve new resource combinations as markets emerge, collide, split, evolve, and die."[21]

Understanding Strategic Fit

A central theme throughout this book is the notion of *strategic fit*. The basic framework for strategy analysis presented in Chapter 1 (Figure 1.2) emphasized how strategy must *fit* with the business environment and with the firm's resources and capabilities. We subsequently viewed the firm as an *activity system* where all the activities of the firm fit together (Figure 1.3). In Chapter 6, we introduced *contingency approaches* to organizational design: the idea that the structure and management systems of the firm must fit with its strategy and its business environment. In Chapter 8, we saw how this fit between strategy, structure, and management systems can act as a barrier to change. In recent years our understanding of fit (or contingency) has progressed substantially as a result of two major concepts: complementarity and complexity. These concepts offer new insights into linkages within organizations.

Complementarity Research Complementarity research addresses the linkages among a firm's management practices. Thus, in the transition from mass manufacturing to lean manufacturing it has been observed that reorganizing production processes tends to be counterproductive without simultaneously adapting human resource practices.[22] Similarly, a six-sigma quality program needs to be accompanied by changes in incentives, recruitment policies, product strategy, and capital budgeting practices.[23]

The complementarity of management practices makes generalization about strategy very difficult: every firm is unique and must create a unique configuration of strategic variables and management practices. In practice, strategic choices tend to converge around a limited number of *configurations*. Thus, successful adaptation among large European companies was associated with a small number of configurations of organizational structure, processes, and boundaries.[24]

Complexity Theory Organizations—like the weather, flocks of birds, human crowds, and seismic activity—are *complex systems* whose behavior results from the interactions of a large number of independent agents. This behavior of complex systems has interesting features that have important implications for the management of organizations:

- *Unpredictability*: The behavior of complex adaptive systems cannot be predicted in any precise sense: there is no convergence toward stable equilibria, cascades of change are constantly interacting to reshape competitive landscapes, and small changes typically have minor consequences but may also trigger major movements.[25]
- *Self-organization*: Complex biological and social systems have a capacity for self-organizing. Bee colonies and shoals of fish show coordinated responses to external threats and opportunities without anyone giving orders. Quite sophisticated synchronized behavior can be achieved through adopting just a few simple rules. There are three main requirements for **self-organization**: *identity* that permits a common sense-making process within the organization, *information* that provides the possibility of synchronized behavior, and *relationships* that are the pathways through which information is transformed into intelligent, coordinated action.[26]
- *Inertia, chaos, and evolutionary adaptation*: Complex systems can stagnate into inertia (stasis) or become disorderly (chaos). In between is an intermediate region where the most rapid evolutionary adaptation occurs. Positioning at this *edge of chaos* results in both small, localized adaptations and occasional

evolutionary leaps that allow the system to attain a higher *fitness peak.*[27] Kaufman's *NK model,* which allows the behavior of complex systems to be simulated, has been widely applied to the study of organizations.[28]

The Contextuality of Linkages within the Firm   The implications of both complementarity and complexity approaches depends upon *contextuality* of the linkages among activities—the extent to which the benefits from any particular activity depend upon which other activities are taking place.[29] There are two dimensions of this contextuality. First, the *contextuality of activities:* whether the performance effects of an activity are dependent or independent of the other activities that a firm undertakes. Second, *contextuality of interactions:* whether the interactions between activities are the same for all firms, or whether they are specific to individual contexts.[30]

Acknowledging the different ways in which a firm's activities interact offers insight into some of the complexities of strategic management. In particular, it helps us to understand why a strategy that has worked well for one company is a dismal failure when adopted by a competitor; it points to the risks in attempting to transfer "best practices" either from another firm or even from another part of the same firm; it allows us to see why piecemeal adaptations to external change often make the situation worse rather than better; and it reveals why post-merger integration is so treacherous.

Redesigning Organizations

A more complex, more competitive business environment requires that companies perform at higher levels with broader repertoires of capabilities. Building multiple capabilities and pursuing multiple performance dimensions presents dilemmas: producing at low cost while also innovating, deploying the massed resources of a large corporation while showing the entrepreneurial flair of a small start-up, achieving reliability and consistency while also adapting to individual circumstances. We addressed one of these dilemmas: the challenge of *ambidexterity*—optimizing efficiency and effectiveness for today while adapting to the needs of tomorrow—in Chapter 8. In reality, the problem reconciling incompatible strategic goals is much broader: the challenge of today is reconciling *multiple* dilemmas—this requires *multi-dexterity.*

Implementing complex strategies with conflicting performance objectives takes us to the frontiers of organizational design. We know how to devise structures and systems that drive cost efficiency; we know the organizational conditions conducive to innovation; we know a good deal about the characteristics of *high-reliability organizations,* we are familiar with the sources of entrepreneurship. But how on earth do we achieve all of these simultaneously?

Multi-Dimensional Structures

Organizational capabilities, we have learned (Chapter 5), need to be embodied in processes and housed within organizational units that provide the basis for coordination between the individuals involved. The traditional matrix organization allows capabilities to be developed in relation to products, geographical markets, and functions. And the more capabilities an organization develops, the more complex its organizational structure becomes.

- The total quality movement of the 1980s resulted in companies creating organizational structures to implement quality management processes.
- The adoption of social and environmental responsibility by companies has resulted in the creation of structures devoted to these activities.
- The dissemination of knowledge management during the 1990s resulted in many companies setting up knowledge management structures and systems.
- The need to develop and exercise capabilities to meet the needs of large global customers has resulted in multi-national corporations establishing organizational units for managing key accounts.[31]
- The quest for innovation and organizational change has resulted in the establishment of organizational units that conduct "exploration" activities (see the discussion on ambidexterity in Chapter 8). These include project teams for developing new products, incubators for developing new businesses, and communities-of-practice for sharing knowledge and solving problems. They also include organizational change initiatives such as General Electric's "Work-Out" program and innovation structures such as IBM's Innovation Jam and Whirlpool's "innovation pipeline."

Coping with Complexity: Making Organizations Informal, Self-Organizing, and Permeable

If firms expand their range of capabilities, the implications for organizational complexity are alarming. In Chapter 6, we observed that traditional matrix structures which combined product, geographical, and functional organizations proved unwieldy for many corporations. Yet, developing additional capabilities has involved adding further organizational dimensions!

Informal Organization   The key to increasing organizational complexity while maintaining agility and efficiency is to shift from formal to informal structures and systems. The organizational requirements for coordination are different from those required for compliance and control. Traditional hierarchies with bureaucratic systems are based upon the need for control. Coordination requires structures that support modularity, but within each module, team-based structures are often most effective in supporting organizational processes; and coordination between modules does not necessarily need to be managed in a directive sense—coordination can be achieved by means of standardized interfaces, mutual adjustment, and horizontal collaboration (see discussion of "The Coordination Problem" and "Hierarchy in Organizational Design" in Chapter 6.

The scope for team-based structures to reconcile complex patterns of coordination with flexibility and responsiveness is enhanced by the move toward project-based organizations. More companies are organizing their activities less around functions and continuous operations and more around time-designated projects where a team is assigned to a specific project with a clearly defined outcome and a specified completion date. While construction companies and consulting firms have always been structured around projects, a wide range of companies are finding that project-based structures featuring temporary cross-functional teams charged with clear objectives are more able to achieve innovation, adaptability, and rapid learning than more traditional structures. A key advantage of such temporary organizational forms is that they can avoid the ossification of structures and concentrations of power that more permanent structures encourage. W. L. Gore, the supplier of Gore-tex and other hi-tech fabric products, is an example of a team-based, project-focused structure that integrates a broad range of highly sophisticated capabilities despite an organizational structure that is almost wholly informal: there are no formal job titles and leaders are selected by peers. Employees ("associates") may apply to join particular teams, and it is up to the team members to choose new members. The teams are self-managed and team goals are not assigned from above but agreed through team commitments. Associates are encouraged to work with multiple teams.[32]

Reducing complexity at the formal level can foster greater variety and sophisticated coordination at the informal level. In general, the greater the potential for reordering existing resources and capabilities in complex new combinations, the greater the advantages of *consensus-based hierarchies*, which emphasize horizontal communication, over *authority-based hierarchies*, which emphasize vertical communication.[33]

Self-Organization   I identified three factors that are conducive to self-organization: identity, information, and relationships. They can play a key role in substituting for traditional management practices.

- *Identity*: In the absence of top-down direction, coordination requires shared understanding of what the organization is and an emotional attachment toward what it represents. These form *organizational identity*—a collective view of what is distinctive and enduring about the character of an organization.[34] A clear and coherent identity offers a stable bearing in navigating the cross-currents of the 21st century business environment. Coherence at the core allows an organization to face the world with greater confidence.[35]

  Of course, organizational identity, because it is permanent, can impede rather than facilitate change. The key challenge for organizational leaders is to reinterpret organizational identity in a way that can support and legitimate change. Michael Eisner at Disney, Lou Gerstner at IBM, and Franck Riboud at Danone all initiated major strategic changes, but within the constancy of their companies' identities. Organizational identity creates an important linkage between a firm's internal self-image and its market positioning. With the increase of symbolic influences on consumer choices, the linkage between product design, brand image, and organizational identity becomes increasingly important. For companies such as Apple, Alessi, and Lego product design is a vehicle for communicating and interpreting organizational identity.[36]

- *Information*: The information and communication revolution of the past two decades has transformed society's capacity for self-organization, as evident from the role of social media in the "Arab Spring" of 2011, the Ferguson and Baltimore riots of 2014/14, and the election of Jeremy Corbyn as leader of Britain's Labor Party in 2015. Within companies, information and communication networks support spontaneous patterns of complex coordination with little or no hierarchical direction.

● *Relationships*: According to Wheatley and Kellner-Rogers, "Relationships are the pathways to the intelligence of the system. Through relationships, information is created and transformed, the organization's identity expands to include more stakeholders, and the enterprise becomes wiser. The more access people have to one another, the more possibilities there are. Without connections, nothing happens ... In self-organizing systems, people need access to everyone; they need to be free to reach anywhere in the organization to accomplish work."[37] There is increasing evidence that a major part of the work of organizations is achieved through informal social networks.[38]

Breaking Down Corporate Boundaries   Even with informal coordination mechanisms, modular structures, and sophisticated knowledge management systems, there are limits to the range of capabilities that any company can develop internally. Hence, in order to expand the range of capabilities that they can deploy, firms collaborate in order to access the capabilities of other firms. This implies less distinction between what happens within the firm and what happens outside it. Strategic alliances, as we have already seen, permit stable yet flexible patterns for integrating the capabilities of different firms while also sharing risks. While localized networks of firms—such as those that characterize Italy's clothing, furniture, and industrial machinery industries—offer potential for building trust and interfirm routines, web-based technologies permit much wider networks of collaboration. The open innovation efforts described in this book—Procter & Gamble's "Connect & Develop" approach to new product development and IBM's "Innovation Jam"—both point to the power of ICT technologies to enable firms to draw upon ideas and expertise across the globe. The collaborative potential of the internet is most strongly revealed in open-source communities that build highly complex products, such as Linux and Wikipedia, through global networks of individual collaborators.[39]

The Changing Role of Managers

Changing external conditions, new strategic priorities, and different types of organization call for new approaches to management and leadership. In the emerging 21st century organization, the traditional role of the CEO as peak decision-maker may no longer be feasible, let alone desirable. As organizations and their environments become increasingly complex, the CEO is no longer able to access or synthesize the information necessary to be effective as a peak decision maker. Recent contributions to the literature on leadership have placed less emphasis on the role of executives as decision makers and more on their role in guiding organizational evolution. Gary Hamel is emphatic about the need to redefine the work of leadership:

> The notion of the leader as a heroic decision maker is untenable. Leaders must be recast as social-systems architects who enable innovation ... In Management 2.0, leaders will no longer be seen as grand visionaries, all-wise decision makers, and ironfisted disciplinarians. Instead, they will need to become social architects, constitution writers, and entrepreneurs of meaning. In this new model, the leader's job is to create an environment where every employee has the chance to collaborate, innovate, and excel.[40]

Jim Collins and Jerry Porras also emphasize that leadership is less about decision making and more about cultivating identity and purpose:

> If strategy is founded in organizational identity and common purpose, and if organizational culture is the bedrock of capability, then a key role of top management is to clarify, nurture and communicate the company's purpose, heritage, personality, values, and norms. To unify and inspire the efforts of organizational members, leadership requires providing meaning to people's own aspirations. Ultimately this requires attention to the emotional climate of the organization.[41]

These views are supported by empirical research by McKinsey & Company into the characteristics of effective leaders. They identify four attributes that "explained 89 percent of the variance between strong and weak organizations in terms of leadership effectiveness": solving problems effectively, operating with a strong results orientation, seeking different perspectives, and supporting others.[42]

This changing role also implies that senior managers require different knowledge and skills. Research into the psychological and demographic characteristics of successful leaders has identified few consistent or robust relationships—successful leaders come in all shapes, sizes, and personality types. However, research using *competency modeling* methodology points to the key role of personality attributes that have been referred to by Daniel Goleman as *emotional intelligence*.[42] These attributes comprise: *self-awareness*, the ability to understand oneself and one's emotions; *self-management*, control, integrity, conscientiousness, and initiative; *social awareness*, particularly the capacity to sense others' emotions (empathy); and *social skills*, communication, collaboration, and relationship building. Personal qualities are also the focus of Jim Collins' concept of "Level 5 Leadership," which combines personal humility with an intense resolve.[43]

A similar transformation is likely to be required throughout the hierarchy. Informal structures and self-organization have also transformed the role of middle managers from being administrators and controllers into entrepreneurs, coaches, and team leaders.

The insights provided by complexity theory also offer more specific guidance to managers, in particular:

- *Rapid evolution requires a combination of both incremental and radical change*: While stretch targets and other performance management tools can produce pressure for incremental improvement, more decisive intervention may be needed to stimulate radical change. At IBM, Sam Palmisano's leadership between 2002 and 2012 refocused IBM upon research and innovation, expanded IBM's presence in emerging markets, and inaugurated a new era of social and environmental responsibility.[45]

- *Simple rules can be effective in coordinating decentralized decision making.* For instance, rather than plan strategy in any formal sense, rules of thumb in screening opportunities (*boundary rules*) can locate the company where the opportunities are richest. Thus, Cisco's acquisition strategy is guided by the rule that it will acquire companies with fewer than 75 employees of which 75% are engineers. Second, rules can designate a common approach to how the company will exploit opportunities (*how-to rules*).[46]

● *Managing adaptive tension*: If too little tension produces inertia and too much creates chaos, the challenge for top management is to create a level of adaptive tension that optimizes the pace of organizational change and innovation. This is typically achieved through imposing demanding performance targets, but ensuring that these targets are appropriate and achievable.

Summary

The dynamism and unpredictability of today's business environment presents difficult challenges for business leaders responsible for formulating and implementing their companies' strategies. Not least, businesses need to compete at a higher level along a broader front.

In responding to these challenges, business leaders are supported by two developments. The first comprises emerging concepts and theories that offer both insight and the basis for new management tools. Key developments include complexity theory, the principles of self-organization, real option analysis, organizational identity, network analysis, and new thinking concerning innovation, knowledge management, and leadership.

A second area is the innovation and learning that results from adaptation and experimentation by companies. Long-established companies such as IBM and P&G have embraced open innovation; technology-based companies such as Google, W. L. Gore, Microsoft, and Facebook have introduced radically new approaches to project management, human resource management, and strategy formulation. In emerging-market countries we observe novel approaches to government involvement in business (China), new initiatives in managing integration in multibusiness corporations (Samsung), new approaches to managing ambidexterity (Infosys), and new forms of employee engagement (Haier).

At the same time, it is important not to overemphasize either the obsolescence of existing principles or the need for radically new approaches to strategic management. Many of the features of today's business environment are extensions of well-established trends rather than fundamental discontinuities. Certainly our strategy analysis will need to be adapted and augmented in order to take account of new circumstances; however, the basic tools of analysis—industry analysis, resource and capability analysis, the applications of economies of scope to corporate strategy decisions— remain relevant and robust. One of the most important lessons to draw from the major corporate failures that have scarred the 21st century— from Enron and WorldCom to Royal Bank of Scotland and Eastman Kodak—has been the realization that the rigorous application of the tools of strategy analysis outlined in this book might have helped these firms to avoid their misdirected odysseys.

Notes

1. "A Conversation with Gary Hamel and Lowell Bryan," *McKinsey Quarterly* (Winter 2008).
2. W. B. Arthur, "The Second Economy," *McKinsey Quarterly* (October 2011).
3. "The Future of Work," *Economist* (January 3, 2015): 17–20.
4. C. M. Christensen, D. Wang, and D. van Bever, "Consulting on the Cusp of Disruption," *Harvard Business Review* 91 (October 2013): 106–114.
5. J. Alceler and J. Oxley, "Learning by Supplying," *Strategic Management Journal* 35 (2014): 204–223.

6. N. N. Taleb, The Black Swan: *The Impact of the Highly Improbable* (New York: Random House, 2007).

7. D. Hiro, *After Empire: The Birth of a Multipolar World* (New York: Nation Books, 2012).

8. A. Y. Lewin, C. B. Weigelt, and J. D. Emery, "Adaptation and Selection in Strategy and Change," in M. S. Poole and A. H. van de Ven (eds), *Handbook of Organizational Change and Innovation* (New York: Oxford University Press, 2004): 108–160.

9. "Why is News Corp Splitting in Two?" *Economist* (June 23, 2013).

10. P. F. Drucker, *Managing in the Next Society* (London: St. Martin's Press, 2003); S. Ghoshal, C. A. Bartlett, and P. Moran, "A New Manifesto for Management," *Sloan Management Review* (Spring 1999): 9–20; C. Handy, *The Age of Paradox* (Boston: Harvard University Press, 1995).

11. T. Piketty, *Capital in the 21st Century* (Cambridge, MA: Harvard University Press, 2014).

12. *The One Percent* is a 2006 documentary produced by Jamie Johnson and Nick Kurzon and premiered on HBO in 2008.

13. "Background Paper on Cooperatives." http://www.un.org/esa/socdev/social/cooperatives/documents/survey/background.pdf, accessed July 20, 2015.

14. J. Moizer and P. Tracey, "Strategy Making in Social Enterprise: The Role of Resource Allocation and its effects on Organizational Sustainability," *Systems Research and Behavioral Science* 27 (2010): 252–266.

15. M. E. Porter and M. R. Kramer, "Creating Shared Value," *Harvard Business Review* (January 2011): 62–77 (see Chapter 2 for a discussion).

16. R. P. Rumelt, "The Perils of Bad Strategy," *McKinsey Quaerly* (June 2011).

17. R. G. McGrath, "Transient Advantage," *Harvard Business Review* (June/July 2013): 62–70.

18. I. Berlin, *The Hedgehog and the Fox* (New York: Simon & Schuster, 1953).

19. J. Collins, *Good to Great* (New York: HarperCollins, 2001).

20. See: N. J. Foss and T. Saebi (eds) *Business Model Innovation: The Organizational Dimension* (Oxford: Oxford University Press, 2015).

21. K. M. Eisenhardt and J. A. Martin, "Dynamic Capabilities: What Are They?" *Strategic Management Journal* 21 (2000): 1105–1121.

22. K. Laursen and N. J. Foss, "New Human Resource Management Practices, Complementarities and the Impact on Innovation Performance," *Cambridge Journal of Economics* 27 (2003): 243–263.

23. Six sigma is a quality management methodology first developed by Motorola in 1986 that aims to reduce defects among products and processes to less than 3.4 per million. See C. Gygi, N. DeCarlo, and B. Williams, *Six Sigma for Dummies* (Hoboken, NJ: John Wiley & Sons, Inc., 2005).

24. R. Whittington, A. Pettigrew, S. Peck, E. Fenton, and M. Conyon, "Change and Complementarities in the New Competitive Landscape," *Organization Science* 10 (1999): 583–600.

25. P. Bak, *How Nature Works: The Science of Self-organized Criticality* (New York: Copernicus, 1996).

26. M. J. Wheatley and M. Kellner Rogers, *A Simpler Way* (San Francisco: Berrett-Koehler, 1996).

27. P. Anderson, "Complexity Theory and Organizational Science," *Organization Science* 10 (1999): 216–232.

28. S. McGuire, B. McKelvey, L. Mirabeau, and N. Oztas, "Complexity Science and Organization Studies," in S. Clegg (ed.), *The SAGE Handbook of Organizational Studies* (Thousand Oaks, CA: SAGE Publications, 2006): 165–214.

29. M. E. Porter and N. Siggelkow, "Contextuality within Activity Systems and Sustainable Competitive Advantage," *Academy of Management Perspectives* 22 (May 2008): 34–56.

30. These issues are discussed in greater depth in Porter and Siggelkow op. cit.

31. G. S. Yip and A. J. M. Bink, *Managing Global Customers: An Integrated Approach* (Oxford: Oxford University Press, 2007).

32. G. Hamel, *The Future of Management* (Boston: HBS Press, 2007): 84–99.

33. J. A. Nickerson and T. R. Zenger, "The Knowledge-based Theory of the Firm: A Problem-solving Perspective," *Organization Science* 15 (2004): 617–632.

34. D. A. Gioia, M. Schultz, and K. G. Corley, "Organizational Identity, Image and Adaptive Instability," *Academy of Management Review* 25 (2000): 63–81.

35. M. J. Wheatley and M. Kellner-Rogers, "The Irresistible Future of Organizing," (July/August 1996), http://margaretwheatley.com/articles/irresistiblefuture.html, accessed July 2015.

36. D. Ravasi and G. Lojacono, "Managing Design and Designers for Strategic Renewal," *Long Range Planning* 38, no. 1 (February 2005): 51–77.

37. Wheatley and Kellner-Rogers, op. cit.

38. L. L. Bryan, E. Matson, and L. M. Weiss, "Harnessing the Power of Informal Employee Networks," *McKinsey Quarterly* (November 2007).

39. A. Wright, "The Next Paradigm Shift: Open Source Everything," http://forum.brighthand.com/threads/the-next-paradigm-shift-open-source-everything.261646/. accessed July 20, 2015.

40. G. Hamel, "Moon Shots for Management?" *Harvard Business Review* (February 2009): 91–98.

41. J. C. Collins and J. I. Porras, *Built to Last* (New York: Harper Business, 1996).

42. C. Feser, F. Mayol, and R. Srinivasan, "Decoding Leadership: What Really Matters," *McKinsey Quarterly* (January 2015).

43. D. Goleman, "What Makes a Leader?" *Harvard Business Review* (November/December 1998): 93–102.

44. J. Collins, "Level 5 Leadership: The Triumph of Humility and Fierce Resolve," *Harvard Business Review* (January 2001): 67–76.

45. "IBM's Sam Palmisano: A Super Second Act," *Fortune* (March 4, 2011).

46. For discussion of the role of rules in strategy making, see K. M. Eisenhardt and D. Sull, "Strategy as Simple Rules," *Harvard Business Review* (January/February 2001): 107–116.

CASES TO ACCOMPANY CONTEMPORARY STRATEGY ANALYSIS

NINTH EDITION

CASES

the company and its strategy, providing the basis for an analysis of the nature and sources of Chipotle's competitive advantage. The case offers insight into Chipotle's business system and considers the sustainability of Chipotle's competitive advantage given the ease with which its business model can be imitated by rivals.

24 W. L. Gore & Associates: Rethinking Management?

W. L. Gore, the manufacturer of Gore-Tex, has a unique organizational structure and management style built around its "lattice" principle. The result is a remarkable lack of hierarchy and exceptional decentralization of decision making, which is devolved to self-managing teams. The case offers the opportunity to consider the advantages and disadvantages of Gore's management system, and whether its radical approach to management can be applied more widely.

Case 1 Tough Mudder Inc.: The Business of Mud Runs

Really tough. But really fun. When I got back to the office on Monday morning, I looked at my colleagues and thought: "And what did you do over the weekend?"

—TOUGH MUDDER PARTICIPANT

Tough Mudder Inc. is a Brooklyn-based company that hosts endurance obstacle events—a rapidly growing sport also known as "mud runs." During 2015, about 600,000 participants will each pay between $180 and $260 to tackle a 10- to 12-mile Tough Mudder course featuring 15 to 20 challenging obstacles. The obstacles include wading through a dumpster filled with ice (the "Arctic Enema"), crawling through a series of pipes part-filled with mud ("Boa Constrictor"), and dashing through live wires carrying up to 10,000 volts ("Electroshock Therapy"). The 2015 schedule comprises 46 two-day Tough Mudder events (a separate run on each day) in the US, Canada, the UK, Ireland, Germany, and Australia. Tough Mudder's website describes the experience as follows:

> Tough Mudder events are team-based obstacle course challenges designed to test your all around strength, stamina and mental grit, while encouraging teamwork and camaraderie. With the most innovative courses and obstacles, over two million inspiring participants worldwide to date, and more than $8.7 million raised for the Wounded Warrior Project by US participants, Tough Mudder is the premier adventure challenge series in the world. But Tough Mudder is more than an event; it's a way of thinking. By running a Tough Mudder challenge, you'll unlock a true sense of accomplishment, have a great time and discover a camaraderie with your fellow participants that's experienced all too rarely these days.[1]

Tough Mudder was founded in 2010 by former British school pals Will Dean and Guy Livingston. While a Harvard MBA student, Dean entered Harvard Business School's annual business plan competition using Tough Guy, a UK obstacle race based upon British Special Forces training, as the basis for his plan.[2] On graduating from Harvard, Dean and Livingstone launched their first Tough Mudder event. On May 21, 2010 at Bear Creek ski resort, Pennsylvania 4,500 participants battled through a grueling 10-mile course.

This case was prepared by Robert M. Grant. ©2015 Robert M. Grant.

The Market for Endurance Sports

The origins of endurance sports can be traced to the introduction of the modern marathon race in 1896, the triathlon in the 1920s, orienteering in the 1930s, and the first Ironman triathlon in 1974. In recent years, a number of new endurance sports have appeared, including:

- adventure races—off-road, triathlon-based events which typically include trekking/orienteering, mountain biking, and paddling;
- obstacle mud runs—cross-country running events with a variety of challenging obstacles;
- novelty events—fun events such as 5K races in which competitors are doused in paint (Color Run), running with real bulls (Great Bull Run), and food fights (Tomato Royale).

Tough Mudder used several strategic variables to map the market and position the different products (Figure 1).

Obstacle mud runs were initiated in the UK in 1987 with the annual Tough Guy race organized by ex-British soldier Billy Wilson (which provided the inspiration for Tough Mudder). In the US, Warrior Dash launched in July 2009, followed by Tough Mudder and Spartan Races in May 2010. A flood of new entries followed. During 2011–2013, new entrants included: Mud Mingle, Play Dirty Adventure Runs, Dirty Girl, Mudslayers, Gritty Goddess Runs, Alpha Warrior, Big Nasty Mud Run, Survival Race, Udder Mud Run, Fugitive Mud Run, Hot and Dirty Mud Run, and many more. During 2013, there were 3.4 million participants in US obstacle mud runs paying a total of $290.1 million.[3] By comparison, triathlons attracted about two million participants in 2013. In 2013, close to 350 organizations offered obstacle mud runs. The surging popularity of mud runs pointed to the desire of the young (and not so young) to turn away from video screens and virtual experiences and test their physical and mental limits in the Great Outdoors.

FIGURE 1 The market for endurance sports

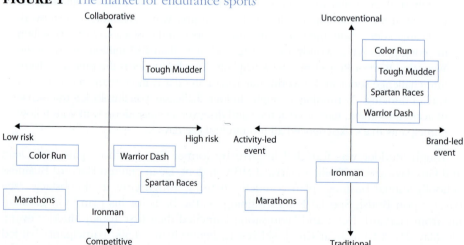

Source: Adapted from a presentation by Nick Horbaczewski to Strategic Planning Innovation Summit, New York, December 2013.

TABLE 1   Tough Mudder's leading competitors

	Spartan races	Warrior Dash
Founding	Started by Joe De Sena in 2010 Expanded overseas through franchising	Red Frog Events LLC launched Great Urban Race in 2007, Warrior Dash in 2009, and Firefly Music Festival in 2012
2015 events	US: 108 mostly 1-day events Overseas: 76 events in 26 countries	US: 27 1-day events Canada: 1 event (No overseas events after 2014)
The product	3 types of race: Sprint (3 miles, 15 obstacles), Super (8 miles, 20 obstacles), Beast (12 miles, 25 obstacles)	3- to 4-mile race with 12 obstacles followed by post-race party (beer, bbq, live music)
Sponsors	Reebok, Clif Bar, Paleo Ranch Jerky, Bodybuilding.com, PursuitRx	Shock Top Brewing, Vibram, Anytime Fitness, Gold Bond, Rockin' Refuel

The psychology of mud runs (and other endurance sports) is complex. The satisfaction participants derive from overcoming their perceived physical and mental limits combines with identification with warrior role models and the nourishing of camaraderie. The *New York Times* referred to the "Walter Mitty weekend-warrior complex," noting that, while the events draw endurance athletes and military veterans, "the muddiest, most avid, most agro participants hail from Wall Street."[4] A psychologist pointed to the potential for "misattributed arousal": the tendency among couples participating in endurance events to attribute increased blood pressure, heart rate, and sensory alertness to their emotional relationship with their partner. Bottom line: "Want your boyfriend or girlfriend to feel intense feelings of love and desire for you? Put yourselves through a grueling, 12-mile obstacle course!"[5]

During 2013–2015, the mud run industry experienced a shake-out as many weaker organizers were unable to attract sufficient participants to cover their costs. At the same time new entry continued—new obstacle race series were launched by BattleFrog in the US and Swedish-based Nexthand's "Toughest" obstacle races in Scandinavia and the UK. By 2015, the industry leaders were Tough Mudder, Spartan Races, and Warrior Dash (Table 1).

Growing the Company, Building the Brand

Tough Mudder's strategic priority was to establish leadership within an increasingly crowded market. How to position Tough Mudder in relation both to other endurance sports and to other obstacle runs was the critical strategic issue for CEO Will Dean. Dean believed that compared to traditional endurance sports—such as marathons and triathlons—the key attributes of obstacle course races were that they presented significant personal risk, of injury, hypothermia, or extreme exhaustion; they could be collaborative rather than competitive events; and they were more engaging by allowing a variety of experiences and challenges.

However, combining the various attributes of the mud run experience—exhaustion, camaraderie, fun, and fear—was challenging in terms of product design. In trading off individual achievement against collaboration, Dean emphasized the collaborative dimension—Tough Mudder would be untimed and team-based;

the individual challenge would be to complete the course. A more complex challenge was the need for Tough Mudder to present itself as formidable ("Probably the Toughest Event on the Planet") while attracting a wide range of participants. Making it a team-based event and giving participants the option to bypass individual obstacles helped reconcile these conflicting objectives. Appealing to military-style principles of esprit de corps ("No Mudder left behind") also helped reconcile this dilemma. This combination of personal challenge and team-based collaboration also encouraged participation from business enterprises and other organizations seeking to build trust, morale, and motivation among teams of employees.

The principle of collaboration was not only within teams but extended across all participants. Before each Tough Mudder event, the participants gather at the start line to recite the Tough Mudder pledge:

- I understand that Tough Mudder is not a race but a challenge.
- I put teamwork and camaraderie before my course time.
- I do not whine—kids whine.
- I help my fellow Mudders complete the course.
- And I overcome all my fears.

As psychologist Melanie Tannenbaum observes: "this pledge is setting a very powerful descriptive norm … a very powerful determinant of our behavior … More than anything else, though, there's a little part of our brains that hasn't quite left the 'Peer Pressure' halls of high school. We want to fit in, and we want to do what others are doing."[6]

The spirit of unity and collaboration provides a central element of Tough Mudder's marketing strategy. Tough Mudder has relied almost exclusively on Facebook for building its profile, encouraging participation, and building community among its participants. Its Facebook ads target specific locations, demographics, and "likes" such as ice hockey and other physical sports. Tough Mudder also makes heavy use of "sponsored stories," which appear on users' Facebook "news feeds" when their friends "Like" Tough Mudder. Most important, Facebook is the ideal media for Tough Mudder to exploit its greatest appeal to participants: the ability for them to proclaim their courage, endurance, and fighting spirit. As the *New York* magazine observes: "the experience is perfect for bragging about on social media, and from the outset Tough Mudder has marketed to the boastful."[7] By March 2015, Tough Mudder had four million Facebook "likes."

Establishing leadership within the obstacle mud run market was a key strategic goal for the company. The tendency for the market to coalesce around a few leading firms would be reinforced by the ability of the market leader to set industry standards—to establish norms of the key attributes of an authentic mud run. Hence, Dean envisaged Tough Mudder playing a similar role as the World Triathlon Corporation and its Ironman brand in triathlon racing.

Early-mover advantage combined with rapid growth (Figure 2) gave Tough Mudder market leadership in North America. However, staying ahead of the competition required delivering an experience that people would want to come back for, time and time again. This involved three major activities at Tough Mudder:

- Meticulous attention to customer feedback was achieved through customer surveys, on-site observations (including employee participation in mud runs),

FIGURE 2 Tough Mudder: Growth 2010–2015

Note: Participant numbers are case writer's estimates. Data for 2015 are projections.

and close attention to social media. Tough Mudder continually sought clues as to how it might make improvements that would allow it to match the energy, determination, and gung-ho spirit of the participants.

- Continuous development of obstacles and course design involved generating ideas for new obstacles while on retreats, developing and testing prototypes at the Brooklyn HQ, and learning from participant experiences. Tough Mudder continually increased its investment in product development with new and improved obstacles announced each year. In January 2015, Tough Mudder announced that "its entire obstacle menu has been revamped" including "ten exhilarating new obstacles," "2.0 versions" of its classic challenges, and off-course "Mudder Village" obstacles for participants and spectators to experience.

- Efforts to extend brand leadership focused heavily on social media and maximizing traffic to Tough Mudder's website, but also included extensive outreach to the online and print media.

Partnering

Partnering with other organizations has been a central feature of Tough Mudder's growth. Its partnerships have been important for building market momentum, providing resources and capabilities that Tough Mudder lacked, and generating additional sources of revenue.

Since its inaugural run in 2010, Tough Mudder has been an official sponsor of the Wounded Warriors Project, a charity that offers support to wounded veterans. The relationship reinforces Tough Mudder's military associations and helps legitimize Tough Mudder's image of toughness, resilience, and bravery. Military connections were further reinforced by sponsorship from the US Army Reserve, which viewed Tough Mudder events as an opportunity for promotion and recruitment.

Commercial sponsors include Under Armour, Shock Top beer, General Mills' Wheaties brand, Radisson hotels, Cellucor nutrition products, MET-Rx food supplements, and Oberto Beef Jerky.

Expanding the Product Range

Reconciling aspirations for toughness and difficulty with breadth of participation and market appeal, encouraged Tough Mudder to introduce several new products between 2011 and 2015:

- *World's Toughest Mudder* was introduced in 2011 to reinforce the brand's reputation for toughness. The annual run featured individuals and teams competing to complete the greatest number of course laps during a 24-hour period. The *Financial Times* described the event: "Le Mans on foot, through a Somme-like landscape with Marquis de Sade-inspired flourishes."[8]
- *Mudderella* is a "5–7 mile obstacle course, designed by women for women. The event is all about working together, having fun, and owning your strong!"[9] Nine Mudderella events were planned for 2015.
- *Urban Mudder* a 5- to 6-mile city-based obstacles course debuted on Randall's Island New York City on July 25, 2015. Participants were required "to scale brick walls, hurtle between platforms and fling themselves into giant air bags" and perform "*Mission Impossible*-like contortions to avoid breaking a beam in a field of lasers." The event was designed to be a "festival-like party with DJs and street performers, food trucks and a beer garden."[10]
- *Fruit Shoot Mini Mudder* is a mile-long adventure course for children aged 7 to 12 years old. Like Mudderella, it accompanies the main Tough Mudder events in order to create family involvement. According to Product Director Daniella Sloane, "We've created a bunch of obstacles that will work whether you're short or whether you're tall. If you're at least 42 inches you're going to have a good time and you're going to have to work with your fellow teammates to make it through." The obstacles were developed through children's focus groups and test events.

Management

As CEO of Tough Mudder, Will Dean focuses upon key priorities. "There are only two things a leader should worry about," he told *Inc.* magazine, "strategy and culture … We aspire to become a household brand name, so mapping out a long-term strategy is crucial. I speak with Cristina DeVito, our chief strategy officer, every day, and I meet with the entire five-person strategy team once a week … We go on retreats every quarter to a house in the Catskill Mountains … There's no phone coverage, and the internet connection is slow … We started the retreats to get everyone thinking about the future."[11]

At the core of Tough Mudder's strategy is its sense of identity, which is reinforced through the culture of the company: "Since Day 1, we've had a clear brand and mission: to create life-changing experiences. That clear focus means that every employee is aligned on the same vision and knows what they're working toward."[12] "We know who we are and what we stand for," he added. To sustain the culture,

Tough Mudder has established a list of core values to guide the actions and behavior of the management team.

An additional key responsibility of Dean's is hiring: Tough Mudder grew from eight employees at the end of 2010 to around 250 by the end of 2014. His observation that "a business is only as good as the people who build it" is reflected in meticulous talent seeking aimed at hiring executives who combine professional achievement with the pursuit of adventure and share Dean's passion and values.

Tough Mudder in 2015

In 2015, Tough Mudder was reckoned to hold a narrow lead over Spartan Races in terms of revenue and numbers of participants—a result of astute strategic positioning, effective brand building, careful product design, meticulous operational planning, and obsessive focus on the customer experience. However, sustaining the company's growth and market leadership in the endurance sports sector would be an ongoing challenge as the market began to mature. While the consolidation of the industry around the three leading players would assist the stability and reputation of obstacle mud runs as an endurance sport, competition among the leading players was becoming increasingly intense as the market leaders became ever-more sophisticated in course design, marketing, and operations management—and increasingly adept at imitating one another's innovations.

Market positioning became a key issue for Tough Mudder: was the firm's attempt to reconcile toughness with breadth of participation sustainable or would the market segment between the organizers of extreme events (such as Tough Guy in the UK and BattleFrog Races in the US) and those offering events more oriented toward fun and recreation (Mud Factor, Zombie Mud Run)?

Finally, there was the long-run future of the industry as a whole: would obstacle courses establish themselves as a continuing sport or were they a passing fad?

Notes

1. http://toughmudder.com/about/, accessed July 20, 2015.
2. An acrimonious legal dispute between Will Dean and Tough Guy Challenge founder Billy Wilson over the alleged theft of trade secrets was resolved by Dean paying $725,000 to Wilson in an out-of-court settlement.
3. "Obstacle Race World: The State of the Mud Run Business (June 2014)", http://www.obstacleusa.com/obstacle-race-world-the-state-of-the-mud-run-business-details-the-size-and-reach-of-the-ocr-market-as-the-sports-first-ever-industry-report/, accessed July 20, 2015.
4. "Forging a Bond in Mud and Guts," *New York Times* (December 7, 2012).
5. M. Tannenbaum, "The Making of a Tough Mudder" (January 15, 2015), http://blogs.scientificamerican.com/psysociety/2015/01/15/mud-running/, accessed July 20, 2015.
6. Ibid.
7. "Tough Mudder: There are riches in this mud pit," *New York Magazine* (September 29, 2013), http://nymag.com/news/business/boom-brands/tough-mudder-2013-10, accessed July 20, 2015.
8. "Tough Mudder," *Financial Times* online edition (January 18, 2013), http://www.ft.com/cms/s/2/7a80e610-603d-11e2-b657-00144feab49a.html#ixzz2nFzd1Xx4, accessed July 20, 2015.
9. http://mudderella.com/, accessed July 20, 2015.
10. http://urbanmudder.com/, accessed July 20, 2015.
11. "The Way I Work: Will Dean, Tough Mudder," *Inc.*, Magazine, http://www.inc.com/magazine/201302/issie-lapowsky/the-way-i-work-will-dean-tough-mudder.html, accessed July 20, 2015.
12. "On the Streets of SoHo. Will Dean, Tough Mudder," http://accordionpartners.com/wp-content/uploads/2013/02/QA-Will-Dean.pdf, accessed July 20, 2015.

Case 2   Starbucks Corporation, May 2015

Howard Schultz, chairman and CEO of Starbucks Corporation, opened the company's annual shareholders meeting in Seattle on March 18, 2015 with the following words:

> 2014 was a remarkable year: record revenue, record profit, record stock price. But, I must say, when I think about the year and what we've accomplished, what I'm most proud of is our consistent ability to balance profitability and social impact.[1]

Schultz went on to elaborate some of Starbucks' accomplishments in relation to both financial and social performance and, in doing so, noted that a $10,000 investment in Starbucks' stock at the time of its 1992 IPO would currently be worth almost $2 million.

Starbucks' rise from a single Seattle coffee store to a global chain of over 22,000 coffee shops employing almost 200,000 people and generating revenues that would top $18 billion in 2015 was one of the wonders of American entrepreneurial capitalism. Its founder, Howard Schultz, was a legend among US business leaders, his heroic status enhanced by the fact that, having built a hugely successful corporation and relinquishing the CEO position in 2000, he returned in 2008 to restore Starbucks' flagging performance. Within two years, profits and share price had set new records (Table 1 and Figure 1).

For many observers, including the owners of the Milanese cafés that had provided the inspiration for Schultz, the Starbucks story was little short of miraculous. America's first coffeehouse had opened in Boston in 1676. How could brewing a better cup of coffee in the 1980s produce a company with a market value of $78 billion? Given the ubiquity of good coffee, could Starbucks possibly sustain its success?

The Starbucks Story

Starbucks Coffee, Tea and Spice had been founded by college buddies Gerald Baldwin and Gordon Bowker. In 1981, Howard Schultz, a coffee filter salesman, visited their store. The coffee he sampled was a revelation: "I realized the coffee I had been drinking was swill." Captivated by the business potential that Starbucks offered, Schultz encouraged the founders to hire him as head of marketing. Shortly afterwards, Schultz experienced a second revelation. On a

---

This case was prepared by Robert M. Grant assisted by Gautham T. ©2015 Robert M. Grant.

TABLE 1   Starbucks Corporation: Financial data for 2007–2014 ($million)

12 months to end-September	2014	2013	2012	2011	2010	2009	2008	2007
Income Statement Items								
Total net revenues of which	16,448	14,892	13,300	11,700	10,707	9,775	10,383	9,412
—company-operated stores	12,978	11,793	10,534	9,632	8,964	8,180	8,772	7,998
—licensed stores	1,589	1,360	1,210	1,007	1,744	1,595	1,611	1,413
—CPG,[a] food service, other	1,881	1,739	1,555	1,061				
Cost of sales	6,859	6,382	5,813	4,916	4,459	4,325	4,645	3,999
Store operating expenses	4,638	4,286	3,918	3,595	3,551	3,425	3,745	3,216
Other operating expenses	450	457	430	393	293	264	330	294
Depreciation and amortization	710	621	550	523	510	535	549	467
General and administrative expenses	991	938	801	636	570	453	456	489
Special charges[b]	—	2,784	—	—	53	3,324	266.9	—
Total operating expenses	13,635	15,469	11,513	10,176	9,436	9,335	9,993	8,466
Operating income	3,081	(325.4)	1,997	1,729	1,419	562	504	1,054
Net earnings	2,068	8	1,384	1,246	946	391	315	673
Net cash from operations	608[c]	2,908	1,750	1,612	1,705	1,389	1,259	1,331
Capital expenditures (net)	1,161	1,411	974	1,019	441	446	985	1,080
Balance Sheet Items								
Working capital (deficit)	690	94	1,990	1,719	977	455	(442)	(459)
Total assets	10,752	11,516	8,219	7,360	6,386	5,577	5,673	5,344
Short-term borrowings		—	—	—	—	—	713	713
Long-term debt	2,048	1,299	550	549	549	549	550	551
Shareholders' equity	5,272	4,482	5,115	4,385	3,675	3,046	2,491	2,284

Notes:
[a]Consumer Products Group.
[b]The special charge in 2013 comprised a payment to Kraft Foods arising from litigation. Special charges in other years were restructuring costs.
[c]Operating cash flow was reduced by the $2.8 billion payment made to Kraft.

trip to Italy, he discovered the joys of the Milanese coffee houses which offered a combination of good coffee, ambiance, social interaction, and the artistry of the barista. His ideas for recreating Starbucks to be a place where people would come to share the experience of drinking great coffee rather than to buy coffee beans failed to persuade the founders. Schultz left to open his own Italian-styled coffee bar, Il Giornale. In 1987, he acquired the Starbucks chain of six stores, merged it with his three Il Giornale bars, and adopted the Starbucks name for the enlarged company.[2]

FIGURE 1 Starbucks' share price ($), May 2005 to May 2015 (adjusted for splits)

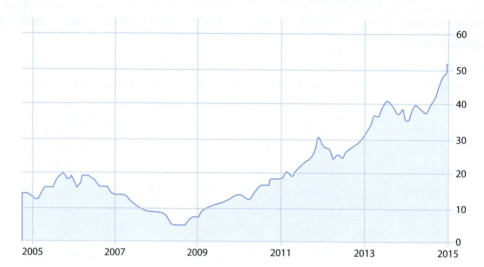

Schultz's original idea of replicating Italian coffee bars (where customers mostly stand to drink coffee) was adapted to "the American equivalent of the English pub, the German beer garden and the French café."[3] With the addition of wi-fi, Starbucks' stores became a place to work as well as to socialize. By 1992, Starbucks, with 165 outlets, went public. With $27 million from the stock offering, Schultz accelerated growth. Expansion followed a cluster pattern: opening multiple stores in a single metro area in order to increase local brand awareness and to help customers make a Starbucks' visit part of their daily routine. International expansion began with Japan in 1996 and the UK in 1998. Starbucks relied mainly on organic growth, but with occasional acquisitions: the UK-based Seattle Coffee Company in 1998, Seattle's Best Coffee and Torrefazione Italia in 2003, and Diedrich Coffee in 2006.

The Starbucks Experience

Starbucks' mission "to inspire and nurture the human spirit" required not just serving excellent coffee but also engaging customers at an emotional level. As Schultz explained: "We're not in the coffee business serving people, we are in the people business serving coffee."

Central to Starbucks' strategy was Schultz's concept of the "Starbucks Experience," which centered on the creation of a "third place"—somewhere other than home and work where people could engage socially while enjoying the shared experience of drinking good coffee. The Starbucks Experience combined several elements:

- Coffee beans of a high, consistent quality and the careful management of a chain of activities that resulted in their transformation into the best possible espresso coffee: "We're passionate about ethically sourcing the finest coffee beans, roasting them with great care, and improving the lives of the people who grow them."

- Employee involvement. Starbucks' counter staff—the baristas—played a central role in delivering the Starbucks Experience. Their role was not only to brew and serve coffee but also to engage customers in the ambiance of the Starbucks coffee shop. This was supported by human resource practices based upon a distinctive view about the company's relationship with its employees. Employees needed to be committed and enthusiastic communicators of the principles and values of Starbucks, which implied treating employees as business partners. Starbucks' human resource practices were tailored, first, to attracting and recruiting people whose attitudes and personalities were consistent with the company's values and, second, to foster trust and loyalty that facilitated their engagement with the Starbucks experience. Starbucks' employee selection emphasized adaptability, dependability, capacity for teamwork, and willingness to further Starbucks' principles and mission. Its training program extended beyond basic operational and customer-service skills and placed particular emphasis on educating employees about coffee. Unique among catering chains, Starbucks provided health insurance for almost all regular employees, including part-timers. In 2014, Starbucks introduced its College Achievement Plan, providing tuition reimbursement for employees taking online degree programs from Arizona State University.

- Community relations and social purpose. Schultz viewed Starbucks as redefining the role of business in society: "I wanted to build the kind of company my father never had the chance to work for, where you would be valued and respected wherever you came from, whatever the color of your skin, whatever your level of education … We wanted to build a company that linked shareholder value to the cultural values that we want to create with our people."[4] Schultz's vision was of a company that would earn good profits but would also do good in the world. This began at the local level: "Every store is part of a community, and we take our responsibility to be good neighbors seriously. We want to be invited in wherever we do business. We can be a force for positive action—bringing together our partners, customers, and the community to contribute every day."[5] It extended to Starbucks' global role: "we have the opportunity to be a different type of global company. One that makes a profit but at the same time demonstrates a social conscience." Starbucks' sponsoring of social causes was not without controversy: its March 2015 "Race Together" campaign, which encouraged employees to discuss racism with customers, was hit by a "cascade of negativity" on Twitter and was soon abandoned.[6]

- The layout and design of Starbucks' stores were critical elements of the experience. Like everything else at Starbucks, store design was subject to meticulous planning, following Schultz's dictum that "retail is detail." While every Starbucks store is adapted to its unique neighborhood, all stores reflect some common themes. "The design of a Starbucks store is intended to provide both unhurried sociability and efficiency on-the-run, an appreciation for the natural goodness of coffee and the artistry that grabs you even before the aroma. This approach is reflected in the designers' generous employment of natural woods and richly layered, earthy colors along with judicious high-tech accessorizing ... No matter how individual the store, overall store design seems to correspond closely to the company's first and evolving influences: the clean, unadulterated crispness of the Pacific Northwest combined with the urban suavity of an espresso bar in Milan."[7]

- Starbucks' location strategy—its clustering of 20 or more stores in each urban hub—was viewed as enhancing the experience both in creating a local "Starbucks buzz" and in facilitating loyalty by Starbucks' customers. Starbucks' analysis of sales by individual store found little evidence that closely located Starbucks stores cannibalized one another's sales. To expand sales of coffee-to-go, Starbucks began adding drive-through windows to some of its stores and building new stores adjacent to major highways.

Broadening the Experience

Delivering the Starbucks Experience encouraged Starbucks to broaden its product range. "The overall strategy is to build Starbucks into a destination," explained Kenneth Lombard, then head of Starbucks Entertainment. This involved adding food, music, books, and videos. In music publishing, Starbucks' "Artists Choice" CDs, for which well-known musicians chose their favorite tracks, were particularly successful. "I had to get talked into that one," says Schultz. "But then I began to understand that our customers looked to Starbucks as a kind of editor. It was like, 'We trust you. Help us choose.'"

Starbucks also diversified its business model to include other ownership and management formats, additional products, and different channels of distribution. These included:

- Licensed coffee shops and kiosks. The desire to reach customers in a variety of locations eventually caused Starbucks to abandon its policy of only selling through company-owned outlets. Its first licensing deal was with Host Marriot, which owned food and beverage concessions in several US airports. This was followed by licensing arrangements with Safeway and Barnes & Noble for opening Starbucks coffee shops in their stores. Overseas, Starbucks increasingly relied upon licensing arrangements with local companies.
- Distribution of Starbucks retail packs of Starbucks coffee through super-markets and other retail food stores.
- Licensing of Starbucks brands to PepsiCo and Unilever for the supply of Starbucks bottled drinks (such as Frappuccino and Tazo Tea).
- Starbucks' involvement in financial services began with its Starbucks prepaid store card, which was later combined with a Visa credit card (the Starbucks/Bank One Duetto card). The Starbucks card allowed entry to the Starbucks reward program, which offered free drinks and other benefits to regular customers.

Adjusting the Strategy

Crisis and Retrenchment, 2007–2009

Starbucks' downturn of 2007–2009 was triggered by slowing growth of same-store sales and operating profits and exacerbated by the financial crisis. Amidst concerns over Starbucks' strategy and future prospects, chairman and founder Howard Schultz returned as CEO at the beginning of 2008.

Schultz's turnaround strategy comprised two initiatives. First, retrenchment: Schultz cancelled new store openings and revised operational practices to improve cost efficiency. In the summer of 2008, he announced the closure of 600 US stores and most Australian stores; 6,000 jobs were lost in the stores and 700 positions in corporate and support activities. Savings in operating costs of $500 million in 2009 included Schultz cutting his own salary from $1.2 million to $10,000 and selling two of Starbucks' three corporate jets.[8]

The second thrust was the reaffirmation of Starbucks' values and business principles, including revitalizing the "Starbucks Experience" and reconnecting with its customers. Reinvigorating Starbucks' social commitment played a central role in the rediscovery process. During 2008, a company-wide reconsideration of Starbucks' purpose and principles resulted in a revised mission statement and a stronger commitment to corporate social responsibility. Initiatives included participation in the New Orleans clean-up after Hurricane Katrina and launching Starbucks' Shared Planet: an environmental sustainability and community service program.

Schultz's review of operating practices to assess their consistency with the Starbucks Experience and Starbucks' image resulted in reducing the automation of coffee making. To speed up coffee making, Starbucks had replaced its La Marzocco espresso machines, which required grinding coffee for each cup, with automatic machines that required baristas to press a button. During 2008, Starbucks began replacing these automated machines with new coffee machines that made individual servings from freshly ground beans. Revisions to Starbucks' food menu included withdrawing toasted breakfast sandwiches whose aromas masked that of the coffee: "The breakfast sandwiches drive revenue and profit but they are in conflict with everything we stand for in terms of the coffee and the romance of the coffee," noted Schultz.[9]

Reconnecting with customers involved the extensive use of new digital media. Starbucks was a leader in the use of Facebook and Twitter for promotional and loyalty-building purposes. Starbucks also pioneered new payment methods to facilitate transactions and build customer loyalty. The original Starbucks Card, an in-store debit card, was launched in 2002 and was subsequently linked to a loyalty program offering rewards based upon cumulative purchases. The loyalty program was relaunched in 2011 as "My Starbucks Rewards" and was linked to an innovative cell phone payment system. Customers displayed a two-dimensional barcode on their cell phones which was scanned at the point-of-sale. By 2015, ten million customers had downloaded the Starbucks app and mobile transactions accounted for 14% of its US sales.

Most of all, Schultz traveled extensively meeting with employees ("partners") to reignite their drive and enthusiasm and reinforce Starbucks' values. At a series of meetings held in concert halls and other venues, Schultz recounted inspiring tales that exemplified the "humanity of Starbucks" and challenged his store managers to return to the values and practices that had made Starbucks a special place.[10]

Diversification within the US, 2009–2015

With operational efficiency, customer connections, and core values and principles restored, Starbucks returned to growth. In the US market the primary emphasis was on exploiting new revenue opportunities. Overseas, it was building Starbucks' presence in emerging markets,

Major US initiatives included:

- The introduction of Via, a new type of instant coffee, launched in February 2009 at $2.95 for a pack of three individual servings and $9.95 for 12 servings. Via used a patented process which allowed the company to "absolutely replicate the taste of Starbucks coffee." In less than two years, sales of Via reached $200 million.
- Entry into single-serve pod coffee systems. In 2011, Starbucks began producing Starbucks' K-cup pods for Keurig machines. In 2012, Starbucks introduced its own pod-based home espresso system.
- In November 2011, Starbucks acquired premium juice maker Evolution Fresh Inc. with a view to expanding the retail distribution of fruit juices both within its own stores and to the grocery trade.
- In June 2012, Starbucks acquired San Francisco bakery La Boulange, with a view to distributing pastries and baked goods to 2,500 Starbucks stores by the end of 2013.
- In November 2012, Starbucks acquired Teavana Holdings, Inc. for $620 million with a commitment "to grow and extend Teavana's already-successful 300 mall-based stores as well as add a high-profile neighborhood store concept that will accelerate Teavana's domestic and global footprint." Schultz anticipated over 1,000 Teavana stores and argued that "the tea category is ripe for reinvention and rapid growth. The Teavana acquisition now positions us to disrupt and lead, just as we did with espresso starting three decades ago."[11]
- In June 2014, Starbucks introduced its Fizzio Handcrafted Sodas: individually prepared soda drinks in three flavors made from all-natural ingredients.

Several of these initiatives involved growing Starbucks' sales to the grocery sector. Under Schultz's leadership Starbucks' Channel Development (previously the Consumer Products Group) became the fastest-growing part of the company. The strategy was based upon exploiting complementarities between Starbucks' coffeehouses and the grocery trade:

> Starbucks can seed and introduce new products and new brands inside our stores. We introduced Via instant coffee in our stores. Instant coffee is a $24 billion global category that has not had any innovation in over 50 years. And no growth. If we took Via and we put it into grocery stores and it sat on a shelf, it would have died. But we can integrate Via into the emotional connection we have with our customers in our stores. We did that for six to eight months and succeeded well beyond expectations. And as a result of that, we had a very easy time convincing the trade, because they wanted it so badly.[12]

FIGURE 2 Starbucks' "Blueprint for Profitable Growth"

This use of Starbucks' stores to lead sales through traditional grocery channels became Starbucks' "Blueprint for Profitable Growth" (Figure 2). At the base of the model were Starbucks' values and business principles. As Schultz explained: "We have built the Starbucks brand with a goal of staying true to our values and our guiding principles with a deep sense of humanity. Going forward, we will continue to focus on what made us a different kind of company, one that balances profitability and social conscience while providing exceptional shareholder value."[13] These values were the basis for Starbucks' emotional engagement with its customers. Increasingly, Starbucks augmented face-to-face customer contact within its stores with its use of social media to extend and deepen its relationships with customers. Starbucks' social media team connects with consumers through over 30 accounts on 12 different social platforms— the most important being Facebook, Twitter, Instagram, Google+, and Pinterest. This online engagement has greatly facilitated Starbucks' expansion into new overseas markets and the introduction of Starbucks-branded products in the grocery trade.

International Expansion, 2009–2015

Schultz saw emerging markets, China in particular, as a huge opportunity for Starbucks:

> The big opportunity, in terms of total stores, is what's happening in China; we've got 800 stores in greater China, 400 in the mainland. When all is said and done, we'll have thousands. We're highly profitable there. We've been there 12 years, and I would say that the hard work—in terms of building the foundation to get access to real estate, design stores, and operate them—is well in place.[14]

India was next. In January 2012, Starbucks announced a 50/50 joint venture with Tata Global Beverages to establish a chain of Starbucks coffeehouses. By July 2014, Tata Starbucks Ltd. had 50 outlets in India, mainly in airports, malls, and commercial complexes.

Other new market entries during 2012–2014 included Morocco, Colombia, Vietnam, Monaco, Brunei, Costa Rica, Finland, and Norway. In 2014, Starbucks took full ownership of Starbucks Japan, buying out its Japanese partner for $915 million. Table 2 shows store information by region.

TABLE 2   Starbucks Corporation: Store information, 2007–2014

	2014	2013	2012	2011	2010	2009	2008	2007
Percentage change in same store sales								
Americas	6	7	8	8	7	(6)	(5)	42
EMEA[a]	5	0	0	3	5	(3)		
China/Asia-Pacific	7	9	15	22	11	2	21	71
Consolidated	6	7	7	8	7	(6)	(3)	5
Stores opened during the year (net of closures)								
Americas								
Company-operated								
stores	317	276	228	32	32	(419)	4,452	10,652
Licensed stores	381	404	280	215	101	110	4,382	7,232
EMEA								
Company-operated								
stores	(9)	(29)	10	25	(64)	20	2,361	2,861
Licensed stores	180	129	101	79	100	98	5,501	497
China/Asia-Pacific								
Company-operated								
stores	250	240	154	73	30	24	n.a.	n.a.
Licensed stores	492	348	294	193	79	129	n.a.	n.a.
All other segments								
Company-operated								
stores	12	343	0	6	(1)	(2)	n.a.	n.a.
Licensed stores	(24)	(10)	(4)	(478)	10	(5)	n.a.	n.a.
Total	1,599	1,701	1,063	145	223	(45)	1,669	2,571
Total number of stores at year-end								
Americas								
Company-operated								
stores	8,395	8,078	7,802	7,574	7,542	7,574	72,382	67,932
Licensed stores	5,796	5,415	5,011	4,731	4,516	4,415	43,292	38,912
EMEA								
Company-operated								
stores	817	853	882	872	847	911	2,093	1,831
Licensed stores	1,323	1,116	987	886	807	707	3,020	2,496
China/Asia-Pacific								
Company-operated								
stores	1,132	906	666	512	439	409	n.a.	n.a.
Licensed stores	3,492	2,976	2,628	2,334	2,141	2,062	n.a.	n.a.
All other segments								
Company-operated								
stores	369	357	14	14	8	9	n.a.	n.a.
Licensed stores	42	66	76	80	558	548	n.a.	n.a.
Total	21,366	19,767	18,066	17,003	16,858	16,635	16,680	15,011

Note:
[a]Europe, Middle East, and Africa.
n.a. = not available.
Source: Starbucks Corporation, 10-K reports.

TABLE 3 Seven strategies for growth

	Theme	Action	Notes
1	Be the Employer of Choice	Invest in partners capable of delivering a superior customer experience	First and foremost, Starbucks is a people business: customers' relationship with Starbucks employees is a key determinant of customer loyalty
2	Coffee Leadership	Build our leadership position around coffee	Central to Starbucks' commitment to quality coffee is close control of its supply chain right back to the grower During 2015, 99% of Starbucks' coffee would be ethically sourced and sustainably produced
3	Grow the Store Portfolio	Increase the scale of the Starbucks store footprint with disciplined expansion	Number of stores in China Asia-Pacific to double during 2015–2019, including growth from 1,600 to 3,400 stores in China India would become one of Starbucks' top-five markets In N. America new retail formats include small stores, Starbucks' mobile trucks for college campuses, and "Reserve" roasteries
4	Create New Occasions	Grow store usage throughout the day with new product offers	New food offerings to include hot breakfast items, lunchtime meals, and evening snack and alcoholic drinks
5	Consumer Product Brand Growth	Focus on the Starbucks brand to unlock industry-leading profitable growth	Starbucks to grow sales of packaged coffee and ready-to-drink coffee beverages by 60% by 2019 Growth will come primarily for Asia-Pacific—especially China where Starbucks partnering with Tingy
6	Build Teavana	Create a second major business in tea	Teavana to spearhead Starbucks' growth within the $125 billion global market for tea Starbucks' tea revenues to double by 2019
7	Extend Digital Engagement	Drive convenience and brand engagement through mobile commerce platforms	Starbucks' growth to be underpinned by its Rewards program and its mobile payments platform New features to the Starbucks mobile app include advance ordering and payment prior to pick-up at a Starbucks store

Source: Starbucks 2015 Annual Meeting of Shareholders, Growth Strategy Panel Discussion.

Starbucks' Strategy, 2015

By 2015, these themes had been developed into a seven-part strategy that was outlined by Beto Guajardo, senior vice president for global strategy. The "Seven Strategies for Growth" are summarized in Table 3.

The Market for Coffee

Coffee was the most popular beverage of North America and Europe, with Northern Europeans the heaviest consumers (Table 4).

The US was the world's biggest market for coffee with expenditure (for consumption at home, at work, and at catering establishments) of $52.5 billion in 2013. In terms of expenditure, the market was split roughly equally between sales for

TABLE 4 Coffee consumption per head of population, 2014

Rank	Country	Kilograms	Rank	Country	Kilograms
1	Finland	9.6	11	Bosnia-Herzegovina	4.3
2	Norway	7.2	12	Estonia	4.2
3	Netherlands	6.7	13	Switzerland	3.9
4	Slovenia	6.1	14	Croatia	3.8
5	Austria	5.5	15	Dominican Republic	3.7
6	Serbia	5.4	16	Costa Rica	3.7
7	Denmark	5.3	17	Macedonia	3.6
8	Germany	5.2	18	Italy	3.4
9	Belgium	4.9	19	Canada	3.4
10	Brazil	4.8	20	Lithuania	3.3

Source: Euromonitor (www.caffeineinformer.com/caffeine-what-the-world-drinks).

the home-brewed coffee and sales of ready-brewed coffee. However, in terms of consumption, 80% of the coffee consumed in the US was at home. Sales of home-brewed coffee had recently reversed their long-term decline due to the popularity of single-serve coffee makers.

The US market could also be segmented between "ordinary" coffee and "specialty" coffee (also known as "premium" or "gourmet" coffee). Although specialty coffeehouses had existed for many decades, especially on the east and west coasts of the US, Starbucks' achievement had been to bring quality coffee to the mass market. Sales of premium brewed coffee were estimated to have grown from about $3.5 billion in 2000 to about $13 billion in 2013, with the number of coffee shops roughly doubling over the same period to reach 29,000.

Although Starbucks had been the primary driver of this growth, its success had spawned many imitators. These included both independent coffeehouses and chains, most of which were local or regional, although some aspired to grow into national chains (Table 5).

In addition to specialty coffeehouses, most catering establishments in the US, whether restaurants or fast-food chains, served coffee as part of a broader menu of food and beverages. Increasingly, these outlets were seeking to compete more directly with Starbucks by adding premium coffee drinks to their menus. McDonald's had introduced a premium coffee to its menuv but had reconfigured its outlets to include McCafés which highlighted its premium coffee drinks. Burger King and Dunkin' Donuts had also moved upmarket in their coffee offerings. Both McDonald's and Dunkin' Donuts had targeted Starbucks in their advertising, characterizing Starbucks as overpriced and snobbish.

Outside of the US, Starbucks' competitive situation varied by country. In many, competition was even more intense than in the US. For example, Starbucks' withdrawal from Australia was a consequence of a highly sophisticated coffee market developed by southern European and Middle Eastern immigrants. Throughout continental Europe, Starbucks had to deal with well-developed markets with high standards of coffee preparation and strong local preferences. In the UK, where Starbucks was second to Costa in terms of outlets, it was barely profitable.

TABLE 5 Leading chains of coffee shops in the US, 2014

Company	No. of outlets	Headquarters
Starbucks	10,780	Seattle, WA
Tim Hortons	714	Oakville, Ontario
Caribou Coffee	415	Brooklyn Center, MN
Coffee Bean and Tea Leaf	296	Los Angeles, CA
Peet's Coffee & Tea	193	Emeryville, CA
Tully's Coffee Shops	180	Seattle, WA
Coffee Beanery	131	Flushing, MI
It's A Grind Coffee House	105	Long Beach, CA
Gloria Jean's	90	Chicago, IL
Dunn Bros Coffee	85	St Paul, MN
PJ's Coffee	50	New Orleans, LA
Port City Java	32	Wilmington, NC

Source: Multiple web sources.

As well as competition from the bottom (McDonald's, Dunkin' Donuts), Starbucks faced competition from the top. The upmarket Italian coffee roaster Illycaffè SpA was expanding in the US through franchise arrangements with independent coffee-houses. Some observers believed that once Starbucks had educated North Americans about the joy of good coffee consumers of gourmet coffee would go on to seek superior alternatives to Starbucks.

The home-brewed coffee market was also being revolutionized. Sales of Italian-style espresso coffee makers, which used highly pressurized hot water to make coffee, had grown rapidly since 2000. The key stimulus had been the popularity of single-serve coffee pod systems pioneered by Nestlé's Nespresso subsidiary. In the US, Keurig Green Mountain with its K-Cup system was the market leader. Other major entrants were the Senseo system launched by Philips and Sara Lee, Kraft's Tassimo system, Lavazza's Espresso Point system, and Illy's Iperespresso system. In March 2012, Starbucks joined the fray by launching its own single-serve, home coffee makers under its Verismo brand. Starbucks also supplied K-Cups for Keurig coffee makers. By 2014, Starbucks was US brand leader in retail sales of both premium packaged coffee and single-cup capsules (Table 6).

TABLE 6 Brand market shares of packaged coffee shops in the US, 2014

Premium roast ground coffee		Single cup servings	
Brand	Market share (%)	Brand	Market share (%)
Starbucks	26.1	Starbucks	16.3
Dunkin' Donuts	14.8	Green Mountain	15.9
Private label	8.5	Private label	11.2
Peet's Coffee & Tea	7.7	Folgers Select	9.5
Eight O'clock	7.6	Coffee People	6.5

Source: Multiple web sources.

Looking Ahead

The credibility of the growth projections revealed by Beto Guajardo, head of global strategy, at Starbucks' 2015 shareholders meeting was reinforced by the release of the company's quarterly financial results on April 26, 2015. For the quarter ended March 26, 2015, revenues were 18% higher than the corresponding quarter in 2014 and operating profit was 21% higher. Among 30 investment analysts polled by the *Financial Times* on April 24, 2015, 23 assessed Starbucks as a "buy" or "outperform."

Yet amidst the acclaim for Starbucks' resumption of its growth path since 2009 and confidence in its expansion strategy for the future, doubts existed over the company's ability to sustain its outstanding performance record. Several of these risks were identified in Starbucks' 10-K report for 2014, including:

- Risks to Starbucks' brand reputation resulting from "business incidents, whether isolated or recurring and whether originating from us or our business partners, that erode consumer trust, such as actual or perceived breaches of privacy, contaminated food, recalls or other potential incidents…"[15]

- Growing competition in all of Starbucks' markets: "In the US, the ongoing focus by large competitors in the quick-service restaurant sector on selling high-quality specialty coffee beverages could lead to decreases in customer traffic to Starbucks … Similarly, continued competition from well-established competitors in our international markets could hinder growth … Increased competition in the US packaged coffee and tea and single-serve and ready-to-drink coffee beverage markets, including from new and large entrants to this market, could adversely affect the profitability of the Channel Development segment. Additionally, declines in general consumer demand for specialty coffee products for any reason, including due to consumer preference for other products, could have a negative effect on our business."[16]

- Saturation of the US market: "because the Americas segment is relatively mature and produces the large majority of our operating cash flows, such a slowdown or decline could result in reduced cash flows…"[17]

- In international markets, Starbucks' future growth was heavily dependent upon China and Asia Pacific. Here risk factors included political and regulatory uncertainties, difficulties of protecting intellectual property and enforcing contracts, reliance upon foreign partners, and the challenge of adapting to differences in consumer tastes and business and employment practices.

Some observers expressed concern over Starbucks' growing diversification—both its widening range of food and beverage products and its entry supplying the grocery trade, about which Barclays Capital analyst Jeff Bernstein observed: "They're starting a new chapter from scratch … the question has to be: Do you realize the magnitude of the task you're taking on?"[18] Other commentators expressed concern over the possible erosion of the Starbucks Experience and Starbucks' identity as it extended into tea, soda drinks, hot food, instant coffee, and drive-through stores.

Appendix: Starbucks' Country and Segment Data
Starbucks' Stores by Country

TABLE A1   Starbucks' company operated stores

	2014	2012
US	7,303	6,856
Canada	983	874
Brazil	89	53
Puerto Rico	20	19
UK	506	593
Germany	152	157
France	78	67
Switzerland	55	50
Austria	17	12
Netherlands	7	3
China	823	408
Thailand	203	155
Singapore	106	80
All other[a]	369	14
Total	10,711	9,327

Note:
[a]Includes Seattle's Best Coffee, Teavana, and Evolution Fresh.
Source: Starbucks Corporation 10-K reports.

TABLE A2   Starbucks' licensed stores

	2014	2012
US	4,659	4,189
Mexico	434	356
Canada	462	300
Other Americas	241	166
UK	285	168
Turkey	220	171
United Arab Emirates	115	99
Spain	86	78
Kuwait	72	65
Saudi Arabia	67	64
Russia	87	60
Other EMEA[a]	391	282
Japan	1,060	965
China	544	292
South Korea	700	467
Taiwan	323	271
Philippines	240	201
Other CAP	625	432
Other licensed	42	76
Total licensed	**10,653**	**8,702**

Note:
[a]EMEA: Europe, Middle East, and Africa.
Source: Starbucks Corporation 10-K reports.

Starbucks' Segment Results, 2013 and 2014

TABLE A3   Starbucks' Americas segment ($million)

	2014	2013
Net revenues:		
Company-operated stores	10,866.5	10,038.3
Licensed stores	1,074	915.4
CPG, food service and other	39.1	47.1
Total net revenues	**11,979.6**	**11,000.8**
Cost of sales including occupancy costs	4,487.0	4,214.9
Store operating expenses	3,946.8	3,710.2
Other operating expenses	100.4	96.9
Depreciation and amortization expenses	469.5	429.3
General and administrative expenses	167.8	186.7
Total operating expenses	9,171.5	8,638.0
Income from equity investees	—	2.4
Operating income	**2,808.1**	**2,365.2**

Source: Starbucks Corporation, 10-K report for 2014.

TABLE A4   Starbucks' EMEA[a] segment ($million)

	2014	2013
Net revenues:		
Company-operated stores	1,013.8	932.8
Licensed stores	238.4	190.3
CPG, food service and other	42.6	36.9
Total net revenues	**1,294.8**	**1,160.0**
Cost of sales including occupancy costs	646.8	590.9
Store operating expenses	365.8	339.4
Other operating expenses	48.2	38.5
Depreciation and amortization expenses	59.4	55.5
General and administrative expenses	59.1	71.9
Total operating expenses	1,179.3	1,096.2
Income from equity investees	3.7	0.4
Operating income	**119.2**	**64.2**

Note:
[a]EMEA is Europe, Middle East, and Africa.
Source: Starbucks Corporation, 10-K report for 2014.

TABLE A5 Starbucks' China/Asia Pacific segment ($million)

	2014	2013
Net revenues:		
Company-operated stores	859.4	671.7
Licensed stores	270.2	245.3
Total net revenues	**1,129.6**	**917.0**
Cost of sales including occupancy costs	547.4	449.5
Store operating expenses	221.1	170.0
Other operating expenses	48.0	46.1
Depreciation and amortization expenses	46.1	33.8
General and administrative expenses	58.5	48.4
Total operating expenses	921.1	747.8
Income from equity investees	164.0	152.0
Operating income	**372.5**	**321.2**

Source: Starbucks Corporation, 10-K report for 2014.

TABLE A6 Starbucks' Channel Development segment

	2014	2013
Net revenues:		
CPG	1,178.8	1,056.0
Food service	367.2	342.9
Total net revenues	1,546.0	1,398.9
Cost of sales	882.4	878.4
Other operating expenses	187.0	179.4
Depreciation and amortization expenses	1.8	1.1
General and administrative expenses	18.2	21.1
Total operating expenses	1,089.4	1,080.0
Income from equity investees	100.6	96.6
Operating income	**557.2**	**415.5**

Note:
Channel Development comprises sales of packaged coffee, packaged beverages, and other products to the grocery and food service trades.
Source: Starbucks Corporation, 10-K report for 2014.

Notes

1. Starbucks' 2014 Annual Shareholders' Meeting, March 18, 2015. Opening remarks by Howard Schultz, http://investor.starbucks.com/phoenix.zhtml?c=99518&p=irol-irolhome, accessed July 20, 2015.
2. Howard Schultz, *Pour Your Heart Into It: How Starbucks Built a Company One Cup at a Time* (New York: Hyperion, 1997).
3. J. Wiggins "When the Coffee Goes Cold," *Financial Times* (December 13, 2008).
4. Quoted in: *Howard Schultz: Building the Starbucks Community* (Harvard Business School Case No. 9-406-127, 2006).
5. "The Way We Do Business," http://gr.starbucks.com/en-US/_About+Starbucks/Mission+Statement.htm, accessed July 20, 2015.
6. "Starbucks hit by 'cascade of negativity' after ordering staff to talk racism with customers: Vice President forced off Twitter as angry public turns on 'patronizing' project," www.dailymail.co.uk/news/article-3000260/Starbucks-PR-fail-Twitter-mockery-causes-coffee-executive-delete-account-customers-say-NOT-want-talk-racism-ordering-coffee.html#ixzz3YTz4jXh5, accessed July 20, 2015.

7. "Starbucks: A Visual Cup o' Joe," *@Issue: Journal of Business and Design* 1, (2006): 18–25.

8. Starbucks Corporation, press release, Starbucks Reports First Quarter Fiscal 2009 Results (January 28, 2009).

9. M. Allison, "Schultz Concerned about Consumers, Not Competitors," *Seattle Times* (January 31, 2008), http://seattletimes.com/html/businesstechnology/2004155269_starbucksadd31.html, accessed July 20, 2015.

10. A meeting at London's Barbican Center is described in J. Wiggins, "When the Coffee Goes Cold," *Financial Times* (December 13, 2008).

11. "Starbucks' Quest for Healthy Growth: An Interview with Howard Schultz," *McKinsey Quarterly* (March 2011).

12. Ibid.

13. Ibid.

14. "Starbucks Outlines Blueprint for Profitable Growth at Annual Shareholders Meeting," Starbucks Corporation press release (March 23, 2011).

15. Starbucks Corporation 10-K report for 2014: 10.

16. Ibid.: 12.

17. Ibid.: 13.

18. "Latest Starbucks Concoction: Juice," *Wall Street Journal* (November 11, 2011).

Case 3 Kering SA: Probing the Performance Gap With LVMH

In March 2013, the French fashion and retail giant Pinault-Printemps-Redoute (PPR) changed its name to Kering. According to CEO François-Henri Pinault: "Kering is a name with meaning, a name that expresses both our purpose and our corporate vision. Strengthened by this new identity, we shall continue to serve our brands to liberate their potential for growth." The change in name followed the transformation in the business of the company.

PPR was primarily a retailing company: it owned the department store chain Au Printemps, the mail-order retailer La Redoute, and the music and electronics chain Fnac. However, the acquisition of 40% of the Gucci Group in 1999 (later increased to 99.4%) marked the beginning of a transformation from being a retailing company to a fashion and luxury goods company. Table 1 shows the main acquisitions and divestments of PPR/Kering.

This was not the first transformation that the company had undergone. PPR/Kering was the creation of the French entrepreneur Francois Pinault who had established Pinault SA as a timber trading company before acquiring retailers Au Printemps and La Redoute. In March 2005, Francois Pinault was replaced by his son, François-Henri Pinault—a graduate of HEC School of Management—as chairman and CEO of Kering. The Pinaults' dominance of Kering is ensured through the role of the Pinault family's holding company, Groupe Artémis, which owns 40.9% of Kering. (Artemis also owns Christie's, the auction house, and the Château Latour vineyards.)

In recreating itself as a diversified fashion and luxury goods company, Kering has been widely viewed as modeling itself on LVMH—the world's leading purveyor of luxury goods. However, despite the close parallels between the two companies—and their leading families, the Pinaults and the Arnaults—Kering has underperformed LVMH. During the ten-year period under the leadership of François-Henri Pinault (March 2005 to March 2015), Kering's share price growth was 121% compared to 271% for LVMH. Kering's revenues had declined by 41% over the period, compared to LVMH's growth of 100%, while operating profit had grown by 21%, compared with 67% for LVMH. (Figure 1 charts changes in Kering's share price.) It was widely believed that LVMH's superior performance would continue: of the investment analysts surveyed by the Financial Times during summer 2015, 62% rated LVMH as a "buy" or "outperform" as compared with 36% for Kering.

Efforts to boost Kering's performance included a shakeup of the management of Gucci—chief executive Patrizio di Marco was replaced by Marco Bizzarri and Creative Director Frida Giannini by Alessandro Michele—and exploring the

This case was prepared by Robert M. Grant. ©2015 Robert M. Grant.

TABLE 1   Kering's principal acquisitions and divestments, 2000–2014

Year	Business
2000	Acquisition of Boucheron (jewelry and perfumes)
2001	Acquisition of Bottega Veneta and Balenciaga
	Launch of Stella McCartney and Alexander McQueen brands
2004	Ownership of Gucci Group increased to 99.4%
	Sale of Facet (financial services), Rexel (distributors of electrical equipment)
2006	Sale of Printemps
2007	Acquisition of 62% of Puma
2009	Acquisitions of Dobotex (manufacturer of Puma socks and apparel) and Brandon (corporate merchandising)
2010–2011	Acquisitions of Cobra and Volcom (sports equipment suppliers) and luxury menswear supplier, Brioni
2012	Divestment of Fnac
	Sale of Redcats online businesses
	Joint venture formed with Yoox for online sales of luxury brands
2013	Acquisition of Christopher Kane (fashion clothing), Pomellato (jewelry) and France Croco (processor of crocodile skins)
	Sale of La Redoute and Relais Colis (parcel delivery)
2014	Acquisition of Ulysse Nardin (watches)

Source: Tables 1, 2, 3, A1 and A2 are based upon information in Kering Financial Documents for 2014, 2012, and 2010.

possible sale of its sportswear company, Puma. However, if Kering was to close the performance gap between itself and LVMH, a critical first step was to understand the sources of that performance differential.

Kering in 2015

In 2015, Kering SA operated in two segments:

- Luxury: designs, manufactures, and markets ready-to-wear clothing, leather goods, shoes, watches, jewelry, fragrances, and cosmetic products through a number of high-profile brands.

FIGURE 1   The share price of PPR/Kering, 2000–2015

€ (log Scale)

Source: Yahoo! Finance.

FIGURE 2 Kering Group: Simplified organizational chart, January 2015

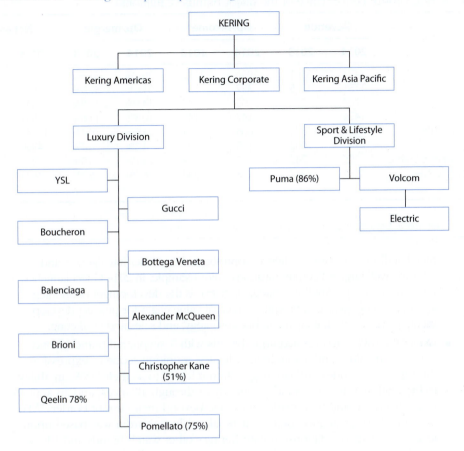

Source: Kering Financial Document, 2014.

- Sport & Lifestyle: designs and develops footwear, apparel, and accessories under the Puma, Volcom, and Electrics brands.

Figure 2 shows Kering's organizational structure. Table 2 shows the performance of major brands.

Table 3 shows revenue by geographical region.

Kering's states that its mission is "To offer products that enable its customers to express their personality. To reach this goal, the Group empowers an ensemble of powerful, complementary brands to reach their full potential, while ensuring that each of them stays true to its own values and identity—this is what Kering calls *Empowering Imagination.*"[1]

Kering's strategy comprises a combination of organic and external growth:

- Organic growth involves "(i) launching new product categories and continuously refining existing lines; (ii) strengthening distribution channels through selective expansion of directly-operated store networks, close relationships with third-party retailers, and implementation of a dynamic e-commerce strategy; (iii) enhancing sales performance, notably through increasingly efficient

TABLE 2   Kering Group: Performance of the major brands (€ millions)

Brand	Revenue		Op. Income[a]		Op. margin		Net assets	
	2014	2013	2014	2013	2014	2013	2014	2013
Gucci	3497	3561	1056	1132	30.2%	31.8%	6373	6355
Bottega Veneta	1131	1015	357	331	31.6%	32.5%	1072	532
Saint Laurent	707	557	105	77	14.9%	13.8%	547	1005
Other luxury brands	1424	1337	147	144	10.3%	11.6%	2551	1935
Total Luxury Division	6759	6378	1666	1684	24.6%	26.4%	10542	9826
Puma	2990	3002	128	192	4.3%	6.4%	4399	4335
Other sport/lifestyle brands	255	245	10	9	3.7%	3.5%	277	418
Total Sport & Lifestyle Division	3245	3247	138	200	4.2%	6.2%	4675	4753

Note:
[a]Recurrent operating income. Excludes impairment of goodwill, restructuring costs, etc.

merchandising, in-store excellence, sophisticated customer intelligence, and relevant, well-targeted communications."[2] For example, in 2014 Gucci launched a range of cosmetics. Another strategic initiative is the development of an integrated approach to eyewear comprising an internal value chain for product development, supply chain management, brand strategy, and sales and marketing.

- External growth involves acquiring brands with "exceptional brand identity, well-rooted values and a sought-after legacy; a unique scope of expression through lasting codes and language, often referred to as their DNA; an ability to broaden their territories independently or through alliances; and an aptitude to gradually expand their market coverage beyond their current borders."[3] For example, Kering's acquisition of watchmaker Ulysse Nardin was based upon its complementary relationship with Kering's other watch brands and Ulysse Nardin's potential for geographical expansion, especially in Asia-Pacific.

Synergies across Kering's businesses are achieved through:

- Talent development and deployment: "The idea behind the HR strategy is for the brands to flourish through access to a shared talent pool [which] primarily targets the top 200 managers of the Group."[4]

TABLE 3   Kering Group: Sales revenue by geographical region

	2014 €million	2013 €million	Reported change (%)	Comparable change (%)[a]
Western Europe	3,152	3,022.0	+4.3	+1.6
North America	2,147	2,032	+5.7	+5.5
Japan	963	968	−0.5	+7.3
Eastern Europe, Middle East and Africa	728	710	+2.7	+4.9
South America	465	475	−2.2	+9.0
Asia-Pacific (excluding Japan)	2,583	2,449	+5.4	+5.3
Total revenue	**10,038**	**9,656**	**+4.0**	**+4.5**

Note:
[a]Change in revenue after correcting for changes in exchange rates.

- An e-business strategy developed initially for Gucci but then extended to each of Kering's brands.
- A group-wide approach to sustainability that "represents long-term differentiation and competitive advantage by offering new business development opportunities, stimulating innovation and in many cases helping to reduce costs. It is also a motivating factor for the employees … The Kering sustainability department acts as a platform of resources to accompany the brands' own activities."[5]

Appendix 1: Kering SA: Selected Financial Data[6]

TABLE A1   Selected items from the financial statements of Kering SA, year to 31 December (€million)

	2014	2013	2012	2011	2010
INCOME STATEMENT					
Total revenue	10,038	9,656	9,736	8,062	11,008
Cost of sales	3,742	3,615	3,776	3,087	5,639
Selling, general and admin. expenses	1,545	1,516	1,494	1,229	1,637
Non-recurring net expenses	112	441	25	24	98
Other operating expenses, total	3,087	2,774	2,675	2,245	2,405
Total operating expense	8,486	8,345	7,970	6,584	9,779
Operating income	1,552	1,311	1,766	1,478	1,229
Net income from continuing operations	1,008	874	1,324	968	709
Net income from discontinued operations	(479)	(825)	(276)	18	255
Net income	529	50	1048	986	965
BALANCE SHEET					
Assets					
Cash and short-term investments	1,196	1,527	2,168	1,316	1,449
Total receivables, net	1,168	1,069	1,061	1,183	1,317
Total Inventory	2,235	1,806	1,737	2,203	2,227
Total current assets	5,273	4,925	5,460	5,277	6,940
Property, plant, and equipment	1,887	1,677	1,376	1,372	1,424
Goodwill, net	4,040	3,770	3,871	4,215	4,540
Brands and other intangibles	10,748	10,703	10,490	10,331	10,200
Total assets	23,254	22,811	25,257	24,954	24,695
Liabilities					
Accounts payable	983	766	685	1,536	1,928
Notes payable/short-term debt	1,254	540	362	892	372
Current portion long-term debt/capital leases	1,247	1,310	1,223	1,095	1,799
Total current liabilities	5,780	4,559	4,381	7,072	6,495
Total long-term debt	3,195	3,133	2,989	3,066	3,148
Total debt	5,696	4,982	4,212	5,053	5,319
Total liabilities	12,620	12,224	13,843	14,029	14,095
Total shareholders' equity	10,634	10,587	11,414	10,925	10,599
CASH FLOWS					
Net cash from operating activities	1261	1521	1366	1,332	1,264
Total cash from investing of which	(903)	(966)	259	402	79
—Capital expenditures	(551)	(675)	(442)	(325)	(305)

TABLE A2   Kering Group: Divisional information

	Luxury		Sport & Lifestyle	
Brand	**2014**	**2013**	**2014**	**2013**
Brand value (€m)	6578	6629	3887	2523
Goodwill (€m)	2944	2523	1096	1247
Number of stores	1173	1088	677	608
Number of production & logistic units	140	110	44	51
Divisional revenue by product	6759	6378	1666	1684
Apparel (%)	16	16	40	43
Footwear (%)	12	13	40	39
Leather goods (%)	53	54	--	--
Watches & jewelry (%)	10	9	--	--
Other (%)	9	8	20	18
Divisional revenue by region				
W. Europe (%)	32	33	30	30
N. America (%)	19	19	26	25
Asia Pacific (%)	31	31	14	13
Japan (%)	10	10	9	10
Other (%)	8	7	21	22

Appendix 2: LVMH: Selected Financial Data

LVMH Moet Hennessy Louis Vuitton SA (LVMH) is a Paris-based luxury goods company. Tables A3 to A5 show financial data for the company and its main businesses.

TABLE A3   LVMH's businesses and brands[a]

	Revenue (€million)		Op. profit (€million)		
Division	**2014**	**2013**	**2014**	**2013**	**Major brands**
Wines and Spirits	3,973	4,187	1,147	1,370	Moët & Chandon, Dom Pérignon, Veuve Clicquot, Krug, Ruinart, Mercier, Château d'Yquem, Château Cheval Blanc, Hennessy, Glenmorangie, Ardbeg, Wen Jun, Belvedere, Chandon, Cloudy Bay
Fashion and Leather Goods	10,828	9,882	3,189	3,140	Louis Vuitton, Céline, Loewe, Kenzo, Givenchy, Thomas Pink, Fendi, Emilio Pucci, Donna Karan, Marc Jacobs, Berluti, Nicholas Kirkwood, Loro Piana
Perfumes and Cosmetics	3,916	3,717	415	414	Christian Dior, Guerlain, Parfums Givenchy, Parfums Kenzo, Loewe Perfumes, Benefit Cosmetics, Make Up For Ever, Acqua di Parma
Watches and Jewelry	2,782	2,784	283	375	Bulgari, TAG Heuer, Chaumet, Dior Watches, Zenith, Fred, Hublot, De Beers Diamond Jewellers Ltd (a joint venture)
Selective Retailing	9,534	8,938	882	901	DFS, Sephora, Le Bon Marché, la Samaritaine, Royal Van Lent

Note:
[a]Net assets by business in 2014 were: Wines and Spirits €10,543m; Fashion and Leather €9,484m; Perfumes and Cosmetics €1,397m; Watches and Jewelry €7,196m; Selective Retailing €4,849m.
Source: Tables A3, A4, and A4 are based upon LVMH Annual Reports for 2014, 2012, and 2010.

TABLE A4   LVMH's revenues by geographical region, 2014 (€million)

France	3,212
Europe (excluding France)	5,830p
Asia (excluding Japan)	8,740
Japan	2,107
United States	7,262
Other countries	3,487

TABLE A5   Selected items from financial statements of LVMH (€million)

	2014	2013	2012	2011	2010
INCOME STATEMENT ITEMS					
Total revenue	30,638	29,016	27,970	23,659	20,320
Cost of sales	10,801	9,997	9,863	8,092	7,184
Selling, general, and admin. expenses	14,117	12,979	12,164	10,304	8,815
Non-recurring net expenses	289	116	174	95	155
Operating income	5,431	5,898	5,742	5,154	4,169
Net income	5,648	3,436	3,425	3,065	3,032
BALANCE SHEET ITEMS					
Cash and short-term investments	4,091	3,397	2,187	2,448	2,511
Total receivables, net	2,628	3,132	2,173	2,750	2,155
Inventory	9,475	8,492	7,994	7,510	5,991
Total current assets	18,110	15,971	14,167	13,267	11,199
Property, plant, and equipment	10,387	9,621	8,694	8,017	6,733
Goodwill, net	8,810	9,058	7,709	6,957	5,027
Brands and other intangibles	13,031	12,596	11,322	11,482	9,104
Total assets	53,362	56,176	49,850	47,113	37,164
Accounts payable	3,606	3,297	3,118	2,952	2,298
Notes payable/short-term debt	—	3,661	—	1,825	823
Current portion long-term debt/capital leases	4,189	1,013	2,950	1,219	1,011
Total current liabilities	12,175	11,639	9,405	9,594	7,060
Total long-term debt	5,054	4,149	3,825	4,132	3,432
Total debt	9,243	8,823	6,775	7,176	5,266
Total liabilities	31,599	29,297	25,426	24,742	19,966
Shareholders' equity	21,763	26,879	24,424	22,371	17,198
CASH FLOWS					
Net cash from operating activities	4,607	4,714	4,115	3,907	4,049
Total cash from investing of which	(2,007)	(3,917)	(1,690)	(3,016)	(2,691)
—Capital expenditures	(1,775)	(1,657)	(1,694)	(1,749)	(1,002)

Notes

1. Kering Financial Document 2014: 8.
2. Ibid.: 8.
3. Ibid.: 9.
4. Ibid.: 10.
5. Ibid.: 11.
6. LVMH 2014 Annual Report.

Case 4 Pot of Gold? The US Legal Marijuana Industry

During the early months of 2015, the US venture capital industry was waking up to the opportunities offered by the legalization of marijuana in several US states. Several specialist investment firms had been established to invest in marijuana-related businesses. An early leader was Seattle-based Privateer Holdings, which sought "to cement a leading position within the legal cannabis industry by consolidating market share through strategic investments"—these included Marley Natural, established in collaboration with Bob Marley's daughter. Another pioneer was Emerald Ocean Capital, founded by Justin Hartfield, which sought to "own and operate the 'Starbucks' and 'Bacardi' of the marijuana industry." Mainstream interest in the industry was triggered by the news in January that Founders Fund, led by PayPal co-founder Peter Theil, and a major investor in Airbnb, Lyft, and Spotify, was investing in Privateer Holdings. The Cannabis Capital Summit held in Denver during June 2015 organized by the Rockies Venture Capital Club provided a further boost to the marijuana industry by linking the growing number of potential investors with the many entrepreneurs seeking to exploit the business opportunities that legalization had made available.

However, amidst the "new gold rush" hype that surrounded the rapid growth of the legal marijuana industry—especially in Colorado—were perplexing questions over the industry's potential to generate attractive profits. Would the industry offer the sustained high profitability associated with the two other heavily regulated industries supplying recreational drugs—alcohol and tobacco—or would the industry be associated with the squeezed margins and low returns typical of the agricultural sector?

Legalization

Legalization of the sale of marijuana by the states of Colorado and Washington in 2014 was a milestone in the transition of America's marijuana business from a clandestine activity—where growers, dealers, and consumers risked fines and jail sentences—to a legitimate economic activity, which many believed would increasingly resemble tobacco and alcoholic beverages. By the beginning of 2015, Colorado, Washington, Oregon, and Alaska allowed the sale of marijuana for recreational use, 12 other states and the District of Colombia permitted its sale for medical use, and

---

This case was prepared by Robert M. Grant. ©2015 Robert M. Grant.

six states (Massachusetts, Maine, Rhode Island, California, Nevada, and Hawaii) were expected to legalize recreational use by 2018.

Yet, amidst continuing concerns over the physical and psychological ill effects of marijuana consumption, the impetus to change federal law was weak. Continuing illegality of the production, sale, and possession of marijuana under federal law was a major handicap for the industry, even if the federal government did not seek to counter or overturn legalization by individual states. In particular, firms engaged in producing and selling marijuana had very little access to the US financial system. Banks were fearful that involvement with the industry might contravene drug-racketeering or money-laundering rules. In the US as a whole, law enforcement against consumers and suppliers of marijuana continued to be active. In 2013, there were 693,481 arrests throughout the US on marijuana-related charges—88% of them for possession.

The Market for Marijuana

The US market for marijuana may be segmented between legal and illegal sectors and between medical and recreational use. Table 1 provides some data.

There were various estimates as to the extent of marijuana consumption in the US. A US government survey found that:

Marijuana was the most commonly used illicit drug in 2013. There were 19.8 million past month users in 2013 (7.5 percent of those aged 12 or older), which was similar to the number and rate in 2012 (18.9 million or 7.3 percent). The 2013 rate was higher than the rates in 2002 to 2011 (ranging from 5.8 to 7.0 percent). Marijuana was used by 80.6 percent of current illicit drug users in 2013.[1]

One suggested that 7.5% of adult Americans were regular users. A 2013 study by Pew Research found that 12% of adult respondents had used marijuana in the previous 12 months: 30% of which were for medical reasons, 47% "just for fun," and the remainder for both reasons.

TABLE 1   The US marijuana market

Market feature	Data
Numbers of users, 2014	Total users 19.5m (of which, legal users 1.5m)
Marijuana sales, 2014	Legal: $2.7bn (of which 82% medical, 18% recreational) Illegal: between $18bn and $30bn
Top six states for legal marijuana sales, 2014	California $1.32bn; Colorado $0.81bn; Washington $0.22bn; Arizona $0.16bn; Michigan $0.11bn; Oregon $0.05bn
Rate of annual growth of US legal marijuana sales	2012—18%; 2013—35%; 2014—74%; 2015E—31%; 2016E—23%
Estimate of US annual sales of marijuana with full legalization	Between $20bn and $46bn

Sources: Houston Chronicle, ArcView Market Research, Medical Marijuana Business Daily.

The Colorado Legal Marijuana Industry

Because Colorado was the first state to legalize recreational marijuana, it was seen as a bellwether for how the legal marijuana industry might develop elsewhere—even though the structure and conduct of the industry would depend greatly upon how each state framed its regulations.

From January 2014, Colorado residents were allowed to possess up to one ounce of marijuana, and could make purchases not exceeding one ounce per transaction. Initially, recreational marijuana licenses were only available to existing medical marijuana dispensaries and retail dispensaries had to produce at least 70% of the marijuana they sold. From July 2014, newcomers could apply for a license and separate cultivation and retailing licenses were issued—thus allowing the development of a wholesale market.

All marijuana facilities had to have elaborate security equipment installed, including surveillance camera and RFID tagging and tracking of every plant.

Costs included a $5000 application fee plus a licensing fee of $4000–$15000. Separate, lower-cost, licenses were issued for companies producing food and drink products with marijuana as an ingredient.

By the end of 2014, Colorado had approved 833 recreational licenses (322 of which were for retail stores) and 1416 medical licenses (505 of which were for retail dispensaries). There were many times more applications than this. Cannabis sales during 2014 comprised 109,578 lb to the medical market and 38,660 lb to the recreational market.

The companies engaged in cultivation and retailing varied greatly in size from tiny owner-proprietorships growing a few hundred plants to industrial-scale operations. In 2014, Garden of the Gods produced about 280 lb a month from dozens of 1,000-square-foot growing and flowering rooms. Medicine Man, "the Costco of weed," generated revenues in the region of $11 million during 2014.[2]

Around the core cultivation and retail distribution businesses, a variety of other businesses had emerged providing services to the industry and complementary products:

- MJ Freeway offered "seed-to-sale" tracking software that met states' regulatory requirements and assisted operations management.
- Advanced Cannabis Solutions leased real estate to large commercial growers.
- Waste Farmers supplied soils for cannabis growing.
- ArcView Group was the industry's premier hub for investment, data, and progress, including market research and a network of venture capitalists and entrepreneurs to facilitate investment in marijuana-related businesses.
- Denver-based Dixie Elixirs & Edibles offered a range of THC-infused chocolates and drinks—one of 92 businesses with licenses for producing edible marijuana products at the end of 2014.

The Economics of the Marijuana Business

Growing marijuana, whether for the medical or the recreational market, required, first, a license, then investment in a growing facility. Most of these were indoor, climate-controlled buildings with artificial light, but could also be secure greenhouses. The growing process involved the following stages:

1 Establishing stage: cloning new plants from existing female plants and allowing the new plants 7–12 days to become established.

2 "Veg" (or growing) stage: two months under constant light.

3 Flowering stage: about two months of a cycle of 12 hours of light followed by 12 hours of darkness.

4 Processing stage: hanging the plants upside down then harvesting their buds and leaves.

5 Curing stage: drying the buds and leaves.

Most published sources suggested that marijuana was a highly profitable crop. For example, Motley Fool estimated that a 10,000-square-foot growing facility with five annual growing cycles could produce 1250 lb a year with a wholesale value of $2.75 million. With production costs of $1.25 million (i.e., $1000/lb), this implied a profit margin of 55%.[3] Estimates of production costs were highly variable: one study estimated a range of $70–$400/lb[4] another study put them as high as $1606/lb.[5]

Legalization had impacted production costs. Technological advances and greater operational efficiencies had reduced production costs to around $802/lb, according to one estimate. It was predicted that costs could fall further: to $602/lb for indoor and $400/lb for greenhouse-grown marijuana. However, the costs of the required initial investment were rising. In addition to the long and arduous process of obtaining a license and fees that could be as high as $20,000, capital costs were typically between $100 and $150 per square foot, implying an investment of $600,000 to $900,000 for a modest-sized facility of 60,000 square feet. For some of Colorado's largest facilities, initial capital costs amounted to around $15 million. Real estate prices for facilities suitable for marijuana cultivation had risen sharply during 2014. Figure 1 shows the layout of a typical growing facility.

FIGURE 1 Layout of a typical marijuana indoor cultivation facility

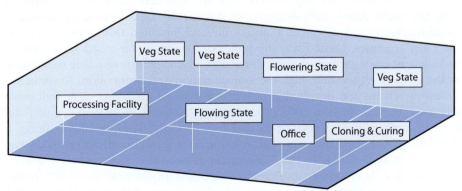

Source: J. Maxfield, "More Legalized Drug Dealing: An Inside Look at Colorado's Massive Marijuana Industry," *Motley Fool* (January 5, 2014).

Most estimates of the profit margins on marijuana growing failed to take account of risks: diseases and other sources of crop failure were common; in a cash-based business, crime was an ever-present risk; finally, there was the risk of closure or loss of license from failure to comply with state or local regulations. As a result, most Colorado marijuana businesses reported modest margins: La Conte's Clone Bar & Dispensary estimated its margin to be just 6% on revenues of $4.2 million.

Future profit margins depended upon the trends in costs and prices. On the cost side, electricity prices, tax rates, and wage rates were the key variables—workers in licensed facilities required occupational licenses, and hourly rates tended to be significantly above those in similar horticultural and retail sectors. As for prices, most predictions were for a downward trend. Colorado Pot Guide's Denver price survey found an average retail price of recreational marijuana of $327 in mid-November 2014 and commented: "The amount of marijuana grown in Colorado is expected to increase 200–300% over the next year, as more 'grow only' operations get up and running. This is going to result in an oversupply, which can only mean lower prices for consumers."[6] In mid-March 2015, the *Price of Weed* reported retail marijuana prices in Colorado as $242.20 per ounce for high-quality and $197.07 for medium-quality marijuana.[7]

Competition

Competition among the 800+ outlets supplying marijuana to the retail market in Colorado was limited by two factors: first, the market was segmented between medical and recreational markets—the medical market was open only to Colorado citizens with the necessary medical approval; second, suppliers were differentiated by geographical location and their offerings. In terms of offerings, marijuana comprised two species: *Cannabis indica* and *Cannabis sativa*, each with distinctive characteristics and each comprising many different strains. Leafly.com ("The World's Cannabis Information Resource") listed and reviewed some 800 strains. Individual dispensaries used quality and customer service to build loyalty. Although individual firms established and promoted their own brands of marijuana, the potential for brand differentiation was limited by the inability to register trademarks for marijuana-based products with the US Patent Office.

Competition extended beyond the boundaries of the legal market for marijuana. Users, both medical and recreational, had the option of growing their own (in Colorado adults could cultivate up to six plants) or could buy illegal marijuana. Illegal marijuana was produced domestically and imported from Mexico, Canada, and other countries. Mexico was the principal foreign source: outdoor production and low-cost labor gave producers a huge cost advantage that was only partly offset by the costs of clandestine, high-risk transportation and distribution. Nevertheless, the supply chains and distribution networks for illegal marijuana were well established and the lack of sales tax and regulatory compliance more than compensated for their inefficiencies. According to data from *Price of Weed*, marijuana prices in states where marijuana laws were lightly enforced (e.g., California and Florida) were similar to those in Colorado and Washington. However, in states where marijuana laws were heavily enforce (e.g., Texas and Georgia), prices were about 40% higher.

Marijuana also competes with a host of other recreational drugs. These include cocaine, amphetamine, methamphetamine, ecstasy, and a number of other organic and synthetic drugs.

The Future

The primary determinant of the development of the US marijuana industry in the coming years would be government policy. While in 2015 the forces for legalization had the upper hand at the state level, the widely predicted expansion of legal marijuana to new states would depend greatly upon the success of legalization in Colorado and Washington—in particular the impact of legalization on overall consumption, the incidence of health and social problems, and the economic impact—especially in terms of tax revenues. However, as far as the industry's development was concerned, what happened at the federal level was critical. So long as marijuana remained classified as an illegal drug, the industry would be excluded from the banking system and intellectual property protection, and business enterprises would find it difficult to expand across state boundaries. Certainly it would be impossible for established corporations selling intoxicating and addictive products—tobacco and alcoholic beverages—to enter the industry. However, the tobacco and alcoholic beverages industries did offer some pointers to how the marijuana industry might evolve over the longer term. In the case of tobacco it was interesting that, despite falling consumption, tight regulation, and heavy taxation, tobacco remained one of the most profitable industries in the US, with the major cigarette suppliers (Altria, Reynolds American, BAT, and Lorillard) earning an average return on equity of 64% during 2012–2014. However, there were major differences in structure between the tobacco and marijuana industries: while the former was highly concentrated with strongly entrenched brands, the latter was fragmented and brands had yet to emerge.

Notes

1. Substance Abuse and Mental Health Services Administration, *Results from the 2013 National Survey on Drug Use and Health: Summary of National Findings*, (Rockville, MD: SAMHSA, 2014).

2. "Family Bonds Holding Marijuana Business Together Showing Strains," *Denver Post* (April 13, 2014).

3. "More Legalized Drug Dealing: An Inside Look at Colorado's Massive Marijuana Industry," *Motley Fool* (January 5, 2014), http://www.fool.com/investing/general/2014/01/05/legalized-drug-dealing-an-inside-look-at-colorados.aspx, accessed July 20, 2015.

4. J. P. Caulkins, "Estimated Cost of Production for Legalized Cannabis," RAND Corporation (July 2010), http://www.rand.org/pubs/working_papers/WR764.html, accessed July 20, 2015.

5. PBS Frontline, "Marijuana Economics 101," http://www.pbs.org/wgbh/pages/frontline/the-pot-republic/marijuana-economics/, accessed July 20, 2015.

6. "Marijuana prices in Denver and Colorado: Fall 2014 Update," *Colorado Pot Guide* (November 20, 2014), www.coloradopotguide.com/colorado-marijuana-blog/2014/november/20/marijuana-prices-in-denver-and-colorado-fall-2014-update/, accessed July 20, 2015.

7. "Price of Weed: A Global Price Index for Marijuana," http://www.priceofweed.com/prices/United-States/Colorado.html, accessed July 20, 2015.

Case 5   The US Airline Industry in 2015

During the first quarter of 2015, it was clear the strong upswing in the profitability of US airlines that had begun in 2012 was continuing into 2015. The turnaround in the industry's fortunes was reflected in the airlines stock market values: Figure 1 shows the airline industry's index of share prices.

Airline profitability was benefiting from the fall in oil prices and the revival of the US economy. However, whether this was a temporary upturn or a more fundamental transformation in the fortunes of the industry was unclear. The major carriers had done much to reduce the cost gap between themselves and the low-cost carriers (LCCs), such as Southwest. They had won substantial concessions on pay, benefits, and working practices from their labor unions and gained efficiency benefits from outsourcing, better use of IT, and investment in new, fuel-efficient planes. Moreover, the consolidation in the industry as a result of mergers and acquisitions had created the conditions for a more restrained price competition. Meanwhile, the major airlines were showing unusual restraint by allowing increased demand to fill existing capacity rather than rushing to add new capacity.

Others were less sanguine. The US airline industry had been plagued by intense competition and dismal profitability since it was deregulated in 1978. All the major airlines, with the exception of Southwest, had been in Chapter 11 bankruptcy—some multiple times. Legendary investor Warren Buffett had observed: "The money that had been made since the dawn of aviation by all of this country's airline companies was zero. Absolutely zero." Even with the recent revival, the profit margins of the major US carriers remained thin (Table 1). The airlines' financial weakness was also evident from their credit ratings: Southwest was the only US airline whose debt was not classified as "speculative."

The financial woes of the airline industry were not restricted to the US: the global airline industry had consistently failed to earn returns that covered its cost of capital (Figure 2). Of the hundreds of airlines surveyed by IATA over the period 2000–2009, only 15 earned a return on capital that exceeded their cost of capital. Among these were Ryanair, Emirates, Singapore Airlines, and Southwest Airlines.[1]

The airline companies' propensity to invest in overcapacity that triggered a new round of fare wars was noted by the *Financial Times*' Lex column which suggested that, "Perhaps the newfound confidence in US airlines was misguided." The US airlines' response the revival in their profits and share prices had been to add capacity at a rate that far outstripped demand growth. Particularly ominous was the warning by Doug Parker, CEO of American Airlines Group, that his airlines would not cede market share to discount rivals such as Southwest.[2]

This case was prepared by Robert M. Grant. ©2015 Robert M. Grant.

FIGURE 1   Dow Jones Index of Airline Stocks, ten years to April 13, 2015

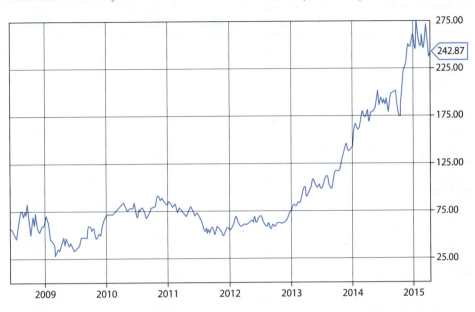

From Regulation to Competition

The history of the US airline industry comprises two eras: the period of regulation up until 1978 and the period of deregulation thereafter.

The first scheduled airline services began in the 1920s: mail rather than passengers was the primary business. In the early 1930s, a transcontinental route structure was built around United Airlines in the north, American Airlines in the south, and TWA through the middle. To counter the threat of instability from growing competition (notably from Delta and Continental), the Civil Aeronautics Board (CAB) was established in 1938 to administer the industry and competition within it. The CAB awarded interstate routes to the existing 23 airlines, established safety guidelines, approved mergers and acquisitions, and set fares and airmail rates. Industry structure ossified: despite more than 80 applications, not a single new carrier was approved between 1938 and 1978.

During the 1970s, the impetus for deregulation were supported by new developments in economics which undermined the conventional view that scale economies and network effects caused the industry to be a natural monopoly. The *theory of contestable markets* proposed that an industry did not need to be competitively structured in order to result in competitive outcomes. So long as barriers to entry and exit were low then the potential for hit-and-run entry would cause established firms to charge competitive prices and earn competitive rates of return.[3] The outcome was the Airline Deregulation Act, which, in October 1978, abolished the CAB and inaugurated a new era of competition in the airline industry.

The height of barriers to entry into the airline industry is unclear. While capital costs of setting up an airline can be modest (a single leased plane will suffice), establishing a scheduled airline service requires setting up a complex system comprising gates, airline and aircraft certification, airport facilities, baggage handling services,

TABLE 1 Revenues and profitability of the largest US airlines, 2009–2014

	2014	2013	2012	2011	2010	2009
Revenue ($bn)						
United[a]	38.3	38.9	37.2	37.1	23.3	16.3
Delta	40.4	37.8	36.2	35.1	31.8	28.1
American[b]	42.6	26.7	24.9	24.0	22.2	19.9
Southwest	18.6	17.7	—	12.1	15.6	10.4
Net margin (%)						
United[a]	2.9	1.5	(1.9)	2.7	1.1	(4.0)
Delta	1.6	6.7[d]	2.7	2.4	1.9	(4.4)
American[b]	10.0	(4.7)	(8.3)	(8.2)	(2.1)	(7.4)
Southwest	6.1	4.2	2.5	1.1	3.8	1.0
ROA (%)[c]						
United[a]	3.0	1.6	(1.9)	2.2	0.6	(3.5)
Delta	1.2	4.8[d]	2.3	2.0	1.4	(2.8)
American[b]	9.7	(3.0)	(8.8)	(8.3)	(2.1)	(5.8)
Southwest	5.7	3.9	2.3	1.0	3.0	0.7

Notes:
[a]AMR until 2014, after American Airlines Group.
[b]UAL Corp. until 2010, there after United Continental Holdings.
[c]Net income/End of period total assets.
[d]Based upon pre-tax net income.

FIGURE 2 Return on invested capital (ROIC) and weighted average cost of capital (WACC) for the world airline industry, 1993–2014

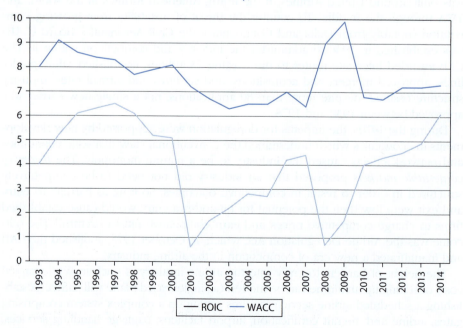

Source: IATA.

FIGURE 3 Profitability of the US airline industry, 1978–2014

Source: Bureau of Transportation Statistics.

and the marketing and distribution of tickets. At some airports, the dominance of gates and landing slots by the major carriers made entry into particular routes difficult. Nevertheless, immediately following deregulation, 20 new carriers—including People Express, Air Florida, and Midway—had set up, and new entry into the industry has continued—one of the most recent entrants being Virgin America in 2007.

Since deregulation, the industry has been subject to turbulence caused by external shocks and internal competition. During 1979–1983, high oil prices, recession, and strong competition triggered bankruptcies (over 100 carriers went bust) and a wave of mergers. Further profit slumps occurred in 1990–1994, 2001–2003, and 2008–2010. Figure 3 shows industry profitability since deregulation. Profitability is acutely sensitive to the balance between demand and capacity: losses result from industry load factors falling below the breakeven level (Figure 4). The role of competition in driving efficiency is evident from the near-continuous decline in real prices over the period (Figure 5).

Firm Strategy and Industry Evolution

Changes in the structure of the airline industry during the past three decades were primarily a result of the strategies of the airlines as they sought to adjust to the conditions of competition in the industry and to gain competitive advantage.

Route Strategies: The Hub-and-Spoke System

During the 1980s, the major airlines reorganized their route networks. Systems of point-to-point routes were replaced by hub-and-spoke systems where each airline concentrated its routes on a few major airports. These hubs were linked by frequent services using large aircraft. Smaller cities were connected to these hubs by shorter routes using smaller aircraft. The hub-and-spoke system offered two major benefits:

- It allowed greater efficiency through reducing the total number of routes needed to link the airports within a network and concentrating traveler and

FIGURE 4 Load factor in the US airline industry, 1978–2014

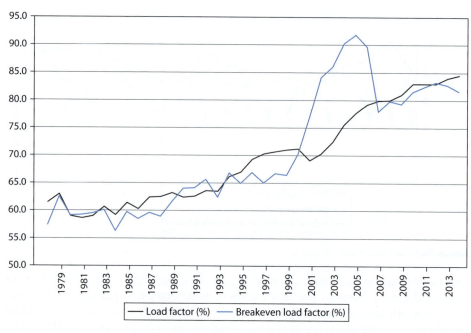

Source: Air Transport Association, annual economic reports (various years); Bureau of Transportation Statistics.

    maintenance facilities into fewer locations. It permitted the use of larger, more cost-efficient aircraft for interhub travel. The efficiency benefits of the hub-and-spoke system were optimized by scheduling flights so that incoming short-haul arrivals were concentrated at particular times to allow passengers to be pooled for the longer-haul flights on large aircraft.

- It allowed major carriers to establish dominance in regional markets and on particular routes. Table 2 shows airports where a single airline held a dominant market share in 2014. The hub-and-spoke system also created a barrier to the entry of new carriers, who often found it difficult to obtain gates and landing slots at the major hubs.

    The hub-and-spoke networks of the major airlines also involved alliances with local commuter airlines. American Eagle, United Express, and Delta Shuttle were franchise systems established by AMR, United Airlines, and Delta, respectively, whereby regional airlines used the reservation and ticketing systems of the major airlines and coordinated their operations and marketing policies with those of their bigger partners.

Mergers

The effect of continued new entry in reducing seller concentration in the industry has been offset by mergers and acquisitions between existing players (Figure 6). Since 2007, as a result of a more permissive attitude from the Department of Justice, the pace of consolidation in the industry accelerated with several mergers among leading airlines—Delta acquiring Northwest, United merging with Continental, and

FIGURE 5 Average fares in the US airline industry (cents per revenue passenger mile), 1960–2015

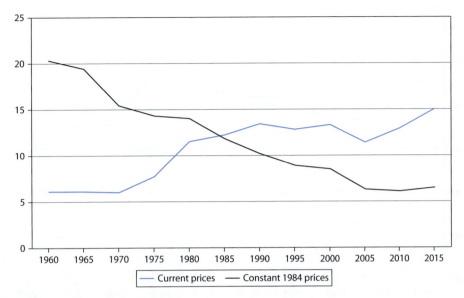

Source: Bureau of Transportation Statistics.

American merging with US Airways (Figure 7). Yet, despite consolidation, there is limited evidence that competition has been significantly affected. As a result of capacity reduction by the biggest airlines and market share gains by smaller carriers—notably Alaska, JetBlue, Frontier, and Virgin America—concentration has continued to decline since 2000. A report by the US General Accounting Office concluded that:

TABLE 2 Local market share of largest airline for selected US airports (by domestic passenger numbers), 2014

City	Airline	Share of passengers (%)
Miami	American[a]	80.8
Dallas/Fort Worth	American[a]	73.5
Atlanta	Delta	73.4
Baltimore	Southwest	68.8
Charlotte	American[a]	60.2
Houston	Continental	53.5
Minneapolis–St. Paul	Delta	53.0
Newark	United	48.3
Detroit	Delta	47.2
Seattle	Alaska	40.7
San Francisco	United	39.3
Chicago (O'Hare)	Delta	26.0

Note:
[a]Includes US Airways.
Source: Bureau of Transportation Statistics.

FIGURE 6   Concentration in the US Airline Industry (four-firm concentration ratio) 1970–2015

Note:
The four-firm concentration ratio (CR4) measures the share of the industry's passenger miles accounted for by the four largest companies. During 1970–1981, the four biggest companies were United, American, TWA, and Eastern. During 1982–2005, the four biggest companies were American, United, Delta, and Northwest. During 2006–2015, the four biggest were American, United, Delta, and Southwest.
Source: US Department of Transportation.

In recent years, the average number of competitors has not substantially changed in markets traveled by the majority of passengers, despite several major airline mergers. From 2007 through 2012, the average number of effective competitors (defined as airlines with more than a 5 percent market share) ranged from 4.3 to 4.5 in the markets with the most passengers.[4]

However, this conclusion did not take account of the 2014 merger between American and US Airways.

Pricing

The intensification of competition that followed deregulation was typically led either by established airlines becoming financially distressed or by LCCs. People Express, Braniff, New York Air, and Southwest all used their highly efficient cost structures and a bare-bones service to aggressively undercut the legacy airlines. Although most new budget airlines failed within a few years of entry, there seemed to be an inexhaustible supply of aviation entrepreneurs enthralled with the opportunity to run their own airlines. Among recent entrants, JetBlue and Virgin America have been the most successful.

FIGURE 7 Mergers and acquisitions among major US passenger airlines, 1981–2012

Price cutting by the major carriers tends to be highly selective, with airlines seeking to separate price-sensitive leisure customers from price-inelastic business travelers. As a result, fare bands widened: advanced-purchased economy fares with Saturday night stays were as little as one-tenth of the first-class fare for the same journey.

Price cuts were also selective by route. Typically, the major airlines offered low prices on those routes where they faced competition from low-cost rivals. Southwest, the biggest and most successful of the LCCs, complained continually of predatory price cuts by its larger rivals. However, the ability of the major airlines to compete against the budget airlines was limited by the majors' cost structures, including infrastructure, restrictive labor agreements, old airplanes, and commitments to extensive route networks. To meet the competition of low-cost newcomers, several of the majors set up new subsidiaries to replicate the strategies and cost structures of the budget airlines. These included Continental's Continental Lite (1994), UAL's Shuttle by United (1995), Delta's Song (1993), and United's Ted (1994): all were expensive failures.

The quest for cost efficiency among the legacy airlines involved them adopting many of the operational practices of the LCCs. They also renegotiated union contracts, terminated inefficient working practices, abandoned unprofitable routes, and reduced staffing levels. In many instances, radical cost cutting was preceded by Chapter 11 bankruptcy. Major airlines entering Chapter 11 bankruptcy since 2000 have included: TWA (2001), US Airways (2002–2003), United (2002–2005), Northwest (2005–2007), Delta (2005–2007), and American (2011–2013).

The legacy airlines also adopted many of the pricing practices of the LCCs: notably charging separately for baggage, seat preferences, refreshments, and boarding priority. Baggage and reservation change fees collected by US airlines increased from about $1.4 billion in 2007 to $6.1 billion in 2013. The overall tendency was for the legacy carriers and LCCs to become increasingly similar in their strategies:

> What was once a clear division between network, low-cost, and charter models is now less clear, with network carriers operating low-cost, short-haul subsidiaries; LCCs providing frequencies and services to attract business passengers; and charter carriers venturing into single-seat sales. LCCs are even starting long-haul service, competing with network carriers on point-to-point routes.[5]

The Quest for Differentiation

Under price regulation, competition among airlines focused upon branding, customer service, and in-flight food and entertainment. Deregulation brutally exposed the myth of customer loyalty: most travelers found little discernible difference among the offerings of different major airlines and their choice of airline on a particular route became increasingly dependent upon price. As airlines cut back customer amenities, efforts at differentiation became primarily focused upon business and first-class travelers. The high margins on premium fares provided a strong incentive to attract these customers by offers of spaciousness and in-flight pampering.

The most widespread and successful initiative to build customer loyalty was the introduction of frequent-flyer schemes. American's frequent-flyer program was launched in 1981 and was soon followed by all the other major airlines. By offering free tickets and upgrades on the basis of miles flown, and setting threshold levels for rewards, the airlines encouraged customers to concentrate their air travel on a single airline. Airlines' unredeemed frequent-flyer miles represented liabilities running into billions of dollars by 2015. At the same time, by involving other companies as partners—car-rental companies, hotel chains, credit card issuers—frequent-flyer programs became an important source of additional revenue for the airlines.

The Industry in 2015

The Airlines

At the beginning of 2015, the US airline industry (including air cargo firms) comprised 151 companies, many of them local operators. Table 3 lists those with annual revenues exceeding $100 million. The industry was dominated by five major passenger airlines: United, American, Delta, US Airways, and Southwest. The importance of the leading group was enhanced by its networks of alliances with smaller airlines. In addition to these domestic alliances with regional airlines, the Big 3, were also core members of international alliances: United with Star Alliance, American with the oneworld alliance, and Delta with SkyTeam.

Market for Air Travel

Airlines were the dominant mode of long-distance travel in the US. For shorter journeys, cars provided the major alternative. Alternative forms of public transportation—bus and rail—accounted for a small proportion of journeys in excess of a hundred miles. Only on a few routes (notably Washington–New York–Boston) did trains provide a viable alternative to air travel.

Most forecasts pointed to continued growth in the demand for air travel, but at a much slower rate than in earlier decades. During the last two decades of the 20th century, North American air travel had grown by almost 5% per annum. Between 2013 and 2033, Boeing predicted that North American airline traffic would grow by an average of 2.9% a year (in terms of passenger miles). Some observers thought this overoptimistic, citing the increasing discomfort of air travel and the upsurge in video conferencing, suggesting that the long-anticipated shift from face-to-face to virtual business meetings had finally arrived.

Changes were occurring within the structure of demand. Of particular concern to the airlines was evidence that the segmentation between business and leisure

TABLE 3   The leading US airlines, 2014[a]

Airline	Market share (%)[a]	Passenger numbers (million)	Load factor (%)
Southwest	16.90	26.0	82.8
Delta	16.85	106.2	86.8
United	15.07	64.7	86.1
American	12.40	66.4	85.0
US Airways	8.32	50.6	85.4
JetBlue	5.12	26.4	84.7
Alaska	4.28	19.2	85.6
SkyWest	2.33	26.0	83.5
ExpressJet	2.33	28.0	81.4
Spirit	2.13	12.6	86.8
Frontier	1.65	11.3	89.8
Hawaiian	1.62	9.1	85.0
Envoy	1.16	14.7	77.5
Endeavor	0.96	11.4	78.7
Mesa	0.69	8.3	83.3
Horizon	0.33	6.5	79.2
Air Wisconsin	0.33	5.6	78.2
Chautauqua	0.19	3.1	75.8

Note:
[a]Based upon revenue passenger miles.
Source: Bureau of Transportation Statistics.

customers was breaking down. Conventional wisdom dictated that the demand for air tickets among leisure travelers was fairly price elastic; that of business travelers was highly inelastic. Hence, the primary source of airline profit was high-margin business fares. However, following the 2008–2009 financial crisis, growing numbers of companies were limiting or eliminating employee access to premium-class air travel.[6]

Changes in the distribution of airline tickets contributed to increased price competition. The advent of the internet had decimated traditional travel agencies—retailers that specialized in the sale of travel tickets, hotel reservations, and vacation packages. Airline tickets were increasingly sold by online travel agents such as Expedia, Priceline, and Orbitz, or through airlines' own websites. By 2015, the traditional travel agency industry was dominated by a few global leaders such as American Express and Carlson Wagonlit. Although airlines had benefited from the cuts in travel agents' commission rates (commissions paid by airlines to resellers fell from 6 to 1% of operating expenses between 1992 and 2013), the key impact of the internet was providing consumers with unparalleled price transparency, greatly increasing their responsiveness to fare differentials.

Cost Conditions

The structure of operating costs is shown in Table 4. A key feature of the industry's cost structure was the high proportion of fixed costs. In the short term, most costs varied little with fluctuations in demand. For example, because of union contracts, it was difficult to reduce employment and hours worked during downturns. Similarly, the need to maintain flight schedules meant that planes flew even when occupancy was very low. The desire to retain the integrity of the entire network made the airlines reluctant to shed unprofitable routes during downturns. An important implication of the industry's cost structure was that, at times of excess capacity, the marginal costs of filling empty seats on scheduled flights was extremely low.

The industry's labor costs were boosted by high levels of employee remuneration: average pay in the airline industry was $72,634 in 2013, compared to an average for US employees generally of $44,888. Pilots and co-pilots earned an average of $141,306.[7] Pension and other benefits were also more generous than in most other industries. Labor costs for the major network airlines were boosted by low labor productivity resulting from rigid working practices that were part of the employment contracts agreed with unions. The industries main labor unions were the Association of Flight Attendants, the Air Line Pilots Association, and the International Association of Machinists and Aerospace Workers. Despite these unions' tradition of militancy and past successes in pay negotiation, since 2001 the precarious financial state of the airlines and the flexibility offered by Chapter 11 bankruptcy have enabled the airlines to impose pay restrictions and more flexible working practices.

Fuel Expenditure on fuel depended on the age of an airline's fleet, average flight length, and oil prices. Newer planes and longer flights led to higher fuel efficiency. Fuel-efficiency considerations had encouraged plane manufacturers to develop long-distance, wide-body planes with two rather than four engines. Fuel represented the most volatile and unpredictable cost item for the airlines due to fluctuations in crude oil prices.

TABLE 4 Operating costs in the US airline industry, 2006 and 2014

Cost item	Increase in cost 2000–2014 (%)	% of total operating expenses	
		2006	2014
Labor	62[a]	23.8	24.7
Fuel	233[b]	25.5	28.0
Professional services	20[c]	7.8	7.5
Food and beverage	(38)[d]	1.5	1.5
Landing fees	72[e]	2.0	1.9
Maintenance material	8[f]	1.4	1.9
Insurance	0[g]	0.1	0.3
Passenger commissions	(78)[h]	1.3	0.9
Communication	(28)[i]	0.9	0.8
Advertising and promotion	(46)[j]	0.8	0.6
Other operating expenses	86	34.5	31.9

Notes:
[a]Compensation per employee; [b]cost per gallon; [c]per available seat mile; [d]per revenue seat mile; [e]per ton landed; [f]per aircraft block hour; [g]aircraft and non-aircraft; [h]as % of passenger revenue; [i]per enplanement; [j]per revenue passenger mile.
Source: Airlines for America, "Passenger Airline Cost Index: US. Passenger Airlines."

In principle, an airline can use forward contracts and options to hedge against fluctuations in fuel prices. In practice this is difficult: futures and options in jet fuel are not widely traded, hence airlines typically use crude oil and heating oil derivatives to hedge. However, the differential between jet fuel and crude oil prices tend to fluctuate greatly.

The extent of hedging varied between airlines according to their expectations about the future direction of prices and whether they have the financial resources for hedging. Southwest has historically hedged most of its fuel purchases; US Airways has traditionally left its fuel cost unhedged. The decline in oil prices during 2014 encouraged most airlines to reduce their hedging.

Delta Airlines took its fuel hedging one step further by becoming an active trader of jet fuel and crude oil. In 2011, it moved its jet fuel procurement unit into its treasury services department and hired oil traders from Wall Street. However, its most audacious move was buying the Trainer oil refinery in Pennsylvania from ConocoPhillips for $180 million. The refinery would be supplied with crude by BP, which would also exchange refined products from the refinery for jet fuel. Delta believed that its fuel-trading activities would benefit from having a physical product to trade and access to detailed information on production costs.[8]

Equipment Aircraft were the biggest capital expenditure item for the airlines. In 2015, with list prices for commercial jetliners ranging from $64 million for a Boeing 737 to $428 million for an Airbus A380, the purchase of new planes represented a major source of financial strain for the airlines. While Boeing and Airbus competed fiercely for sales of new aircraft through discounts and generous financing terms, their major source of profits was aftermarket sales. Even with the huge delays and cost overruns on its 787 development, Boeing's return on equity during 2005–2014 averaged 54%. Airbus's return on equity averaged 9%. Regional jets were supplied by Bombardier and Embraer, both of which had developed larger aircraft which were increasingly competing with the smaller planes offered by Boeing and Airbus.

The airlines' weak finances and high borrowing costs meant a preference for leasing rather than purchasing planes. The world's two biggest aircraft owners were both leasing companies: GECAS (a subsidiary of General Electric) with 1732 planes and ILFC (a subsidiary of AIG) with 1031.

Airport Facilities   Airports play a critical role in US aviation industry. They are hugely complex, expensive facilities and few in number. Only the largest cities are served by more than one airport. Despite the growth in air transport, Denver International Airport is the only major new airport to have been built since 1978. Most airports are owned by municipalities and generate substantial revenue flows for their owners. In 2013, the airlines paid over $2.5 billion to US airports in landing fees and a further $3 billion in passenger facility charges. Landing fees were set by contracts between the airport and the airlines and were usually based on aircraft weight. New York's La Guardia airport has the highest landing fees in the US, charging about $7000 for a Boeing 777 to land.

Four US airports—JFK and La Guardia in New York, Newark, and Washington's Reagan National—are officially "congested" and takeoffs and landings there are regulated by the government. At these airports, slots were allocated to individual airlines, who subsequently assumed de facto ownership and engaged in trading them. According to Jeff Breen of Cambridge Aviation Research, "Slots are a lot like baseball franchises. Once you have one, you have it for life."[9]

Cost Differences Between Airlines   One of the arguments for deregulation had been that there were few major economies of scale in air transport, hence large and small airlines could coexist. Subsequently, little evidence has emerged of large airlines gaining systematic cost advantages over their smaller rivals. However, there are economies associated with network density: the greater the number of routes within a region, the easier it is for an airline to gain economies of utilization of aircraft, crews, and passenger and maintenance facilities. In practice, cost differences between airlines reflect managerial, institutional, and historical factors rather than the influence of economies of scale, scope, or density. The industry's traditional cost leader, Southwest, created the LCC business model comprising point-to-point service from minor airports, single-class planes, limited customer service, a single type of airplane, and job flexibility by employees. Southwest, JetBlue, and Spirit Airlines continue to have the industry's lowest operating costs per available seat mile (ASM), despite flying relatively short routes. However, as shown in Table 5, the cost gap between the legacy carriers and the LCCS has narrowed.

Managing costs requires meticulous attention to capacity utilization: the primary source of losses is load factors falling below the breakeven level. Moreover, excess capacity creates incentives to cut prices in order to fill empty seats. Adjusting fares to optimize load factors and maximize the revenue for each flight is the goal of the airlines' *yield management systems*—highly sophisticated computer models that combine capacity, sales data, and demand forecasts to continually adjust pricing.

TABLE 5   Operating data for the larger airlines, 2006 and 2014

Airline	ASMs (billion)		Load factor (%)		Operating revenue per ASM (cents)		Operating expense per ASM (cents)	
	2006	2014	2006	2014	2006	2014	2006	2014
American	175.9	154.4	82.0	85.0	12.5	17.3	12.5	15.8
United	139.8	104.1	82.1	86.1	13.1	18.2	13.1	17.3
Delta	133.5	115.5	77.8	86.8	13.0	19.0	13.6	16.8
Southwest	85.2	120.5	73.0	80.9	9.5	13.0	8.5	12.4
US Airways	83.9	58.0	77.6	85.4	15.7	19.5	15.2	17.7
JetBlue	23.8	36.0	82.5	84.7	7.6	12.9	7.5	11.9
Alaska	23.2	29.8	76.4	85.6	11.3	16.7	11.5	14.0

Source: Bureau of Transportation Statistics.

Looking to the Future

At the end of April 2015, the US airline industry presented a mixed picture. Despite the sustained upturn in profitability, the balance sheets of most airlines remained weak. Among the leading airlines only Southwest had a ratio of long-term debt to equity of less than one. Delta's ratio of long-term debt to ratio was 106, for American Airlines Group it was 685, and for United Continental Holdings it was 408.

Looking ahead, the critical issue was whether the recent improvement in industry profitability was a cyclical phenomenon driven by weak oil prices, an improving domestic economy, and the impact of higher load factors in moderating price competition, or whether it was supported by a more fundamental shift in industry structure and competitive behavior.

The success of the major network airlines in reducing their cost base through productivity improvements and reductions in compensation and benefits provided one source of optimism. As a result, the LCCs no longer had a substantial cost advantage. However, a key issue for the airlines was whether the beneficiaries from improvements in cost efficiency were the airlines' shareholders (through higher profits) or their customers (through lower fares).

Previous revivals in airline industry profitability ended either as a result of external events or by the industry's own propensity to overinvest. In the case of the two previous upturns (1996–1999 and 2006–2008), external events were the critical factors (the September 11, 2001 terrorist attacks and the financial crisis of 2008–2009). In the absence of external shocks, the critical issue will be the willingness of the airlines to avoid overinvesting in new capacity. The revival of 2012–2015 was driven by rising load factors. This was the result not only of an improving economy but also of capacity restraint. During 2007–2009, the industry's ASMs fell from 744 to 667 billion. Subsequent capacity additions during 2009–2014 were modest. As a result, the legacy carriers had substantially less capacity in 2014 than in 2006 (see Table 5). As the disruptions caused by bankruptcy and merger faded into the past, would the airlines resume their traditional propensity to compete for market share through new planes and fare reductions?

One factor favoring moderation in price competition was the reduction in the number of legacy carriers from six in 2000 (American, United, Delta, Continental, Northwest, and US Airways) to three in 2015. Although expansion by LCCs—especially Southwest and Jet Blue—had partly filled the gap, by 2015 there were fewer airlines competing on most routes than in 2000. Yet, fewer major airlines did not necessarily translate into capacity discipline. During 2015 and 2016, the industry was expected to expand capacity by between 4 and 6% in each year, with the LLCs leading the way with capacity growth of over 10% annually.[10] Moreover, the US airline industry would not be isolated from the international situation where Asian and Middle East airlines were continuing to add capacity on international routes.

Notes

1. International Air Transport Association, *Vision 2050* (Singapore: IATA, February 2011).
2. Lex, "US Airlines: Here We Go Again," *Financial Times* (May 28, 2015).
3. S. Martin, "The Theory of Contestable Markets," Department of Economics, Purdue University (July 2000).
4. United States Government Accountability Office, *Report to Congressional Requestors: Airline Competition* (June 2014).
5. Boeing Company, "About Our Market: Current Market Outlook 2014–15," http://www.boeing.com/commercial/market/, accessed July 20, 2015.
6. "CEOs Fly Coach? Business Travel Turns Frugal," *Wall Street Journal* (February 12, 2013).
7. US Dept. of Transportation, *Form 41 via BTS*, Schedule P6 and P10.
8. "Delta Buys Refinery to Combat Fuel Costs," *Financial Times* (April 30, 2012).
9. "Airlines' Control of Landing Slots Affects Ticket Prices," *Seattle Times* (October 12, 2010).
10. Lex, op. cit.

Case 6 Wal-Mart Stores, Inc., June 2015

If you don't want to work weekends, you shouldn't be in retail.

—SAM WALTON (EXPLAINING THE SATURDAY CORPORATE MEETING)

In 2015, Wal-Mart Stores, Inc. was the world's biggest company in terms of revenue—a position it had first attained in 2000 and had held for most of the intervening years.

Since going public in 1972, Walmart's record of growth and profitability was remarkable. It had increased in revenue in every single year and its return on equity had never fallen below 19%—despite the turmoil of economic recessions, war, and political crises, and the rise of e-commerce.

External circumstances had created challenges of each of Walmart's CEOs. For Doug McMillon, Walmart's fourth CEO since founder Sam Walton stepped down in 1988, the key challenges of his first year as CEO included the growing competition from online retailers—Amazon in particular—and the growing criticism that Walmart's success was built upon the efforts of underpaid employees. McMillon, at 48 the youngest CEO since Walton, had responded resolutely to both challenges. He increased investment in Walmart's Silicon Valley e-commerce development centers and, in February 2015, announced that Walmart's minimum starting pay would rise to $9 an hour—$1.75 above the federal minimum wage.[1]

Yet, sustaining Walmart's phenomenal record of growth and profitability would be an ever more daunting challenge. As Walmart continued to expand its range of goods and services—into groceries, fashion clothing, music downloads, online prescription drugs, financial services, and health clinics—it was forced to compete on a broader front. While Walmart could seldom be beaten on price, it faced competitors that were more stylish (T.J.Maxx), more quality-focused (Wholefoods), more service-oriented (Lowe's, Best Buy), and more focused in terms of product range. In its traditional area of discount retailing, Target was proving an increasingly formidable competitor, while in warehouse clubs, its Sam's Clubs ran a poor second to Costco.

Increasing its size boosted Walmart's buying power but also brought problems. Walmart's success had rested heavily upon its ability to combine huge size with speed and responsiveness. Critical to Walmart's agility was its short chain of command and close relationship between the top management team and individual store managers. A key component in this linkage had been Walmart's Saturday-morning

This case was prepared by Robert M. Grant. ©2015 Robert M. Grant.

meeting at its Bentonville HQ. In January 2008, the growing size of the meeting and increasing difficulty of getting all Walmart executives back to Bentonville resulted in the company changing these meetings, which the company had described as "the pulse of our culture," from weekly to monthly.[2] In 2014, McMillon made attendance voluntary.[3]

Increased size also made Walmart a bigger target for opponents. For years Walmart had been under attack by organized labor seeking to unionize Walmart's two million employees. More recently, "The Beast of Bentonville" had attracted the ire of environmentalists, anti-globalization activists, women's and children's rights advocates, small-business representatives, and a growing number of legislators of varying political hues. In response, Walmart had become increasingly image-conscious and was a late, but enthusiastic, convert to social and environmental responsibility. The result was a series of senior appointments to new executive positions—a head of global ethics and a new executive vice president of government relations—plus more top management time spent in Washington and with the media.

Walmart's expanding global reach also raised complex strategic and organizational issues. Unlike other successful global retailers (such as IKEA and H&M), Walmart did not have a consistent approach to different national markets: it had different strategies and operated under different names in different countries. Its performance, too, varied greatly from country to country. Although its international operations delivered most of Walmart's growth, their profitability was inferior to that of the US business. Underlying these contrasts was the incongruity that the world's biggest company had its roots in Bentonville, Arkansas—a town which, when Walmart became a public company, had a mere 5,508 inhabitants.

Given these challenges, how could Walmart possibly sustain its remarkable performance in the brutally competitive, fast-paced world of discount retailing?

History of Walmart

Discount stores—large retail outlets offering a broad range of products—began appearing in the US after World War II. Conventional wisdom held that cities with at least 100,000 inhabitants were needed to support a discount store. Sam Walton—an operator of Ben Franklin variety stores in Arkansas—believed that, with low prices, discount stores could be viable in smaller communities: "Our strategy was to put good-sized stores into little one-horse towns that everyone else was ignoring."[4] His first Walmart opened in 1962; by 1970, there were 30 Wal-Mart Stores in small and medium-sized towns in Arkansas, Oklahoma, and Missouri.

Distribution was a problem for Walmart:

> Here we were in the boondocks, so we didn't have distributors falling over themselves to serve us like our competitors in larger towns. Our only alternative was to build our own distribution centers so that we could buy in volume at attractive prices and store the merchandise.[5]

In 1970, Walton built his first distribution center, which was financed by taking the company public. Replicating this structure of large distribution hubs serving up to 100 discount stores formed the basis of Walmart's expansion strategy. Entering a new area, Walmart built a few stores that were served initially from a nearby distribution center. Once a critical mass of stores had been established, Walmart would build a new distribution center. By 1995, Walmart was in all 50 states.

Inevitably, this expansion took Walmart from small and medium-sized towns to major conurbations, where it met stronger competition from other discount chains.[6]

Different Store Formats

Sam Walton experimented continually with alternative retail formats—this continued under Walmart's subsequent CEOs:

- Sam's warehouse clubs were wholesale outlets which required membership: they offered products in multipacks and catering-size packs with minimal customer service.
- Supercenters were large-format stores (averaging a floor space of 178,000 square feet, compared with 105,000 square feet for a Walmart discount store and 129,000 square feet for a Sam's Club). They combined a discount store with a grocery supermarket, plus other specialty units such as an eyeglass store, hair salon, dry cleaners, and photo lab. They were open 24 hours a day, seven days a week.
- Neighborhood Markets were supermarkets with an average floor space of 42,000 square feet.
- Walmart Express convenience stores of about 12,000 square feet were launched in 2013.
- Walmart also built a substantial online business through its websites www. walmart.com and www.samsclub.com. Its online presence was extended through its online pharmacy and music download service. A key feature of Walmart's online strategy was its integration of web-based transactions with its physical presence allowing online customers to pick up at their local Walmart store—with same-day pickup for items that were in stock.

International Expansion

Walmart's international expansion began in 1991 with a joint venture with Mexico's largest retailer, Cifra SA, to open discount stores and Sam's Clubs in several Mexican cities. By 2000, Walmart had entered six overseas countries. Table 1 summarizes Walmart's international development.

Walmart's overseas expansion followed no standard pattern: sometimes it entered through greenfield entry, sometimes through joint venture, and in some countries it acquired an existing retailer. Its overseas operations have met with varying degrees of success. In the adjacent countries of Mexico and Canada, Walmart was highly successful. In Germany, Walmart sold its 85 stores to Metro after eight years of losses. Walmart also withdrew from South Korea in 2006. In Japan, its Seiyu chain has found profitability elusive. In October 2014, Walmart announced the closure of 30 of its Japanese stores.[7]

China presented Walmart with its biggest opportunity and greatest challenge. The perils of China's highly politicized market became apparent to Walmart in 2011 when the now-deposed regional leader, Bo Xilai, closed 13 Wal-Mart Stores in Chongqing for alleged mislabeling of meat. Despite ambitious growth plans—in April 2015 CEO

TABLE 1 Walmart stores by country, January 2015

Country	Stores	Notes
US	5,163	Included 3,407 Supercenters, 470 discount stores, 647 Sam's Clubs, 639 Neighborhood Markets, and other small formats
Mexico	2,290	In 1991 formed JV[a] with Cifra. Chains include Walmart, Bodegas, Suburbia, VIPS, and Mercamas. In 2000, Walmart acquired 51% of Cifra and took control of the JV. By 2003, Walmart Mexico was the country's biggest retailer
Canada	394	Entered in 1994 by acquiring 120 Woolco stores from Woolworth and converting them to Walmart discount stores
Argentina	105	Entered 1995: greenfield venture
Brazil	557	Entered 1995: JV with Lojas Americana, includes Todo Dia, Bompreço, and Sonae stores
China	411	In 1996, built a Supercenter and Sam's Club in Shenzhen. Continued to grow organically, then in 2006 acquired Trust-Mart with its 102 stores
UK	592	Entered 1999 by acquiring Asda. Operates Walmart superstores, and Asda supermarkets and discount stores
Japan	431	Entered 2002: acquired 38% of Seiyu; 2008, Seiyu became a wholly owned subsidiary of Walmart. Mainly small stores, some superstores
Central America	690	Acquired CARHCO, a subsidiary of Royal Ahold in 2005 with stores throughout Central America
Chile	404	Entered January 2009 by acquiring Distribución y Servicio SA
India	20	Entered May 2009; JV with Bharti Enterprises
Africa	396	Entered 2011, acquiring 51% of Massmart Holdings Ltd; 305 stores in South Africa, also stores in Botswana, Ghana, Lesotho, Malawi, Mozambique, Namibia, Nigeria, Swaziland, Tanzania, Uganda, and Zambia
Total	11,453	

Note:
[a] JV = joint venture.
Source: www.walmartstores.com.

Doug McMillon announced plans to open 115 more Walmart's in China by 2017—finding sites for new Wal-Mart Stores was an ongoing problem. Walmart's China strategy also involved integrating its growing network of stores with its online presence through its 51% stake in online retailer Yihaodianh.[8]

In every country Walmart entered, it was forced to adapt its retailing system to the specific circumstances of each country's consumer habits and preferences, infrastructure, competitive situation, and the political and regulatory environment.

Sam Walton and His Legacy

Walmart's strategy and management style was inseparable from the philosophy and values of its founder. Until his death in 1992, Sam Walton was the embodiment of Walmart's unique approach to retailing. After his death, Sam Walton's beliefs and business principles continued to guide Walmart's identity and its development.

For Walton, thrift and value for money were a religion. Undercutting competitors' prices was an obsession that drove his unending quest for cost economies. Walton established a culture in which every item of expenditure was questioned. Was it necessary? Could it be done cheaper? He set an example that few of his senior colleagues could match: he walked rather than took taxis, shared rooms at budget motels while on business trips, and avoided any corporate trappings or manifestations of opulence or success. For Walton, wealth was a threat and an embarrassment rather than a reward and a privilege. His own lifestyle gave little indication that he was America's richest person (before being eclipsed by Bill Gates). He was equally disdainful of the display of wealth by colleagues: "We've had lots of millionaires in our ranks. And it drives me crazy when they flaunt it … I don't think that big mansions and flashy cars is what the Walmart culture is supposed to be about."[9]

His attention to detail was legendary. As chairman and CEO, his priorities lay with his employees ("associates"), customers, and the operational details through which the former created value for the latter. He shunned offices in favor of spending time in his stores. Much of his life was spent on the road (or in the air, piloting his own plane) making impromptu visits to stores and distribution centers. He collected information on which products were selling well in Tuscaloosa, why margins were down in Santa Maria, how a new display system for children's clothing in Carbondale had boosted sales by 15%. His passion for detail extended to competitors' stores: as well as visiting their stores, he was known to count cars in their parking lots.

Central to his leadership role was his relationship with his employees, the Walmart associates. In an industry known for low pay and tough working conditions, Walton created a unique spirit of motivation and involvement. He believed fervently in giving people responsibility, trusting them, but also continually monitoring their performance.

After his death in 1992, Sam Walton's habits and utterances became enshrined in Walmart's operating principles. The "10-foot attitude" pledge reflected Sam Walton's request to an employee that: "I want you to promise that whenever you come within 10 feet of a customer, you will look him in the eye, greet him and ask if you can help him."[10] The "Sundown Rule"—that every request, no matter how big or small, gets same-day service—become the basis for Walmart's fast-response management system. "Three Basic Beliefs" became the foundation for Walmart's corporate culture:

- *Service to our customers*: "Every associate—from our CEO to our hourly associates in local stores—is reminded daily that our customers are why we're here. We do our best every day to provide the greatest possible level of service to everyone we come in contact with."
- *Respect for the individual*: Walmart's emphasis on "respect for every associate, every customer, and every member of the community" involves valuing and recognizing the contributions of every associate, owning "what we do with a sense of urgency" and empowering "each other to do the same," and "listening to all associates and sharing ideas and information."
- *Striving for excellence*: this comprised innovating by continuous improvement and trying new ways of doing things, pursuing high expectations, and working as a team by "helping each other and asking for help."[11]

Sam Walton's iconic status owed much to his ability to generate excitement and fun within the seemingly sterile world of discount retailing. Walmart's replacement of its mission slogan—"Everyday Low Prices" by "Save Money, Live Better"—was intended to reflect Walton's insistence that Walmart play a vital role in the happiness and well-being of ordinary people.

Walmart in 2015

The Business

Walmart described its business as follows:

> Wal-Mart Stores, Inc. … helps people around the world save money and live better—anytime and anywhere—in retail stores or through our e-commerce and mobile capabilities. Through innovation, we are striving to create a customer-centric experience that seamlessly integrates digital and physical shopping. Physical retail encompasses our brick and mortar presence in each market where we operate. Digital retail is comprised of our e-commerce websites and mobile commerce applications. Each week, we serve nearly 260 million customers who visit our over 11,000 stores under 72 banners in 27 countries and e-commerce websites in 11 countries.
>
> Our strategy is to lead on price, invest to differentiate on access, be competitive on assortment and deliver a great experience. Leading on price is designed to earn the trust of our customers every day by providing a broad assortment of quality merchandise and services at everyday low prices ("EDLP"), while fostering a culture that rewards and embraces mutual respect, integrity and diversity. EDLP is our pricing philosophy under which we price items at a low price every day so our customers trust that our prices will not change under frequent promotional activity. Price leadership is core to who we are. Everyday low cost ("EDLC") is our commitment to control expenses so those cost savings can be passed along to our customers. Our digital and physical presence provides customers access to our broad assortment anytime and anywhere. We strive to give our customers and members a great digital and physical shopping experience.

Currently, our operations comprise three reportable business segments:

- Walmart U.S. is our largest segment and operates retail stores in all 50 states in the U.S., Washington D.C. and Puerto Rico, with three primary store formats, as well as digital retail. Walmart U.S. generated approximately 60% of our net sales in fiscal 2015, and of our three segments, Walmart U.S. is the largest and has historically had the highest gross profit as a percentage of net sales…

- Walmart International consists of operations in 26 countries outside of the US … and includes numerous formats including supercenters, supermarkets, hypermarkets, warehouse clubs, including Sam's Clubs, cash & carry, home improvement, specialty electronics, restaurants, apparel stores, drug stores and convenience stores, as well as digital retail. Walmart International generated approximately 28% of our fiscal 2015 net sales. The overall gross profit rate for Walmart International is lower than that of Walmart U.S. because of its merchandise mix.

- Sam's Club consists of membership-only warehouse clubs and operates in 48 states in the US … Sam's Club accounted for 2% of our fiscal 2015 net sales … [M]embership income is a significant component of the segment's operating income. As a result, Sam's Club operates with a lower gross profit

TABLE 2   Walmart: Performance by segment (year ending January 31)

	2005	2006	2007	2008	2009	2010	2011	2012	2013	2014	2015
Sales ($billion)											
Wal-Mart Stores	191.8	209.9	226.3	239.5	255.7	259.9	260.3	264.2	274.4	279.4	288.0
Sam's Clubs	37.1	39.8	41.6	44.4	46.9	47.8	49.4	53.7	56.4	57.2	58.0
International	56.3	62.7	77.1	90.6	98.6	97.4	109.2	125.9	134.7	136.5	136.2
Change in sales (%)											
Wal-Mart Stores	10.1	9.4	7.8	5.8	6.8	1.6	0.1	1.5	3.9	1.8	3.1
Sam's Clubs	7.5	7.3	4.5	6.7	5.6	1.9	3.5	8.8	4.9	1.3	1.5
International	18.3	11.4	30.2	17.5	9.1	(1.2)	12.1	15.2	7.4	1.3	0.3
Operating income ($billion)											
Wal-Mart Stores	14.2	15.3	16.6	17.5	18.8	19.3	19.9	20.3	21.1	21.8	21.3
Sam's Clubs	1.3	1.4	1.5	1.6	1.6	1.5	1.7	1.8	1.9	1.8	2.0
International	3.0	3.3	4.3	4.8	4.9	4.9	5.6	6.2	6.4	5.1	6.2
Operating margin (%)											
Wal-Mart Stores	7.4	7.3	7.3	7.3	7.3	7.4	7.6	7.7	7.7	7.8	7.4
Sam's Clubs	3.5	3.5	3.6	3.6	3.4	3.1	3.4	3.4	3.3	3.2	3.4
International	5.3	5.3	5.5	5.2	5.0	4.5	5.1	4.9	4.7	3.8	4.5

Source: Wal-Mart Stores, Inc. 10-K reports.

rate and lower operating expenses as a percentage of net sales than our other segments.[12]

Table 2 shows sales and profits for these three business segments.

Performance

Table 3 summarizes some key financial data for Walmart during 2003–2015. Table 4 compares Walmart to its leading competitors.

Wal-Mart Stores' Operations and Activities

Purchasing and Vendor Relationships

The size of Walmart's purchases and its negotiating ability made it both desired and feared by suppliers. As a Walmart vendor, a manufacturer gained unparalleled access to the US retail market. At the same time, Walmart's buying power and cost-cutting fervor meant razor-thin margins for most suppliers. Purchasing was centralized. All dealings with US suppliers took place at Walmart's Bentonville headquarters. Would-be suppliers were escorted to one of the spartan cubicles on "Vendor Row" where they prepared themselves for an intimidating and grueling encounter: "Expect a steely eye across the table and be prepared to cut your price," counselled one supplier.[13] Another observed: "All normal mating rituals are verboten. Their highest priority is making sure everybody at all times in all cases knows who's in charge … They talk softly, but they have piranha hearts, and if you aren't totally prepared when you go in there, you're in deep trouble."[14] To avoid dependence on individual suppliers, Walmart limited the total purchases it obtained from any one supplier. The result was an asymmetry of

TABLE 3 Wal-Mart Stores, Inc.: Financial summary 2003–2015 (year ended January 31; $billion unless otherwise stated)

	2003	2004	2005	2006	2007	2008	2009	2010	2011	2012	2013	2014	2015
Net sales	230	256	285	312	345	375	401	405	419	444	469	476	486
Net sales increase (%)	5.5	12.0	11.3	9.5	11.7	8.6	7.2	1.0	4.4	5.9	5.0	1.6	2.0
US same-store sales increase (%)	6.0	4.0	3.3	3.4	2.0	1.6	3.5	(0.8)	(0.6)	1.6	2.4	(0.5)	0.5
Gross margin (%)	22.6	22.3	22.8	23.1	23.5	24.1	24.3	24.9	24.8	24.5	24.3	24.3	24.3
SG&A[a] expense as % of sales	17.4	17.5	18.0	18.2	18.5	19.1	19.4	19.7	19.4	19.2	19.0	19.3	19.4
Interest, net	0.8	0.7	0.9	1.2	1.6	1.8	1.9	1.9	2.0	2.1	2.1	2.2	2.3
Income taxes	4.4	5.1	5.6	5.8	6.2	6.9	7.1	7.4	7.5	7.9	8.0	8.1	8.0
Operating income	13.3	15.2	17.3	18.7	20.5	22.0	22.8	24.0	25.5	26.5	27.7	26.9	27.1
Net income	8.0	9.1	10.3	11.2	11.3	12.7	13.4	14.4	16.9	16.3	17.0	16.0	16.4
Current assets	30.7	34.5	38.9	43.8	47.6	47.6	48.8	48.8	52.0	54.9	58.8	61.2	63.3
Inventories	24.4	26.6	29.8	32.2	33.7	35.2	34.5	32.7	36.4	40.7	43.8	44.9	45.1
Property and equipment	51.4	58.5	68.1	79.3	88.4	97.0	95.7	102	105	110	113	115	114
Total assets	94.8	105	120	138	152	164	163	170	181	193	200	205	204
Current liabilities	32.5	37.4	43.2	48.8	52.2	58.5	55.3	56.8	58.6	62.3	67.2	69.3	65.3
Long-term debt[b]	19.6	20.1	23.3	30.1	30.7	33.4	34.5	39.5	43.7	47.0	41.4	44.6	43.7
Shareholders' equity	39.5	43.6	49.4	53.2	61.6	64.6	65.3	70.5	68.5	71.3	76.3	76.3	81.4
Current ratio	0.9	0.9	0.9	0.9	0.9	0.8	0.9	0.8	0.9	0.9	0.9	0.9	1.0
Return on assets[c] (%)	9.0	9.0	9.3	8.9	8.8	8.5	8.4	8.7	9.3	8.4	9.1	8.2	8.4
Return on equity[d] (%)	21.0	21.0	22.6	22.5	22.0	21.0	21.2	21.2	24.6	22.8	23.0	21.0	20.8
Other data (units)													
US stores[e]	3393	3551	3702	3856	4022	4141	4258	4314	4418	4479	4625	4835	5173
International units[f]	1272	1355	1587	2285	2757	3121	3615	4099	4587	5287	5783	6107	6290
Employees (millions)	1.4	1.4	1.6	1.8	2.1	1.9	2.1	2.1	2.1	2.2	2.2	2.2	2.2

Notes:
[a]SG&A: sales, general, and administration (cost of doing business).
[b]Including long-term lease obligations.
[c]Net income before minority interest/average assets.
[d]Net income/average shareholders' equity.
[e]For 2012–2015 includes overseas Sam's Club outlets.
[f]For 2012–2015 excludes overseas Sam's Club outlets.
Source: Wal-Mart Stores, Inc. 10-K reports.

TABLE 4 Walmart and its competitors: Performance comparisons ($billion unless otherwise stated)[a]

	Walmart		Target		Dollar General		Costco	
	2013	2014	2013	2014	2013	2014	2013	2014
Sales revenue	476.3	485.7	71.3	72.6	17.5	18.9	105.2	112.6
Operating Income	26.9	27.1	5.2	4.5	1.7	1.8	3.1	3.2
Total net income	16.0	16.4	2.0	(1.6)	1.0	1.1	2.0	2.1
Inventories	44.9	45.1	8.8	8.8	2.6	2.8	7.9	8.5
Total current assets	61.2	63.3	11.6	14.1	3.2	3.5	15.8	17.6
Total assets	204.8	203.7	44.6	41.4	10.9	11.2	30.3	33.0
Total current liabilities	69.3	65.3	12.8	11.7	1.8	2.0	13.3	14.4
Long-term debt	41.8	41.1	12.6	12.7	0.0	2.6	5.0	5.1
Total liabilities	128.5	122.3	28.3	27.4	5.5	5.5	19.5	20.7
Shareholder's equity	76.3	81.4	16.2	14.0	5.4	5.7	10.8	12.3
Financial ratios								
Gross profit margin (%)	24.8	24.8	29.5	29.4	31.1	30.7	12.6	12.6
Operating margin (%)	5.6	5.6	7.3	6.2	9.7	9.45	2.9	2.9
Net profit margin (%)	5.2	5.1	2.8	1.2	5.7	5.8	1.9	1.9
SG&A[b] expense/sales (%)	19.2	19.2	21.2	20.2	21.1	21.3	9.7	9.7
Depreciation and amortization/ sales (%)	0.03	0.03	0.02	0.02	0.08	0.09	0.07	0.07
Total asset turnover	2.3	2.4	1.6	1.7	1.7	1.7	3.7	3.6
Inventory turnover	8.1	8.1	6.1	5.8	4.9	4.9	12.3	12.0
Long-term debt/equity	0.6	0.5	0.8	0.9	0.5	0.5	0.5	0.4
Current ratio	0.9	1.0	0.9	1.2	1.8	1.8	1.2	1.2
Operating income/assets (%)	13.4	13.3	11.2	10.5	15.7	16.2	10.4	10.1
Return on equity (%)	21.0	20.8	12.5	10.6	18.7	19.8	18.9	18.1

Notes:
[a]The table shows data for the financial years that correspond most closely to calendar years 2013 and 2014.
[b]SG&A: sales, general, and administration (cost of doing business).
Sources: Company 10-K reports.

bargaining power: Walmart's biggest supplier, Procter & Gamble, accounted for about 3% of Walmart's sales, but this represented 18% of P&G's revenues.

However, Walmart's relationships with its suppliers were anything but arm's-length, Walmart involved itself in its suppliers' employment and environmental policies, imposing detailed requirements monitored through third-party audits. By 2012, Walmart's *Standards for Suppliers Manual* ran to 46 pages.

Collaboration involved a constant quest for efficiencies through enhanced cooperation—though Walmart received a disproportionate share of the resulting cost savings. Walmart's arrangements with P&G were a model for these relationships. Electronic data interchange (EDI) began in the early 1990s and within two years there were 70 P&G employees based at Bentonville to manage sales and deliveries to Walmart.[15] EDI was extended to almost all Walmart's US vendors. Through Walmart's "Retail Link," suppliers could log onto the Walmart database for real-time store-by-store information on sales and inventory for their products. This collaboration allowed suppliers and manufacturers within the supply chain to synchronize their demand projections under a collaborative planning, forecasting, and replenishment scheme, resulting in Walmart achieving faster replenishment, lower inventory, and a product mix more closely tuned to local customer needs.

Warehousing and Distribution

Since the 1980s, Walmart has been a world leader in distribution logistics. While most discount retailers rely heavily on their suppliers and third-party distributors for distribution to their individual stores, 82% of Walmart's purchases are shipped to Walmart's own distribution centers from where they are distributed in Walmart trucks. The efficiency of the system rests on Walmart's hub-and-spoke configuration. Distribution centers (the hubs) are typically over a million square feet, operate 24/7, and serve between 75 and 110 stores within a 200-mile radius. Deliveries into distribution centers are made either in suppliers' trucks or Walmart trucks, then deliveries are made to Walmart stores. The grouping of Walmart stores allows trucks to deliver partial loads to several Walmart stores on a single trip. On backhauls, Walmart trucks bring returned merchandise from stores and pick up from local vendors, allowing trucks to be over 60% full on backhauls.

Walmart continuously adapts its logistics system to increase speed and efficiency:

- Cross-docking allows goods arriving on inbound trucks to be unloaded and reloaded on outbound trucks without entering warehouse inventory.
- "Remix" adds an additional tier to Walmart's distribution system: third-party logistic companies made small frequent pick-ups from suppliers allowing Walmart a five-day rather than a four-day week ordering cycle from suppliers.
- The international extension of Walmart's procurement system involves direct purchases from overseas suppliers, rather than through importers, giving Walmart direct control of import logistics. In 2002, it established a global purchasing center in Shenzhen and another in Shanghai. In Baytown, Texas it created a four-million square foot import distribution center.[16]
- Walmart pioneered the use of radio frequency identification (RFID) for logistics management and inventory control.
- In 2008, Walmart introduced a new system of packing trucks—allowing a better use of their capacity.

The fact that Amazon's warehousing and supply chain system was built almost entirely by logistics managers poached from Walmart is indicative of Walmart's leadership in this area.[17]

In-store Operations

Walmart's management of its retail stores was based upon satisfying customers by combining low prices, a wide range of quality products carefully tailored to customer needs, and a pleasing shopping experience. Walmart's store management was distinguished by the following characteristics:

- *Merchandising*: Wal-Mart Stores, Inc. offered a wide range of nationally branded products. Between 2006 and 2009, it had expanded its range of brands, focusing in particular on upscale brands. Traditionally, Walmart had placed less emphasis on own-brand products than other mass retailers; however, after 2008, Walmart greatly increased its range of private-label products. Its "Store of the Community" philosophy involved tailoring its range of merchandise to local market needs on a store-by-store basis—a goal that was facilitated by Walmart's meticulous analysis of point-of-sale data for individual stores (see below).

- *Decentralization of store management*: Individual store managers were given greater decision-making authority in relation to merchandise, product positioning within stores, and pricing than was typical in discount retailing where such decisions were concentrated at head office or at regional offices. Similar decentralized decision-making was apparent within stores, where the department managers (e.g., toys, health and beauty, consumer electronics) were expected to develop and implement their own ideas for increasing sales and reducing costs.

- *Customer service*: Discount stores were open from 9am to 9pm weekdays, with shorter hours on weekends. Supercenters were open continuously. Despite the primacy of low costs allowing low prices, Walmart sought to engage with its customers at a personal level. Within stores, employees were expected to look customers in the eye, smile at them, and offer a verbal greeting. Walmart's "Satisfaction Guaranteed" program assured customers that Walmart would accept returned merchandise on a no-questions-asked basis.

Marketing and External Relations

At the core of Walmart's strategy was Sam Walton's credo that "There is only one boss: the customer" and the belief that value for customers equated to low prices. Hence, Walmart's marketing strategy was built upon its slogan "Everyday Low Prices." Unlike other discount chains, Walmart did not engage in promotional price-cutting.

"Everyday Low Prices" also permitted Walmart to spend less on advertising and other forms of promotion than its rivals. Its advertising/sales ratio in 2012 was 0.55%—most of its rivals had advertising/sales ratios of between 1.5 and 3.0% (Target's was 2.0%). Nevertheless, Walmart advertising budget of over $2 billion exceeded that of any other retailer.

The image that Walmart communicated was grounded in traditional American virtues of hard work, thrift, individualism, opportunity, and community. This identification with core American values was reinforced by a strong emphasis on patriotism and national causes.

However, as Walmart became a target for pressure from politicians, NGOs, and labor unions, it was increasingly forced to adapt its image and business practices. In 2005, Walmart committed itself to a program of environmental sustainability and set ambitious targets for renewable energy, the elimination of waste, and a shift in product mix toward environmentally friendly products.[18] Two years later, Walmart published the first of its annual sustainability reports.

Commitment to social and environmental responsibility was part of a wider effort by Walmart to broaden its consumer appeal and counter the attempts by activist groups to characterize Walmart as a heartless corporate giant whose success was built upon exploitation and oppression. The desire to reposition and renew Walmart's relationship with its customers and with society culminated in a 2008 company-wide image makeover that included a new corporate logo, a program of store redesign, and the replacement of its "Everyday Low Prices" tagline with "Save Money. Live Better."[19]

Human Resource Management

Walmart's accommodation of external pressures also extended to changes in its human-resource practices. Walmart's approach to human resource management reflected Sam Walton's beliefs about relations between the company and its employees and between employees and customers. All employees, from corporate executives to checkout clerks, are known as "associates." Walmart claims that its relations with its associates are based on respect, high expectations, close communication, and clear incentives.

In common with other discount retailers, Walmart's employees received low pay. In April 2015, full-time employees earned an average of $13 an hour; part-time employees, $10. However, starting pay was about $8 an hour for in-store employees. Benefits included a company health plan that covered almost all employees and a retirement scheme for employees with a year or more of service. Performance-based bonuses extended to hourly as well as salaried employees and a stock purchase plan was also available.

Walmart's decision, in February 2015, to increase hourly rates for about 500,000 of its US employees to a base rate of $9 an hour in 2015 and $10 by 2016 (costing about $1 billion annually) was in response to external and internal pressures. Labor unions had long sought to recruit Walmart employees. Walmart resisted unionization in the belief that union membership created a barrier between the management and the employees in furthering the success of the company and its members. However, at several of its overseas subsidiaries Walmart worked closely with local unions.[20] Internal pressures were of greater concern. Walmart's rates of pay and employee scheduling practices were attacked by OUR Walmart—an association of current and former Walmart employees formed in 2011.

The careers page of Walmart's website opens with the words: "Innovation. Collaboration. Transformation. And lots of fun." Orchestrating employee enthusiasm and involvement was a central feature of Walmart's management style. Opportunity for advancement was a key incentive: 75% of Walmart managers (including CEO Doug McMillon) had started as hourly employees. Close collaboration between managers and front-line employees infused every aspect of Walmart's operations. Employees were encouraged to use their initiative and to be flexible, especially in relation to serving customers and identifying opportunities for cost saving. They received continual communication about their company's performance and about store operations.

Walmart's human resource practices are an ongoing paradox. The enthusiasm it generates among employees helps to generate a level of involvement and empowerment that is unusual among large retail chains. Yet, the intense pressure for cost reduction and sales growth frequently results in cases of employee abuse. In several adverse court decisions, Walmart has been forced to compensate current and former employees for unpaid overtime work and for failure to ensure that workers received legally mandated rest breaks. However, a class action suit alleging systematic discrimination against Walmart's female employees was rejected by the Supreme Court in 2011.

Information Technology

Walmart was a pioneer in applying information and communications technology to support decision making and promote efficiency and customer responsiveness. Walmart was among the first retailers to use computers for inventory control, to initiate EDI with its vendors, and to introduce bar code scanning for point-of-sale and inventory control. To link stores and cash register sales with supply chain management and inventory control, Walmart invested $24 million in its own satellite in 1984. By 1990, Walmart's satellite system was the largest integrated private satellite network in the world, providing two-way interactive voice and video capability, data transmission for inventory control, credit card authorization, and enhanced EDI. During the 1990s, Walmart pioneered the use of data mining for retail merchandising,

> The result, by now, is an enormous database of purchasing information that enables us to place the right item in the right store at the right price. Our computer system receives 8.4 million updates every minute on the items that customers take home—and the relationship between the items in each basket.

> Data analysis allows Walmart to forecast, replenish, and merchandise on a product-by-product, store-by-store level. For example, with years of sales data and information on weather, school schedules and other pertinent variables, Walmart can predict daily sales of Gatorade at a specific store and automatically adjust store deliveries accordingly.[21]

Analyzing purchasing patterns also led to continual adjustments in store layout (e.g., creating "baby aisles that include infant clothes and children's medicine alongside diapers, baby food and formula—but at the same time plac[ing] higher-margin products among the staples."[22]

Even before the onset of web-based computing, IT had played a central role in integrating Walmart's entire value chain with point-of-sale data forming the basis for inventory replenishment, deliveries from suppliers, and top management decision making:

> Combine these information systems with our logistics—our hub-and-spoke system in which distribution centers are placed within a day's truck run of the stores—and all the pieces fall into place for the ability to respond to the needs of our customers, before they are even in the store. In today's retailing world, speed is a crucial competitive advantage. And when it comes to turning information into improved merchandising and service to the customer, Walmart is out in front.[23]

Unlike most retailers, Walmart outsourced little of its IT requirements. Walmart's IT function was split between two groups: Walmart Technology, at the corporate headquarters in Bentonville, developed and managed technology for the stores and logistical systems, while Global eCommerce, employing over 2000 developers and engineers in Silicon Valley, developed customer-focused technologies and ran Walmart websites. Walmart's commitment to IT was indicated by its hiring of IT professionals and its acquisition of 14 technology-based companies between February 2010 and May 2015. However, not all Walmart's IT initiatives were successful. It was the prime mover behind the much-delayed mobile payments platform CurrentC, which was losing out to ApplePay and Google Wallet.[24]

Organization and Management Style

Walmart's management structure and management style reflected Sam Walton's principles and values—especially his belief that all managers, including the CEO, needed to be closely in touch with customers and store operations. The result was a structure in which communication between individual stores and the Bentonville headquarters was both close and personal. Traditionally, Walmart US's regional vice presidents were each responsible for supervising between ten and 15 district managers (later designated "market managers") who, in turn, were in charge of eight to 12 stores. The key to Walmart's fast-response management system was the close linkages in this system which ensured speed of communication and decision making between the corporate headquarters and the individual stores and warehouses. The critical links in this system were the regional vice presidents. Most large retailers had regional offices; Walmart's regional VPs had no offices. Their time was spent visiting stores and warehouses in their regions Monday to Thursday, then returning to Bentonville on Thursday night for Friday and Saturday meetings. On Friday, the 7 a.m. management meeting was followed by the merchandising meeting, which dealt with stockouts, excess inventory, new product introductions, and various merchandising errors. At the Saturday meeting, weekly sales data would be reviewed and the regional VPs would contact their district managers about actions for the coming week. According to former CEO David Glass: "By noon on Saturday we had all our corrections in place. Our competitors, for the most part, got their sales results on Monday for the week prior. Now, they're already ten days behind."

The two-and-a-half-hour Saturday morning meetings beginning at 7 a.m. were a manifestation of Walmart's unique management style—described by *The Economist* magazine as "part evangelical revival, part Oscars, part Broadway show."[25] Meetings began with a review of the week's performance data, involved question-and-answer sessions targeting examples of good and bad performance, and included presentations that focused on merchandising best practices or new product lines. Then came guest appearances—guests had included CEOs, such as Carlos Ghosn, Steve Jobs, and Steve Ballmer; celebrity entertainers; and sports stars. The meetings closed with a talk from Walmart's CEO. The meetings were relayed to Walmart offices worldwide.

However, Walmart's growing size necessitated changes to its structure and management systems. In 2010, it introduced an additional layer of management, dividing the US into three regions: North, South, and West. As already noted, the legendary Saturday meetings were also downgraded. Did these changes mean that the unique spirit and drive that had been the basis of Walmart's success for four decades were finally being overwhelmed by the size and complexity that were the products of this success?

Notes

1. "Wal-Mart Raising Wages as Market Gets Tighter," *Wall Street Journal* (February 19, 2015).
2. "Wal-Mart Alters Regular Saturday Meeting," *Northwest Arkansas Democrat Gazette* (January 14, 2008).
3. "Walmart's new CEO has made its iconic Saturday morning meeting optional," http://qz.com/272018/walmarts-new-ceo-has-made-its-iconic-saturday-morning-meeting-optional/, accessed July 20, 2015.
4. S. Walton, *Sam Walton: Made in America* (New York: Bantam Books, 1992).
5. "How Sam Walton Does It," *Forbes* (August 16, 1982): 42.
6. *Wal-Mart Stores, Inc.*, Harvard Business School Case No. 9–974–024 (1994).
7. "Wal-Mart: US retail giant to close 30 stores in Japan," http://www.bbc.co.uk/news/business-29844379, accessed July 20, 2015.
8. "Walmart Accelerates China Expansion," *Financial Times* (April 29, 2015).
9. S. Walton, op. cit.
10. "Sam's Way," www.walmart.com/cservice/aw_samsway.gsp, accessed July 20, 2015.

11. "Culture," http://corporate.walmart.com/our-story/work-ing-at-walmart/culture, accessed July 20, 2015.

12. Wal-Mart Inc., 2015 10-K report: 7–8.

13. "A Week aboard the Wal-Mart Express," *Fortune* (August 24, 1992): 79.

14. Ibid.

15. "Lou Pritchett: Negotiating the P&G Relationship with Wal-Mart," Harvard Business School Case No. 9-907-011 (2007).

16. "Inside the World's Biggest Store," *Time Europe* (January 20, 2003).

17. B. Stone, *The Everything Store: Jeff Bezos and the Age of Amazon* (New York: Little Brown, 2013): 68–76.

18. "The Green Machine," *Fortune* (July 31, 2006).

19. "Wal-Mart Moves Upmarket," *Business Week* (June 3, 2009).

20. "Wal-Mart Works with Unions Abroad, but not at Home," *Washington Post* (June 7, 2011).

21. Wal-Mart Stores, *Annual Report, 1999*: 9.

22. Ibid.: 9.

23. Ibid.: 11.

24. "Apple Pay Is Creaming Walmart in the Mobile Payment Wars," *Money Magazine* (May 11, 2015), http://time.com/money/3848698/apple-pay-walmart-mcx-currentc/, accessed July 20, 2015.

25. "Wal-Mart's Weekly Meeting: Saturday Morning Fever," *Economist* (December 6, 2001).

Case 7 Harley-Davidson, Inc., May 2015

> For us and for our loyal customers, the motorcycles we build aren't just motor-cycles. They are living pieces of American history, mystique on two wheels. They are the vehicle with which our riders discover the power, the passion, and the people that define the Harley-Davidson Experience.
>
> —HARLEY-DAVIDSON, INC.[1]

On May 1, 2015, Matt Levatich took over as CEO of Harley-Davidson, Inc.. Levatich was 48 years old and had joined Harley as a management trainee in 1994. He held an engineering degree from Rensselaer Polytechnic Institute and an MBA from Northwestern. The company he was taking charge of was not among the world's biggest motorcycle companies—it shipped 270,726 bikes in 2014 compared to Honda's 17 million. However, it was the world's most financially successful motorcycle manufacturer: it earned a higher sales margin and a higher return on equity than any of its rivals.

Levatich's predecessor was Keith Wandell, who had stabilized Harley after the financial crisis of 2008–2009 and returned the company to its growth path. During Wandell's six-year tenure, Harley's cumulative total return to shareholders was 280%, compared to 172% for the S&P 500 as a whole.

The road ahead, however, looked distinctly bumpy. On Levatich's first day as CEO, investment advisor James Berman published a newsletter that asked the question: "Is the long, classic American love affair with Harleys a thing of the past?"[2] Harley's profit growth depended on its ability to keep expanding the sales of its high-priced, heavyweight motorcycles. While no other company could replicate the emotional attachment of riders to the "Harley Experience," there was always the risk that motorcycle riders might seek a different type of experience and become more attracted to the highly engineered models produced by European and Japanese manufacturers. Equally worrying was the fear that motorcycles might lose their appeal both as a leisure activity and as a male status symbol. Such concerns were fueled by demographic trends. Harley's core market was the baby-boomer generation—and this cohort was moving more toward retirement homes than outdoor sports. Would the next cohorts—Generation X and Generation Y—have the same affinity for noisy, heavyweight motorcycles and the cultural values that Harley-Davidson

This case was prepared by Robert M. Grant. ©2015 Robert M. Grant.

represented? Moreover, with consumer spending weak in both North America and Europe—Harley's two biggest markets—the demand for luxury leisure products costing between $7000 and $38,000 was likely to be subdued.

The History of Harley-Davidson

From Birth to Maturity, 1903–1981

Harley-Davidson, Inc. was founded in 1903 by William Harley and the three Davidson brothers: William, Arthur, and Walter. In 1909, Harley introduced its two-cylinder, V-twin engine with its deep, rumbling sound: this engine type would be the characteristic feature of Harley-Davidson motorcycles for the next hundred years. At that time there were about 150 US motorcycle producers in the US; by 1953, Harley-Davidson was the sole survivor.

The postwar affluence and the rise of youth culture created a growing demand for motorcycles. This was satisfied primarily by imports: first the British (BSA, Triumph, and Norton) and then the Japanese (led by Honda). Harley benefitted from the rebirth of motorcycling as a leisure activity. However, its acquisition by the leisure conglomerate AMF in 1969 was followed by quality problems and financial losses.

Rebirth, 1981–2008

In 1981, Harley's senior managers led a leveraged buyout of the company. Despite a perilous financial condition, the management team embarked upon rebuilding production methods and working practices. Managers visited Japanese automobile plants and introduced their own version of Toyota's just-in-time (JIT) system called "MAN" (materials-as-needed). Harley's manufacturing plants adopted collaborative processes of quality management.

The 1986 initial public offering of Harley-Davidson's shares fueled investment in new models, plants, and dealerships. Harley's share of the market for heavyweight motorcycles (over 500cc) grew steadily. During the 1990s, Harley's biggest challenge was satisfying the surging demand for its products. In 1996, Harley announced its Plan 2003 to dramatically increase production capacity in the period preceding its 100th anniversary in 2003. In 2004, Harley sold more than 300,000 motorcycles, a tenfold increase on 1983. From 1984 to 2008, Harley's output and revenue had grown in every single year (Figure 1).

Downturn and Readjustment, 2008–2014

The financial crisis of 2008 put an abrupt end to growth. After decades of customer waiting lists and a shortage of production capacity, Harley faced plummeting sales, excess inventory, and problems of bad debts as customers defaulted on their loan repayments. In the shrinking motorcycle markets of North America and Europe, Harley—with the highest average retail price of any major manufacturer—suffered disproportionately. Amidst the credit crunch, Harley-Davidson Financial Services (HDFS), which supplied credit, insurance, and extended warranties to Harley dealers and customers, was unable to securitize its customer loans and was forced to retain them on its own books.

FIGURE 1 Annual shipments of motorcycles by Harley-Davidson

Sources: Harley Davidson annual reports and Harley-Davidson archives.

When Keith Wandell took over as Harley's CEO in May 2009, his priorities were to restore funding for Harley's consumer lending, align production and employment with lower demand, and refocus on the core Harley-Davidson brand—which involved closing Buell Motorcycles[3] and selling Italian subsidiary MV Agusta.[4] In 2009, Harley posted a net loss for the year—its first as a public company. (Appendix Table A1 provides details of Harley-Davidson's financial performance.)

During 2010–2014, Wandell established "a bold, clear strategic direction that would maximize our opportunities going forward and restore the company as a strong business that could consistently grow over the long haul."[5] The resulting transformation of Harley included:

- Rethinking and restructuring of manufacturing operations including reducing capacity and increasing flexibility to allow a wider range of models to be produced and to match production to seasonal fluctuations in demand—what Harley called its "surge production system."

- Expanding international sales. The primary focus for Harley's overseas sales had been Europe—the world's biggest market for heavyweight motorcycles. With Europe mired in recession, emphasis shifted to building distribution and growing sales in the emerging markets of Asia and Latin America. In 2011, Harley opened an Asia-Pacific regional headquarters in Singapore, and an assembly plant in India.[6]

- Expanding the customer base. To reestablish growth in North America, Harley needed to broaden its customer base from its core demographic of white males of 45 years or more. Targeted groups included: women riders, "Harlistas" (Latino riders), "Iron Elite" (African-American riders), "Harley's Heroes" (military and veteran riders), and, most of all, younger riders through new models. The result was a major investment in new product development. During 2013, Harley launched its "Project Rushmore" motorcycles: "The first to come through our new, world-class product development pipeline and introduce major innovation and design improvements. They were developed with a level of consumer input that brought the voice of the customer to product design in an unparalleled way for us."[7] They were followed by the "Street" models—lighter, sports motorcycles featuring new, liquid-cooled 500cc and 750cc engines.

The Heavyweight Motorcycle Market

Until the financial crisis of 2008–2009, the heavyweight segment had been the most rapidly growing part of the world motorcycle market, with the US accounting for a major portion of this growth. Worldwide sales of heavyweight motorcycles trebled between 1990 and 2008. However, during 2008–2010, sales dropped sharply in North America and Europe and the subsequent recovery has been slow.

In North America, Harley was the leader in heavyweight bikes, with over half the market (Table 1). Overseas, Harley had been unable to replicate this market dominance, despite strong sales in a few markets. Harley achieved the remarkable feat of becoming heavyweight market leader in Japan. It held similar leadership in Australia and Brazil. The European market was more fragmented, with Harley one among a leading group that included Honda, BMW, Suzuki, Yamaha, Kawasaki, and Triumph, each with market shares in heavyweight motorcycles of between 8 and 15%.

The heavyweight motorcycle market comprised three segments:

- *Cruiser motorcycles*: These were "big, noisy, low riding, unapologetically macho cycles,"[8] typically with V-twin, large displacement engines and an

TABLE 1   Retail sales (registrations) of heavyweight motorcycles (601+ cc), 2005–2014 (thousands of units)

	2005	2006	2007	2008	2009	2010	2011	2012	2013	2014
North America										
Total market	554	579	555	477	304	260	271[a]	299[a]	306[a]	316[a]
Harley-Davidson	265	282	267	235	174	154	152[a]	161[a]	168[a]	167[a]
Market share (%)	47.8	48.6	48.7	49.3	53.2	54.9	55.7	53.8	54.9	52.8
Europe										
Total market	351	377	372	384	314	301	293	300	282	320
Harley-Davidson[b]	30	34	42	45	40	41	44	36	36	39
Market share (%)	8.5	9.1	11.3	11.7	12.0	12.7	13.7	12.1	12.8	12.0
Asia-Pacific										
Harley-Davidson	11	13	23	25	23	21	21[c]	25[c]	27[c]	30[c]
Latin America										
Harley Davidson	n.a.	n.a.	3	8	6	6	7	9	11	12

Notes:
[a]US only.
[b]Includes Middle East and Africa for 2005–2011.
[c]In each year, sales in Japan were between 10,000 and 11,000.
n.a. = not available.
Source: Harley-Davidson 10-K reports.

upright riding position. Their design reflected the dominance of styling over either comfort or speed. For the urban males (and some females) in congested cities such as Los Angeles, New York, Paris, and Tokyo, the cruiser motorcycle, while a practical mode of transportation, was primarily a statement of style. The cruiser segment was practically created by Harley and represented over two-thirds of the heavyweight market in the US. Most of Harley's competitors in this segment had imitated the main features of the traditional Harley design.

● *Touring motorcycles*: These included cruisers especially equipped for longer-distance riding and bikes especially designed for comfort over long distances (including the Honda Goldwing and the bigger BMWs). These tourers featured luxuries such as audio systems, two-way intercoms, and heaters. While Harley led this segment on the basis of style and image, Honda and BMW had engineered their motorcycles for greater smoothness and comfort over long distances through the use of multi-cylinder, shaft-drive engines and advanced suspension systems.

● *Performance motorcycles*: These were based on racing bikes, with high-technology, high-revving engines offering speed, acceleration, race-track styling, and minimal concessions to rider comfort. The segment was the most important in the European and Asia-Pacific markets, representing 62 and 65% of total heavyweight bike sales respectively. The segment was dominated by Japanese motorcycle companies, with a strong representation of European specialists, such as Ducati and Triumph. Harley had competed in this segment during 1993–2010 through Buell Motorcycles.

Unlike its Japanese competitors, Harley was highly market focused: its Harley's models were concentrated on the "super-heavyweight" segment (over 850cc) and within this on cruiser and touring motorcycles.

Harley-Davidson in 2015

The Brand

Harley-Davidson's image and the loyalty the company engendered among its customers were seen as its greatest assets. The famed spread eagle signified not just the brand of one of the world's oldest motorcycle companies but also an entire lifestyle with which it was associated. Harley has been described as "the ultimate biker status symbol … a quasi religion, an institution, a way of life."[9] Harley had a unique relationship with American culture. The values that Harley represented—individuality, freedom, and adventure—could be traced back to the cowboy and frontiersman of yesteryear, and before that to the quest that brought people to America in the first place. As the sole surviving indigenous motorcycle company, Harley-Davidson represented a once-great tradition of American engineering and manufacturing.

The Harley brand was central not just to the company's marketing but also to its strategy as a whole. The central thrust of the strategy was reinforcing and extending the relationship between the company and its consumers. Harley-Davidson had long recognized that it was not selling motorcycles: it was selling the Harley Experience, which formed the central theme in almost all its external communications:

> A chill sweeps through your body, created by a spontaneous outburst of pure, unadulterated joy. You are surrounded by people from all walks of life and every corner of the globe. They are complete strangers, but you know them like your own family. They were drawn to this place by the same passion—the same dream. And they came here on the same machine. This is one place you can truly be yourself. Because you don't just fit in. You belong.[10]

Customers and Customer Relations

If the appeal of the Harley motorcycle was the image it conveyed and the lifestyle it represented, the company's challenge was to ensure that the experience matched the image. Harley's involvement in its consumers' riding experience was through the Harley Owners' Group (HOG), which organized social and charity events. Employees, from the CEO down, were encouraged to take an active role in attending HOG shows, rallies, and rides. "The feeling of being out there on a Harley-Davidson motorcycle links us like no other experience can. It's made HOG like no other organization in the world … more family reunion than organized meeting."[11] Customer loyalty led to their continuing reinvesting in Harley products: Harley-branded accessories and apparel, customizing their bikes, and eventually trading them in for a new (typically more expensive) model. About half of bike sales were to repeat customers.

Financial success involved Harley's repositioning from blue-collar youngsters to middle-aged and upper-income buyers, many of whom had never ridden a motorcycle before. Harley's core demographic was Caucasian males aged 35 and over. The average age of Harley's customers was believed to be 47.[12] In his final letter to shareholders, retiring CEO Keith Wandell reported success in expanding Harley's customer base:

> For the third straight year, Harley-Davidson grew U.S. retail sales to outreach customers, which includes young adults, women, African Americans and Hispanics, at more than twice the rate of the growth in sales to core customers. International retail sales of new Harley-Davidson motorcycles grew more than 5 percent and accounted for more than 36 percent of total retail Harley-Davidson motorcycle sales, with dealers in the Asia Pacific, EMEA and Latin America regions posting their highest new retail motorcycle sales on record for each region.[13]

The Products

Broadening Harley's market appeal had major implications for product policy and design. Ever since its disastrous foray into small bikes during the AMF years, Harley had recognized that its competitive advantage lay with super-heavyweight bikes. Here it stuck resolutely to the classic styling that had characterized Harleys since the company's early years. At the heart of the Harley motorcycle was the air-cooled V-twin engine that had been Harley's distinctive feature since 1909. Harley's frames, handlebars, fuel tanks, and seats also reflected traditional designs.

Harley's commitment to traditional design features may be seen as making a virtue out of necessity. Its smaller corporate size and inability to share R & D across cars and bikes (unlike Honda and BMW) limited its ability to invest in technology and new products. As a result, Harley lagged far behind its competitors in the application of automotive technologies: not only did its motorcycles look old-style, much of their technology was old-style. Since the Evolution engine launched in 1984, Harley has introduced just four entirely new engines.

Yet, even in its 2015 models, Harley's commitment to tradition was clear. Long after other manufacturers had moved to multiple valves per cylinder, overhead camshafts, liquid cooling, and electronic ignition, most Harley bikes featured air-cooled push-rod engines with two valves per cylinder. In suspension systems, braking systems, and transmissions, Harley was also a laggard.

Nevertheless, Harley was engaged in constant upgrading—principally incremental refinements to its engines, frames, and gearboxes—aimed at improving power delivery and reliability, increasing braking power, and reducing vibration. Harley automotive technology alliance partners included Porsche, Ford, and Gemini Racing.

Although technological innovation was limited, Harley was very active in new product development. By 2015, Harley offered 38 different models. Its Product Development Center and Prototyping Lab were among the most important units within the company. Most of Harley's product development efforts were limited to style changes, new paint designs, and engineering improvements; however, after 2000, Harley accelerated technological development. Milestones included the V-Rod model introduced in October 2001, which featured innovative styling and an all-new liquid-cooled engine; the Twin Cam 96 engine in 2006, which featured electronic ignition and a six-speed gearbox; the Street models in 2015; and Harley's prototype all-electric motorcycle. Among the 218 US patents awarded to Harley during 2000–2014, a large proportion related to the design of peripheral items: saddlebag mounting systems, footpegs, seats, backrests, electrical assemblies, and motorcycle music systems. Over the same period Honda was awarded 10,982 US patents, Kawasaki 2002, and Suzuki 625.

Central to Harley's product strategy was the belief that every Harley rider should own a unique, personalized motorcycle—hence the offer of a wide range of pre-sale and post-sale customization opportunities. New bikes offered multiple options for seats, bars, pegs, controls, and paint jobs, with over 7000 accessories, and special services such as "Chrome Consulting."

TABLE 2   Harley-Davidson shipments of motorcycles, 2003–2014

	2003	2004	2005	2006	2007	2008	2009	2010	2011	2012	2013	2014
US[a]	237.7	260.6	266.5	273.2	241.5	206.3	144.4	131.6	152.2	160.5	167.0	174.0
International[a]	53.5	56.7	62.5	76.0	89.1	97.2	78.5	78.8	80.9	87.1	93.4	96.7
Product mix[b]												
Sportster[c]	19.7	22.0	21.3	18.5	21.8	20.0	21.4	19.5	21.3	20.5	19.3	21.0
Custom	52.0	48.6	45.2	46.2	43.7	46.4	40.9	41.4	39.2	39.1	39.5	33.8
Touring	28.4	29.4	33.5	35.4	34.5	33.6	37.7	39.0	39.5	40.4	41.2	45.2
Buell	10.0	9.9	11.2	12.5	11.5	13.1	9.5	2.6	0.2	—	—	—
Company total[a]	301.2	327.2	340.2	361.6	342.1	316.4	232.4	213.0	233.2	247.6	260.5	270.7

Note:
[a]Thousands of units.
[b]Percentage of total shipments.
[c]Includes sales of Street motorcycles for 2014.
Source: Harley-Davidson 10-K reports.

Reconciling product differentiation with scale economies was a continuing challenge for Harley. The solution was to offer a wide range of customization options while standardizing key components. Thus, Harley's broad model range involved "permutations of four": four engine types, four basic frames, four styles of gas tank, and so on.

The Harley product line also covered a wide price range. The Street 500 model was priced as an entry-level bike, beginning at $6799, less than one-fifth of the price of the CVO Limited, at $39,349. Table 2 shows Harley's motorcycle output by product type.

Distribution

Upgrading Harley's distribution network was central to its resurgence during the 1980s and 1990s. At the time of the buyout, many of Harley's 620 US dealerships were operated by enthusiasts, with erratic opening hours, a poor stock of bikes and spares, and indifferent customer service. If Harley was in the business of selling a lifestyle and an experience, then dealers played a pivotal role in delivering that experience. Moreover, if Harley's target market had shifted toward mature, upper-income individuals, Harley needed to provide a retail experience commensurate with the expectations of this group.

Harley's dealer development program increased support for dealers while imposing higher standards of pre- and after-sales service, and requiring better dealer facilities. Dealers were obliged to carry a full line of Harley replacement parts and accessories and to offer an expanding range of services: in addition to traditional services such as service and repair and financing, dealers offered test ride facilities, rider instruction classes, motorcycle rental, consulting services for customizing bikes through dealer-based design centers and Chrome Consultants, and insurance services. Harley-Davidson Authorized Tours offered vacation packages with bikes supplied by Harley dealers. Over 90% of Harley dealerships in the US were exclusive: most other motorcycle manufacturers sold through multi-brand dealerships.

Dealer relations were a continuing strategic priority for Harley. Its Retail Environments Group established a meticulous set of performance standards and guidelines for dealers that covered every aspect of managing the showroom and interacting with actual and potential customers. Harley-Davidson University was established to "enhance dealer competencies in every area, from customer satisfaction to inventory management, service proficiency, and front-line sales."[14]

Expanding international sales required Harley to extend its dealer network into countries where it had little or no distribution presence. As Table 3 shows, emerging

TABLE 3 Harley-Davidson's dealership network, 2008–2014

	US		Canada		EMEA		Asia-Pacific		Latin America	
	2008	2014	2008	2014	2008	2014	2008	2014	2008	2014
Full-service dealerships	686	669	71	69	383	369	201	273	32	55

Note:
In addition, there were 152 non-traditional dealerships in 2014: US 96, Canada 4, EMEA 11, Asia-Pacific 12, and Latin America 29.
Source: Harley Davidson 10-K reports.

TABLE 4   Harley-Davidson's non-motorcycle sales, 2005–2014 ($million)

	2005	2006	2007	2008	2009	2010	2011	2012	2013	2014
Parts and accessories	815.7	862.3	868.3	858.7	767.2	749.2	816.5	836.7	873.1	875.0
General merchandise	247.9	277.5	305.4	313.8	282.2	259.1	274.1	282.5	295.9	284.8
Financial services	331.6	384.9	416.2	377.0	494.7	682.7	649.4	650.1	641.6	660.8

Source: Harley Davidson 10-K reports.

markets accounted for the whole of the increase in Harley's dealerships between 2008 and 2014.

Other Products and Services

Sales of parts, accessories, "general merchandise" (clothing and collectibles), and financial services represented 28% of Harley's total revenue in 2014 (Table 4)—much higher than for other motorcycle companies. Clothing sales included not just traditional riding apparel but also a wide range of men's, women's, and children's leisure apparel.

Most of the "general merchandising" business represented licensing of the Harley-Davidson name and trademarks to third-party manufacturers of clothing, giftware, jewelry, toys, and other products. Most of these were sold through channels other than the Harley dealership network. To expand sales of licensed products, Harley opened "non-traditional" dealerships: retail outlets selling clothing, accessories, and giftware but not motorcycles.

Manufacturing

As already noted, Harley-Davidson's development during the 1980s and 1990s focused heavily on upgrading its manufacturing operations: capacity expansion permitted investment in new plants and equipment and the introduction of more advanced process technologies. Particular emphasis was placed on developing manufacturing capabilities through total quality management, JIT scheduling, CAD/CAM, and the devolution of responsibility and decision making to the shop floor.

Despite the constant development of its manufacturing facilities and operational capabilities, Harley's low production volume relative to Honda and the other Japanese manufacturers imposed significant cost disadvantages, especially in the purchase of components. Despite this lack of bargaining muscle, Harley sought close, collaborative relations with key suppliers. Its Supplier Advisory Council (SAC) served "not only to improve purchasing efficiency, but also to provide a forum to share information, ideas, and strategy."[15]

Harley's capacity for efficiency was also limited by its dispersed manufacturing operations: engine manufacture in Milwaukee, Wisconsin and assembly in York, Pennsylvania and Kansas City, Missouri. During 2009–2014, Harley reorganized its manufacturing plants and manufacturing systems. A program of plant consolidation involved combining the two Milwaukee-area powertrain plants into a single facility and merging the separate paint and frame operations at York, Pennsylvania.

New agreements negotiated with unions allowed for more flexible employment arrangements and working practices, which supported the introduction of a new enterprise resource planning (ERP) system at the York plant. Combined with Harley's "surge production," the new system meant customer demand would drive manufacturing, every production line would have the flexibility to build every model, and inventories could be reduced.

Human Resource Management

Central to Harley-Davidson's remarkable growth between 1981 and 2007 was the creation of a new relationship between management and employees that was forged following the buyout from AMF. The new approach to human resource management was built on participation, self-management, open communication, and team-based organization. Team-based organization extended from eight- to 15-member work groups at plant level right up to senior management where three functional teams—the Create Demand Circle (CDC), the Produce Product Circle, and the Provide Support—were coordinated by the Strategic Leadership Council.[16]

Despite Harley's commitment to employee participation and development, the production cutbacks and cost-cutting pressures during 2009–2012 created tensions between the company and its employees. These were resolved by the 2012 labor agreement, which created a new framework for workplace flexibility.[17]

Competition

Despite Harley's insistence that it was supplying a unique Harley experience rather than competing with other motorcycle manufacturers, the more it took market share from other manufacturers and expanded its product range and geographical scope, the more it came into direct competition with other producers. The clearest indication of direct competition was imitation: Honda, Suzuki, Yamaha, and Kawasaki had long been offering V-twin cruisers styled closely along the lines of the classic Harleys, but at lower prices and with more advanced technologies (Table 5). In competing against Harley, the Japanese manufacturers' key advantage was the scale economies that derived from vastly greater volume. However, despite their price premium, Harley-Davidson motorcycles benefitted from a lower rate of depreciation than other brands.

Almost all of Harley's competitors were, compared to Harley, highly diversified. Honda, BMW, and Suzuki were important producers of automobiles, and more than one-third of Yamaha's turnover came from boats and snowmobiles. These companies could share technologies, engineering capabilities, distribution, and brand awareness across their different vehicle divisions. Moreover, sheer size conferred purchasing power.

Imitators of Harley's retro-styled, V-twin cruisers were not only the Japanese motorcycle companies but also domestic competitors—including new entrants Excelsior, Polaris (Victory), and a resuscitated Indian. Their heavyweight cruisers typically sold at prices exceeding those of Harley.

Appendix Table A2 compares the financial performance of leading motorcycle companies.

TABLE 5 Recommended retail prices for V-twin, cruiser motorcycles, 2015

Model	Specifications	Price ($)
Harley-Davidson		
Sportster 883 Low	V-twin, air-cooled, 883cc	8,249
VRSC V-Rod Muscle	V-twin, liquid-cooled, OHC, 1247cc	16,649
Fat Boy	V-twin, air-cooled, 1690cc	17,699
Heritage Softail Classic	V-twin, air-cooled, 1690cc	18,349
Honda		
Shadow 750 Aero	V-twin, liquid-cooled, OHC, 745cc	7,499
Fury	V-twin, liquid-cooled, OHC, 1312cc	9,999
Interstate ABS	V-twin, liquid-cooled, OHC, 1312cc	10,999
Suzuki		
C50	V-twin, liquid-cooled, OHC, 805cc	8,199
C90T	V-twin, liquid-cooled, OHC, 1462cc	12,899
Boulevard C90 B.O.S.S.	V-twin, liquid-cooled, 1462cc	12,389
Kawasaki		
Vulcan 900 Classic	V-twin, liquid-cooled, 8-valve, OHC, 903cc	7,499
Vulcan 900 Custom		8,499
Yamaha		
V-Star Custom	V-twin, OHC, 4-valve, air-cooled, 649cc	6,990
Stryker	V-twin, OHC, 8-valve, liquid-cooled, 1304cc	11,690
Polaris		
Victory Vegas 8-Ball	V-twin, 8-valve, air-cooled, 1731cc	14,999
Victory Hammer 8-Ball		17,899

Note:
OHC = overhead camshaft.
Source: Websites of different motorcycle manufacturers.

Meeting the Challenges of Tomorrow

Harley's first-half results for 2015 reinforced fears over the sustainability of Harley's top-line growth. Profits were 8% lower than in the year-ago period, sales revenue was 6% lower, and unit sales were down by 1.4%. Wandell's strategy had been strongly orientated around expanding sales to "non-core" customer segments. Among these were younger riders in the US and potential customers in overseas markets.

The need to attract younger riders was driven by unfavorable US demographic trends—the aging of the baby boomers and the smaller number of white males entering the 40–55 age band. However, would the Harley Experience have the same appeal for Generation X and Y as it did for the baby-boomers? As the *New York Times* noted, "BMW, Honda and Yamaha are attracting younger customers who seem less interested in cruising on what their old man rides."[18]

International markets also presented a major challenge: should Harley adapt to the different requirements of these markets or should it remain faithful to the traditional Harley image? "The US and Harley are tied together," observed Britain's *Bike* magazine, "the guy who's into Harleys here is also the guy who owns cowboy boots. You get a Harley and you're buying into the US mystique."[19]

Harley claimed that its new Street 500 and Street 750 models had met with an enthusiastic response both in the US and in India (the two countries where this model was manufactured). However, Harley's previous incursions into smaller motorcycles—including Buell—had not been successful.

A Milwaukee blogger summarized Harley's dilemma:

So what does Harley do? One tack would be to stay focused on what it does best: big bikes. While that strategy may make sense on some fronts (focus on what you know, stay loyal to the brand identity, etc.), that approach will mean greatly reduced growth prospects and could doom it if the current consumer spending environment holds out long term. And meanwhile its core audience just gets older.

Or it could do what people have been saying what it should do for years: Make smaller, more affordable bikes. That's harder than it sounds, as it would force Harley to compete against the Japanese manufacturers on their own turf. But if the market is moving away from Harley, does it have a choice?[20]

Appendix: Financial Data

TABLE A1   Selected Items from Harley-Davidson financial statements, 2005–2014 ($million)

	2005	2006	2007	2008	2009	2010	2011	2012	2013	2014
Income statement items										
Net sales	5,342	5,801	5,727	5,594	4,781	4,859	5,311	5,581	5,900	6,229
R & D	179	178	186	164	143	136	145	137	152	138
Selling, administrative, and engineering expense	762	846	901	985	979	1,020	1,061	1,111	1,127	1,160
Operating income, of which:	1,470	1,603	1,426	1,029	197	559	829	1,000	1,154	1,281
–Financial services	192	211	212	83	(117)	181	268	259	283	278
Interest income/(expense)	23	27	22	9	(22)	(90)	(45)	(46)	(45)	(4)
Income before taxes	1,488	1,624	1,448	1,034	178	390	792	961	1,114	1,283
Income taxes	528	581	514	379	108	130	244	338	380	439
Net income	960	1,043	934	655	(55)	146	599	624	734	845
Balance sheet items										
Cash	141	238	403	594	1,630	1,021	1,526	1,327	1,067	907
Finance receivables	1,943	2,101	1,575	1,378	1,436	1,080	1,168	1,344	1,774	1,917
Accounts receivable, net	122	143	181	296	269	262	219	255	261	248
Inventories	221	288	350	401	323	326	418	428	425	449
Total current assets	3,145	3,551	3,467	5,378	4,341	4,066	4,542	4,216	3,989	3,948
Property, plant, and equipment, net	1,012	1,024	1,061	1,094	906	815	809	819	842	883
Total assets	5,255	5,532	5,657	7,829	9,155	9,430	9,674	9,513	9,405	9,528
Current portion of long-term debt	205	832	398	0	1,332	0	399	682	1,176	1,011
Accounts payable	271	763	300	324	162	225	255	248	240	197
Total current liabilities	873	1,596	1,905	2,604	2,268	2,013	2,698	0	2,510	2,389
Long-term debt	1,000	870	980	2,176	4,144	2,516	2,396	2,936	3,417	3,762
Post-retirement healthcare liability	61	201	193	274	264	254	268	258	216	203
Stockholders' equity	3,084	2,757	2,375	2,116	2,108	2,207	2,420	2,558	3,009	2,909
Cash flow items										
Operating activities	961	762	798	2,685	609	1,163	885	801	977	1,147
Capital expenditures	(2,198)	(2,220)	(2,242)	(2,232)	(116)	(170)	(189)	(189)	(208)	(232)
Total investing activities	(177)	(2,35)	(3,91)	(2,393)	(863)	145	(63)	(261)	(569)	(745)
Financing activities	1,272	2,637	1,038	1,293	1,381	(1,856)	(309)	(990)	(393)	(536)
Net increase in cash	2,134	97	164	191	1,134	(542)	(505)	(459)	(2)	(160)

TABLE A2 Comparative financial data for Honda, Yamaha, and Harley-Davidson

	Honda Motor Co.[a]		Yamaha Motor Co.[b]		Harley-Davidson	
	2013	2014	2013	2014	2013	2014
Revenue ($bn)	117.8	115.0	14.9	14.1	5.9	6.2
Operating income ($bn)	7.5	5.9	0.6	0.8	1.2	1.3
Net income after tax ($bn)	5.7	4.8	0.5	0.6	0.7	0.8
Gross margin (%)	26	25	35	25	39	40
Operating margin (%)	6.3	5.2	3.9	5.7	19.6	20.6
Net margin (%)	4.8	4.2	4.0	4.5	12.4	13.6
Operating income/total assets (%)	4.8	3.9	1.7	3.4	12.3	13.4
Return on equity (%)	9.4	7.9	11.8	14.3	24.4	29.0
Inventory turnover	8.5	8.5	5.2	4.8	13.9	13.9
Debt/equity ratio	0.52	0.53	0.31	0.36	1.14	1.29
Capital expenditure ($bn)	6.4	6.0	5.1	5.5	0.2	0.2
—of which motorcycles ($bn)	0.6	0.6	3.0	3.8	0.2	0.2
R & D expenditure ($bn)	6.5	6.1	0.8	0.8	0.2	0.1
Advertising expenditure ($bn)	2.7	2.8	1.0	0.9	0.1	0.1
Motorcycles shipped (thousands of units)	10,343	10,742	6,010	5,800	213	233.2

Notes:

[a]Honda's data relates to the whole company (motorcycles account for about 14% of Honda's total sales). Financial year 2013 covers 12 months to March 31, 2014; financial year 2014 covers 12 months to March 31, 2015.
[b]Yamaha's data relates to the whole company (motorcycles account for about 65% of Yamaha's total sales).
Sources: Company annual reports.

Notes

1. "The Company," http://www.harley-davidson.com/content/h-d/en_GB/company/becoming-a-dealer/the-company.html, accessed July 20, 2015.
2. "Harley-Davidson: Running Out of Road?" http://www.forbes.com/newsletters/the-berman-value-folio/2015/05/01/harley-davidson-running-out-of-road/, accessed July 20, 2015.
3. Buell Motor Company, founded by Harley engineer Erik Buell, built performance motorcycles using Harley engines and other components, and targeted younger riders. The Buell range included a 490cc single-cylinder bike with a price tag of $4,595—Harley's cheapest motorcycle. However, Buell's sales both in the US and overseas had been disappointing.
4. Harley acquired MV Agusta, an Italian manufacturer of premium, high-performance motorcycles in July 2008. On August 6, 2010, Harley sold it back to its previous owner for €3 ($3.90).
5. "Letter to Shareholders," Harley-Davidson, Inc. annual report for 2009.
6. The Indian plant was its second overseas assembly plant; the first was established in Brazil in 1999.
7. K. Wandell, "Chairman's Annual Letter," Harley-Davidson 2013 annual report.
8. G. Strauss, "Born to be Bikers," *USA Today* (November 5, 1997).
9. M. Ballon, "Born to be Wild," *Inc.* (November, 1997): 42.
10. Harley-Davidson, Inc., annual report (2000).
11. "Welcome Letter," Blackstone Valley HOG Chapter, http://www.blackstonevalleyhog.com/HTML/Welcome.php, accessed July 20, 2015.
12. "Analysis: As Boomers Age, Harley Hunts for Younger Riders," *Reuters*, June 21, 2013, http://uk.reuters.com/article/2013/06/21/us-harleydavidson-boomers-analysis-idUSBRE95K0GU20130621, accessed July 20, 2015.
13. "Letter to Shareholders," Harley-Davidson 2014 annual review.
14. Harley-Davidson, Inc., "Knowledge is Horsepower," annual report (2003).
15. K. R. Fitzgerald, "Harley's Supplier Council Helps Deliver Full Value," *Purchasing* (September 5, 1996).

16. C. Fessler, "Rotating Leadership at Harley-Davidson: From Hierarchy to Interdependence," *Strategy and Leadership* (July 17, 1997).

17. "Harley-Davidson Workers Brace for Big Change," *Business Journal*, Milwaukee (April 27, 2012).

18. "Harley, You're Not Getting Any Younger," *New York Times* (March 21, 2009).

19. Reported in Marco della Cava, "Motorcycle Maker Caters to the Continent," *USA Today* (April 22, 1998): 8B.

20. "Screw it, let's ride is not a strategy," *Brew City Brawler*, January 23, 2009, http://brewcitybrawler.typepad.com/brew_city_brawler/2009/01/screw-it-lets-ride-is-not-a-strategy.html, accessed July 20, 2015.

Case 8   BP: Organizational Structure and Management Systems

When John Browne stepped down as CEO at BP plc in January 2007, he was credited with having transformed a formerly inefficient, bureaucratic, state-owned oil company into the world's most dynamic, entrepreneurial, performance-focused, and environmentally aware oil and gas major. Since taking up the job in 1995, BP's market capitalization had increased fivefold and its earnings per share by 600%.

Even before Browne's departure, BP's fall from grace had already commenced. Concerns over BP's HSE (health, safety, and environmental) management had been circulating for years. However, in March 2005 disaster struck: an explosion at BP's Texas City refinery killed 15 employees. This was the first of a series of catastrophes that destroyed the company's reputation and threatened its very survival.

In 2006, a corroded pipeline from BP's huge Alaskan oilfield caused a leakage of 4800 barrels of oil. Then in March 2009, BP was fined for safety violations at its Toledo refinery. The next month, an explosion on Transocean's *Deepwater Horizon* oilrig drilling BP's Macondo oil well in the Gulf of Mexico killed 11 workers and caused one of the worst environmental disasters in US history. The company took an accounting charge of $37.2 billion to cover the likely costs of the cleanup, compensation, and legal penalties, but by 2013 these costs had already exceeded $42 billion.

BP's troubles extended beyond its safety and environmental mishaps. Between 2003 and 2013, BP's trading activities in the crude oil, gasoline, propane, and natural gas markets were investigated by US regulators, resulting in a series of fines being imposed. In its core exploration and production business, BP experienced continuing problems from its large investment in Russia, first from difficult relations with its joint venture partner, TNK, and then from the declining value of its 20% stake in Rosneft following Western sanctions on Russia and the declining value of the ruble.

In the recriminations that followed the Texas City and Gulf of Mexico disasters, attention increasingly focused upon the organizational structure, management systems, and corporate culture that had developed at BP during John Browne's tenure. The management system developed by Browne had produced what the *Financial Times* described as "the most swashbuckling, the most entrepreneurial, the most creative" of the world's biggest oil companies.[1] Was it also the most accident prone?

This case was prepared by Robert M. Grant. ©2015 Robert M. Grant.

A Brief History of BP

BP began as the Anglo-Persian Oil Company, which had been founded in 1909 to exploit a huge oilfield that had been discovered in Iran. At the outbreak of the First World War the British government acquired a controlling interest in the company, which it held until the company (by then renamed British Petroleum) was privatized by Margaret Thatcher's government in 1979.

Under a series of chief executives—Peter Walters, Bob Horton, and David Simon—BP went from being a highly centralized, bureaucratic organization to becoming less hierarchical and more financially oriented. However, it was under John Browne that BP's transformation gathered pace. Under Browne's leadership, BP grew rapidly: its acquisitions of Amoco, Atlantic Richfield, and Burmah Castrol not only made BP the world's third biggest petroleum major after Exxon and Shell but also precipitated an industry-wide wave of consolidation. Browne refocused BP's exploration efforts around frontier regions including deep waters (the Gulf of Mexico in particular), Angola, Siberia, and the Arctic. Browne also broke away from industry convention by acknowledging climate change, supporting the Kyoto Protocol, and rebranding BP as "Beyond Petroleum." This strategic transformation was accompanied by radical changes to BP's structure, systems, and culture.

The Atomic Structure

In 1997, the *Harvard Business Review* commented upon the changes occurring at BP:

> Organizationally, BP is much smaller and simpler than it was a decade ago. It now has 53,000 employees–down from 129,000. Before, the company was mired in procedures; now it has processes that foster learning and tie people's jobs to creating value. Before, it had a multitude of baronies; now it has an abundance of teams and informal networks or communities in which people eagerly share knowledge.[2]

At the heart of Browne's transformation of BP were high aspirations. According to Nick Butler, former head of strategy at BP:

> When Browne stepped in as CEO in 1995, we knew we had to create something different. We looked at the ROACE [return on average capital employed]: we were all operating within a limited space. We realized that to break out we had to redefine ourself. It was not about beating Exxon, it was about how to beat the ROACE of Microsoft. We wanted to create [a] company with sufficient scale to take regional knocks with enough reach to survive in almost any circumstances.[3]

Through a series of mergers and acquisitions, Browne created a company with the scale he believed was essential to become a leader in the petroleum industry. But it also created the challenge of how to organize such a huge company—by

2000, BP was the world's seventh biggest company in terms of revenues. Browne's management philosophy embodied three principles:

- BP operates in a decentralized manner, with individual business unit leaders (such as refinery plant managers) given broad latitude for running the business and direct responsibility for delivering performance.
- The corporate organization provides support and assistance to the business units (such as individual refineries) through a variety of functions, networks, and peer groups.
- BP relies upon individual performance contracts to motivate people.[4]

At the time, most of the oil majors had a corporate head office that coordinated and controlled a few major divisions. These were, typically, upstream businesses (exploration and production), downstream businesses (refining and marketing), and petrochemicals. BP had been similar; it had been described as a "collection of fiefdoms."

The structure created by Browne was radically different: the divisions ("sectors") were dismantled and the company was organized around 150 business units each headed by a business unit leader who reported directly to the corporate center. According to the deputy CEO, this was "an extraordinarily flat, dispersed, decentralized process of delivery" that reflected a division of responsibility between the business unit heads who were responsible for operational performance and senior management who were responsible for strategic direction and managing external relations—especially with governments. The 150 business units were organized into 15 "peer groups"—networks of similar businesses that could share knowledge, cooperate on matters of common interest, and challenge one another.

The Performance Management System

A basic principle of BP's management system was decentralized, personalized responsibility:

> Under the Management Framework, authority is delegated, but accountability is not. Delegations of authority flow from the shareholders to the Board of Directors to the Group Chief Executive and down throughout BP. BP's philosophy is to delegate authority to the lowest appropriate point in the organization—a single point of accountability. The single point of accountability is always a person, as opposed to an organization, committee, or other group of people, who manages performance through monitoring and intervention. Those higher in the chain of delegation monitor this performance and report up the line of delegation to meet their accountabilities. This structure reflects BP's philosophy that leadership monitors but does not supervise the business; leadership only supervises the people who report directly to them. BP's Management Framework is evident at every level of the organization. Its concepts of delegation and accountability begin with the shareholders and extend through each level of the organization.[5]

The relationship between top management and the business units was governed by a "performance contract": an agreement between the head of the business unit and the corporate center over the performance that the business would deliver in the year ahead. While the performance targets included strategic and operational goals—including HSE objectives—the primary emphasis was on four financial targets: profit before tax, cash flow, investment, and return on invested capital.

Performance goals for the year were proposed by the business unit head after discussions, first with his/her own management team and, second, with the other business unit heads within the peer group. BP encouraged the business unit heads within each peer group to support and encourage one another. There was a particular responsibility for the top three units in each peer group to assist the performance of the bottom three.

Each business unit then discussed its performance targets with top management. The outcome was a performance contract. Once a performance contract was agreed, the business unit leader was free to pursue them in whatever way he or she found appropriate. The monitoring of performance targets involved a quarterly meeting between top management and the business unit leader. "There is an understanding here … that this is a performance culture and either you deliver or you don't," explained one senior executive. Failure to achieve performance targets often meant reassignment to another job or termination.

Performance contracts were given to all managers within BP from the CEO down and were a key determinant of a manager's annual bonus.

BP as a Learning Organization

At the same time as driving financial and operational performance, Browne was determined to recreate BP as a "learning organization." According to Browne:

> In order to generate extraordinary value for shareholders, a company has to learn better than its competitors and apply that knowledge throughout its business faster and more widely than they do. Any organization that thinks it does everything the best and that it need not learn from others is incredibly arrogant and foolish.[6]

Turning BP into a learning organization involved redefining the role of top management. The primary role of top management was strategic thinking, which involved a quest for knowledge and a commitment to analysis and sharing ideas. Browne espoused an intellectualism that was foreign to the senior executives of most oil companies:

> This company is founded on a deep belief in intellectual rigor. In my experience, unless you can lay out rational arguments as the foundation of what you do, nothing happens. Rigor implies that you understand the assumptions you have made: assumptions about the state of the world, of what you can do, and how your competitors will interact with it, and how the policy of the world will or will not allow you to do something.[7]

This openness involved BP's executives fostering links outside their own company and outside the petroleum business. Browne was a board member of both Intel and Goldman Sachs.

The same culture of interaction and communication was encouraged among peer groups and supported by a number of intranet-based knowledge management and groupware tools. It also involved increased emphasis on career development within BP through training and mentoring.

Social and Environmental Responsiveness

Browne sought to distance BP from the common perception of oil companies as being powerful, secretive organizations complicit with the corrupt, autocratic practices of many leaders of oil-producing countries. Browne envisaged the "new BP" as being more open and responsive to the interests of its employees and the needs of society:

> To build the reputation, we picked four areas. First, safety: when you invite someone to come and work, you should send them home in the same shape as when they arrived—that is a minimum requirement for respect of a person, and you have to take that terribly seriously. Second, you have to take care of the natural environment. It is important because people do not want companies to make a mess and leave them behind. Third, everyone wants a place in the ideal which is free of all discrimination; it doesn't matter what you stand for in terms of your race, gender, sexual orientation or religious beliefs. All that matters is merit. Fourth, the company has to invest in the community from which the people have come, so as to narrow the gap between life within the company and life outside the company.

The key initiative was Browne's endorsing of the link between greenhouse gases and climate change and his commitment to a path of environmental responsibility for BP. The resulting effort to reposition BP in the minds of consumers, governments, and NGOs involved a host of initiatives, including renaming British Petroleum as simply "BP" and replacing its shield logo with a sunburst. The effectiveness of BP's newfound environmentalism was indicated by references to BP and Exxon as "beauty and the beast"[8] and the *Oil & Gas Journal*'s lauding of the company:

> Among the top 10 [oil and gas companies] there is one striking example of a company driven by a different vision. BP has designated corporate citizenship and being forward-thinking about the environment, human rights and dealing with people and ethics as the new fulcrum of competition between the oil companies.[9]

Adapting the Management Model, 2001–2008

In 2001 and again in 2003, BP's organizational structure underwent significant revisions designed to address excessive decentralization and to improve coordination and control.

Instead of the individual business units reporting directly to top management, the peer groups were replaced by "strategic performance units," which were more formalized organizational units with their own budgets and with responsibility for the business units beneath them.

The strategic performance units were organized within three business segments: exploration and production; refining and marketing; and gas, power, and renewables. Thus, while BP's individual refineries remained as separate business units, they reported to refining, which itself was one of the three strategic performance units that comprised the refining and marketing segment.

In addition to the business structure there was also a regional structure. BP had four broad geographic areas: (1) Europe; (2) the Americas; (3) Africa, the Middle East, Russia, and the Caspian; and (4) Asia, the Indian subcontinent, and Australasia. The head of each region was responsible for ensuring regional consistency of the businesses within that region, managing BP's relations with governments and other external parties, and conducting certain administrative functions relating to tax and compliance with local laws.

Further changes took place when Tony Hayward took over from John Browne in 2007. A consulting report from Bain and Co. declared that BP was the most complicated organization that the consultants had ever encountered. Bain identified more than 10,000 organizational interfaces. Hayward's "forward agenda" emphasized cost cutting and simplification. Regional structures were eliminated, functional structures streamlined, and the number of senior executives was reduced from 650 to 500.

Findings of the Baker Panel

An independent investigation by a panel led by former Secretary of State James Baker into the Texas City refinery explosion offered penetrating insights into the role that BP's culture and management system had played in the events leading up to the disaster. Among the findings of the Panel were the following:

- From board level downwards, "BP has not provided effective process safety leadership and has not adequately established process safety as a core value across all its five US refineries."[10]

- Inappropriate performance metrics. Establishing and monitoring performance targets can reconcile individual decision making with overall coordination— but only if the targets encourage the right decisions. In safety, BP's key performance metric was the number of days lost through injury. While conducive to improvements in personal safety, this metric did not help BP in improving its process safety. According to the Panel: "BP's corporate process safety management system does not effectively translate corporate expectations into measurable criteria for management of process risk or define the appropriate role of qualitative and quantitative risk management criteria."[11]

- Inadequate resources. On this issue of whether BP's emphasis on cost reduction and profit performance caused inadequate resources to be devoted to safety, the Panel was agnostic. However, it did observe that: "the company did not always ensure that adequate resources were effectively allocated to support or sustain a high level of process safety performance. In addition, BP's corporate management mandated numerous initiatives that applied to the US refineries and that, while well-intentioned, have overloaded personnel at BP's US refineries. This 'initiative overload' may have undermined process safety performance."[12]

- Failure of board oversight: "BP's Board of Directors has been monitoring process safety performance of BP's operations based on information that BP's corporate management presented to it. A substantial gulf appears to have existed, however, between the actual performance of BP's process safety management systems and the company's perception of that performance … [T]he Panel believes that BP's Board can and should do more to improve its oversight of process safety at BP's five US refineries."[13]

Similar allegations surfaced following the Deepwater Horizon tragedy. A study by the Center for Catastrophic Risk Management observed that BP lacked a 'functional safety culture'; there were "gross imbalances between the system's provisions for production and those for protection"; a potent driving force was "BP management's desire to "close the competitive gap" and "improve bottom-line performance." In addition to "incentives that provided increases in productivity without commensurate increases in protection" and "inappropriate cost and corner cutting," the study pointed to BP's emphasis on "worker safety" and its failure to address "system safety."[14]

However, these inquiries into the Texas City and Deepwater Horizon disasters focused entirely on BP's performance in relation to safety. A broader issue concerned the appropriateness of BP's organization structure and management systems to overall corporate performance. It was notable that BP's organizational delayering and system of performance management had not been imitated by other oil and gas majors. Exxon Mobil for example remained organized around 10 global businesses, and maintained a management system that was dominated by its emphasis on disciplined processes. Its management style had been described as "no-nonsense," "conservative," "detail-oriented," "engineering-based," and "military." Yet, Exxon Mobil had maintained the best financial performance in the industry and was widely admired for its operational excellence—including its safety record: it had not suffered any major incident since the Exxon Valdez oil spill in 1989.

Notes

1. "BP: The Inside Story," *Financial Times* (July 3, 2010).
2. "Unleashing the Power of Learning: An Interview with British Petroleum's John Browne," *Harvard Business Review* (September–October 1997).
3. *The Transformation of BP*, London Business School (March 2002): 2–3.
4. See *The Report of the BP U.S. Refineries Independent Safety Review Panel* (January 2007).
5. Ibid.: 27. Note that the "Management Framework" refers to the company's description of its management system, produced in 2003.
6. *The Transformation of BP*, London Business School (March 2002): 5.
7. Ibid.: 7.
8. I. H. Rowlands, "Beauty and the Beast? BP's and Exxon's Positions on Global Climate Change" *Environment and Planning: Government and Policy* 18 (2000): 339–54.
9. "Common Financial Strategies Found among Top-10 Oil and Gas Firms," *Oil & Gas Journal* (April 20, 1998).
10. *The Report of the BP U.S. Refineries Independent Safety Review Panel* (January 2007): xii.
11. Ibid.: xv.
12. Ibid.: iii.
13. Ibid.: xv.
14. Deepwater Horizon Study Group, *Final Report on the Investigation of the Macondo Well Blowout* (Center for Catastrophic Risk Management, March 1, 2011).

Case 9   AirAsia: The World's Lowest-cost Airline

By 2009, AirAsia had established itself as Asia's most successful low-cost airline. Between January 2002 and March 2009, AirAsia had expanded from two aircraft and 200,000 passenger journeys to 79 aircraft and 11.8 million passenger journeys. Its route network had grown beyond Malaysia to cover ten Southeast Asian countries. In addition to its hub in Kuala Lumpur (KL), Malaysia, it had replicated its system by establishing associated airlines in Thailand and Indonesia.

By 2007, UBS research showed that AirAsia was the world's lowest-cost airline with costs per available seat kilometer (ASK) significantly below those of Southwest, Jet Blue, Ryanair, or Virgin Blue (Figure 1). It was also one of the world's most profitable airlines. In 2008, when very few of the world's airlines made any profit at all, AirAsia earned a return on assets of 4%.[1] In 2009, it won the Skytrax Award as "The World's Best Low Cost Airline."

AirAsia had built its business on the low-cost carrier (LCC) model created by Southwest Airlines in the US and replicated throughout the world by a host of imitators. AirAsia had adapted the basic LCC model to the market, geographical, and institutional features of Southeast Asia while preserving the principal operational features of the strategy. However, in 2007, AirAsia embarked upon a major departure from the LCC model: expansion into long-haul flights by inaugurating routes to Australia and China and then, in 2009, to India and the UK. The conventional wisdom was that the efficiency of the LCC model was dependent upon short and medium-distance flights with a single type of aircraft and minimal customer amenities—intercontinental flights required contravening these basic conditions. Very few LCCs had ventured into long-haul; even fewer had made a success of it.

To evaluate AirAsia's potential to expand from being a regional carrier to an international airline would require a careful analysis of the basis of its existing cost advantage and an evaluation of the transferability of these cost advantages to the long-haul market.

The History of AirAsia

The growth of AirAsia is closely associated with the entrepreneurial effort of Tony Fernandes. Son of a Malaysian doctor, Fernandes was sent to boarding school in

Written by Robert M. Grant. The case draws upon a report written by Sara Buchholz, Nadia Fabio, Andrés Ileyassoff, Laurent Mang, and Daniele Visentin: *AirAsia: Tales from a Long-haul Low Cost Carrier*, Bocconi University (2009), and from an earlier case by Thomas Lawton and Jonathan Doh: *The Ascendance of AirAsia: Building a Successful Budget Airline in Asia* (Ivey School of Business, Case No. 9B08M054 2008). Used by permission of the authors. © 2012, Robert M. Grant.

FIGURE 1 Costs in US cents per available seat kilometer for different low-cost airlines

Source: AirAsia Presentation, CLSA Forum, Hong Kong, September 2007.

Britain with a view to following his father's footsteps into the medical profession. Tony had other ideas and, after an accounting degree at the London School of Economics, he went into music publishing, first with Virgin, then Time Warner. He describes his decision to start an airline as follows:

> I was watching the telly in a pub and I saw Stelios [Haji-Ioannou] on air talking about easyJet and running down the national carrier, British Airways. (Sound familiar? Hahaha.) I was intrigued as I didn't know what a low cost carrier was but I always wanted to start an airline that flew long haul with low fares.

> So I went to Luton and spent a whole day there. I was amazed how people were flying to Barcelona and Paris for less than ten pounds. Everything was organized and everyone had a positive attitude. It was then at that point in Luton airport that I decided to start a low cost airline.[2]

He subsequently met with Conor McCarthy, former operations director of Ryanair. The two developed a plan to form a budget airline serving the Southeast Asia market.

Seeking the support of the Malaysian government, Fernandes was encouraged by Prime Minister Mahathir Mohammad to acquire a struggling government-owned airline, AirAsia. With their own capital and support from a group of investors, they acquired AirAsia for one Malaysian ringgit (RM)—and assumed debts of RM40 million (about $11 million). In January 2002, AirAsia was relaunched with just three planes and a business model that McCarthy described as: "a Ryanair operational strategy, a Southwest people strategy, and an easyJet branding strategy."[3]

Fueled by rising prosperity in Malaysia and its large potential market for leisure and business travelers seeking inexpensive domestic transportation, AirAsia's domestic business expanded rapidly. In January 2004, AirAsia began its first international service from KL to Phuket in Thailand; in February 2004, it sought to tap the Singapore market by offering flights from Johor Bahru, just across the border from Singapore, and in 2005 it began flights to Indonesia.

International expansion was financed by its initial public offering (IPO) in October 2004, which raised RM717 million. Airline deregulation across Southeast Asia greatly facilitated international expansion. To exploit the market for budget travel in Thailand and Indonesia, AirAsia adopted the novel strategy of establishing joint-venture companies in Thailand (Thai AirAsia) and Indonesia (Indonesia AirAsia) to create new hubs in Bangkok and Jakarta. In both cases, the operations of these companies were contracted out to AirAsia, which received a monthly fee from these associate companies.

From the beginning, Fernandes had set his sights on long-haul travel, guided by the example of his hero, Freddie Laker, the pioneer of low-cost transatlantic air travel. However, this risked his good relations with the Malaysian government because it put AirAsia into direct competition with the national airline, Malaysia Airlines. Hence, Fernandes established a separate company, AirAsia X to develop its long-haul business. AirAsia X is owned 16% by AirAsia (with an option to increase to 30%), 48% by Aero Ventures (co-founded by Tony Fernandes), 16% by Richard Branson's Virgin Group, with the remaining 20% owned by Bahrain-based Manara Consortium and Japan-based Orix Corporation. Operationally, AirAsia and AirAsia X are closely linked.

In 2007, flights began to Australia, followed by China. By July 2009, AirAsia X had flights from KL to the Gold Coast, Melbourne, and Perth in Australia; Tianjin and Hangzhou in China; and Taipei and London using five Airbus A340s, with three more to be delivered by year-end. Planned future routes included Abu Dhabi (October 2009), India (2010), and later Sydney, Seoul, and New York. At Abu Dhabi, AirAsia X planned to have a hub that would serve Frankfurt, Cairo, and possibly East Africa too: "You just can't get to East Africa from Asia," observed Fernandes.[4] To support its expansion, AirAsia X ordered ten Airbus A350s for delivery in 2016.

AirAsia's Strategy and Culture

Strategy

AirAsia described its strategy as follows:

- Safety first: partnering with the world's most renowned maintenance providers and complying with world airline regulations.
- High aircraft utilization: implementing the region's fastest turnaround time at only 25 minutes, assuring lower costs and higher productivity.
- Low fare, no frills: providing guests with the choice of customizing services without compromising on quality and services.
- Streamline operations: making sure that processes are as simple as possible.
- Lean distribution system: offering a wide and innovative range of distribution channels to make booking and traveling easier.
- Point-to-point network: applying the point-to-point network keeps operations simple and costs low.[5]

Prior to its expansion into long-haul, AirAsia identified its geographical coverage as encompassing three-and-a-half hours' flying time from its hubs. Fernandes' confidence in his growth strategy rested on the fact that "This area encompasses a population of about 500 million people. Only a small proportion of this market regularly travels by air. AirAsia believes that certain segments of this market have been under-served historically and that the Group's low fares stimulate travel within these market segments."[6] Its slogan "Now Everyone Can Fly!" encapsulated AirAsia's goal of expanding the market for air travel in Southeast Asia.

To penetrate its target market, AirAsia placed a big emphasis on marketing and brand development. "The brand is positioned to project an image of a safe, reliable low-cost airline that places a high emphasis on customer service while providing an enjoyable flying experience." For an LCC, AirAsia had comparatively large expenditures on TV, print, and internet advertising. AirAsia used its advertising expenditures counter-cyclically: during the SARS outbreak and after the Bali bombings, AirAsia boosted its spending on advertising and marketing. In addition, it sought to maximize the amount of press coverage that it received. AirAsia also built its image through co-branding and sponsorship relationships. A sponsorship deal with the AT&T Williams Formula 1 race car team resulted in AirAsia painting one of its A320s in the livery of a Williams race car. Its sponsorship of Manchester United encouraged it to paint its planes with the portraits of Manchester United players. It also sponsored referees in the English Premier League. A cooperative advertising deal with *Time* magazine resulted in an AirAsia plane being painted with the *Time* logo.

Its internet advertising included banner ads on the Yahoo mobile homepage and a Facebook application for the Citibank–AirAsia credit card. The overall goals were increasing visibility, encouraging interaction, and allowing users to immerse themselves in the AirAsia brand.

This heavy emphasis on brand building provided AirAsia with a platform for offering services that met a range of traveler needs. AirAsia offered an AA express shuttle bus connecting airports to city centers with seats being bookable simultaneously with the online booking of plane tickets. Fernandes also founded Tune Hotels, a chain of no-frills hotels co-branded with AirAsia. Tune Money offered online financial services—again co-branded with AirAsia.

Culture and Management Style

AirAsia's corporate culture and management style reflected Tony Fernandes' own personality: informal, friendly, and cheerful. In the same way that culture and brand identity of Southwest Airlines and the Virgin airlines (Virgin Atlantic, Virgin Blue, and Virgin America) reflect the personalities of founders Herb Kelleher and Richard Branson, respectively, Fernandes has used his personality and personal style to create a distinct identity for AirAsia. His usual dress of jeans, open-neck shirt, and baseball cap provide a clear communication of AirAsia's unstuffy, open culture. Its team spirit, commitment to job flexibility, and lack of hierarchy were reinforced from the top: Fernandes worked one day a month as a baggage handler, one day every two months as cabin crew, and one day every three months as a check-in clerk.

The share offer prospectus described AirAsia's culture as follows:

> The Group prides itself on building a strong, team-orientated corporate culture. The Group's employees understand and subscribe to the Group's core strategy and actively focus on maintaining low costs and high productivity. AirAsia motivates its employees by awarding bonuses based upon each employee's contribution to AirAsia's productivity, and expects to increase loyalty through its ESOS [employee

share ownership scheme] which will be available to all employees. The Group's management encourages open communication which creates a dynamic working environment, and meets all its employees on a quarterly basis to review AirAsia's results and generate new ways to lower costs and increase productivity. Employees . . . frequently communicate directly with AirAsia's senior management and offer suggestions on how AirAsia can increase its efficiency or productivity. . .

In addition to the above, AirAsia:

- inculcates enthusiasm and commitment among staff by sponsoring numerous social events and providing a vibrant and friendly working environment
- strives to be honest and transparent in its relations with third parties. . .
- fosters a non-discriminatory, meritocratic environment where employees are offered opportunities for advancement, regardless of their education, race, gender, religion, nationality or age, and
- emphasizes maintaining a constant quality of service throughout all of AirAsia's operation through bringing together to work on a regular basis employees based in different locations.[7]

AirAsia's Operations

AirAsia's operations strategy comprised the following elements:

- *Aircraft*: In common with other LCCs, AirAsia operated a single type of aircraft, the Airbus A320. (It switched from Boeing 737s in 2005.) A single aircraft type offered economies in purchasing, maintenance, pilot training, and aircraft utilization.
- *No-frills flights*: AirAsia offered a single class, which allowed more seats per plane. For example, when it was operating its Boeing 737s, these were equipped with 148 seats, compared to 132 for a typical two-class configuration. Customer services were minimal: complimentary meals and drinks were not served on board—but snacks and beverages could be purchased, passengers paid for baggage beyond a low threshold, and there was no baggage transfer between flights. AirAsia did not use aerobridges for boarding and disembarking passengers, which was another cost-saving measure. Flights were ticketless and there was no assigned seating. Such simplicity allowed quick turnaround of planes, which permitted better utilization of planes and crews.
- *Sales and marketing*: AirAsia engaged in direct sales through its website and call center. As a result, it avoided paying commission to travel agents.
- *Outsourcing*: AirAsia achieved simplicity and cost economies by outsourcing those activities that could be undertaken more effectively and efficiently by third parties. Thus, most aircraft maintenance was outsourced to third parties, contracts being awarded on the basis of competitive bidding. Most of AirAsia's information technology requirements were also outsourced.

- *Information technology*: AirAsia used Navitair's Open Skies computer reservations system (CRS), which linked Web-based sales and inventory system, which also linked with AirAsia's call center. The CRS was integrated with AirAsia's yield management system (YMS) that priced seats on every flight according to demand. The CRS also allowed passengers to print their own boarding passes. In 2006, AirAsia implemented a wireless delivery system which enabled customers to book seats, check flight schedules, and obtain real-time updates on AirAsia's promotions via their mobile phones—an important facility in the Asia-Pacific region because of the extensive use of mobile phones. The YMS helped AirAsia to maximize revenue by providing trend analysis and optimize pricing; it also gave information on future passenger numbers that was used by AirAsia's Advanced Planning and Scheduling (APS) system to minimize operational costs by optimizing supply chain and facilities management. These two IT systems allowed AirAsia to reduce costs in logistics and inbound activities. During 2005, AirAsia adopted an ERP (enterprise resource planning) system to support its processes, facilitate month-end financial closing, and speed up reporting and data retrieval.[8] This was superseded by an advanced planning and scheduling system, which optimized AirAsia's supply chain management and forecasted future resource requirements.

- *Human resource management*: Human resource management had been a priority for AirAsia since its relaunch under Tony Fernandes. A heavy emphasis was given to selecting applicants on the basis of their aptitudes, then creating an environment and a system which developed employees and retained them. AirAsia's retention rates were exceptionally high, which it regarded, first, as an indicator of motivation and job satisfaction and as a cost-saving measure—because employees were multi-skilled, AirAsia's training costs per employee tended to be high. Job flexibility at all levels of the company, including administration, was a major source of productivity for AirAsia.

AirAsia: Cost Information

To offer a comparative view of AirAsia's operational efficiency and cost position, Table 1 provides operating and financial information on Malaysia's two leading airlines: Malaysia Airlines and AirAsia. Although Malaysia Airlines' route network was very different from that of AirAsia's (Malaysia Airlines had a larger proportion of long-haul routes), it was subject to similar cost conditions as AirAsia.

For the first time since its relaunch in 2002, AirAsia made a loss in 2008. This was the result of Fernandes' decision to unwind AirAsia's futures contracts for jet fuel purchased. When crude oil prices started to tumble during the latter half of 2008, Fernandes believed that AirAsia would be better off taking a loss on its existing contracts in order to benefit from lower fuel prices.

Going Long-haul

Fernandes was aware that expanding from short-haul flights in Southeast Asia to flights of more than four hours to China, Australia, Europe, and the Middle

TABLE 1 Comparing operational and financial performance between AirAsia and Malaysia Airlines, 2008

	AirAsia	Malaysia Airlines
Operating data		
Passengers carried (millions)	11.81	13.76
Available seat kilometers (billions)	18.72	53.38
Revenue passenger kilometers (billions)	13.49	36.18
Seat load factor (%)	75.0	67.8
Cost per available seat kilometers (sen[a])	11.66	22.80
Revenue per available seat kilometers (sen)	14.11	20.60
Number of aircraft in fleet December 31, 2008	78.0	109.0
Number of employees	3,799	19,094
Aircraft utilization (hours per day)	11.8	11.1
Financial data (RM, millions)[a]		
Revenue	2,635	15,035
Other operating income	301.8	466.0
Total operating expense	2,966.0	15,198.3
of which:		
—Staff costs	236.8	2,179.9
—Depreciation	347.0	327.9
—Fuel costs	1,389.8	6,531.6
—Maintenance and overall	345.1	1,146.4
—Loss on unwinding derivatives	830.2	—
—Other operating expenses[b]	139.2	5,020.0
Operating profit	(351.7)	305.5
Finance cost (net)	517.5	60.8
Pre-tax profit	(869.2)	264.7
After-tax profit	(496.6)	245.6
Total assets	9,520.0	10,071.6
of which:		
—Aircraft, property, plant and equipment	6,594.3	2,464.8
—Inventories	20.7	379.7
—Cash	153.8	3,571.7
—Receivables	694.4	2,020.1
Debt	6,690.8	433.4
Shareholders' equity	1,605.5	4,197.0

Notes:
[a]RM: Malaysian ringgit; 1 ringgit: 100 sen (cents). During 2008/9 the average exchange rate was US$1 • RM3.43.
[b]For AirAsia the main components were aircraft lease expenses and loss on foreign exchange. For Malaysia Airlines the main components were hire of aircraft, sales commissions, landing fees, and rent of buildings.
Sources: Company annual reports.

East required major changes in operating practices and major new investments, primarily in bigger planes. The creation of AirAsia X was intended to facilitate a measure of operational independence for the long-haul flights while also spreading the risks of this venture among several investors. The investors in AirAsia X also contributed valuable expertise: Virgin Group had experience in establishing and operating four airlines (Virgin Atlantic, Virgin Express, Virgin Blue, and Virgin USA), and the chairman of Air Ventures was Robert Milton, the former CEO of Air Canada.

TABLE 2 Comparing AirAsia and AirAsia X

	AirAsia	**AirAsia X**
Concept	Low cost short-haul, no-frills	Low cost long-haul, no frills
Flying range	Within four hours' flying time from departing city	More than four hours' flying time from departing city
Aircraft	Airbus A320 with 180 seats	Airbus A330 with more than 330 seats
Cabin configuration	Single class	Economy and Premium (previously known as XL)
Seat option	Unassigned seating, plus Xpress Boarding option	Assigned seating with seat request option
In-flight dining	Range of light meals and snacks available for purchase onboard	Pre-ordered full meals available including Asian, Western, vegetarian, and kids' meal; light snacks also available for purchase onboard

Source: AirAsia websites www.airasia.com and www.airasiax.com.

Table 2 shows the principal differences in AirAsia and AirAsia X's operations and services.

Kuala Lumpur to London: Price and Cost Comparisons

A comparison of prices and costs allows a clearer picture of AirAsia's ability to compete in the long-haul market—a market in which AirAsia had to establish itself against some of the world's major airlines. Between KL and London, AirAsia was in competition with at least six international airlines, the closest of which were Malaysia Airlines, Emirates, and British Airways.

A comparison of economy, round-trip airfares between the two cities is shown in Table 3. As Table 4 shows, these fare differentials reflected differences in cost between AirAsia and its long-haul competitors. These cost differences do not take account of differences in load factors, which can have a major effect on the average cost per passenger. AirAsia reported that its KL–London flights had a load factor in excess of 90%. For the airlines as a whole, Table 5 shows load factors.

TABLE 3 Fare comparisons: AirAsia and its competitors between Kuala Lumpur and London

	AirAsia X[a] (US$)	Cheapest other airline[b] (US$)	AirAsia price advantage (%)	Cheapest other airlines
KL–London round trip	433.96[c]	683.68	36.5	1. Gulf Air 2. Qatar Air 3. Emirates
London–KL round trip	433.96[c]	530.35	18.2	1. Emirates 2. Etihad 3. Gulf Air

Notes:
[a] Average fare between September 1 and October 1, 2009.
[b] Average of lowest airline fare on each day between September 1 and October 1, 2009.
[c] Average outbound fare: $187.87; average inbound fare: $209.48; meals and baggage charges: $36.61.

TABLE 4 Flight operating cost comparison: Kuala Lumpur to London (in US$)

	AirAsia	British Airways	Malaysia Airlines	Emirates	
Aircraft type	Airbus 340-300	Boeing 747-400	Boeing 747-400	Boeing 777-300	
Route[a]	KUL–STN	KUL–LHR	KUL–LHR	KUL–DXB–LHR	
Maximum passenger capacity	286	337	359	360	
				KUL–DXB	DXB–LHR
Flight fuel cost	79,299	159,522	159,522	77,525	80,822
Leasing costs	5,952	0	0	0	0
En route navigation charges	7,949	12,294	12,294	1,435	6,613
Terminal navigation arrival charges	419	645	645	0	645
Landing/parking	1,100	2,200	2,200	2,200	2,200
Departure handling	6,000	12,000	12,000	12,000	12,000
Arrival handling	6,000	12,000	12,000	12,000	12,000
Segment totals				105,160	114,280
Total cost per flight[b]	106,719	198,661	198,661	219,440	
Average cost per passenger[b]	373.14	589.50	553.37	609.56	

Notes:

[a]KUL = Kuala Lumpur, STN = London Stansted, LHR = London Heathrow, DXB = Dubai.

[b]Excluding maintenance, depreciation, meal services, and crew salaries.

Source: S. Buchholz, N. Fabio, A. Ileyassoff, L. Mang, and D. Visentin, *AirAsia: Tales from a Long-haul Low Cost Carrier* (Bocconi University, 2009). Data based on NewPacs Aviation Tool Software. Used by permission of the authors.

The Outlook for Long-haul

There can be little doubt that AirAsia had been remarkably successful in building a budget airline in Southeast Asia. Its cost efficiency, growth rate, brand awareness, and awards for customer service, airline management, and entrepreneurship all pointed to outstanding achievement, not simply in replicating the LCC business model pioneered by Southwest Airlines but in adapting that model and augmenting it with innovation, dynamism, and marketing flair that derived from Tony Fernandes' personality and leadership style.

However, its AirAsia X venture presented a whole set of new challenges. AirAsia had successfully transferred several of its competitive advantages from AirAsia to AirAsia X. The low costs associated with fuel-efficient new planes, secondary airports, and human resources practices had allowed AirAsia X to become the low-cost

TABLE 5 Difference between airlines in load factors (%)

	2004	2005	2006	2007	2008
AirAsia	77.0	75.0	78.0	80.0	75.5
Emirates	73.4	74.6	75.9	76.2	79.8
British Airways	67.6	69.7	70.0	70.4	71.2
Malaysia Airlines	69.0	71.5	69.8	71.4	67.8

Source: S. Buchholz, N. Fabio, A. Ileyassoff, L. Mang, and D. Visentin, "AirAsia: Tales from a Long-haul Low Cost Carrier," (case report, Bocconi University, 2009). Used by permission of the authors.

operator on most of its routes. The AirAsia brand and corporate reputation provided AirAsia X with credibility on each new route it inaugurated. By sharing web-based and telephone flight booking systems along with administrative and operational services between the two airlines, AirAsia X was able to secure cost efficiencies that would not be possible for an independent start-up.

Nevertheless, doubts remained over AirAsia X's ability to compete with established international airlines. Unlike AirAsia, which was attracting a whole new market for domestic and regional air travel, AirAsia X would have to take business away from the established international airlines whose business models offered some key competitive advantages over that of long-haul LCCs. In particular, the dense domestic and regional route networks of the established carriers offered feeds for their intercontinental flights. These complementarities were supported by through-ticketing, baggage transfer, and frequent-flyer schemes. Their sources of profit were very different from the LCCs: most of their profit was earned from first- and business-class travelers, which permitted subsidization of economy-class fares.

These challenges pointed to the advantages of closer integration of AirAsia X with AirAsia. AirAsia X's CEO, Azran Osman-Rani, had argued for the operational and financial rationale of merging AirAsia X into AirAsia: "It would be difficult for AirAsia in the future if it did not have trunk routes as [this] is where the traffic volumes come from, so AirAsia needs growth from AirAsia X and the merger allows it to tap growth opportunities in the long-haul markets." Responding to allegations that the real rationale for the merger was to allow AirAsia to finance AirAsia X's losses, Azran said: "Rubbish, we can clearly dispute that. For the first quarter ended March 31, 2009 our net profit was RM 18 million and we are net cash flow positive. We even had a little cash at RM 3 million. We are in a very good position and on a much firmer footing and now is an interesting time to talk about a merger."[9]

Notes

1. Operating profit before depreciation, amortization, and interest as a percentage of average total assets.
2. See www.tonyfernandesblog.com, accessed June 3, 2009. Website no longer available.
3. Quoted by T. Lawton and J. Doh, *The Ascendance of AirAsia: Building a Successful Budget Airline in Asia* (Ivey School of Business, Case No. 9B08M054, 2008).
4. "AirAsia X to Hub in Abu Dhabi: AirAsia CEO," *Khaleej Times* (August 5, 2009).
5. "Corporate Profile," http://www.airasia.com/ot/en/about-us/corporate-profile.page, accessed July 20, 2015.
6. "AirAsia Berhad," *Offering Circular* (October 29): 3.
7. Ibid.: 5.
8. C. Cho, S. Hoffman Arian, C. Tjitrahardja, and R. Narayanaswamy, *AirAsia: Strategic IT Initiative* (student report, Faculty of Economics and Commerce, University of Melbourne, 2005).
9. "AirAsia X CEO backs Merger with AirAsia Bhd," *The Star Online* (July 23, 2009), http://www.thestar.com.my/Story/?file=%2F2009%2F7%2F23%2Fbusiness%2F4369512, accessed July 20, 2015.

Case 10 Chipotle Mexican Grill, Inc.: Disrupting the Fast-food Business

Chipotle Mexican Grill was the most successful new restaurant chain to be established in the US since 1990. From a single restaurant in 1993, Chipotle was expected to have 1988 restaurants by the end of 2015 that would generate sales of about $1.3 billion. Strong top-line and bottom-line growth—during 2010–2014 revenues had grown by 22% annually and net income by 26% annually—had made Chipotle the best-performing stock in its sector (Figure 1).

Compared with industry leaders such as McDonald's and Yum! Brands, Chipotle was still a small player. Yum! Brands had 41,000 KFC, Pizza Hut, and Taco Bell restaurants generating sales of $34 billion. Yet, Chipotle's market capitalization was $21 billion compared to $34 billion for Yum! Brands: a clear indication of investors' favorable expectations for Chipotle's future growth and profitability.

Chipotle's Founding and Growth

Steve Ells graduated from a New York culinary school in 1990. Working at a San Francisco restaurant, he developed a passion for fresh ingredients and became intrigued by the combination of high-quality cuisine, fast service, and low prices offered by the local *taqueria*—tiny restaurants serving tacos and burritos. He opened his first Chipotle Mexican Grill in a former ice cream parlor in his home town of Denver in 1993. He described the birth of the concept as follows:

> The inspiration came from the little *taqueria* in the Mission district of San Francisco. What fascinated me about these burritos was that they were made in this great tortilla and everything was on the inside—the rice, the beans, the meat, the salsas— then wrapped in foil … So the idea was that I could use these authentic ingredients but then put my own twist to them … I noticed customers formed a line and how small the place was and how few people were behind the counter. So the economic model that was happening occurred to me.[1]

His father provided the initial capital:

> Steve said he needed $75,000. So I said, "OK, you've got to write a business plan." It was one page and it said, "Worst-case, best-case and mid-case." He put down

This case was prepared by Robert M. Grant. ©2015 Robert M. Grant.

FIGURE 1 Chipotle Mexican Grill Inc.: Share Price, 2006–2015 ($)

"number of burritos sold per day," and then he went through the cost of the burrito and the cost of electricity, utilities, rent, and repaying my loan. The break-even was he had to sell 114 burritos a day.[2]

By 1998, Chipotle had 16 restaurants and, for its next stage of expansion, was seeking venture capital. Steve Ells' father recounts:

We sent the business plan to 13 venture capital or investment banker-type companies that specialize in the restaurant business. We got rejected by all 13.[3]

Venture capital came from a surprising source: McDonald's Corporation invested $380 million for a minority stake, fueling Chipotle's national expansion. When Chipotle went public in 2006, McDonald's sold its shareholding for $1.5 billion. Ells' friend and legal adviser Monty Moran joined Chipotle in 2005 and in 2009 was appointed co-CEO with Steve Ells.

Ells' passion for fresh, wholesome ingredients extended to increasing concern over environmental sustainability and animal welfare. The result was the launch of Chipotle's "Food with Integrity" initiative in 2001. This involved sourcing organically produced foodstuffs, including meat from free-range, hormone-free animals, and an emphasis on local sourcing. Chipotle's commitment to humane, sustainable farming became a key theme in its marketing and brand development. In 2011, a commercial video entitled *Back to the Start* featuring Willie Nelson singing a song about a farmer embracing organic farming became hugely popular.

Chipotle explained that its vision "is to change the way people think about and eat fast food. We do this by avoiding a formulaic approach when creating our restaurant experience, looking to fine-dining restaurants for inspiration. We use high-quality raw ingredients, classic cooking methods and a distinctive interior design and have friendly people." This vision was not necessarily limited to Mexican food. As far as Steve Ells was concerned: "The model is cuisine agnostic. It can be applied to any kind of food." Chipotle's director of concept development, Tim Wilding, was eager to exploit this opportunity:

> Hearing Steve say that many cuisines could work in the Chipotle format, I basically pitched him this idea. I said, "Steve, we have to do a Southeast Asian restaurant." He miraculously said, "OK, let's do this." So I set up a trip for us and we went to Bangkok and Singapore, and we spent a little over a week just eating like crazy.[4]

The result was the first Shop House Southeast Asian Kitchen opening in Washington, DC in 2011.

During 2011, Ells began collaborating with Denver restaurateurs Bobby Stuckey and Lachlan Mackinnon-Patterson to create a fast-food version of their gourmet pizza restaurant, Pizzeria Locale. With Chipotle as the major investor, two Pizzeria Locales opened in Denver and a number of other openings were planned for 2015. In February 2015, Chipotle reiterated its belief that:

> The fundamental principles on which Chipotle restaurants are based—finding the very best sustainably raised ingredients, prepared and cooked using classical methods in front of the customer, and served in an interactive format by special people dedicated to providing a great dining experience—can be adapted to cuisines other than the food we serve at Chipotle.[5]

Restaurant Operations

Chipotle's distinctive product offering—based upon freshly prepared, organic ingredients that allowed a maximum of choice within a limited-item menu—required an operational model that was distinctively different from that which operated throughout the fast-food industry.

Ingredients formed a much higher percentage of total costs than were typical in the industry, hence, if prices were to be kept low, this required cost efficiencies elsewhere. If each customer was to be allowed to customize his/her order, it required restaurant staff to engage with customers during the preparation of their order.

Chipotle restaurants are all company owned and operated and are between 1,000 and 2,800 square feet—much smaller than a typical fast-food restaurant. Chipotle's emphasis on simplicity and functionality is reflected in the design and decor of its restaurants. The layout is designed to optimize space utilization and maximize the efficiency of customer service. The decor is minimalist with concrete floors, exposed piping, natural colors, and a plentiful use of wood and stainless steel.

At Chipotle, customers order from a pared-down menu of tacos and burritos, then watch the kitchen staff prepare their meal from fresh, sustainably raised ingredients. "We don't say on the menu board that we have fresh guacamole," says founder and co-CEO Steve Ells. "As a customer, you can see it being made right in front of you."

Chipotle's menu is based upon the principle of "A Few Things, Thousands of Ways." The menu comprises only burritos (also served without the tortilla as a "burrito bowl"), tacos, and salads. Because customers can choose among four different meats or tofu, two types of beans, and various extras, the menu offers "countless choices." The ingredients are freshly prepared, by hand, each day.

The restaurants feature open kitchens and customers form a line which moves along the serving counter, selecting the ingredients for their chosen dish. Speed of service is achieved through focusing upon the "four pillars of throughput": a dedicated "expeditor," who works just before the cashier to get drink and side orders and bag to-go orders; a dedicated "linebacker," who ensures the serving line is always stocked; *mise en place,* meticulous attention to having everything placed and ready for serving; and "aces in their places," the best employees at each position during peak periods. Chipotle regards itself as an industry leader in speed of service: some of Chipotle's fastest restaurants run more than 350 transactions per hour at lunchtime.

Human Resource Management

The fact that all employees engage with customers has important implications for human resource management. Chipotle's 2014 annual report states:

> All of our restaurant employees are encouraged to interact with customers no matter their job, whether preparing food or serving customers during our busiest period. We focus on attracting and retaining people who can deliver that experience for each customer. We provide each customer with individual attention and make every effort to respond to customer suggestions and concerns in a personal and hospitable way. We believe our focus on creating a positive and interactive experience helps build loyalty and enthusiasm for our brand among general managers, crew members and customers alike.[6]

Chipotle was committed to training its employees and promoting from within. Its website declared: "No Experience Preferred":

> Many restaurant companies hire "professional" managers to run their restaurants and almost never look to their crews for new leaders. But at Chipotle, most of our general managers were promoted from our crews and because our company is growing, there's plenty of opportunity.[7]

Chipotle's focus on developing its managers resulted in its "restaurateur program." Restaurateurs are general managers specially selected for their management abilities—especially for their ability to develop their staff. When selected, they get a one-time bonus and stock options. And after that they receive an extra $10,000 each time they train a crew member to become a general manager. Restaurateurs have greater discretion in running their own restaurants and, in some cases, manage more than one restaurant.

Co-CEO Monty Moran identified its approach to human resource management as a key element of Chipotle's competitive advantage:

> Our strong People culture continues to drive our success in attracting loyal customers and delivering exceptional results. Our restaurant teams are ambitious, passionate, and dedicated to delivering the best dining experience possible. Our efforts to hire and develop top performing crews will continue to lead to stronger

future leaders running our restaurants, and ensure our customers will enjoy the best customer service possible."[8]

Marketing

Chipotle went to great efforts to distinguish itself from established perceptions of fast food. Its corporate profile positioned itself within the "fast-casual" rather than the "fast-food" segment (Exhibit 1). Its distinctive approach extends to its marketing where it eschews most traditional marketing in favor of social media and non-traditional means of promotion. Chipotle emphasizes communicating "what differentiates Chipotle from other fast food companies," especially with regard to its "Food with Integrity" mission:

> [W]e are continuing to explore and pioneer new avenues of branded content aimed at making consumers more curious about issues that are important to us, and explaining why and how we are working to drive positive change in the nation's food supply. In addition, we continue to generate considerable media coverage…
>
> [W]e have been developing more "owned media," including new video and music programs, a more visible event strategy that includes our "Cultivate" food, music and ideas festivals, and participation in relevant events in markets around the country. Many of these newer programs allow us to tell our story with more nuance than is afforded by traditional advertising, and help forge stronger emotional connections with our customers.[9]

Within social media, Chipotle was widely viewed as the most engaged and responsive of fast-food companies in terms of frequency of tweets and responses to Facebook posts. This allowed it to build strong one-to-one engagement with its core demographic group of 18- to 24-year-olds.

Challenges

The restaurant business is fiercely competitive and Chipotle faced competition on multiple fronts. By 2015, Chipotle had established itself among the leading fast-food chains in the US (Table 1), although among those specializing in Mexican cuisine, Chipotle was a distant second to Yum! Brand's Taco Bell (Table 2).

Taco Bell's response to Chipotle's success was to introduce a new, upscale menu under the "Cantina Bell" name. Second, Taco Bell launched a new chain of casual dining restaurants, US Taco Company. When, in 2012, David Einhorn, founder of hedge fund Greenlight Capital, recommended shorting Chipotle because of Taco Bell's resurgence, Chipotle's share price fell by 7%. Einhorn's case against Chipotle was supported by a Zagat comparison of steak burritos: although Chipotle's was declared superior to that of Cantina Bell, Chipotle's was priced at $10.34 compared to $5.99 for the Cantina Bell product.

EXHIBIT 1

Chipotle Corporate Profile

When Chipotle (pronounced chi-POAT-lay) opened its first store in 1993, the idea was simple: demonstrate that food served fast didn't have to be a "fast-food" experience. We use high-quality raw ingredients, classic cooking methods and a distinctive interior design, and have friendly people to take care of each customer—features that are more frequently found in the world of fine dining. When we opened, there wasn't an industry category to describe what we were doing. Some 20 years and more than 1500 restaurants later, we compete in a category of dining now called "fast-casual," the fastest growing segment of the restaurant industry, where customers expect food quality that's more in line with full-service restaurants, coupled with the speed and convenience of fast food…

Our focus has always been on using the kinds of higher-quality ingredients and cooking techniques used in high-end restaurants to make great food accessible at reasonable prices. But our vision has evolved. While using a variety of fresh ingredients remains the foundation of our menu, we believe that "fresh is not enough, anymore." Now we want to know where all of our ingredients come from, so that we can be sure they are as flavorful as possible while understanding the environmental and societal impact of our business. We call this idea *Food With Integrity*, and it guides how we run our business.

◆ Using higher-quality ingredients. We use a variety of ingredients that we purchase from carefully selected suppliers. We concentrate on where we obtain each ingredient … and we continue to investigate using even more naturally raised, organically grown and sustainably grown ingredients…

◆ A few things, thousands of ways. We only serve a few things: burritos, burrito bowls (a burrito without the tortilla), tacos and salads. We plan to keep a simple menu, but we'll always consider sensible additions.

Source: Chipotle corporate website, http://ir.chipotle.com/phoenix.zhtml?c=194775&p=irol-homeProfile&t=&id=&, accessed July 20, 2015.

Chipotle also inspired a wave of imitators among new start-ups. As *Forbes* magazine noted in 2014:

> Chipotle is the most influential and game changing restaurant in America. They are spawning countless imitators… Practically every chain in the United States is trying to be the next Chipotle—or the Chipotle of fried chicken, the Chipotle of pizza, the Chipotle of barbecue.[10]

Chipotle's success also encouraged a flood of venture capital into new casual dining start-ups—a segment that had emerged as a result of Chipotle's "reinvention of fast food." When the shares of Shake Shack—billed as the "Chipotle of burgers"—began trading on January 29, 2015, the chain of 63 burger joints was valued at $1.8 billion, representing a price/earnings ratio of 700. In April 2012, Ruby Tuesday bought Florida-based start-up Lime Fresh Mexican Grill for $24 million with plans to expand the chain from 15 to 65 outlets—by April 2015 there were only 26 outlets.

TABLE 1   Leading US restaurant chains, 2015

Company	Principal brands	Total outlets (% company-owned)	Sales, 2014 ($bn)	Market cap. March 25, 2015 ($bn)	Op. margin (%)	ROA (%)	Employees, including part-time (,000s)
McDonald's Corp.	McDonald's	14,278 (11)	27.4	94.8	29.0	13.4	420
Starbucks Corp.	Starbucks	11,457 (62)	17.0	73.0	21.0	22.2	191
Yum! Brands	KFC, Pizza Hut, Taco Bell	16.027 (11)	13.3	34.4	11.7	12.0	537
Darden Restaurants	Olive Garden, LongHorn Steakhouse, + 5 others	2,259 (97)	6.5	8.6	4.5	1.9	206
Chipotle	Chipotle	1,780 (100)	4.1	21.1	17.3	19.6	53
Wendy's Co.	Wendy's	5,791 (22)	2.1	4.1	12.2	2.9	31
Panera Bread	Panera	1,777 (49)	2.5	4.3	10.9	13.9	26

Note: Excludes privately owned chains such as Subway, Burger King, and Dunkin' Donuts.
Sources: Company websites, company 10-K reports, and Financial Times.

Stock analysts were largely positive about Chipotle's potential to generate continuing value for shareholders. In March 2015, 18 of the 30 investment analysts covering Chipotle recommended the stock as a "buy" or "strong buy"; the remaining 12 rated the stock as a "hold." Beyond the brokerage community opinions were more diverse. Seeking Alpha noted that "Chipotle's brand is the source of its intangible asset moat with its uniquely customizable menu structure and upscale restaurant environments." Also its sustainably sourced, organic produce allowed it to "attract a largely affluent clientele."[11] Similarly, NYU Stern Investment Management and Research observed that "CMG's total addressable market is still huge," and predicted that "Brand equity and unique business model should preserve pricing power and ROIC over the long term."[12] Others were less sanguine, pointing to the difficulty that Chipotle would have to sustain its remarkable earnings growth in the face of increased competition and the challenges of managing its increased size

TABLE 2   Leading US restaurant chains specializing in Mexican cuisine, 2015

Company	Headquarters and start year	Approx. no. of outlets
Taco Bell	California, 1962	6,500
Chipotle Mexican Grill	Colorado, 1993	1,900
Del Taco	California, 1964	547
Qdoba Mexican Grill	Colorado, 1995	641
Moe's Southwest Grill	Georgia, 2000	540
El Pollo Loco	California, 1980	410
On the Border Mexican Grill & Cantina	Texas, 1982	122
Green Burrito	California, 1980	300
Rubio's Coastal Grill	California, 1993	159

Source: Companies' websites.

and complexity (especially in relation to food sourcing), and the risk of consumers becoming bored with its limited menu.

There were also signs of shareholders becoming less infatuated with the management team: in 2014, shareholders voted down a remuneration package for the co-CEOs, Ells and Moran, which would have paid them $285 million over three years.

Appendix 1

TABLE A1   Chipotle Mexican Grill, Inc. financial data, 2010–2014

	2014	2013	2012	2011	2010
Sales ($mn)	4,108	3,215	2,731	2,269	1,836
Operating income ($mn)	710	533	456	351	288
Net income ($mn)	445	327	278	215	179
Total assets ($mn)	2,546	2,009	1,669	1,425	1,122
Shareholders' equity ($mn)	2,012	1,538	1,246	1,044	811
Operating margin (%)	17.3	16.6	16.8	15.5	15.7
Net margin (%)	10.8	10.2	10.2	9.5	9.7
Operating income/average total assets (%)	31.2	29.0	29.5	27.6	28.3
Return on average equity (%)	25.1	23.4	24.3	23.2	23.4
Current ratio	3.6	3.3	2.9	3.4	3.3

Source: Chipotle Mexican Grill, Inc. 10-K report for 2014.

TABLE A2   Performance comparison: Chipotle vs. Yum! Brands, 2014

	Chipotle Mexican Grill	Yum! Brands, Inc.[a]	Taco Bell[b]
Number of restaurants	1,780	41,000	926
Revenues ($mn)	4,108	13,279	1,452
Gross margin (%)	65.4	72.3	70.3
Operating margin (%)	17.3	11.7	18.5
Net margin (%)	10.8	7.9	n.a.
Food, drink, packaging/operating cost (%)	41.8	31.4	36.6
Labor costs/operating cost (%)	26.6	22.0	35.1
Occupancy costs /operating cost (%)	6.8	15.4[c]	12.6[c]
General and admin/operating cost (%)	8.1	12.2	15.7[d]
Depreciation and amortization/operating cost (%)	3.2	8.7	4.5[d]
Advertising/operating cost (%)	1.7	5.1	n.a.
Sales/total assets	1.61	1.59	n.a.
Sales/fixed assets	3.71	2.95	n.a.
Sales/inventories	26.8	37.7	n.a.
Long-term debt/equity	0	1.92	n.a.

Notes:
[a]These corporate data relate to Taco Bell, Pizza Hut, and KFC.
[b]These data (unless otherwise indicated) relate to the company-owned restaurants of Yum! Brands' Taco Bell division.
[c]This ratio is for "occupancy and other operating expenses."
[d]This ratio is for the Taco Bell division as a whole (both company owned and franchised restaurants).
n.a. = not available.
Source: Chipotle Mexican Grill and Yum! Brands' 10-K reports for 2014.

Notes

1. "Chipotle Story: How it all started," http://www.chipotle. com/en-US/fwi/videos/videos.aspx?v=5, accessed July 20, 2015.
2. "Chipotle: The definitive oral history," http://www. bloomberg.com/graphics/2015-chipotle-oral-history/, accessed July 20, 2015.
3. Ibid.
4. Ibid.
5. Chipotle Mexican Grill Inc. 10-K report for 2014 (filed February 4, 2015).
6. Ibid.
7. "We're growing quickly," http://www.chipotle.com/ en-US/careers/get_rolling/get_rolling.aspx, accessed July 20, 2015.
8. Chipotle Mexican Grill, Inc. Press Release: First Quarter 2012 Results (April 19, 2012).
9. Chipotle Mexican Grill Inc. 10-K report for 2014 (filed February 4, 2015).
10. "Fast Food Goes Custom," *ForbesLife*, http://www. forbes.com/sites/andrewbender/2014/12/31/top-10- food-trends-of-2014/?slide=5, accessed July 20, 2015.
11. "Chipotle Mexican Grill: A Multi-Decade Growth Opportunity," http://seekingalpha.com/article/3026406- chipotle-mexican-grill-a-multi-decade-growth-opportu- nity, accessed July 20, 2015.
12. "A Great Entry Point for Chipotle," http://seekingalpha. com/article/3020946-a-great-entry-point-for-chipotle, accessed July 20, 2015.

Case 11   Ford and the World Automobile Industry in 2015

Addressing Ford's shareholders for the first time since his appointment as CEO in July 2014, Mark Fields expressed optimism about Ford's future.

> The past five years mark one of the most consistently profitable periods in our recent history. Now we are poised to accelerate our progress in all areas of our business. Put simply, Ford is a growth company in a growing global industry.[1]

Ford was the only one of the US "Big Three" automakers to survive the financial crisis of 2008–2009 without the need for a bailout either from the federal government or from a foreign competitor. This was a result of the "One Ford" strategy that Mark Fields' predecessor, Alan Mulally, had inaugurated at Ford soon after his appointment in 2006. The One Ford strategy had closed plants; cut employment from 295,000 to 181,000; divested Jaguar, Land Rover, Volvo, and Mazda; and focused the company around its core brand, around global integration, and fast-cycle new product development.

Fields, too, was committed to the One Ford strategy. By 2016, Ford's 50+ models would be built on just nine global platforms (in 2007, Ford had 27 platforms). By the end of 2015, 97% of Ford's production would be from its global platforms and by 2019 each global platform would support an average of 6.6 models. The One Ford strategy also embodied ambitious goals for quality improvement and innovation. By 2015, Ford was already a leader in semi-autonomous driving technologies through its parking assistance and collision avoidance systems and in connectivity through its Sync 3 communications and entertainment system.

However, despite forecasting that Ford would increase its pre-tax profit by between 35 and 50% during 2015, Field realized that the world's automobile industry was on the threshold of wrenching changes that would have profound effects on whether and how Ford would be able to earn profit in the future. Exhibit 1 discusses some of forces that would drive the industry's transformation.

Yet even before these forces came into play, the industry in its present state was hardly in robust health. The collapse in industry profitability during 2007–2009 was not wholly a consequence of the financial crisis. It also reflected the long-term problems of the industry, most notably too many firms with too much capacity chasing too little demand. The financial crisis had been expected to trigger a major industry restructuring. Yet, despite predictions that 2009 would be a "Darwinian year," the auto industry's pre-crisis structure survived almost intact. The *Financial Times* commented:

Instead of natural selection, something else happened: governments around the world, from Canada and Brazil to Russia and South Korea, stepped in with prodigious amounts of cash to keep car plants open and assembly lines running … The money has prevented a necessary shake-out in an industry that has long had too many producers.[2]

The industry's recovery since 2010 had been supported by economic recovery in North America, Japan, and Europe, growing demand in emerging market economies—especially China and India—and lower oil prices. Yet the underlying structure of the industry was far from attractive: there were 32 companies in the world with the capacity to produce over half a million cars annually, and despite only 77% utilization of the industry's capacity in 2015, all the major automakers had committed themselves to sizable capital expenditure for the coming years.

EXHIBIT 1
The Future of the Automobile Industry

According to the consultants from McKinsey & Company's automotive practice, "transformative change is on the way." A number of forces would be driving this change, including:

◆ **Competition.** The world auto industry had been transformed by the entry onto the world stage of Japanese automakers in the 1970s, then Korean automakers, now it was the turn of the Chinese. "With strong local demand as a base, a number of Chinese automakers will probably consolidate, become better able to serve their domestic market, and then seek to achieve an international impact."

◆ **Regulation.** "We expect vehicle-use restrictions to grow more stringent as the level of urbanization increases … [T]he automotive industry should expect to remain under regulatory scrutiny and future emissions standards will probably require OEMs to adopt some form of electrified vehicle. Indeed, we believe that regulatory pressures, technology advances, and the preferences of many consumers will make the end of the internal combustions engine's dominance more a matter of 'when' rather than 'if.'"

◆ **Digital disruption.** "The car of the future will be connected—able not only to monitor, in real time, its own working parts and the safety of conditions around it but also to communicate with other vehicles and with an increasingly intelligent roadway infrastructure." Will the opportunities offered for the creation of new services be captured by the automakers or by Apple, Google, and other leaders in digital innovation?

◆ **Rethinking ownership.** "Technology and connectivity pose the question of whether it's necessary to own an automobile." However, as the McKinsey consultants observed: "increased car sharing does not necessarily translate into fewer car sales … The average distance driven per person probably will not decrease; in fact, it may creep up." Increased use of shared vehicles of essential travel may mean that some consumers still have their personal cars for fun driving and as symbols of identity and status.

Source: Adapted from P. Gao, R. Hensley, and A. Zielke, "A Road Map to the Future of the Auto Industry," *McKinsey Quarterly*, October 2014.

FIGURE 1 US motor vehicle production, 1900–2014

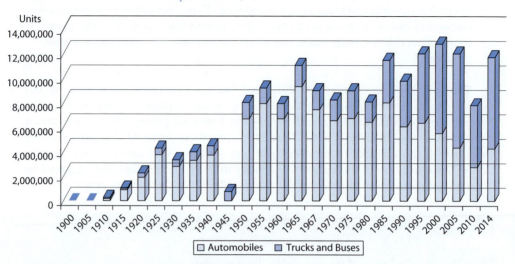

Development of the World Automobile Industry

The Growth of Demand and Production

Vehicles powered by internal combustion appeared in Europe during the 1880s. By the end of the 19th century, hundreds of small companies were producing automobiles both in Europe and in America.

During the 20th century, the industry followed different development paths in different parts of the world. The US auto industry grew rapidly during 1910–1928 and 1946–1965 before reaching market saturation (Figure 1). In Western Europe, growth was most rapid during the 1950s and 1960s, and in Japan during the 1970s and 1980s. In both, production peaked around 1990. In all the advanced industrial countries, the increased longevity of cars dampened market demand (Figure 2).

The world automobile industry has continued to grow (Figure 3) fueled by growing demand and output among the newly industrializing countries, notably Korea, China, Brazil, and India (Table 1). As a result, the proportion of world output contributed by the traditional production centers—the US, Western Europe, and Japan—fell from 77% in 1994 to 42.8% in 2014 (Table 2).

The Evolution of the Automobile

The early automobiles featured diverse designs and technologies. The first "horse-less carriages" were precisely that: they followed design features of existing horse-drawn carriages and buggies while embodying a variety of competing technologies. The internal-combustion engine vied with steam-propulsion and electric motors, and automakers experimented with different approaches to transmission, steering, and brakes.

Gradually, technologies and designs converged. The Ford Model T with its front-mounted, water-cooled, four-cylinder engine represented the first dominant design in automobiles. Convergence continued throughout the 20th century. Power trains

FIGURE 2 Median age of US automobiles, 1941–2012

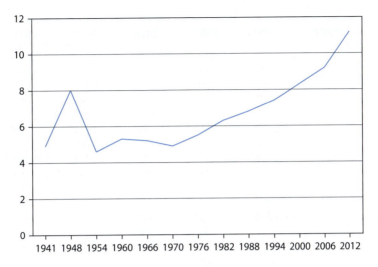

standardized around four-cylinder, water-cooled, in-line engines, plus V-6 and V-8 engines for big cars and three-cylinder engines for some small cars. Front-wheel drive became standard on smaller cars; suspension, steering, braking systems, and body shapes all became increasingly similar. Technological progress became incremental: new materials (plastics, carbon fiber), new safety features, multi-valve cylinders, and electronic systems for traction control, fuel injection, suspension, navigation, and intelligent monitoring.

Convergence also occurred across countries. The distinctive differences that once distinguished American, French, and Japanese cars largely disappeared, partly due to the manufacturers' promotion of global models. The same market segments are

FIGURE 3 World motor vehicle production (cars and trucks), 1985–2011

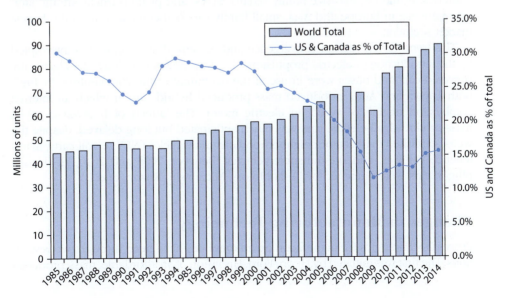

TABLE 1 The world's top-20 automobile-producing countries in 2014 (thousands of cars; excludes trucks)

	1987	1990	1995	2000	2005	2010	2014
China	n.a.	79	356	620	3,118	13,897	19,920
Japan	7,891	9,948	7,664	8,363	9,017	8,310	8,277
Germany	4,604	4,805	4,360	5,132	5,350	5,552	5,604
S. Korea	793	987	1,893	1,881	2,195	3,866	3,158
India	n.a.	n.a.	394	541	999	2,832	4,253
US[a]	7,099	6,077	6,338	5,542	4,321	2,731	4,124
Brazil	789	663	1,312	1,348	2,009	2,585	2,315
France	3,052	3,295	3,051	2,883	3,113	1,924	1,528
Spain	1,403	1,679	1,959	2,445	2,098	1,914	1,495
Russia[b]	1,329	1,260	834	967	1,288	1,208	1,898
Mexico	266	346	710	1,130	846	1,386	1,684
UK	1,143	1,296	1,532	1,641	1,596	1,270	1,915
Czech Rep.	n.a.	n.a.	193	428	599	1,070	1,247
Indonesia	n.a.	n.a.	n.a.	257	333	496	1,011
Slovakia	n.a.	n.a.	n.a.	182	218	562	993
Iran	n.a.	n.a.	n.a.	275	924	1,367	926
Canada	810	1,072	1,339	1,551	1,356	967	913
Thailand	n.a.	n.a.	n.a.	97	278	554	743
Turkey	n.a.	n.a.	233	297	454	603	733
Malaysia	n.a.	n.a.	164	280	405	522	547

Notes: [a]The production data for the US do not include the large volumes of pick-up trucks and SUVs produced by the automobile companies classed as trucks.
[b]USSR in 1987 and 1990.
n.a. = not available.
Source: International Organization of Motor Vehicle Manufacturers.

present in different countries, though the sizes of these segments vary greatly across countries. In the US, mid-size family sedans, SUVs, and pick-up trucks are the largest segments; in Europe and Asia, small family cars (subcompacts) form the largest market segment.

This trend toward design convergence and piecemeal innovation was interrupted by the introduction of electric propulsion—hardly a new technology: the electrically powered cars and buses were in use at the beginning of the 20th century. In 1997, both Toyota and Audi introduced mass-produced hybrid cars in which an internal combustion engine powered an electric motor. The launch of highway-capable, mass-produced, all-electric cars was much anticipated but long delayed, despite the well-established markets for neighborhood electric vehicles (NEVs): golf carts, maintenance vehicles, and site-transport vehicles. Between 2008 and 2010, all-electric, plug-in cars were launched by Tesla Motors, Mitsubishi, Nissan, and BYD.

Changes in Manufacturing Technology

Process technologies for manufacturing automobiles have been through two revolutions. The first was initiated by Henry Ford. His vision of an affordable, mass-produced

TABLE 2   World motor vehicle production by countries and regions (% of world total)[a]

	1960	1989	1994	2000	2005	2008	2010	2012	2014
US	52.0	23.8	24.5	22.2	20.0	18.6	12.9	12.3	13.0
European Union	38.0	31.7	31.2	29.9	28.4	20.7	14.6	19.3	18.9
Japan	1.0	18.2	21.2	17.7	17.0	16.7	12.6	11.8	10.9
South Korea	n.a.	1.8	4.6	5.0	5.3	5.5	5.6	5.4	5.0
China	n.a.	n.a.	2.7	3.5	5.7	13.3	23.6	22.9	26.4
India	0.2	0.7	1.3	1.5	2.5	4.0	4.6	5.0	4.3
World total (million units)	12.8	49.5	50.0	57.4	66.8	69.4	76.1	84.1	89.7

Note:

[a]Motor vehicles include automobiles, trucks, and buses.

n.a. = not available.

Source: International Organization of Motor Vehicle Manufacturers.

automobile resulted in his system of mass production. The key was his development of more precise machine tools that permitted interchangeable parts. This allowed components to be produced either in batches or continuously to be assembled on moving assembly lines by semi-skilled workers. The productivity gains were enormous. In 1912, it took 23 hours to assemble a Model T; 14 months later, after the introduction of his new system, it took just four.

The second was Toyota's system of *lean production* which was developed in postwar Japan where shortages of key materials encouraged extreme parsimony and avoidance of inventories and waste. Lean production combined statistical process control, just-in-time scheduling, quality circles, teamwork, and flexible production (multiple models were manufactured on a single production line). During the 1980s and 1990s, all the world's car manufacturers redesigned their manufacturing processes to incorporate aspects of the Toyota system.

Flexible, lean plants reduced the importance of scale economies in assembly. Minimum efficient scale was once believed to be around 400,000 units a year. After 1990, most new assembly plants had capacities of between 150,000 and 300,000 units per annum. However, scale economies remained important in components and subassemblies: the minimum efficient scale for an engine plant was around one million units annually.

New Product Development

The increasing complexity of new cars in terms of electronics, and new safety and environmental requirements, caused new product development costs to rise steeply. Developing an entirely new mass-production model, including plant tooling and launch costs, typically cost between $2 billion and $6 billion. To spread development costs over a greater volume of production, all the leading automakers adopted global models.

The costs of developing new models put great pressure on smaller manufacturers: they could join rivals—either through alliance or merger—or seek niche positions. Geographically focused manufacturers such as Tofas of Turkey and Proton of Malaysia licensed designs from the global automakers; Chinese car makers tended to form joint ventures. A few remained independent: the tiny British sports car maker Morgan made the same handcrafted car it had designed in the late 1930s.

To economize on new product development and exploit scale economies in purchasing costs, the automakers increasingly adopted a single *platform* for multiple models. A platform comprised a vehicle's architecture, including its floorplan, suspension system, and layout of engine, gearbox, and major components. Volkswagen aimed to reduce its number of platforms to just four. Similarly with major components: in engines, Ford had moved to three engine families: the V-8/V-10, the V-6, and the I-4 (four in-line cylinders). The I-4 engine had over 100 variations, an annual volume of 1.5 million, and was built at three different plants—one in North America, one in Europe, and one in Japan.

The World Auto Industry in 2015

The Manufacturers

The world's leading producers were US, Japanese, and Western European companies, plus Hyundai of Korea (Table 3). All had broad product lines and were multinational (Toyota, GM, and Ford each produced more vehicles outside their home countries than within). The next tiers of companies were either geographically focused (Dongfeng, FAW, AvtoVAZ) or had narrower product lines (BMW, Mazda, Subaru).

Despite many mergers and acquisitions (Table 4), the industry remained fragmented: the four-firm concentration ratio (CR_4) was only 42%. The trend toward consolidation was offset by the rapid growth of emerging market automakers, notably Chinese and Indian companies.

Within most national markets, seller concentration had declined over the period 1980 to 2014. Internationalization had meant that domestic champions had lost their dominance of their home markets: all the world's major auto companies were competing in one another's home markets (see Appendix Table A1).

The Quest for Cost Reduction

The quest for cost efficiency was a key feature of the strategies of all the world's automobile companies and the major driver of structural change in the industry.

The major sources of scale economies were in new product development and purchases of components. Sergio Marchionne, the CEO of Fiat, believed that viability required producing at least six million cars a year: companies producing fewer would struggle to survive.[3] As a result volume car makers needed to serve the world market. Renault's merger with Nissan, Fiat's with Chrysler, and PSA's with General Motors were driven by this logic.

These scale economies also encouraged the automakers to widen their product ranges—especially when a common platform could be used across multiple product segments. For example, Volkswagen's MQB platform was used for the VW Golf, VW Passat, the Audi A3, the Audi TT, the VW Touran, and several other models. One result was that few specialists could survive as independent car makers: VW had

TABLE 3 The world's top-20 automobile producers by volume (millions of units)[a]

		1992	1996	2002	2007	2010	2014
Toyota	Japan	4.25	4.79	6.63	8.53	8.56	10.23
Volkswagen	Germany	3.86	3.98	5.02	6.27	7.34	10.14
GM	US	6.76	8.18	8.33	9.35	8.48	9.92
Nissan	Japan	2.96	2.71	2.72	3.77	4.21	8.47
Renault[b]	France	1.93	1.76	2.33	2.67	2.63	
Hyundai[c]	S. Korea	0.87	1.40	2.64	3.99	5.77	7.71
Ford	US	5.74	6.61	6.73	6.25	5.52	6.32
SAIC[d]	China	n.a.	n.a.	n.a.	n.a.	3.58	5.62
Fiat	Italy	1.80	2.55	2.19	2.68	2.08	4.75
Chrysler	US	2.48	2.96	n.a.	1.58	1.86	
Honda	Japan	1.76	2.02	2.99	3.91	3.64	4.36
PSA	France	2.44	1.98	3.26	3.46	3.60	2.94
Suzuki	Japan	0.89	1.39	1.70	2.60	2.89	2.88
Dongfeng Motor[d]	China	n.a.	n.a.	n.a.	—	2.62	2.73
FAW[d]	China	n.a.	n.a.	n.a.	1.44	2.56	2.65
Daimler	Germany	0.61	0.99	4.46	4.64	1.94	2.53
Changan Auto[d]	China	n.a.	n.a.	n.a.	n.a.	1.90	2.53
Beijing Auto[d]	China	n.a.	n.a.	n.a.	n.a.	1.50	2.15
BMW	Germany	0.60	0.64	1.09	1.54	1.48	2.12
Mitsubishi	Japan	1.60	1.45	1.82	1.41	1.17	1.08
Mazda	Japan	1.25	0.98	1.04	1.29	1.10	1.38
Tata Motors	India	n.a.	n.a.	n.a.	0.59	0.84	0.97
Fuji Heavy Industries	Japan	0.65	0.53	0.54	0.59	0.62	0.89

Notes:
[a]For some companies the figures show total units produced; for others it shows total units sold.
[b]Includes Dacia and Samsung Motors.
[c]Includes Kia.
[d]Includes the entire output of the joint ventures in which the company is a partner.
n.a. = not available.
Source: Company websites.

acquired Bentley, Lamborghini, Bugatti, and Porsche; BMW owned the Rolls-Royce brand.

The quest for cost efficiency also encouraged outsourcing. Henry Ford's system of mass production involved extensive backward integration: Ford had once produced its own steel and owned rubber plantations in the Amazon basin. By the end of the 20th century, the automobile companies had outsourced most of their components and many services. Relationships with suppliers also changed. The Japanese model of close, collaborative, long-term relationships with their first-tier suppliers has displaced the US model of contract-based, arm's-length relationships. The new system resulted in component suppliers growing in size, global reach, and technological capability. Bosch, Denso, and Johnson Controls were of similar size to mid-tier auto companies such as PSA, Renault, and BMW (Table 5).

Yet, despite their quest for cost efficiency through scale and automation, locational factors remained critical determinants of unit costs. Wage rates varied greatly between countries (Table 6) with the result that costs of assembly were far lower in emerging-market counties. Tata Motors' 2009 launch of its Nano model—a

TABLE 4 Mergers and acquisitions among automobile manufacturers, 1986–2014

Year	Acquirer	Target	Notes
2013	Daimler AG (Germany)	BAIC Motor Co. Ltd. (China)	12% stake acquired for $873mn
2012	Porsche AG (Germany)	Volkswagen AG (Germany)	Acquired for $8.9bn
	PSA Peugeot Citroën (France)	General Motors (US)	7% stake acquired for $399mn
2010	Geely (China)	Volvo (Sweden)	Sold by Ford for $1.3bn
2009	Volkswagen (Germany)	Suzuki (Japan)	Acquires 20% stake
	Fiat (Italy)	Chrysler (US)	Acquires 35% stake, later increased to 100%
	Volkswagen	Porsche (Germany)	Acquires 49%
	Beijing Auto (China)	Fujian Motor; Changfeng Motor (China)	
2008	Tata (India)	Jaguar Land Rover (UK)	Sold by Ford
	SAIC Motor Group (China)	Nanjing Automobile (China)	SAIC combines MG and Rover brands
2005	Nanjing Automobile	Rover (UK)	
	Toyota (Japan)	Fuji Heavy Industries (Japan)	Acquired 8.7% stake from GM
2002	GM (US)	Daewoo (S. Korea)	42% of equity acquired
2000	Renault (France)	Samsung Motors (S. Korea)	70% of equity acquired
	GM	Fiat	20% of equity acquired
	DaimlerChrysler (Germany)	Hyundai (S. Korea)	10% of equity acquired
	DaimlerChrysler	Mitsubishi Motors (Japan)	34% of equity acquired
1999	Renault (France)	Nissan (Japan)	38.6% of equity acquired
	Ford (US)	Volvo	Acquires car business only
	Ford	Land Rover	Acquired from BMW
	Toyota	Daihatsu	51% stake acquired
1998	Daimler-Benz (Germany)	Chrysler	Biggest auto merger ever
	VW (Germany)	Rolls Royce Motors (UK)	Acquired from Vickers PLC
	Hyundai (S. Korea)	Kia (S. Korea)	
	Daewoo (S. Korea)	Ssangyong Motor (S. Korea)	
	Daewoo (S. Korea)	Samsung Motor (S. Korea)	
1997	Proton (Malaysia)	Lotus (UK)	
	BMW (Germany)	Rover (UK)	
1996	Daewoo (S. Korea)	FSO (Poland)	
	Daewoo (S. Korea)	FS Lublin (Poland)	
	Ford (US)	Mazda (Japan)	Increases stake from 25 to 33%
1995	Fiat (Italy)	FSM (Poland)	
1994	Daewoo (S. Korea)	Oltcit/Rodae (Romania)	
1991	Volkswagen	Skoda (Czech Rep.)	31% stake later increased to 100%
1990	GM	Saab-Scandia (Sweden)	50% of equity acquired
	Ford	Jaguar	
1987	Ford	Aston Martin (UK)	
	Chrysler	Lamborghini (Italy)	
1986	Volkswagen	Seat (Spain)	

Sources: Financial Times; www.autonews.com.

four-seater, 623cc city car, with fuel consumption of 70 miles per gallon and priced at a mere $2200—was a great shock to the major automakers. However, the subsequent difficulties that the Nano encountered in terms of production, safety, and market acceptance pointed to the sheer complexity of bringing an innovative new model to market and the challenges facing emerging-market automakers in rivaling the experience and expertise of the established leaders.[4]

TABLE 5 Revenues and profitability of the top-ten automotive component suppliers

	Revenues ($billion)				ROA (%)	ROE (%)
	1994	2000	2011	2014	2010–2014	2010–2014
Robert Bosch (Germany)	19.6	29.1	67.3	65.7	4.4	7.9
Johnson Controls (US)	7.1	17.2	41.7	42.8	5.2	15.2
DENSO Corp. (Japan)	11.0	18.2	37.7	41.0	5.9	8.1
Magna International (Canada)	n.a.	10.5	24.1	36.6	8.2	18.2
Aisin Seiki (Japan)	7.3	8.9	26.4	27.9	3.8	7.6
Eaton Corp. plc (Ireland)	4.4	8.3	13.7	22.3	5.5	12.1
TRW Automotive Holdings (US)	n.a.	n.a.	16.2	—	10.2	37.0
Delphi Automotive (UK)	n.a.	29.1	13.8	17.0	8.9	21.6
Lear Corp (US)	3.1	14.1	14.2	17.7	7.3	21.8
Valeo (France)	3.8	8.9	14.1	16.2	5.7	22.5

Notes:
ROA: Return on assets = net income/total assets.
ROE: Return on equity = net income/shareholders' equity.
n.a. = not available.
Sources: Company financial statements.

Excess Capacity

The greatest structural problem of the industry was excess capacity. Ever since the early 1980s, the growth of production capacity had outstripped the growth in the demand for cars. Import restrictions had exacerbated the problem. During the 1980s and early 1990s, North American and European production capacity grew substantially as Japanese automakers built greenfield "transplants." Internationalization by Korean automakers resulted in further big additions to world production capacity.

The eagerness of Western and Japanese automakers to exploit growing demand in emerging markets was a further source of new capacity. As a result, excess

TABLE 6 Hourly compensation for motor vehicle workers ($/hour, including benefits)

	1975	1984	1994	2004	2006	2012
Germany	7.9	11.9	34.7	44.0	45.9	59.0
US	9.6	19.0	27.0	33.9	35.1	37.4
UK	4.1	7.4	16.0	29.4	30.0	35.0
France	5.1	8.2	18.8	26.3	29.4	42.4
Japan	3.6	7.9	25.9	27.4	27.8	41.7
Spain	3.7	5.3	15.4	21.5	24.2	32.2
S. Korea	0.5	1.7	7.8	15.8	19.0	25.7
Italy	5.2	8.0	16.3	21.7	18.6	36.9
Mexico	2.9	2.6	3.0	3.5	3.7	7.8

Note: Compensation includes direct pay, social insurance, and labor-related taxes.
Source: US Bureau of Labor Statistics.

TABLE 7 Capacity utilization in automobile production (%)

	2007	2009	2011	2014
North America	79	44	69	91
South America	82	62	75	71
Europe	82	61	72	70
Japan and Korea	86	72	81	84
China and SE Asia	89	83	76	65
Global	84	67	75	74

Source: Author's estimates based upon data from OECD, US Federal Reserve System, HIS Automotive, and press articles.

capacity was not only a problem in the mature markets—it was also a huge problem in China, where the large number of domestic car makers and the influx of foreign auto companies resulted in capacity growing faster than demand. By 2014, Ford had five plants in China, Volkswagen had eight, and 45% of the country's automobile capacity was unused. Table 7 shows the percentage of the automobile industry's capacity being utilized.

Outlook for the Future

The greatest source of long-term uncertainty for the industry was the direction of technology. The imminent death of the internal combustion engine had been predicted since the early 1980s, yet in 2014 only about 0.5% of the automobiles sold in the world were plug-in electric vehicles.

If oil prices remained low, the chances of a large-scale, consumer-driven shift to all-electric cars seemed remote. The ascendancy of electric cars would likely be the result of government action. Until 2015, government action to promote electric vehicles had occurred mainly through subsidies (including tax incentives and regulatory exemptions).[5] In the future, growing restrictions on petroleum-fueled vehicles would be driven by environmental concerns. This was particularly likely in China where air pollution in some cities had reached crisis levels.

The implications for Ford and the other automobile companies of a shift to electric vehicles remained unclear. All-electric cars offered opportunities to serve a new wave of demand, but would also allow newcomers to establish themselves in the market. Despite the huge investments by the leading automakers in electric cars, it was Californian-based Tesla Motors and the Chinese company BYD that were seen as market leaders. A further concern was that the critical technology and biggest cost item in all-electric cars—the batteries—would be provided by outsiders.

The implications of developments in digital technologies were likely to have even broader implications for the automobile industry. A report by IBM identified some of the fundamental changes that would reshape the industry between 2015 and 2025:

[T]he dynamics of the consumer-vehicle-enterprise relationship are starting to change drastically as traditional industry boundaries disappear. Automotive (auto) enterprises must adapt to how consumers can access vehicles in new ways and use them in their digital lives — and how cars now fit into an increasingly complex web of transportation options. Interconnectedness is the essence of the creative disruption ahead: between consumers and automakers; between consumers and vehicles; and among traditional and non-traditional participants in the industry ecosystem.[6]

The disruptive forces identified in the study included:

- Consumer expectations: "Digital technologies and lifestyle changes are creating new expectations in how auto consumers buy, own and use vehicles," noted the report. Consumers will expect to actively participate in the creation of new products and service and are likely to seek new ownership models.
- Intelligent vehicles would "be able to learn, heal, drive, and socialize with other vehicles and its surrounding environment … The vehicle will be an integrated component in the Internet of Things. It will collect and use information concerning traffic, mobility, weather, and other events." The development of mobility services would conflict with the traditional car companies' model of selling vehicles.
- The ecosystem: new models of personal mobility would involve many more types of business enterprise. Already Apple and Google had positioned themselves as leaders in the application of digital technologies to driving experiences. The implication was that car companies would need to seek non-traditional partners from outside the automotive sector in seeking to deliver new services to consumers.

At Ford, Mark Fields was reinforcing his predecessor's emphasis on Ford becoming a technological leader in the industry. One initiative was to engender "A Silicon Valley Mindset" which required the company to "challenge industry norms and take nothing for granted." A major initiative related to leadership in urban mobility, where "Ford's goal is to make mobility affordable—economically, environmentally, and socially—and provide seamless mobility for all."[7]

However, if the industry's potential for generating profits was to deteriorate, to what extent was it feasible for Ford to devote the resources needed to keep abreast of the many technologies likely to impinge upon the industry and, even if it did, was there a realistic and viable business model that could justify such investment?

Appendix: Market Share and Company Performance

TABLE A1 Automobile market share in individual countries (%)

	1988	2006	2010	2014
US[a]				
GM	36.3	23.5	19.1	17.8
Ford	21.7	16.7	16.5	14.7
Chrysler	11.3	8.8	9.3	13.2
Toyota	6.9	13.9	15.3	15.1
Honda	6.2	8.8	10.7	9.6
France				
Renault	29.1	24.8	22.1	25.4
PSA	34.2	28.2	32.4	29.9
VW/Audi	9.2	11.6	11.0	13.2
Ford	7.1	6.0	5.1	4.2
Italy				
Fiat	59.9	28.5	30.1	27.6
VW/Audi	11.7	10.8	11.6	14.0
Ford	3.7	7.8	9.1	6.7
PSA	n.a.	9.6	10.3	9.3
Renault	7.1	6.4	5.2	12.5[b]
Germany				
VW/Audi	28.3	27.8	30.1	38.9
GM (Opel)	16.1	9.7	8.9	7.5
BMW	7.1	8.9	9.7	8.8
Daimler	9.2	11.3	10.8	9.7
UK				
Ford	26.3	18.5	15.8	14.5
GM (Vauxhall)	13.7	12.7	12.8	10.7
PSA	8.7	10.0	8.8	7.4
VW/Audi	5.9	12.9	16.0	18.8
BMW	15.0	4.6	6.9	5.9
Japan				
Toyota	43.9	40.4	34.4	39.9
Nissan	23.2	14.0	12.8	12.0
Honda	10.8	12.2	14.2	15.3
Suzuki	n.a.	12.1	11.4	14.1
Korea				
Hyundai	55.9	50.0	37.6	41.2
Kia	25.0	23.3	28.2	28.0
GM/Daewoo	19.1	10.0	22.7	9.3

(continued)

TABLE A1 Automobile market share in individual countries (%) (*Continued*)

	1988	2006	2010	2014
China				
Shanghai GM	n.a.	n.a.	10.4	8.6
Shanghai VW	n.a.	n.a.	9.7	9.8
FAW-Volkswagen	n.a.	n.a.	8.9	9.4
Beijing Hyundai	n.a.	n.a.	6.1	5.8
Dongfeng Nissan	n.a.	n.a.	4.8	5.3
Changan Ford	n.a.	n.a.	1.8	4.5
Chery	n.a.	n.a.	5.1	3.6

Notes:

[a]US data relate to automobiles and light trucks.

[b]Includes Nissan.

n.a. = not available.

Sources: Japan Automobile Manufacturers Association; Korean Automobile Manufacturers Association; www.best-selling-cars.com.

TABLE A2 Sales revenues of the leading automobile manufacturers (annual averages, $billion)

	1980–1984[a]	1985–1989[a]	1990–1994[a]	1995–1999[a]	2000–2004[a]	2005–2009[a]	2010–2014
Toyota	18	42	82	107	125	205	229
VW	16	28	48	64	96	143	168
GM	68	110	128	169	186	167	135
Ford	42	77	96	149	166	155	129
Daimler[b]	12	34	59	71	166	153	129
Honda	8	18	35	50	62	94	104
Nissan	16	26	51	57	58	90	102
Hyundai Motor	n.a.	n.a.	n.a.	18	38	70	97
Fiat Chrysler[c]	18	27	42	50	59	72	92.8
BMW	5	10	21	34	45	70	80
Peugeot	13	19	28	35	58	73	74
Mitsubishi	12	14	25	32	27	43	61
Renault	15	31	31	37	44	52	52
Mazda	n.a.	12	21	18	19	27	27

Notes:

[a]Annual average.

[b]Daimler-Chrysler 2000–2006.

[c]Prior to 2010-2014, the data refer to Fiat only.

n.a. = not available.

Source: Companies' financial statements; Hoovers.

TABLE A3 Company profitability (return on equity, %)

	1980–1984[a]	1985–1989[a]	1990–1994[a]	1995–1999[a]	2000–2004[a]	2005–2009[a]	2010–2014
Toyota	12.6	10.6	6.1	6.8	10.1	7.0	9.4
VW	1.6	6.3	(0.4)	11.1	6.8	5.5	17.5
GM	11.4	11.8	3.2	27.5	11.7	n.a.[b]	15.9
Ford[c]	0.4	21.8	5.9	35.4	(7.7)	(10.4)	51.2
Daimler	24.3	18.3	6.9	22.1	7.7	4.8	15.0
Honda	18.1	11.8	5.3	15.1	13.2	8.0	8.1
Nissan	10.3	4.7	3.6	(0.1)	29.3	7.4	9.7
Hyundai Motor	n.a.	n.a.	n.a.	4.4	10.6	12.0	16.6
Fiat Chrysler[d]	10.9	18.7	6.8	7.6	(24.2)	9.9	9.6
BMW	14.8	10.4	9.7	(4.0)	15.4	10.8	15.8
Peugeot	(15.2)	36.7	12.5	3.0	13.4	(1.4)	(21.3)
Mitsubishi	10.0	7.9	4.8	(5.3)	(113.3)	(12.7)	14.7
Renault	(152.4)	51.1	9.1	11.0	14.7	14.4	8.2
Mazda	n.a.	4.8	5.0	6.3	(34.2)	9.6	5.5

Notes:
[a]Annual average.
[b]GM's ROE was not calculable during 2005–2010 because its shareholders' equity was negative. Its losses over this period (excluding 2009 reorganization gains) were $96 billion.
[c]Ford's ROE was volatile between 2005 and 2015 because of a narrow equity base: Ford's debt/equity ratio over this period was 16:1.
[d]Prior to 2010-2014, the data refer to Fiat only.
n.a. = not available
Source: Companies' financial statements; Hoovers.

Notes

1. "Letter from our President and CEO," Ford Motor Company Annual Report for 2014.
2. "U.S. Car Industry: Back on the Road," *Financial Times* (June 17, 2009).
3. "Fiat's Marchionne sees auto-industry consolidation," *MarketWatch* (September 9, 2011), http://www.market-watch.com/story/fiats-marchionne-sees-auto-industry-consolidation-2011-09-09, accessed July 20, 2015.
4. "Tata's Nano: Stuck in low gear," *Economist* (August 20, 2011).
5. For example, in Norway electric vehicles were exempt from annual road tax, public parking fees, and toll payments, and were allowed to use bus lanes. In London electric cars were exempt from congestion charges.
6. IBM Institute for Business Value, *Automotive 2025: Industry without Borders* (January 2015).
7. "Trends and Strategies," Ford Motor Company 10-K report for 2014: 31–6.

Case 12 Eastman Kodak's Quest for a Digital Future

When Eastman Kodak Company declared bankruptcy ("voluntary Chapter 11 business reorganization") on January 19, 2012, CEO Antonio Perez was emphatic that this was not the end of the road for Kodak:

> Kodak is taking a significant step toward enabling our enterprise to complete its transformation....We look forward to working with our stakeholders to emerge a lean, world-class, digital imaging and materials science company.[1]

Yet, despite Perez's brave words, most observers saw little likelihood that Kodak would emerge as a significant player in the imaging sector. The reality was that after billions of dollars of investment in new technologies and new products, Kodak had failed to build a viable digital imaging business.

Kodak's strategy of transitioning from traditional photography into digital imaging had been in place for over two decades. In 1990, Kodak had launched its Photo CD system for storing photographic images; in 1991, it had introduced its first digital camera and, in 1994, its new CEO, George Fisher, had declared: "We are not in the photographic business . . . we are in the picture business."

With senior executives recruited from Motorola, Apple, General Electric, Silicon Graphics, and Hewlett-Packard, Kodak's digital imaging efforts had established some notable successes. In digital cameras, Kodak was US market leader for most of 2004–2010; globally, it ranked third after Canon and Sony. It was a technological leader in megapixel image sensors. It was global leader in retail printing kiosks and digital minilabs.

Financial performance was a different story. In 1991, Eastman Kodak was America's 18th-biggest company by revenues; by 2011, it had fallen to 334th: over the same period its employment had shrunk from 133,200 to 17,100. During 2000–2011 its operating losses totaled $5.2 billion.

As Antonio Perez prepared for his weekly meeting with Kodak's chief restructuring officer, James Mesterharm, he reflected on Kodak's two decades of decline. How could a company that had been a pioneer of digital imaging and had invested so heavily in building digital capabilities and launching new digital imaging products have failed so miserably to generate income from its efforts? And what did the future hold for Kodak?

This case was prepared by Robert M. Grant. ©2015 Robert M. Grant.

Kodak's History, 1901–1993

George Eastman transformed photography from a professional, studio-based activity into an everyday consumer hobby. His key innovations were silver halide roll film and the first fully portable camera. The Eastman Kodak Company established in Rochester, New York in 1901 offered a full range of products and services for the amateur photographer: "You push the button, we do the rest" was its first advertising slogan. By the time George Eastman died in 1932, Eastman Kodak was one of the world's leading multinational corporations with production, distribution, and processing facilities throughout the world and with one of the world's most recognizable brand names.

After the Second World War, Kodak entered a new growth phase with an expanding core business and diversification into chemicals (its subsidiary, Eastman Chemical, exploited its polymer technology) and healthcare (Eastman Pharmaceutical was established in 1986). Kodak also faced major competitive challenges. In cameras, Kodak's leadership was undermined by the rise of the Japanese camera industry; in film, Fuji Photo Film Company embarked on a strategy of aggressive international expansion. In addition, new imaging technologies were emerging: Polaroid pioneered instant photography; Xerox led the new field of electrostatic plain-paper copying; while the advent of the personal computer ushered in new image management and printing technologies.

Early Moves into Electronics

Kodak's top management was well aware of technological developments in imaging during the 1980s. Kodak's R & D resulted in a number of products that embodied new imaging technologies:

- The world's first megapixel electronic image sensor (1986), followed by a number of new products for scanning and electronic image capture.
- Computer-assisted image storage and retrieval systems for storing, retrieving, and editing graphical and microfilm images.
- Data storage products included floppy disks (Verbatim was acquired in 1985) and 14-inch optical disks (1986).
- Plain-paper office copiers (Kodak acquired IBM's copier business in 1988).
- The Photo CD system (1990) allowed digitized photographic images to be stored on a compact disk, which could then be viewed and manipulated on a personal computer.
- Kodak's first digital camera, the 1.3 megapixel DCS-100, priced at $13,000 launched in 1991.

Committing to a Digital Future

Kodak's commitment to a digital imaging strategy was sealed with the appointment of George Fisher as CEO. Fisher had a doctorate in applied mathematics, ten years of R & D experience at Bell Labs, and had led strategic transformation at Motorola. To focus Kodak's efforts on the digital challenge, Fisher's first moves were to divest Eastman Chemical Company and most of Kodak's healthcare businesses (other than medical imaging) and to create a single digital imaging division headed by newly hired Carl Gustin (previously with Apple and Digital Equipment).

Kodak's Digital Strategy

Under three successive CEOs—George Fisher (1993–1999), Dan Carp (2000–2005), and Antonio Perez (2005–2012)—Kodak developed a digital strategy intended to transform Kodak from a traditional photographic company to a leader in the emerging field of digital imaging. The scale and scope of this transformation was clearly recognized by all three CEOs. In 2005, Antonio Perez summarized the "fundamental challenges" that Kodak was engaged in (Figure 1).

During 1993–2011, Kodak's strategy embodied four major themes:

- an incremental approach to managing the transition to digital imaging;
- different strategies for the consumer market and for the professional and commercial markets;
- external sourcing of knowledge through hiring, alliances, and acquisitions;
- an emphasis on printed images;
- harvesting the traditional photography business.

An Incremental Approach

"The future is not some harebrained scheme of the digital information highway or something. It is a step-by-step progression of enhancing photography using digital

FIGURE 1 Eastman Kodak's "Fundamental Challenges"

Source: Based upon Bob Brust, "Completing the Kodak Transformation," Presentation, Eastman Kodak Company, September 2005. © Kodak. Used with permission.

technology," declared Fisher in 1995.[2] This recognition that digital imaging was an evolutionary rather than a revolutionary change would be the key to Kodak's ability to build a strong position in digital technology. If photography was to switch rapidly from the traditional chemical-based technology to a wholly digital technology where customers took digital pictures, downloaded them onto their computers, edited them, and transmitted them through the internet to be viewed electronically, Kodak would face an extremely difficult time. Not only would the new digital value chain make redundant most of Kodak's core competitive advantages (its silver halide technology and its global network of retail outlets and processing facilities): most of this digital value chain was already in the hands of computer hardware and software companies.

Fortunately for Kodak, during the 1990s digital technology made only selective incursions into traditional photographic imaging. As late as 2000, digital cameras had achieved limited market penetration; the vast majority of photographic images were still captured on traditional film.

Hence, central to Kodak's strategy, was a hybrid approach where Kodak introduced those aspects of digital imaging that could offer truly enhanced functionality for users. Thus, in the consumer market, Kodak recognized that image capture would continue to be dominated by traditional film for some time (digital cameras offered inferior resolution compared with conventional photography). However, digital imaging offered immediate potential for image manipulation and transmission.

If consumers continued to use conventional film while seeking the advantages of digitization for editing and emailing their pictures, this offered a valuable opportunity for Kodak's vast retail network. Kodak had installed its first self-service facility for digitizing, editing, and printing images from conventional photographs in 1988. In 1994, Kodak launched its Picture Maker, a self-service kiosk located in retail stores where customers could edit and print digital images from a variety of digital inputs, or from digital scans of conventional photo prints. Picture Maker allowed customers to edit their images (zoom, crop, eliminate red-eye, and add text) and print them in a variety of formats. George Fisher emphasized the central role of retail kiosks in Kodak's digital strategy:

> Four years ago, when we talked about the possibilities of digital photography, people laughed. Today, the high-tech world is stampeding to get a piece of the action, calling digital imaging perhaps the greatest growth opportunity in the computer world. And it may be. We surely see it as the greatest future enabler for people to truly "Take Pictures. Further." We start at retail, our distribution stronghold . . . We believe the widespread photo-retailing infrastructure will continue to be the principal avenue by which people obtain their pictures. Our strategy is to build on and extend this existing market strength which is available to us, and at the same time be prepared to serve the rapidly growing, but relatively small, pure digital market that is developing. Kodak will network its rapidly expanding installed base of Image Magic stations and kiosks, essentially turning these into nodes on a massive, global network. The company will allow retailers to use these workstations to bring digital capability to the average snapshooter, extending the value of these images for the consumers and retailers alike, while creating a lucrative consumable business for Kodak.[3]

Despite growing ownership of inkjet printers, a very large proportion of consumers continued to use photo-print facilities in retail stores. By the beginning of 2004, Kodak was the clear leader in self-service digital printing kiosks, with 24,000 installed Kodak Picture Makers in the US and over 55,000 worldwide.

Kodak also used digital technology to enhance the services offered by photofinishers. Thus, the Kodak I.Lab system offered a digital infrastructure to photofinishers that digitized every film negative and offered better pictures by fixing common problems in consumer photographs.

Despite the inferior resolution of digital cameras, Fisher recognized their potential and pushed Kodak to establish itself in this highly competitive market. In addition to high-priced digital single reflex lens cameras for professional use, Kodak developed the QuickTake camera for Apple: at $75 it was the cheapest digital camera available in 1994. In March 1995, Kodak introduced the first full-featured digital camera priced at under $1,000.

The Consumer Market: Emphasizing Simplicity and Ease of Use

Kodak pursued different approaches to consumer and professional/commercial markets. While the commercial and professional market offered the test-bed for Kodak's advanced digital technologies, the emphasis in the consumer segment was to maintain Kodak's position as mass-market leader by providing simplicity, quality, and value. Kodak's incremental strategy was most evident in the consumer market, providing an easy pathway for customers to transition to digital photography while exploiting Kodak's core brand and distribution strengths. This transition path was guided by Kodak's original vision of "You push the button, we do the rest." Kodak envisages itself as the mass-market leader in digital imaging, providing security, reliability, and simplicity for customers bewildered by the pace of technological change. Thus, Kodak would offer an array of services that would allow consumers to digitize conventional photographs, edit digitized images, and obtain printed photographs in a variety of formats.

Simplicity and mass-market leadership also implied that Kodak provided the fully integrated set of products and services needed for digital photography. "For Kodak, digital photography is all about ease of use and helping people get prints—in other words, getting the same experience they're used to from their film cameras," noted Martin Coyne, head of Kodak's Photographic Group.[4] A systems approach rather than a product approach recognized that most consumers had neither the time nor the patience to read instructions and to integrate different devices and software. Kodak believed that its integrated system approach would have particular appeal to women, who made up the major part of the consumer market.

The result was Kodak's EasyShare system, launched in 2001. According to Willy Shih, head of digital and applied imaging, EasyShare's intention was to:

> provide consumers with the first easy-to-use digital photography experience . . . Digital photography is more than just about digital cameras. This is just the first step . . . People need to get their pictures to their PCs and then want to share by printing or e-mail. So we developed a system that made the full experience as easy as possible.[5]

The result would be a comprehensive digital system within which consumers could take digital pictures on digital cameras or phone-cameras (or have conventional photographs digitized), view their images on a variety of devices, and print their digital images at home, at retail kiosks, or through Kodak's online processing service. Figure 2 shows Kodak's conceptualization of its EasyShare system.

By 2005, most of the main elements of the EasyShare system were in place:

- Kodak's range of EasyShare digital cameras had carved out a strong position in a crowded market (by 2005 some 40 companies were offering digital cameras).

- EasyShare software allowed the downloading, organization, editing, and emailing of images and the ordering of online prints. EasyShare software was bundled with Kodak's cameras as well as being available for downloading for free from Kodak's website.

- The EasyShare printer dock introduced in 2003 was the first printer which incorporated a camera dock allowing the "one touch simple" thermal-dye printing direct from a camera. Antonio Perez's arrival in 2003 reinforced Kodak's push into printers: "If a company wants to be a leader in digital imaging, it necessarily has to participate in digital output."[6]

- Online digital imaging services: Kodak had been quick to recognize the potential of the internet for allowing consumers to transmit and store their photographs and order prints. Kodak's Picture Network was launched in 1997. Consumers could have their conventional photographs digitized by a retail photo store, then uploaded to a personal internet account on Kodak's Picture Network. The following year Kodak launched its online printing service, *PhotoNet*, enabling consumers to upload their digital photo files and

FIGURE 2   Kodak's EasyShare Network: "Your Pictures—Anytime, Anywhere"

Source: Based upon Bob Brust, "Completing the Kodak Transformation," Presentation, Eastman Kodak Company, September 2005. © Kodak. Used with permission.

order prints of them. Kodak also partnered with AOL to offer *You've Got Pictures*. By acquiring Ofoto in 2001, Kodak became the leader in online photofinishing and online image storage. In January 2005, Kodak renamed Ofoto "Kodak EasyShare Gallery."

By 2005, therefore, Kodak was present across the entire digital value chain—this integrated presence was underpinned by technological strengths at each of these stages (Figure 3).

Professional, Commercial, and Healthcare Markets

The commercial and professional markets were important to Kodak for two reasons. First, they were lead customers for many of Kodak's cutting-edge digital technologies: news photographers were early adopters of digital cameras; the US Department of Defense pioneered digital imaging for satellite imaging, weather forecasting, and surveillance activities; NASA used Kodak cameras and imaging equipment for its space missions, including the Mars probe and the IKONOS Earth-orbiting satellite. For many commercial applications ranging from real estate brokerage to security systems, digital imaging offered huge advantages because of its ability to transmit images (especially through the internet) and link with sophisticated IT management systems for image storage and retrieval. The huge price premium of commercial consumer products (up to 100 times that of a basic consumer version) made it attractive to focus R & D on these leading-edge users in the anticipation of trickle-down to the consumer market.

In commercial printing and publishing (which became the Graphic Communications Group in 2005), Kodak assembled a strong position in commercial scanning, formatting, and printing systems for the publishing, packaging, and

FIGURE 3 Kodak's technological position within the digital imaging chain data processing industries. Kodak's opportunity was to exploit the transition from traditional offset printing to digital, full-color, variable printing. This opportunity built on two key strengths: first, Kodak's proprietary inkjet technology (including its technically superior inks) and, second, its leadership in variable-data printing— printing that permitted individually customized output (as in personalized sales catalogues or bills). Kodak built its commercial printing business on both internally developed technologies and acquisitions—notably Heidelberg's Nexpress and Digimaster businesses, and Scitex, supplier of Versamark high-speed inkjet printers. Kodak also built a presence in pre-press and workflow systems used by commercial printers.

In medical imaging, Kodak also faced the decline of its sales of X-ray film and in related chemicals and accessories. Through a series of acquisitions and internal developments, Kodak established a portfolio of products for digital X-rays, laser imaging, picture archiving and communications systems—including systems for digitizing and storing conventional X-rays. Kodak also built up a strong position in dental imaging systems comprising hardware, software, and consumables. Kodak sold its Health Group to Onex Healthcare Holdings in 2007 for $2.55 billion.

Kodak's capability in creating integrated imaging and information solutions was of particular value in certain public sector projects. Kodak's digital scanning and document management systems were used in national censuses in the US, the UK, France, Australia, and Brazil. At the German post office, a Kodak team achieved a world record, creating digitized copies of 1.7 million documents in 24 hours.

Hiring, Alliances, and Acquisitions

Kodak's business system had been based upon vertical integration and self-sufficiency: at its Rochester base, Kodak developed its own technology, produced its own products, and supplied them worldwide through its vast global network. In digital imaging, not only did Kodak lack much of the expertise needed to build a digital imaging business but also the pace of technological change was too rapid to rely on in-house development. Hence, as Kodak transformed its capability base from chemical to digital imaging, it looked outside for the knowledge it required.

Kodak had traditionally been a lifetime-employment company that grew its own senior executives. The arrival of George Fisher from Motorola changed all that. Under Fisher's leadership Kodak launched a major hiring campaign to put in place the executives and technical specialists it needed for its new digital strategy. Key executives who relocated from Silicon Valley to Rochester included Kodak's first head of its digital imaging division, Willy Shih, whose prior experience included Silicon Graphics and IBM. Kodak also brought in senior hires from Xerox, Hewlett-Packard, Lexmark, Apple, GE Medical Electronics, Olympus Optical, and Lockheed Martin. Table 1 shows the backgrounds of Kodak's top management team.

Kodak acknowledged that the digital imaging chain already included companies that were well established, sometimes dominant, in particular activities. For example, Adobe Systems dominated image-formatting software; Hewlett-Packard, Epson, and Canon were leaders in inkjet printers for home use; and Microsoft dominated PC operating systems. Willy Shih, head of Kodak's digital imaging products from 1997 to 2003, observed: "We have to pick where we add value and commoditize where we can't."[7] The challenge was to identify activities and products where Kodak could add value.

TABLE 1 Eastman Kodak's senior management team, April 2012

Name	Position	Joined Kodak	Prior company experience
Robert L. Berman	Senior Vice President	1982	Kodak veteran
Philip J. Faraci	President and COO	2004	Phogenix Imaging, Gemplus
Stephen Green	Director, Business Development, Asia-Pacific	2005	Creo Inc.
Pradeep Jotwani	President, Consumer Business	2010	Hewlett-Packard
Brad W. Kruchten	President Film and Photofinishing Systems Group	1982	Kodak veteran
Antoinette McCorvey	CFO and Senior Vice President	1999	Monsanto/Solutia
Gustavo Oviedo	Chief Customer Officer	2006	Schneider Electric
Antonio M. Perez	Chairman and CEO	2003	Hewlett-Packard
Laura G. Quatela	General Counsel and Chief Intellectual Property Officer	1999	Clover Capital Management, Inc., SASIB Railway GRS, and Bausch & Lomb Inc.
Isidre Rosello	General Manager, Digital Printing Solutions	2005	Hewlett-Packard
Eric H. Samuels	Chief Accounting Officer and Corporate Controller	2004	KPMG, Ernst & Young
Patrick M. Sheller	Chief Administrative Officer, General Counsel and Secretary	1993	McKenna, Long & Aldridge, Federal Trade Commission
Terry R. Taber	Vice President	1980	Kodak veteran

Note:
Includes corporate officers, senior vice presidents, and division heads.
Source: www.kodak.com. © Kodak. Used with permission.

In many cases this meant partnering with companies that were already leaders in digital technologies and hardware and software products. Kodak forged a web of joint ventures and strategic alliances with Canon (for developing and manufacturing digital, SLR cameras), AOL (You've Got Pictures service for uploading, storing, and sharing digital photographs), Intel (development of digital image storage media and ASP system for archiving and downloading medical images), Hewlett-Packard (technology exchange; Phogenix Imaging joint venture to develop inkjet solutions for Kodak photo-finishing labs), Olympus (sharing digital camera technology), Sanyo Electric Co. (joint development of OLED displays), and IBM (manufacturing alliance to produce CMOS imaging sensors).

Kodak made acquisitions where it believed that a strong proprietary position was essential to its strategy and in technologies where it needed to complement its own expertise. Although Kodak's profits were under pressure for most of the period, its size and balance-sheet strength meant that it was still one of the financially strongest firms in the industry. The bursting of the stock-market bubble in technology stocks in 2000 allowed Kodak to make a number of key acquisitions for modest outlays. Its major acquisitions over the period are shown in Table 2.

Emphasis on Printed Images

A consistent feature of Kodak's digital strategy from 1993 to 2012 was the belief that digital technology would not eliminate printed images. Kodak's emphasis on printed images was reinforced by its own capabilities: the printing of photographic

TABLE 2 Kodak's major acquisitions, 1994–2011

Date	Company	Description
1994	Qualex, Inc.	Provider of photo-finishing services; acquired to complement Kodak's online photofinishing service
1997	Wang Laboratories	Acquisition of Wang's software unit
1997	Chinon Industries	Japanese camera producer; majority stake acquired; outstanding shares purchased in 2004
1998	PictureVision, Inc.	Provider of PhotoNet online digital imaging services and retail solutions; complement to Kodak's Picture Network business
1998	Shantou Era Photo Material, Xiamen Fuda Photographic Materials	Strengthened Kodak's position in photographic film in China
1999	Imation	Supplier of medical imaging products and services
2000	Lumisys, Inc.	Provider of desktop computed radiography systems and X-ray film digitizers
2001	Bell & Howell	Imaging businesses only acquired
2001	Ofoto, Inc.	Leading US online photofinisher
2001	Encad, Inc.	Wide-format commercial inkjet printers
2003	PracticeWorks	Digital dental imaging and dental practice management software
2003	Algotec Systems Ltd.	Developer of picture archiving systems
2003	Lucky Film Co., Ltd.	Acquisition of 20% of China's leading photographic film supplier
2003	LaserPacific Media Corporation	Provider of post-production services for filmmakers
2004	NexPress	Acquired Heidelberg's 50% of this joint venture, which supplied high-end, on-demand color printing systems and black-and-white variable-data printing systems
2004	Scitex Digital Printing	A leader in high-speed variable data inkjet printing (renamed Kodak Versamark, Inc.)
2004	National Semiconductor	Acquisition of National's imaging sensor business
2005	Kodak Polychrome Graphics LLC	Kodak acquires Sun Chemical's 50% stake in the joint venture, which is a leader in graphic communication
2005	Creo Inc.	Leading supplier of pre-press and workflow systems used by commercial printers
2008	Design2Launch	Developer of collaborative end-to-end digital workflow solutions for transactional printing
2008	Intermate A/S	Danish supplier of Intelligent Print Data Stream software for managing high speed printers
2009	Böwe Bell & Howell	Acquisition of document scanner division
2011	Tokyo Ohka Kogyo Co., Ltd.	Acquisition of TOK's relief printing plates business

Source: Eastman Kodak 10-K reports, various years.

and other images onto paper and other media lay at the heart of Kodak's traditional chemical and chromatic know-how. Throughout the Fisher/Carp/Perez era, Kodak continued to invest heavily in its printing know-how and in printers: both commercial and consumer. Under Perez, the impetus behind photographic printers for the consumer market intensified, reflecting Perez's own background as former head of Hewlett-Packard's printer division.

Perez's decision to make a major investment to build Kodak's presence in the market for consumer inkjet printers has been the most widely criticized of all Kodak's digital imaging initiatives. Even with Kodak's "treasure trove" of inkjet technologies and its tweaking of the traditional "razors-and-blades" model by charging low prices for ink and higher prices for printers, establishing Kodak in such a mature, intensely competitive market would be a struggle. By 2011, Kodak held only 6% of the US market, compared to 60% for Hewlett-Packard.

Harvesting the Traditional Photography Business

On the basis that the transition to digital photography would be gradual, Kodak believed that the transition period would give it the opportunity to generate cash flows from its legacy film business while investing in digital imaging technologies and products. Kodak's prediction of a gradual transition from film to digital imaging was largely correct. Through the 1990s, film sales continued to grow in the US, reaching a peak of 800 million rolls in 1999. However, the decline that began in 2000 accelerated during the first decade of the 21st century. By 2004, sales had halved to under 400 million. By 2011, sales had fallen to below 100,000.

Kodak's forecasts proved wrong in relation to emerging market demand. Kodak's acquisitions of Chinese photographic film producers were based on the assumption that sales of roll film would continue to increase into the 21st century. In reality, the transition to digital imaging occurred at much the same pace in emerging markets as in the mature industrialized countries.

Under Perez, Kodak accelerated its withdrawal from film. During 2011 and 2012, it withdrew several film products, including film for slides. It also withdrew from other unprofitable markets (including cameras) and divested other businesses, including its Kodak EasyShare Gallery to rival Shutterfly. Retrenchment was accompanied by accelerated job cutting.

Eastman Kodak in 2012

Eastman Kodak's business was organized around three business segments. Exhibit 1 describes each of these segments.

Competition

In most of the markets where it competed, Kodak was subject to intense competition: as with most forms of digital hardware, the dominant forces were many players, low entry barriers, falling real prices, and commoditization. In the case of digital cameras, phones incorporating cameras had decimated all but the quality segment of the market. Online photographic services were also ferociously competitive: Kodak's Gallery was the market leader, but it competed with a host of other online competitors, including: Shutterfly, Snapfish, Walmart.com's Photo Center, Fujifilmnet.com, Yahoo Photos, and Sears.com.

Kodak's highest margins were earned on consumables, notably photographic paper. However, Kodak faced strong competition, mainly from Xerox, Hewlett-Packard, 3M, and Oji, as well as from many minor brands. In supplying photo-finishers and commercial printers, Kodak was able to benefit from its leadership in retail kiosks and labs. To fight commoditization in printing paper, Kodak pioneered a number of technical advances, particularly in inkjet printing paper,

EXHIBIT 1
Eastman Kodak's business segments

CONSUMER DIGITAL IMAGING GROUP ("CDG") SEGMENT

CDG's mission is to enhance people's lives and social interactions through the capabilities of digital imaging and printing technology. CDG's strategy is to drive profitable revenue growth by leveraging a powerful brand, a deep knowledge of the consumer, and extensive digital imaging and materials science intellectual property.

- **Digital Capture and Devices** includes digital still and pocket video cameras, digital picture frames, accessories, and branded licensed products. These products are sold directly to retailers or distributors, and are also available to customers through the Internet ... As announced on February 9, 2012, the Company plans to phase out its dedicated capture devices business...

- **Retail Systems Solutions'** product and service offerings to retailers include kiosks and consumables, Adaptive Picture Exchange ("APEX") drylab systems and consumables, and after sale service and support ... Kodak has the largest installed base of retail photo kiosks in the world.

- **Consumer Inkjet Systems** encompasses Kodak All-in-One desktop inkjet printers, ink cartridges, and media ...

- **Consumer Imaging Services**: Kodak Gallery is a leading online merchandise and photo sharing service ...

GRAPHIC COMMUNICATIONS GROUP ("GCG") SEGMENT

GCG's strategy is to transform large graphics markets with revolutionary technologies and customized services that grow our customers' businesses and Kodak's business with them.

- **Prepress Solutions** is comprised of digital and traditional consumables, including plates, chemistry, and media, prepress output device equipment and

including its Colorlast technology, designed to preserve the fidelity and vibrancy of photographic prints. However, across all markets, Kodak was suffering from the growing trend for consumers to view their photographs on screens rather than in printed form.

In commercial markets, competitive price pressures were less severe than in the consumer sector, in particular the opportunity for Kodak to differentiate its offering through packaging hardware, software, and services into customized "user solutions."

Kodak's Resources and Capabilities

Digital imaging was a classic "disruptive technology."[8] For traditional photographic companies it was "competence destroying"[9]—the new technological regime meant that many of their resources and capabilities became close to useless. For the camera companies—Nikon, Canon, Olympus, and Pentax, for example—digital imaging related services, and proofing solutions. Prepress solutions also include flexographic packaging solutions, which is one of Kodak's four digital growth initiative businesses.

◆ **Digital Printing Solutions** includes high-speed, high-volume commercial inkjet printing equipment, consumables, and related services, as well as color and black-and-white electrophotographic printing equipment . . .

◆ **The Business Services and Solutions** group's product and service offerings are composed of high-speed production and workgroup document scanners, related services, and digital controllers for driving digital output devices, and workflow software and solutions. Workflow software and solutions, which includes consulting and professional business process services, can enable new opportunities for our customers to transform from a print service provider to a marketing service provider . . .

FILM, PHOTOFINISHING AND ENTERTAINMENT GROUP ("FPEG") SEGMENT

FPEG provides consumers, professionals, and the entertainment industry with film and paper for imaging and photography. Although the markets . . . are in decline . . . due to digital substitution, FPEG maintains leading market positions for these products. The strategy of FPEG is to provide sustainable cash generation by extending our materials science assets in traditional and new markets.

◆ **Entertaining Imaging** includes origination, intermediate, and color print motion picture films, special effects services, and other digital products and services for the entertainment industry.

◆ **Traditional Photofinishing** includes color negative photographic paper, photochemicals, professional output systems, and event imaging services.

◆ **Industrial Materials** encompasses aerial and industrial film products, film for the production of printed circuit boards, and specialty chemicals, and represents a key component of FPEG's strategy of extending and repurposing our materials science assets.

◆ **Film Capture** includes consumer and professional photographic film and one-time-use cameras.

Source: Eastman Kodak 10-K report, 2011: pp. 5–8. Reproduced by permission of Eastman Kodak Company.

was not such a threat: digital backs could be added to standard camera architectures; optical capabilities remained important. For the film companies—Kodak, Fujifilm, and Agfa—digital imaging rendered chemical capabilities obsolete. This is why the transition period between traditional and digital imaging was so important for Kodak. During the transition period, Kodak could exploit its brand loyalty and vast distribution system to offer hybrid solutions, while building the resources and capabilities required for digital imaging. The problem for Kodak was that it was now competing with companies that had well-developed microelectronics and software engineering capabilities: Canon, Hewlett-Packard, Sony, Adobe Systems, to mention just a few.

By the time it had entered bankruptcy in January 2012, Kodak was clearly in a weakened state; nevertheless, it had maintained, and accumulated, potentially valuable resources and capabilities.

● *Brand*: Kodak's traditional resource strengths had been its brand and its global distribution presence. Two decades of decline and wrenching technological changes had weakened both. Yet, as late as 2011, MPP Consulting had ranked Kodak the 77th most valuable US brand. Yet, for all Kodak's brand recognition, the key issue was the extent to which it added value and market appeal to Kodak's consumer and commercial products.

● *Distribution*: Kodak's distribution presence was still unrivalled in the industry. However, as demand for printed photographs declined, so this too was a depreciating asset.

● *Technology*: For two decades Kodak had maintained one of the world's biggest research efforts in imaging. During 2000–2005, its research labs in the US, the UK, France, Japan, China, and Australia had employed more than 5000 engineers and scientists, including more than 600 PhDs. Between 1975 and 2011, Kodak had been issued 16,760 patents. During 2011–2012, it sought to sell its patents in order to raise capital. Table 3 identifies some of Kodak's principal areas of technological strength.

TABLE 3   Kodak's technical capabilities

Area of technology	Kodak capabilities
Color science	Kodak is a leader in the production, control, measurement, specification, and visual perception of color, essential to predicting the performance of image-capture devices and imaging systems. Kodak has pioneered *colorimetry*—measuring and quantifying visual response to a stimulus of light.
Image processing	Includes technologies to control image sharpness, noise, and color reproduction. It is used to maximize the information content of images and to compress data for economical storage and rapid transmission. Kodak is a leader in image processing algorithms for automatic color balancing, object and text recognition, and image enhancement and manipulation. These are especially important in digital photo-finishing for image enhancement, including adjustments for scene reflectance, lighting conditions, sharpness, and a host of other conditions.
Imaging systems analysis	Provides techniques to measure the characteristics of imaging systems and components. Predictive system modeling is especially important in Kodak's new product development, where it can predict the impact of individual components on the performance of the entire system.
Sensors	A world leader in image sensor technology, with 30 years' experience in the design and manufacture of both CCD and CMOS electronic image sensors used in cameras, machine vision products, and satellite and medical imaging.
Ink technology	A world leader in dyes and pigments for color printing. Pioneer of micro-milling technology (originally invented for drug delivery systems). It has advanced knowledge of humectants (which keep print-head nozzles from clogging), and surface tension and viscosity modifiers (which control ink flows).

(continued)

TABLE 3 Kodak's technical capabilities (*Continued*)

Area of technology	Kodak capabilities
Inkjet technology	Innovations in the electronic and thermal control of inkjet heads coupled with innovation in inks have given Kodak technological advantages in inkjet printing. In commercial printing, Kodak's continuous inkjet technology has permitted the flexibility of inkjet printing to be matched with substantial improvements in resolution and color fidelity.
Microfluidics	Microfluidics, the study of miniature devices that handle very small quantities of liquids, is relevant to film coating, fluid mixing, chemical sensing, and liquid inkjet printing.
Print media	A leader in applying polymer science and chemical engineering to ink-receiving materials. Expertise in specially constructed inkjet media in which layers of organic/inorganic polymers are coated onto paper or clear film and multi-layer coated structures of hydrogels and inorganic oxides.
Electronic display technology	Through its joint venture with Sanyo, Kodak pioneered organic light-emitting diode (OLED) technology for self-luminous flat panel displays. Kodak's OLED display panels extended from small-screen devices to larger displays.
Software	EasyShare software focused on ease of image manipulation, printing, and storage (even without a computer). Commercial software leads in workflow solutions (Kodak EMS Business Software), scanning software (Perfect Page), and printing software (Kodak Professional Digital Print Production Software); strengths in control software and printing algorithms that overcome technical limitations of inkjet printing and optimize color and tone reproduction (e.g. the Kodak One Touch Printing System).

Source: www.kodak.com.

- *New Product Development*: Despite Kodak's strengths in basic and applied research and its long history of successful new product launches, the company had struggled to move away from its traditional long and meticulous product development process to embrace the fast-cycle world of electronics.

- *Financial Resources*: Chapter 11 had given Kodak freedom from its creditors and allowed it to cut retiree health benefits. However, it offered little escape from its pension obligations. While its US pension scheme was judged fully funded, its UK pension fund required an additional $800 million top-up. By the end of the first quarter of 2012, Kodak's financial position was showing some improvements: with selling, general and administrative expenses down by $84 million and investment in unprofitable businesses cut, Kodak's cash balance was $1.4 billion, up $500 million from the end of 2011. However, under Chapter 11 protection, Kodak would not be able to seek new sources of financing and would be tightly constrained as to any strategic initiatives that required significant capital expenditure.

Table 4 shows financial data for Eastman Kodak, while Table 5 shows data for its business segments.

TABLE 4 Eastman Kodak: Selected financial data, 2006–2011 ($million)

	2011	2010	2009	2008	2007	2006
From income statement						
Sales	6,022	7,167	7,609	9,416	10,301	10,568
Cost of goods sold	5,135	5,221	5,850	7,247	7,757	8,159
Selling, general, and admin.	1,159	1,275	1,298	1,606	1,802	1,950
R & D costs	274	318	351	478	525	578
Operating earnings	(600)	(336)	(28)	(821)	(230)	(476)
Interest expense	156	149	119	108	113	172
Other income (charges)	(2)	26	30	55	86	65
Restructuring costs	121	70	226	140	543	416
Income taxes	9	114	115	(147)	(51)	221
Net earnings	(764)	(687)	(210)	(442)	676	(601)
From balance sheet						
Total current assets	2,703	3,786	4,303	5,004	6,053	5,557
Including:						
Cash	861	1,624	2,024	2,154	2,947	1,496
Receivables	1,103	1,196	1,395	1,716	1,939	2,072
Inventories	607	746	679	948	943	1,001
Property, plant, and equipment	895	1,037	1,254	1,551	1,811	2,602
Other long-term assets	803	1,109	1,227	1,728	4,138	3,509
Total assets	4,678	6,226	7,691	9,179	13,659	14,320
Total current liabilities	2,150	2,820	2896	3,438	4,446	4,554
Including:						
Payables	706	959	2,811	3,267	3,794	3,712
Short-term borrowings	152	50	62	51	308	64
Other liabilities:						
Long-term borrowings	1,363	1,195	1,129	1,252	1,289	2,714
Post-employment liabilities	3,053	2,661	2,694	2,382	3,444	3,934
Other long-term liabilities	462	625	1,005	1,119	1,451	1,690
Total liabilities	7,028	7,301	7,724	8,191	10,630	12,932
Shareholders' equity	(2350)	(1075)	(33)	988	,3029	1,388
From cash flow statement						
Net cash from operating activities	(998)	(219)	(136)	168	328	956
Net cash used in investing activities	(25)	(112)	(22)	(188)	2408	(225)
Net cash flows from financing activities	246	(74)	33	(746)	(1294)	(947)
Number of employees	17,100	18,800	20,250	24,400	26,900	40,900

Source: Eastman Kodak annual reports.

Reflections

As Perez reflected upon Kodak's two decades of digital transformation, he was struck by the paradox of Kodak's progress. In terms of adapting to a highly disruptive technological revolution, Kodak had been surprisingly successful. For a company that had dominated its traditional market for so long and so thoroughly as Kodak had, to survive the annihilation of its core technology, and to build the capabilities needed to become a significant player in a radically different area of technology was unusual. Yet, in terms of financial performance, Kodak had failed: for all of Kodak's

TABLE 5   Eastman Kodak: Results by business segments, 2007–2011 ($million)

	2011	2010	2009	2008	2007
Net sales from continuing operations					
Consumer Digital Imaging Group	1,739	2,731	2,626	3,088	3,247
Film, Photofinishing, and Entertainment Group	1,547	1,762	2,262	2,987	3,632
Graphic Communications Group	2,736	2,674	2,718	3,334	3,413
All other	—	—	3	7	9
Consolidated total	6,022	7,167	7,609	9,416	10,301
Earnings (losses) from continuing operations					
before interest and taxes					
Consumer Digital Imaging Group	(349)	278	(10)	(177)	(17)
Graphic Communications Group	(191)	(95)	(107)	31	104
Film, Photofinishing, and Entertainment Group	34	91	187	196	281
All other	—	(1)	(16)	(17)	(25)
Total of segments	(506)	273	54	33	343
Segment total assets:					
Consumer Digital Imaging Group	929	1,126	1,198	1,647	2,442
Graphic Communications Group	1,459	1,566	1,734	2,190	3,723
Film, Photofinishing, and Entertainment Group	913	1,090	1,991	2,563	3,778
All other	—	1	—	8	17
Total of segments	3,301	3,782	4,923	6,408	9,960

Source: Eastman Kodak 10-K reports.

technical and market achievements, Perez and his two predecessors, Dan Carp and George Fisher, had been unable to build a financially viable digital imaging business. Where had they gone wrong?

- It was difficult to argue that Kodak had been too slow or that it had failed to recognize the digital threat—as early as 1979 Kodak produced a remarkably accurate forecast of the evolution of digital imaging and it had been a pioneer of digital cameras.[10]
- It was also difficult to argue that Kodak had failed in implementing its digital strategy in terms of being a laggard in developing the capabilities needed to compete in digital imaging. Kodak's market leadership in digital cameras pointed to its ability to build technological know-how, apply that know-how to develop attractive new products, and market those products in fiercely competitive digital markets.
- Perhaps Kodak's emphasis had been on the wrong markets and wrong products? Kodak's biggest losses had been in the consumer market, Kodak's traditional stronghold. Was this market simply too unattractive because of intense competition? Had Perez's emphasis on printing been misplaced? Might Kodak's scarce resources been better spent on other parts of the digital value chain (such as image capture through cameras and sensors and displays)?
- A further possibility was that Kodak's vision of establishing itself as a leader in digital imaging was misconceived. In 2000, Kodak had announced its intention to be at the center of the $225 billion "infoimaging" industry. But did this "infoimaging" industry really exist? While some products were specific to digital imaging—editing software such as Adobe's Photoshop, sensors

EXHIBIT 2

Fujifilm Holdings Corporation

	1992			2011		
	Sales ($million)	Net income ($million)	Employees	Sales ($million)	Net income ($million)	Employees
Fujifilm Holdings[a]	9,126	593	24,868	27,440	1,412	35,274
Eastman Kodak[b]	20,577	1,146	132,600	6,022	(764)	17,100

Notes:
[a]2011 data are for financial year to March 31, 2012.
[b]2011 data are for year ended December 31, 2011.

Despite the strong similarities between Fujifilm and Kodak—both companies were heavily dependent on film during the early 1990s and both had diversified into other imaging technologies (Fujifilm had a major position in plain-paper copiers through its Fuji/Xerox joint venture)—the two companies responded to the digital revolution with different strategies which led to very different financial results.

Like Kodak, Fujifilm recognized the implications of digital imaging for its core business and struggled to adapt its strategy. However, a key difference was Fuji's recognition that digital imaging alone would be unlikely to support the business of a large company, hence its emphasis on diversification. Under its chief executive, Shigetaka Komori, Fujifilm underwent a major restructuring between 2000 and 2010 (especially during 2005/6 and 2009/10) involving business closures, employee layoffs, and financial write-downs.

Comparing Fujifilm and Kodak in 2012, the most obvious difference is Fujifilm's business diversity. Its three business segments comprise a variety of different businesses:

Imaging solutions (14.8% of total sales) included traditional photo imaging products (photographic paper, film, and supplies) and electronic imaging (mainly digital cameras).

Information solutions (40.5% of total sales) included medical systems, pharmaceuticals, cosmetics, flat panel display materials, graphic arts materials, data storage tapes, industrial X-rays, and optical devices.

Document solutions (44.8% of total sales) comprised office supplies, office printers, and document product services.

Fujifilm's diversification has combined selective acquisitions (since 2000, $9 billion has been spent on 40 acquisitions) and internal development based upon Fujifilm's existing technical capabilities. In particular, it has built upon its chemical and coatings expertise to diversify into cosmetics, pharmaceuticals (especially drug delivery systems), components for LCD panels, and a variety of plastics products. The quest to exploit technical capabilities in "functional compound molecular design, chemical reaction control, and organic synthesis technologies" resulted in several discoveries. For example, human skin was observed to be similar to photographic film: it contained collagen and was about the same thickness. Fujifilm discovered that many of the antioxidants used to preserve photographic film could be used for skin care products.

Sources: www.fujifilm.com; "The last Kodak moment?" *Economist,* January 14, 2012; Stefan Kohn, "Disruptive innovations applied: A review of the imaging industry," http://www.iande.info/wp-content/uploads/2011/03/ StefanKohnDisruptiveInnovationsFujifilm.pdf, accessed September 20, 2012.

for image scanning, online imaging archive—for the most part, digital imaging was part of the overall computing and communication sector. It comprised smartphones and tablet computers, broadband services, data storage devices, printers, and social networking services.

Finally, Perez wondered as to what lessons could be drawn from the comparative success of Fujifilm. For all of Fuji's similarities to Kodak, its performance had been radically different: its revenues had grown (in terms of US dollars), and it had been consistently profitable (Exhibit 2).

Perez's reflections on Kodak's past were cut short by the arrival of James Mesterharm, from turnaround consultants AlixPartners, who had been appointed Kodak's chief restructuring officer. Together Perez and Merterham would discuss the implications of Chapter 11 bankruptcy for Kodak's corporate strategy for 2012 and beyond.

Notes

1. "Eastman Kodak Company and its U.S. Subsidiaries Commence Voluntary Chapter 11 Business Reorganization," Press Release (January 19, 2012).
2. "Kodak's New Focus," *Business Week* (January 30, 1995): 62–68.
3. Eastman Kodak Company, "Kodak Leaders Outline Road Ahead to get Kodak 'Back on Track'," press release (November 11, 1997).
4. Eastman Kodak Company, "The Big Picture: Kodak and Digital Photography," www.Kodak.com/US/en/corp/presscenter/presentations/020520mediaforum3.shtml. Website no longer available.
5. See www.Kodak.com/US/en/corp/presscenter/presentations/020520mediaforum3.shtml, accessed October 29, 2009. Website no longer available.
6. Interview with Antonio Perez, President and COO, Kodak, *PMA Magazine* (February 2004).
7. "Why Kodak Still Isn't Fixed," *Fortune* (May 11, 1998).
8. J. L. Bower and C. M. Christensen, "Disruptive Technologies: Catching the Wave," *Harvard Business Review* (January/February 1995).
9. M. Tushman, and P. Anderson, "Technological Discontinuities and Organizational Environments," *Administrative Science Quarterly* 31 (1986): 439–465.
10. Andrew Hill of the *Financial Times* observed: "In 1979, the company put together a graphic timeline laying out roughly when Kodak's customers would make the transition to digital imaging, starting with government clients, moving through graphic businesses and ending, in about 2010, with retail consumers. In 1991, the group drew up a digital strategy . . . Even the potential threat from camera-enabled mobile phones was 'war-gamed' by Kodak executives in the early 2000s." ("A Victim of Its Own Success," *Financial Times*, April 2, 2012.)

Case 13 Tesla Motors: Disrupting the Auto Industry

Tesla Motors' strategy was no secret: in 2006 the chairman and CEO, Elon Musk, announced:

> So, in short, the master plan is:
>
> - Build a sports car.
> - Use that money to build an affordable car.
> - Use that money to build an even more affordable car.
> - While doing above, also provide zero emission electric power generation options.
> - Don't tell anyone.[1]

The remarkable thing was that by 2015, Tesla had kept to that strategy and executed it almost flawlessly. Phase 1 ("Build a sports car") was realized with the launch of its Roadster in 2007. Phase 2 ("Use that money to build an affordable car") began in 2013 with the launch of the Model S.

The acclaim that greeted both cars had propelled Tesla's reputation and its share price. Since its initial public offering in June 2010, Tesla's share price had followed an upward trajectory. On June 12, 2015, Tesla's stock market value was $31.7 billion. By comparison, Fiat Chrysler was valued at $20.5 billion despite that fact that Fiat Chrysler would sell about 2.5 million cars in 2015 against Tesla's 55,000. The optimism that supported Tesla's valuation reflected the company's remarkable achievements during its short history and investors' faith in the ability of Elon Musk to realize his vision "to accelerate the advent of sustainable transport by bringing compelling mass market electric cars to market as soon as possible."[2]

Indeed, Musk's vision for Tesla extended beyond revolutionizing the automobile industry: Tesla's battery technology would also provide an energy storage system that would change "the fundamental energy infrastructure of the world."

A central issue in the debate over the appropriate market valuation of Tesla was whether Tesla should be valued as an automobile company or as a technology company. In practice, these two issues could not be separated: Tesla's principal source of revenue would be its cars, but realizing the expectations of earnings growth that were implicit in Tesla's share price required Tesla to maintain technological leadership in electric vehicles. Given that Tesla's rivals were some of the world's largest

This case was prepared by Robert M. Grant. ©2015 Robert M. Grant.

industrial companies—Toyota, General Motors, Ford, Volkswagen, and Renault–Nissan, to name a few—this was a daunting prospect.

Electric Cars

The 21st century saw the Second Coming of electric cars. Electric cars and buses were popular during the 1890s and 1900s, but by the 1920s they had been largely displaced by the internal combustion engine.

Most of the world's leading automobile companies had been undertaking research into electric cars since the 1960s, including developing electric "concept cars." In the early 1990s, several automakers introduced electric vehicles to California in response to pressure from the California Air Resources Board. However, the first commercially successful electric cars were hybrid electric vehicles (HEVs). Sales of HEVs in the US grew from 9,350 in 2000 to 352,862 in 2007. By far the most successful HEV, both in the US and globally, was the Toyota Prius, which by early 2010 had sold 1.6 million units worldwide.

Mass production, plug-in electric vehicles (PEVs) were first launched in 2008. There were two types of PEV: all-electric cars—of which the pioneers were the Tesla Roadster (2008), the Mitsubishi i-MiEV (2009), the Nissan Leaf (2010), and the BYD e6 (launched in China in 2010)—and plug-in hybrid electric vehicles (PHEVs) which were fitted with an internal combustion engine in order to extend their range. General Motors' Chevrolet Volt, introduced in 2009, was a PHEV.

However, there were also a number of other types of battery electric vehicles (BEVs). Some of these were highway-capable, low-speed, all-electric cars such as the Renault Twizy and the city cars produced by the Reva Electric Car of Bangalore, India. There were also various types of neighborhood electric vehicles (NEVs) intended for off-road use—these included golf carts and vehicles for university campuses, military bases, industrial plants, and other facilities. Global Electric Motorcars, a subsidiary of Polaris, was the US market leader in NEVs. Most NEVs used heavier, but cheaper, lead–acid batteries.

Electric motors had very different properties from internal combustion engines—in particular they delivered strong torque over a wide range of engine speeds, thereby dispensing with the need for a gearbox. This range of torque also gave them rapid acceleration. Although electric motors were much lighter than internal combustion engines, the weight advantages were offset by the need for heavy batteries—which were also the most expensive part of an electric car, costing from $10,000 to $25,000.

Electric cars were either redesigns of existing gasoline-powered models (e.g., the Ford Focus Electric and Volkswagen's e-Golf) or newly designed electric cars (e.g., the Tesla Roadster and Nissan's Leaf). Complete redesign had major technical advantages: the battery pack formed part of the floor of the passenger cabin, which saved on space and improved stability and handling due to a lower center of gravity.

Predictions that electric cars would rapidly displace conventionally powered cars had proved false. In 2009, Frost & Sullivan had predicted that the market for electric vehicles (including hybrid electric vehicles) would grow to 0.6 million units worldwide in 2015—about 14% of new vehicles sold.[3] In 2014, global registrations of electric cars totaled 340,000. Although this was a 70% increase on 2013, it was a tiny fraction of the total automobile market. The US was market leader in terms of

TABLE 1   Sales of leading models of plug-in electric cars in the US during January to May (units)

	2015	2014
Tesla S (estimated)	9,200	9,000
Nissan Leaf	7,742	8,301
Chevrolet Volt	4,400	5,290
BMW i3	3,900	336
Ford Fusion PHEV	3,563	3,553
Ford C-max Energi PHEV	2,900	2,415
Toyota Prius PHEV	2,426	5,988
Chevy Spark	1,559	454

Source: evobsession.

numbers sold, yet electric cars accounted for a mere 0.74% of total car sales. During 2015, the market for electric cars, especially in the US, was adversely affected by lower oil prices: total sales for the first five months of 2015 were little changed from the year-ago period (Table 1). However, electric car sales in China grew rapidly, overtaking the US as the largest market for electric cars.

While oil prices were an important factor influencing consumer choice between gasoline and electric cars, government incentives were even more important. Norway had the highest penetration of electric cars (14% of the market in 2014). This reflected incentives that included exemption from purchase taxes on cars (including VAT), road tax, and fees in public car parks; electric cars were also allowed to use bus lanes.

"Range anxiety"—the threat of running out of battery charge and the limited availability of charging stations were seen as the primary obstacles to the market penetration of all-electric PEVs. However, both issues were being resolved. Between 2015 and 2018, the range of EVs was expected to double—most EVs would then have a range of close to 200 miles (though still far from the 265-mile range of the Tesla S (with an 85 kWh battery pack). Charging stations were widely available in most urban areas, but they were sparse in many rural areas.

While most experts expected the plug-in electric car to be the primary threat to conventional cars, it was not the only zero-emission technology available to automakers. Fuel cells offered an alternative to plug-in electrical power. Fuel cells are powered by hydrogen which reacts with oxygen from the air to create electricity that then drives an electric motor. Fuel cell technology was developed during the space program and became applied to experimental land vehicles during the 1960s. Although a number of automakers had developed prototypes of fuel cell cars, only Toyota, Hyundai, and Honda had marketed cars powered by fuel cells. Since fuel cells consume hydrogen, a key factor limiting the adoption of fuel cells was the absence of a network of hydrogen fueling stations.

Tesla Motors: Product Launches

Elon Musk was a South African-born, serial entrepreneur with interests in e-commerce, renewable energy, and space travel. He had co-founded Zip2, which provided web-based software to publishing companies, and then PayPal, which earned him $165 million when it was acquired by eBay. His next start-ups were SpaceX, which would develop space launch vehicles, and SolarCity, which aimed to become "the Walmart of solar panel installations."

Tesla Motors Inc., founded in 2003, was named after Nikola Tesla, the pioneer of electric motors and electrical power systems in the late 19th century. In 2004, Musk became lead shareholder and chairman of Tesla Motors. He took over as CEO in 2008, and two years later Tesla Motors' shares began trading on the NASDAQ market.

Tesla's first car, the Roadster, launched in 2007, was a sensation. Priced at $109,000, it was a luxury sports car. Capable of accelerating from 0 to 60 miles per hour in less than four seconds, it was faster than most Ferraris. Its range of 260 miles on a single charge far exceeded that of the plug-in cars being developed by other automakers. The car became a favorite of Hollywood celebrities and a statement of environmental responsibility by the super-rich. The car's battery was built by Tesla from lithium-ion battery units supplied by Panasonic, its body was built by Lotus in the UK, and it was delivered direct to the final customer without using dealers. Only 2,500 Roadsters were produced between 2007 and 2012, but it attracted huge publicity and is credited with changing public perceptions of electric cars.

The Model S was Tesla's first mass production car. A prototype was displayed in March 2009 and the car was launched in 2013. The Tesla S was a four-door, five-seater sedan (with an additional third seat to accommodate two children) that came with different battery options (up to 85 kilowatt-hours) and a list price between $52,400 and $72,400. The car had a modular design developed on a flexible platform that would support multiple variants. Despite its high price (compared to other mass-market sedans), Tesla claimed that the Model S's overall user cost was about $1,800 per year—similar to that of comparable gasoline cars—as a result of Tesla's higher purchase price being offset by savings on fuel and maintenance.

The car was built at the former NUMMI plant at Fremont, California that Tesla had acquired from Toyota for $42 million. It was sold directly to consumers without using franchised dealers—the standard approach to sales and after-sales services in the auto business. Instead, Tesla opened its own directly managed showrooms in major cities throughout the world. This direct sales model conflicted with the laws of several US states, which required retail sales of automobiles to be undertaken through independent dealers. Tesla was soon involved in a flurry of legal battles. In New Jersey, New York, Maryland, Ohio, and Pennsylvania, Tesla was successful in getting state laws changed to allow it to directly sell its cars to the public; in Texas, it failed.

The Tesla S was greeted by a torrent of rave reviews. Tesla's 2014 Annual Report observed:

> Since its launch, Model S has won several awards, including the prestigious Motor Trend Car of the Year for 2013. Surveys by Consumer Reports gave Model S the highest customer satisfaction score of any car in the world in 2013 and gave Tesla Service the best overall satisfaction rating in the entire automotive industry in 2015. Model S also earned the highest safety rating in the United States by the National Highway Traffic Safety Administration.[4]

In addition to unsurpassed range and remarkable acceleration, it was praised for its stability and handling. The car's electronics were considered an advance upon those available from any other automaker. The driver's console featured a touch-screen that controlled almost all the car's functions, eliminating the need for most knobs and other controls; the car used a wireless fob instead of a key; and its software allowed the driver to adjust the car's suspension and steering behavior.

The Model S was to be followed by the Model X, a crossover between a sedan and an SUV (sport utility vehicle), built upon the same platform as the Model S, and to be launched in the third quarter of 2015.

Tesla's Technology

Tesla regarded itself as a technological leader within electric vehicles:

> Our battery pack and electric powertrain system has enabled us to deliver market-leading range capability on our vehicles at what we believe is a compelling battery cost per kilowatt-hour. Our battery packs use commercially available lithium-ion battery cells and contain two to three times the energy of any other commercially available electric vehicle battery pack, thereby significantly increasing the range capabilities of our vehicles. Designing an electric powertrain and a vehicle to exploit its energy efficiency has required extensive safety testing and innovation in battery packs, motors, powertrain systems and vehicle engineering.
>
> Our proprietary technology includes cooling systems, safety systems, charge balancing systems, battery engineering for vibration and environmental durability, customized motor design and the software and electronics management systems necessary to manage battery and vehicle performance under demanding real-life driving conditions.

However, Tesla's Sportster and Model S had, for the most part, combined existing automotive, electric motor, and battery technologies with little radically new innovation. In terms of electric motors, the technology was mature and well diffused. Tesla produced its electric motors in-house and possessed several patents relating to refinements in their design (e.g., a liquid-cooled rotor). However, the critical technical advantages of Tesla's electric motors related to their overall integration within the electrical powertrain and the software that managed that system.

Batteries

Electrical storage represented the most formidable challenge facing electrical vehicle manufacturers. The lithium-ion battery was first introduced by Sony in 1991, and soon became the dominant type of battery for laptop computers and other rechargeable electronic devices. By 2005, all the automakers developing electric vehicles had adopted lithium-ion batteries because of their superior power to weight ratio as compared with alternative battery types. For electric cars, lithium-ion cells are first combined into modules then the modules are combined into battery packs. Battery packs are controlled by software that monitors and manages their charging, usage, balancing, and temperature. The leading producers of lithium-ion batteries are shown in Table 2.

The leading automakers had each partnered with a battery producer to develop and supply batteries for their electric cars. Renault–Nissan, under the leadership

TABLE 2 The world's top-ten producers of lithium-ion batteries (in megawatt-hours)

	1st Quarter 2015	2014
Panasonic	888	2,726
AESC	361	1,620
BYD	196	461
Mitsubishi/GS Yuasa	135	451
LG Chem	114	886
Samsung	105	314
Wanxiang	62	0
Beijing Pride Power	47	121
Tianneng	38	77
SB LiMotive	37	0
Total	1,983	6,656

Source: http://cleantechnica.com/2015/05/06/10-biggest-electric-car-battery-manufacturers-are/, accessed July 20, 2015.

of Carlos Ghosn, was the most enthusiastic pioneer of electric vehicles, investing over $5.6 billion in its electrical vehicle program (which included the Nissan Leaf). This investment included a battery plant in Tennessee developed in collaboration with NEC. General Motors had partnered with LG for its supply of lithium-ion batteries.

Investments in battery plants were motivated by two factors, first, projection of a shortage of capacity for lithium-ion batteries for electric vehicles and, second, by the presence of a steep learning curve in battery production. This meant that there were substantial savings in unit costs for those producers able to expand their battery production the fastest.

Unlike Nissan, which had collaborated with NEC to develop a lithium-ion battery for its cars from scratch, Tesla used off-the-shelf lithium-ion cells bought from Panasonic. The cells were considerably smaller than those used by Nissan, hence requiring a much larger number (7,000) for the Roadster as compared with 192 for the Nissan Leaf, but avoiding some of the problem of overheating associated with lithium-ion cells.[5]

In July 2014, Tesla announced an agreement with Panasonic to build the world's biggest manufacturing plant for lithium-ion batteries. By 2020, the plant would have the capacity to manufacture 35 gigawatt-hours of battery cells and 50 gigawatt-hours of battery packs. The facility, the "Gigaplant," would cost about $5 billion—of which Tesla would invest $2 billion, Panasonic between $1.5 billion and $2 billion, and the state of Nevada would provide $1.25 billion in grants and tax breaks. The plant was located near Reno, Nevada and would begin production during 2017. The plant's annual output would exceed the entire global output of lithium ion batteries in 2013. Tesla's goal in building the plant was, first, to ensure sufficient supply of battery packs for its cars and, second, to bring down the cost of lithium-ion batteries from a cost of about $260 per kilowatt-hour in early 2015 to about $120 by 2020.

The Gigaplant would also allow Tesla to expand its sales of storage batteries for homes and businesses. At a product launch event on April 30th, 2015, Elon Musk announced its Powerwall—a battery pack for home use. Tesla offered two types of Powerwall: one to provide storage for solar-generated power (the 7 kWh model costing $2000) the other as emergency backup (the 10 kWh model costing $3500). With solar panels from SolarCity, Musk could now offer a total home generation system. In addition, Tesla would launch its Powerpack—a large capacity power storage unit for business and utilities at a cost of $250 per kilowatt-hour. Only a week after their launch, Bloomberg estimated that Tesla had taken $179 million in orders for Powerwalls and $635 million for Powerpacks. As a result, all Tesla's 2016 scheduled production of these two products had been pre-sold.[6]

Of Tesla's patents and patent applications up to the end of 2012, one-third related to batteries and another 28% to battery charging.[7] Its battery patents related mainly to the configuration of batteries, their cooling and temperature management, and systems for their monitoring and management. Tesla undertook limited research into battery chemistry, but monitored closely developments elsewhere (see Exhibit 1). Musk was skeptical of claims of major breakthroughs in battery technology, noting that most battery inventors were "long on promises and short on delivery." However, in May 2015, Tesla hired Jeff Dahn of Dalhousie University, one of the inventors of the nickel-manganese-cobalt battery.[8]

Despite widespread excitement that Tesla's revenues from batteries could outstrip those from cars, *Scientific American* noted that, first, Tesla did not possess any breakthrough technology in batteries and, second, while Tesla had some cost advantages over other suppliers of battery packs, it was not clear that this cost advantage was sustainable.[9]

EXHIBIT 1
The Quest for a Better Battery

The quest for a cheaper way of storing electricity was viewed as one of the greatest challenges in industrial R & D, most efforts focused upon improving lithium-ion batteries. Technical developments included:

♦ developing electrodes that combined lithium with other elements (Electromechanical Technologies Group at Berkley Livermore National Laboratories);

♦ providing thin-film coatings for the positive electrode (Stanford University);

♦ Using solid or gel-like electrolytes (Oak Ridge National Laboratory).

Innovatory battery technologies were also being developed by start-up companies:

♦ The British appliance maker Dyson, together with General Motors, had invested in Sakti3, which was developing solid-state batteries that had a potential cost-to-power ratio of $100 per kilowatt.

♦ EOS Energy Solutions was producing huge zinc-based batteries whose cost of $160 per kilowatt-hour made it viable for utilities to store electricity.

Sources: "Charge of the Lithium Brigade," *The Economist Technology Quarterly* (May 30, 2015); "Battery Revolution: A Clean Leap Forward," *Wall Street Journal* (March 16, 2015).

Battery Charging

If the range of its cars was one clear advantage that Tesla had over its competitors, the other was in battery charging. Tesla's Superchargers offered the world's fastest recharging of electric vehicle batteries. A Supercharger delivered up to 120 kWh of direct current directly to the battery. As a result, a 30-minute charge from a Supercharger offered 170 miles' driving, compared to just 10 miles with a 30-minute charge from a public charging station. The speed of the Supercharger is a result of the technology embodied in the Supercharger, the architecture of Tesla's car battery packs, the high voltage cables that feed the battery, and the computer system that managed the charging process. At the end of 2014, Tesla had 380 Supercharger stations in North America, Europe, and Asia which provided free charging to Tesla owners. In addition, there were 1000 locations in hotels and other locations in North America and Asia with Tesla wall connectors for free charging of Tesla cars.

In June 2015, Tesla had about 64 patents relating to its charging system. These related to the design of connectors and cables, systems for voltage and optimal charge rates, management systems for charging stations that charged multiple vehicles, and several other aspects of the charging process.

However, despite the superiority of Tesla's proprietary changing system, this did little to assist the general inadequacies of the electric vehicle charging infrastructure. The critical problem was not a shortage of charging stations but multiple systems. There were two problems:

1 There were two competing technical standards for fast charging: the CHAdeMO standard supported by Nissan, Mitsubishi, and Toyota and the SAE J1772 standard supported by GM, Ford, Volkswagen, and BMW. Tesla's proprietary charging system was not compatible with either, hence to use the large number of CHAdeMO and SAE J1772 charging stations, Tesla owners needed to buy special adapters.

2 Multiple networks of charging stations with different systems of payment. In the US the biggest network of fast-charging stations was owned by ChargePoint, which required users to purchase an annual subscription. In China, the leading provider of charging stations was the State Grid, a major electricity supplier. However, its charging stations could not charge Tesla cars. In several European countries, leading automakers (notably Renault–Nissan and Daimler) had collaborated with national power utilities (e.g., EDF in France and ENEL in Italy) and national governments to provide national networks of charging stations in each country. Tesla had built its own network and bundled the cost of charging into the price of the car.

Tesla Opens Its Patents

From its earliest days, Tesla had taken a rigorous approach to protecting its intellectual property. In its 2012 Annual Report it stated:

> Our success depends, at least in part, on our ability to protect our core technology and intellectual property. To accomplish this we rely on a combination of patents, patent applications, trade secret, including know-how employee and third party non-disclosure agreements, copyright laws, trademarks, intellectual property

licenses and other contractual rights to establish and protect our proprietary rights in our technology.[10]

Hence the amazement when, on June 12, 2014, Elon announced:

Tesla Motors was created to accelerate the advent of sustainable transport. If we clear a path to the creation of compelling electric vehicles, but then lay intellectual property landmines behind us to inhibit others, we are acting in a manner contrary to that goal. Tesla will not initiate patent lawsuits against anyone who, in good faith, wants to use our technology.[11]

The announcement was followed by a flurry of speculation as to the reasons why Tesla would want to relinquish its most important source of competitive advantage in the intensifying battle for leadership in electric vehicles. In the ensuing debate, four possible rationales emerged:

- Elon Musk's personal commitment to the displacement of petroleum fueled automobiles by electric vehicles;
- a calculated judgment that Tesla's interest would be better served by speeding the development of an electric vehicle infrastructure and a bigger, more efficient set of firms supplying parts and services to Tesla than by holding on to its proprietary technologies;
- an attempt to influence the emergence of standards in the industry so that Tesla's approaches to battery design, charging technology, electric powertrains, and control systems would dominate the electrical vehicle industry;
- the desire to boost Tesla's visibility and reputation within the industry.

Professor Scott Shane of Case Western University expressed surprise over Tesla's decision: typically the only way that startups can offset the resource advantages that incumbent firms possess is by building a strong patent portfolio. However, Shane went on to observe that the biggest challenge facing Tesla was not competition but the slow adoption of electric cars, hence, "the benefits of spurring customer adoption of electric cars outweigh the costs of strengthening competitors."[12]

Writing in the *Harvard Business Review*, Paul Nunes and Joshua Bellin probed the strategic considerations motivating Tesla's opening-up of its intellectual property. They pointed first to Tesla's view of its business environment as an interactive ecosystem rather than as a traditional industry. Tesla's view was more Silicon Valley than Detroit, including its abandoning of traditional dealer networks in favor of selling direct to consumers and its patterns of collaborative interactions with the suppliers of electronic hardware and software. Within its ecosystem, Tesla's primary role was as an innovator of electrical storage and battery solution, by adopting an open-source approach to its technology, Tesla could strengthen its centrality within its ecosystem.[13]

However, the fact remained that Tesla's technical strengths were not primarily its patent portfolio—indeed, Tesla's patent portfolio was smaller than those of most major auto companies (Table 3). Tesla's strengths were much more in the know-how needed to combine existing technologies in order to optimize vehicle performance, design, add-on features, and the overall user experience.

TABLE 3 Automobile companies' patents relating to electric vehicles, 2012

Company	Number of US patents
General Motors	686
Toyota	663
Honda	662
Ford	446
Nissan	238
Daimler	194
Tesla Motors	172
Hyundai	109
BMW	41

Sources: M. Rimmer, "Tesla Motors: Intellectual Property, Open Innovation, and the Carbon Crisis," Australian National University College of Law (September 2014); M. Shah, "Auto Industry May Ignore Tesla's Patents," Envision IP (June 26, 2014).

Disrupting the Auto Industry

Tesla's willingness to share its patents only added to the uncertainty over the extent to which Tesla represented a disruptive force within the auto industry.

Tony Seba, a prominent advocate of clean energy, argued that "the electric vehicle will disrupt the gasoline car industry (and with it the oil industry) swiftly and permanently … Even worse from the standpoint of gasoline and diesel cars, the EV [electric vehicle] is not just a disruptive technology; the whole business model that the auto industry has built over the past century will be obliterated."[14]

Others downplayed the whole issue on the basis, first, that Tesla's patents did not represent a significant barrier to other companies and, second, it probably did not make much sense for Tesla to devote time and money to litigating infringements of its patents. Professor Karl Ulrich of Wharton Business School stated: "I don't believe Tesla is giving up much of substance here. Their patents most likely did not actually protect against others creating similar vehicles." He suggested that patents are increasingly less about protecting innovations from imitation as strategic bargaining chips: "Big technology-based companies amass patent portfolios as strategic deterrence against infringement claims by their rivals … Tesla is essentially deciding it doesn't want to spend money litigating patents, which is a great decision for its shareholders and for society."[15]

In the debate over, whether or not the electric automobile represented a disruptive innovation, Clay Christensen and his team at Harvard Business School, were emphatic that Tesla's electric cars were definitely not such a disruptive force. While classic disruptive innovations typically target overserved customers with lower-performance products at a lower price (or open up entirely new market segments), Tesla offered incrementally higher performance at higher prices. A further feature of disruptive innovation is that incumbents typically have low incentives to adopt the disruptive innovation—yet all the major auto firms had been working on developing electric cars for years. If Tesla is not a disruptive force, who is in the automobile market? A more likely source, according to Professor Christensen's associate Tom

Bartman, was the neighborhood electric vehicle: a cheap, low-powered, easy-to-park vehicle that is well suited to urban transportation and can readily be upgraded for use on public roads.[16]

If Tesla Motors was going to meet strong competition from exceptionally well-resourced competitors—companies such as GM, Renault–Nissan, Ford, Daimler, VW, and BMW—it lacked clear technological advantages over these firms, and if it also was likely to meet competition from the manufacturers of NEVs in mass-market electric cars, how feasible was Elon Musk's goal that Tesla would be "a leading global manufacturer and direct seller of electric vehicles and electric vehicle technologies"?

Appendix

TABLE A1   Tesla Motors Inc. financial data ($million)

	2014	2013	2012	2011	2010
Revenues	3,198	2,013	413	204	117
Gross profit	882	456	30	62	31
Research and development	465	232	274	209	93
Operating profit	(187)	(61)	(394)	(251)	(147)
Net profit	(294)	(74)	(396)	(254)	(154)
Total assets	5,849	2,417	1,114	713	386
Total long-term obligations	2,772	1,075	450	298	93
Capital investment	970	264	239	198	105

Notes

1. Elon Musk, "The Secret Tesla Motors Master Plan (Just between You and Me)," (August 2, 2006), http://www.teslamotors.com/en_GB/blog/secret-tesla-motors-master-plan-just-between-you-and-me, accessed July 20, 2015.
2. "The Mission of Tesla," (November 18, 2013), http://www.teslamotors.com/en_GB/blog/mission-tesla, accessed July 20, 2015.
3. Quoted in Tesla Motors, Inc. *IPO Prospectus* (January 29, 2010): 2–3.
4. Tesla Motors, Inc. 10-K report for 2014: 4.
5. See Tesla Motors, HBS Case No. 9-714-913 (2014): 7.
6. "Tesla Has Already Received an Estimated $800 Million Worth of Battery Orders," www.bgr.com/2015/05/08/tesla-powerpack-powerwall-battery-sales-estimate, accessed July 20, 2015.
7. "How to Build a Tesla, According to Tesla," *Washington Post* (June 23, 2014), http://www.washingtonpost.com/blogs/the-switch/wp/2014/06/23/how-to-build-a-tesla-according-to-tesla, accessed July 20, 2015.
8. "Elon Musk wants inventors to stop pitching his battery ideas," www.ecomento.com/2015/05/14/elon-musk-stop-pitching-battery-ideas, accessed July 20, 2015.

9. "Will Tesla's Battery for Homes Change the Energy Market?" *Scientific American* (May 4, 2015).
10. Tesla Motors, Inc. 10-K report for 2012.
11. "All Our Patent Are Belong To You," http://www.tesla-motors.com/en_GB/blog/all-our-patent-are-belong-you, accessed July 20, 2015.
12. "Tesla's New Patent Strategy Makes Sense," *Entrepreneur* (July 8, 2015), www.entrepreneur.com/article/25408, accessed July 20, 2015.
13. "Elon Musk's Patent Decision Reflects Three Strategic Truths," https://hbr.org/2014/07/elon-musks-patent-decision-reflects-three-strategic-truths, accessed July 20, 2015.
14. T. Seba, *Clean Disruption of Energy and Transportation: How Silicon Valley Will Make Oil, Nuclear, Natural Gas, Coal, Electric Vehicles and Conventional Cars Obsolete by 2030*, Clean Planet Ventures (2014): 102–3.
15. "What's Driving Tesla's Open Source Gambit?" *Knowledge@Wharton* (June 25, 2014), http://knowledge.wharton.upenn.edu/article/whats-driving-teslas-open-source-gambit/, accessed July 20, 2015.
16. "Idea Watch: Tesla's Not as Disruptive as You Might Think," *Harvard Business Review* (May 2015).

Case 14 Video Game Console Industry in 2015

The latest round of competition in the market for video game consoles kicked off in November 2012 when Nintendo launched its Wii U. A year later, Sony launched its PlayStation 4 and Microsoft its Xbox One. The new generation of video game consoles—the eighth since the beginnings of the industry in 1972—presented considerable uncertainty for all three companies.

The first six generations of consoles had established a clear consensus as to key success factors in this industry. The strategies of all the leading players were focused upon establishing market leadership that would then generate network effects in gaining support both from users and game developers. To establish early market leadership the key was to target early adopters—the "hardcore gamers," who were primarily males aged between 13 and 30.

However, the conventional wisdom had been upset by the outcome of the last round of competition. Among seventh-generation consoles the winner had been Nintendo. Its Wii was a technologically unsophisticated, easy-to-use console targeted at the casual user. It had outsold the more technologically advanced machines from Sony and Microsoft. Moreover, while Sony and Microsoft had focused upon turning their consoles into multifunctional home entertainment devices, the Wii was a dedicated games console.

At the same time the home video game console was under threat. Increasingly game playing was shifting to mobile, multifunctional devices, such as smartphones and tablet computers.

Increasing competition between different types of hardware—home video game consoles, PCs, portable game consoles (such as the Nintendo 3DS and the PlayStation Vita), mobile phones, and tablet computers—had implications for the console makers' market positioning. The success of the Wii was built upon its appeal to causal game players. However, these casual players were migrating to playing games on mobile devices such as smartphones, and tablet computers.[1] If consoles were to lose casual game players to other hardware devices, the console makers might be inclined to return to their traditional focus: the hard core gamer for whom the video game console offered unparalleled speed and graphical realism.

History of the Video Game Industry, 1972–2015

The history of the video game console comprised a series of product generations, each lasting about five years and each defined primarily by the power of the microprocessors used by the consoles (Figure 1).

This case was prepared by Robert M. Grant. ©2015 Robert M. Grant.

FIGURE 1   Global sales of video game consoles by product generation (millions of units)

The First and Second Generations, 1972–1985: The Atari Era

The home video game market emerged during the 1970s as an extension of arcade video games. The first generation of home video consoles were dedicated machines that embodied a single game. The second generation of players featured inter-changeable cartridges. Industry pioneer Atari with its Atari 2600 unleashed a craze for video games driven by *Space Invaders* (released in 1979) and *Pac-Man* (1981). Atari failed to protect its proprietary technology and was overwhelmed by competition from suppliers of Atari-compatible consoles and a flood of unauthorized games from independent software developers.

The Third Generation, 1985–1990: The Nintendo Era

Nintendo, the leading Japanese supplier of arcade video games, released its Nintendo Entertainment System (NES) home video console system in Japan in 1983 and two years later in the US. By 1988, Nintendo held 80% the US market, due to hugely popular games such as *Donkey Kong*, *Legend of Zelda*, and *Super Mario Brothers* created by its legendary games developer, Shigeru Miyamota.

Nintendo's market dominance and huge profits rested upon its careful management of the relationship between hardware and software. Nintendo kept a tight control of the supply of games, managing their quality and releases. Developers were required to follow strict rules for the creation and release of games for the NES console. Cartridges incorporated a security chip that ensured that only cartridges manufactured by Nintendo could run on the NES. Nintendo charged game publishers a 20% royalty and a manufacturing fee of $14 per cartridge. The minimum order—10,000 cartridges for the Japanese market and 50,000 for the US market—had to be paid in advance. Any game developed for the NES could not be released on a competing system for two years.

By 1991, Nintendo's sales exceeded $4.4 billion, its stock market value exceeded that of Sony, and about one-third of US and Japanese households owned an NES.

The Fourth Generation, 1991–1995: Sega vs. Nintendo

Sega, like Atari and Nintendo, began in arcade games. In October 1988, it launched its 16-bit Genesis home video system in Japan, and next year in the US. With the introduction of *Sonic the Hedgehog* in 1991 and, with strong support from independent games developers, sales of Genesis took off.

Nintendo countered with its 16-bit Super-NES, in September 1991. But despite maintaining market leadership in Japan, Sega's bigger library of 16-bit titles (by January 1993 it offered 320 games, compared to 130 for Nintendo) allowed it to take a small lead in Europe and the US.

The Fifth Generation, 1995–1998: Sony PlayStation

With the launch of its 32-bit Saturn console in November 1994, Sega sought to extend the success of its Genesis console. However, a month later, Sony introduced its PlayStation console, the result of a six-year development effort led by Ken Kutaragi, Sony's video game guru. Like Saturn, PlayStation used CD-ROMs rather than cartridges. However, PlayStation possessed some key advantages: by courting top games developers, providing them with comprehensive software development tools and financing game development, PlayStation entered with a range of high-quality games. Moreover, Sony possessed a strong brand, global distribution capability, and content from its movie division. Sega's ill-coordinated Saturn introduction paled beside PlayStation's well-orchestrated, big budget launch, which was preceded by cryptic prelaunch advertisements that fueled a buzz of anticipation within the gamer community. Meanwhile, Nintendo attempted to recapture market leadership by leapfrogging Sony in technology. Its 64-bit N-64 console was released in June 1996 at a low price ($199 compared to $299 for a PlayStation), but it retained its cartridge system, which involved higher manufacturing costs and less flexibility in meeting unexpected demand for hit games. The lower costs of producing and distributing CDs allowed Sony to offer a much bigger library of games than Nintendo could, many of which targeted niche markets and minority interests.[2] By 1998, PlayStation was the leader in most of the world's major markets.

The Sixth Generation, 1999–2005: Sony vs. Microsoft

With the sixth generation of consoles, the global market was transformed. Although Sega led with its Dreamcast console in November 1998, the company was unable to establish market leadership and in 2001 exited hardware to focus on games development. Its nemesis was Sony, which launched its PlayStation 2 (PS2) early in 2000. Kutaragi's brief had been to design a games machine with performance that exceeded any PC and with graphics processing power ten times that of the original PlayStation. With cinematic-style graphics, a DVD player, and the potential for internet connectivity, the PS2 aspired to be a multifunctional entertainment device. However, the technical complexity of the PS2 created problems both for the supply of key components and the development of new games. As a result, the launch of the PS2 was marred by a shortage of consoles and a lack of new games.

In 2001, Microsoft joined the fray. Despite having just 19 games and a poor reception in Japan, Xbox combined three key strengths: its technological advances (an internal hard disk, a 733 MHz processor, 64 MB of memory, a DVD player, and an ethernet port), the hit game *Halo,* and Microsoft's online capabilities. In 2002, Microsoft launched Xbox Live, which allowed online interactive gaming and the direct downloading of games.

Nintendo, with its GameCube console, was the last to join the new generation of consoles.

By 2004, Sony was the clear market leader, with Microsoft a strong second in the US and Europe, and Nintendo a strong second in Japan.

The Seventh Generation, 2006–2012: Nintendo's Renaissance

Microsoft led the new generation of consoles with its Xbox 360 released on November 25, 2005: the first ever console with a simultaneous global launch as opposed to a phased rollout. Xbox 360 involved a shift in market positioning by Microsoft: while the original Xbox emphasized processing power and focused on hardcore gamers, Xbox 360 emphasized versatility, design, and its multiplicity of entertainment and online capabilities.

Sony's PS3 was launched on November 11, 2006 after a long delay, caused by Sony's technological ambitiousness—notably its decision to make the PS3 the flagship for the Blu-ray DVD drive and its adoption of an advanced multicore-cell microprocessor developed jointly with IBM and Toshiba. The losses incurred by the PS3 were the result not only of huge development and launch costs but also of the component cost of each unit sold (estimated at over $800) exceeding the retail price ($499).[3] In addition, the complexity and high cost of developing games for the PS3 meant that there were few games that fully exploited its technical capabilities.

Nintendo's launch of its Wii console coincided with that of the PS3. Despite its technological modesty—it lacked the speed and graphical capabilities of the PS3 and Xbox 360 as well as a hard drive, DVD player, and ethernet port—it was a sensation. Its innovative feature was its remote wand-like controller that was sensitive to a range of hand movements. This allowed Wii to be used for a variety of new sport and exercise applications—*Wii Fit* was one of the biggest-selling titles of 2008–2010. The accessibility and ease of use of the Wii allowed it to target a very broad demographic, including older people. But although Wii established a clear market lead over the PS3 and Xbox 360 in terms of unit sales, in terms of revenue it was overtaken by both Sony and Microsoft.

The Video Game Industry in 2015

The Market for Video Games

At the beginning of 2015, video games continued to be a growth industry (Figure 2). Worldwide sales of video game software and dedicated hardware (both consoles and handheld game players) were about $70 billion in 2014 and PwC expected them to grow to $93 billion by 2019.[4] Most of this growth would be in emerging markets. China offered particularly interesting prospects. The prohibition of video game consoles was lifted in 2014 and Microsoft's Xbox One and Sony's PS4 were being distributed by the state-controlled Shanghai Media Group whose primary interest was in encouraging home-developed games for these platforms.[5]

FIGURE 2   Projected worldwide sales of video game hardware and software to 2017

However, video games were played on an increasingly wide variety of hardware: home video consoles, personal computers, and various mobile devices—smartphones in particular. All the recent growth had been in gaming on mobile devices. In mature markets, notably in the US, sales of video game consoles had been in decline for several years (Figure 3). Nevertheless, video game consoles faced little prospect of total displacement. User experience had been continually enhanced by graphical realism, multiplayer online gaming, and the personalization of games, 3-D visual displays, and virtual reality.

The shift in the distribution of games from boxed DVDs to downloads, subscriptions, and cloud access fostered the emergence of new business models. The online distribution of video games through console makers' websites had facilitated the sale of add-ons and accessories. In-game advertising also offered additional sources of revenue. Most video games for mobile devices were offered free and supported by advertising. Increasingly, the developers of mobile games adopted "freemium" models: the games could be downloaded for free, but additional features and enhancements had to be purchased.

In terms of demographics, a major development of the past decade had been the broadening user base of video game players. Once the preserve of teenage boys and young adult men, by 2014 the majority of the US population aged 18–49 played video games, and even among 55- to 65-year-olds 30% played video games. Female participation had also increased strongly—especially in mobile gaming. However, gaming on dedicated consoles remained primarily the pursuit of teenage boys and young men aged between 20 and 35. The broadening of the market had also led to its segmentation—both demographically and in terms of game genres.[6]

Software

Each video game console supplier ("platform provider") licensed third-party software companies to develop and distribute games for its system. Two types of

FIGURE 3   US sales of home video game consoles and associated software ($billion)

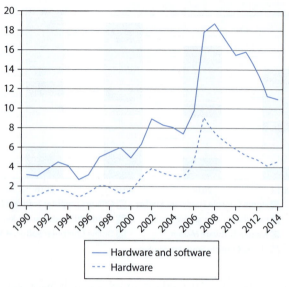

Source: Author's estimates based upon multiple sources.

company were involved in video game software: video game publishers, which were responsible for financing, manufacturing, marketing, and distributing video games; and video game developers, which developed the software. Publishing was increasingly dominated by a few large companies (Table 1). Typically, the software publisher submitted a proposal or a prototype to the console maker for evaluation and approval. The licensing agreement between the software company and the hardware provider gave the console maker the right to approve game content and control of the release date, and provided for a royalty payment from the software company. Game developers were paid a royalty, typically between 5 and 15%, based on the publisher's revenues from the game. The console makers were also the major developers and publishers responsible for some of the most popular video games (Table 2).

Escalating game development costs were a result of the demand for multi-featured, 3-D, cinematic-quality games that could utilize the potential of increasingly powerful consoles. Atari's *Pac-Man* released in 1982 was created by a single developer and cost about $100,000. Activision's *Destiny* released in September 2014 involved a budget of over $500 million—though this included marketing costs as well as development costs. *Grand Theft Auto V* cost an estimated $265 million. In terms of cost and revenue patterns, video games increasingly resembled movies: they incurred substantial upfront costs and a mere few became money-spinning blockbusters. Their production processes were increasingly similar—even to the point of using Hollywood actors not just to voice characters but also to make appearances: Kevin Spacey played a character in *Call of Duty: Advanced Warfare*. Like movies, too, many of the most successful new releases were sequels to earlier games—this

TABLE 1 Top-20 suppliers of video games ranked by sales of game software

Rank	Company	2014 ($million)	Change over 2013
1	Tencent	7,211	+37%
2	Sony*	6,040	+27%
3	Microsoft*	5,023	+3%
4	Electronic Arts	4,453	+22%
5	Activision Blizzard	4,409	−4%
6	Apple*	3,199	+35%
7	Google*	2,623	+89%
8	King.com	2,260	+20%
9	Nintendo	2,092	−13%
10	Ubisoft	1,806	+33%
11	NetEase	1,586	+11%
12	GungHo Entertainment	1,447	−7%
13	Nexon	1,446	−2%
14	Disney	1,280	+9%
15	DeNA	998	−38%
16	TakeTwo Interactive	978	−60%
17	Facebook*	974	+10%
18	Square Enix	949	+13%
19	GREE	883	−34%
20	Konami	841	−18%

Note:
*Estimated. Estimates include all non-hardware, game-related revenues.
Source: Newzoo.

created valuable brand franchises such as *Super Mario Brothers, Grand Theft Auto, Call of Duty*, and *Halo*).

Recent generations of consoles had seen a major shift in the balance of power between console makers and game publishers. In earlier generations, the console

TABLE 2 Top-ten console games in the US, 2014 (units sold)

Rank	Title/platform	Publisher
1	*Call of Duty: Advanced Warfare* (PS3, PS4, X360, Xbox1)	Activision Blizzard
2	*Madden NFL 15* (PS3, PS4, X360, Xbox1)	Electronic Arts
3	*Destiny* (PS3, PS4, X360, Xbox1)	Activision Blizzard
4	*Grand Theft Auto V* (PS3, PS4, X360, Xbox1)	Take 2 Interactive
5	*Minecraft* (PS3, PS4, X360, Xbox1)	Mojang
6	*Super Smash Bros.* (WiiU)	Nintendo
7	*NBA 2K15* (PS3, PS4, X360, Xbox1)	Take 2 Interactive
8	*Watch Dogs* (PS3, PS4, X360, Xbox1)	Ubisoft
9	*FIFA 15* (PS3, PS4, X360, Xbox1, Wii)	Electronic Arts
10	*Call of Duty: Ghosts* (PS3, PS4, X360, Xbox1, WiiU)	Activision Blizzard

Source: NPD.

makers were dominant, enforcing exclusivity and imposing heavy royalty payments on the publishers. Consolidation among publishers (caused by rising development costs) and more intense competition among the different hardware platforms had changed all that. Exclusivity ties had disappeared from most licensing contracts— most leading games titles were cross-platform—and were often launched simultaneously on both PlayStation and Xbox. The only popular games exclusive to a single platform were typically those developed in-house by the console makers (e.g., Microsoft's *Halo*).

At the same time, game publishers were also facing new pressures. The licensing fees paid by software publishers for exclusive rights to the intellectual property of media companies and sports organizations grew substantially between 1998 and 2002. The rights to a game based on a hit movie (e.g., *Harry Potter*) could cost several million dollars. For sports games, the major leagues (NFL, NHL, MLB, NBA, and FIFA) required an upfront payment, plus a royalty of 5–15% of the publisher's revenue from the game.

Not only did software sales exceed hardware sales; software was responsible for virtually all of the industry's profit. The console makers followed a "razors and blades" business model: the consoles were sold at a loss; profits were recouped on software sales (both games developed internally and royalties received from third-party game publishers). The result was strongly cyclical earnings for the platform providers: the launch of a new console would result in massive cash outflows; only with a substantial installed base would the platform provider begin to recoup the investment made.

The Console Makers

For the console suppliers, the period 2006–2014 had been a difficult one. The razors-and-blades model worked less well when the games were no longer exclusive to specific platforms. The loss of software exclusivity also undermined network effects: the tendency for consumers and software developers to gravitate toward the market-leading platform.

The new dynamics of the market were evident from the financial performance of the companies (see the Appendix). Despite Nintendo's success with its Wii, only during 2007–2010 did the company earn high profits; by 2012, it had fallen back into losses. For Sony, its technological ambition for its PS3 bestowed high costs which ate up potential margins. Sony's games division incurred substantial losses during 2007–2015. While Microsoft had the satisfaction of achieving its goal of establishing itself as a major force within the video game business, the costs were high: although the financial results for the Xbox were buried in the aggregated financial data it published, it believed that Microsoft's video game business had accumulated billions of dollars of losses between 2001 and 2015.

One consequence of deteriorating profitability was the desire to extend product cycles. Reluctance to incur the costs of developing new models was the major motivation behind Sony and Microsoft's desire to extend the lives of their current models. Eight years had elapsed between the launch of Microsoft's Xbox 360 and its replacement by Xbox One—previous cycles tended to have a duration of five or six years.

When the companies did launch their eighth-generation models, they each pursued a differentiated strategy.

- Nintendo's Wii U was essentially an upgraded Wii. It had limited computing power and its innovatory features were focused upon its controllers—notably an embedded touchscreen.

- With the PS4, Sony returned to the industry's traditional focus on hardcore gamers—its tagline "4 the players" was designed to emphasize this focus. However, Sony also envisaged a ten-year life cycle for the PS4 and over that lifetime it would broaden its market appeal and expand its functionality. The appeal to core gamers was primarily through technical capabilities—notably in graphics, its second screen and remote playing capability, and upgraded online services through the PlayStation network. Sony also committed to a continuous upgrading of the game playing experience—notably through its Morpheus project to deliver virtual reality.

- Microsoft's Xbox One shared many of the same technical features of the PS4—many of the core components including the AMD CPU were identical. However, its initial market position was different from that of Sony. Xbox One's design and launch were influenced by Microsoft's "One Microsoft" strategy, which sought greater integration across the company's products and divisions. According to Microsoft's VP for hardware: "It's more than a gaming platform. We're thinking about our devices as a stage for all of Microsoft."[7] In particular, the Xbox One was seen as a platform for a broad array of Microsoft's streaming and cloud services.

During 2014, it was apparent that Sony's PS4 had established a clear market lead. The Xbox One had been launched at $499 in the US, compared to $399 for the PS4, which put Microsoft at an immediate disadvantage. It was also clear that Microsoft's emphasis on home entertainment and online capabilities had alienated many gamers—especially in relation to always-on internet connectivity and restrictive digital rights on boxed games. During 2015, Microsoft was busily back-pedaling and reformulating its Xbox One strategy. By the end of June 2015, lifetime sales of the PS4 were 25.3 million, Xbox One 14.3 million, and Wii U 10 million.

Looking to the Future

The evolution of the video game industry had greatly impacted both the profit potential of the industry and the sources of competitive advantage within it.

The rise of mobile platforms and the shift in power from the suppliers of hardware to the suppliers of software had greatly undermined the industry's capacity to generate profits for the console makers. The weakening of network effects had meant that video games were no longer a winner-takes-all industry with a dominant strategy for the competitors within the industry.

Moreover, the expanding number and variety of video game players suggested that the market was segmenting, for example the Wii appealed to different users than the Xbox and PlayStation.

For Sony and Microsoft, their game consoles were part of their broader corporate strategies. Both companies envisaged their video game consoles as multifunctional home entertainment devices, but where Sony was primarily a consumer electronics company with a strong emphasis on hardware and entertainment—and movies in particular—Microsoft's Xbox was an integral part of a home-based digital strategy based upon the online provision of software and services. The willingness of Sony and Microsoft to devote so many resources to a business that yielded them such low returns on their investments could only be justified by broader strategic considerations.

Nintendo was the closest to a "pure play" in video games—its business comprised hardware and software both for home and mobile game playing. Its portable game players (the Nintendo 3DS) comprised a much larger proportion of its revenues and profit than its home consoles (Wii). However, as a specialist, it lacked the financial and technological resources of Sony and Microsoft and was most threatened by the trend to multifunctional hardware—especially in mobile devices.

Appendix: Financial Data for the Leading Console Makers

TABLE A1   Nintendo (year ending March 31; ¥billion)

	2004	2005	2006	2007	2008	2009	2010	2011	2012	2013	2014	2015
Sales	514	515	509	966	1,672	1,838	1,434	1,014	648	635	572	550
Operating income	110	113	91	226	487	555	357	171	(37)	(36)	(46)	25
Net income	33	87	98	174	257	279	229	78	(43)	7	(23)	42
Operating income/ Average total assets (%)	10.5	9.7	7.9	19.5	27.0	31.7	21.0	10.1	(2.4)	(2.2)	(3.1)	1.8
Return on equity (%)	3.7	9.6	10.4	16.8	11.0	19.9	16.8	5.7	(4.2)	0.6	(2.0)	3.7

Source: The financial data in Tables A1, A2, and A3 is derived from the companies' annual reports.

TABLE A2   Sony Corporation (year ended March 31; ¥billion)

	2004	2005	2006	2007	2008	2009	2010	2011	2012	2013	2014	2015
Sales	7,496	7,160	7,475	8,296	8,871	7,729	7,214	7,181	6,403	5,691	6,682	7,036
of which												
–Games	754	703	918	974	1,219	1,685[a]	1,512[a]	1,493[a]	3,137[b]	750[c]	1,044[c]	1,388[c]
Operating income	99	114	191	150	475	(227)	32	200	(67)	227	26	40
of which												
–Games	68	43	9	(232)	(124)	(87)[a]	(83)[a]	36[a]	(230)[b]	(4)	(19)	48
Net income	89	164	124	126	369	(98)	(41)	(259)	(457)	42	(128)	(126)
Operating income/ Average total assets (%)	1.1	1.2	1.9	0.6	2.9	(1.8)	0.3	1.6	(0.5)	1.6	0.0	0.3
Return on equity (%)	3.6	6.3	4.1	3.9	10.8	(3.1)	(1.4)	(9.4)	(15.6)	0.3	(4.6)	(4.1)

Notes:
[a]For 2009–2011, the segment data for Sony are for "Networked Products and Services." This includes both game consoles and PCs.
[b]For 2012, the segment data are for "Consumer Products and Services."
[c]For 2013–2015, the segment data are for "Game and Network Services."

TABLE A3   Microsoft (year ending June 30; $billion)

	2003	2004	2005	2006	2007	2008	2009	2010	2011	2012	2013	2014
Sales	32.2	36.8	39.8	44.3	51.1	60.4	58.4	62.5	69.9	73.7	77.8	86.8
of which												
—Entertainment and devices	2.75	2.73	3.11	4.29	6.07	8.14	6.42	6.22	8.16	32.44[a]	32.10[a]	37.67[a]
Operating income	13.2	9.0	14.6	16.5	18.5	22.5	20.4	24.1	27.2	21.8	21.9	22.1
of which												
—Entertainment and devices	(0.92)	(1.01)	(0.45)	(1.28)	0.43	(1.97)	0.29	0.57	1.14	6.05[a]	9.42[a]	8.71[a]
Net income	10.0	8.2	12.3	12.6	14.1	17.7	14.6	18.8	23.2	17.0	21.9	22.1
Operating income/ Average total assets (%)	17.9	10.3	17.6	23.6	29.3	30.9	27.2	27.8	27.9	18.0	18.8	16.0
Return on equity (%)	17.6	11.7	19.9	28.6	16.45	42.47	38.5	43.7	44.8	25.6	27.8	24.7

Note:
[a]The segment data for 2012–2014 relate to "Devices and Consumer," of which "Computing and Gaming Hardware" comprises less than 25%.

Notes

1. The rise of smartphones for playing video games was revealed by the success of *Angry Birds*. Launched in 2009 for the Apple iPhone, 300 million copies of *Angry Birds* had been downloaded by the end of 2011.
2. In 1997, the average PlayStation game sold 69,000 copies; the average N-64 title sold over 400,000 copies.
3. "Delays Likely for Sony's PlayStation 3," *Financial Times* (February 20, 2006).
4. PwC, *Global Entertainment and Media Outlook, 2015–2019*, http://www.pwc.com/gx/en/global-entertainment-media-outlook/global-data-insights.jhtml, accessed July 20, 2015.
5. "The End of Console Competition and the New Game Development Era in China," *Forbes Asia* (January 30, 2015).
6. Genres included: action games, shooter games, adventure games, role-playing games, simulation games, strategy games, and sports games.
7. "Xbox is a Test for the One Microsoft Strategy," *Bloomberg Business Week* (November 21, 2013).

Case 15 New York Times: The Search for a New Business Model

When Mark Thompson joined the New York Times Company (NYT) as its CEO in November 2012, expectations were low. During the previous six years, the company, which published the *New York Times, Boston Globe*, and *International Herald Tribune*, had made an overall loss and suffered declining revenues in each year. Several commentators pointed to the likely demise of the company: Henry Blodget of *Business Insider* predicted a continuing decline in the company's revenues as news readership and advertising moved online.[1] Eric Jackson of Ironfire Capital LLC predicted that declining advertising revenues, rising pension costs, and limits on further cuts in operating costs would mean that NYT would be unable to continue as a standalone business by 2015.[2]

Moreover, Mark Thompson's ability to focus on his new job was hampered by controversy arising from his previous one. During 2004–2012, Thompson had been Director-General of the British Broadcasting Corporation (BBC). The scandal over Jimmy Savile, a popular BBC presenter who was later revealed as a blatant sexual predator had generated criticism of Thompson's leadership.

Nevertheless, during his first two-and-a-half years at NYT (to June 2015), Thompson led a strategic and organizational transformation of the company that accelerated its move into digital media and stabilized the company's finances. Even the NYT's share price showed signs of revival after years of decline (Figure 1).

Despite promising signs of growing online subscriptions and online advertising revenues, the future of NYT was far from assured. Results for the first quarter of 2015 pointed to the size of the challenge that Thompson and his team faced: revenues were lower than during the same quarter of 2014 and the company had slipped back into losses (Table 1).

The US Newspaper Industry

The US newspaper industry—like that of other countries—had been in decline for over two decades. The reason was competition from online media both for news readership and for advertising. Although print newspapers had diversified into online news provision, they met powerful competition in this field from other suppliers of digital news content, including online newspapers such as Huffington Post

This case was prepared by Robert M. Grant. © 2015 Robert M. Grant.

FIGURE 1 New York Times Company's share price, May 2005 to May 2015

Source: NYSE

and BuzzFeed and TV news suppliers with their own websites (ABC, CNN, and Fox). Moreover, newspapers' digital content was heavily reliant upon other online players for distribution—including portals such as Yahoo and MSN and search engines such as Google and Bing, and social media such as Facebook and Twitter. The shift of the internet access toward mobile devices further weakened newspapers by increasing the power of platform owners such as Apple (iPhone, iPad) and Google (Android). As a result, the decline in print readership (Figure 2) translated into an even steeper decline in advertising revenues for printed newspapers, which were only partly compensated by increased digital advertising revenues (Figure 3).

Most US newspapers served local markets—individual cities and metropolitan regions. Some had a broader market, for example, the *Los Angeles Times* served southern California and the *San Francisco Chronicle* served northern California.

TABLE 1 New York Times Company, Inc.: Financial results for the first quarter of 2014 and 2015 ($million)

	2015	2014
Revenues	384.2	390.4
of which		
—Circulation	211.5	209.7
—Advertising	149.9	159.2
—Other	22.9	21.5
Operating costs	350.3	365.8
Pension and termination charges	45.1	2.6
Operating profit	(11.1)	22.1
Net income	(14.4)	1.9

Source: New York Times Company: 2015 First-Quarter Results, March 30, 2015.

FIGURE 2   Annual changes in US newspaper circulation, 2002–2014

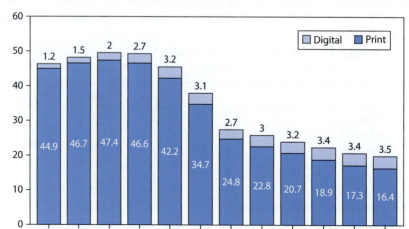

Source: "State of the News Media 2015," Pew Research Center, Washington, DC (April, 2015) http://www
.journalism.org/files/2015/04/FINAL-STATE-OF-THE-NEWS-MEDIA1.pdf.

Few cities had more than one daily newspaper and New York City was unique in
having three: the *Times, Daily News*, and *Post*. Only three newspapers could claim
to be national (or even international) in their distribution: *USA Today*, the *Wall Street
Journal*, and the *New York Times*.

While most newspapers were able to cover their operating costs, net margins—
after interest, taxes, and special charges—were typically razor-thin. Maintaining
profitability had required constant cost cutting. Independent news gathering had
been a key casualty of cost cutting—most newspapers relied upon agencies such as
Reuters, Associated Press, and Agence France-Presse. Sunday print sales were more
resilient than Monday–Friday sales.

FIGURE 3   US newspaper advertising revenues from print and digital media,
2003–2014 ($billion)

Source: "State of the News Media 2015," Pew Research Center, Washington, DC (April, 2015) http://www
.journalism.org/files/2015/04/FINAL-STATE-OF-THE-NEWS-MEDIA1.pdf.

TABLE 2   Top-ten US news websites by number of unique visitors for January 2015 (in millions)

Website	Visitors
Yahoo/ABC News	128
CNN Network	102
NBC News Digital	101
Huffington Post	100
CBS News	84
USA Today sites	79
BuzzFeed	78
The New York Times	57
Fox News Digital Network	57
Mail Online/Daily Mail	51

Source: Pew Research Center, State of the News Media 2015.

NYT had few delusions as to the fiercely competitive nature of its industry:

We operate in a highly competitive environment. Our print and digital products compete for advertising and circulation revenue with both traditional and new content providers, and this competition has intensified as a result of new digital media technologies and new media providers offering news and other online content. Competition among companies offering online content is intense; new competitors can quickly emerge, and some competitors may have greater resources or better competitive positions than we do.[3]

Competitors included: "paid and free newspapers, digital media, broadcast, satellite and cable television, broadcast and satellite radio, magazines, other forms of media and direct marketing." In printed media, the *Times'* competitors included: "national newspapers such as *The Wall Street Journal* and *USA Today*; newspapers of general circulation in New York City and its suburbs;" while the *International New York Times* was in competition with "all international sources of English-language news, including *The Wall Street Journal's* European and Asian Editions, the *Financial Times, Time, Bloomberg Business Week* and *The Economist*."[4] In digital news: "NYTimes.com faces competition from sources such as WSJ.com, Google News, Yahoo! News, huffingtonpost.com, MSNBC and CNN.com."[5] For advertising, the scope of competition was even broader. Table 2 shows America's leading digital news sources; Table 3 shows America's leading print newspapers.

The *New York Times'* Quest for Survival

Focus on the *Times*

Since 1896, the NYT was under the control of the Ochs/Sulzberger family. The family's control of the company was ensured by their ownership of a special category of shares that elected the majority of board members. Hostile takeover was

TABLE 3 US daily newspapers ranked by weekday circulation, 2013

	Print	Digital	Total average circulation
Wall Street Journal	1,480,725	898,102	2,378,827
New York Times	731,395	1,133,923	1,865,318
USA Today	1,424,406	249,900	1,674,306
Los Angeles Times	432,873	177,720	610,593
New York Daily News	360,459	155,706	516,165
New York Post	299,950	200,571	500,521
Washington Post	431,149	42,313	473,462
Chicago Tribune	368,145	46,785	414,930
Denver Post	213,830	192,805	406,635
Newsday	265,782	111,962	377,744
Newark Star-Ledger	180,271	160,507	340,778
Houston Chronicle	231,233	102,341	333,574
Cleveland Plain Dealer	216,122	95,483	311,605
Minneapolis Star Tribune	227,694	73,651	301,345
Phoenix Republic	285,927	7,048	292,975
Chicago Sun-Times	184,801	77,660	262,461
Tampa Bay Times	241,020	17,099	258,119
Dallas Morning News	190,613	65,912	256,525
Philadelphia Inquirer	184,827	67,958	252,785
Boston Globe	172,048	73,524	245,572

Source: Alliance for Audited Media.

impossible: any family member wishing to sell their shares had to first offer them to other family members or convert them to the ordinary shares that were traded on the NYSE. Arthur Sulzberger Jr.—a member of the fourth generation of the newspaper dynasty—was appointed chairman in 1996 and since then had exercised control over strategy and senior appointments. Under his leadership, the *Times* was committed to delivering the highest standards of journalism while recognizing that from the outset that the company could not restrict itself to print:

> At the heart of this presentation are plans for ensuring that, a decade from now and a century from now, *The New York Times* will still be the leader in its field of quality journalism, regardless of how it is distributed. These plans entail our moving from a strategy focused on the specific products we produce to one built around our audience—*a quality audience strategy*. Our goal is to know our audience better than anyone else; to meet their informational and transactional needs—by ourselves where we can; in partnership with others when necessary; and to serve them in print and digitally, continuously and on-demand.[6]

Pursuing this strategy meant an increasing focus upon a single title: the *Times*. During 2007, NYT sold nine local television stations and, in 2009, its WQXR radio station. In January 2012, its Regional Media Group of 16 daily newspapers in six different states was sold for $143 million, then in August 2013, the loss-making *Boston*

Globe was sold for $70 million—93% less than the $1.1 billion that the NYT had acquired the paper for in 1993. At the same time, the Paris-published *International Herald Tribune* was renamed the *International New York Times.*

The central role of the *Times* reflected the unique status of the newspaper in terms of its national distribution and unrivalled reputation for journalism. Its journalists had earned more than double the number of Pulitzer prizes than any other newspaper. Its columnists included Nicholas Kristof, Thomas Friedman, Maureen Dowd, and Nobel Prize-winning economist Paul Krugman. The company attributed its ability to raise the cover price of the *Times* (up from $1 to $2.50 between July 2007 and January 2012) to the appeal of its quality journalism.

Declining Revenues

The NYT's revenues were derived from users (circulation revenue) and from advertisers. Both had been in decline since a high of $3.4 billion in 2005, reflecting reduced numbers of print copies of the NYT's newspapers and the shift in advertising budgets from print media. The latter had been a bigger source of lost revenue than the former. The composition of NYT's revenue is shown in Table 4. Financial data for the company are shown in Table 5.

Cost Cutting

The main response by NYT's management to shrinking revenues was to cut costs. Cost economies included:

- Consolidating operations to eliminate duplication, e.g., the *Times* had consolidated two New York printing plants into a single facility, saving $30 million annually.
- Closing loss-making businesses, e.g., the City & Suburban, New York retail and newsstand distribution business was closed in 2009.

TABLE 4 New York Times Company: Revenue and cost components ($million)

	2014	2013	2012	2011	2010	2009	2008
Total revenues	1,589	1,577	1,595	2,323	2,394	2,440	2,949
of which							
—Advertising	662	667	712	1,222	1,300	1,336	1,780
—Circulation	837	824	795	942	932	937	910
—Other	89	86	88	160	162	168	259
Total production costs	644	627	651	958	962	1,021	1,315
of which							
—Raw materials	89	93	106	162	160	166	251
—Wages and benefits	358	332	331	496	498	525	623
—Other	197	202	214	300	303	330	442
Selling, general, and administrative costs	761	706	711	1,020	1,054	1,153	1,332
Depreciation and amortization	79	78	79	116	121	134	144
Total operating costs	1,485	1,412	1,411	2,093	2,137	2,308	2,792

Source: New York Times Company, Inc., 10-K reports, 2011 and 2014.

TABLE 5 New York Times Company, Inc.: Selected financial data for 2007–2014

	2014	2013	2012	2011	2010	2009	2008	2007
Revenues	1,589	1,577	1,595	2,323	2,393	2,440	2,948	3,195
Operating costs	1,484	1,412	1,441	2,093	2,137	2,308	2,792	2,928
Operating (loss)/profit	91.9	156.1	103.7	56.7	23.4	74.1	(40.6)	227.4
Interest expense, net	53.7	58.1	62.8	85.2	85.1	81.7	47.8	39.8
Gain on sale of investments	—	—	220	71	9	5	—	—
Post-tax income from continuing operations	33.4	56.9	163.9	(40.2)	108.7	1.6	(66.1)	(108.9)
Post-tax income from discontinued operations	(1.1)	7.9	(27.9)	—	—	(1.2)	8.3	99.8
Net income	33.3	65.1	135.8	(40.2)	108.7	19.9	(57.8)	208.7
Property, plant, and equipment	666	713	773	1,085	1,157	1,250	1,354	1,468
Total assets	2,566	2,573	2,807	2,883	3,286	3,089	3,402	3,473
Total debt and lease obligations	650	683	697	698	996	769	1,059	1,035
Stockholders' equity	726	843	662	506	656	604	504	978
ROE (%)	4.2	8.6	23.2	(6.9)	17.3	3.6	(11.9)	26.7
Debt/equity ratio	0.89	0.81	1.05	1.38	1.52	1.27	2.10	1.07
Operating margin (%)	5.8	9.9	6.5	2.4	1.0	3.0	(1.4)	7.1
Current assets to current liabilities	1.90	3.36	2.45	1.46	1.7	1.00	0.60	0.68
Employees (full-time equivalent)	3,588	3,529	5,363	7,273	7,414	7,665	9,346	10,231

Source: New York Times Company, Inc. 10-K reports.

- Outsourcing functions such as advertising service, circulation telemarketing, customer service, and financial back-office functions.
- Reducing newsprint and production costs by eliminating some newspaper sections (e.g., TV guides, the Metro section, regional sections, and the Sunday automobiles section) and shrinking the page size of the *Times*.
- Cutting jobs: positions were eliminated both in production activities and in administrative and marketing activities. Despite a high level of unionization (over one-half of employees) and complex union agreements (there were ten different unions), employment reduction accelerated during 2012 and 2013—one consequence was that severance payments increased sharply.
- Controlling pension costs and retiree benefits. These were major expenses that were not amenable to cost cutting—and had tended to grow over time. NYT sought to control its pension liabilities by making lump sum payments to certain retirees.

In Search of an Online Business Model

NYT Digital

NYT was an early mover in recognizing the potential—and the threat—of the internet. Its NYTimes.com website was launched in 1996 by a small team whose primary role was adapting content from the print edition for web display. As with most web-based media businesses, the revenue model was to provide content free and to attract paid advertising.

In 1999, New York Times Digital was established as a separate business unit within NYT, responsible not only for the websites of the *Times, Globe,* and *International Herald Tribune* but also for other online ventures. The new unit operated separately from the rest of the company—if NYT was to be a serious player in cyberspace, it believed that it needed to have the people, systems, and culture of a dot.com start-up rather than of a century-old newspaper.

User Subscriptions

Despite its success in attracting online visitors, the advertising revenues generated by the website were disappointing. As a result, the company became increasingly attracted to user charges. The first online subscription, launched in 2005, was Times Select, which charged an annual $49.95 fee for premium content and access to online archives. It generated a mere $10 million a year and was discontinued in 2007. In March 2011, NYT introduced its "metered access" model, which allowed web visitors free access to a limited number of articles each month, after which a paid subscription was required. By the end of 2011, there were 390,000 paid digital subscribers to subscription packages and, by the end of 2014, there were 910,000 digital-only subscribers.

Although digital advertising revenues grew—by 2014, digital accounted for 27% of NYT's advertising revenues. The growth in digital advertising failed to offset declining revenues from print advertising. Moreover, for all the progress that had been made in improving NYTimes.com, other news websites tended to lead in terms of innovation and new user features.

Some industry observers saw the hybrid model—print and digital editions—as doomed to failure. Rick Wartzman, Director of the Drucker Institute, argued: "Dead-tree editions must immediately yield to all-internet operations. The presses need to stop forever, with the delivery trucks shunted off to the scrapyard." He proposed the *Huffington Post* (owned by AOL) as the model for an online newspaper and suggested that if the *Los Angeles Times* went online only it could operate with a staff of 275 and earn a net margin of 10%.[7] Eric Schmidt, chairman of Google, argued only where content was unique would users be willing to pay—and most news was available from many online sources. The opportunity for online newspapers was to offer targeted advertising linked to customized content—that's where he saw Google becoming an essential partner for the newspaper companies.[8]

The 2014 Innovation Report

One of the main initiatives of the incoming CEO, Mark Thompson, was to initiate a fundamental rethink of NYT's digital strategy. In May 2014, a committee headed by Arthur Gregg Sulzberger, son of the chairman, delivered a report entitled *Innovation* that provided a probing diagnosis of NYT's weakness in "the art and science of getting our journalism to readers" and offering ideas for audience development.

Among the many challenges and opportunities the report identified were:

- Creating a fully digital newsroom. With Jeff Bezos funding advanced technological development at the *Washington Post,* BuzzFeed and Yahoo increasing their investments in news gathering and delivery, and new entrants such as Flipboard and First Look Media entering the business—NYT was at risk of disruption.

- Fewer and fewer readers are accessing the *Times* through the NYTimes.com home page. The NYT needed to take its journalism to the reader: at NYT "the story is done when you hit publish. At Huffington Post, the article begins its life when you hit publish."[9] Taking NYT journalism to readers' "digital door-steps" would require the news side and the business side of the company working together.

- Exploit the archive: "We have an archive of 14,723,933 articles extending back to 1851 that can be resurfaced in useful or timely ways. Yet we rarely think to mine our archive, largely because we are so focused on news and new features."[10]

- Experimentation—especially in finding new ways of packaging existing content that are conducive to sharing on social networks.

- Personalization: "using technology to ensure that the right stories are reaching the right readers in the right places and the right times. For example, letting you know when you are walking past a restaurant we have just reviewed."[11]

- User-generated content. The *Times'* audience is its "most underutilized resource. We can count the world's best-informed and most influential people among our readers. And we have a platform to which many of them would be willing and honored to contribute."[12]

Several of the digital initiatives launched in 2014 proved highly successful:

- Paid Posts were NYT's entry into "native advertising" and involved content created by NYT's T Brand Studio displayed on the company's own websites and mobile apps. For example, a Paid Post advertising Netflix's *Orange is the New Black* series featured an article on women prison inmates together with videos of interviews with women convicts.

- NYT Cooking was a mobile app allowing access to the *Times'* library of over 17,000 recipes.

- NYT Now offered a quick way for iPhone users, particularly younger readers, to access the news.

Organizational and Personnel Changes

The innovation report was a prelude to a flurry of top management and organizational changes at NYT. A week after the distribution of the report, the executive editor of the *Times*, Jill Abramson, was fired. She was replaced by Dean Baquet, the managing editor of the *Times*. One factor in her dismissal was her perceived opposition to the greater integration of the news and business sides of the NYT—a key objective of CEO Thompson, but contrary to the long tradition of the independence of the *Times'* journalism.

Her dismissal was followed by the elimination of about one hundred positions in the company's newsroom: "the most extraordinary collection of talent, of human knowledge that has ever left the *New York Times* in a single day," according to reporter David Dunlap.[13]

Under Dean Baquet the newsroom leadership was reorganized around four deputy editors. On both the news and the business side of the company, the major emphasis was on promoting and bringing in talent that could propel the *Times'* digital efforts—especially within mobile. Arthur Gregg Sulzberger, fifth-generation family member and prime author of the innovation report, was appointed head of strategy.

Looking to the Future

The innovation report produced in 2014 highlighted weaknesses in NYT's commitment to digital media and failings in the execution of its digital strategy. While pointing the way forward for the company, it also highlighted key differences in digital capabilities between NYT and some of its leading competitors that would be difficult to solve.

The combination of flexibility, innovation, and cost efficiency that characterized online news providers such as BuzzFeed, Vox, Yahoo News, and Huffington Post was difficult to match by established newspaper companies which had their long heritages to contend with. As the *Times* report observed: "The vast majority of our content is still published late in the evening, but our digital traffic is busiest early in the morning."

Similar observations were made in a report by the Duke Reporters' Lab, which examined the slow adoption in US newsrooms of digital tools that enable journalists to report and present their work.[14]

Even if NYT were successful in executing its digital strategy, would the revenues from subscriptions and advertising support the high costs of high-quality, global journalism? If not then NYT needed to explore alternative models that might support its financial viability. One possibility was that NYT could become a social enterprise: either explicitly, through enlisting charitable support or establishing an endowment that could support news gathering and analysis, or implicitly, through seeking a wealthy backer (as in the case of the *Washington Post* with Jeff Bezos).[15]

Alternatively, should NYT view itself less as a supplier of news to consumers and more as a supplier of customized intelligence to corporations and other organizations?

Notes

1. "The Incredible Shrinking *New York Times*," *Business Insider* (February 4, 2012).
2. "End Game of the *New York Times*," Ironfire Capital LLC (April 5, 2012).
3. The New York Times Company, 10-K report for 2014: 23.
4. Ibid.: 5.
5. Ibid.: 5.
6. New York Times Company, Inc., annual meeting of stockholders (April 23, 2009).
7. "Out with the Dead Wood for Newspapers," *Business Week* (March 10, 2009).
8. "View from the Top: Eric Schmidt of Google," *Financial Times* (May 21, 2009).
9. *New York Times* Innovation Report (May 2014): 24.
10. Ibid.: 28.
11. Ibid.: 37.
12. Ibid.: 49.
13. "In One Day, The Times Lost a World of Knowledge" *Times Insider* (December 16, 2014), http://www.nytimes.com/times-insider/2014/12/16/1925-in-one-day-the-times-lost-a-world-of-knowledge/?_r=1, accessed July 20, 2015.
14. Duke Reporters' Lab, "The Goat Must Be Fed: Why Digital Tools Are Missing in Most Newsrooms" (May 2014), www.goatmustbefed.com, accessed July 20, 2015.
15. See, for example, P. M. Abernathy, "A Nonprofit Model for the New York Times?" Duke Conference on Nonprofit Media (May 4–5, 2009), http://www2.sanford.duke.edu/nonprofitmedia/documents/dwcabernathyfinal.pdf, accessed July 20, 2015.

Case 16 Eni SpA: The Corporate Strategy of an International Energy Major

On May 13, 2015, Claudio Descalzi opened the annual meeting of shareholders' of Eni SpA. It had been little more than a year since the 59-year-old petroleum executive had been appointed as CEO of Italy's largest company. Yet, during that time a series of events had shaken Eni and raised troubling questions over its strategic direction.

Over two and a half decades, Eni had been transformed from a widely diversified, loss-making, state-owned company into an international oil and gas major with the highest market capitalization of any Italian company. Under Descalzi's three predecessors, Eni had developed a distinctive, well-integrated strategy that comprised a:

- near exclusive focus on oil and gas, with a primary focus on exploration and production, especially in Africa which accounted for more than half of Eni's oil and gas production;
- vertically integrated natural gas strategy where Eni's major gas fields were linked to its downstream markets in Europe by pipelines and LNG (liquefied natural gas) facilities.

During 2014, the security and profitability of Eni's upstream operations were threatened by a series of political and economic developments. The Arab Spring had unleashed chaos across much of North Africa and the Middle East. That year, instability and violence were especially acute in Libya and Egypt—Eni's two most important sources of hydrocarbons. Further problems for Eni ensued from the tensions between Europe and Russia that followed Russia's annexation of Crimea and intervention in Ukraine. Eni's relations with Russia extended back to the Soviet era: Eni was a key customer of Gazprom, a partner of Gazprom in several major pipeline projects, and was pursuing several upstream projects in Russia. In December 2014, Vladimir Putin announced the cancellation of the South Stream gas pipeline from Russia to Western Europe, which was to have been built by Eni's subsidiary Saipem.

In terms of its impact on Eni's bottom line, the most catastrophic event was the collapse of crude oil prices during the latter half of 2014. The effect of low oil prices became clear on April 28, 2015 when Descalzi presented Eni's financial results for

---

This case was prepared by Robert M. Grant. ©2015 Robert M. Grant.

the first quarter of the year. Net profit was 46% lower than in the year-ago quarter with upstream operating profit down by more than 70%.

The History of Eni

Mattei and Eni as a State-owned Enterprise, 1926–1992

In 1926, Italian Prime Minister Benito Mussolini established Agip (Azienda Generali Italiana Petroli) as a state-owned oil company. At the end of the Second World War, Enrico Mattei, a former partisan, was appointed head of Agip and instructed to dismantle this relic of fascist economic intervention. Contrary to instructions, Mattei renewed Agip's exploration efforts and, in 1948, discovered a substantial gas field in northern Italy's Po Valley. Mattei also took over the management of Snam SpA, the Italian gas distribution company and in 1953, the government merged Agip, Snam, and other state-owned energy activities to form Ente Nazionale Idrocarburi (Eni) with the task of "promoting and undertaking initiatives of national interest in the fields of hydrocarbons and natural gases." Mattei became its first chairman and chief executive. Eni's 36 subsidiaries extended well beyond oil and gas to include engineering services, chemicals, soap, and real estate.

Mattei's vision was for Eni to become an integrated, international oil and gas company that would ensure the independence of Italy's energy supplies and make a substantial contribution to Italy's postwar regeneration. In doing so he became a national hero: "He embodied great visions for postwar Italy—antifascism, the resurrection and rebuilding of the nation, and the emergence of the 'new man' who had made it himself, without the old boy network."[1]

Eni's international growth reflected Mattei's daring and resourcefulness. The international oil majors, which Mattei referred to as the "Seven Sisters," had tied up most of the world's known sources of oil in the Middle East and Latin America. The production-sharing agreement that Mattei signed with the Shah of Iran in 1957 marked the beginning of a fundamental shift of power from the oil majors to producer governments and established Eni as the *enfant terrible* of the oil business. The Iranian agreement was revolutionary. It created a jointly owned exploration and production company headed by an Iranian chairman and with the proceeds shared between Eni and the Iranian National Oil Company. This "Mattei formula" was replicated in Libya, Egypt, Tunisia, and Algeria. Mattei also concluded a barter deal to acquire crude oil from the Soviet Union.

At home, Mattei built political support within Italy. He rescued struggling companies to meet the political needs of government ministers and politicians. By 1962, Eni was "engaged in motels, highways, chemicals, soap, fertilizers, synthetic rubber, machinery, instruments, textiles, electrical generation and distribution, contract research, engineering and construction, publishing, nuclear power, steel pipes, cement, investment banking, and even education, to mention only a few."[2]

Mattei died in a plane crash on October 27, 1962 at the age of 56. He left a sprawling corporate empire whose strategy had been Mattei's own vision and whose integrating force had been Mattei's charisma and personal authority.[3] Without his leadership, power shifted to the politicians and Eni became an instrument of government economic, industrial, and employment policies: the boards and chief executives of Eni's subsidiaries were appointed by government.[4] Nevertheless, Eni continued to

FIGURE 1 The Development of Eni, 1985–2014

Note: BOE = barrels of oil-equivalent.
Source: Eni annual reports for various years.

expand its oil and gas interests, though financial performance remained weak: Eni earned significant profits only during 1988–1990 (Figure 1).

The Bernabè Era: Privatization and Transformation, 1992–1998

Pressured from the European Commission to cut the public-sector deficit and reduce state intervention, reformist Prime Minister Giuliano Amato granted Eni greater autonomy in 1992 and appointed Franco Bernabè, a 44-year-old economist, as CEO. Though lacking line management experience, Bernabè possessed a clear vision for Eni's future as a privatized, integrated energy company, shorn of its various diversified businesses.[5] The corruption scandal that swept Italy in 1993 resulted in Eni's chairman together with several board members and executives being arrested on corruption charges. Bernabè now seized the opportunity to launch a radical transformation of Eni.

Bernabè's corporate strategy was "to reduce Eni from being a loose conglomerate to concentrate on its core activity of energy."[6] During 1993, 73 Eni businesses were closed or sold and employment was cut by 15,000. Cost savings and asset sales resulted in a profit of almost $2 billion in 1994.[7]

Eni's initial public offering on the Milan, London, and New York stock exchanges in November 1995 marked the beginning of a new era. After four decades of looking to politicians in Rome for direction, Eni's top management had a new set of masters: the global investment community.

The new creed of shareholder value creation encouraged further refocusing: "Eni's strategy is to focus on businesses and geographical areas where, through size, technology, or cost structure, it has a leading market position. To this end, Eni intends to implement dynamic management of its portfolio through acquisitions, joint ventures, and divestments. Eni also intends to outsource non-strategic activities."[8] Investment was concentrated upon upstream activities with divestment of refining, marketing, and petrochemical assets.

The results were striking (see Figure 1). Between 1992 and 1998, Eni halved its debt, turned a loss into a substantial profit, and reduced employment by 46,000. In 1998, Bernabè was appointed to lead another newly privatized giant: Telecom Italia.

Eni's Strategy Under Mincato and Scaroni, 1998–2014

Eni's next two CEOs had very different backgrounds. Vittorio Mincato was a veteran line manager with 42 years' service at Eni. Paolo Scaroni, who succeeded Mincato in 2005, had pursued a diverse international career and had been CEO of British glassmaker Pilkington, and of Enel, Italy's dominant electricity supplier. Nevertheless, the two followed similar strategies for Eni.

Upstream Strategy: "Disciplined Growth"   Eni's primary strategic goal was to grow its production of oil and gas. Expanding oil and gas reserves and production was achieved primarily by organic growth—finding new oil and gas fields and more effectively exploiting existing reserves. Both CEOs were skeptical of growth through mergers and acquisitions and chose to limit themselves to small acquisitions that could be integrated within Eni's existing upstream activities. These included British Borneo (2000, €1.3 billion), LASMO (2000, €4.1 billion), Fortum's Norwegian oil and gas assets (2002, $1.1 billion), and Dominion Exploration and Production's Gulf of Mexico oilfields (2007, $4.8 billion), Maurel & Prom's Congo oilfields (2007, $1.4 billion), and Burren Energy (2008, €2.36 billion).

Between 1998 and 2014, Eni's capital expenditure more than tripled (in US$ terms) with 82% of it going into exploration and production (E&P). Major upstream projects included:

- Kazakhstan: Eni's giant Kashagan oilfield with upward of 15 billion barrels of oil was the world's biggest oil find of the past three decades and the most expensive to develop. Eni held a 16.8% stake and was the field's operator. As well as being Eni's biggest upstream project, it was also the most troublesome with huge cost overruns, an eight-year delay in start-up, and fierce disputes with the Kazakh government.
- In Russia, Eni built upon its status as a major, long-term customer for Soviet gas, to broaden its relationship with Gazprom (including joint ventures to build the Greenstream and South Stream gas pipelines) and initiated several exploration ventures with Rosneft.
- In Congo, Eni's approach was widely viewed as a model for oil company relations with host governments. In addition to onshore and offshore E&P projects, Eni built power plants using associated gas from the M'Boundi oilfield to provide the majority of Congo's electricity needs. Eni also initiated a biofuels plant, while the Eni Foundation established health clinics and a vaccination program for children.
- In Libya, Eni built on its status as Libya's oldest and biggest petroleum partner by extending its concessions to 2047 and maintaining production despite the chaos that followed the overthrow of the Gaddafi regime.

- In deep waters off Mozambique, Eni discovered in 2011–2013 the world's fourth-largest gas field with about 2,650 billion cubic meters (or 93.6 trillion cubic feet) of gas. Eni and its partner Anadarko were planning an LNG plant which would begin operations in 2018.
- Eni extended its E&P activities into Asia—including Australia, East Timor, Indonesia, and Pakistan.

A further feature of Eni's upstream strategy was its preference to take the role of operator in oil and gas fields in which it held a major stake. This allowed Eni greater control over development and costs and helped it to build its production capabilities.

As Eni extended the geographical extent of its gas fields beyond its core Mediterranean region, it looked increasingly to LNG as a means of monetizing these reserves. LNG allowed Eni to develop gas production far from its core European market and to expand its sales of gas to Asia. By 2014, Eni held equity interests in LNG trains in Egypt, Libya, Nigeria, Angola, Oman, Trinidad, Indonesia, and Australia.

Table 1 shows the geographical distribution of Eni's production and reserves. This distribution contrasted sharply with that of most other petroleum majors. Their major sources of hydrocarbons were North America and the Middle East. Eni's focus on Africa and the former Soviet Union reflected, first, its comparative youth and, second, its capacity to build cordial relations in countries that were viewed as difficult places to do business. Energy commentator Steve LeVine observed: "Italy's Eni continues to pioneer a successful path to survival in Big Oil's treacherous new world—get in bed, don't compete with the world's state-owned oil companies … Where its brethren bicker with Hugo Chavez and Vladimir Putin, Eni has found a comfortable embrace."[9] Others viewed Eni's willingness to engage with the autocratic and

TABLE 1   Eni's petroleum production and reserves by region, 2014[a]

	Hydrocarbon production[b]	Liquids production[c]	Gas production[d]	Reserves[e]
Italy	179	73	541	503
Rest of Europe	149	93	498	544
North Africa	528	253	1,536	1,756
Sub-Saharan Africa	307	230	418	1,320
Kazakhstan	96	52	181	1,069
Rest of Asia	135	37	297	290
Americas	114	84	205	960
Australia and Oceania	299	6	106	160
TOTAL	1,537	828	3,782	6,602

Notes:
[a]Production/reserves data include both consolidated subsidiaries and equity-accounted entities.
[b]Thousands of barrels of oil equivalent per day.
[c]Thousands of barrels per day.
[d]Millions of cubic feet per day.
[e]Millions of barrels of oil equivalent (includes both developed and undeveloped reserves).
Source: Eni 20-F report for 2014.

unrepresentative governments of Algeria, Nigeria, Angola, Kazakhstan, and Russia as opportunistic and unprincipled. Scaroni's response was matter-of-fact: "We deal with countries that have gas. If Switzerland had gas, we would deal with Switzerland." At the root of Eni's flexible approach to host government relationships was its recognition that the balance of power had shifted in favor of the producer countries: "The fact is, the oil is theirs … If you are looked at as a partner, you are allowed to exploit their oil; if not, you are pushed aside."[10] A key component of Eni's engagement with host countries was investing in electricity supplies. In Nigeria, the Okpai power plant and electricity from other industrial plants supplied 10.5 million customers.

Downstream: Building the European Gas Business   In possessing a large downstream gas business, Eni was unique among the majors—though vertically integrated in oil, gas distribution had historically been in the hands of regulated monopolies: state-owned companies such as British Gas and Gaz de France in Europe or regulated local utilities in the US.

Eni's downstream gas and power business (it had forward integrated into producing electricity from its gas supplies) was a consequence of Eni's historical roots in natural gas and its belief that its integrated gas chain was a key competitive advantage. As Paolo Scaroni observed:

> Eni has a very distinctive way of dealing with the gas in Europe. We are both upstream with our E&P division, and downstream in distribution, transport and sales. Just to give you an idea of how integrated these two divisions are, 35% of our equity gas is sold through our Gas and Power division, so we are already where most of our competitors in the midstream and downstream business of gas would like to be: integrated upstream, and generating our sales from our own equity gas … Then of course we have a wide portfolio of sourcing of gas, which goes from Algeria to Libya, Poland, Norway, and of course, Russia … There is no other player that has such a privileged position in the European market.[11]

Marco Alvera, in charge of gas supplies, added further explanation of these advantages:

> Our gas, be it equity or contracted, comes from ten different countries. This gives us considerable diversity and security of supply. Second, we can leverage on a growing integrated LNG business. Third, we have attractive contractual structures and terms. Fourth, we have access to a very large set of transportation and storage assets across Europe from north to south and east to west. Finally, we have significant commercial flexibility that allows us to vary, on a daily basis, the amounts of gas produced or drawn from each of our contracts. Summing up, I would say that no other operator in the European gas market can claim to have the same scale and asset backed flexibility as Eni's Gas and Power division.[12]

International pipelines played a key role in linking Eni's gas supplies with its Italian distribution network. The Trans Austria Pipeline (TAP) brought Russian gas from Slovakia; the Trans Europa Naturgas Pipeline (TENP) carried North Sea gas from the Netherlands; the Trans-Mediterranean pipeline brought Algerian gas; the Greenstream pipeline linked Libya to Italy; the Bluestream pipeline, owned jointly with Gazprom, linked Russia and Turkey across the Black Sea. The South Stream pipeline, begun by Eni and Gazprom in 2012, was intended to take Russian gas to Germany and Italy. Saipem, an oilfield services, engineering, and construction company, 43% owned by Eni, played a key role in building Eni's subsea pipelines.

The key threat to Eni's integrated gas strategy was the European Commission's goal of a competitive European gas market. Eni was required to reduce its share of the Italian downstream gas market to 50% and divest its gas transmission, storage, and distribution. These were transferred to Snam, which was separated from Eni in 2012. Eni's ownership and operation of international gas pipelines were also targeted by the European Commission: Eni was forced to sell its stakes in the TAP and TENP pipelines.

While divesting its gas storage and distribution system in Italy, Eni acquired equity stakes in downstream gas companies in Spain (Union Fenosa Gas), Germany (GVS), Portugal (Galp Energia), Belgium (Distrigas and Nuon), Hungary, Greece, and Croatia.

Refining, Marketing, and Chemicals   Downstream oil was a different story. Unlike most other oil and gas majors, the refining and marketing of oil products was a comparatively minor part of Eni's overall business, accounting for a mere 5% of Eni's fixed assets. Refining and marketing were heavily focused on Italy, where Eni held 31% of the market for fuels. Under Mincato and Scaroni, Eni shrank its refining capacity, closed retail outlets, and exited from downstream markets outside of Italy. Despite cost cutting and asset sales, Eni's refining and marketing sector lost money during 2009–2013.

Chemicals, where Eni lacked scale and distinctive technological advantages, were an even greater challenge. Chemicals had been a loss maker for Eni for decades. Despite creating a business into a separate chemical company, Polimeri Europa, Eni had been unable to find a buyer. In 2012, Eni embarked upon a new strategy for its chemicals business focusing on specialty chemicals and seeking licensing, alliances, and joint ventures. Bio-chemicals—including plant-based plastics, lubricants, and additives—were one target area. To emphasize the strategy shift, Polimeri was renamed Versalis.

Eni's vertical chains for oil and gas are shown in Figure 2.

Organizational Changes   Both Mincato and Scaroni sought to make Eni a more integrated corporation. The first stage of this was transforming it from a holding company into a multidivisional corporation with three key divisions: exploration and production, gas and power, and refining and marketing. The new structure permitted stronger corporate-level functions, especially finance and human resources.

Achieving greater integration involved stronger financial control, more rigorous internal auditing, and risk management procedures, establishing a code of ethics, and company-wide procedures for sustainability reporting.

To forge a clearer stronger identity and image for Eni, the slogan "Eni's Way" was adopted as the company's tagline in advertising and corporate communication. The key themes that "Eni's Way" conveyed were technological strength, a spirit of adventure, and social and environmental responsibility.

The organizational changes continued under Descalzi with a further integration across the divisions and centralization of functional areas. The divisional structure was broken up and reorganized around capabilities (Figure 3).

FIGURE 2 Eni's vertical chains in oil and gas

OIL (millions of tonnes)

NATURAL GAS (billion cubic meters)

Source: Eni Fact Book.

FIGURE 3 Eni's organizational structure, March 2015

Source: www.eni.com/en_IT/company/organisation-chart/organisation-chart.shtml.

The Petroleum Industry in 2015

The Industry Sectors

The petroleum sector comprises two major segments: upstream and downstream. Upstream undertakes the exploration and production of oil and gas; in the downstream, gas and oil have separate value chains. In oil the primary activities are refining and marketing (where marketing includes both wholesale and retail distribution of fuels). In gas the primary downstream activities are distribution and marketing. Linking upstream and downstream are mid-stream activities: transportation of oil and gas and trading.

Exploration and Production The rise in the price of crude from around $22 in 2002 to over $100 during 2010–14, reinforced the conventional wisdom that industry's primary source of profit was oil and gas production. During 2006–2013, the majors earned a return on capital employed in E&P at least double what they earned in refining and marketing. Although upstream activities accounted for only one-fifth of their revenues, they contributed about three-quarters of overall profits during this period. In response, all the majors greatly increased the proportion of their capital investment toward E&P.

High oil prices were the result of rising world demand—especially from India and China—and limits on oil production—not because of declining reserves—but because of political instability in Libya, Egypt, Iraq, and Nigeria and underinvestment in Venezuela, Russia, and Mexico. Production quotas imposed by the Organization of Petroleum Exporting Countries (OPEC) also helped to support prices. However,

FIGURE 4 The price of Brent crude, 1987–2015 ($ per barrel)

the costs of finding and developing oil and gas fields were also rising, causing upstream profitability to decline during 2011–2013.

Between June 2014 and January 2015, the price of Brent crude declined from $115 to $47 per barrel (Figure 4). The principal cause was a remarkable expansion in US oil production: as a result of horizontal drilling and hydraulic fracturing, increased output of US "tight" oil would result in the US displacing Saudi Arabia as the world's biggest oil producer during 2015 (Table 2). In response to falling oil prices, the Saudis abandoned their traditional role as "swing producer" and refrained from cutting production to support prices.

The result was a transformation in the finances of the oil majors. During the first quarter of 2015, the pretax profits of the majors declined by between 32 and 63%.

To contain rising upstream costs, the oil and gas companies had outsourced more and more of their E&P activities. Drilling, seismic surveys, rig design, platform construction, and oilfield maintenance were increasingly undertaken by oilfield service companies. As these companies developed their expertise and their proprietary technologies, and grew through mergers and acquisitions, so sector leaders such as Schlumberger, Baker Hughes, Halliburton, and Diamond Offshore Drilling emerged as powerful players within the petroleum industry.

Refining and Marketing The main refined products in order of importance were: gasoline, diesel fuel, aviation fuel, heating oil, liquefied petroleum gas (LPG), and petrochemical feedstock (e.g., naphtha). Historically, downstream was less profitable than upstream: in their refining and marketing businesses, the majors typically earned rates of return that barely covered their costs of capital. As a result, all the majors had divested refining and marketing assets to concentrate increasingly on their upstream businesses (Table 3).

TABLE 2 Oil and gas production and reserves by country

	Oil production (mn barrels/day)			Gas production (bn cubic meters)			Oil reserves (bn barrels)	Gas reserves (tn cubic meters)
	2013	2007	1991	2013	2007	1991	2013	2013
Saudi Arabia	11.5	10.4	8.8	103	76	35	266	8.2
Russia	10.8	10.0	9.3	605	607	600	93	31.3
US	10.0	6.9	9.1	688	546	510	44	9.3
China	4.2	3.7	2.8	117	69	15	18	3.3
Canada	3.9	3.3	2.0	155	184	105	174	2.0
Iran	3.6	4.4	3.5	167	112	26	157	33.8
UAE	3.6	2.9	2.6	56	49	24	98	6.1
Kuwait	3.1	2.6	0.2	16	13	1	102	1.8
Iraq	3.1	2.1	0.3	1	1	n.a.	150	3.6
Mexico	2.9	3.5	3.1	57	46	28	11	0.3
Venezuela	2.6	2.6	2.5	28	29	22	298	5.6
Norway	2.1	2.6	1.9	109	90	27	9	2.0
Nigeria	1.8	2.4	1.9	36	28	4	37	5.1
Brazil	2.1	1.8	0.8	21	14	6	16	0.5
Qatar	2.0	1.3	0.5	159	63	12	25	24.7
Kazakhstan	1.8	1.5	0.5	19	15	4	30	1.5
Angola	1.8	1.7	0.2	—	—	—	13	—
Algeria	1.6	2.0	1.4	79	83	53	12	4.5

Notes:
mn = million; bn = billion; tn = trillion.
n.a. = not available.
Source: BP Statistical Review of World Energy, 2008 and 2014.

The main problem in refining was excess capacity. Demand for refined products was declining in Europe and North America and new refining capacity was coming on stream in the Middle East and Asia as a result of downstream investments by national oil companies (NOCs). Excess capacity and thin margins were also the norm in gasoline retailing.

Downstream Gas and Power Unlike Eni, whose origins lay in gas rather than oil, the other petroleum majors were relative newcomers to natural gas. The rising demand for natural gas caused all the majors to reorient their upstream activities toward gas, while the privatization and liberalization of downstream gas and power markets offered opportunities to market gas to end users and to become generators of electricity. However, the downstream gas and power did not offer the petroleum majors rates of return comparable to those earned upstream.

Chemicals Petrochemicals displayed many of the same structural features as oil refining: capital-intensive processes producing commodity products, many competitors, and a tendency toward excess capacity (mainly resulting from new investment by Asian and Middle Eastern producers). Competitive advantage in chemicals depended upon scale economies, technological advantages (such as patented products and

TABLE 3 Capital expenditures among the majors, 2003–2011

	Average annual capex ($billion)			Capex on E&P as % of total		
	2003–2007	2008–2011	2012–2014	2003–2007	2008–2011	2012–2014
ExxonMobil	17.0	30.5	38.4	78.2	82.6	80.5
Royal Dutch/Shell	16.4	26.6	40.6	68.0	78.2	83.6
BP	17.9	24.9	23.5	69.3	79.1	81.3
Total	12.2	23.9	26.0	72.3	65.2	69.2
Chevron	10.8	21.9	35.0	77.0	90.2	92.1
Conoco Phillips	11.4	11.3	16.3	57.9	86.7	98.0[a]
Eni	9.6	16.1	15.7	65.7	69.8	90.3

Note:
[a]Estimated
Source: Company annual reports.

processes), and low costs of feedstock. Lower feedstock costs gave Middle Eastern and North American producers a big advantage over European producers. Among the oil and gas majors there were two distinct views about chemicals. Some, like Eni and BP, saw chemicals as a fundamentally unattractive industry and believed that chemical plants were better run by chemical companies. Others (including ExxonMobil, Shell, and Total) viewed chemicals as part of their core business and believed that integration between refining and petrochemicals offered them a cost advantage.

The Companies

The petroleum sector featured three main types of company:

- The *oil and gas majors* were characterized by their age, size, international scope, and vertical integration. Between 1998 and 2002, a wave of mergers and acquisitions resulted in the emergence of an elite group of "super majors" comprising ExxonMobil, BP, Royal Dutch Shell, Chevron, ConocoPhillips, and Total (Table 4). The extent of economic benefits from these mergers and acquisitions remains unclear. The costs of developing oil and gas fields and building LNG facilities were huge, but typically these were undertaken as joint ventures, not by single firms. The main benefits of a large portfolio of upstream projects were spreading risks and infrastructure costs and accelerating learning. However, there was little evidence that scale economies continued up to the size of companies such as ExxonMobil or Shell. The majors differed in the geographical and sector balance of their businesses. Although all the majors had shifted their capital expenditure upstream, only ConocoPhillips had gone as far as spinning off its downstream businesses entirely.
- The *NOCs* were the state-owned enterprises created by producer governments to manage their countries' petroleum reserves. In terms of production and reserves, they dominated the industry (Table 5). Most had been created

TABLE 4 Mergers and acquisitions among the petroleum majors, 1998–2013[a]

Major oil companies, 1995	Revenues, 1995 ($billion)	Date merged	Major oil companies, 2013	Revenues, 2013 ($billion)
Exxon	124	1999	Exxon Mobil Corp.	392.6
Mobil	75			
Royal Dutch Petroleum	66			
Shell Transport & Trading	44	2004	Royal Dutch Shell	448.1
Enterprise Oil	1	2002		
British Petroleum	56	1998	BP	337.2
Amoco	28	2000		
Arco	16			
Chevron	31	2001	Chevron	208.4
Texaco	36			
Total	28	1999	Total	223.4
Petrofina	18	2000		
Elf Aquitaine	37			
Conoco	15	2002	ConocoPhillips	54.4
Philips Petroleum	13	2001		
Tosco	14			
Eni	36		Eni	160.0
Repsol	21	1999	Repsol	77.6
YPF	5	(demerged 2012)		

Note:
[a]Only includes acquisitions of companies with revenues exceeding $1 billion.
Source: Reports in the financial press.

between 1965 and 1982 by nationalizing the assets of the majors. During 2000–2015, the relationship between the majors and the NOCs shifted substantially. High crude prices and growing nationalism among oil-producing countries resulted in the desire for greater control over their countries' hydrocarbon resources and bigger shares of production and revenues. In Venezuela, Bolivia, and Russia, foreign oil companies were forced to transfer upstream assets to the national government or to NOCs. Elsewhere higher taxes were imposed and participation agreements renegotiated. Different NOCs followed different strategies. Petróleo Brasileiro SA (Petrobras), Statoil, PetroChina and CNOOC, became important international players. Others, such as Saudi Aramco, Kuwait Petroleum, and Petróleos de Venezuela SA (PDVSA), invested heavily in refining and petrochemical businesses. With the help of oil service companies, many NOCs became less dependent upon the majors for technology and know-how.

- *Independents*: At all vertical levels, specialist companies played an important role. In exploration and production, companies such as Devon Energy, Anadarko Petroleum, Cairn Energy, and Woodside Petroleum were important players, especially in exploring frontier regions. Their operational and financial success contradicted the arguments of the majors that huge size was an essential requirement in the petroleum industry. In refining, independent refiners such as Valero in the US grew as the majors sold off downstream

TABLE 5 The world's top-30 petroleum companies by size of reserves

Company	State ownership	Reserves (million BOE)
National Iranian Oil Company (Iran)	100%	315,757
Saudi Arabian Oil Company (Saudi Arabia)	100%	307,143
Petróleos de Venezuela SA (Venezuela)	100%	241,744
Qatar General Petroleum Corporation (Qatar)	100%	178,508
Iraq National Oil Company (Iraq)	100%	135,503
Abu Dhabi National Oil Company (UAE)	100%	128,439
Kuwait Petroleum Corporation (Kuwait)	100%	112,269
Nigerian National Petroleum Corporation (Nigeria)	100%	69,145
National Oil Company (Libya)	100%	55,767
Sonatrach (Algeria)	100%	39,379
OAO Gazprom (Russia)	50%	29,261
OAO Rosneft (Russia)	75%	22,885
PetroChina Co. Ltd (China)	87%	22,475
BP Corporation (United Kingdom)	0%	17,829
Egyptian General Petroleum Corporation (Egypt)	100%	17,597
Exxon Mobil Corporation (United States)	0%	17,420
Petróleos Mexicanos (Mexico)	100%	13,319
OAO Lukoil (Russia)	0%	13,029
Royal Dutch/Shell (Netherlands)	0%	12,585
Petróleo Brasileiro SA (Brazil)	37%	12,531
Sonangol (Angola)	100%	11,370
Chevron Corporation (United States)	0%	10,648
Petroleum Development Oman LLC (Oman)	100%	10,628
Total (France)	5%	10,395
ConocoPhillips (United States)	0%	6,733
Eni (Italy)	30%	6,680
Petróleos de Ecuador (Ecuador)	90%	6,558
Petronas (Malaysia)	100%	5,986
Statoil (Norway)	67%	5,195
Suncor Energy Inc. (Canada)	0%	4,920

Note:
BOE: barrels of oil equivalent.
Source: "OGJ 200/100," *Oil & Gas Journal* (October 1, 2011).

assets. (In the Appendix, Table A4 lists the world's largest oil and gas companies with publicly traded shares.)

Vertical Integration Strategies

Vertical integration throughout the value chain from exploration through to retailing refined products was a key feature of the strategies of majors. The rationale for vertical integration had been to secure supply and market outlets. However, in the case of oil, the development of a global infrastructure of transportation and storage, competitive markets for both crude and refined products, and the presence of specialist companies at every stage of the value chain had reduced (if not eliminated) the advantages of vertical integration. Most majors remained vertically integrated, but few had close operational linkages between their oilfields and refineries, and all had withdrawn from some stages of the value chain (e.g., outsourcing oilfield services and marine transportation). When ConocoPhillips spun off its downstream businesses into a separate company, Phillips 66, in 2011, CEO Jim Mulva stated:

> Looking forward over time, we believe that pureplay companies will deliver greater value because the complex, integrated business model is no longer a strategic advantage in gaining resource and market access…repositioning into two separate companies will be the best way to compete and grow and to attract, retain and develop talent.[13]

In gas the situation was different. The physical difficulties of transporting and storing gas meant that monetizing gas reserves required dedicated investments in transportation, liquefaction, and storage to link production to consumption. The lack of an integrated global market in gas was indicated by the wide geographical price differences—prices in Asia were often five times those in the US. The desire to exploit their upstream gas resulted in all the majors making substantial investment in LNG. Most had also integrated further downstream through directly supplying large industrial customers or establishing relationships with gas marketing companies.

Technology and Knowledge Management

The quest for reserves had taken the petroleum majors to the Arctic and the depths of the ocean. It had encouraged companies to develop enhanced recovery techniques in order to extend the lives of mature fields. It resulted in the production of synthetic crudes from sulfur-heavy petroleum, from coal, and from tar sands and oil shale. Gas-to-liquids technologies were being deployed to produce gasoline from natural gas.

The result was increased dependence upon technology. Nevertheless, investments in R & D by the majors were modest (less than 0.3% of revenues in recent years). Increasingly, the majors outsourced technology-intensive activities to other companies. Upstream, the technological leaders in directional drilling, 4-D seismic modeling, and "intelligent oilfield" management were generally the oil service companies, and Schlumberger in particular.

However, the knowledge requirements of the petroleum business extended beyond technology. The technical, logistical, political, and financial complexities of the business meant that a critical driver of competitive advantage was the ability to learn from experience and transfer that learning throughout the company. By the early years of the new century, all the leading oil and gas companies had adopted some form of knowledge management to increase the efficiency of their knowledge capture, storage, and utilization. Many of the new knowledge management systems relied heavily on web-based technology, distributed computing, and digital wireless communication to enhance the speed and quality of decision making.

TABLE 6   Key elements of Eni's strategic plan for 2015–2018

Strategic guidelines to use and develop our assets	Assets for delivering sustainable value	Principles for delivering sustainable value
Profitable, selective upstream growth Focus on core areas Partnership with NOCs Reduction in time to market Operatorship Gas supply contracts renegotiation Development of green fuels and chemical products Trading in energy commodities Customer retention in gas and fuel markets Efficiency and cost control Reduction of capacity in downstream businesses.	Solid and competitive resource base Conventional oil and gas assets with low breakeven Skills in exploration activities and upstream operations Gas supply portfolio aligned to market conditions Large and loyal customer base Bio-refineries and green chemical plants Eni brand	Integrity in business management Support countries' development Excellence in conducting operations Innovation in developing competitive solutions to address complexity Inclusiveness of Eni's people and development of know-how and skills Integration of financial and non-financial issues in the company's plans and processes

Source: "Eni's Business Model," *Eni Fact Book 2014*: 10.

The Outlook for Eni in 2015

Despite the tumultuous events of 2014 and early 2015 and the profound challenges they presented for Eni's long-term strategy, Claudio Descalzi's presentation of Eni's strategy for 2015–2019 on March 13, 2015 gave little indication of any major rethink of Eni's strategic direction. Apart from reducing capital expenditure and accelerating cost reduction and asset sales, the broad thrust of Eni's strategy was maintained—including its heavy emphasis on the upstream sector, its focus on Africa, and its commitment to vertical integration in gas. Some of the key components of Eni's strategy for 2015–2018 are shown in Table 6. Eni's projections for 2015–2018 included a rise in the price of crude oil from $55 to $90 a barrel and Eni sustaining a growth of petroleum output of 3.5% each year (which would continue at more than 3.5% to 2024). In view of the uncertain geopolitical situation, continuing growth in the production of tight oil and gas, and the depressed state of Eni's home market, were these forecasts unduly optimistic, and did Eni need to reconsider the fundamentals of its strategic direction?

Appendix

TABLE A1   Eni SpA: Financial highlights, 2008–2014 (€billion unless otherwise indicated)

	2008	2009	2010	2011	2012	2013	2014
Exchange rate ($/€)	1.473	1.394	1.326	1.393	1.285	1.328	1.329
Net sales from operations	108.1	83.2	98.5	109.6	127.1	114.7	109.8
Operating profit	18.5	12.1	16.1	17.4	15.2	8.9	7.9
Adjusted operating profit	21.5	13.0	17.5	17.9	20.7	12.6	11.6
Net profit	8.8	4.4	6.3	6.9	7.8	5.1	1.3
Adjusted net profit	10.2	5.2	6.9	7.0	7.3	4.4	3.7
Net cash from operating activities	21.8	11.1	14.7	14.4	12.4	11.0	15.1
Capital expenditures	14.6	13.7	13.9	13.4	13.5	12.8	12.2
R & D expenditures	0.32	0.29	0.29	0.27	—	—	—
Total assets at year-end	116.7	117.5	131.9	142.9	140.2	138.3	146.2
Shareholders' equity (including minority interests)	44.4	46.1	51.2	55.5	62.4	61.0	62.2
Short- and long-term debt	20.8	24.8	27.8	29.6	24.2	25.6	25.9
Leverage	0.38	0.46	0.47	0.46	0.24	0.25	0.22
Net capital employed	66.9	73.1	81.8	88.4	78.2	76.6	75.9
Average share price (€)	21.4	16.6	16.4	16.0	17.2	17.6	17.8
Adjusted ROACE (%)	15.7	12.3	16.0	17.2	17.6	13.5	–

Source: Reports in the financial press.

TABLE A2   Eni's operating performance, 2008–2014

	2008	2009	2010	2011	2012	2013	2014
Employees	71,714	71,461	73,768	72,574	77,838	82,289	84,405
Proved hydrocarbon reserves (million BOE)	6,600	6,571	6,843	7,086	7,166	6,535	6,602
Reserve life index (years)	10.0	10.2	10.3	12.3	11.5	11.1	11.3
Hydrocarbon production (thousand BOE/day)	1,797	1,769	1,815	1,581	1,701	1,619	1,598
Worldwide gas sales (bn m³)	104.2	103.7	97.1	96.8	95.3	93.2	89.2
Finding and development cost per BOE ($)	n.a.	28.9	19.3	18.8	17.4	19.2	21.5
Electricity sold (TWH)	29.9	34.0	39.5	40.3	42.6	35.1	33.6
Refinery throughput (mn tonnes)	35.8	34.6	34.8	32.0	30.0	27.4	25.0
Refinery capacity (m barrels/day)	544	747	757	767	767	787	617
Sales of refined products (mn tonnes)	50.7	45.6	46.8	45.0	48.3	43.5	44.4
Retail sales (mn tonnes)	12.7	12.0	11.7	11.4	10.9	9.7	9.2
Number of service stations	5,956	5,986	6,167	6,287	6,384	6,386	6,220
Av. service station throughput (m liters/year)	2,502	2,477	2,353	2,206	2,064	1,828	1,725
Engineering and construction: orders acquired (€bn)	13.9	9.9	12.9	12.5	13.4	10.7	18.0
Order backlog (€bn)	19.1	18.7	20.5	20.4	19.7	17.5	22.1

Source: Reports in the financial press.

TABLE A3   Eni: Financial performance by business segment, 2010–2014 (€million unless otherwise indicated)

	2010	2011	2012	2013	2014
Sales					
E&P	29,479	29,121	35,874	31,264	28,488
Gas & Power	27,806	33,093	36,198	32,212	28,250
Refining & Marketing	43,190	51,219	62,531	57,238	56,153
Versalis	6,143	6,491	6,418	5,859	5,284
Engineering & Construction	10,581	11,834	12,799	11,598	12,873
Operating profit					
E&P	13,866	15,887	18,470	14,643	11,551
Gas & Power	896	(326)	(3,125)	(2,967)	186
Refining & Marketing	149	(273)	(1,264)	(1,492)	(2,229)
Versalis	(86)	(424)	(681)	(725)	(704)
Engineering & Construction	1,302	1,422	1,453	(98)	18
Operating margin (%)					
E&P	47.7	54.6	51.5	46.8	40.5
Gas & Power	3.2	(1.0)	(8.6)	(9.2)	0.6
Refining & Marketing	(0.3)	(0.5)	(2.0)	(2.6)	(4.0)
Versalis	(1.3)	(6.5)	(10.9)	(13.0)	(13.2)
Engineering & Construction	20.5	20.4	19.7	17.5	22.1
Net capital employed					
E&P	37,636	42,024	42,369	45,699	47,629
Gas & Power	12,931	12,367	10,597	9,201	7,776
Refining & Marketing	8,321	9,188	8,871	7,998	7,993
Versalis	1,978	2,252	2,557	2,656	2,973
Engineering & Construction	7,610	8,217	9,937	9,554	8,644
Operating profit/Capital employed (%)					
E&P	37.0	37.9	43.6	32.0	24.2
Gas & Power	7.0	2.9	(29.5)	(32.3)	2.4
Refining & Marketing	1.8	(2.9)	(14.2)	(18.6)	27.9
Versalis	(4.3)	(18.8)	(26.6)	(29.3)	(23.7)
Engineering & Construction	14.6	17.3	14.6	(1.0)	0.2

Source: Reports in the financial press.

TABLE A4   World's leading publicly traded oil and gas companies, 2014 (ranked by stock market capitalization)

Company	Country	Market value ($billion)	Sales ($billion)	ROA (%)
ExxonMobil	US	357	376	9.3
PetroChina	China	335	333	4.5
Chevron	US	201	192	7.2
Royal Dutch Shell	Netherlands	195	420	4.2
BP	UK	121	353	1.2
Sinopec	China	121	428	3.3
Total	France	120	211	1.8
ConocoPhillips	US	81	52	5.4
Eni	Italy	64	146	1.0
CNOOC	China	64	45	9.2
Gazprom	Russia	63	158	6.7
Occidental Petroleum	US	59	19	1.1
Statoil	Norway	58	121	2.7
Indian Oil	India	52	74	2.6
Rosneft	Russia	51	129	6.0
Suncor Energy Inc.	Canada	45	36	3.5
Petrobras	Brazil	44	144	(2.5)
Lukoil	Russia	44	121	4.3
BG Group	UK	44	19	(1.8)
PTT PCL	Thailand	44	87	3.1
Reliance Industries	India	43	72	4.8
Phillips 66	US	43	150	9.9
Canadian Natural Resources	Canada	35	17	6.9
Chesapeake	US	35	20	2.6
Ecopetrol	Colombia	34	34	6.4
Husky Energy	Canada	32	22	3.1
Valero	US	31	131	7.5
Anadarko Petroleum	US	29	16	
Repsol YPF	Spain	27	61	3.5
Devon Energy	US	26	18	3.1
Inpex	Japan	24	12	
Surgutneftegas	Russia	24	27	11.8
Marathon	US	21	12	8.1
Oil & Natural Gas	India	21	29	7.4
Woodside Petroleum	Australia	19	7	10.1
EOG Resources	US	16	17	8.4
YPF	Argentina	16	17	4.7
Hess	US	21	14	6.0

Source: "The World's Biggest Companies," *Forbes* (2015).

Notes

1. D. Yergin, *The Prize* (Simon & Shuster, New York, 1992): 23.
2. Ibid.: 23.
3. *L'Eni di Fronte a un Bivio* (Eni SpA, 2002).
4. D. Votaw, *The Six-Legged Dog: Mattei and ENI: A Study in Power* (University of California Press, Berkeley, CA, 1964): 71.
5. *Franco Bernabè at Eni*, Harvard Business School Case 9-498-034 (April 7, 1998).
6. "Eni Savors the Taste of Freedom," *Financial Times* (June 9, 1994).
7. Eni SpA, Securities and Exchange Commission, Form 20F (1996).
8. Ibid.: 3.
9. S. LeVine, *The Oil and the Glory: The Pursuit of Empire and Fortune on the Caspian Sea* (New York: Random House, 2007).
10. "How Italy's ENI Vastly Boosted Oil Output," *Business Week* (April 20, 2009).
11. Eni SpA Gas seminar conference call (December 1, 2006).
12. Eni SpA Gas seminar conference call (December 1, 2006).
13. "Creating Two Leading Energy Companies," *Spirit Magazine* (ConocoPhillips, 3rd quarter, 2011): 6.

Case 17 American Apparel: Vertically Integrated in Downtown LA

The dismissal of American Apparel's founder, Dov Charney, as CEO in June 2014 did little to stem the company's decline in financial performance that had begun in 2010 (Figure 1). American Apparel's share price reflected the gloom that had engulfed the company (Figure 2).

Paula Schneider had been appointed CEO at the beginning of 2015. The turn-around strategy launched by the new management team emphasized operational improvements and substituting formal internal processes for Dov Charney's free-wheeling management style. Initiatives included:

- aligning American Apparel's product range with customer preferences;
- closing unprofitable stores;
- expanding American Apparel's online presence, especially through opening online stores in additional countries (including China);
- growing wholesale sales;
- improving production planning;
- improving manufacturing capabilities in order to be faster in introducing new products and reacting to changing trends;
- upgrading distribution logistics to improve wholesale, retail, and online order fulfillment.[1]

However, American Apparel's results for the first half of 2015 (Table 1) revealed a continuing deterioration of the company's performance. On October 5, 2015 American Apparel filed for Chapter 11 bankruptcy protection in order to implement a financial restructuring. The existing stock, including that of Mr. Charney, would be wiped out and creditors would swap their debt for new equity.

Under Dov Charney's leadership, American Apparel had defied the conventional wisdom of the rag trade. Instead of outsourcing production to low-wage countries, it had followed a Los Angeles-based, vertical integration strategy. Charney believed that the higher costs of manufacturing in the US could be offset by the price premium from superior quality, styling, and image, and by the benefits of speed to market.

CEO Paula Schneider had initially embraced American Apparel's vertical integration strategy: "The beauty of what we have is we have all of our own manufacturing ... The competitive advantage that American Apparel has is there is no one else that

This case was written by Robert M. Grant assisted by Ellen A. Drost and Stephen J. J. McGuire. ©2015 Robert M. Grant.

FIGURE 1   American Apparel sales and profits, 2005–2014 ($million)

can do what we do. We have it right in our house. We have the ability to look at what's selling … and make sure we create more of it or different colors of it or … sister versions of it, that then can drive market share."[2]

However, the opportunity for strategic change that financial restructuring under Chapter 11 offered, Schneider wondered whether American Apparel should follow almost every other US supplier of leisure apparel by outsourcing production to contract manufacturers in Asia or Central America.

The T-Shirt Business

T-shirts, like denim jeans, are quintessential items of American clothing. About 1.4 billion cotton T-shirts are sold in North America annually with a retail value of about $20 billion. Originally underwear garments, T-shirts are the most common summer outerwear garment for weekend Americans. The designs and words they carry are statements of personal identity, indicating affiliation with a sports team, college, political movement, religion, charity, or specific social event. Yet despite the T-shirt's

FIGURE 2   American Apparel share price, March 2006 to May 2015 ($)

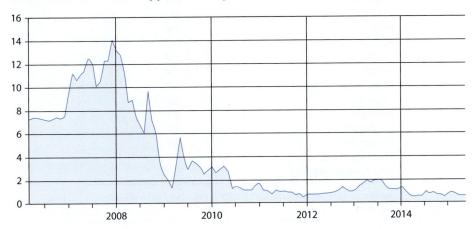

TABLE 1 American Apparel: Financial results for the first six months of 2015 and 2014 ($million)

	2015	2014
Net sales	258.7	299.5
Cost of sales	149.6	145.1
Gross profit	109.0	154.4
Selling and distribution expenses	90.9	106.5
General and administrative expenses	50.9	52.0
Operating profit/(loss)	(35.9)	(4.9)
Interest expense	20.2	20.0
Net income/(loss)	(45.8)	(21.7)

Source: American Apparel Inc. 10-Q Report, August 17, 2015.

place in American culture, the vast majority are imported (Table 2). Major US producers, such as Gildan Activewear, Hanesbrands, and Delta Apparel, supply the US from plants in Central America and the Caribbean. Many imported T-shirts are made from cotton grown in the US, the world's largest exporter of cotton fiber.[3] The average import price of a T-shirt in 2013 was $3.10. Imports from low-cost overseas production centers have caused employment in the US garment industry to shrink from 1.4 million in 1974 to 151,800 in 2011.

The US T-shirt market features a wide variety of suppliers. At the wholesale level, blank T-shirts are sold by major suppliers (such as Gildan Activewear, Hanesbrands, Russell Athletic, and Fruit of the Loom) to screen printers that add their own designs or corporate and club logos. At the retail level, many different types of retailer supply T-shirts: independent specialty stores; department stores; and chains such as Gap, Urban Outfitters, H&M, and American Eagle; and market stalls. The price dispersion

TABLE 2 Major sources of US Imports of knitted shirts, 2014

Source country	Value of imports, HTS codes 6105 and 6106 ($million)
Vietnam	625
China	501
Indonesia	281
India	236
Pakistan	147
Cambodia	114
Jordan	114
Guatemala	89
Sri Lanka	68
Honduras	59
El Salvador	50
Philippines	44
Other countries	672
Total from all countries	3000

Source: US International Trade Commission, Interactive Tariff and Trade DataWeb.

TABLE 3   Sales and profits of leading fashion apparel companies, 2014[a]

	Sales ($billion)	Operating margin (%)	Return on equity (%)
Inditex (Spain)	23.7	17.6	25.4
H&M (Sweden)	17.9	16.8	40.1
Gap (US)	16.4	16.8	40.1
VF (US)	12.3	11.6	19.5
Next (UK)	6.2	10.6	29.2
Hanesbrands (US)	5.3	0.27	31.4
Abercrombie & Fitch (US)	3.7	3.0	3.2
American Eagle (US)	3.3	5.7	9.9
Esprit Holdings (China)	3.0	10.6	1.0
J. Crew (US)	2.6	(22.7)	(73.0)
Gildan Activewear (US)	2.4	11.0	13.6
American Apparel (US)	0.6	(7.2)	(57.2)[b]

Notes:
[a]The data are for the financial year that most closely approximates calendar year 2014.
[b]Shareholders' equity was negative, hence ROE was not calculable. The figure shown here is for ROCE.
Source: Financial Times.

is wide: at Walmart, a Hanes T-shirt retails at $4.45, while at Nordstrom, a Versace Collection T-shirt sells for $395. Table 3 shows some leading suppliers of casual clothing.

Dov Charney and the Development of American Apparel

The Early Days

Dov Charney has been described as "a brilliant entrepreneur," "an exhibitionist," "a champion of social liberation," "a sleaze-ball," and "a pervert." In other respects he was a traditionalist: emphasizing his Jewish roots, his affection for the *shmata* business, and his desire to recreate America as a manufacturing nation.

Charney was born in Montreal in 1969. He started his first T-shirt business in 1990 and in 1997 moved to Los Angeles, where he joined Sam Lim and an associate of Lim's to form a garment company named "Two Koreans and a Jew." This later became American Apparel.[4]

Under Charney's leadership, American Apparel developed as a vertically integrated T-shirt manufacturer whose activities extended from knitting cotton yarn, through cutting and sewing, to dyeing and finishing. The main customers were screen printers who printed their own designs and logos and retailed the products. Compared to blank T-shirt giants Hanes (owned by Hanesbrands) and Fruit of the Loom, American Apparel differentiated itself by quality and design. In contrast to the standard loose-fitting, heavy-knit T-shirts, American Apparel offered closely fitting women's and men's T-shirts with finer thread and a denser knit.

In October 2003, American Apparel opened its first retail store in Los Angeles. Within 14 months, American Apparel was operating 34 stores in North America and three in the UK. By 2005, American Apparel was the largest garment manufacturer in the US—a position it has held to this day.

In December 2007, American Apparel was listed on the New York Stock Exchange. During 2008, American Apparel expanded rapidly opening 80 stores and entering five new countries (Austria, Belgium, Spain, Brazil, and Australia). It also won a number of awards as a trendsetting brand and an innovative retailer.

The Controversial Mr Charney

Dov Charney's key fashion innovation was in turning T-shirts into garments that enhanced the physical attractiveness of the wearer. Sexuality also played a wider role in the marketing and culture of American Apparel. In addition to its sexually provocative advertising, the company had a culture that acknowledged the sexual drives of its customers and its employees and embraced sexual conduct and sexual content as part of openness and creativity.

Charney's sexual openness provided the basis for multiple sexual harassment lawsuits from former employees and triggered a wider investigation by the Los Angeles office of the Equal Employment Opportunity Commission into sexual harassment at American Apparel.[5] Charney attributed the lawsuits to disgruntled employees seeking personal gain by exploiting California's litigious culture.[6] As a result of the lawsuits, American Apparel required employees to sign a document that acknowledged the "sexually charged" character of the company's products and marketing and sales activities.[7]

American Apparel also reflected Charney's social and political beliefs—notably his support for immigration reform and the wellbeing of illegal immigrants within the US. However, in 2009, American Apparel was found to be employing illegal immigrants and was forced to dismiss 1,500 workers.

Problems Mount, 2010–2014

American Apparel's reversal of fortunes in mid-2010 was sudden and sharp. In July 2010, the company's auditor, Deloitte & Touche, resigned after discovering "material weaknesses" in the company's financial controls. Amidst warnings of declining sales and an operating loss, American Apparel's share price crashed: it hit 66 cents in September 2010, down from a high of $16.80 in December 2007. Mounting losses during 2010 resulted in the company breaching its loan covenants, forcing American Apparel to issue a bankruptcy warning.

The result was a sudden shift of strategy from expansion to retrenchment and cost cutting. During the latter part of 2010, experienced senior managers were hired from Gap, Ralph Lauren, and Blockbuster Entertainment; turnaround specialist FTI Consulting was hired; and new sources of finance were sought. Cost reduction involved store closures, staff reduction, logistical improvements, and cuts to overhead costs. The financial weakness of the company was reflected in its cost of debt: an interest rate of 15% on its senior secured notes and 17% on its loan from the hedge fund Standard General.

Despite some success at expanding sales and cutting overheads, the effectiveness of the turnaround strategy was undermined by increasing rancor in the top ranks of the company. As American Apparel's finances deteriorated, so did the board's tolerance for Mr. Charney's eccentricities. In June 2014, after an internal investigation found evidence of "misconduct" by Charney, the American Apparel board replaced him as chairman and CEO. However, Mr. Charney did not go quietly: during the summer of 2014 he sought to regain control of the company and in May 2015 began legal proceedings against the American Apparel board for defamation.

Table 4 shows American Apparel's waning financial performance.

American Apparel's Strategy and Operations

American Apparel was a leading supplier of T-shirts to the US market, both blank T-shirts sold to screen printers and final products supplied through its retail stores. Its Los Angeles manufacturing plant was by far the biggest garment-manufacturing facility in the US. This reflected the dominance of imported garments in the US market: most fashion clothing companies concentrated on design, marketing, and distribution, with manufacturing outsourced and offshored.

The distinctive feature of American Apparel was its high level of vertical integration: not only did it undertake most stages of production at its Los Angeles headquarters but also it performed its own design, marketing, and advertising, and

TABLE 4   Selected financial data for American Apparel, 2008–2014 ($million)

	2014	2013	2012	2011	2010	2009	2008
Income statement items							
Net sales	608.9	633.9	617.3	547.3	533.0	558.8	545.1
Cost of sales	299.8	313.1	289.9	252.4	253.1	238.9	245.9
Gross profit	309.1	320.9	327.4	294.9	279.9	319.9	299.2
Total operating expenses	—	—	—	318.2	330.0	295.5	263.1
Selling and distribution costs	212.6	241.7	227.4	209.8	218.2	198.5	168.5
General and administrative	121.4	107.0	97.3	104.1	103.2	93.6	78.9
Income from operations	(27.6)	(29.3)	1.0	(23.3)	(50.1)	24.4	36.1
Interest expense	39.9	39.3	41.6	33.2	23.8	22.6	13.9
Net income	(68.8)	(106.3)	(37.3)	(39.3)	(86.3)	1.1	14.1
Balance sheet items							
Current assets	199.0	215.3	224.4	230.7	216.5	186.3	187.0
Inventories	147.6	169.4	174.2	185.8	178.1	141.2	148.2
Total assets	294.4	333.8	328.2	324.7	328.0	327.6	333.0
Current liabilities	162.3	162.0	161.7	143.4	213.2	64.9	74.3
Overdraft and current bank debt	40.0	38.0	60.6	52.3	141.8	3.7	3.8
Accounts payable	35.6	38.3	38.2	33.9	31.5	19.7	26.3
Long-term debt	217.4	213.5	110.0	98.9	5.6	71.4	100.0
Total liabilities	409.9	411.2	306.1	276.6	252.9	170.2	196.6
Stockholders' equity	(115.5)	(77.4)	22.1	48.1	75.0	157.3	136.4
Cash flow items							
Net cash from/(used in) operations	(5.2)	(12.7)	23.6	2.0	(32.0)	45.0	21.2
Net cash from/(used in) investing activities	(9.6)	(25.1)	(24.9)	(10.8)	(15.7)	(20.9)	(72.2)
Net cash provided by financing activities	15.6	34.2	4.2	12.6	48.2	(25.5)	41.2

Source: American Apparel Inc. 10-K Reports.

owned and operated all its retail stores, even its overseas stores. As a result, American Apparel's business system achieved remarkable speed and flexibility:

> Our vertically integrated business model, with manufacturing and various other elements of our business processes centered in downtown Los Angeles, allows us to play a role in originating and defining new and innovative trends in fashion, while enabling us to quickly respond to market and customer demand for classic styles and new products. For our wholesale operations, being able to fulfill large orders with quick turn-around allows American Apparel to capture business. The ability to swiftly respond to the market means that our retail operations can deliver on-trend apparel in a timely manner and maximize sales of popular styles by replenishing product that would have otherwise sold out.[8]

American Apparel's product development cycle—from design concept to store rack—took as little as two weeks. Within a day, a designer could come up with an idea, design a garment, create a pattern, cut it, and have it sewn together. By the evening, the garment could be photographed on a model and emailed for approval by the CEO. After test marketing in a few American Apparel retail stores, customer purchases were tracked and analyzed, and then, if successful, the garment would go into full production for shipping to the rest of American Apparel's retail locations.

Product Development and Design

Recreating the T-shirt as a fashion garment was at the heart of American Apparel's business proposition. Design required careful attention to fit, texture, shape-retention, and color. "We've fashionized and brought fashion to the commodity setting," Charney explained, arguing that his main achievement was "feminizing the blank T-shirt industry."[9] Previously, T-shirts were "bulky, one-size-fits-all" garments that were not gender specific.

American Apparel employed an in-house team of designers at its Los Angeles headquarters. The team didn't read fashion magazines and paid little attention to catwalk fashion trends. It developed "updated versions of timeless, iconic styles" and took "inspiration from classic styles of the past, as well as the latest emerging fashion trends"—notably, style trends among young, urban bohemians in cities such as Los Angeles, London, and New York.[10] The clothing represented a retro urban-chic style with a 1970s flavor. Designers often went to vintage clothing stores to find inspirations for new designs. Until his departure, the design team was led by Dov Charney, who hired each member on the basis of whether the designer had "an eye for what's next."[11]

By 2009, the company had expanded its product range well beyond the T-shirt. It offered over 20,000 stock keeping units (SKUs), including fabric shirts, dresses, denim jeans, sweaters, jackets, swimwear, babywear, and a variety of accessories, such as bags, hats, scarves, and sunglasses—even sweaters for dogs. American Apparel intended to continue to introduce new merchandise to complement its existing products and draw in new customers.

Manufacturing

American Apparel's headquarters and main manufacturing facility comprised 800,000 square feet of floor space that occupied the former Southern Pacific Railroad depot in downtown Los Angeles. Dyeing and finishing were at a separate facility in California. Capacity shortage at its Los Angeles facility resulted in American Apparel expanding production to nearby locations. The company described its production operations as follows:

> Purchased yarn is sent to knitters to be knit into "greige" fabric, which is fabric that is not dyed or processed … As of December 31, 2011, our knitting facilities knit approximately 85% of the total fabric used in our garments and had approximately 80 employees.

> Knitted greige fabric … is batched for bleaching and dyeing and transported to our dyeing and finishing facilities, or other commissioned dye houses…

> Most fabric is shipped to our primary manufacturing facility in downtown Los Angeles, where it is inspected and then cut on manual and automated cutting tables, and subsequently sewn into finished garments … Garments are sewn by teams of sewing operators typically ranging from five to fifteen operators, depending on the complexity of a particular garment. Each sewing operator performs a different sewing operation on a garment before passing it to the next operator. Sewing operators are compensated on a modified piece-rate basis. Quality control personnel inspect finished garments for defects and reject any defective product.[12]

Retail and Wholesale Distribution

In May 2015, American Apparel owned and operated 252 retail stores in 20 countries (Table 5). The company described its retail operations as follows:

> Our retail operations principally target young adults aged 20 to 32 via our unique assortment of fashionable clothing, accessories and compelling in-store experience. We have established a reputation with our customers who are culturally sophisticated, creative, and independent minded. Our product offerings include basic apparel and accessories for men and women, as well as apparel for children. Stores average approximately 2500–3000 square feet of selling space. Our stores are located in large metropolitan areas, emerging neighborhoods, and select university communities. We strive to instill enthusiasm and dedication in our store managers and sales associates through regular communication with the stores.[13]

American Apparel favored locations away from traditional main streets using nontraditional retail buildings with unique environments. Store selection and design had been undertaken by Jordan Parnass, a lifelong friend of Dov Charney, whose

TABLE 5 American Apparel: Number of retail outlets at year-end

	2014	2013	2012	2011	2010	2009	2008	2007	2006
US	136	139	140	143	157	160	147	105	93
Canada	31	32	35	37	40	40	37	30	26
International	75	77	76	69	76	81	75	47	30

Source: American Apparel, 10-K reports.

location scouts searched cities for areas that were populated by artists and musicians and for the hangouts of young adults. Store designs sought to incorporate the location's "regional flavor" together with the characteristics of the building's structure.[14] Stores included a converted movie theater and a former auto-garage.[15]

American Apparel's wholesale business sold to about a dozen authorized distributors and over 10,000 screen printers. The latter printed blank products with corporate logos, brands, and other images. Wholesale customers were served by a call center at its Los Angeles headquarters. The company prided itself on the fast turnaround of orders: orders received before 6 pm were shipped the same day.

American Apparel offered online retail sales through its www.americanapparel.com website. There were localized websites for the US, Canada, the UK, Europe, Switzerland, Japan, South Korea, Australia, Mexico, Brazil, and, from late 2014, China.

Table 6 and Table 7 show American Apparel's sales and profits by segment and by country.

Employee Relations: A "Sweat-Shop" Free Environment

American Apparel summarized its approach to human resource management as follows:

> We view our employees as long-term investments and adhere to a philosophy of providing employees with decent working conditions in a technology driven environment which allows us to attain improved efficiency, while promoting employee loyalty.[16]

Rates of pay exceeded the going rates for the job: even the lowest-paid workers earned around double the minimum wage. Workers were offered subsidized healthcare for themselves and their families, subsidized lunches, free parking, bus passes, and low-cost auto insurance. There were on-site massage therapists who provided regular services for all employees. Yoga classes were also available, along with a health-and-wellness specialist who provided counseling. Workers could take bathroom breaks at any time and use their cell phones for quick personal calls during working hours. Workers received training to improve their job and management skills as well as English and math classes. The human resources department also assisted employees in completing their tax returns and in opening bank accounts.

Marketing and Social Responsibility

American Apparel's approach to marketing was radically different from that of most fashion clothing companies. It developed all of its marketing and advertising in-house. Its advertisements were striking. The photographs used in advertising and promotion had traditionally been taken by Charney and other amateur photographers. Models were all amateurs—employees, customers, and friends—who posed without makeup or fancy hair-dos. They did not conform to conventional notions of style and beauty: they often featured skin blemishes and asymmetrical features. Not only were the models natural and ordinary, so too were the poses and locations: American Apparel ads depicted young men and women sitting on the floor, lying

TABLE 6   American Apparel: Financial results by business segment ($million)

	2014	2013	2012	2011	2010	2009	2008
US wholesale							
Sales	208.9	201.3	185.4	156.5	149.0	141.5	162.7
Gross profit	60.2	49.9	53.2	42.6	32.0	36.2	46.9
Operating income[a]	31.1	12.0	27.9	22.4	11.2	15.5	21.0
Capital expenditure	2.4	10.1	9.8	3.6	4.7	4.6	7.1
US retail							
Sales	191.4	205.0	198.9	174.8	177.6	191.3	168.7
Gross profit	123.7	131.9	130.5	117.2	117.5	136.4	127.9
Operating income[a]	(0.8)	(2.7)	4.2	(4.7)	(18.5)	17.3	33.5
Capital expenditure	4.0	11.2	6.6	4.9	7.6	11.2	30.9
Canada							
Sales	51.5	60.1	63.7	61.9	65.6	69.0	67.3
Gross profit	28.0	34.7	37.5	35.8	43.3	43.2	40.1
Operating income[a]	3.8	3.7	(0.1)	(3.7)	5.1	14.0	10.8
Capital expenditure	1.7	1.2	1.6	0.4	1.5	1.4	4.7
International							
Sales	156.9	167.5	169.4	154.2	140.7	156.9	146.4
Gross profit	97.2	104.4	106.2	99.3	87.1	104.0	84.2
Operating income[a]	(1.4)	3.6	10.7	8.4	(5.1)	15.3	8.0
Capital expenditure	3.0	4.6	3.6	2.1	2.0	3.8	18.3

Note:
[a]Before corporate expense, interest, other income, and foreign currency adjustment.
Source: American Apparel, 10-K reports.

on a bed, or lounging on a sofa. As the *New York Times* observed: the advertisements have a "flashbulb-lighted, lo-fi sultriness to them" looking more like photos on Facebook than ads on a billboard or glossy magazine.[17]

They were also sexually suggestive. In April 2012, Britain's Advertising Standards Authority banned eight images on American Apparel's website, objecting to the

TABLE 7   Geographical distribution of sales, 2009–2014 ($million)

	2014	2013	2012	2011	2010	2009
United States	400.4	406.3	384.2	331.3	326.6	332.8
Canada	51.5	60.1	63.7	61.9	65.6	70.0
Europe (excluding UK)	64.8	70.3	66.9	68.1	69.0	81.3
United Kingdom	42.6	44.2	47.7	40.0	32.5	34.2
Japan	12.8	18.1	20.3	14.2	10.7	14.1
South Korea	12.7	10.4	10.7	9.7	9.5	9.4
Australia	9.3	10.2	11.5	11.6	9.5	9.1
China	7.6	6.9	5.3	n.a.	n.a.	n.a.
Other foreign countries	7.1	7.4	7.0	10.5	9.5	8.8
Total net sales	608.9	633.9	617.3	547.3	533.0	558.8

Note:
n.a. = not available.
Source: American Apparel, 10-K reports.

"voyeuristic and amateurish quality to the images which served to heighten the impression that the ads were exploitative of women and inappropriately sexualized young women."[18]

American Apparel made heavy use of billboards but avoided mainstream media. Its advertising was directed mainly to online sites and alternative newspapers, such as *The Village Voice*, *LA Weekly*, and *The Onion*, and online fashion magazines. It also used its social and political activism in its marketing communications emphasizing its "sweatshop free" credentials, its support for immigrant rights, and its commitment to environmental sustainability.

Under Paula Schneider, American Apparel sought to sustain its edgy appeal while toning down its overt sexuality. Britain's *Independent* newspaper commented: "Editing the photos of lingerie models on its website seems to be the first attempt by the brand to distance itself from the racy advertising it's well known for. However, by photoshopping out some of the models' exposed nipples and pubic hair makes them look like plastic mannequins."[19]

The Road Ahead

While Chapter 11 offered American Apparel breathing space, Paula Schneider realized that its room for maneuver was limited. The most obvious way to cut costs was to offshore manufacture. Monthly wages for production workers in Los Angeles were about $1,500; in Bangladesh they were about $69. However, American Apparel's Los Angeles manufacturing base was central to its brand identity and its business model. Design too presented intractable problems. While still commanded a loyal following from many consumers, American Apparel's 1980s vibe appealed to less and less of the late-teens to early 30s demographic segment. The continuing decline in sales during 2015 suggested that Schneider had yet to articulate and convey a clear and appealing image for the American Apparel brand.

Notes

1. "New CEO Paula Schneider: How I'll Fix American Apparel," Forbes (January 22, 2015).
2. Ibid.
3. P. Rivoli, *The Travels of a T-Shirt in the Global Economy: An Economist Examines the Markets, Power, and Politics of World Trade*, 2nd edn (John Wiley & Sons, Ltd, Chichester, 2009).
4. The early history of American Apparel is described in A. A. Nieder, "The Branding of Blank Tees," https://www.americanapparel.net/presscenter/articles/20000818caapparelnews.html, accessed July 20, 2015.
5. American Apparel, 10-K report for 2008 (2009): 31.
6. "Living on the Edge at American Apparel," *Business Week* (July 27, 2007).
7. J. Wolf, "And You Thought Abercrombie & Fitch Was Pushing It?" *New York Times Magazine* (April 23, 2006).
8. American Apparel, 10-K report for 2011: 7.
9. D. Charney, interview, "Worldwide," Chicago Public Radio (November 13, 2003).
10. American Apparel, 10-K report for 2011: 10.
11. D. Charney, interview, "Charlie Rose," KQED9 (TV broadcasting station) (July 2006).
12. American Apparel, 2011, op. cit.: 8–9.
13. Ibid.
14. A. DiNardo, "The Anti-Brand," *Visual Store* (December 4, 2006).
15. Ibid.
16. American Apparel, 2011, op. cit.: 11.
17. J. Wolf, op. cit.
18. "American Apparel Ads Banned for Using Overtly Sexual Images," http://www.theguardian.com/media/2013/apr/10/american-apparel-ad-banned, accessed July 20, 2015.
19. "American Apparel Tones Down Ads by Airbrushing Models' Nipples and Pubic Hair," *The Independent* (March 20, 2015).

Case 18 Chipotle Mexican Grill, Inc.: The International Challenge

Since its founding in Denver, Colorado in 1993, Chipotle Mexican Grill had grown to a chain of 1783 fast-food restaurants by the end of 2014. Yet, of these, a mere 17 were outside the US (of which seven were in Canada). Chipotle's US focus was unusual for a major US-based restaurant chain, most of which had sought to exploit growth opportunities in overseas markets relatively early in their development. Table 1 shows the international presence of some of the larger chains. Was Chipotle missing out on a huge growth opportunity and, if so, what strategy should Chipotle adopt to expand its overseas presence?

Chipotle Ventures Abroad

Chipotle first ventured beyond the United States in 2008, when it opened a restaurant in Toronto, Canada. In 2010, it opened a restaurant in London, England. This was followed by restaurants in Paris, France (2012) and Frankfurt, Germany (2013). However, compared to its pace of US expansion, Chipotle's international growth was tentative (Table 2).

The choice of London for Chipotle's first restaurant outside of North America was for cultural and economic reasons: London was perceived as similar to the urban environments where Chipotle had thrived. According to communications director, Chris Arnold:

> When we started in the U.S., we've primarily been in large cities. Almost all of our restaurants are in major metropolitan areas or suburbs of major metropolitan areas … There's a great appreciation there for local and sustainably raised ingredients. Culturally, that aligns with what we do more than most options here in the U.S. do.[1]

Founder and co-CEO Steve Ells was similarly optimistic about Chipotle's UK prospects:

This case was prepared by Robert M. Grant. ©2015 Robert M. Grant.

TABLE 1 The total and international outlets of leading US fast-food chains, 1994 and 2014

	Total outlets		International outlets	
	2014	**1994**	**2014**	**1994**
Subway	42,230	8,450	9,300	179
McDonald's	36,258	15,950	21,919	5,712
Starbucks	21,366	425	9,655	18
KFC	14,197	9,407	9,827	4,258
Pizza Hut	13,602	11,325	5,739	2,925
Burger King	12,947	7,684	6,224	1,357
Domino's	10,913	5,079	5,846	840
Wendy's	6,515	4,411	780	413
Taco Bell	6,199	5,614	278	162
Little Caesars	5,110	4,855	1,238	155
Hardee's	1,721	3,516	274	72

Source: Company websites.

We are very encouraged by the prospects for Chipotle in the UK. London has become an important food city over the years, especially because of the awareness of and desire for things like locally sourced, seasonal, and artisanal ingredients. These are all core values of Chipotle and we have been instrumental in bringing this kind of thinking to fast food in the U.S. We call it "Food with Integrity" and it is how we are changing the way people think about fast food. We believe Londoners will appreciate our efforts to serve food that is raised right and in a way that is so accessible.[2]

When Chipotle opened on London's Charing Cross Road in April 2010, it followed its US model almost exactly: the same menu, the same assembly line operations, the same grassroots marketing efforts. According to Chris Arnold: "We really don't see why it needs to be any different going into Europe. It will all be the same. Part of the beauty of Chipotle is its simplicity."

Developing a supply chain was not perceived as a major challenge: the European food culture was seen as friendly to Chipotle's policy of "Food with Integrity" policies. However, getting tortillas made to Chipotle's specification proved a challenge.

TABLE 2 Chipotle restaurants by location (at year-end)

	2014	**2013**	**2012**	**2011**	**2010**
US	1,766	1,556	1,399	1,226	1,079
Canada	7	7	5	2	2
UK	6	6	5	2	1
France	3	2	1	—	—
Germany	1	1	—	—	—
Total international	17	16	11	4	3
Total	1,783	1,572	1,410	1,230	1,082

Source: Company websites.

Chipotle also applied the same human resource policies, particularly with regard to nurturing local talent. Start-up of the London store was led by managers and operations personnel from North America. After an initial period, locally trained staff would replace most of the US-based managers.

Subsequent Chipotle restaurants were opened in Baker Street, Soho, Covent Garden, Islington, and Wimbledon.

Chipotle's International Experiences

Chipotle's progress in London was slow in terms of both sales growth and brand awareness. According to Bloomberg, Chipotle's market research showed that only 1% of Londoners was familiar with the brand as compared with 16% for Pret A Manger and 23% for McDonald's. "It looks likely that London will be a developing market for a while, until our awareness is raised there," Steve Ells said during the earnings call.[3]

Chipotle's Chris Arnold attributed Chipotle's low brand awareness in London to its handful of restaurants—six compared to 40 in New York City. He explained that Chipotle's approach was "to build up the business organically, [which] gives us a chance to build up our crews and operations in a new location."[4]

A further challenge for Chipotle was Europeans' lack of familiarity with Mexican cuisine, compared to other non-European cuisines, such as Thai, Indian, Vietnamese, and Chinese. Taco Bell's experience was salutary: it entered the UK market in the late 1980s, only to withdraw some seven years later. In 2010, it made a second attempt to enter the UK, but by March 2015 it had only five UK outlets.

Yet, even in London—one of the world's most multi-ethnic cities with a huge diversity of cuisines—Chipotle had clearly failed to make much of an impact. In Trip Advisor's March 28, 2015 listing of 161 Mexican/Southwestern restaurants in London, Chipotle's highest-ranked restaurant came in at #19. In terms of numbers of outlets, Chipotle lacked the market presence of other chains serving Mexican cuisine: Tortilla had 16 London restaurants and several elsewhere in Britain, Wahaca had 14 London restaurants.

Chipotle's own reservations about its potential for profitable expansion outside the US were apparent from its discussion of "Risk Factors" in its 2014 annual report:

> Our expansion into international markets may present increased risks due to lower customer awareness of our brand, our unfamiliarity with those markets and other factors … As a result of our small number of restaurants outside the U.S. and the relatively short time we have been operating those restaurants, we have lower brand awareness, lower sales and/or transaction counts, and less operating experience in these markets. The markets in which we've opened restaurants outside the U.S., and any additional new markets we enter outside the U.S. in the future, have different competitive conditions, consumer tastes and discretionary spending patterns than our U.S. markets. As a result, new restaurants outside the U.S. may be less successful than restaurants in our existing markets [they] may take longer to ramp up and reach expected sales and profit levels, and may never do so, thereby affecting our overall growth and profitability. To build brand awareness in international markets, we may need to make greater investments in advertising and

promotional activity than we originally planned, which could negatively impact the profitability of our operations in those markets.

We may also find it more difficult in international markets to hire, motivate and keep qualified employees who can project our vision, passion and culture, and labor costs may be higher in international markets due to increased regulation or local market conditions. In addition, restaurants outside the U.S. have had higher construction, occupancy and food costs than restaurants in existing markets, and we may have difficulty finding reliable suppliers or distributors or ones that can provide us, either initially or over time, with adequate supplies of ingredients meeting our quality standards. Markets outside the U.S. may also have regulatory differences with the U.S. with which we are not familiar, or that subject us to significant additional expense or to which we are not able to successfully adapt, which may have a particularly adverse impact on our sales or profitability in those markets and could adversely impact our overall results.[5]

Chipotle's direct ownership and management of its restaurants also handi-capped the profitability of its international operations. Motley Fool questioned whether the Chipotle concept translated well to international markets and observed that:

Chipotle has impressive margins, with its 16.5% operating margin besting that of Panera by about 3.5 percentage points. Looking at McDonald's metrics, it would appear that Chipotle still has plenty of room to grow its margins. McDonald's managed an operating margin in excess of 30% in 2013, nearly twice that of Chipotle. However, McDonald's has a very different business model than Chipotle, with a large portion of its restaurants franchised. Chipotle owns all of its restaurants, so the company will never even come close to McDonald's margins. McDonald's makes a lot its money by collecting franchise fees and rent, not selling burgers, and that's why the company's margins are so high. If anything, the difficulty in sourcing quality ingredients will lead to higher food prices and lower margins for Chipotle in the future.[6]

Overseas Expansion by US Restaurant Chains

The international market offered substantial growth opportunities for US restaurant chains. Among the leading chains—notably Subway, McDonald's, Starbucks, and KFC—international sales accounted for up to one-half of total sales and a growing proportion of total profit. However, the more traditional of the "casual dining" chains—such as Denny's, Applebee's, T.G.I. Friday's, and Tony Roma's—had a much weaker presence outside the US and Canada.

The attraction of overseas markets was that their restaurant markets were typically less saturated than those of the US and most of the local competition was made up of independent, family-owned restaurants rather than large chains. In overseas markets it was anticipated that market trends would follow those of the US, in particular that greater affluence and a declining role of family life would result in increased eating away from home.

By contrast, the US restaurant market appeared mature and saturated—it was estimated that there were 192,000 franchised fast-food and restaurant outlets at the beginning of 2014.[7]

However, overseas markets also represented a substantial management challenge. These included:

- *Market demand*: The extent to which market demand existed for a particular type of restaurant depended on levels of disposable income, urbanization, demographics, and a host of other social, economic, and lifestyle factors. Most critical to a specific company were national preferences with regard to cuisine and dining conventions. Even McDonald's, whose name had become synonymous with global standardization, had made substantial adaptations of its menu and business practices to local conditions.

- *Cultural and social factors* are critical influences on customer preferences with regard to menus, restaurant facilities, and overall ambiance; they are also important with regard to employee management practices and entrepreneurial potential.

- *Infrastructure*: Transportation and communication, basic utilities such as power and water, and locally available supplies were important elements in the decision to introduce a particular restaurant concept. A restaurant must have the ability to get resources to its location. Easy access to the raw materials for food preparation, equipment for manufacture of food served, and mobility for employees and customers were essential.

- *Raw material supplies*: Overseas restaurant chains needed local supplies of food and drink. In 1995, the US International Trade Commission noted that: "International franchisers frequently encounter problems finding supplies in sufficient quantity, of consistent quality, and at stable prices. Physical distance also can adversely affect a franchise concept and arrangement. Long distances create communication and transportation problems, which may complicate the process of sourcing supplies, overseeing operations, or providing quality management services to franchisees."[8] In 2015, these problems remained critical challenges to fast food chains seeking to expand internationally. While a franchiser could develop its own supply chain (e.g., McDonald's when it entered the Soviet Union), the investment of management time and money could be substantial.

- *Regulations and trade restrictions*: The principal challenges were national regulations relating to food standards, business licensing, and business contracts. Establishing new businesses in most countries involves far more regulation than within the US. Franchise agreements are an especially difficult area because they involve complex contractual agreements between franchisor and franchisee regarding trademark licensing, royalty payments, and requirements for quality control and quality monitoring. In some countries some usual terms of franchise agreements have been viewed as restraints on commerce. Employment law was also important, particularly with regard to restrictions on employers' ability to dismiss or lay off employees and requirements for union recognition and national collective bargaining arrangements over wages and working conditions.

US-based chains also faced powerful local competitors when they entered overseas markets. For example, in the UK, Chipotle's leading competitor was Tortilla, UK's largest Mexican fast-casual chain with 21 restaurants in March 2015. It was founded in 2007 by American-born Brandon Stephens and backed by private equity investors Quilvest and Clapham House Group.

Notes

1. "Chipotle: London Calling," http://www2.qsrmagazine.com/articles/features/138/global_growth-3.phtml, accessed July 20, 2015.
2. "Chipotle Finalizes London Location," Chipotle Mexican Grill, Inc., press release (November. 17, 2009), http://ir.chipotle.com/phoenix.zhtml?c=194775&p=irol-newsArticle&ID=1356314, accessed July 20, 2015.
3. "Why Chipotle Sales Lag in London," http://www.bloomberg.com/bw/articles/2013-02-26/why-chipotle-sales-are-low-in-london, accessed July 20, 2015.
4. Ibid.
5. Chipotle Mexican Grill, Inc., 10-K report for 2014: 13.
6. "Why Chipotle Is Severely Overvalued," http://www.fool.com/investing/general/2014/03/31/why-chipotle-is-severely-overvalued.aspx, accessed July 20, 2015.
7. IHS Global Insight, *Franchise Business Economic Outlook for 2014* (January 2014).
8. *US International Trade Commission, Industry and Trade Summary: Franchising* (Washington, DC, 1995): 15–16.

Case 19 Haier Group: Internationalization Strategy

The transformation of the bankrupt Qingdao General Refrigerator Factory into the Haier Group, one of the world's biggest and most successful household appliance companies, is an epic tale that symbolized China's rise to become the world's dominant manufacturing center and a major source of foreign direct investment. In the process, Haier's CEO, Zhang Ruimin, had become a national hero and internationally renowned business leader that *Fortune* magazine listed among "The World's 50 Greatest Leaders" for 2014.

Yet, the story of Haier is also atypical of China's industrial development. By 2015, Haier had achieved a global position that had eluded most other Chinese state-owned enterprises. Within the appliance industry, Haier had established itself as a major global brand, a frontrunner in terms of innovation and product design, and, without the help of large-scale acquisitions, had built a strong presence in the sophisticated and intensely competitive appliance markets of North America, Europe, and Japan. Haier views its development as comprising a sequence of phases each lasting about seven years (Figure 1).

What lessons can other emerging market multinationals learn from Haier's remarkable achievements and does Haier's unconventional approach to strategy and management also offer lessons for the leaders of Western multinational corporations?

And what about the future of Haier? Its global presence has been built upon a combination of opportunism, ambition, and determination. As it consolidates its position as a leading multinational corporation, does Haier need a more orderly and integrated approach to global strategy?

Building Leadership in the Home Market

When Zhang Ruimin was appointed general manager of the Qingdao General Refrigerator Factory in 1984, it was a cooperative enterprise with about 800 workers operating under the control of the Qingdao city government. Zhang's early effort concentrated upon collaborating with foreign appliance makers—including Liebherr of Germany, Merloni of Italy, and Mitsubishi and Sanyo of Japan—in order to improve product design and process technology. In 1985, Qingdao Refrigerator formed a joint venture with Liebherr for producing refrigerators for the Chinese

---

This case was prepared by Robert M. Grant assisted by Ayan Chakraborty. ©2015 Robert M. Grant.

FIGURE 1   Haier Group: Strategy phases, 1984–2015

Brand Building Strategy	Diversification Strategy	Internationalization Strategy	Global Brand Strategy	Networking Strategy
Haier builds presence within the Chinese market though quality and customer service	Haier acquires other Chinese enterprises to expand product range	Haier enters 19 other national markets and becomes the world's biggest domestic appliance company in terms of units of output	Transformation from a product-driven to a user-driven "on-demand" mode. Globalization uses global resources to create localized mainstream brands.	Haier's networked enterprise strategy embodies: a border-free enterprise, manager-free management, and a scale-free supply chain
1984	1991	1998	2005	2012

Source: www.haier.net/en/about_haier/haier_strategy/, accessed July 20, 2015.

market. A key challenge was changing employees' attitudes to product quality. In one—now famous—intervention, Zhang ordered defective refrigerators to be removed from the production line and smashed to pieces.[1] The company's efforts at quality management were also greatly assisted by the decision in 1992 to apply for ISO9001 authentication. Achieving this international quality standard required a total reformulation and upgrading of processes.[2]

At the heart of Zhang's efforts to build the Haier brand was emphasis on customer service. Haier's efforts to build an after-sales service network were helped in 1990 by establishing a computerized service center to keep track of its customers.

Under the leadership of Zhang Ruimin and his close colleague Yang Mianmian, the company developed rapidly. Improved product quality fueled strong demand and, between 1984 and 1989, revenues climbed from 3.5 million to 410 million yuan. In 1992, a new factory complex and head office were built on the outskirts of Qingdao and in the same year the company adopted the name Haier Group. In 1995, its refrigerator division was listed on the Shanghai Stock Exchange and in 2005 its subsidiary, Haier Electronics Group, was listed on the Hong Kong Stock Exchange.

During the 1990s, Haier acquired 16 other Chinese companies with the result that it became a supplier not only of a broad range of domestic appliances but also televisions, telecommunications equipment, and other consumer electronics products.

As a result of Haier's cultivation of brand image through its emphasis on product quality and customer service, not only did it become a leading manufacturer of domestic appliances in China but it was also able to sell its products at a price premium to other domestic brands.

Haier's Management System

Governance

Formally, Haier was a collective under the supervision of Qingdao municipal government. In practice, the ownership, organizational structure, and governance of the Haier Group were unclear.[3] The group's two public companies—Qingdao Haier

Company Ltd listed in Shanghai and Haier Electronics Group Company Ltd listed in Hong Kong—had opaque relationships with one another and with their parent company. The list of directors and senior managers of Qingdao Haier Company made no mention of Mr. Zhang Ruimin. No consolidated financial statements were available for the group. The Haier website gave the group's revenues as 200 billion yuan in 2014; however, the revenues of the two listed companies totaled 155 billion yuan, implying that another 45 billion yuan were attributable to other business entities within Haier.

Zhang Ruimin

Despite its opaque governance structure—or perhaps because of it—power within the Haier Group was concentrated in the hands of Zhang Ruimin. This power derived partly from his formal position as chairman and CEO, partly from his informal authority and reputation as the architect of Haier's remarkable development, and partly from his political ties. In addition to being the secretary of the Communist Party Committee of the Haier Group, he was also a member of the party's Central Committee. His political connections gave Haier independence from municipal interference and valuable support from central and provincial government.

Zhang was born in Qingdao in 1949. Despite a lack of formal education, he was an avid reader. His ideas about management developed during his career at Haier, where he began as deputy plant manager at the age of 33. His management philosophy combined Chinese traditions from Confucius and Sun Tzu to Mao Zedong and Western ideas he derived from Joseph Schumpeter, Peter Drucker, Jack Welch, and Jim Collins and Jerry Porras (*Built to Last*).[4]

Zhang's management thinking developed in parallel with his strategy for Haier. His early focus was on building Haier's capabilities in relation to quality management, customer focus, brand building, and new product development. Gradually, Zhang's priorities shifted toward fundamentally rethinking Haier's structure and management systems. For example, customer orientation became the principle of "market chains" around which Haier's internal relationships were reformulated.

The idea behind "market chains" was that, in the same way that Haier's fundamental purpose was to serve its final customers, all interactions within the company could be redefined around supplier–customer relationships:

> Every unit, every operation and everyone was linked to a customer and every unit/operation/body was someone else's customer. In this way everyone within the enterprise, no matter how deeply inside the firm, felt market pressure directly.[5]

Developments in information and communications technology, especially the internet, greatly influenced Zhang's thinking about internal organization. Increasingly, he devoted himself to moving Haier from a hierarchy to a decentralized, team-based structure. For example, Haier's sales organization for China was completely restructured:

> We used to have a pyramid-style structure for our sales in China. The people in charge of sales had to manage business at the national, provincial, and city level. After the arrival of the internet age, we realized that under this triangular hierarchical structure, people had a difficult time adapting to the requirements of the times.

So we reorganized ourselves as an entrepreneurial platform. We flattened every-thing out, taking out all the middle management. We decentralized the structure to one with more than 2,800 counties. Each county organization has seven people or fewer.[6]

His notion of a platform-based enterprise also embodied the concept of a border-less enterprise:

We are using digital technology to connect everyone ... there is no "inside" the company versus "outside" anymore. As a Haier executive, my goal is no longer to be a maker of home appliances, but to be an agent of interaction and network-ing among people who might be anywhere. I want to turn the company into an Internet-based company, a company unrestricted by borders. Whoever is capable, come and work with us ... In the long run, there won't be any company employees to speak of—only the Haier platform. We involve customers in a similar way. In the past, users would hear through advertising which Haier products were good, then they'd go buy those products. Now we bring in users to participate in the whole process of product development.[7]

Central to Zhang's approach to management was commitment to innovation, adaptation, and continuous improvement. This was captured in the slogan: "today's work must be finished today; today's accomplishment must be better than yester-day's; and tomorrow's goal must be higher than today's." Increasingly, this meant adopting a totally different conception of what Haier was and what it was trying to achieve. According to an interview with Zhang conducted by Reuters:

The ultimate aim, Zhang says, is for Haier to become a full services company for the wireless age, where customers place orders for tailor-made appliances, and communicate directly with their home appliances via smartphone or controlling device.[8]

In pursuit of this goal, Haier became the first home appliance maker to partner with Apple on its smart home platform.

Performance Management

A feature of the management system Zhang introduced at Haier was commitment to performance enforced through accountability and backed by individual incentives—an approach that was unusual among Chinese companies.

At the heart of this system was "Overall, Every, and Control and Clear"—also known as Haier's "OEC" principle. According to Haier's head of human resources, Wang Yingmin: "O stands for Overall; E stands for Everyone, Everything, and Every day; C stands for Control and Clear. OEC means that every employee has to accom-plish the target work every day. The OEC management-control system aims at over-all control of everything that every employee finishes on his or her job every day with a 1% increase over what was done the previous day."[9]

OEC became part of a performance management system that began each December with performance targets set by corporate headquarters for every division. Each division submits a divisional action program. This becomes the basis for a month-by-month system of performance management where actual performance is compared to the previous month's performance and targets for the current month. Monthly divisional performance management is disaggregated into daily performance management assessment for every employee. Each day begins with team leaders briefing team members and each day ends with each worker completing a self-checking assessment against specific OEC criteria. These assessments are linked to employee compensation through a system of bonuses and penalties.

Innovation and New Product Development

Haier's product development was driven primarily by its responsiveness to customer needs. A Harvard Business School case study reports on how, in response to frequent breakdowns of washing machines in rural China, Haier technicians discovered that its washing machines were being used to clean sweet potatoes and other vegetables. Haier responded with design changes to its washing machines together with advice to rural customers on their use for cleaning vegetables and peanuts.[10]

Providing design modifications to meet the preferences of specific customer groups were facilitated through flexible modular design. According to Zhang Ruimin, "Our products are based on modules and sub-systems, and on basic platforms that we can vary. Periodically we will add some new features, but the basic model is there."[11] Simple design modifications included freezers with separate compartments that kept ice cream at a slightly higher temperature to permit ease of serving, and Korean refrigerators with separate compartments for kimchee.

Haier's commitment to enhancing consumers' experiences also extended to providing internet connectively for it appliances. In 2014, it launched its "Smart Living" appliances with Broadcom' embedded wireless connectivity allowing customers to monitor and control their appliances remotely including home appliance controls, managing lighting and curtains, multimedia entertainment, and security alarm monitoring.

Building the Networked Enterprise

Zhang Ruimin's ideas about market responsiveness, entrepreneurial initiative, and team-based organization eventually became crystallized in his concept of the networked enterprise. Central to the transformation of Haier into a new type of organization was the creation of some 2000 self-managed teams called "ZZJYTs"—an acronym for Zi Zhuu Jing Ying Ti, meaning "autonomous business unit." Professor Bill Fischer and colleagues described the ZZJYTs as follows:

> Each comprises a team of 10 to 20 people—sometimes located in one place, other times virtual—who come from various functional roles and are brought together for a specific mission, and who are given profit and loss responsibility and accountability. They have their own independent accounting systems and complete autonomy in hiring and firing employees, setting internal rules about expenses and determining bonus distribution, and making almost any operational decision that typically would be made by an independent functional organization.

Haier organizes its ZZJYTs in three tiers. First-tier ZZJYTs have the task of directly facing the market, understanding customer needs, and providing customers with the right products. Second-tier ZZJYTs are responsible for supporting the first-tier ones, providing them with the resources and the guidance they need. Third-tier ZZJYT managers are the business division managers or functional managers who set corporate strategies and direction for the whole group. A typical first-tier ZZJYT is composed of sales, R&D, marketing, and finance people. Everyone, whatever their function, is expected to talk to consumers regularly.[12]

The transition from hierarchy to self-managed teams is one phase in Haier's transformation into a network of microenterprises where each team becomes an entrepreneurial business unit responsible for its own success. Within this model, the team members are not necessarily Haier employees. During 2014 and 2015, Haier's eliminated thousands of jobs then encouraged displaced employees to seek opportunities as self-employed members of micro-enterprises collaborating within the Haier network. According to Zhang Ruimin:

Employees used to obey their superiors and now they create value for users. They must become entrepreneurs and makers. The makers set up micro-enterprises, and the micro-enterprise owners jointly create users and the market. However, micro-enterprise owners are not appointed by the enterprise but elected by makers, and micro-enterprise owners can also select makers. After a period of time, if a micro-enterprise owner is considered incompetent by micro-enterprise members, he/she will be removed from the post, which actually often happens in Haier. More importantly, micro-enterprise owners are not limited to Haier employees but can come from external resources as well. The micro-enterprises plus social resources form an ecosystem to jointly create different markets.[13]

Internationalization

International Strategies in Domestic Appliances

Internationalization in the domestic appliance industry has attracted considerable interest from business school scholars. In an influential article, Harvard professor Ted Levitt argued that the success of Italian appliance manufacturers such as Indesit and Merloni was the result of the economies of scale they were able to exploit through producing large volumes of standardized models for world markets.[14] Subsequent research, however, showed not only that scale economies were modest in appliance manufacture but also that the most profitable producers were typically those that differentiated their products and their marketing strategies to meet the preferences of individual national markets.[15]

By the beginning of the 21st century, the domestic appliance industry was dominated by multinational firms whose operations spanned most continents of the world: Electrolux (of Sweden), Whirlpool (of the US), LG and Samsung (of South Korea), and Bosch-Siemens (of Germany). However, there were still major players whose markets were predominantly either national or regional: General Electric and Maytag (of the US); Merloni (of Italy); and Haier, Hisense Kelon, and Wuxi LittleSwan (of

China). However, during the first decade of the 21st century, several of these national players either internationalized or sold out to multinational players (e.g., Maytag was acquired by Whirlpool and GE's appliance division was acquired by Electrolux).

Haier's Initial Internationalization

Haier began its internationalization in, what appeared to be, a fairly haphazard fashion. Between 1992 and 1997, Haier entered a number of overseas markets:

- In South-East Asia, initially Indonesia, Philippines, and Malaysia, Haier established joint ventures with local companies to manufacture and sell refrigerators and air conditioners.
- In the US, Haier began supplying compact refrigerators to an importer, Welbilt Appliances, initially for sale under a retailer's brand, subsequently under the Haier brand. Compact refrigerators were followed by wine coolers. Sales were concentrated on large chains—notably Walmart.
- In 1997, Haier began exporting appliances to Germany, the Netherlands, and Italy for sale by importers mainly under the Haier brand name. Haier achieved significant sales in Germany, where Liebherr was its sales agent and distributor.

However, Zhang soon made it clear that Haier's goal in expanding overseas was not to seek export revenues through exploiting Haier's low manufacturing costs in China but to build a global brand: "making Haier the most respected brand in the world is the most important goal in the global strategy."[16] While this was partly a matter of national pride—"China should have world famous brands of its own"—it was also about challenging Haier to raise its standards of product development, manufacturing, marketing, and customer service to world-class levels. Yet, building a global brand would be achieved through focusing on local markets: "All success relies on one thing in overseas markets—creating a localized brand name," noted Mr. Zhang. "We have to make Americans feel that Haier is a localized US brand rather than an imported Chines brand. The same goes for the European market."[17]

Haier's "locally designed, locally made, locally sold" approach involved three stages of development:

- First, *seeding*—getting its products established in an overseas market and building brand recognition, initially through using local distributors and sales agents.
- Second, *rooting*—building market share and establishing manufacturing plants in the foreign market.
- Third, *harvesting*—establishing R & D facilities and conducting a full range of activities within the foreign market.

It also meant a focus on challenging markets. Rather than following conventional wisdom and focusing on entering nearby markets which were at a similar (or lower) stage of economic development than China, Haier chose to tackle developed markets with sophisticated consumers—North American, Europe, and Japan. As

Mr. Zhang remarked: "If one wants to improve one's chess skills, then one must play with the top players."[18]

Success in these markets required hiring experienced local managers to head Haier's overseas subsidiaries. "We want to use local people and local thinking to satisfy the needs of the customer," explained Yang Mianmian. Haier typically targeted experienced executives who had worked with leading appliance companies to head up its foreign operations. Chinese expatriates were primarily technical staff sent from headquarters.

Haier America

Haier America was established at the initiative of Michael Jemal, a partner of Haier's US distributor, Wellbilt Appliances. Under Jemal's leadership Haier penetrated niche markets—notably small refrigerators for offices and students' dorm rooms and wine coolers. In both categories Haier became the market leader, before expanding into window air conditioners and full-size appliances. In 2000, it opened a manufacturing plant in South Carolina and in 2001 moved into its New York headquarters on Broadway.

Haier's US production and marketing focused initially on refrigerators, where Haier positioned itself at similar price points to the market leaders, Whirlpool, GE, and Electrolux (Frigidaire), but sought differentiation advantage through innovative design features targeted at specific customer needs. Thus, Haier's product development and marketing of appliances were built around a segmentation of four demographic groups: 18- to 25-year-old dwellers in dorms or small apartments, 22- to 30-year-old apartment dwellers, 28- to 35-year-old first-time homebuyers, and 35- to 55-year-old "step-up" home dwellers.

In 2006, Haier introduced its upmarket range of Italian-designed appliances under the Casarte brand name. The Casarte line of products was subsequently introduced into other markets, including China.

Haier's US product development capability was enhanced by the creation of an R & D center at its South Carolina industrial park in 2012. In 2013, Haier America became a fully owned subsidiary of Haier Group after minority shareholders were bought out. In 2014, Adrian Micu, formerly head of engineering with Whirlpool, was appointed CEO of Haier America.

Haier Europe

In 2000, Haier established a European sales office in Varese in the north of Italy to coordinate its European appliance sales. In the following year, Haier acquired Meneghetti Equipment, which owned a refrigerator plant in Padua and a distribution network.

Over time, Haier repositioned itself from the lower price band to the middle of the market, where it sought to capture market share through aesthetics and design—drawing upon its Italian design center (in Varese) and German R & D center (in Frankfurt). In refrigerators, Haier Europe put a special emphasis on three-door models and novel color options. In 2010, Haier Europe moved its headquarters to Paris and, in 2015, Yannick Fierling, another recruit from Whirlpool, was named CEO of Haier Europe.

Haier in Asia-Pacific

Most of Haier's market entries into Asian countries were through joint ventures. In India, Haier partnered with Fedder Lloyd Corporation; in Pakistan, with the Ruba Group. The most important collaboration was with Sanyo Electric Company of Japan. The 2002 agreement with Sanyo involved the distribution by Haier of Sanyo products in China, the supply of technology and components from Sanyo to Haier, and the creation of Sanyo Haier to produce and market Haier appliances in Japan.

In 2012, Haier acquired Sanyo's domestic appliance business from its parent, Panasonic, for $132 million. As explained in a *Financial Times* case study, transferring Haier's management system to the newly acquired Sanyo employees was a major challenge given Haier's emphasis on individual responsibility for performance targets and Sanyo's traditions of collective responsibility and deference to seniority.[19]

Later in 2012, Haier acquired New Zealand-based Fisher & Paykel, an upmarket appliance maker specializing in dishwashers, washing machines, and cookers, for $751 million. Fisher & Paykel had plants in New Zealand, Australia, US, Thailand, Mexico and Italy.

Haier's Future as a Global Company

For all Haier's remarkable success under Zhang Ruimin's leadership, the effectiveness of its international strategy is difficult to assess. Clearly, Haier had done a brilliant job in exploiting the greatest opportunity available to the appliance industry for the past three decades: the rapid rise in the living standards of Chinese households. By 2015, it had become the world's biggest supplier of major home appliances with a unit market share of over 9%—ahead of rivals LG, Electrolux, Samsung, and Whirlpool. In terms of domestic appliance revenues, Haier was either third or fourth.

However, the great majority of Haier's sales was in its home market, where it was market leader. In refrigerators it held 36% of the Chinese market; in washing machines, 46%. Outside of China, Haier's performance was less consistent. In the US it had performed spectacularly well taking market leadership from Whirlpool in 2014, but in Europe, Japan, and most emerging-market countries, its performance was much less impressive.

This uneven performance raised questions about the overall cohesiveness of Haier's international strategy and the rationale upon which it was based. Despite the effectiveness with which Zhang Ruimin articulated Haier's strategy and management system, Haier's international strategy seemed inconsistent and haphazard. In some countries Haier set up new subsidiaries; in others, it used joint-venture to access an existing business system. Its product strategies, market positioning, and brand identity all varied considerably from country to country.

Given the likelihood that Haier's home market would experience slower growth in the next five years than the last five, and that the global market would experience slow growth, did Haier need to reformulate its international strategy?

Appendix: Financial Data for Haier

TABLE A1 Selected financial data for Qingdao Haier and Haier Electronics

	2010	2011	2012	2013	2014
Qingdao Haier					
Revenue ($million)	9,743	11,638	12,628	14,102	14,422
Operating margin (%)	4.9	5.5	6.6	7.1	8.7
Net margin (%)	3.36	3.65	4.09	4.82	5.62
ROE (%)	27.61	35.03	33.59	32.57	27.5
Return on invested capital (%)	17.93	18.35	17.23	16.94	14.89
Employees	53,412	59,814	57,977	55,726	54,286
Haier Electronics Group					
Revenues ($billion)	5,802	7,893	8,819	10,199	12,452
Operating margin (%)	4.01	3.75	4.18	4.36	4.89
Net margin (%)	2.69	2.82	3.05	3.27	3.64
ROE (%)	48.30	42.80	35.48	30.72	25.47
Return on invested capital (%)	47.58	39.07	31.74	28.11	23.05
Employees	18,204	18,406	17,304	16,506	15,637

Sources: Annual reports of Qingdao Haier Company Ltd. and Haier Haier Electronics Group Co., Ltd.

Notes

1. The early history of Haier is outlined in the Harvard Business School case "Haier: Taking a Chinese Company Global," Case No. 9-706-401 (2006).
2. See "Yang Mianmian: President of Haier," CEIBS Case No. 307-015 (2007): 5.
3. Haier's corporate governance is discussed in N. Kumar and J.-B. E. M. Steenkamp, *Haier: The Quest to Become the First Chinese Global Consumer Brand* (University of North Carolina, Kenan-Flagler Business School, December 2013): 4–5.
4. Zhang's intellectual influences are discussed in Kumar and Steenkamp, ibid.: 5–6.
5. IMD/CEIBS, "Building Market Chains at Haier," IMD Case No. 3-0939 (August 2003).
6. A. Kleiner, "China's Philosopher: CEO Zhang Ruimin," *strategy+business*, Issue 77, (Winter 2014).
7. Ibid.
8. "Fridge Magnate: Zhang Shifts Haier Focus for Wireless Age," (May 12, 2015), http://www.reuters.com/article/2015/05/12/us-haier-elec-strategy-idUSKBN-0NX2IN20150512, accessed July 20, 2015.
9. T. W. Lin, "OEC Management-Control System Helps China Haier Group Achieve Competitive Advantage," *Management Accounting Quarterly* (Spring 2005).
10. "Haier: Taking a Chinese Company Global," HBS Case No. 9-706-401 (2006): 6.
11. Ibid.
12. B. Fischer, U. Lago, and F. Liu, "The Haier Road to Growth," *strategy+business* (April 27, 2015).
13. Z. Ruimin "Nine Years' Exploration of Haier's Business Models for the Internet Age," www.haier.net/en/about_haier/news/201502/t20150225_262109.shtml, accessed July 20, 2015.
14. T. Levitt, "The Globalization of Markets," *Harvard Business Review* (May/June 1983).
15. C. Baden-Fuller and J. Stopford, *Rejuvenating the Mature Business*, revised edition (Boston: Harvard Business School Press, 1994).
16. Kumar and Steenkamp, op. cit.: 7.
17. Kumar and Steenkamp, op. cit.: 14.
18. "Haier's Aim: Develop Our Brand Overseas," *Bloomberg Business Week* (March 30, 2003), http://www.bloomberg.com/bw/stories/2003-03-30/online-extra-haiers-aim-develop-our-brand-overseas, accessed July 20, 2015.
19. "Case Studies: How Haier Handled Foreign Traditions," *Financial Times* (April 1, 2013): 3.

Case 20   The Virgin Group in 2015

On July 18, 2015, Sir Richard Branson celebrated his 65th birthday. There was little in his appearance or behavior that suggested a man who had reached normal retirement age. His enthusiasm for his business ventures seemed little dimmed. During the early months of 2015, he announced the launch of a Virgin cruise line, he accompanied the Virgin Racing team to a Formula E race at Miami where he expressed an interest in launching a Virgin electric automobile to compete with Tesla, in Chicago he opened the first of a US chain of Virgin hotels, and announced a major investment in OneWeb—a satellite internet service company whose satellites would be launched by Virgin Galactic's LauncherOne spacecraft.

However, the Virgin Group's investment in new ventures was dwarfed by its recent divestments. During 2014–2015, these included the sale of Virgin Mobile France, the flotation of Virgin America and Virgin Money, and the sale of the major part of Virgin's stake in Virgin Active.

Yet, even after these sales, the Virgin Group remained a highly diversified business empire. Bloomberg described Virgin as follows:

> Virgin Group Ltd., through its subsidiaries, engages in the businesses of mobile telephony, travel, financial services, leisure, music, holidays, and health and wellness in the United Kingdom and internationally. Its mobile telephony business includes IP-VPN, Wi-Fi, phones, phone plans, mobile broadband, TV phone, broadband services, and SIM cards. The company's travel business comprises airlines, leisure and travel Websites, travel booking services, travel information, flying clubs, commercial spaceline services, holiday services, hotel services, holiday cruise services, hotels, private islands, mountain retreats, game reserves, catamarans, lodges, tented camps, vineyards, restaurants, private members clubs, trains, and tour operating services. Its financial services include credit cards, home loans, insurance, savings, superannuation, fundraising services, and small business funding. The company's leisure businesses comprise balloon rides, corporate gifts, competition prizes and promotions, benefits, rewards and incentives, corporate events and hospitality, PR events and photography/filming, advertising balloons, book publishing, employee rewards, gift cards, electric vehicle championships, wine production, and online wine retail. Its health and wellness business includes health clubs, fitness clubs, NHS and social care services, health banks, and employee wellness services. The company also engages in entertainment businesses, such as casinos, bingo, slots, and radio stations.[1]

The complexity of the Virgin Group was also reflected in its structure. In May 2015, there were 312 Virgin companies registered at Britain's Companies House (113 of

---

This case was prepared by Robert M. Grant. ©2015 Robert M. Grant.

which had been identified as "converted/closed" or "recently dissolved"). In addition, there were Virgin companies registered in about 28 other countries. The Virgin companies were linked through a complex network of parent–subsidiary relations—many of which were identified as "holding companies." For most of the Virgin companies the ultimate parent was identified as Virgin Group Holdings Ltd., registered in the British Virgin Islands. Some Virgin companies where wholly or majority owned; in others, Virgin Group held minority stakes. In some, such as Virgin Media, a subsidiary of Liberty Global, Virgin Group owned no equity and simply licensed the Virgin brand.

The dispersed ownership and control structure of the Virgin Group had facilitated its dynamic, entrepreneurial growth. But now that Branson's business empire had matured and was consolidating around fewer businesses, did its structure and management systems still match the strategy? And was the strategy attuned to the changing conditions the group faced?

The maturing of Virgin had been accompanied by greater formalization of structure and management systems. The appointment of co-CEOs in 2011 marked the beginning of a more conventional management structure and Branson's transition to a more peripheral role, where he remained the inspiration, public face, and unifying force for the group but was less involved in Virgin's business activities and more committed to environmental and charity activities. However, the future of the Virgin Group remained uncertain—would Virgin remain an entrepreneurial organization committed to launching new business ventures designed to upset the status quo in different industries or was Virgin transitioning to a more conventional financially based holding company along the lines of Warren Buffet's Berkshire Hathaway or the Wallenberg family's Investor AB group? Perhaps, the string of divestments pointed to the fact that Virgin—like Branson himself—was entering an era of old age and decline where the break-up of the group was the best option.

Development of the Virgin Group, 1968–2015

Richard Branson's first business venture was a magazine, *Student*, which was first published on January 26, 1968 when he was a student at Stowe, a private boarding school. The magazine displayed features that would characterize many of Branson's subsequent entrepreneurial initiatives. It targeted the baby-boomer generation; embodied the optimism, irreverence, and anti-authoritarianism of the 1960s; combined fashion, popular music, and avant-garde culture; and filled a "gaping hole in the market." The success of the magazine encouraged Branson to leave school at the age of 17, before taking final exams.

Virgin Records

Branson's next venture, mail-order record sales, saw the birth of the Virgin brand name. In 1971, Virgin Records opened its first retail store, on London's busy Oxford Street and, in 1973, Virgin created its own record label. Its first release, *Tubular Bells*, by an unknown musician, Mike Oldfield, was a huge hit eventually selling over five million copies. Virgin Records went on to sign up a series of new artists such as Phil Collins, Human League, Simple Minds, and Boy George's Culture Club—including several that had been shunned by the major record companies, most notably the Sex Pistols.

Virgin Atlantic Airways

Virgin Atlantic began with a phone call from Randolph Fields, a Californian lawyer, suggesting a transatlantic, budget airline. To the horror of his colleagues at Virgin Records, Branson was enthralled with the idea. On June 24, 1984, Branson appeared in a First World War flying outfit to celebrate the inaugural flight of Virgin Atlantic in a second-hand 747 bought from Aereolíneas Argentinas. Unlike Branson's other businesses, the airline business was highly capital-intensive and heavily regulated; it also required a completely new set of business skills, including collaboration with governments, banks, and aircraft manufacturers.

Virgin Atlantic's massive financing needs encouraged Branson to seek an initial public offering for most of Virgin's other businesses. In 1985, 35% of Virgin Group PLC was listed on the London and NASDAQ stock markets and Branson began an unhappy few years as the chairman of a public corporation—a role which ill-fitted his own personality and leadership style. Following the October 1987 stock market crash, Branson took the opportunity to raise £200 million to buy out external shareholders.

Virgin Everywhere, 1988–2004

Between 1988 and 2004, Virgin launched a near-continuous stream of new businesses. These were concentrated around a few main areas of opportunity:

- *Travel*: The success of Virgin Atlantic encouraged Branson to launch other airlines. The Virgin approach was to mesh the business model of the low-cost carriers with Virgin's distinctive approach to enhancing customers' experience in novel ways. New airlines included the Brussels-based Virgin Express, Virgin Australia (originally Virgin Blue and Pacific Blue), and Virgin America. Other aviation ventures included Vintage Air Tours, Virgin Lightships (blimp advertisements), Virgin Galactic, and Virgin Balloons. Virgin Rail was established in 1997 to operate two passenger rail franchises awarded in the privatization of Britain's rail system. In 1998, Virgin sold 49% of Virgin Rail to the Stagecoach travel group.
- *Holidays*: Linked to Virgin's airline interests were investments in hotels and vacation services, including a lodge and wildlife park in South Africa and Branson's own Necker Island resort in the Caribbean.
- *Retailing*: Virgin's record stores provided a platform for internationally expanding retail interests. The Our Price chain of UK record stores was a joint venture between Virgin and WHSmith. Virgin Megastores pioneered "experience-based retailing" not just in the UK but also in Japan, the US, Australia, and Europe. Virgin Bride was a UK chain of bridal stores.
- *Information and communication technology*: Developments in digital technologies offered a broad new field of opportunity to Virgin. The internet allowed Virgin to expand its retail interests into the online retailing of cars, motorcycles, wine, and music downloads. The most successful of these was Virgin Direct (later renamed Virgin Money), a joint venture with Norwich Union, which offered credit cards and other personal financial products. The start of cellular communication encouraged the launch of Virgin Mobile, a joint venture with Deutsche Telekom, which pioneered the "virtual network

operator" model of wireless service (Virgin Mobile purchased network access from other providers). The Virgin Mobile strategy was then replicated in the US, Australia, South Africa, and South-East Asia. Virgin.net, an internet service provider, was a joint venture with cable operator NTL. NTL subsequently acquired both Virgin.net and Virgin Mobile UK to create Virgin Media Inc., the UK's first "quadruple play" provider offering TV, broadband internet, mobile, and fixed-line phone services. Virgin Group held a 10.6% shareholding in Virgin Media.

- *Leisure and entertainment.* From its origins in music and magazine publishing, Virgin entered video games (Virgin Games, 1991), book publishing (Virgin Publishing, 1991), radio broadcasting (Virgin Radio, 1992), cinemas (Virgin Cinemas, 1995), and health clubs (Virgin Active, 1998).

- *International expansion*: Virgin's expansion outside the UK began with its Megastores. After 2000, Virgin replicated several of its successful UK businesses overseas, including Virgin Mobile, Virgin Active, and Virgin Money.

Other new ventures defied categorization; they were the result of opportunism and Branson's whims. These included biofuels (Virgin Fuels, Virgin Bioverda), video games (Virgin Interactive), beverages (Virgin Drinks, Virgin Cola), clothing (Victory Corporation), cosmetics (Virgin Vie), and Virgin Health Bank, where parents could store the stem cells from their newly born babies.

Focusing the Group, 2004–2015

Throughout its history, Virgin has divested businesses, either wholly or partially, in order to release equity for other business ventures or simply to take advantage of the high valuations that others placed on Virgin businesses. In 1992, it sold its music business to EMI and, in 1999, sold 49% of Virgin Atlantic to Singapore Airlines. From 2005, the pace of divestment increased with the sale or closure of financially unsuccessful businesses—such as Virgin Vie, Virgin Cosmetics, Virgin Cars, Virgin Bikes, Virgin Brides, Virgin Cola, Virgin Drinks, and Virgin Money USA—and the sale or floatation of some of its most successful businesses, including Virgin Media, Virgin Money, and Virgin America. Many of Virgin's new initiatives during this period reflected Branson's increased commitment to environmental and charitable causes. Virgin Unite was established by The Virgin Foundation, the charitable arm of Virgin, to channel efforts by Virgin Group companies, Virgin employees, and contributions from Virgin customers toward charitable causes. Virgin Green Fund was established as a private equity fund to invest in renewable energy and resource conservation businesses.

One indication of Virgin's shifting view of itself was when, in 2012, the Virgin website described itself as a "branded venture capital organization"; by 2015, it proclaimed: "Virgin is a leading international investment group" and described its corporate executives as "Virgin's Senior Investment Team."[2]

The Virgin Group of Companies in 2015

Among the several hundred companies that are part of the Virgin Group, the Virgin website lists 59, which it groups into seven categories. These are shown in Figure 1.

FIGURE 1   Virgin's business portfolio[a]

Entertainment	Health and Wellness	Leisure
Virgin Casino	Virgin Active (separate	Virgin Balloon Flights
Virgin Festival	cos. in Australia, Italy,	Virgin Experience Days
Virgin Games	Portugal, South Africa,	Virgin Gift Cards
Virgin Megastore	Spain, UK)	Virgin Megastore
Virgin Produced	Virgin Care	Virgin Racing
Virgin Radio	Virgin Health Bank	Virgin Wines (UK, US,
	Virgin Pulse	Australia)
	Virgin Pure	

Entertainment
Virgin Casino
Virgin Festival
Virgin Games
Virgin Megastore
Virgin Produced
Virgin Radio

Telecom and Tech
Virgin Connect
Virgin Media
Virgin Media Business
Virgin Mobile
 (Australia, Canada,
 Chile, Columbia,
 France, India, Mexico,
 Poland, South Africa,
 UK, USA, Saudi Arabia)

Health and Wellness
Virgin Active (separate
 cos. in Australia, Italy,
 Portugal, South Africa,
 Spain, UK)
Virgin Care
Virgin Health Bank
Virgin Pulse
Virgin Pure

Planet and People
Virgin Earth Challenge
Virgin Green Fund
Virgin Unite

Money
Virgin Money UK
Virgin Money Australia
Virgin Money S. Africa
Virgin Money Giving
Virgin Start-up

Leisure
Virgin Balloon Flights
Virgin Experience Days
Virgin Gift Cards
Virgin Megastore
Virgin Racing
Virgin Wines (UK, US,
 Australia)

Travel
Virgin America
Virgin Atlantic
Virgin Australia
Virgin Galactic
Virgin Holidays
Virgin Holidays + Hip
 Hotels
Virgin Limited Edition
Virgin Trains
Virgin Vacations

Note:
[a]Includes only those companies listed on the Virgin website.
Sources: http://www.virgin.com/company.

Most Virgin companies were not wholly owned by Virgin Group. Virgin Atlantic and Virgin Trains were 51% owned, Virgin Money 34%, and Virgin Active 20%. Virgin had sold off Virgin Media, Virgin Mobile and Virgin Wines entirely, licensing the brand to the new owners.

Virgin's Financial Performance

Financial reporting by the Virgin companies was fragmented, hard to locate, and difficult to interpret. No consolidated accounts were available for the group as a whole and tracking financial results for individual companies was complicated by Virgin's tendency to transfer its investments in operating companies between group companies. Among the several hundred British-registered Virgin companies filing their financial statements with the UK's Companies House, the closest to an overall parent company was Virgin Wings Ltd. Table 1 shows financial data for Virgin Wings, Table 2 shows data for its main business segments, and Table 3 shows its principal subsidiaries.

Doubts had frequently been expressed about the overall financial health of the group.[3] Branson was dismissive of such speculation, claiming that analysts and journalists misunderstood his business empire, emphasizing that the financial performance goals of a private company were different from a public corporation: "Short-term taxable profits with good dividends are a prerequisite of public life. Avoiding short-term taxable profits and seeking long-term capital growth is the best

TABLE 1   Consolidated financial data for Virgin Wings Ltd.

	9 months to 31/12/2013 (£million)	12 months to 31/03/2013 (£million)
Turnover	3,548	4,046
Operating profit	70	99
Pre-tax profit	62	86
Net profit	60	106
Fixed assets	880	853
Current assets	1,383	1,668
Total assets	2,263	2,521
Total liabilities	1,977	2,316
Net assets	286	205
Shareholders' equity	285	204

Source: Virgin Wings Ltd. and Subsidiary Companies: Strategic Report, Directors' Report and Financial Statements (December 31, 2013).

approach to growing private companies."[4] The observation that few Virgin companies were generating significant profits was reinforced by concerns over the balance sheet strength of the group. The complex financing arrangements between Virgin companies made it difficult to estimate the overall financial position—it is notable that many Virgin companies operated with negative shareholder equity and liabilities exceeding current assets. Also, the accounts for UK companies did not take account of the cash drain from Virgin Galactic. Galactic had absorbed over $600 million by November 2014, $380 million of which was provided by Abu Dhabi's state investment agency.[5]

The Virgin Brand

The Virgin brand was the group's greatest single asset. Compared to most other consumer brands, it was unusual in the range of products it encompassed. Could a

TABLE 2   Segment financial data for Virgin Wings Ltd.

	Revenue (£million)		Operating profit (£million)		Net operating assets (£million)	
	9 months to 31/12/2013	12 months to 31/03/2013	9 months to 31/12/2013	12 months to 31/03/2013	9 months to 31/12/2013	12 months to 31/03/2013
Air travel	2,554	2,854	20	(78)	(123)	(247)
Rail	716	898	8	31	(33)	(43)
Mobile telecoms	120	211	(3)	1	(23)	(20)
Financial services	25	29	(2)	(4)	(5)	(8)
Hotels	22	28	(2)	(5)	(11)	(8)
Healthcare	153	156	(3)	(5)	(11)	(8)
Other trading	22	30	8	10	32	30
Management services	59	55	44	149	423	159
TOTAL	3,671	4,261	70	99	311	159

Source: Virgin Wings Ltd. and Subsidiary Companies: Strategic Report, Directors' Report and Financial Statements (December 31, 2013).

TABLE 3   **Virgin Wings Ltd. subsidiary companies**

Subsidiary	Country	Activity	Ownership (%)
Virgin Holdings Ltd.	UK	Investment holding co.	100
Classboss Ltd.	UK	Investment holding co.	100
Virgin Rail Group Holdings Ltd.	UK	Train operator	51
Virgin Management SA	Switz.	Management services	100
Virgin Healthcare Holdings Ltd.	UK	Health service provider	94
VML 2 Ltd.	BVI	Investment holding co.	100
Virgin Atlantic Ltd.	UK	Flight and holiday operator	51
Barfair Ltd.	UK	Investment holding co	100
Vanson Developments Ltd.	UK	Investment holding co.	100
Virgin Management Ltd.	UK	Management services	100
Virgin Models Ltd.	UK	Investment holding co.	100
Voyager Group Ltd.	UK	Investment holding co.	100
Necker Island BVI	BVI	Hotel operator	100
Virgin Life Care Investments Ltd.	UK	Health and rewards program	91
Virgin Management USA Inc.	USA	Management services	100
Virgin Sky investments Ltd.	UK	Investment holding co.	100
Vexair Ltd.	UK	Investment holding co.	100
Virgin Management Asia Pacific Pty Ltd.	Australia	Management services	100
Bluebottle UK Ltd.	UK	Investment holding co.	100
Bluebottle Investment (UK) Ltd.	UK	Investment holding co.	100
Virgin Cinemas Group Ltd.	UK	Investment holding co.	100
VEL Holdings Ltd.	UK	Investment holding co.	100
Virgin Enterprises Ltd.	UK	Brand licensing	100
Virgin Hotels Group Ltd.	UK	Hotel operator	100
Virgin Insight Ltd.	UK	Procurement services	100

Note:
For all but two of the companies listed above, Virgin Wings' investments are held indirectly.
Source: Virgin Wings Ltd. and Subsidiary Companies: Strategic Report, Directors' Report and Financial Statements (December 31, 2013).

brand that extended from rail travel to streamed music have any meaningful identity? The Virgin website offered the following explanation:

> All the markets in which Virgin operates tend to have features in common: they are typically markets where the customer has been ripped off or under-served, where there is confusion and/or where the competition is complacent. In these markets, Virgin is able to break into the market and shake it up. Our role is to be the consumer champion, and we do this by delivering to our brand values, which are:

- Value for Money.
- Good Quality.
- Brilliant Customer Service.
- Innovative.
- Competitively Challenging.
- Fun.[6]

These attributes were conveyed to customers through Virgin's distinctive approach to differentiation. For example, Virgin Atlantic pioneered a range of innovative customer services (principally for its business class passengers). These included inflight massages, hair stylists, aroma therapists, and limousine and motorcycle transportation to and from the airport—even a speedboat service along the Thames from Heathrow to the London financial center. British Airways provided the ideal adversary against which Virgin Atlantic could position itself as the plucky upstart with customers' interests at heart.

Some of Branson's ventures seemed to be inspired more by a sense of fun and eagerness to "stick it to the big boys" than by commercial logic. When Virgin Cola was introduced in 1994, the goal, according to Branson, was to "drive Coke out of the States."[7] By 1997, Virgin Cola was losing £5 million on revenues of £30 million.

The Virgin brand was inseparable from Richard Branson's persona as entrepreneur, joker, and the "acceptable face of capitalism." The affection of the British public for Branson, and the appeal of the Virgin brand, reflected the alignment between Branson's values and sense of fair play with some of the traditional values that defined the British character. In battling huge, anonymous corporations, Branson recalled the legendary heroes of yesteryear who fought tyranny and evil: King Arthur, Robin Hood, and St. George. His willingness to appear in outlandish attire reflected a British propensity for eccentric dressing-up. But this distinctiveness also raised questions as to the appeal of the Virgin brand outside of Britain. It was unclear whether Branson and the Virgin brand could achieve the same rapport with consumers in other countries as they did in Britain.

Virgin's diversity presented several risks to the Virgin brand: overextension, entry into businesses where the Virgin/Branson identity offered limited differentiation appeal, and the danger that customer dissatisfaction in a single business might contaminate the entire brand. There was also the risk that Branson's popular appeal might be waning. A critical biography highlighted some of the contradictions in Branson's image and behavior: flying his private jet to climate change summits, lecturing on transparency and accountability while presiding over an impenetrably opaque business empire, promoting the interests of the underprivileged while protecting his own wealth in offshore family trusts.[8]

The Virgin Business Development Model

Most of Virgin businesses were start-ups. From the founding of *Student* magazine through to the formation of Virgin Galactic, Branson's strength as a businessman was in conceiving and implementing new business ideas—though the ideas behind most of Virgin's new business ventures came from other people: Branson acted as a magnet for would-be entrepreneurs from both inside and outside the Virgin Group. Virgin's website encouraged the submission of new business ideas to its corporate development office.

Virgin's approach to business start-ups reflected Branson's values of innocence, innovation, and irreverence for authority. His business ventures, just like his sporting exploits, reflected a "just live life" attitude and a "bigger the challenge, greater the fun" belief. He was particularly drawn to markets where stodgy, incumbent firms resulted in underserved customers and Virgin could offer a better alternative. Financial services were one sector where Branson hoped to bring a breath of fresh air.

Over time Virgin's approach to business development had become more systematized:

> When we start a new venture, we base it on hard research and analysis. Typically, we review the industry and put ourselves in the customer's shoes to see what could make it better. We ask fundamental questions: Is the customer confused or badly served? Is this an opportunity for restructuring a market and creating competitive advantage? What are the competitors doing? Is this an opportunity for building the Virgin brand? Can we add value? Will it interact with our other businesses? Is there an appropriate trade-off between risk and reward?

> We are also able to draw on talented people from throughout the Group. New ventures are often steered by people seconded from other parts of Virgin, who bring with them the trademark management style, skills and experience. We frequently create partnerships with others to combine industry specific skills, knowledge, and operational expertise…

> Once a Virgin company is up and running, several factors contribute to making it a success. The power of the Virgin Brand; Richard Branson's personal reputation; our unrivalled network of friends, contacts and partners; the Virgin management style; the way talent is empowered to flourish within the group. To some traditionalists, these may not seem hard headed enough. To them, the fact that Virgin has minimal management layers, no bureaucracy, a tiny board and no massive global HQ is an anathema. But it works for us! The proof of our success is real and tangible.

> Our companies are part of a family rather than a hierarchy. They are empowered to run their own affairs, yet the companies help one another, and solutions to problems often come from within the Group somewhere. In a sense we are a commonwealth, with shared ideas, values, interests and goals.[9]

Typically, Virgin was able to use the Virgin brand and Branson's celebrity status to obtain 51% or more of the equity of new ventures while contributing a minority of the equity capital. For example, Virgin's stake in Virgin Direct (which later became Virgin Money) required an initial outlay of only £15 million; its partner, AMP, put £450 million into the joint venture. At Virgin Blue, Branson's initial investment was a mere £12 million.

The Virgin Group's Management Structure and Style

The complexity of the legal and ownership structure of the Virgin Group is indicated by the following examples:

- West Coast Trains Ltd, Virgin's main UK rail franchise, was owned by Virgin Rail Group, which was owned by Virgin Rail Group Holdings Ltd, the majority of which was owned by Virgin Holdings Ltd, which was a subsidiary of Virgin Wings Ltd.
- Virgin Atlantic Airways was run through 11 companies, most of which were financial holding companies with no operational activities; others provided management and leading services.

These holding companies were, for the most part, ultimately owned by Virgin Group Holdings Limited, a private company registered in the British Virgin Islands and owned by a series of family trusts, the beneficiaries of which were Richard Branson and his family. The offshore domicile of the group's ultimate parent company made financial performance difficult to assess, disguised the identity of minority shareholders through the use of bearer shares, and cloaked the Virgin empire in a thick veil of secrecy.[10]

Branson's approach to management reflected his values and personality. Informality and disrespect for convention were central to Branson's way of business. He resisted any separation between work, family, and leisure reflecting a view of business as part of life which, like life, should involve excitement, creativity, and fun. Equally he was happy to involve cousins, aunts, childhood friends, and dinner-party acquaintances in business relationships. His hands-off approach to his business empire was based upon giving autonomy and incentives to managers he trusted. Once a new Virgin business was up and running, it was handed over to a trusted managing director and financial controller. The top management team were rewarded with equity stakes or options and expected to develop the company.

Branson's approach to business also reflected the social changes during his formative years. To many of his generation he embodied the spirit of the "New Britain"—a country identified more by its vibrant culture than by its colonial heritage and rigid class system. In a country where business leaders were conventionally part of "the establishment," Branson was seen as a revolutionary. Despite a privileged family background, Branson had the ability to transcend the social classes that traditionally divided British society and segmented consumer markets.

Branson's antipathy toward authority and convention was also reflected in his disrespect for conventional business principles. He argued that Virgin's network of small companies combined "small is beautiful" with "strength through unity." Claiming to have never read a management book, he developed his own principles of management. His business maxims have included: "Staff first, then customers and shareholders," "Shape the business around the people," "Be best, not biggest," "Pioneer, don't follow the leader," "Capture every fleeting idea," and "Drive for change."

Increasingly, Branson's freewheeling management philosophy was at odds with the growing formalization of the Virgin Group's management structure. This included:

- Establishing Virgin Management Ltd. as the center for the group's management capability. As the Virgin website explained:

  > At the center, Virgin Management Ltd. (VML) provides advisory and managerial support to all of the different Virgin companies and our specialist Sector teams around the world. Our people in London, New York and Sydney offer regional support and between us and the Sector teams we manage Virgin's interests across the whole of the Virgin Group.

  > VML's fastidious number-crunchers get to manage Virgin's financial assets in the group, our witty marketeers and intelligent communicators get to protect and maximise the value of the Virgin brand and our touchy-feely people teams ensure Virgin is an employer of choice.[11]

- Sector teams, each headed by a managing partner, provided oversight to companies within a particular area of business: "The specialists keep our companies on their toes and ensure we keep developing better experiences and world beating products."[12]

- Centralizing ownership and control of the Virgin brand within Virgin Enterprises Ltd. Neil Hobbs, intellectual property lawyer for Virgin Enterprises, explained: "Our role is both to optimize and enhance the value of the brand and to protect that by ensuring that value is not diminished through infringement by third parties."[13] During 2013, royalties from licensing the Virgin brand to members of the group and to other companies amounted to about £52 million.

- Establishing a top-management team. The appointment of Peter Norris as non-executive chairman of Virgin Group Holdings in 2009 was followed, in July 2011, with the appointment of Josh Bayliss, formerly Virgin's general counsel, as CEO.[14]

Nevertheless, formal structures and process formed a minor part of the Virgin management system. At the heart were two critical components of the system: culture and personal relations.

Despite structural formalization, the group endeavored to sustain the Virgin culture—an organizational embodiment of Branson's eccentricity, sense of fun, disrespect for hierarchy, informality, commitment to employees and consumers, and belief in creativity and individual effort. While the working environment was determinedly unstuffy and anti-corporate, expectations were high in relation to commitment, personal accountability, hours of work (when required), and performance goals.

The cohesiveness of Virgin's business empire was critically dependent on the relationships and collaboration among the group's senior management team. In 2015, these comprised the executives listed in Table 4. Each of these individuals held board positions in multiple Virgin companies.

Looking to the Future

In 2015, the strategic direction of the Virgin Group was unclear. While Richard Branson continued to espouse—and pioneer—bold entrepreneurial ventures, the businesses owned and controlled by the Virgin Group were primarily established ventures in regulated industries: airlines, trains, and healthcare. The group's profit was increasingly dependent not on its own businesses but on brand royalties and dividends from associated companies.

This raised the issue of the appropriate business model for Virgin Group. For much of its history Virgin had been primarily a business incubator, initiating and developing entrepreneurial new ventures. As already noted, Virgin had previously described itself as a "branded venture capital organization"; however, the typical venture capital firm invested in other entrepreneurs' start-ups: Virgin created its own businesses, typically using other people's money.

As the company established a number of major businesses in the travel, entertainment, and retail sectors, Virgin increasingly became a diversified holding company—along the lines of Berkshire Hathaway, Koch Industries, or the Tata Group. Branson himself had likened Virgin to a Japanese *keiretsu*—like Mitsubishi

TABLE 4 Virgin's senior executives, 2015

Executive	Role at Virgin	Prior career
Josh Bayliss	CEO since 2011, previously Virgin's General Counsel	Lawyer (Slaughter & May)
Peter Norris	Non-executive Chairman since 2009	Investment banker (Goldman Sachs, Barings)
Patrick McCall	Senior Partner, previously with Virgin Rail and Virgin Active	Investment banker (S.G. Warburg)
Evan Lovell	Investment Partner, on the boards of several Virgin investment holding companies	Private equity (TPG)
J. P. Moorhead	CFO, investment management at Virgin since 2005	Investment banker (Goldman Sachs)
Keith Roberts	Partner and Head of Corporate Development and Strategy	Management consultant (Bain & Co.)
Peter Stephens	Investment Partner, responsible for the development and expansion of Virgin's media and telecom	Investment banker, (Merrill Lynch, CSFB, Salomon Brothers)
Jean Oelwang	Partner and CEO of Virgin Unite, previously with Virgin Mobile Australia	Manager/entrepreneur in (telecom and not-for-profit enterprises)
Ian Woods	Partner, General Counsel and COO	Lawyer (Slaughter & May)
Nick Fox	Director of External Relations	Journalist (*Sunday Telegraph*, *Sunday Times*), business development (Granada, Jordan Co., M Communications)

Source: www.virgin.com/about-us.

or Mitsui, the Virgin Group featured equity linkages, interlocking directorships, collaboration between member companies, and a focus on long-term development.

However, as Virgin increasingly sold off or floated majority equity stakes in its core businesses, so it increasingly became more like a private equity fund. Certainly, the preponderance of investment bankers and lawyers among Virgin's top executive team was reminiscent of private equity firms.

Yet, what distinguished Virgin from the typical private equity firm was the central role of the Virgin brand. In markets where brand differentiation has proved elusive—airlines, rail travel, wireless communication, and healthcare—the Virgin brand was widely viewed as conferring substantial value. This raises the issue of whether the appropriate business model for Virgin was as a brand licensing company. However, the Virgin brand, because it is linked to an individual rather than to a particular product or business enterprise, appears vulnerable. "Every day that Richard gets older the issue of the Virgin brand becomes a bigger one because so much of it is tied to him," noted Jez Frampton, chief executive of Interbrand, the brand consultancy.[15] The use of high-profile new ventures to expand Virgin's brand awareness has also proved risky. In the US, where Branson and Virgin had relatively low profiles, Virgin Galactic was seen as a vehicle for boosting brand awareness. However, the crash of Galactic's SpaceShipTwo in October 2014 had wide repercussions. According to the *Financial Times*: "Sir Richard had hoped Galactic would have a 'halo effect' on the rest of the company. The risk is that it will have the opposite impact and threaten the value of the brand upon which the whole edifice depends."[16]

Whichever strategic model Virgin followed, it seemed likely that it would need to continue to make changes to its structure and management system. The informal, collaborative approach that had allowed the Virgin Group to survive and develop despite a turbulent economic environment had depended greatly upon Richard Branson and his personal leadership. Inevitably, his role within the group would diminish over time.

Notes

1. "Company Overview of Virgin Group Ltd.," http://www.bloomberg.com/research/stocks/private/snapshot.asp?privcapId=36312, accessed July 20, 2015. In fact, Bloomberg overstated the diversity of the Virgin Group, since it included a number of companies in which the Virgin parent company, Virgin Group Holdings Ltd., had no equity stake.

2. "About Us," https://www.virgin.com/about-us, accessed July 20, 2015.

3. "The future for Virgin," *Financial Times* (August 13, 1998): 24–5; M. Wells, "Red Baron," *Fortune* magazine (July 3, 2000).

4. R. Branson, letter to the *Economist* (March 7, 1998): 6.

5. Virgin Group Funds Tapped for Delayed Space Venture," *Financial Times* (November 2, 2014).

6. "Virgin Group: Brand it like Branson," *Financial Times* (November 5, 2014).

7. P. Robison, "Briton Hopes Beverage Will Conquer Coke's Monopoly," *Bloomberg News* (December 14, 1997).

8. T. Bower, *Branson: Behind the Mask* (London: Faber & Faber, 2014).

9. "The Virgin Brand," http://www.virgin.com/about-us, accessed September 27, 2012. Reproduced with permission.

10. By registering in the British Virgin Islands, Virgin Group Holdings Ltd. was not liable to local taxes and was allowed "maximum confidentiality and anonymity"; see http://www.offshorecorporation.com/bvi-company, accessed July 20, 2015.

11. "The Virgin Brand," http://www.virgin.com/about-us, accessed September 27, 2012. Reproduced with permission.

12. Ibid.

13. "Consolidating and Protecting the Licensed Virgin Brand," http://www.chrispatmore.com/wp-content/uploads/2011/12/virgin_case_study.pdf, accessed July 20, 2015.

14. Initially, Josh Bayliss and David Baxby were appointed co-CEOs. Baxby left his job in 2014.

15. "Virgin Group: Brand it like Branson," *Financial Times* (November 5, 2014).

16. Ibid.

Case 21 Google Is Now Alphabet—But What's the Corporate Strategy?

On August 10, 2015, Google's CEO, Larry Page, announced that Google Inc. would become Alphabet Inc., a holding company of which Google (comprising the company's search and internet businesses) would be the biggest operating company. Extracts of the announcement are reproduced in Exhibit 1.

The announcement led to a flurry of online debate among Google-watchers. Some saw the creation of Alphabet as Google's top management finally acceding to investors' demands for greater transparency by separating Google's primary source of profits, its search business, from Google's other businesses. Others regarded the announcement as confirmation that Google's founders, Larry Page and Sergey Brin, were prioritizing reckless technology-based diversification over shareholder interests.

Clear to all observers, however, was that Google had formally acknowledged it was no longer simply a search company. Since the introduction of its email system, Gmail, in April 2004 to the launch of its Project Fi wireless service in April 2015, Google had continually expanded its scope. Its products and services included YouTube's video-sharing website; the Android mobile operating system; online translation; the Chrome web browser and computer operating system; the Google+ social network; streaming and downloading books, music, movies and games; business productivity software; Android's smart TV platform; Google Fit's health-tracking system; Google Drive's cloud storage; Google Wallet's mobile payment system; and Google Flights online travel service—to mention but a few. Then there was Google's growing range of hardware products: smartphones, laptop and tablet computers, digital eyewear, intelligent watches, and home security devices. Finally, Google's development projects included driverless cars, intelligent contact lenses, robotics, a wireless internet service using air balloons (Project Loon), and extending the human life span (Google Calico).

The creation of Alphabet had done little to clarify the identity of the company-formally-known-as-Google. One online comment on the *New York Times*'s report on Google's new name asked:

This case was prepared by Robert M. Grant. ©2015 Robert M. Grant.

What kind of company does Google—er, Alphabet—want to become? I doubt they know, beyond the vague idea of "innovate."[1]

The same bewilderment had been expressed six years earlier:

Google increasingly feels like a company running in a thousand different directions at once … The problem is that in expanding into so many different areas, the identity of Google itself has become muddled … it's getting harder every day to articulate what Google is. Is it a Web company? A software company? Something else entirely?[2]

However, by creating Alphabet Inc., Google had addressed one of the questions the *Economist* magazine had posed: "whether Google can knit the diverse businesses it is developing and acquiring into an even more profitable engineering colossus."[3] Alphabet's holding company structure was designed to offer greater independence to Google's different businesses—making it clear that greater integration was not Google's chosen direction.

Beyond confirming Google's identity as a highly diversified, technology company and aligning its structure with that diversity, the creation of Alphabet did little to address the challenges arising from Google's expanding realm. In particular, entry into so many markets brought Google into direct competition with more and more companies: Apple in mobile platforms; Microsoft in browsers, operating systems, and office software; Facebook in social media; Amazon in online retailing; Honeywell in control systems for the home; Expedia in online travel services; Netflix in video streaming; AT&T and Verizon in wireless communication—and many more. Google had become a bigger target for regulators as well as competitors. The Federal Trade Commission found that Google had used anticompetitive tactics and abused its monopoly power, yet required only voluntary changes to Google's business practices.[4] European competition authorities took a harder line, accusing Google of abusing its dominant market position in web search and investigating possible anticompetitive practices in relation to Android.[5]

Was the creation of Alphabet a sound response to the range of opportunities and threats that Google faced and, within its new identity and legal structure, what kind of corporate strategy should Google/Alphabet adopt?

The History of Google, 1996–2015

The Google Search Engine

Larry Page and Sergey Brin met as PhD students at Stanford University. Their investigation of the linkage structure of the World Wide Web led them to develop a page-ranking algorithm that used backlink data (references by a web page to other web pages) to measure the importance of any web page. They called their search engine "Google" and in September 1998 incorporated Google Inc. in Menlo Park, California. Google's "PageRank" algorithm received a patent on September 4, 2001.

Search engines met the need of the growing number of people who were turning to the World Wide Web for information and commercial transactions. As the number of websites grew, locating relevant content became essential. Early web search engines included WebCrawler, Lycos, Excite, Infoseek, Inktomi, Northern Light, and

EXHIBIT 1

Google Announces Plans for New Operating Structure August 10, 2015

As Sergey and I wrote in the original founders' letter 11 years ago, "Google is not a conventional company. We do not intend to become one." … From the start, we've always strived to do more, and to do important and meaningful things with the resources we have.

We did a lot of things that seemed crazy at the time. Many of those crazy things now have over a billion users, like Google Maps, YouTube, Chrome, and Android. And we haven't stopped there. We are still trying to do things other people think are crazy but we are super excited about.

We've long believed that over time companies tend to get comfortable doing the same thing, just making incremental changes. But in the technology industry, where revolutionary ideas drive the next big growth areas, you need to be a bit uncomfortable to stay relevant.

Our company is operating well today, but we think we can make it cleaner and more accountable. So we

are creating a new company, called Alphabet. I am really excited to be running Alphabet as CEO with help from my capable partner, Sergey, as President.

What is Alphabet? Alphabet is mostly a collection of companies. The largest of which, of course, is Google. This newer Google is a bit slimmed down, with the companies that are pretty far afield of our main internet products contained in Alphabet instead. What do we mean by far afield? Good examples are our health efforts: Life Sciences (that works on the glucose-sensing contact lens), and Calico (focused on longevity). Fundamentally, we believe this allows us more management scale, as we can run things independently that aren't very related.

Alphabet is about businesses prospering through strong leaders and independence. In general, our model is to have a strong CEO who runs each business, with Sergey and me in service to them as needed. We will rigorously handle capital allocation and work to

AltaVista. Several of them became *portal sites*—websites that offered users their first port of entry to the web. Other portal sites soon recognized the need to offer a search facility. Yahoo! First licensed AltaVista's search engine, then replaced it with Inktomi.

The Google search engine attracted a rapidly growing following because of its superior page ranking and simple design. In 2000, Google began selling advertisements—paid web links associated with search keywords. These "sponsored links" were brief, plain text ads with a click-on URL, which appeared alongside web search results for specific keywords. Advertisers bid for keywords; it was these "cost-per-click" bids weighted by an ad's click-through rate (CTR) that determined the order in which a sponsored link would appear. In May 2002, AOL adopted Google's search engine and its paid listings service. By 2004, Google became the US market leader in web search.

Google became a public company on August 19, 2004: an IPO of about 7% of Google's shares raised $1.67 billion, valuing Google at $23 billion.

make sure each business is executing well. We'll also make sure we have a great CEO for each business, and we'll determine their compensation. In addition, with this new structure we plan to implement segment reporting for our Q4 results, where Google financials will be provided separately than those for the rest of Alphabet businesses as a whole…

Sergey and I are seriously in the business of starting new things. Alphabet will also include our X lab, which incubates new efforts like Wing, our drone delivery effort. We are also stoked about growing our investment arms, Ventures and Capital, as part of this new structure.

Alphabet Inc. will replace Google Inc. as the publicly-traded entity and all shares of Google will automatically convert into the same number of shares of Alphabet, with all of the same rights. Google will become a wholly-owned subsidiary of Alphabet … We liked the name Alphabet because it means a collection of letters that represent language, one of humanity's most important innovations, and is the core of how we index with Google search! We also like that it means *alpha-bet* (Alpha is investment return above benchmark), which we strive for! I should add that we are not intending for this to be a big consumer brand with related products—the whole point is that Alphabet companies should have independence and develop their own brands.

We are excited about…

♦ Getting more ambitious things done.

♦ Taking the long-term view.

♦ Empowering great entrepreneurs and companies to flourish.

♦ Investing at the scale of the opportunities and resources we see.

♦ Improving the transparency and oversight of what we're doing.

♦ Making Google even better through greater focus.

♦ And hopefully … as a result of all this, improving the lives of as many people as we can.

What could be better? No wonder we are excited to get to work with everyone in the Alphabet family. Don't worry, we're still getting used to the name too!

Larry Page, CEO, Alphabet

Source: Google Investor Relations, Press Releases, https://investor.google.com/releases/2015/0810.html, accessed July 20, 2015.

Organizing the World's Information

In addition to developing its core web search business through seeking to improve users' search experiences and finding ways to better monetize web search through advertising, Google also expanded beyond web search. This expansionism reflected the company's raison d'être: it had never seen itself just as an internet search engine—its mission was "to organize the world's information and make it universally accessible and useful." Google's IPO prospectus elaborated this intent:

We serve our users by developing products that enable people to more quickly and easily find, create and organize information. We place a premium on products that matter to many people and have the potential to improve their lives, especially in areas in which our expertise enables us to excel.

Search is one such area. People use search frequently and the results are often of great importance to them. For example, people search for information on medical conditions, purchase decisions, technical questions, long-lost friends and other topics about which they care a great deal. Delivering quality search results requires significant computing power, advanced software and complex processes—areas in which we have expertise and a high level of focus.[6]

The result was a series of new products that allowed access to information from diverse sources. New sources of information included images (Google Image Search), maps (Google Maps), academic articles (Google Scholar), books (Google Book Search), satellite imagery (Google Earth), panoramic street photographs of most of the world's cities (Google StreetView), news (Google News), patents (Google Patent Search), video (YouTube), finance (Google Finance), and web logs (Google Blog Search).

However, Google's entrepreneurial and technological dynamism caused the company to venture far beyond its mission to organize and make accessible the world's information. Beginning with Gmail in 2004, Google introduced a widening array of software and services for communicating, creating, and manipulating 2D and 3D images, producing documents, creating web pages, managing time, and social networking.

Although most of these new products and services offered limited revenue opportunities for Google, Google was expanding its advertising-based revenue model. Google's primary source of advertising revenue was AdWords, launched in 2000. Advertisers specify the words that should trigger their ads and the maximum amount they are willing to pay per click. When a user searches google.com, short text advertisements appear as "sponsored links" on the right side of the screen.

AdSense uses an advertisement placement technology developed by Applied Semantics (acquired in 2003) that allows Google to place ads on third-party websites. During 2010–2014, about 24% of Google's advertising revenues were derived from non-Google websites (see Table 3).

In 2007 and 2008, Google's diversification efforts took a dramatic new turn with Google's entry into mobile telephony and web browsers.

Android and Mobile Telephony

Google acquired Android Inc. in 2005 and in November 2007 launched the development of it Android software platform, a Linux-based operating system for mobile devices. *PC Advisor* commented:

> Google's announcement of the Android mobile development platform … is yet another example of the lengths the company will go to keep its advertising business growing at a jaw-dropping rate. It is also another awe-inspiring—or terrifying, depending on one's perspective—display of the engineering and business resources Google can unleash and of the power it has to influence, disrupt and rearrange markets.[7]

Android was a spectacular success: in establishing market leadership (Table 1), it prevented Apple from dominating the smartphone and tablet market. Android's success was the result of attracting, first, a large number of handset manufacturers (the

TABLE 1   Shipments of smartphones: Market share by operating system

	2015ª (%)	2013ª (%)	2011ª (%)
Android (Google)	78.0	75.5	36.1
iOS (Apple)	18.3	15.9	18.3
Blackberry OS (RIM)	0.3	2.9	13.6
Windows (Microsoft)	2.7	3.2	2.6
Other	0.7	1.5	29.4ᵇ
TOTAL	100.0	100.0	100.0

Notes:
[a]The data are for the first quarter of each year.
[b]In 2011, "Other" comprised Symbian with 26.0%, Linux with 3.1% and other systems 0.3%.
Source: IDC.

most important being Samsung) and, second, vast numbers of application developers
—by May 2015, there about 1.5 million Android apps.

Chrome

Google's Chrome web browser announced on September 2, 2008 generated huge
publicity, but little surprise. Google's then head of product development (later CEO
of Google within Alphabet), Sundar Pichai, explained: "Google's entire business is
people using a browser to access us and the web." Google's website added: "Google
Chrome is a browser that combines a minimal design with sophisticated technology
to make the web faster, safer, and easier." By contrast, Microsoft's Internet Explorer
(IE) was constrained by the legacy of its 15-year history.

Google's goal for Chrome was not simply a superior user experience. Version 8 of
Microsoft's IE launched in 2008, allowed an "InPrivate" protection mode that would
delete cookies, making it more difficult to track users' browsing habits. This would
limit Google's ability to use such information to target advertising.

Others saw Google's primary intention as not so much to protect its search engine
but more to attack Microsoft's dominance of personal computing and to speed the
transition of computing to a new online environment:

> [Google Chrome] is an explicit attempt to accelerate the movement of computing
> off the desktop and into the cloud—where Google holds advantage. And it's an
> aggressive move destined to put the company even more squarely in the crosshairs
> of its rival Microsoft.[8]

The announcement ten months later that Google would add an operating system to its Chrome browser was seen as confirmation of Google's aggressive intent
toward Microsoft.

Google in Hardware

As internet access transitioned toward mobile devices, Google sought to build technological strength in that sphere. In July 2011, a consortium of technology companies led by Apple and Microsoft purchased more than 6000 mobile-device-related

patents from Nortel Networks for about $4.5 billion. Believing its Android platform was vulnerable, Google acquired the struggling handset maker Motorola Mobility. Motorola's rich portfolio of patents relating to wireless communication would give Google a bigger bargaining chip and help it counter legal challenges from competitors —Apple in particular.

Owning Motorola would also permit Google closer integration of hardware and software development in smartphones and tablet computers. According to Phil McKinney of Hewlett-Packard: "Everyone is figuring out that if you want to survive, you really want to control the experience end to end. The ability to control both the hardware platform and operating system is absolutely critical."[9]

However, becoming a handset maker put Google into competition with some of its major customers, including Samsung, which had begun developing its own operating system to replace Android. In 2012, Google sold Motorola to Lenovo, but continued to develop and market mobile devices, including the Nexus brand of smartphones (build by HTC) and a range of notebook and tablet computers based upon its Chrome operating system.

Google's involvement in hardware was also apparent in some of its recent diversifications:

- Google Glass, an internet-enabled, optical head-mounted display controlled by natural language voice commands, was marketed on an experimental basis between April 2013 and January 2015.
- With the acquisition of Nest in January 2014, Google became a supplier of home security and control devices. This was to build Google's position as a central player in the "smart home." In May 2015, Google announced Project Brillo, an operating system to link home devices, such as door locks, light bulbs, and security cameras. Another development project, Project Weave, would allow these devices to communicate with other products and web services.[10]

Google+

Google's foray into social networking began with Orkut in January 2004 and continued with Google Friend Connect and Google Buzz. However, all were eclipsed by Facebook. When, in March 2010, Facebook overtook Google as the most visited website within the US, Google became fully aware of the threat posed by Facebook to its online advertising revenue:

> If you were an advertiser, who would you rather place your ads with? On the one hand, you have a company that will attempt to gear ads to things like the search history of users. On the other hand, you have a company that knows where its users went to college, where they work, who they are friends with, what they're reading and sharing, and their favorite bands, books, foods, and colors. Advertisers want to target their ads to the people most likely to be receptive to them, and information is the key to targeting. The more information available, the better the targeting.[11]

Facebook's threat was accentuated by the likelihood it would launch its own search engine to compete with Google. In 2011, Facebook had received a patent for a search algorithm and in December 2014 it dropped Microsoft's Bing as its licensed search engine.[12]

Launched in June 2011, Google+, the company's fourth venture into online social networking, had 540 million users by October 2013. However, their level of engagement (as measured by time spent online) was low and users have declined since that peak.

Google X

The experimental projects mentioned so far—driverless cars, Google Glass, and Project Loon (internet provision via airborne balloons)—are all located within Google X: a corporate lab for developing experimental technologies known as "moonshots." Other projects being undertaken at Google X during May 2015 included:

- Project Wing—package delivery via airborne drones;
- Makani Power—generating electrical power through wind turbines mounted on tethered kites;
- development of a revolutionary, miniature battery for powering mobile devices;
- a number of life sciences projects relating to Parkinson disease, intelligent contact lens for diabetics, synthetic skin, and genetic database analysis.

Google's Management and Capabilities

Google's phenomenal growth and capacity for innovation rested upon a management system that was unique, even by the unorthodox standards of Silicon Valley. Some of the key features of this system included:

- *Hiring policy*: From its earliest days, Google committed itself to hiring only the "brightest of the bright." Google's targets were not simply the highly intelligent. They were "smart creatives"—people who were "not confined to specific tasks … not adverse to taking risks … not hemmed in by role definitions … don't keep quiet when they disagree … get bored easily and shift jobs a lot … combine technical depth with business savvy and creative flair."[13] As founders Page and Brin explained: "Our employees, who have named themselves Googlers, are everything. Google is organized around the ability to attract and leverage the talent of exceptional technologists and business people … Because of our employee talent, Google is doing exciting work in nearly every area of computer science … Talented people are attracted to Google because we empower them to change the world."[14]
- *A "dramatically flat, radically decentralized" organization*: Google structure and systems were designed around the simple notion of "What do smart creatives need in order to be productive?" The answer was primarily about the aspects of traditionally managed organizations that should be avoided: authority, rules, formality, defined job roles, and hierarchical privileges. Google was a flat organization because its smart creatives needed easy access to key decisions in order to get things done. To minimize hierarchy,

Google used a "rule of seven": each manager must have at least seven direct reports. Google also maintained a function-based structure, avoiding business units based upon products or customer groups on the basis that once businesses have their own profit-and-loss accounts they tended to become silos.

- *Small, self-managing teams*: The majority of Google's employees, including all those involved in product development, worked in small teams. Most engineers were in teams of three or four. Team size was limited by the "two-pizza rule"—teams should be small enough to be fed by two pizzas. Teams appointed their own leaders, and engineers could switch teams without the need for permission from the HR department.

- *An environment that fosters creativity*: For employees to be productive required a working environment that stimulated and fostered their interaction. Google's workplaces were typically cramped cubicles that minimized separation from colleagues, Google's opulent eating and sports facilities were similarly designed to increase human interaction. Creativity and innovation were institutionalized through Google's "70–20–10" rule, which stipulated that Google would devote 70% of its engineering resources to developing the core business, 20% to extend that core into related areas, and 10% allocated to fringe ideas. As a result, Google employees were able to spend time working on pet projects of their own choosing.

- *Rapid, low-cost experimentation*: According to Gary Hamel: "Evolutionary adaptation isn't the product of a grand plan, but of relentless experimentation … Google's 'just-try-it' philosophy is applied to even the company's most daunting projects, like digitizing the world's libraries … Google Book Search began with a makeshift experiment aimed at answering a critical question; in this case: how long does it take to digitize a book?" To find out the team rigged up a prototype system that was subsequently adapted and improved. Hamel observed: "That kind of step-wise, learn-as-you-go approach has repeatedly helped Google to test critical assumptions and avoid making bet-the-farm mistakes."[15]

Underlying Google's capacity for innovation and the effective implementation of new initiatives was a set of resources that few other technology-based companies could match. With an operating cash flow of $22.4 billion in 2014 and a cash pile of $64.4 billion, Google was a financial powerhouse matched only by few other companies in the technology sector. This financial strength allowed Google to buy its way through acquisition into almost any market or area of technology. Most of the time Google did not need to buy its way into a new market: it was the world's most valuable brand after Apple[16] and possessed the strongest user base of any IT company—with 3.5 billion searches performed on Google each day, Google held close to 70% of the world market for internet search. (Second was Baidu with about 9%; Yahoo and Microsoft (Bing) each held between 3 and 4%.[17])

Alphabet: The New Structure

In the transition from Google Inc. to Alphabet Inc., Google's businesses remained the same. The difference was in the structuring of the company. While Google was an integrated corporation with internal functional departments, product groups, and project teams, Alphabet was a holding company with separate subsidiaries—by far the biggest being Google. The press release announcing Google's transition into Alphabet offered few details of this structure beyond identifying some of the constituent companies. These would include:

- Google, which would comprise search, advertising, maps, YouTube, and Android;
- Calico, an anti-aging biotech company;
- Sidewalk, a company focused on smart cities;
- Nest, a maker of internet-connected devices for the home;
- Fiber, high-speed internet service in a number of American cities;
- investment arms, such as Google Ventures and Google Capital;
- incubator projects, such as Google X, which is developing self-driving cars and delivery drones.

The result would be greater independence for the individual subsidiaries. However, the gains from greater autonomy and flexibility would be at the cost of less integration—notably in human resources in terms of less mobility across the company.

Corporate governance was largely unchanged. Google's board became the Alphabet board and Alphabet retained Google's dual-class share structure, which meant that founders Page and Brin retained about two-thirds of shareholder votes, in effect insulating their company from pressures from Wall Street.

Performance

Google's financial performance is summarized in Table 2.

As Table 3 shows, the vast majority of Google's revenues were derived from advertising—primarily from advertisements carried on its own websites. However, as Google diversified, so its non-advertising revenues grew. These "other revenues" comprised revenues for digital content—such as apps, music, and video from the Google Play store—and sales of hardware—notably Nexus and Chromecast products. The slowing growth of Google's advertising revenues was mainly due to a declining cost-per-click paid by advertisers to Google. This was primarily the result of the shift of internet access to small-screen mobile devices which were less conducive to presenting advertising and to making online purchases.

The Future of Alphabet

Although Alphabet Inc. would comprise the same businesses and have the same revenues and cash flows as Google Inc., the new name and structure implied significant changes for the company's identity and its management. The fact that the search business, which generated most of Google's revenue and all its profits, would be one of several subsidiaries implied greater prominence for diversified businesses, such as Nest and Calico.

TABLE 2 Google Inc.: Selected financial data, 2006–2014 ($billion)

	2006	2007	2008	2009	2010	2011	2012	2013	2014
Revenues	10.6	16.6	21.8	23.7	29.3	37.9	43.7	50.5	59.1
Cost of revenues	4.2	6.6	8.6	8.8	10.4	13.2	17.2	22.0	25.7
R & D	1.2	2.1	2.8	2.8	3.8	5.2	6.1	7.1	9.8
Sales and marketing expense	0.9	1.5	1.9	2.0	2.8	4.6	5.5	6.6	8.1
General and admin. expense	0.8	1.3	1.8	1.7	2.0	2.7	3.5	4.4	5.9
Income from operations	3.6	5.1	6.6	8.3	10.4	11.7	13.8	15.4	16.5
Net interest income	0.5	0.6	0.3	0.1	0.4	0.6	0.6	0.5	0.8
Income before income taxes	4.0	5.7	5.9	7.1	10.8	12.3	14.5	15.9	17.3
Net income	3.1	4.2	4.2	6.5	8.5	9.7	10.7	12.9	14.4
Cash and marketable securities	11.2	14.2	28.4	24.5	35.0	44.6	48.1	58.7	64.4
Long-term liabilities	0.1	0.6	1.2	1.7	1,6	5.5	7.7	7.7	9.8
Total stockholders' equity	17.0	22.7	28.2	36.0	46.2	58.1	71.7	87.3	104.5

Source: Google Inc. 10-K reports.

The holding company structure also conferred greater autonomy to the businesses, giving them greater freedom to develop and grow. This would resolve many of the problems arising from Google's increasing size and complexity. Between 2004 and 2014, Google had grown from 2840 to 53,600 employees, inevitably putting strain upon Google's famously informal management processes. As Google had acknowledged in its annual report for 2012: "If we do not effectively manage our growth, the quality of our products and services could suffer."[18] These risks had been amplified by the strains of integrating Google's many acquisitions, which had caused a "[d]iversion of management time and focus from operating our business to acquisition integration challenges."[19] However, the new holding company structure would also limit the potential for exploiting synergies between the different businesses.

TABLE 3 Google's revenue sources, 2006–2014 ($billion)

	2006	2007	2008	2009	2010	2011	2012	2013	2014
Advertising revenues of which	10.5	16.4	21.1	22.9	28.2	36.5	46.0	56.5	66.0
—Google websites	6.3	10.6	14.4	15.7	19.4	26.1	31.2	37.4	45.1
—Google network members' websites	4.2	5.8	6.7	7.2	8.8	10.4	12.5	13.1	14.0
Other revenues	0.1	0.2	0.7	0.8	1.1	1.4	2.4	5.0	6.9
Total revenues	10.6	16.6	21.8	23.7	29.3	37.9	46.0	55.5	66.0

Source: Google Inc., 10-K reports.

The new structure would also facilitate adding new businesses—either by acquisition or internal development—thereby setting the scene for further diversification. This raised concerns among investors as to whether the new company would provide greater opportunity for Page and Brin to pursue their ambitions of using technology to change the world. In an interview with the *Financial Times* in October 2014, Larry Page declared, "The societal goal is our primary goal," and outlined the main challenge as: "How do we use all these resources … and have a much more positive impact on the world?"[20] The answer seemed to be to use the money generated by Google's search advertising business to make bets on technologies that offered long-term solutions to some of the world's most pressing problems. Many of these initiatives grew out of the curiosity and personal interests of the two founders. For example, the inspiration for Calico came from the interests of Larry Page's wife, Lucy, in bioinformatics and the diseases of old age.

Beyond the notion of creating a "21st century, technology-based conglomerate," there was little indication of the boundaries that would be established around Alphabet's ambitions or its activities. *Forbes* contributor Dan Diamond pointed to healthcare as a major area of future growth for Alphabet.[21]

The implications of the new company for Google's core search and advertising business were far from clear. While investors hoped the holding company structure would allow greater transparency and bottom-line focus for management, there was limited evidence to support this optimism. The new Google subsidiary would include YouTube and Android; there was no indication that financial data would be available for the individual lines of businesses within Google.

Nor was it clear what the new structure would mean for the company's ability to address the challenges it faced from competitors and regulators. One regulatory challenge was antitrust: Google's dominant share of internet search and Android's share of mobile operating systems meant it was a monopoly in terms of the competition laws of many countries of the world. The other was privacy: concerns included the scanning of emails sent through Gmail, the use of cookies to track an individual's search history, the aggregation of an individual's data across Google's various services, the depiction of private residences on Google's StreetView, and the release of user data to national government agencies.[22]

Given the breadth of the challenges Google faced, had the time come for Google's leading trio—CEO and founder Larry Page, founder and director Sergey Brin, and executive chairman Eric Schmidt—to scale back Google's ambitions and draw boundaries around Google's corporate strategy?

Notes

1. "Google to Reorganize as Alphabet to Keep Its Lead as an Innovator," comment by "Eric," http://www.nytimes.com/2015/08/11/technology/google-alphabet-restructuring.html?ref=technology&_r=0, accessed July 20, 2015.
2. "Google's Growing Identity Crisis," (July 19, 2009), http://www.mercurynews.com/ci_12853656?IADID, accessed July 20, 2015.
3. "The New GE: Google, Everywhere," *Economist* (January 18, 2014).
4. "FTC Staff Wanted to Sue Google," *Wall Street Journal* (March 26, 2015).
5. European Commission, Press Release, "Antitrust: Commission sends Statement of Objections to Google," (Brussels, April 15, 2015).
6. Google Inc. SEC form 424B3 (filed November 23, 2004).
7. "Analysis: Google's Android Mobile Strategy Explained," *PC Advisor* (November 6, 2007), http://www.pcadvisor.

co.uk/news/mobile-phone/analysis-googles-android-mobile-strategy-explained-11248/, accessed July 20, 2015.

8. "Inside Chrome: The Secret Project to Crush IE and Remake the Web," *Wired* (October 16, 2008).

9. "What Google Gobbling Motorola Mobility Means For The Way We Think About Smartphones," (August 17, 2011), http://www.fastcompany.com/1774008/what-google-gobbling-motorola-mobility-means-way-we-think-about-smartphones, accessed July 20, 2015.

10. "Google Reveals Project Brillo and Weave to Power Internet of Things," *Fast Company* (May 28, 2015).

11. "Why Facebook Is a Threat to Google's Earnings," (April 12, 2012), http://www.cnbc.com/id/47030496, accessed July 20, 2015.

12. "Facebook Drops Microsoft's Bing in Favor of Its Own Search Tool," http://betanews.com/2014/12/14/facebook-drops-microsofts-bing-in-favor-of-its-own-search-tool/, accessed July 20, 2015.

13. E. Schmidt and J. Rosenberg, *How Google Works* (London: J. Murray, 2014): 17.

14. Letter from the Founders, "An Owner's Manual," for Google's Shareholders, http://investor.google.com/ipo_letter.html, accessed July 20, 2015. Reproduced with permission from Google Inc.

15. G. Hamel, *The Future of Management* (Boston: Harvard Business School Press, 2007).

16. "Apple beats Google to be named world's most valuable brand," *The Guardian* (May 26, 2015).

17. "Google Search Statistics,"http://www.internetlivestats.com/google-search-statistics/, accessed July 20, 2015.

18. Google Inc., 10-K report to the SEC for 2011: 16. Reproduced with permission from Google Inc.

19. Google Inc., 10-K report to the SEC for 2014: 7.

20. "FT Interview with Google Co-founder and CEO Larry Page," *Financial Times* (October 31, 2014).

21. "Google is now Alphabet, and that Spells Big Things for Healthcare," *Forbes* (August 11, 2015), http://www.forbes.com/sites/dandiamond/2015/08/11/google-is-now-alphabet-and-it-could-spell-big-things-for-healthcare/, accessed July 20, 2015.

22. In May 2014, the European Court of Justice established "the right to be forgotten": individuals could require Google to remove links to any content that was inadequate or irrelevant; "Google sets up 'right to be forgotten' form after EU ruling," http://www.bbc.co.uk/news/technology-27631001, accessed July 20, 2015.

Case 22 Jeff Immelt and the New General Electric

When Jeff Immelt got up to welcome shareholders to General Electric Company's annual general meeting in Oklahoma City on April 22, 2015, it was the 14th annual general meeting of the company he had presided over since his appointment as chairman and CEO in 2001. Yet his address to the meeting also made it very clear that General Electric (GE) was still a work in progress.

In his address, Immelt outlined his vision of GE as a "connected industrial company" that stood at the intersection of the physical and digital worlds and blended "the best elements of speed, scale and flexibility."[1] To further this vision, GE would be undertaking major adjustments to its business portfolio during 2015: completing its biggest ever acquisition, Alstom's power equipment and grid businesses, and divesting the major part of its financial services company, GE Capital.

The recreation of GE under Immelt's leadership had been a turbulent process.

When in September 2001 Immelt took over from his predecessor, Jack Welch—"living legend" and "best manager of the 20th century"—he knew that leading GE would be a difficult challenge. Little did he know just how tough his job would be.

Four days after Immelt took over the chairman's suite, two hijacked airliners crashed into New York's World Trade Center, setting off a train of events that would profoundly affect GE's business environment. A month later, Enron's collapse precipitated a crisis of confidence over ethics, corporate governance, and financial reporting, which soon engulfed GE, forcing it to restate earnings and reveal the details of Jack Welch's staggeringly generous retirement package. Then came the financial crisis of 2008–2009, which, due to GE Capital's position as one of America's leading financial institutions, threatened GE's survival, forcing it to seek a $3 billion equity injection from Warren Buffett's Berkshire Hathaway group.

Despite the turbulent circumstances of 2001 to 2015, during this period Immelt had systematically put in place a long-term transformation strategy for GE. This strategy had involved reconfiguring GE's business portfolio, reorienting its performance goals toward revenue growth, refocusing GE's competitive advantage around technological innovation and customer service, and adjusting GE's structure, management processes, and corporate culture. The April 2015 decision to sell off most of GE Capital was the culmination of that strategy.

The changing shape of GE's overall business makeup is shown in Figure 1. However, for all of Immelt's success in transforming GE's business model and guiding

This case was prepared by Robert M. Grant. ©2015 Robert M. Grant.

FIGURE 1 General Electric's changing business portfolio, 2001 and 2015

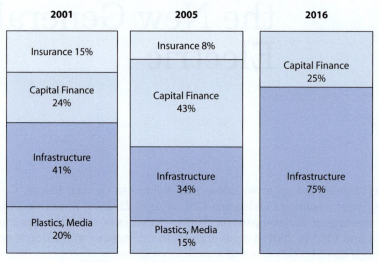

Source: General Electric shareowners meeting (April 25, 2012) and Annual Letter to GE Shareholders (2014).

GE through the challenges of the 21st century, the company's financial performance had lagged. Early in his tenure, Immelt had set ambitious performance targets for GE: sales growth at 2–3 times that of global GDP, 10% plus earnings growth, and a 20% plus return on total capital.[2] GE's performance had fallen well short of these targets (Table 1). GE's share price told the story: when Immelt's appointment had been announced late in 2000, GE's stock was trading at $53: since taking office, GE's share price had never regained these heights (Figure 2).

Throughout his 15 years at GE, Immelt had been haunted by the question of whether GE's shareholders would be better off if the company were broken up altogether. Since the early 1990s, highly diversified companies had been deeply unpopular with investors and investment analysts and were subject to a "conglomerate discount": diversified companies had stock market values that were below the estimated aggregate valuation of their individual businesses. As a result, most conglomerates (including ITT, Tyco International, General Mills, Fortune Brands, and Vivendi Universal) had been broken up—or, in the case of Danaher, were proposing

TABLE 1 General Electric: Performance indicators, 2001 and 2014

Year	Sales ($billion)	Net income ($billion)	Return on equity (%)	Return on invested capital (%)[a]	Market capitalization, 31st Dec. ($billion)	Employees (thousand)	Non-US employees (%)
2001	125.9	13.7	26.0	27.0	397.9	310	49
2014	148.6	15.3	11.9	10.6	187.8	305	57

Note:
[a]Industrial businesses only (excludes GE Capital).
Source: General Electric, 10-K reports.

FIGURE 2   General Electric share price, 1995–2015 ($)

to do so. The trend had spread to other diversified companies: Kraft Foods had split into two, Kraft, a processed foods company, and Mondēlez International, a chocolate and snacks company.

The case against highly diversified companies was reinforced by the growing recognition of the need for in-depth domain expertise for senior managers. Andrew Hill of the *Financial Times* raised the question: "If the demand is now for depth over breadth, will there be enough 'serial masters' capable of understanding, let alone running, companies of the scale and scope of General Electric?"[3] In a subsequent article he addressed the broader question: "Have some companies become too big to manage?"[4]

The challenge for Jeff Immelt, therefore, was not only reinventing GE, it was also reinventing the management model of the diversified corporation. He rejected the description of GE as a conglomerate—"That word does not apply to us"[5]—and argued:

> GE is … bound together by common operating systems and initiatives, and a common culture with strong values. Because of these shared systems, processes, and values, the whole of GE is greater than the sum of its parts.[6]

The challenge for Immelt was to create the systems, processes, and values that could demonstrate that GE was more valuable as a single entity than as a number of separate businesses.

Table 2 summarizes GE's financial performance during 2008–2014.

The History of GE

The GE that Jeff Immelt inherited in 2001 was the world's most valuable company (in terms of market capitalization) and was widely regarded as the world's most successful. It was the only company to have remained a member of the Dow Jones

TABLE 2 General Electric: Selected financial data, 2008–2014 ($billion unless otherwise indicated)

	2014	2013	2012	2011	2010	2009	2008
GE Consolidated							
Revenues	148.6	146.0	146.7	147.3	150.2	156.8	182.5
Net earnings	15.3	15.2	14.6	14.2	11.6	11.0	17.4
R & D expenditure[a]	4.2	4.6	4.5	5.4	4.9	4.4	4.3
Cash from operating activities	27.5	29.0	31.0	33.4	36.1	24.6	48.6
Cash from (used in) investing activities	(5.0)	29.1	11.3	19.9	32.4	43.0	(35.4)
Return on average equity (%)	11.6	12.2	12.1	11.9	12.1	11.6	15.9
Stock price range ($)	27.94–23.69	28.09–20.68	23.18–18.02	21.65–14.02	19.70–13.75	17.52–5.87	38.52–12.58
Year-end closing stock price ($)	25.27	28.03	20.99	17.91	18.29	15.13	16.20
Total assets	648.3	656.6	681.7	717.2	747.8	781.8	797.8
Long-term borrowings	200.4	221.7	236.1	243.5	293.3	336.2	330.1
Total employees (thousands)	305	307	305	301	287	304	323
GE data (industrial businesses)							
Short-term borrowings	3.9	1.8	6.0	2.2	0.5	0.5	2.4
Long-term borrowings	12.5	11.5	11.4	9.4	9.6	11.7	9.8
Shareowners' equity	128.2	130.6	123.0	116.4	118.9	117.3	104.7
Total capital invested	145.3	144.8	141.3	129.0	133.1	135.3	123.5
Return on average capital invested (%)	10.6	11.3	11.7	11.6	11.8	10.6	14.8
Borrowings as % of capital invested	11.2	9.2	12.4	9.0	7.6	9.0	9.9
Working capital				(0.0)	(1.6)	(1.6)	3.9
GECC[b] data (financial services)							
Revenues	42.7	44.1	45.4	49.1	49.91	51.8	71.3
Net earnings	7.2	6.2	6.2	16.5	2.2	1.4	7.1
Shareowner's equity	87.5	82.7	81.9	77.1	69.0	70.8	53.3
Total borrowings	349.5	371.1	397.0	443.1	470.5	493.3	514.6
Ratio of debt to equity at GECC	3.99:1	4.49:1	4.85:1	5.75:1	6.82:1	6.96:1	8.76:1
Total assets	500.2	516.8	539.4	584.5	605.3	650.4	660.9

Note:
[a]Includes R & D funded by customers (principally the US government).
[b]GECC = General Electric Capital Corporation, also known as GE Capital.
Source: General Electric 10-K reports.

industrial index since the index was created in 1896. The key to its success had been to combine massive size with constant adaptation. Over the decades, GE had adapted both its business portfolio and its management systems to the demands and opportunities of a changing world.

GE was founded in 1892 from the merger of Thomas Edison's Electric Light Company with the Thomas Houston Company. Its business was based upon exploiting Edison's patents relating to electricity generation and distribution, light bulbs, and electric motors. Throughout the 20th century, GE was not only one of the world's biggest industrial corporations but also "a model of management—a laboratory studied by business schools and raided by other companies seeking skilled executives."[7] Under the leadership of Charles Coffin, between 1892 and 1922, GE successfully married Edison's industrial R & D laboratory to a business system capable of turning scientific discovery into marketable products. After the Second World War, chairman Ralph Cordiner, assisted by Peter Drucker, pioneered new approaches to the systematization of corporate management. Under Fred Borch (CEO 1963–1972), GE's corporate management system based on strategic business units and portfolio analysis became a model for most diversified corporations. Reg Jones, GE's chairman from 1972 to 1981, linked GE's techniques of strategic planning to its systems of financial management.

During his two decades at GE's helm, Jack Welch had led the most comprehensive strategic and organizational upheaval in GE's long history. Welch reformulated GE's business portfolio through exiting low-growth extractive and manufacturing businesses and expanding services—financial services in particular. By the time he retired, GE Capital represented almost half of GE's revenues and the majority of its assets. At the heart of Welch's remaking of GE was the creation of a performance culture supported by comprehensive systems for setting and monitoring performance targets and providing powerful incentives for their achievement:

> Changing the culture—opening it up to the quantum change—means constantly asking not how fast am I going, how well am I doing versus how well I did a year or two before, but rather, how fast and how well am I doing versus the world outside. Are we moving faster, are we doing better against that external standard?

> Stretch means using dreams to set business targets—with no real idea of how to get there … We certainly didn't have a clue how we were going to get to 10 inventory turns [a year] when we set that target. But we're getting there, and as soon as we become sure we can do it—it's time for another stretch.[8]

Welch declared war on GE's elaborate bureaucracy and stripped out layers of hierarchy. His management style was direct, personal, and confrontational: managers were encouraged to commit to ambitious performance targets, after which they and their subordinates were under intense pressure to deliver. Every aspect of GE's management systems was redesigned from the ground up, from strategic planning to human resources. Welch also introduced periodic challenges for the whole organization. These included: "Be #1 or #2 in your global industry"; "Work-out," a process for company meetings that allowed grassroots ideas about organizational change to be implemented; "six sigma," a program of company-wide initiatives to improve quality and reliability; and "Destroy your business dot.com," an initiative to drive the adoption of internet technologies.

Under Welch's leadership, GE enjoyed two decades of outstanding performance. Between 1981 and 2001, revenues grew from $30 billion to $126 billion, net income from under $2 billion to $14 billion, and stock market capitalization from $14 billion to $510 billion: an average annual return to stockholders of 24%.

Jeff Immelt

Jeffrey R. Immelt was appointed CEO of GE at the age of 44. He had previously been head of GE's Plastics business and, most recently, head of Medical Systems. He had a BA from Dartmouth and an MBA from Harvard. He was second-generation GE—his father had spent his entire career at the company. On joining GE from Harvard in 1982, Immelt was identified as a "young high potential," which meant his progress would be carefully tracked by top management at GE. At GE Appliances, GE Plastics, and GE Medical Systems, Immelt acquired a reputation for turning around troubled units, driving customer service and exploiting new technologies. He also demonstrated the ability to motivate others, an aptitude that he had revealed as an offensive tackler for Dartmouth's football team.[9]

In December 1994, the GE board began to consider possible candidates to replace Jack Welch. Between 1995 and 1999, the list had been cut from 20 GE executives to three. The final choice of Immelt was primarily the result of his outstanding leadership of GE Medical Systems.

His personality and leadership style contrasted sharply with that of Welch. "Where Welch ruled through intimidation and thrived as something of a cult figure, Immelt opts for the friendlier, regular-guy approach. He prefers to tease where Welch would taunt. Immelt likes to cheer people on rather than chew them out. That style has given him a very different aura within GE. He may not be a demigod, but it's his man-of-the-people nature that draws praise from the top ranks to the factory floor."[10] This style of leadership had implications for the organizational and management changes that Immelt would introduce; however, it was radical changes in GE's business environment that would be the dominant drivers of GE's strategic and organizational development.

GE's Business Environment, 2001–2015

GE's financial performance under Welch was in an economy effused with optimism, confidence, and growth. The new century presented a new set of challenges. In his first letter to shareholders, Immelt observed: "The exuberance of the late 1990s and the inevitable downturn have created difficult times. Entire industries have collapsed, poor business models have been exposed, large companies have filed for bankruptcy and corporate credibility has been called into question."[11]

In a world of turbulence, Immelt viewed GE's diversified portfolio of businesses as a source of stability over the business cycle. Throughout his 15 years at the helm he emphasized the merits of a portfolio of businesses that smoothed the volatility that afflicted individual businesses. The GE annual report for 2014 emphasized, "Diversity provides strength through disruptive events and commodity cycles," thereby constituting a key source of "value from a Multibusiness Company."[12]

A further key change in the business environment was the discrediting of the 1990s' obsession with shareholder value maximization. From the outset, Immelt was anxious to disassociate himself from cruder versions of shareholder value maximization. In all his communications to shareholders, Immelt was emphatic that the job of the CEO was not to manage the stock price but to manage the company for the long-term earnings growth that would drive the stock price: "We all want the stock to go up. But to do that we have to manage the company. In fact, the only way you can run GE is to believe that performance will ultimately drive the stock."[13]

The critical challenge of the business environment of the 21st century, believed Immelt, was to identify the potential sources of profit for GE. Under Welch, GE had created value through cost reduction, eliminating underperforming assets, and exploiting the opportunities offered by financial services. By the time Immelt took over, these sources of value had been mined out: GE would need to look into new areas. Top-line growth, he reasoned, would have to be the driver of bottom-line returns—despite the generally poor outlook for growth in the world economy.

In identifying opportunities for profitable organic growth, Immelt identified four global trends he believed would offer business opportunities for GE:

- *Demography*: The aging of the world's population would create opportunities for goods and services required by older people, in particular healthcare services. Population growth in the developing world would also offer expanding demand for many of GE's other businesses, including entertainment.
- *Infrastructure*: GE predicted massive investments in infrastructure. GE's positioning in infrastructure products, services, and financing offered it opportunities in energy, aviation, rail transportation, water, and oil and gas production.
- *Emerging markets*: China, India, Eastern Europe, Russia, the Middle East, Africa, Latin America, and South-East Asia would offer rates of GDP growth around three times that of the world as a whole. These countries would be key centers of business opportunity for GE.
- *Environment*: The challenges of global warming, water scarcity, and conservation would become increasingly pressing, creating the need for technologies and innovatory responses to alleviate these problems.

Reshaping GE's Business Portfolio

Growth, organic growth in particular, became the primary goal for Immelt's strategy. In 2002, he committed GE to an organic growth rate of 8% per annum (under Welch organic growth had averaged 5% a year) and to "double digit" earnings growth. This 8% revenue growth was based upon the idea that GE should be able to grow at between two and three times that of world GDP. Profits would grow faster than revenues, explained Immelt, because of reductions in general and administrative expenses as a percentage of sales and higher margins resulting from new products and services. Between 2002 and 2007, GE comfortably met these targets: revenues grew at 13% each year; operating earnings, at 14%. However, during 2008–2009, revenues and profits contracted sharply and during 2010–2014 there was no growth in either.

To position GE for stronger growth, the company would need to exit slow-growth businesses, reallocate resources to businesses where growth prospects were strong, and enter new businesses. A key theme in Immelt's reshaping of GE's business portfolio toward higher growth was the creation of "growth platforms." These could be extensions of existing businesses or entirely new areas of business. Identifying new growth platforms became a central strategic challenge for GE's businesses.

In several cases, GE's growth platforms involved existing businesses where there was potential to greatly expand the company's market presence. For example:

- *Healthcare*: GE was the world leader in diagnostic imaging: X-ray equipment, CT scanners, and MRI scanners. Under Immelt it became a major area of growth for GE, expanding its range of products and services and its geographical presence. Key acquisitions included: Amersham (a UK-based diagnostics and medical equipment company) and Abbott Diagnostics (the world's leading provider of in vitro diagnostics).

- *Energy*: Power generation was GE's oldest business; in addition it had developed a promising business supplying equipment to the oil and gas sector. Immelt viewed energy as a particularly attractive growth platform for GE. One major growth area was alternative energy where key acquisitions included Enron's wind energy business, ChevronTexaco's coal gasification business, and AstroPower, which supplied solar energy products. In conventional power generation, the Alstom acquisition made GE the undisputed world leader in turbines. In oil and gas, a series of acquisitions established GE as a key player in supplying oilfield equipment and services.

- *Broadcasting and entertainment*: During 2001–2007, GE expanded its entertainment activities beyond its NBC broadcasting and cable TV businesses. Key acquisitions were Telemundo, which took GE into the fast-growing market for Spanish-language broadcasting, and Vivendi Universal's entertainment business, which took GE into film studios and theme parks. However, by 2009, it was increasingly evident that NBC Universal did not fit with Immelt's identification of GE as a technology-based industrial company. As a result, NBC Universal was merged with Comcast's cable TV channels, with the new company 49% owned by GE and 51% by Comcast. In 2013, Comcast bought out GE's remaining 49% stake.

- *Technology infrastructure*: Infrastructure provided a valuable umbrella for a number of Immelt's growth initiatives. In 2003, he announced: "We are taking the company to a place where few can follow: big, fundamental, high technology infrastructure industries in which GE can have enormous competitive advantage."[14] In addition to GE's core electrical generation business, with the acquisition of Alstom GE developed new growth platforms such as: security systems; water treatment; and aerospace, where GE built upon its strong position in jet engines to diversify into avionics (Smiths Aerospace was a major acquisition).

Divestments focused on areas either where growth and profit prospects were poor—such as domestic appliances—or that did not fit with GE's capabilities or its management model—such as NBC Universal. GE also exited other businesses, most notably plastics, where it believed high petroleum prices would limit growth opportunities and where it lacked the critical mass of the major petrochemical companies.

However, by far its greatest divestment challenge was its financial services business, GE Capital. Despite Immelt's emphasis on GE as a technology-based industrial company and his commitment to shrinking GE Capital, GE Capital continued to grow during 2001–2007 as a result of organic growth and acquisitions in equipment leasing, commercial finance, credit cards, and consumer finance that were only partly offset by the sale of GE's insurance businesses in 2004 and 2005. In 2006 and 2007, GE Capital accounted for almost half of GE's total net profit (up from 25% in 2001).

With the financial crisis Immelt came under urgent pressure to shrink GE Capital's assets (i.e., reducing its loan exposure), increase its liquidity, improve its risk profile, and redefine its role within GE. Increasingly, GE Capital was reconceived as a supplier of specialist financial services with a particular emphasis on "mid-market lending and leasing, financing in GE domains and a few other specialty finance segments."[15]

In 2013, US financial regulators designated GE Capital as a "systemically important financial institution." The requirement that GE Capital would have to hold higher capital reserves effectively eliminated the competitive advantage of GE Capital as a non-bank supplier of financial services and, combined with the generally poor outlook for the financial services industry in the US, encouraged the decision to break up and dispose of most of GE Capital.[16] The GE Capital businesses that would be retained comprised "vertical financial businesses"—those that were closely linked to GE's core industrial businesses such as GE Capital Aviation services, Energy Financial Services, and Healthcare Equipment Finance.

Table 3 lists GE's principal acquisitions and disposals during Immelt's tenure.

Building GE's Competitive Advantage

A major theme of all Immelt's speeches and strategy presentations as chairman and CEO was his emphasis of the competitive advantages that GE shared across its different businesses. Immelt placed a particular emphasis on three sources of competitive advantage: technology and innovation, customer focus and integrated solutions, and global presence.

Technology and Innovation

Immelt identified technology as a major driver of GE's future growth, emphasizing the need to turn the corporate R & D center into an intellectual hothouse and to speed the internal diffusion of new technologies. His commitment to technology was signaled by expanding GE's R & D budgets. This began with a $100 million upgrade to GE's corporate R & D center in Niskayuna, New York and the construction of new Global Research Centers in Shanghai, Munich, and Rio de Janeiro. By 2015, GE claimed to have about 37,000 technologists working in R & D within its businesses and its eight global research centers in the US, Germany, China, Brazil, Israel, and India.

Under Immelt, GE focused its research upon fewer, bigger, longer-term programs. This emphasis was reflected in GE's Advanced Technology Programs in molecular imaging and diagnostics, nanotechnology, energy conversion, advanced propulsion, and sustainable energy.

TABLE 3 General Electric's principal acquisitions and disposals, 2001–2015

Year	Acquisitions	Disposals
2001	NBC acquires Telemundo, a Spanish language TV network	
2003	GE Healthcare acquires Instrumentarium	
	GE Capital acquires Transamerica Finance from AEGON	
2004	NBC acquires the entertainment assets of Vivendi Universal, to form NBC Universal (80% owned by GE)	Sells 60% of GE Capital International Services (GECIS) for $500mn
	GE Healthcare acquires Amersham PLC for $9.5bn	GE's life and mortgage insurance businesses spun off as Genworth Financial
	GE Capital acquires Dillard's credit card unit for $1.25bn	
	GE Security acquires InVision Technologies, a leading manufacturer of airport security equipment	
2005	GE Commercial Finance acquires the financial assets of Bombardier, for $1.4bn	
2006	GE Healthcare acquires IDX Systems, a medical software firm, for $1.2bn	GE Advanced Materials division is sold to Apollo Management for $3.8bn
	GE Water & Process Technologies acquires Zenon Environmental Systems for $758mn	Sale of GE Insurance Solutions and GE Life to Swiss Re for $6.5bn
2007	GE Aviation acquires Smiths Aerospace for $4.6bn	GE Plastics is sold to Saudi Arabia Basic Industries Corp. for $11.7bn
	GE Oil & Gas acquires VetcoGray for $1.4bn	
	NBC Universal acquires Oxygen Media (cable TV channel)	
2008	GE Co. acquires Vital Signs Inc. for $860mn	
	GE Energy Infrastructure acquires Hydril Pressure Control (oilfield equipment)	
	GE Capital acquires Merrill Lynch Capital, CitiCapital, and Bank BPH	
2009	GE increases its ownership of BAC to 75%	
2010	GE Healthcare acquires Clarient, Inc.	GE Capital sells Regency Energy Partners LP
2011	GE Energy Infrastructure acquires Converteam, Dresser, Inc., the Well Support division of John Wood Group PLC, Wellstream PLC, and Lineage Power Holdings, Inc.	Sells 51% of NBC Universal to Comcast for about $19bn
		GE Capital sells Mexican assets to Santander
2012	GE Capital acquires $7bn bank deposits from Metlife	
2013	Acquires oilfield pump maker, Lufkin Industries, for $3bn	Sells remaining 49% of NBC Universal to Comcast for $16.7bn
2014	Acquires power and grid business of French engineer Alstom for $17bn	Spinoff of retail finance business, Synchrony Financial
		Sale of appliances business to Electrolux for $3.3bn
2015		GE Capital Real Estate sold to Wells Fargo and Blackstone for $26.5 billion
		Announces sale of majority of GE Capital

Sources: General Electric annual reports and press releases.

Immelt was particularly interested in identifying and supporting projects that offered large-scale market potential. "Imagination Breakthroughs" were promising projects with the potential to create $100 million in sales over a three-year period. By mid-2006, some 100 Imagination Breakthroughs had been identified and individually approved by Immelt. Imagination Breakthroughs included:

- *evolution hybrid locomotive*: an energy-saving locomotive that would use energy lost in braking to be stored in batteries;

- *Smart Grid*: a marriage of IT with electrical infrastructure to support 21st-century energy needs;
- *sodium batteries*: a novel, patented battery technology for large-scale electricity storage.

GE's "Ecomagination" was a program of product and business development launched in 2005 as "GE's commitment to address challenges such as the need for cleaner, more efficient sources of energy, reduced emissions, and abundant sources of clean water."[17] The Ecomagination program provided funding and coordination for developing environmentally friendly products and business solutions across GE's different business divisions. In 2011, it was credited with generating $21 billion of clean energy revenue.

During 2013–2015, GE further reconceptualized its technological focus and its approach to innovation. It described its R & D focus as "breakthrough innovations in areas such as molecular imaging and diagnostics, energy conversion, nanotechnology, advanced propulsion and security technologies."[18] One of the most important areas of opportunity for all GE's industrial business lay at the "interface of the physical and digital worlds" through "combining data and physics." Since 2013, GE had used the term "industrial internet" to refer to the linkage between big data analytics and the "internet of things." This created opportunities for all GE's businesses by using embedded sensors on its jet engines, locomotives, oil and gas equipment, healthcare equipment, electricity generators, and so on to link with software that managed maintenance schedules, fuel optimization, accident prevention, factory automation, and enterprise management.

For example, a GE Evolution locomotive contained 6.7 miles of wiring and 250 sensors that put out nine million data points hourly that provided input for software tools such as Trip Optimizer (real-time guidance to train drivers on fuel economy), Remote Diagnostics (predicting equipment failures and scheduling maintenance), Yard Planner (to speed the breakup, sorting, and reformation of trains), and Movement Planner (to optimize the movement of trains on individual tracks and rail networks).

Customer Focus and Integrated Solutions

Throughout his career at GE, Immelt had emphasized customer orientation, the value of spending time with customers, building relationships with them, and working on their problems. Soon after taking over as CEO, Immelt emphasized the primacy of customer focus:

> We're dramatically changing our resource base from providing support to creating value. Every business has functions that add high value by driving growth. These are the functions that deal with the customer, create new products, sell, manufacture, manage the money and drive controllership. Call that the front room. Every business has backroom support functions that sometimes are so large and bureaucratic they create a drain on the system and keep us from meeting our customers' needs and keep us from growing. So we're going to take more of the back-room resources and put them in the front room—more sales people, more engineers, more product designers. We're changing the shape of this company and we're doing it during a recession."[19]

The increased customer focus involved increased investment in GE's marketing function, including hiring talented marketing executives and developing processes for identifying new product and service offerings and unmet customer needs.

A major avenue for translating enhanced customer focus into value creation for GE was through bundling products with support services to offer customized "customer solutions." Expanding the range of customer service offerings included technical services, financial services, training, and other forms of customer support. Creating customer solutions required coordination across GE's businesses. For example, in the case of a new hospital development, there might be opportunities not just for medical equipment but also for lighting, turbines, and other GE businesses as well. To exploit new opportunities that cut across GE's existing divisional structure, GE began to create cross-business, high-visibility marketing campaigns.

Increasing GE's capacity to serve customers better through providing integrated solutions was a key goal of the organizational changes introduced by Immelt (see below).

Global Presence

Immelt believed that some of the biggest payoffs from greater customer orientation would come from GE's increased success in international markets. Positioning GE to compete in growing emerging markets was a central strategic priority for GE. In 2011, Immelt appointed vice chairman John Rice to lead GE's international growth efforts, with particular emphasis on high-growth markets such as China, India, the Middle East, and Brazil. Maximizing GE's potential in these markets required a coordinated approach across GE's businesses:

> A great example is our spectacular success with the Beijing 2008 Olympic Games. This event produced $2 billion of revenues across multiple GE platforms, while building our relationships in China. In 2008, we announced a multifaceted partnership with Mubadala, the commercial investing arm of Abu Dhabi, which includes a commercial finance joint venture, projects in renewable energy, and a training center in Abu Dhabi. Mubadala will also become a "Top 10" GE investor.[20]

This integrated approach to working directly with government to meet host country needs across a range of infrastructure investments was formalized in 2009 as GE's "Company-to-Country" strategy. While China, India, and Brazil were the initial top targets, in 2012, GE announced that "Nigeria should be our next billion-dollar country."[21]

Internationalization involved a fundamental rethink of GE's approach to product development and an overhaul of its products and services to meet local market needs. GE's traditional approach had been to develop products for the US market, then to offer simpler, less costly "de-featured" versions to emerging markets. Combining GE's international emphasis with its increasing customer focus reoriented GE toward a "customer-optimization" approach to product development where local teams were given greater freedom in adapting and innovating products for their own markets. The outcome was "reverse innovation": many of the product concepts developed to meet the needs of emerging-market customers could be subsequently applied to GE's clients of the advanced industrialized nations. For example, a low-cost, portable, battery-operated ultrasound machine designed to meet the needs of physicians in India and China became a commercial success in the US.[22]

Exploiting global opportunities also involved globalizing GE's organization and its talent base. For example, the headquarters of GE Healthcare was moved to the UK, while in 2011 it announced the transfer of its X-ray business from Wisconsin to Beijing, China. Workforce internationalization extended to core corporate functions: a large proportion of GE's audit staff was from India.

Changing the GE Management Model

The management system that Immelt inherited had been reformulated by his predecessor and mentor, Jack Welch, but was also a product of 120 years of continuous development. Immelt respected GE's management systems and processes, and recognized that many of them were so deeply embedded within GE's culture that they were integral to GE's identity and the way it viewed the world. At the core of GE's management system was its management development—its so-called talent machine—and its system of performance management.

Leadership Development and Performance Management

From the early days, GE was committed to internally developed leadership: all of its CEOs were promoted from within the company. GE's meritocratic system of development and promotion was put in place by Charles Coffin, the CEO who succeeded Edison in 1892. Since then, GE had been a "CEO factory," producing top management talent not only for GE but also for corporations worldwide. Its management development system rested on two key pillars: its corporate university at Crotonville, New York and its "Session C" system for tracking managers' performance, planning their careers, and formulating succession plans for every management position at GE from department heads upwards. Under Welch the Session C reviews became all-day events at each of GE's businesses where Welch and the division CEO reviewed the performance and potential of every manager.

GE's management appraisal and development processes together with its financial and strategic planning systems formed the core of GE's performance management system. Under Jack Welch, GE's system of performance management became increasingly based upon quantitative targets that allowed focus and accountability. Immelt was equally committed to GE's metrics-driven approach to performance management: "Nothing happens in this company without an output metric," observed Immelt. All of Immelt's strategic initiatives—from earnings and organic growth targets to productivity improvements, reductions in overhead costs and six-sigma quality—were linked to precise quantitative targets. In 2005, GE standardized its customer satisfaction metrics, focusing on "net promoter scores" (the percentage of customers who would recommend GE to a friend, minus the percentage who wouldn't).

Immelt's strategic initiatives represented a challenge to GE's metrics-based performance management system. Goals such as innovation, enterprise selling, and environmental sustainability tended to be less amenable to quantification and objective measurement than goals of cost efficiency, productivity, and profitability.

The shifting of strategic priorities also had implications for GE's management development system. As with Jack Welch, Immelt saw his most important task as helping to develop GE's managerial talent. Implementing GE's growth strategy required GE's employees to internalize growth as part of their personal mission. This required inculcating among GE's managers the skills and aptitudes needed to become "growth leaders." A benchmarking exercise investigating the management characteristics of 15 companies with outstanding records of revenue growth resulted in the identification of five "growth traits." These included: external focus, imagination and creativity, decisiveness and clear thinking ability, inclusiveness, and deep "domain expertise" (knowledge of the particular business).

These growth traits became part of GE's annual HR review, with each of GE's top 5000 people rated on each of the five traits and the results of the assessment built into their subsequent development plans. Career planning also changed: because of the importance of domain expertise, managers were required to stay longer in each job.

Changing Organizational Structure

The most visible of the management changes introduced by Immelt concerned the overall structure of the organization. Between 2002 and 2008, Immelt reversed several of the major structural changes Welch had introduced during the 1980s. As part of "delayering" and his effort to create a more responsive company, Welch had broken up GE's major industrial sectors into smaller divisions. In order to facilitate greater cross-business integration, the bundling of products and services into "systems," and the creation of new "growth platforms," Immelt progressively reorganized GE's divisions into a smaller number of broad-based sectors. Reorganizations in 2002, 2005, and 2008 reduced the number of business sectors reporting to Immelt from 12 to five; before further reorganizations in 2010 and 2012 increased them to nine (Figure 3).

Innovation and New Business Development

A key challenge for Immelt was to reconcile GE's famous obsession with profitability and cost control with nurturing the innovation needed to drive growth. Innovation, especially when it involved big, long-term projects, involved substantial risk. The danger was that GE's obsession with short- and medium-term performance metrics might discourage business unit heads from making big bets on promising new opportunities. Furthermore, given the fact that many of the biggest opportunities were likely to require cooperation across divisions further increased the likelihood that they would fail to get the support they needed.

The Imagination Breakthroughs initiative (referred to above) was designed to ensure that major innovatory projects would receive the investment and attention needed to exploit their potential. To ensure the rapid development of promising projects, funding decisions were placed not with the business sectors but with Immelt and the top management team. Once approved, these projects were protected from normal budget pressures. About half involved new products and the other half involved changing commercial structure. Immelt saw these Innovation

FIGURE 3 General Electric's organization structure, 2001 and 2015

September 2001

March 2015

Breakthroughs as a means of focusing attention on the goal of business creation and development. Given that some of these projects (GE's hybrid locomotive, for example) involved substantial expenditures, lifting these projects from the business level to the corporate level took pressure off the business heads and helped address the lack of product managers and systems engineers within GE's business to run high-visibility, high-risk programs.

Achieving closer integration of technology development within GE was a major goal of Immelt. This was necessary not only to increase technology transfer across businesses and from corporate R & D to the businesses but also because more and more technologies were common to all GE's businesses (especially digital technologies). Rebranding GE Global Research as "The GE Store for Technology" was intended to enhance the responsiveness of GE's corporate R & D centers to the needs of all the businesses and speed the embodiment of innovation within products. According to Immelt, "It means that every business in GE can share and access the same technology, markets, structure and intellect … it makes the totality of GE more competitive than the parts. No other company has the ability to transfer intellect and technology as GE can through the Store":[23]

> The GE Store is a place where every business can come for technologies, product development and services that no one else can provide. The work of our researchers ties directly into the operational plans and product roadmaps of our businesses. GE business leaders meet with our technical leaders once every quarter to review their portfolios.[24]

Marketing and Sales

Realizing Immelt's goal of a customer-driven company required a revitalization of GE's marketing function: "Marketing was the place where washed-up salespeople went," observed Immelt.[25] Upgrading GE's marketing was achieved through creating the new senior position of chief marketing officer, the recreation of GE's Advanced Marketing Seminar, developing an Experienced Commercial Leadership Program, and requiring that every business appoint a VP-level head of marketing. Most important was the creation of GE's Commercial Council, which brought together GE's leading sales and marketing leaders to develop new business ideas, to transfer best practices, and instill a commercial culture within GE. A key initiative was "At the Customer, For the Customer," a program that deployed six sigma in marketing, sales, and customer relations activities, applied GE's six-sigma methodologies to customers' own businesses, and used new metrics to track customer satisfaction and customer attitudes.

As with all aspects of GE's approach to management, marketing was subject to the same systematized, metrics-driven analysis as all other functions were within the firm, often with some startling revelations:

> We're getting the sales force better trained and equipped with better tools and metrics. A good example is what we're doing to create discipline around pricing. Not long ago, a guy here named Dave McCalpin did an analysis of our pricing in appliances and found out that about $5 billion of it is discretionary. Given all the decisions that sales reps can make on their own, that's how much is in play. It was the most astounding number I'd ever heard—and that's just in appliances. Extrapolating across our businesses, there may be $50 billion that few people are tracking or accountable for. We would never allow something like that on the cost side. When it comes to the prices we pay, we study them, we map them, we work them. But with the prices we charge, we're too sloppy.[26]

Managing Integration

A central theme of the strategic changes initiated by Immelt was the desire to create value through the many parts of GE working together more closely and more effectively. "Working at GE is the art of thinking and playing big; our managers have to work cross-function, cross-region, cross-company. And we have to be about big purposes," observed Immelt.[27]

Implementing Immelt's strategic vision of GE as a technology-based, customer-focused, growth-orientated industrial powerhouse involved changes in GE's organizational structure, its management development and appraisal system, and its marketing and technology functions, and a host of other changes designed to align GE's structure, systems, and processes with the intended strategy. By 2006, these various initiatives had coalesced in Immelt's mind around an integrated system that he referred to as the "GE Growth Process." The approach—establishing a process, setting metrics for measuring the performance of that process, then aligning incentives with those metrics—was quintessentially GE. The difference was that Immelt was designing a process that related to the operation of GE as a whole.

During 2006, Immelt's view of GE's growth engine as an integrated, six-part process was disseminated throughout the organization and became a key part of Immelt's communication to GE's external constituencies (Figure 4).

However, greater integration across GE's different businesses created complex coordination problems. Consider GE's initiatives relating to product bundling and

FIGURE 4   General Electric's six-part growth process

Source: General Electric, annual report, 2005, p. 8.

customer solutions through its "Enterprise Selling" and "Company-to-Country" initiatives. In principle, these strategies were intuitive and straightforward:

> If somebody's building a hospital, that might represent a total package of $1 billion, of which the GE market potential might be $100 million. We're probably already talking to the C-suite because we sell the medical equipment. What we need to do is set things up so that the medical rep can bring in the lighting rep, the turbine rep, and so on.

Similarly with whole countries:

> In Qatar, the emir wants to know everybody doing business in his country. In a dinner set up to talk about oil and gas bids, he might say, "Jeff, I'm going to put $10 billion into a hospital," or he might mention that they're going to buy GE engines for Qatar Airways.[28]

However, the organizational ramifications were complex. Sales and marketing staff were required to focus less upon their particular business and more on the opportunities available to GE as a whole. In practice, this created complex problems of organization, expertise, and incentives. Exhibit 1 describes the difficulties encountered in the apparently simple bundling of medical diagnostic equipment with consulting services.

EXHIBIT 1

General Electric Medical Systems Customer Solutions Initiative

One of the earliest initiatives to exploit opportunities for bundling products and services was to combine the sale of medical imaging equipment with consulting services. In 2001, GE Medical Systems (soon to become GE Healthcare) created a new unit, Performance Solutions, to provide an integrated approach to hospital diagnostic imaging departments by combining equipment with technical support and patient-management systems. A lead customer was Stanford University Medical Center, which transitioned to all-digital imaging for its hospital and outpatient unit.

After a promising start, by 2005 Performance Solutions was in trouble. The medical equipment sales people had limited understanding of the consulting services being offered by the Performance Solutions unit and provided few sales leads for the new integrated offering. They were also reluctant to share their customers with sales personnel from Performance Solutions. Meanwhile, the sales personnel from Performance Solutions considered themselves "solution providers" and felt constrained by having to limit their solutions exclusively to GE offerings.

Source: Based upon R. Gulati, "Silo Busting: How to Execute on the Promise of Customer Focus," *Harvard Business Review* (May 2007).

Immelt reflected on the organizational challenges of a customer-centric collaboration across different businesses:

> I've found that few companies are actually structured to deliver products and services in a synchronized way that's attractive from a customer's perspective. Individual units are historically focused on perfecting their products and processes, and give little thought to how their offerings might be even more valuable to the end user when paired with those of another unit. It's not just that the status quo doesn't reward collaborative behavior—although the right incentives are also critical. It's that the connections literally aren't in place.
>
> One way to forge those connections is to do away with traditional silos altogether and create new ones organized by customer segments or needs. Many companies, however, are understandably reluctant to let go of the economies of scale and depth of knowledge and expertise associated with non-customer-focused silos. A company organized around geographies can customize offerings to suit local preferences, for instance, while a technology-centric firm can be quick to market with technical innovations. In many cases, functional and geographic silos were created precisely to help companies coordinate such activities as designing innovative products or gaining geographic focus. A customer focus requires them to emphasize a different set of activities and coordinate them in a different way.[29]

GE Global Growth and Operations—one of GE's nine business divisions—was created to provide integration and focus across GE's eight other business divisions in developing GE's sales to customers in markets outside the US. Headquartered in Hong Kong, GE Global Growth and Operations was organized with separate units for China, India, South-East Asia, Latin/South America, Russia, Canada, Australia, the Middle East, Africa, Germany, Europe, and Japan/Korea.

As headquarters became increasingly involved in promoting and supporting developmental initiatives (e.g., Imagination Breakthroughs and Enterprise Selling), so the corporate HQ became more of a partner with the business divisions rather than an overseer of divisional performance and interrogator of business strategies.

Looking Ahead

Driving innovation and customer orientation within GE required a level of collaboration across divisional boundaries that was not always compatible with its metrics-based system of performance management and culture of internal competition. A more integrated GE changed the relationship between GE's corporate headquarters and the businesses. Under Welch, there was a clear division of roles and responsibilities between the business divisions and that of the corporate HQ. The business divisions with their individual CEOs were responsible for running their own businesses both operationally and strategically. The role of the corporate headquarters was both to support the businesses through various centralized services and to drive business performance by putting divisional top management under intense pressure to deliver. Immelt's emphasis on creating value through exploiting the linkages among GE's different business had meant that much of the simplicity and directness associated with Jack Welch's management style had been supplanted by an emphasis on managing integration. Could a system that had been built upon management through performance metrics accommodate Immelt's growing number of initiatives intended to foster integrated approaches to innovation and customer service?

Most US companies that had achieved outstanding performance by combining innovation, efficiency, and customer focus in fast-moving business environments—companies such as IBM, Apple, Nike, and Johnson & Johnson—were far more specialized than GE. Certainly the great majority of companies on *Fortune*'s list of "most admired companies" were strongly based on a single core business. Highly successful companies that were both highly diversified and multinational were unusual.

Given GE's comparatively weak performance during the five-year period 2010–2015, the management system that Immelt had built at GE remained unproven. As Immelt reminded his top managers even before the upheaval caused by the financial crisis: "The business book that can help you hasn't been written yet."[30]

Appendix: General Electric Segment Performance (from 10-K reports)

TABLE A1   Revenues ($billion)

	2014	2013	2012	2011	2010
Power & Water	27.6	24.7	28.3	25.7	24.8
Oil & Gas	18.7	17.0	15.2	13.6	9.4
Energy Management	7.3	7.6	7.4	6.4	5.2
Aviation	24.0	21.9	20.0	18.9	17.6
Healthcare	18.3	18.2	18.3	18.1	16.9
Transportation	5.7	5.9	5.8	4.9	3.4
Appliances & Lighting	8.4	8.4	8.0	7.7	8.0
Total industrial	109.9	103.6	102.8	95.2	85.2
GE Capital	42.7	44.1	45.4	48.3	49.2
Total	152.6	147.7	148.2	143.5	134.4
Consolidated	148.6	146.0	146.7	146.5	148.9

TABLE A2   Profit ($billion)

	2014	2013	2012	2011	2010
Power & Water	5.35	4.99	5.42	5.02	5.80
Oil & Gas	2.59	2.18	1.92	1.66	1.41
Energy Management	0.25	0.11	0.13	0.08	0.16
Aviation	4.97	4.35	3.75	3.51	3.30
Healthcare	3.05	3.05	2.92	2.80	2.74
Transportation	1.13	1.17	3.07	0.76	0.32
Appliances & Lighting	0.43	0.38	0.31	0.24	0.40
Total industrial	17.76	16.22	15.49	14.07	14.13
GE Capital	7.02	7.96	7.22	6.48	3.08
Total	24.78	24.18	22.71	20.55	17.21
Consolidated after-tax earnings	15.23	13.06	13.64	14.15	11.64

TABLE A3   Assets and capital investment ($billion)

	Assets			Additions to property, plant and equipment		
	2014	**2013**	**2012**	**2014**	**2013**	**2012**
Power & Water	30.34	29.49	27.14	0.62	0.71	0.66
Oil & Gas	27.26	26.19	20.11	0.65	1.19	0.47
Energy Management	10.98	10.31	9.59	0.18	0.14	0.16
Aviation	33.72	32.27	25.15	1.20	1.18	0.78
Healthcare	29.23	27.86	28.37	0.41	0.32	0.32
Transportation	4.45	4.31	4.20	0.13	0.28	0.72
Appliances & Lighting	4.46	4.31	4.20	0.36	0.41	0.49
GE Capital	500.22	516.83	539.35	10.41	9.98	11.88
Total	648.35	646.56	685.00	13.84	14.39	15.38

Notes

1. Transcript, General Electric annual shareholder meeting (April 22, 2015).
2. "Letter to Stakeholders," General Electric, annual report (2002): 3.
3. "Can a Specialist Run General Electric?" (March 7, 2012), http://blogs.ft.com/businessblog/2012/can-a-specialist-run-general-electric/#axzz1tv41XKUt.
4. "When Is a Company Too Big to Manage?" *Financial Times* (February 28, 2015).
5. Letter to Shareholders, General Electric annual report (2001).
6. Letter to Shareholders, General Electric annual report (2003).
7. "What Makes GE Great?" *Fortune* (March 6, 2006): 90–96.
8. General Electric, annual report (1993): 5.
9. "Running the House that Jack Built," *Business Week* (October 2, 2000).
10. "The Days of Welch and Roses," *Business Week* (April 29, 2002).
11. General Electric, annual report (2002).
12. General Electric, 10-K report for 2014: 7.
13. Address to shareholders, Annual Shareowners' Meeting, Philadelphia (April 26, 2006).
14. Letter to stakeholders," General Electric, annual report (2002): 9.
15. "Letter to shareowners," General Electric, annual report (2011): 5.
16. "GE to Cash Out of Banking Business," *Wall Street Journal* (April 11, 2015).
17. "GE Launches Ecomagination," General Electric press release (May 9, 2005).
18. Global R&D Fact Sheet. http://www.ge.com/about-us/research/factsheet, accessed July 20, 2015.
19. General Electric, 2002 Annual Report to Share Owners.
20. General Electric, Annual Report 2008: 6–7.
21. "Letter to Shareowners," General Electric Annual Report, 2011: 6.
22. J. R. Immelt, V. Govindarajan, and C. Trimble, "How GE is Disrupting Itself," *Harvard Business Review* (October 2009): 56–65.
23. GE Chairman and CEO Jeff Immelt's Annual Letter to GE Shareholders: 2014. http://www.gereports.com/post/113784948030/ge-chairman-and-ceo-jeff-immelts-annual-letter-to, accessed July 20, 2015.
24. "The GE Store for Technology," http://www.genewsroom.com/press-releases/ge-store-technology-279623, accessed July 20, 2015.
25. Reprinted by permission of *Harvard Business Review*. From "Growth as a Process: An Interview with Jeff Immelt," (June 2006): 63. Copyright © 2006 by the Harvard Business School Publishing Corporation; all rights reserved.
26. Ibid.: 64.
27. Ibid.: 69.
28. Ibid.: 64.
29. Ibid.: 67.
30. Ibid.: 61.

Case 23 Bank of America's Acquisition of Merrill Lynch

December 2008

On the afternoon of Monday, December 22, 2008, Ken Lewis, chairman and CEO of Bank of America Corporation, was preparing for a special meeting of Bank of America's board of directors, which would be held by telephone at 4 p.m.

The meeting was critical to the future of Bank of America and to the future careers of Lewis and his top management team. The meeting offered the board its final opportunity to pull the plug on its acquisition of Merrill Lynch & Company, which was to be consummated in ten days' time (January 1, 2009).

The acquisition, announced on September 15, 2008 (see Exhibit 1 for the press release), would create America's biggest financial services company in terms of total assets. It was the culmination of a succession of acquisitions that had transformed North Carolina National Bank first into NationsBank, then, after its 1998 acquisition of San Francisco-based BankAmerica, into Bank of America Corporation. Table 1 shows Bank of America's principal acquisitions.

Despite its size, little planning preceded the merger announcement. It came the same day that Lehman Brothers filed for Chapter 11 bankruptcy protection amidst growing fears that the global financial system was going into meltdown. Anticipating that Merrill Lynch might be the next major financial institution to fail, the acquisition was hastily brokered by the chairman of the Federal Reserve Board, Ben Bernanke, and the US Treasury Secretary, Hank Paulson. Announcing the merger, Bank of America's chairman and CEO, Ken Lewis, stated: "The fact that we could put this transaction together in less than 48 hours is a great statement on the strength of both our teams, but also on the great strategic fit which, from the instant that we talked about it, became clear that this transaction would make a lot of sense."

Others were less convinced that the transaction made sense. The biggest concern was that Bank of America was overpaying. The *Financial Times'* Lex column commented:

> Even if Merrill is being taken out at a third of its 52-week high, it is, in the circumstances, hardly a steal at 1.8 times tangible book value and 12 times 2009 earnings.

This case was prepared by Robert M. Grant. ©2015 Robert M. Grant.

EXHIBIT 1

The Merger Announcement: Extracts from the Press Release

CHARLOTTE (September 15, 2008)—Bank of America Corporation today announced it has agreed to acquire Merrill Lynch & Co., Inc. in a $50 billion all-stock transaction that creates a company unrivalled in its breadth of financial services and global reach. "Acquiring one of the premier wealth management, capital markets, and advisory companies is a great opportunity for our shareholders," Bank of America Chairman and Chief Executive Officer Ken Lewis said. "Together, our companies are more valuable because of the synergies in our businesses." "Merrill Lynch is a great global franchise and I look forward to working with Ken Lewis and our senior management teams to create what will be the leading financial institution in the world with the combination of these two firms," said John Thain, chairman and CEO of Merrill Lynch.

Bank of America expects to achieve $7 billion in pretax expense savings, fully realized by 2012. The acquisition is expected to be accretive to earnings by 2010.

The combined company would have leadership positions in retail brokerage and wealth management.

By adding Merrill Lynch's more than 16,000 financial advisers, Bank of America would have the largest brokerage in the world with more than 20,000 advisers and $2.5 trillion in client assets.

The combination brings global scale in investment management, including an approximately 50% ownership in BlackRock, which has $1.4 trillion in assets under management. Bank of America has $589 billion in assets under management. Adding Merrill Lynch both enhances current strengths at Bank of America and creates new ones, particularly outside of the United States. Merrill Lynch adds strengths in global debt underwriting, global equities and global merger and acquisition advice. After the acquisition, Bank of America would be the number one underwriter of global high yield debt, the third largest underwriter of global equity and the ninth largest adviser on global mergers and acquisitions based on pro forma first half of 2008 results.

Source: http://newsroom.bankofamerica.com/press-release/ corporate-and-financial-news/bank-america-buys-merrill- lynch-creating-unique-financial, accessed October 1, 2012. Reproduced with permission.

Mr. Thain's willingness to accept market realities has enabled Merrill shareholders to escape a total wipe-out. As Jamie Dimon noted after acquiring Bear Stearns, there is a difference between buying a house and buying a house that's on fire. While flames are licking at Merrill's outhouses, Mr. Thain has persuaded BofA's Ken Lewis there is still plenty of time to douse them. But until Mr. Lewis can prove that Merrill has suffered only cosmetic damage, he will struggle to get investors excited about promised savings worth $7bn or 10% of the cost base. BofA's shares fell 15%, destroying $23bn of value.

If the deal proceeds to plan, BofA would secure the Merrill brand and the largest retail broker network in the US, with a 17,000-strong herd of financial advisers as well as a leading investment bank and wealth management franchise. There are, though, two big dangers. First, much of the risk Merrill has "offloaded" in its vendor-financed sale of toxic securities could come back to haunt its new owner. Second, a culture war between two workforces remunerated according to different pay systems seems unavoidable.[1]

TABLE 1 Bank of America's growth by acquisition

Year	Company acquired	Notes
1960	Security National Bank of Greensboro merges with American Commercial Bank of Charlotte	Merged bank named North Caroline National Bank (NCNB)
1982	First National Bank of Lake City (Florida)	First out-of-state acquisition by NCNB
1991	C&S/Sovren of Atlanta	NCNB changes its name to NationsBank
1993	MNC Financial of Maryland	
1998	BankAmerica Corporation of San Francisco	NationsBank renamed Bank of America
2004	Fleet Boston Financial Corporation	Expands into Northeast
2006	MBNA	Bank of America becomes largest US credit-card issuer
2007	US Trust	Bank of America becomes leading US private bank for wealthy individuals
2007	ABN AMRO North America	Major subsidiary: La Salle Bank Corp.
2008	Countrywide Financial	Bank of America becomes US's largest mortgage lender
2008	Merrill Lynch & Company, Inc.	September 15 bid to take effect January 1, 2009

Source: http://about.bankofamerica.com/en-us/our-story/our-history-and-heritage.html

During the final quarter of 2008, pessimism about the merger continued to grow. Bank of America's share price declined from $29.55 on September 16, 2008 to $13.53 on December 22. The main concern was Merrill's balance sheet. On October 16, Merrill reported a third-quarter loss of $5.1 billion resulting mostly from a write-down in the value of its CDOs (collateralized debt obligations) and other real-estate related assets.

By mid-December it was becoming clear that Merrill's fourth-quarter results would be even worse. Bank of America's chief financial officer, Joe Price, estimated that Merrill Lynch's fourth-quarter losses had risen from $9 billion to $12 billion.

These revelations about the full horrors of Merrill's financial position removed any lingering doubts over whether Bank of America had overpaid for Merrill: current losses and future write-downs probably meant that Merrill Lynch was worth absolutely nothing. The issue for Lewis and the board was whether to invoke the "MAC clause" in the merger agreement, which allowed the merger to be called off in the event of a "materially adverse event" occurring.

There followed a flurry of communications between Lewis, Bernanke, Paulson, and officials at the US Treasury. After informing them of Bank of America's desire to exit the merger, Lewis became a target of sustained pressure from the Department of the Treasury in particular.

Paulson reminded Lewis of the risks to the entire US financial system that would result from Bank of America's rescinding of the merger agreement, risks that would inevitably have a major impact upon Bank of America itself. Paulson also indicated that, should Bank of America invoke the MAC clause, the US government would seek the removal of Bank of America's board and top management team. However, if Bank of America went ahead with the merger, the Treasury and Federal Reserve System would provide whatever assistance was needed by Bank of America to restore its capital and to protect it against the adverse impact of "toxic" Merrill Lynch assets.[2]

As Lewis got ready to speak to his fellow board members, he realized that he was faced with the most difficult decision of his entire career. If Bank of America went ahead with the merger, Merrill's appalling financial situation would be a major drag on Bank of America's performance, would depress its share price, and would undoubtedly anger shareholders. However, beyond the short term, probably the next two to three years, he believed that shareholders would reap considerable benefit from the strategic advantages from creating one of the world's biggest universal banks. Rescinding the merger and leaving Merrill Lynch to its fate might also be the trigger for the financial calamity that President Bush had forewarned in his recognition that: "This sucker might go down!"[3]

The potential conflict between Lewis's moral obligations to his shareholders and to his country was further complicated by his legal duties. As chairman and CEO, Lewis was required to inform shareholders of company matters relevant to their interests. Although shareholders had on December 5 approved the acquisition of Merrill Lynch, this was without the new projections of Merrill's fourth-quarter losses. When Lewis had raised issues of disclosure with Bernanke and Paulson, he had been informed that such disclosure would not be conducive to the stability of the US financial system.[4]

The Strategic Issues Arising from the Merger

The strategic arguments in favor of the merger were outlined in a joint press conference by the two CEOs (Ken Lewis and John Thain) made on September 15, 2008. Lewis saw Merrill Lynch as adding critical strengths to Bank of America in relation to both individual financial services and corporate financial services. Figure 1 shows two slides from their presentation.

In terms of individual financial services, Merrill Lynch's US-wide network of local offices and its army of financial advisers would represent a massive extension of Bank of America's existing brokerage and wealth-management services. In addition, Bank of America anticipated that the combination of the largest US wealth-management organization with one of America's biggest retail banks with presence in 31 states would offer considerable opportunity for offering a wider range of financial services to the clients of each.

Merrill Lynch's much bigger presence outside of the US would also offer Bank of America the opportunity to build a truly international wealth-management business.

In terms of Bank of America's corporate and investment banking, the merger would transform Bank of America from a provider of corporate banking services with comparatively small-scale investment banking activities into one of the world's leading investment banks. Not only was Merrill strongly positioned in all the world's major financial centers; it had also established a strong position in the emerging markets of Asia, Eastern Europe, Latin America, Africa, and the Middle East, most notably in the BRIC countries. Appendices 1 and 2 provide information on the businesses and performance of the two companies.

The Costs and Benefits of Universal Banking

With the addition of Merrill Lynch, Bank of America would become one of the world's leading universal banks along with Citigroup and JPMorgan Chase—banks that had taken advantage of the repeal of the Glass–Stegall Act to combine commercial

FIGURE 1 Extract from merger presentation by Ken Lewis and John Thain

Creating the Premier Financial Services Company in the World

Ken Lewis	John Thain
Bank of America	Merrill Lynch
Chairman and CEO	Chairman and CEO

Strategic Rationale

• *Diversify business mix*

• *Significant enhancement to our investment banking capabilities*

   – *Creates leading positions in*

      • *Global Debt Underwriting*
      • *Global Equities*
      • *Global M&A Advisory*

• *Leadership position in retail brokerage and wealth management*

   – *20,000 financial advisors (16,690 Merrill Lynch advisors)*
   – *$2.5 trillion in client assets*

• *Brings global scale in investment management*

   – *50% ownership stake in BlackRock with $1.4 trillion in AUMs*
   – *Columbia funds have $425 billion in AUMs (total BAC AUMs $589 billion)*

(AUM = Assets Under Management)

A Bank of America and Merrill combination yields a diverse business mix

Bank of America Segment Revenue

Global Corporate and Investment Banking 24%
Global Wealth and Investment Management 11%
Global Consumer and Small Business 65%

Merrill Lynch Segment Revenue

Global Markets and Investment Banking 56%
Global Wealth Management 44%

Combined Segment Revenue

Global Consumer and Small Business 48%
Global Corporate and Investment Banking 32%
Global Wealth Management 20%

Merrill Lynch

Bank of America

and investment banking. This so-called universal banking model was common in Europe, where UBS, Deutsche Bank, Credit Suisse, BNP Paribas, Barclays, Royal Bank of Scotland, and UniCredit had long combined conventional banking services with capital market activities, corporate advisory services, market making, and proprietary trading.

The relative merits of diversification and specialization within banking services were a topic of debate and disagreement.

The case for universal banking was based upon the benefits, first, of risk spreading and, second, of synergies among different banking services:

- The risk-spreading benefits of universal banking became apparent during the financial crisis, when most US investment banks either failed or converted into bank holding companies. The stability of the universal banks was their ability to finance themselves through bank deposits rather than relying on wholesale money markets. Within retail banking, the casualties were among specialists such as Washington Mutual, Halifax Bank of Scotland, and Northern Rock. However, apart from 2008–2009, the stability benefits of diversification are less evident. Like other diversified companies, universal banks appear to suffer a "conglomerate discount." Nor are their credit ratings superior to those of specialist banks.

- Synergies within universal banks related to economies of spreading the costs of IT and corporate services over multiple businesses and the benefits of cross-selling services to customers. At the retail level these included selling both banking services and wealth management products and services to the same consumers. For corporate clients it involved providing a wide range of banking, advisory, and corporate finance services. There were also believed to be vertical integration benefits from combining investment banking services—especially underwriting and securitization with a retail distribution network of banks and wealth management advisors.

However, as with risk spreading, the synergy benefits of investment banks tended to exist more in theory than in practice. Cross-selling had long been an elusive goal for financial service companies. It had inspired mergers between banks and insurance firms to create "bancassurance" companies. Yet, there were few companies that could point to major revenue gains from cross-selling financial services.

In terms of other economies of scope, the risk was that any such economies were offset by the added complexity created from integrating functions and establishing coordination among different financial service businesses. Cost-to-income ratios, a key measure of efficiency among financial service companies, tended to be higher in most universal banks than in more specialist institutions.

In principle, universal banks should also derive economies from their ability to use banking deposits to finance their underwriting, market making, and trading activities, thereby giving them greater independence from external capital markets. However, any such potential economies were limited by an ever-tightening regulatory framework that was designed to prevent cheap retail deposits being used to finance riskier investment-banking activities.

However, the greatest disadvantages of complexity relate to the effective management of universal banks. Professor Jordi Canals of IESE argued, "financial conglomerates involve additional problems related to risk management, conflicts of interest and capital allocation."[5] In large universal banks, effective risk management is compromised by the increasing distance of top management from operational decision making. Conflicts of interest arise between individuals engaged in different activities and for different clients. While constraints on reallocating capital often result in a tolerance for underperforming business units.

Finally, this complexity affects the design of management systems—not least compensation systems—and the management of corporate culture. Economic commentator John Kay, observed:

> Within every diversified retail bank, there is evidence of the fundamental tension between the cultures of trading and deal-making— buccaneering, entrepreneurial, grasping—and the conservative bureaucratic approach appropriate for retail banking. It is a conflict in which the investment bankers and traders generally come out on top.[6]

Appendix 1: Bank of America Corporation: Business Activities and Performance (extracts from 10-K report for 2007)

General

Bank of America Corporation ("Bank of America" or the "Corporation") is a Delaware corporation, a bank holding company and a financial holding company under the Gramm-Leach-Bliley Act. Our principal executive offices are located in the Bank of America Corporate Center, Charlotte, North Carolina 28255.

Through our banking subsidiaries (the "Banks") and various nonbanking subsidiaries throughout the US and in selected international markets, we provide a diversified range of banking and nonbanking financial services and products through three business segments: Global Consumer and Small Business Banking, Global Corporate and Investment Banking and Global Wealth and Investment Management. We currently operate in 32 states, the District of Columbia and more than 30 foreign countries. The Bank of America footprint covers more than 82% of the US population and 44% of the country's wealthy households. In the US we serve approximately 59 million consumer and small business relationships with more than 6100 retail banking offices, more than 18,500 ATMs and approximately 24 million active online users. We have banking centers in 13 of the 15 fastest growing states and hold the top market share in six of those states . . .

As of December 31, 2007, there were approximately 210,000 full-time equivalent employees within Bank of America and our subsidiaries. Of these employees, 116,000 were employed within Global Consumer and Small Business Banking, 21,000 were employed within Global Corporate and Investment Banking and 14,000 were employed within Global Wealth and Investment Management . . .

Selected Five Year Summary of Financial Data

($billion, except where indicated)	2007	2006	2005	2004	2003
Income statement					
Net interest income	34.4	34.6	30.7	28.0	20.5
Noninterest income	31.9	38.0	26.4	22.7	18.3
Total revenue, net of interest expense	66.3	72.6	57.2	50.7	38.8
Provision for credit losses	8.4	5.0	4.0	2.8	2.8
Noninterest expense, before merger and restructuring charges	36.6	34.8	28.3	26.4	20.2
Merger and restructuring charges	0.4	0.8	0.4	0.6	—

Selected Five Year Summary of Financial Data

($billion, except where indicated)	2007	2006	2005	2004	2003
Income before income taxes	20.9	32.0	24.5	20.9	15.8
Income tax expense	5.9	10.8	8.0	7.0	5.0
Net income	15.0	21.1	16.5	13.9	10.8
Performance ratios (%)					
Return on average assets	0.94	1.44	1.30	1.34	1.44
Return on average common shareholders' equity	11.08	16.27	16.51	16.47	21.50
Return on average tangible shareholders' equity	22.25	32.80	30.19	28.93	27.84
Total ending equity to total ending assets	8.56	9.27	7.86	9.03	6.76
Total average equity to total average assets	8.53	8.90	7.86	8.12	6.69
Dividend payout	72.26	45.66	46.61	46.31	39.76
Market price per share of common stock					
Closing ($)	41.26	53.39	46.15	46.99	40.22
High closing ($)	54.05	54.90	47.08	47.44	41.77
Low closing ($)	41.10	43.09	41.57	38.96	32.82
Market capitalization	183.1	238.0	184.6	190.1	115.9
Average balance sheet					
Total loans and leases	776.2	652.4	537.2	472.6	356.2
Total assets	1,602.1	1,466.7	1,269.9	1,044.6	749.1
Total deposits	717.2	673.0	632.4	551.6	406.2
Long-term debt	169.9	130.1	97.7	92.3	67.1
Total shareholders' equity	136.7	130.5	99.9	84.8	50.1
Asset quality					
Allowance for credit losses	12.1	9.4	8.4	9.0	6.6
Nonperforming assets measured at historical cost	5.9	1.9	1.6	2.5	3.0
Allowance for loan and lease losses as % of total loans and leases	1.33	1.28	1.40	1.65	1.66
Net charge-offs	6.5	4.5	4.6	3.1	3.1
Net charge-offs as % of average loans and leases	0.84	0.70	0.85	0.66	0.87
Nonperforming loans and leases as % of total loans and leases	0.64	0.25	0.26	0.42	0.77
Nonperforming assets as % of total loans, leases and foreclosed properties	0.68	0.26	0.28	0.47	0.81
Ratio of the allowance for loan and lease losses at December 31 to net charge-offs	1.79	1.99	1.76	2.77	1.98
Capital ratios (period end)					
Risk-based capital:					
Tier 1	6.87	8.64	8.25	8.20	8.02
Total	11.02	11.88	11.08	11.73	12.05
Tier 1 Leverage	5.04	6.36	5.91	5.89	5.86

GLOBAL CONSUMER AND SMALL BUSINESS BANKING

2007 ($billion)	Total	Deposits	Card services	Consumer real estate	ALM[a] and other
Net interest income	28.8	9.4	16.6	2.3	0.5
Non-interest income:					
—Card income	10.2	2.1	8.0	0.0	—
—Service charges	6.0	6.0	—	0.0	—
—Mortgage banking income	1.3	—	—	1.3	—
—All other income	1.3	(0.0)	0.9	0.1	0.4
—Total non-interest income	18.9	8.2	9.0	1.4	0.4
Total revenue, net of interest expense	47.7	17.6	25.5	3.7	0.9
Provision for credit losses	12.9	0.3	11.3	1.0	0.3
Noninterest expense	20.1	9.1	8.3	2.0	0.6
Income (loss) before income taxes	14.7	8.2	5.9	0.6	(0.1)
Income tax expense	5.3	3.08	2.2	0.2	(0.2)
Net income	9.4	5.2	3.7	0.4	0.1
Net interest yield[b] (%)	8.15	2.97	7.87	2.04	n.m.
Return on average equity	14.94	33.61	8.43	9.00	n.m.
Efficiency ratio[b]	42.07	51.81	32.49	55.24	n.m.
Period end—total assets	443.0	358.6	257.0	133.3	n.m.

Notes:

n.m. = not meaningful.

[a]Asset and liability management.

[b]The efficiency ratio measures the costs expended to generate a dollar of revenue; net interest yield evaluates how many basis points we are earning over the cost of funds.

The strategy for GCSBB is to attract, retain and deepen customer relationships. We achieve this strategy through our ability to offer a wide range of products and services through a franchise that stretches coast to coast through 32 states and the District of Columbia. We also provide credit-card products to customers in Canada, Ireland, Spain and the United Kingdom. In the US we serve approximately 59 million consumer and small-business relationships utilizing our network of 6149 banking centers, 18,753 domestic branded ATMs, and telephone and internet channels. Within GCSBB there are three primary businesses:

- *Deposits* provides a comprehensive range of products to consumers and small businesses. Our products include traditional savings accounts, money market savings accounts, CDs and IRAs, and noninterest and interest-bearing checking accounts. Debit card results are also included in Deposits.
- *Card Services* provides a broad offering of products, including US Consumer and Business Card, Unsecured Lending, and International Card. We offer a variety of cobranded and affinity credit-card products and have become the leading issuer of credit cards through endorsed marketing in the US and

Europe. During 2007, Merchant Services was transferred to Treasury Services within GCIB.

- *Consumer Real Estate* generates revenue by providing an extensive line of consumer real estate products and services to customers nationwide. Consumer Real Estate products are available to our customers through a retail network of personal bankers located in 6149 banking centers, mortgage loan officers in nearly 200 locations and through a sales force offering our customers direct telephone and online access to our products. Consumer Real Estate products include fixed and adjustable rate loans for home purchase and refinancing needs, reverse mortgages, lines of credit and home equity loans. Mortgage products are either sold into the secondary mortgage market to investors while retaining the Bank of America customer relationships or are held on our balance sheet for ALM purposes . . . The Consumer Real Estate business includes the origination, fulfillment, sale and servicing of first mortgage loan products, reverse mortgage products and home equity products.

GLOBAL CORPORATE AND INVESTMENT BANKING

2007 ($billion)	Total	Business lending	Capital market and advisory	Treasury services
Net interest income	11.2	5.0	2.8	3.8
Noninterest income:				
—Service charges	2.8	0.5	0.1	2.1
—Investment and brokerage services	0.9	0.0	0.9	0.1
—Investment banking income	2.5	—	2.5	—
—Trading account profits (loss)	(5.2)	(0.2)	(5.1)	0.1
—All other income	1.1	0.8	(1.0)	1.1
—Total noninterest income	2.2	1.2	(2.5)	3.3
Total revenue, net of interest expense	13.4	6.2	0.3	7.1
Provision for credit losses	0.7	0.6	—	0.0
Noninterest expense	11.9	2.2	5.6	3.9
Income (loss) before income taxes	0.8	3.4	(5.3)	3.3
Income tax expense	0.3	1.2	(2.0)	1.2
Net income (loss)	0.5	2.1	(3.4)	2.1
Net interest yield (%)	1.66	2.00	n.m.	2.79
Return on average equity (%)	1.19	13.12	(25.41)	26.31
Efficiency ratio	88.88	34.98	n.m.	54.02
Period end—total assets	776.1	305.5	413.1	180.4

Note:
n.m. = not meaningful.

Global Corporate and Investment Banking provides a wide range of financial services both to our issuer and investor clients, who range from business banking clients to large international corporate and institutional investor clients, using a strategy to deliver value-added financial products and advisory solutions. Global Corporate and Investment Banking's products and services are delivered from three primary businesses: Business Lending, CMAS and Treasury Services are provided to our clients through a global team of client relationship managers and product partners. In addition, ALM/Other includes the results of ALM activities and other GCIB activities (such as commercial insurance business, which was sold in the fourth quarter of 2007). Our clients are supported through offices in 22 countries, which are divided into four distinct geographic regions: US and Canada; Asia; Europe, Middle East and Africa; and Latin America.

- *Business Lending* provides a wide range of lending-related products and services to our clients . . . Products include commercial and corporate bank loans and commitment facilities, which cover our business banking clients, middle market commercial clients and our large multinational corporate clients. Real-estate lending products are issued primarily to public and private developers, homebuilders and commercial real-estate firms. Leasing and asset-based lending products offer our clients innovative financing solutions. Products also include indirect consumer loans, which allow us to offer financing through automotive, marine, motorcycle and recreational vehicle dealerships. Business Lending also contains the results for the economic hedging of our risk to certain credit counterparties utilizing various risk mitigation tools.

- *Capital Markets and Advisory Services* provides financial products, advisory services and financing globally to our institutional investor clients in support of their investing and trading activities. We also work with our commercial and corporate issuer clients to provide debt and equity underwriting and distribution capabilities, merger-related advisory services and risk management solutions using interest rate, equity, credit, currency and commodity derivatives, foreign exchange, fixed income and mortgage-related products. The business may take positions in these products and participate in market-making activities dealing in government securities, equity and equity-linked securities, high-grade and high-yield corporate debt securities, commercial paper, mortgage-backed securities and ABS. Underwriting debt and equity, securities research and certain market-based activities are executed through Banc of America Securities, LLC, which is a primary dealer in the US.

- *Treasury Services* provides integrated working capital management and treasury solutions to clients worldwide through our network of proprietary offices and special clearing arrangements. Our clients include multinationals, middle-market companies, correspondent banks, commercial real estate firms and governments. Our products and services include treasury management, trade finance, foreign exchange, short-term credit facilities and short-term investing options. Net interest income is derived from interest-bearing and noninterest-bearing deposits, sweep investments, and other liability management products. Deposit products provide a relatively stable source of funding and liquidity. We earn net interest spread revenues from investing this liquidity in earning assets through client-facing lending activity and our ALM activities.

GLOBAL WEALTH AND INVESTMENT MANAGEMENT

2007 ($billion)	Total	US Trust	Columbia Management	Premier Banking and Investments
Net interest income	3.9	1.0	0.0	2.7
Noninterest income:				
—Investment and brokerage services	4.2	1.2	1.9	1.0
—All other income	(0.1)	0.1	(0.4)	0.1
—Total noninterest income	4.1	1.3	1.5	1.1
Total revenue, net of interest expense	7.9	2.3	1.5	3.8
Provision for credit losses	14	14	—	27
Noninterest expense	4.6	1.6	1.2	1.7
Income before income taxes	3.3	0.7	0.3	2.0
Income tax expense	1.2	0.3	0.1	0.7
Net income	2.1	0.5	0.2	1.3
Net interest yield (%)	3.06	2.69	n.m.	2.70
Return on average equity (%)	18.87	17.25	11.29	72.44
Efficiency ratio (%)	58.50	68.67	79.39	45.31
Period end—total assets	157.2	51.0	2.6	113.3

Note:

n.m. = not meaningful.

Global Wealth and Investment Management provides a wide offering of customized banking, investment and brokerage services tailored to meet the changing wealth management goals of our individual and institutional customer base. Our clients have access to a range of services offered through three primary businesses:

- *US Trust, Bank of America Private Wealth Management.* In July 2007, we completed the acquisition of US Trust Corporation for $3.3 billion in cash combining it with The Private Bank and its ultra-wealthy extension, Family Wealth Advisors, to form US Trust. The results of the combined business were reported for periods beginning on July 1, 2007. Prior to July 1, 2007, the results solely reflect that of the former Private Bank. US Trust provides comprehensive wealth management solutions to wealthy and ultra-wealthy clients with investable assets of more than $3 million. In addition, US Trust provides resources and customized solutions to meet clients' wealth structuring, investment management, trust and banking services as well as specialty asset management services (oil and gas, real estate, farm and ranch, timberland, private businesses and tax advisory). Clients also benefit from access to resources available through the Corporation including capital markets products, large and complex financing solutions and its extensive banking platform.
- *Columbia Management.* Columbia is an asset-management business serving the needs of institutional clients and individual customers. Columbia provides asset management products and services, including mutual funds and separate accounts. Columbia mutual fund offerings provide a broad array of investment strategies and products including equity, fixed income (taxable and nontaxable) and money market (taxable and nontaxable) funds. Columbia distributes its products and services directly to institutional clients

and distributes to individuals through US Trust, PB&I and nonproprietary channels including other brokerage firms.

- *Premier Banking and Investments.* Premier Banking and Investments includes Banc of America Investments, our full-service retail brokerage business and our Premier Banking channel. Premier Banking and Investments brings personalized banking and investment expertise through priority service with client-dedicated teams. It provides a high-touch client experience through a network of approximately 5600 client-facing associates to our affluent customers with a personal wealth profile that includes investable assets plus a mortgage that exceeds $500,000 or at least $100,000 of investable assets.

Source: 10-K report for 2007. Reproduced with permission.

Appendix 2: Merrill Lynch & Co., Inc.: Business Activities and Performance (extracts from 10-K report for 2007)

The Business

Merrill Lynch was formed in 1914 and became a publicly traded company on June 23, 1971. In 1973, we created the holding company, ML & Co., a Delaware corporation that, through its subsidiaries, is one of the world's leading capital markets, advisory and wealth management companies with offices in 40 countries and territories. In our Global Wealth Management ("GWM") business, we had total client assets in GWM accounts of approximately $1.2 trillion at December 26, 2008. As an investment bank, we are a leading global trader and underwriter of securities and derivatives across a broad range of asset classes and we serve as a strategic advisor to corporations, governments, institutions and individuals worldwide. In addition, as of December 26, 2008, we owned approximately half of the economic interest of BlackRock, Inc. ("BlackRock"), one of the world's largest publicly traded investment management companies with approximately $1.3 trillion in assets under management at the end of 2008 . . .

Our activities are conducted through two business segments: Global Markets and Investment Banking ("GMI") and GWM. In addition, we provide a variety of research services on a global basis.

Global Markets and Investment Banking

The Global Markets division consists of the Fixed Income, Currencies and Commodities ("FICC") and Equity Markets sales and trading activities for investor clients and on a proprietary basis, while the Investment Banking division provides a wide range of origination and strategic advisory services for issuer clients. Global Markets makes a market in securities, derivatives, currencies, and other financial instruments to satisfy client demands. In addition, Global Markets engages in certain proprietary trading activities. Global Markets is a leader in the global distribution of fixed income, currency and energy commodity products and derivatives. Global Markets also has one of the largest equity-trading operations in the world and is a leader in the origination and distribution of equity and equity-related products. Further, Global Markets provides clients with financing, securities clearing, settlement and custody services and also engages in principal investing in a variety of asset classes and private equity investing. The Investment Banking division raises capital for its clients through underwritings and private placements of equity, debt and related securities and loan syndications. Investment Banking also offers advisory services to clients on strategic issues, valuation, mergers, acquisitions and restructurings.

Global Wealth Management

Global Wealth Management, our full-service retail wealth management segment, provides brokerage, investment advisory and financial planning services, offering a broad range of both proprietary and third-party wealth management products and services globally to individuals, small- to mid-size businesses and employee benefit plans. Global Wealth Management comprises Global Private Client ("GPC") and Global Investment Management ("GIM").

Global Private Client provides a full range of wealth management products and services to assist clients in managing all aspects of their financial profile through the Total MerrillSM platform. Total MerrillSM is the platform for GPC's core strategy offering investment choices, brokerage, advice, planning and/or performance analysis to its clients. Global Private Client's offerings include commission and fee-based investment accounts, banking, cash management and credit services, including consumer and small business lending and Visa® cards; trust and generational planning; retirement services and insurance products.

Global Private Client services individuals and small- and middle-market corporations and institutions through approximately 16,090 financial advisors as of December 26, 2008.

Global Investment Management includes our interests in creating and managing wealth management products, including alternative investment products for clients. GIM also includes our share of net earnings from our ownership positions in other investment management companies, including BlackRock.

	GMI	GWM
Clients	Corporations, financial institutions, institutional investors, and governments	Individuals, small- to mid-size businesses, and employee benefit plans
Products and businesses	**Global Markets** (comprising Fixed Income, Currencies and Commodities ("FICC") and Equity Markets) Facilitates client transactions and makes markets in securities, derivatives, currencies, commodities and other financial instruments to satisfy client demands Provides clients with financing, securities clearing, settlement, and custody services. Engages in principal and private equity investing, including managing investment funds, and certain proprietary trading activities	**Global Private Client ("GPC")** Delivers products and services primarily through our Financial Advisors ("FAs") Commission fee-based investment accounts Banking, cash management, and credit services, including consumer and small business lending and Visa cards. Trust and generational planning. Retirement services. Insurance products
	Investment Banking Provides a wide range of securities origination services for issuer clients, including underwriting and placement of public and private equity, debt and related securities, as well as lending and other financing activities for clients globally Advises clients on strategic issues, valuation, mergers, acquisitions and restructurings	**Global Investment Management ("GIM")** Creates and manages hedge funds and other alternative investment products for GPC clients Includes net earnings from our ownership positions in other investment management companies, including our investment in BlackRock

RESULTS BY GEOGRAPHICAL AREA, 2008

($billion)	2008	2007	2006
Net revenues			
Europe, Middle East and Africa	(2.39)	5.97	6.90
Pacific Rim	0.07	5.07	3.70
Latin America	1.24	1.40	1.01
Canada	0.16	0.43	0.39
Total non-US	(0.92)	12.87	11.99
United States	(11.67)	(1.62)	21.79
Total net revenues	(12.59)	11.25	33.78
Pretax earnings from continuing operations			
Europe, Middle East, and Africa	(6.74)	1.211	2.09
Pacific Rim	(2.56)	2.40	1.20
Latin America	0.34	0.63	0.36
Canada	0.0	0.24	0.18
Total non-US	(8.95)	4.48	3.83
United States	(32.88)	(17.31)	5.98
Total pretax earnings from continuing operations	(41.83)	(12.83)	9.810

RESULTS BY BUSINESS SEGMENT

($million)	GMI	GWM	MLIM	Corporate	Total
2008					
Noninterest revenues	(25.42)	10.46	—	(1.68)	(16.63)
Net revenues	(26.46)	12.78	—	1.09	(12.59)
Noninterest expenses	15.08	10.43	—	3.72	29.24
Pretax (loss)/earnings from continuing operations	(41.54)	2.35	—	(2.63)	(41.83)
Year-end total assets	568.87	97.85	—	0.83	667.54
2007					
Noninterest revenues	(4.95)	11.72	—	(1.07)	5.701
Net revenues	(2.67)	14.02	—	(0.10)	11.25
Noninterest expenses	13.68	10.39	—	0.01	24.08
Pretax (loss)/earnings from continuing operations	(16.35)	3.63	—	(0.12)	(12.83)
Year-end total assets	920.39	99.20	—	0.47	1,020.05

Source: 10-K report for 2007. Reproduced with permission.

Notes

1. "BofA/Merrill Lynch," *Financial Times* (September 16, 2008), http://www.ft.com/cms/s/2/d285ebc8-82ff-11dd-907e-000077b07658.html#axzz1yzXSaW3l. Reproduced by permission of the *Financial Times*.

2. See letter from Andrew M. Cuomo (State of New York Attorney General) to Christopher Dodd (Chair, Senate Banking Committee), Barney Frank (Chair, House Financial Services Committee), Mary Schapiro (Chair, SEC), and Elizabeth Warren (Chair, Congressional Oversight Panel), April 23, 2009, concerning "Bank of America -Merrill Lynch Merger Investigation," http://online.wsj .com/public/resources/documents/BofAmergLetter-Cuomo4232009.pdf, accessed July 20, 2015.

3. As discussion of the $700 billion bailout package "dissolved into a verbal brawl in the Cabinet Room of the White House," President Bush warned: "If money isn't loosened up, this sucker could go down," *New York Times* (September 26, 2008).

4. The facts regarding conversations between Lewis and US government officials are disputed. See: "Paulson Threatened Lewis," *Forbes* (July 15, 2009), http://www. forbes.com/2009/07/15/paulson-lewis-fed-markets-equity-bank-america-bernanke.html, accessed July 20, 2015.

5. J. Canals, "Universal Banks Need Careful Monitoring," *Financial Times* (October 19, 2008).

6. J. Kay, "Should We Have 'Narrow Banking'?" *Future of Finance: the LSE Report* (June 2, 2011), http://www. johnkay.com/2011/06/02/should-we-have-narrow-banking, accessed July 20, 2015.

Case 24   W. L. Gore & Associates: Rethinking Management?

> If a man could flow with the stream, grow with the way of nature, he'd accomplish more and he'd be happier doing it than bucking the flow of the water.
>
> —W. L. GORE

Malcolm Gladwell (author of *The Tipping Point* and *Outliers*) described his visit to W. L. Gore & Associates (Gore) as follows:

> When I visited a Gore associate named Bob Hen, at one of the company's plants in Delaware, I tried, unsuccessfully, to get him to tell me what his position was. I suspected, from the fact that he had been recommended to me, that he was one of the top executives. But his office wasn't any bigger than anyone else's. His card just called him an "associate." He didn't seem to have a secretary, one that I could see anyway. He wasn't dressed any differently from anyone else, and when I kept asking the question again and again, all he finally said, with a big grin, was, "I'm a meddler."[1]

The absence of job titles and the lack of the normal symbols of hierarchy are not the only things that are different about Gore. Since its founding in 1958, Gore has deliberately adopted a system of management that contrasts sharply with that of other established corporations. While the styles of management of all start-up companies reflect the personality and values of their founders, the remarkable thing about Gore is that, as a $2.5 billion company with 8500 employees ("associates") in facilities located in 24 countries of the world, its organizational structure and management systems continue to defy the principles under which corporations of similar size and complexity are managed.

The Founding of Gore

Wilbert L. (Bill) Gore left DuPont in 1958 after 17 years as a research scientist. At DuPont, Gore had been working on a new synthetic material called

This case was prepared by Robert M. Grant. ©2015 Robert M. Grant.

polytetrafluoroethylene (PTFE), which it had branded "Teflon." Gore was convinced that DuPont's commitment to a business model based on large industrial markets for basic chemical products had caused it to overlook a whole range of innovative applications for PTFE. In forming a business together with his wife, Vieve, Gore was also motivated by the desire to create the energy and passion that he had experienced when working in small research teams at DuPont on those occasions when they were given the freedom to pursue innovation.

Working out of their own home in Newark, Delaware, and with the help of their son, Bob, the Gore, first product was Teflon-insulated cable (which was used for the Apollo space program among other applications).

The company's biggest breakthrough was the result of Bob Gore's discovery of the potential of Teflon to be stretched and laced with microscopic holes. The resulting fabric had several desirable properties; in particular, it shed water droplets but was also breathable. Gore-Tex received a US patent in 1976. Not only did it have a wide range of applications for outdoor clothing, the fact that Gore-Tex was chemically inert and resistant to infection made it an excellent material for medical applications such as artificial arteries and intravenous bags. The potential to vary the size of the microscopic holes in Gore-Tex made it ideal for a wide range of filtration applications.

Origins of the Gore Management Philosophy

FundingUniverse.com describes the development of Bill Gore's management ideas as follows:

> From their basement office, the Gores expanded into a separate production facility in their hometown of Newark, Delaware. Sales were brisk after initial product introductions. By 1965, just seven years after the business had started, Gore & Associates was employing about 200 people. It was about that time that Gore began to develop and implement the unique management system and philosophy for which his company would become recognized. Gore noticed that as his company had grown, efficiency and productivity had started to decline. He needed a new management structure, but he feared that the popular pyramid management structure that was in vogue at the time suppressed the creativity and innovation that he valued so greatly. Instead of adopting the pyramid structure, Gore decided to create his own system.
>
> During World War II, while on a task force at DuPont, Gore had learned of another type of organizational structure called the lattice system, which was developed to enhance the ingenuity and overall performance of a group working toward a goal. It emphasized communication and cooperation rather than hierarchy of authority. Under the system that Gore developed, any person was allowed to make a decision as long as it was fair, encouraged others, and made a commitment to the company. Consultation was required only for decisions that could potentially cause serious damage to the enterprise. Furthermore, new associates joined the company on the same effective authority level as all the other workers, including Bill and Vieve. There were no titles or bosses, with only a few exceptions, and commands were replaced by personal commitments.

New employees started out working in an area best suited to their talents, under the guidance of a sponsor. As the employee progressed there came more responsibility, and workers were paid according to their individual contribution. "Team members know who is producing," Bill explained in a February 1986 issue of the *Phoenix Business Journal*. "They won't put up with poor performance. There is tremendous peer pressure. You promote yourself by gaining knowledge and working hard, every day. There is no competition, except with yourself." The effect of the system was to encourage workers to be creative, take risks, and perform at their highest level.[2]

Bill Gore's ideas about management were influenced by Douglas McGregor's *The Human Side of Enterprise*, which was published as Gore's own company was in its start-up phase. In it, McGregor identifies two models of management: the conventional model of management, rooted in Taylor's scientific management, and Weber's principles of bureaucracy, which he terms "Theory X." At its core is the assumption that work is unpleasant, that employees are motivated only by money, and that management's principal role is to prevent shirking. "Theory Y" is rooted in the work of the human relations school of management, which assumes that individuals are self-motivated, anxious to solve problems, and capable of working harmoniously on joint tasks.

A key element in Bill Gore's management thinking related to the limits of organizational size. He believed that the need for interpersonal trust would result in organizations declining in effectiveness once they reached about 200 members. Hence, in 1967, rather than expand their Delaware facility, Bill and Vieve decided to build a second manufacturing facility in Flagstaff, Arizona. From then on, Gore built a new facility each time an existing unit reached 200 associates.

According to Malcolm Gladwell, Gore's insistence upon small organizational units is an application of a principle developed by anthropologist Robin Dunbar. According to Dunbar, social groups are limited by individuals' capacity to manage complex social relationships. Among primates, the size of the typical social group for a species is correlated with the size of the neocortex of that species' brain. For humans, Dunbar estimates that 148 is the maximum number of individuals that a person can comfortably have social relations with. Across a range of different societies, Dunbar found that 150 was the typical maximum size of tribes, religious groups, and army units.[3]

Organization Structure and Management Principles

The Gore organization does include elements of hierarchy. For example, as a corporation, it is legally required to have a board of directors—this is chaired by Bob Gore. There is also a CEO, Terri Kelly. The company is organized into four divisions (fabrics, medical, industrial, and electronic products) each with a recognized "leader." Within these divisions there are specific business units, each based upon a group of products. There are also specialized, company-wide functions such as human resources and information technology.

What is lacking is a codified set of ranks and positions. Gore associates are expected to adapt their roles to match their skills and aptitudes. The basic organizational units are small, self-managing teams.

Relationships within teams and between teams are based upon the concept of a lattice rather than a conventional hierarchy. The idea of a lattice is that every organizational member is connected to every other organizational member within the particular facility. In the lattice, communication is peer to peer, not superior to subordinate. For Bill Gore, this was a more natural way to organize. He observed that in most formal organizations it was through informal connections that things actually got done: "Most of us delight in going around the formal procedures and doing things the straightforward and easy way."[4]

New associates are assigned to a "sponsor" whose job is to introduce the new hire to the company and guide him or her through the lattice. The new hire is likely to spend time with several teams during the first few months of employment. It is up to the new associate and a team to find a good match. An associate is free to find a new sponsor if desired. Typically, each associate works on two or three different project teams.

Annual reviews are peer based. Information is collected from at least 20 other associates. Each associate is then ranked against every other associate within the unit in terms of overall contribution. This ranking determines compensation.

The company's beliefs, management principles, and work culture are articulated on its website (Exhibit 1).

Leadership

Leadership is important at Gore, but the basic principle is that of natural leadership: "If you call a meeting and people show up—you're a leader."[5] Teams can appoint team leaders; they can also replace their team leaders. As a result, every team leader's accountability is to the team. "Someone who is accustomed to snapping their fingers and having people respond will be frustrated," says John McMillan, a Gore associate. "I snap my fingers and nobody will do anything. My job is to acquire followership, articulate a goal and get there … and hope the rest of the people think that makes sense."[6]

CEO Terri Kelly compares the conventional approach to leadership with Gore's "distributed leadership model":

> The model of the single powerful leader who operates through command and control is attractive in its simplicity … In reality, it is impractical to expect the single leader to have all the answers, and history has shown that relying upon rigid control mechanisms will not prevent catastrophic outcomes. It's far better to rely upon a broad base of individuals and leaders who share a common set of values and feel personal ownership for the overall success of the organization. And as organizations grow in size and complexity, it becomes even more critical to distribute the leadership load … The capacity of the organization increases when it distributes the leadership load to competent leaders on the ground who can make the best knowledge-based decisions.[7]

She argues that talented newcomers to the workforce adapt much more easily to the distributed leadership than to traditional modes of management. Young people recognize they have choices, are not wedded to a single organization, and will move to where they perceive the best opportunities. As a result companies that persevere with traditional management models will find it difficult to retain the best talent. At the same time, warns Kelly, making the shift to a distributed leadership model is

EXHIBIT 1
What We Believe

Founder Bill Gore built the company on a set of beliefs and principles that guide us in the decisions we make, in the work we do, and in our behavior toward others. What we believe is the basis for our strong culture, which connects Gore associates worldwide in a common bond.

FUNDAMENTAL BELIEFS

Belief in the individual: If you trust individuals and believe in them, they will be motivated to do what's right for the company.

Power of small teams: Our lattice organization harnesses the fast decision-making, diverse perspectives, and collaboration of small teams.

All in the same boat: All Gore associates are part owners of the company through the associate stock plan. Not only does this allow us to share in the risks and rewards of the company; it gives us an added incentive to stay committed to its long-term success. As a result, we feel we are all in this effort together, and believe we should always consider what's best for the company as a whole when making decisions.

Long-term view: Our investment decisions are based on long-term payoff and our fundamental beliefs are not sacrificed for short-term gain.

Guiding Principles

♦ *Freedom*: the company was designed to be an organization in which associates can achieve their own goals best by directing their efforts toward the success of the corporation; action is prized; ideas are encouraged; and making mistakes is viewed as part of the creative process. We define freedom as being empowered to encourage each other to grow in knowledge, skill, scope of responsibility, and range of activities. We believe that associates will exceed expectations when given the freedom to do so.

♦ *Fairness*: everyone at Gore sincerely tries to be fair with each other, our suppliers, our customers and anyone else with whom we do business.

♦ *Commitment*: we are not assigned tasks; rather, we each make our own commitments and keep them.

♦ *Waterline*: everyone at Gore consults with other associates before taking actions that might be "below the waterline"—causing serious damage to the company.

Working in Our Unique Culture

Our founder Bill Gore once said, "The objective of the Enterprise is to make money and have fun doing so." And we still believe that, more than 50 years later.

Because we are all part owners of the company through the associate stock plan, Gore associates expect a lot from each other. Innovation and creativity; high ethics and integrity; making commitments and standing behind them. We work hard at living up to these expectations as we strive for business success.

a challenge to top management that requires a fundamental change in the values, attitudes, and reward systems that are deeply embedded in most organizations:

> It will require a shift within the organization from valuing a key few to valuing the unique contributions of many. Individuals will need to feel they have a voice and can be heard. Leaders will need to recognize that their primary role is to empower others versus build their own power. They will no longer stand behind a title with assumed authority to tell people what to do.

But we also trust and respect each other and believe it's important to celebrate success.

Gore is much less formal than most workplaces. Our relationships with other associates are open and informal and we strive to treat everyone respectfully and fairly. This type of environment naturally promotes social interaction and many associates have made lifelong friends with those they met working at Gore.

Do Something You're Passionate About

At Gore, we believe it's important to have passion for what you do. If you're passionate about your work, you are naturally going to be highly self-motivated and focused. If you feel pride and ownership, you will want to do whatever it takes to be successful and have an impact. So when you apply for an opportunity at Gore, be sure you're going to be passionate about the work you'll be doing.

The Lattice Structure and Individual Accountability

Gore's unique "lattice" management structure, which illustrates a nonhierarchical system based on interconnection among associates, is free from traditional bosses and managers. There is no assigned authority, and we become leaders based on our ability to gain the respect of our peers and to attract followers.

You will be responsible for managing your own workload and will be accountable to others on your team. More importantly, only you can make a commitment to do something (for example, a task, a project, or a new role)—but once you make a commitment, you will be expected to meet it. A "core commitment" is your primary area of concentration. You may take on additional commitments depending on your interests, the company's needs, and your availability.

Relationships and Direct Communication

Relationships are everything at Gore—relationships with each other, with customers, with vendors and suppliers and with our surrounding communities. We encourage people to build and maintain long-term relationships by communicating directly. Of course we all use e-mail, but we find that face-to-face meetings and phone calls work best when collaborating with others.

Sponsors

Everyone at Gore has a sponsor, who is committed to helping you succeed. Sponsors are responsible for supporting your growth, for providing good feedback on your strengths and areas that offer opportunities for development and for helping you connect with others in the organization.

Source: www.gore.com/en_xx/careers/whoweare/about-gore.html, W. L. Gore & Associates: Beliefs, Principles and Culture. Reproduced by permission of W. L. Gore & Associates.

Leaders' focus will shift to creating the right environment and instilling the right values that can enable capable leaders to emerge. They will recognize that they are only leaders if they have willing followers, and that this needs to be earned every day. Ultimately their contributions will be judged by the people they lead.

Most rewards systems depend upon higher-level management to assess the effectiveness of the leader. This view can be somewhat limited and biased by the fact the managers were often the ones who put the leader in the role in the first place.

Those who know their leaders best are typically the individuals they lead. If you want individuals to have a voice in the organization, they must also have a voice in selecting and evaluating their leaders.

In our company, we have found it very useful to adopt a peer ranking system. All associates get the opportunity to rank members of their team, including their leaders. They are asked to create a contribution list in rank order based on who they believe is making the greatest contribution to the success of the enterprise. This approach serves as an excellent form of "checks and balances" when it comes to who is truly recognized for their contributions as well as for overall leadership.[8]

EXHIBIT 2
Examples of Innovation at W. L. Gore & Associates

Change Music

How did the creators of GORE-TEX® products—worn by outdoor enthusiasts and people with active lifestyles all over the world—invent a new kind of guitar string?

Although manufacturers have coated their guitar strings for many years to make them last longer by protecting them from perspiration, oil, and dirt the coating severely compromised the quality of the sound.

Gore had no presence in the music industry until one associate envisioned a completely new type of guitar string that would prevent string contamination, last longer, and be more comfortable for musicians to play. Relying on the company's unique culture and mentoring system to support his efforts, he formed a cross-functional team—including Michael and John—to make it happen.

Each member of the Gore team had the knowledge and know-how needed to develop this exciting new product. With the entrepreneurial spirit characteristic of Gore, they took this innovative concept to the marketplace in less than two years.

But the team's commitment to integrity didn't stop in the lab. They asked 15,000 musicians to test the new

strings for sound quality before the product was introduced. Since then, revolutionary ELIXIR® Strings have inspired a generation of musicians all over the world to pick up their guitars and play. And their ELIXIR® Strings experience and the challenges they overcame have changed their lives too.

Change Lives

How did the creators of GORE-TEX® products—worn by outdoor enthusiasts and people with active lifestyles all over the world—invent material to patch human hearts?

For people with a serious heart problem known as an atrial septal defect, or "hole in the heart," open heart surgery was once the only treatment. The surgeon makes an incision in the chest to expose the heart; a heart-lung bypass machine pumps blood while the heart is stopped and the defect is patched. Many patients with this condition are infants and small children, for whom this surgery poses an even greater risk.

A dedicated team of Gore associates—including Hannah, Nitin, and Sarah—developed a minimally invasive device that physicians implant through a cardiac catheter to permanently close the hole without

Innovation

The success of Gore's unusual management system is its capacity for innovation. Between 1976 and the end of May 2012, Gore received 1026 US patents. Even more remarkable has been its ability to extend its existing technological breakthroughs to a wide variety of new applications. Central to Gore's ability to innovate is its willingness to allow individuals the freedom to pursue their own projects: each associate is allowed a half day each week of "dabble time." The company's website gives examples of the results of these initiatives (Exhibit 2).

Gary Hamel closes his discussion of Gore with the following challenge:

major surgery. Driven by Gore's core values of integrity, innovation, and quality, the team spent years perfecting the device before taking it to market. Patients treated this way experience much less pain, recover much more easily and quickly, and have less scarring.

Since then, the GORE HELEX septal occluder has changed the way doctors treat patients with this heart defect and has helped thousands of patients throughout the world—more than half of them infants and children—lead normal, healthy lives. And the team's experience with the septal occluder product changed their lives, too.

Change Industries

How did the creators of GORE-TEX® products— worn by outdoor enthusiasts and people with active lifestyles all over the world—invent material that protects firefighters from heat, flames, and hazardous chemicals?

Gore makes a line of protective fabrics based on its patented membrane technologies. These fabrics are used by Gore's customers—garment manufacturers—as one layer of protective clothing for military and law enforcement uniforms, medical protective wear, workwear, and turnout gear for fire and safety personnel.

Firefighters rely on protective gear—including boots, pants, jackets, gloves, and headgear— to keep them safe. While already incorporating waterproof and breathable GORE-TEX® fabric to improve the comfort and quality of their gear, the firefighting industry identified a need for barrier fabrics that also protected firefighters against bloodborne pathogens and common fire ground chemicals. Dave, Henri, and Ron were part of a cross-functional team that set out to engineer high-performance CROSSTECH® protective barrier fabric to meet this need.

By building relationships with firefighters, suppliers, and industry experts, the global Gore team came to understand the extreme conditions that firefighters are exposed to. Harnessing deep knowledge of Gore's membrane technologies and their passion for making a difference, they developed Gore protective barrier fabrics that change the way firefighters respond to emergencies. And their fire service experience and the challenges they overcame have changed their lives, too.

Source: "Associates Stories," http://www.gore.com/ en_xx/careers/associatestories/1234722965408.html, accessed October 1, 2012. Reproduced by permission of W. L. Gore & Associates.

Bill Gore was a 40-something chemical engineer when he laid the foundations for his innovation democracy. I don't know about you, but a middle-aged polytetra-fluoroethylene-loving chemist isn't my mental image of a wild-eyed management innovator. Yet think about how radical Gore's vision must have seemed back in 1958. Fifty years later, postmodern management hipsters throw around terms like complex adaptive systems and self-organizing teams. Well, they're only a half century behind the curve. So ask yourself, am I dreaming big enough yet? Would my management innovation agenda make Bill Gore proud?[9]

Notes

1. M. Gladwell, *The Tipping Point* (Little, Brown & Co., London, 2000).
2. "W. L. Gore & Associates, Inc. History," http://www.fundinguniverse.com/company-histories/WL-Gore-amp;-Associates-Inc-Company-History.html, accessed July 20, 2015.
3. Gladwell, op. cit.: 177–81.
4. Quoted by G. Hamel with B. Breen, *The Future of Management* (Harvard Business School Press, Boston, MA, 2007, p. 87).
5. Reprinted by permission of Harvard Business School Press from *The Future of Management* by Gary Hamel. Boston, MA, 2007, p. 100 Copyright © 2007 by the Harvard Business School Publishing Corporation; all rights reserved.
6. "W. L. Gore & Associates, Inc.: Quality's Different Drummer," *IMPO Magazine*, January 14, 2002, http://www.impomag.com/articles/2002/01/wl-gore-associates-inc-qualitys-different-drummer, accessed July 20, 2015.
7. Terri Kelly, "No More Heroes: Distributed Leadership," *Management Inforation eXchange* (April 8, 2010), http://www.managementexchange.com/blog/no-more-heroes, accessed July 20, 2015.
8. Ibid.
9. Reprinted by permission of Harvard Business School Press from *The Future of Management* by Gary Hamel. Boston, MA, 2007, p. 100. Copyright © 2007 by the Harvard Business School Publishing Corporation; all rights reserved.

GLOSSARY

acquisition (or takeover)   The purchase of one company by another.

activity system   A conceptualization of the firm as a set of inter-related activities.

agency problem   An agency relationship exists when one party (the principal) contracts with another party (the agent) to act on behalf of the principal. The agency problem is the difficulty of ensuring that the agent acts in the principal's interest.

alliance   See **strategic alliance**

ambidextrous organization   An organization that can simultaneously exploit existing competences while exploring new opportunities for future development.

balanced scorecard   A tool for linking strategic goals to performance indicators. These performance indicators combine performance indicators relating to financial performance, consumer satisfaction, internal efficiency, and learning and innovation.

barriers to entry   Disadvantages that new entrants to an industry face in relation to established firms.

barriers to exit   Costs and other impediments which prevent capacity from leaving an industry.

benchmarking   A systematic process for comparing the practices, processes, resources and capabilities of other organizations with one's own.

blue-ocean strategy   The discovery or creation of uncontested market space.

bottom of the pyramid   This refers to the poorest people in the world: typically the 3 billion people who live on less than $2 per day.

bounded rationality   The principle that the rationality of human beings is constrained ("bounded") by the limits of their cognition and capacity to process information.

business model   The overall logic of a business and the basis upon which it generates revenues and profits.

business strategy (aka competitive strategy) This refers to how a firm competes within a particular industry or market.

capability More precisely referred to as *organizational capability*, is an organization's capacity to perform a particular task or function.

causal ambiguity The difficulty facing any observer of diagnosing the sources of the competitive advantage of a firm with superior performance. It means that potential rivals face the problem of *uncertain imitability.*

comparative advantage A country's ability to produce a particular product at a lower relative cost than other countries.

competency trap The barrier to change which results from an organization developing high levels of capability in particular activities.

competitive advantage A firm possesses a competitive advantage over its direct competitors when it earns (or has the potential to earn) a persistently higher rate of profit.

consumer surplus The value that a consumer receives from a good or service minus the price that he or she paid.

contingency theory Postulates that there is no single best way to design and manage an organization. The optimal structure and management systems for any organization are contingent upon its context—in particular, the features of its business environment and the technologies it utilizes.

corporate governance The system by which companies are directed and controlled.

corporate planning A systematic approach to resource allocation and strategic decisions within a company over the medium to long-term (typically 4 to 10 years).

corporate restructuring Radical strategic and organizational change designed to improve performance through cost reduction, employment reduction, divestment of assets, and internal reorganization.

corporate social responsibility (CSR) The social responsibilities of a business organization.

corporate strategy A firm's decisions and intentions with regard to the scope of its activities (its choices in relation to the industries, national markets, and vertical activities within which it participates) and the resource allocation among these.

customer relationship management (CRM) A set of tools, techniques, and methodologies for understanding the needs and characteristics of customers in order to better serve them.

dominant design   A product architecture that defines the look, functionality, and production method for the product and becomes accepted by the industry as a whole.

dynamic capabilities   Organizational capabilities that allow an organization to reconfigure its resources and modify its operating capabilities in order to adapt and change.

economic profit   Pure profit: it is the surplus of revenues over all the costs of producing that revenue inputs (including the costs of capital).

economic value added (EVA)   A measure of economic profit. It is the excess of net operating profit after tax over the cost of the capital used in the business.

economies of scale   These exist when increases in the scale of a firm or plant result in reductions in costs per unit of output.

economies of scope   These exist when using a resource across multiple products or multiple markets uses less of that resource than when the activities are carried out independently.

emergent strategy   The strategy that results from the actions and decisions of different organizational members as they deal with the forces which impinge upon the organization.

first-mover advantage   The competitive advantage that accrues to the firm which is first to occupy a new market or strategic niche, or to exploit a new technology. First-mover advantage is a special case of *early-mover advantage*.

functional structure   Organization around specialized business functions such as accounting, finance marketing, operations, etc.

game theory   This analyzes and predicts the outcomes of competitive (and cooperative) situations where each player's choice of action depends upon the choices made by the other players in the game. Game theory has applications to business, economics, politics, international relations, biology, and social relations.

global strategy   A strategy that treats the world as a single, if segmented, market.

globalization   The process through which differences between countries diminish and the world becomes increasingly integrated.

hypercompetition   Competition that is characterized by rapid and intensive competitive moves where competitive advantage is quickly eroded and firms are continually seeking new sources of competitive advantage.

industry life cycle   The pattern of industry evolution from introduction to growth to maturity to decline.

innovation   The initial commercialization of invention by producing and marketing a new good or service or by using a new method of production.

institutional isomorphism   The tendency for organizations that are subject to common social norms and pressures for legitimacy to develop similar organizational characteristics.

intellectual property   Intangible goods that have no physical presence and which are "creations of the mind." It includes ideas, names, symbols, designs, artwork, and writings.

intended strategy   The strategy conceived by top management with the intention of implementing it within the organization.

invention   The creation of new products and processes through the development of new knowledge or from new combinations of existing knowledge.

isolating mechanisms   Barriers that protect the competitive advantage of firms from imitative competition.

key success factors   Sources of competitive advantage within an industry.

knowledge-based view of the firm   This regards the firm as a pool of knowledge assets where the primary challenge for management is to integrate the specialized knowledge of organizational members into the production of goods and services.

matrix structures   Hierarchies that comprise multiple dimensions; these typically include product (or business) units, geographical units, and functions.

merger   The amalgamation of two or more companies to form a new company. In a merger, the owners of the merging companies exchange their shares for shares in the new company.

multidivisional structure   A company structure comprising separate business units, each with significant operational independence, coordinated by a corporate head office that exerts strategic and financial control.

network effects (or network externalities)   Linkages between the users of a product or technology that result in the value of that product or technology being positively related to the number of users.

open innovation   An approach to innovation where a firm seeks solutions from organizations and individuals outside the firm and shares its technologies with other organizations.

organizational ambidexterity   see **ambidextrous organization**

organizational culture An organization's values, traditions, behavioral norms, symbols, and social characteristics.

organizational ecology (aka organizational demography and the population ecology of organizations) This studies the organizational population of industries and the processes of founding and selection that determine entry and exit.

organizational routines Patterns of coordinated activity through which an organization is able to perform tasks regularly and predictably.

parenting advantage A parent company's ability to create more value from owning a particular business than could any other parent company.

path dependency The simple fact that history matters; more specifically, it implies that an organization's strategy and structure and management's options for the future are determined by it's past decisions and actions.

platform A product, technology, or system that provides a foundation for a number of complementary products (or applications). In business, platforms that form an interface between two-sided markets (comprising application suppliers and final users) occupy an especially important role in several technology-based sectors.

prisoner's dilemma A simple game theory model which shows how lack of cooperation results in an outcome that is inferior to that which could have been achieved with cooperation.

profit The surplus of revenues over costs available for distribution to the owners of the firm.

real option analysis This identifies and values possibilities for investment in uncertain opportunities. The two major types of real option are investments in flexibility and investment in growth opportunities.

realized strategy The actual strategy that the organization pursues; it is the outcome of the interaction of intended strategy with emergent strategy.

regime of appropriability The conditions that determine the extent to which a firm is able to capture profits from its innovations.

resources The assets of the firm including tangible assets (such as plant, equipment, land, and natural resources), intangible resources (such as technology, brands and other forms of intellectual property) and human resources.

resource-based view of the firm A conceptualization of the firm as a collection of resources and capabilities that form the basis of competitive advantage and the foundation for strategy.

scenario analysis   A technique for integrating information and ideas on current trends and future developments into a small number of distinctly different future outcomes.

segmentation   The process of disaggregating industries and markets into more narrowly defined sub-markets on the basis of product characteristics, customer characteristics or geography.

self-organization   The tendency for complex systems, both natural and biological, to spontaneously achieve order and adaptation though decentralized interactions without any centralized direction or control.

seller concentration   This measures the extent to which a market is dominated by a small number of firms. The concentration ratio measures the market share of the largest firms e.g., the four-firm concentration ratio (CR4) is the combined market share of the four biggest firms.

stakeholder approach to the firm   This proposes that the firm operates in the interests of all its stakeholders (owners, employees, customers, suppliers and society). Top management has the task of balancing and integrating these different interests.

state capitalism   A market-based economy where a large proportion of leading enterprises are owned by the government.

strategic alliance   A collaborative arrangement between two or more firms involving their pursuit of certain common goals.

strategic fit   The consistency of a firm's strategy with its external environment and with its internal environment, especially with its goals and values, resources and capabilities, and structure and systems.

strategic group   A group of firms within an industry that follow similar strategies.

strategic intent   The goal of an organization in terms of a desired future strategic position.

SWOT framework   The SWOT framework classifies the factors relevant for a firm's strategic decision making into four categories: strengths, weaknesses, opportunities and threats.

technical standard   A specification or requirement or technical characteristic that becomes a norm for a product or process thereby ensuring compatibility.

transaction costs   The costs incurred in researching, negotiating, monitoring and enforcing market contracts.

value   Within management terminology, value is used to refer to two very different concepts. In its plural form, *values* typically refer to ethical precepts and principles.

In its singular form it typically refers to economic value: the monetary worth of a product or asset.

value added Sales revenue minus the cost of bought-in goods and services; it is equal to all the firm's payments to factors of production (i.e., wages and salaries + interest + rent + royalties and license fees + taxes + dividends + retained profit).

value chain A sequence of vertically related activities undertaken by a single firm or by a number of vertically-related firms in order to produce a product or service.

vertical integration A firm's ownership of adjacent vertical activities.

winner-takes-all markets Markets where a single firm is able to capture the great majority of sales and/or profits.

INDEX

Note: Page numbers in *italics* refer to illustrations and tables.

Franco, F. 358
Freeman, C. 272
Freeman, J. 212
FreeMove 403
Frei, F. X. 202
Fried, J. M. 163
Friedlander, A. 271
Friedman, M. 51, 60
Frost, T. S. 340
fuel cells 248
Fujifilm 326, 350, 405
Fujimoto, T. 203, 239, 272
Fuld, L. M. 112
functional classification, capabilities 123
functional organization structures 146, 156
Furrier, W. 61

Gabriel, K. J. 271
Gadiesh, O. 31, 107
Galbraith, J. K. 139, 295, 308
Gale, B. T. 30, 88, 287
Gambardella, A. 272
game theory 13, 30, 93–102, 111, 194–195
Gap 299
García-Castro, R. 60
Garmin 244
Gavetti, G. 31, 238
Gawer, A. 261
Gazprom 71
GE *see* General Electric
Geely 128
Geneen, H. S. 156, 341, 374
General Electric (GE)
    acquisitions 400
    brand value *122*
    business linkages 368
    corporate strategy 361, 363–364, 377, 378
    diversification 349, 351, 354
    exploiting innovation *252*, 254
    GE/McKinsey portfolio planning matrix 364, *364*
    joint ventures 401
    market capitalization *219*
    organizational change 218, 224
    organizational structure *157*, 378, 420
    profitability *40*
    "Work-Out" program 420
General Mills 342
General Motors (GM) 402, 405, 416
    acquisitions 391–392
    competitive advantage 183
    international alliances 403–405, *404*
    internationalization 331
    organizational change 223
    organizational structure 146–147, 147, 156, *157*
    profitability 181
    vertical integration 302
geographical boundaries, markets 81
    see also segmentation
geographical distance 327, *327*
geographical location
    competitive advantage from 185

industry life cycle 214
    international strategies 318–322
geographical scope 292, 293–294
    see also internationalization
George, J. M. 272
Geroski, P. A. 110, 238, 254, 271
Gerstner, Lou 225, 231, 379, 421
Ghadar, F. 339
Ghai, S. 387
Ghemawat, P. 86, 88, 111, 325, 327, *327*, 333, 335, *335*, 339, 340
Ghoshal, S. 159, 160, 163, 331, *332*, 332, 334, *334*, 340, 413, 425
Ghosn, Carlos 185
Gilbert, J. 31, 107
Gilead Sciences *121*
Gillette *122*
Gilmore, J. 287
Ginter, J. L. 203
Gioia, D. A. 425
Gladwell, M. 272
GlaxoSmithKline *121*, 401
Glencore International 397
global industries *313*, 314
global localization 329, 330
globalization *see* internationalization
Glover, V. 202
GM *see* General Motors
goals 5, 36
    identifying competitors' 102
    setting 48–51
    short-term monitoring 48–51
    strategy as 17, 37, 49
    value maximization 39, 51–55, 415–416
Goedhart, M. 60
Goizueta, R. 167
Goldman Sachs 53, 129, *129*
Goldwyn, Samuel 225
Goleman, D. 138, 423, 425
Goodnight, J. 272
Goodwin, Frank 395
Google 72, 424
    acquisitions 397
    Android 94
    brand value *122*
    competitive advantage 416
    diversification 342
    industry standards 256
    industry structure 79
    innovation *252*, 253, 263
    mission 37
    organizational design 153
    platform-based markets 258, 259
    platform investments 58
    strategic alliances 401, 403
    vertical integration 300
Goold, M. 350–351, 358, 359, 363, 375, *376*, 387, 388
Gosman, M. L. 88
Goudzwaard, M. B. 358
Gould, B. W. 111
Gould, S. J. 272